EUROPEAN UNGULATES AND THEIR MANAGEMENT IN THE 21ST CENTURY

This book is the first to explore the diversity of management objectives and the different approaches to wildlife management of large ungulates in a wide range of European countries.

Specialist authors from each country present an analysis of the species present, numerical status and distribution of the different ungulates that occur in their particular country and consider issues which must be addressed by management (whether management for conservation, for control of damaging impacts or for exploitation). Management systems are described (and both legislative and administrative structures) together with an evaluation of how effective current management practices may be in addressing the problems identified – or the extent to which they may contribute to those problems. The book is aimed primarily at those who may be actively involved in research into improving methods of wildlife management; practising wildlife managers and game-keepers; policymakers in local regional or national administrations responsible for formulating policies.

MARCO APOLLONIO is Full Professor at the University of Sassari where he is presently Director of the Department of Zoology and of the Ph.D. School in Natural Science. His main interests are in ungulate behaviour, ecology and genetics, with a specific focus on mating and social behaviour, and predator–prey relationships involving wolves and ungulates. He is President of the Italian Mammalogical Society and was involved in conservation activities as a CITES Scientific Commission Member for Italy and as a member of the board of directors of two national parks in the last 15 years.

REIDAR ANDERSEN is a Professor in conservation biology at the Museum of Natural History and Archaeology at the Norwegian University of Science and Technology. He has been leading several cross-disciplinary research projects focusing on ungulates and large carnivores, always aiming to produce applied knowledge, securing sustainable management of the species involved. Over the last few years he has been focusing on non-native invasive species.

RORY PUTMAN is a freelance environmental consultant and wildlife adviser based in Scotland and he also holds an Emeritus Chair at Manchester Metropolitan University. He has worked widely in the UK and overseas, with research efforts focused on the population ecology of different ungulate species and their interaction with their vegetational environment – always with the explicit aim of using increased understanding to help develop more sensitive and more effective methods of managing those same ungulate populations and their impacts on agriculture, forestry or conservation interests.

Published with support from Ministero dell'Ambiente e Tutela del Territorio e del Mare (the Italian Ministry for the Environment, Land and Sea).

EUROPEAN UNGULATES AND THEIR MANAGEMENT IN THE 21ST CENTURY

Edited by

MARCO APOLLONIO
University of Sassari, Italy

REIDAR ANDERSEN
Museum of Natural History and Archaeology, Trondheim, Norway

RORY PUTMAN
Manchester Metropolitan University, UK

CAMBRIDGE UNIVERSITY PRESS
Cambridge, New York, Melbourne, Madrid, Cape Town, Singapore,
São Paulo, Delhi, Dubai, Tokyo

Cambridge University Press
The Edinburgh Building, Cambridge CB2 8RU, UK

Published in the United States of America by Cambridge University Press, New York

www.cambridge.org
Information on this title: www.cambridge.org/9780521760614

© Cambridge University Press 2010

This publication is in copyright. Subject to statutory exception
and to the provisions of relevant collective licensing agreements,
no reproduction of any part may take place without the written
permission of Cambridge University Press.

First published 2010

Printed in the United Kingdom at the University Press, Cambridge

A catalogue record for this publication is available from the British Library

Library of Congress Cataloguing in Publication data
European ungulates and their management in the 21st century / edited by Marco Apollonio,
Reidar Andersen, Rory Putman.
p. cm.
Includes index.
ISBN 978-0-521-76061-4 (hardback)
1. Ungulates – Europe.   2. Wildlife management – Europe.   I. Apollonio, Marco.
II. Andersen, Reidar.   III. Putman, Rory.   IV. Title.
QL737.U4E97   2009
639.97′96094 – dc22   2009036357

ISBN 978-0-521-76061-4 Hardback

Cambridge University Press has no responsibility for the persistence or
accuracy of URLs for external or third-party Internet websites referred to
in this publication, and does not guarantee that any content on such
websites is, or will remain, accurate or appropriate.

Contents

	Contributors and Affiliations	*page* vii
1	Introduction	1
	Marco Apollonio, Reidar Andersen and Rory Putman	
2	Ungulates and their management in Norway	14
	Reidar Andersen, Erik Lund, Erling Johan Solberg and Bernt-Erik Sæther	
3	Ungulates and their management in Sweden	37
	Olof Liberg, Roger Bergström, Jonas Kindberg and Hans von Essen	
4	Ungulates and their management in Denmark	71
	Reidar Andersen and Vidar Holthe	
5	Ungulates and their management in Finland	86
	Vesa Ruusila and Ilpo Kojola	
6	Ungulates and their management in the Baltics (Estonia, Latvia and Lithuania)	103
	Žanete Andersone-Lilley, Linas Balčiauskas, Jānis Ozoliņš, Tiit Randveer and Juri Tõnisson	
7	Ungulates and their management in Great Britain and Ireland	129
	Rory Putman	
8	Ungulates and their management in the Netherlands	165
	Sipke E. van Wieren and Geert W. T. A. Groot Bruinderink	
9	Ungulates and their management in Belgium	184
	Jim Casaer and Alain Licoppe	
10	Ungulates and their management in Germany	201
	Ulrich Wotschikowsky	
11	Ungulates and their management in Poland	223
	Piotr Wawrzyniak, Włodzimierz Jędrzejewski, Bogumiła Jędrzejewska and Tomasz Borowik	

12	Ungulates and their management in the Czech Republic *Luděk Bartoš, Radim Kotrba and Jan Pintíř*	243
13	Ungulates and their management in Slovakia *Slavomír Finďo and Michaela Skuban*	262
14	Ungulates and their management in Hungary *Sándor Csányi and Róbert Lehoczki*	291
15	Ungulates and their management in Romania *Ion Micu, András Náhlik, Şerban Neguş, Ilie Mihalache and István Szabó*	319
16	Ungulates and their management in Austria *Friedrich Reimoser and Susanne Reimoser*	338
17	Ungulates and their management in Switzerland *Nicole Imesch-Bebié, Hans Gander and Reinhard Schnidrig-Petrig*	357
18	Ungulates and their management in Portugal *José Vingada, Carlos Fonseca, Jorge Cancela, Joana Ferreira and Catarina Eira*	392
19	Ungulates and their management in Spain *Juan Carranza*	419
20	Ungulates and their management in France *Daniel Maillard, Jean-Michel Gaillard, Mark Hewison, Philippe Ballon, Patrick Duncan, Anne Loison, Carole Toïgo, Eric Baubet, Christophe Bonenfant, Mathieu Garel and Christine Saint-Andrieux*	441
21	Ungulates and their management in Italy *Marco Apollonio, Simone Ciuti, Luca Pedrotti and Paolo Banti*	475
22	Ungulates and their management in Slovenia *Miha Adamic and Klemen Jerina*	507
23	Ungulates and their management in Croatia *Josip Kusak and Krešimir Krapinec*	527
24	Ungulates and their management in Greece *Haritakis Papaioannou*	540
25	Ungulates and their management in Serbia *Milan Paunović and Duško Ćirović, with John D. C. Linnell*	563
26	Ungulates and their management in Macedonia *Aleksandar Stojanov, Dime Melovski and Gjorgje Ivanov, with John D. C. Linnell*	572
27	Present status and future challenges for European ungulate management *Marco Apollonio, Reider Andersen and Rory Putman*	578

Contributors and Affiliations

MIHA ADAMIC
University of Ljubljana, Biotechnical Faculty, Department of Forestry and Renewable Forest Resources, Večna pot 83, 1000 Ljubljana, Slovenia

REIDAR ANDERSEN
Norwegian University of Science and Technology, Museum of Natural History and Archaeology, N-7491 Trondheim, Norway

ŽANETE ANDERSONE-LILLEY
Defra, 1/06 Temple Quay House, 2 The Square, Temple Quay, Bristol, BS1 6EB, UK

MARCO APOLLONIO
Department of Zoology and Evolutionary Genetics, University of Sassari, Via Muroni 25, I-07100 Sassari, Italy

LINAS BALČIAUSKAS
Institute of Ecology of Vilnius University, Akademijos 2, LT-08412 Vilnius-21, Lithuania

PHILIPPE BALLON
Cemagref, Unité de Recherche 'Ecosystèmes Forestiers', Domaine des Barres, 45290 Nogent/Vernisson, France

PAOLO BANTI
Tuscany Region, Wildlife Management Unit, Via Di Novoli 26, I-50127 Firenze, Italy

LUDĚK BARTOŠ
Ethology Group, Institute of Animal Science (former Research Institute of Animal Production), Ethology Group, Přátelství 814, Praha 10- Uhříněves, 104 01, Czech Republic

ERIC BAUBET
Office National de la Chasse et de la Faune Sauvage, Direction des Études et de la Recherche, 85 bis avenue de Wagram, 75017 Paris, France

ROGER BERGSTRÖM
Forestry Research Institute of Uppsala, Uppsala Science Park, S-751 83 Uppsala, Sweden

CHRISTOPHE BONENFANT
Laboratoire de Biométrie et Biologie Évolutive, Unité Mixte de Recherche 5558, Université Claude Bernard Lyon 1, Bâtiment 711, 43 boulevard du 11 novembre 1918, 69622 Villeurbanne Cedex, France

TOMASZ BOROWIK
Mammal Research Institute, Polish Academy of Sciences, 17–230 Białowieża, Poland

JIM CASAER
Research Institute for Nature and Forestry, Scientific Institute of the Flemish Governement, Gaverstraat 4, 9500 Geraardsbergen, Beglium

JORGE CANCELA
General Directorate of Forestry Resources (DGRF). R. A. Quental, 167, 3000–032 Coimbra, Portugal

JUAN CARRANZA
Biology and Ethology, University of Extremadura, Cáceres, Spain

DUŠKO ĆIROVIĆ
Faculty of Biology, University of Belgrade, Belgrade, Serbia

SIMONE CIUTI
Department of Zoology and Evolutionary Genetics, University of Sassari, Via Muroni 25, I-07100 Sassari, Italy

SÁNDOR CSÁNYI
Institute for Wildlife Conservation, Szent István University, H-2103 Gödöllő, Hungary
Department of Wildlife Biology and Management, St. Stephen University, H-2103 Gödöllő, Hungary

PATRICK DUNCAN
Centre d'Études Biologiques de Chizé, CNRS UPR 1934, 79 360 Beauvoir-sur-Niort, France

CATARINA EIRA
Portuguese Wildlife Society, University of Minho, Campus de Gualtar, 4710-057 Braga, Portugal

HANS VON ESSEN
Swedish Association for Hunting and Wildlife Management, Sweden

JOANA FERREIRA
Portuguese Wildlife Society, University of Minho, Campus de Gualtar, 4710-057 Braga, Portugal

SLAVOMÍR FIND'O
Carpathian Wildlife Society, St. Tulská 29, SK-960 01 Zvolen, Slovakia

CARLOS FONSECA
Department of Biology/CESAM, University of Aveiro, Campus Santiago, 3810-193 Aveiro, Portugal

JEAN-MICHEL GAILLARD
Laboratoire de Biométrie et Biologie Évolutive, Unité Mixte de Recherche 5558, Université Claude Bernard Lyon 1, Bâtiment 711, 43 boulevard du 11 novembre 1918, 69622 Villeurbanne Cedex, France

HANS GANDER
WildARK, Tillierstrasse 6a, 3005 Bern, Switzerland

MATHIEU GAREL
Office National de la Chasse et de la Faune Sauvage, Direction des Études et de la Recherche, 85 bis avenue de Wagram, 75017 Paris, France Laboratoire de Biométrie et Biologie Évolutive, Unité Mixte de Recherche 5558, Université Claude Bernard Lyon 1, Bâtiment 711, 43 boulevard du 11 novembre 1918, 69622 Villeurbanne Cedex, France

GEERT W. T. A. GROOT BRUINDERINK
Alterra, Wageningen University and Research Centre WUR, P.O. Box 47, 6700 AA Wageningen, the Netherlands

MARK HEWISON
Laboratoire Comportement et Ecologie de la Faune Sauvage, Institut National de la Recherche Agronomique (INRA), BP 52627, F-31326 Castanet-Tolosan Cedex, France

VIDAR HOLTHE
Norwegian University of Science and Technology, Museum of Natural History and Archaeology, N-7491 Trondheim, Norway

NICOLE IMESCH-BEBIÉ
Federal Office for Environment, 3003 Bern, Switzerland

GJORGJE IVANOV
Macedonian Ecological Society, Skopje, Macedonia

BOGUMIŁA JĘDRZEJEWSKA
Mammal Research Institute, Polish Academy of Sciences, 17–230 Białowieża, Poland

WŁODZIMIERZ JĘDRZEJEWSKI
Mammal Research Institute, Polish Academy of Sciences, 17–230 Białowieża, Poland

KLEMEN JERINA
University of Ljubljana, Biotechnical Faculty, Department of Forestry and Renewable Forest Resources, Večna pot 83, 1000 Ljubljana, Slovenia

JONAS KINDBERG
Swedish University of Agricultural Sciences, Umeå, Sweden

ILPO KOJOLA
Finnish Game and Fisheries Research Institute, Finland

RADIM KOTRBA
Ethology Group, Institute of Animal Science (former Research Institute of Animal Production), Ethology Group, Přátelství 814, Praha 10-Uhříněves, 104 01, Czech Republic

KREŠIMIR KRAPINEC
Department of Forest Protection and Wildlife Management, Faculty of Forestry, University of Zagreb, Svetošimunska 25 HR-10002, Zagreb, Croatia

JOSIP KUSAK
Biology Department, Veterinary Faculty, University of Zagreb, Heinzelova 55 HR-10000 Zagreb, Croatia

RÓBERT LEHOCZKI
Institute for Wildlife Conservation, Szent István University, H-2103 Gödöllõ, Hungary

OLOF LIBERG
Swedish University of Agricultural Sciences, Grimsö Wildlife Research Station, S-730 91 Riddarhyttan, Sweden

ALAIN LICOPPE
Centre de Recherche de la Nature, des Forêts et du Bois, Laboratoire de la Faune sauvage et de Cynégétique, avenue Maréchal Juin 23, 5030 Gembloux, Belgium

JOHN D. C. LINNELL
Norwegian Institute for Nature Research, Tungasletta 2, N-7485 Trondheim, Norway

ANNE LOISON
Laboratoire de Biométrie et Biologie Évolutive, Unité Mixte de Recherche 5558, Université Claude Bernard Lyon 1, Bâtiment 711, 43 boulevard du 11 novembre 1918, 69622 Villeurbanne Cedex, France

ERIC LUND
Directorate for Nature Management, Tungasletta 2, N-7485 Trondheim, Norway

DANIEL MAILLARD
Office National de la Chasse et de la Faune Sauvage, Direction des Études et de la Recherche, 85 bis avenue de Wagram, 75017 Paris, France

DIME MELOVSKI
Macedonian Ecological Society, Skopje, Macedonia

ION MICU
Str. Gheorghe Doja, Nr. 21/A, Miercurea Ciuc, Jud. Harghita, Romania

ILIE MIHALACHE
Str. Locotenent Niculescu Romulus Bazar, Nr. 30, Sectorul II. Bucuresti, Romania

ANDRÁS NÁHLIK
Faculty of Forestry, University of West Hungary, Ady E. u. 5, H-9400 Sopron, Hungary

ŞERBAN NEGUŞ (DECEASED)
Str. Constantin Brancoveanu, Nr. 1 Brasov, Jud. Brasov, Romania

JĀNIS OZOLIŅŠ
State Forest Service, 13.Janvara Str. 15, Riga, LV-1932, Latvia

HARITAKIS PAPAIOANNOU
University of Ioannina, Department of Environmental and Natural Resources Management, Laboratory of Ecology and Biodiversity Conservation, Seferi 2, 30100 Agrinio, Greece

MILAN PAUNOVIĆ
Natural History Museum, Belgrade, Serbia

LUCA PEDROTTI
Stelvio National Park, Via Roma 65, I-38024 Cogolo di Peio – Trento, Italy

JAN PINTÍŘ
EUagroservis, Dvůr Svojšice s.r.o., Doudleby nad Orlicí 84, 517 42, Czech Republic

RORY PUTMAN
Keil House, Ardgour, by Fort William, Inverness-shire, PH33 7AH, UK

TIIT RANDVEER
Estonian Agricultural University, Kreutzwaldi 5, Tartu 51014, Estonia

FRIEDRICH REIMOSER
Research Institute of Wildlife Ecology, Vienna Veterinary University, Austria

SUSANNE REIMOSER
Research Institute of Wildlife Ecology, Vienna Veterinary University, Austria

VESA RUUSILA
Finnish Game and Fisheries Research Institute, Finland

BERNT-ERIK SÆTHER
Norwegian University of Science and Technology, Department of Biology, Realfagbygget, N-7491 Trondheim, Norway

CHRISTINE SAINT-ANDRIEUX
Office National de la Chasse et de la Faune Sauvage, Direction des Études et de la Recherche, 85 bis avenue de Wagram, 75017 Paris, France

REINHARD SCHNIDRIG-PETRIG
Federal Office for Environment, 3003 Bern, Switzerland

MICHAELA SKUBAN
Carpathian Wildlife Society, St. Tulská 29, SK-960 01 Zvolen, Slovakia

ERLING JOHAN SOLBERG
Norwegian Institute for Nature Research, Tungasletta 2, N-7485 Trondheim, Norway

ALEKSANDAR STOJANOV
Macedonian Ecological Society, Skopje, Macedonia

ISTVAN SZABO
Directia Silvică Miercurea Ciuc, Regia Națională a Pădurilor – Romsilva, Strada George Cosbuc 78, Miercurea Ciuc, 530211, Romania

CAROLE TOÏGO
Office National de la Chasse et de la Faune Sauvage, Direction des Études et de la Recherche, 85 bis avenue de Wagram, 75017 Paris, France

JURI TÕNISSON
Centre of Forest Protection and Silviculture, Rõõmu tee 2, Tartu 51013, Estonia

JOSÉ VINGADA
Department of Biology, University of Minho, Campus de Gualtar, 4710–057 Braga, Portugal

PIOTR WAWRZYNIAK
Regional Directorate of the State Forests, ul. Lipowa 51, 15–950 Białystok, Poland

SIPKE E. VAN WIEREN
Resource Ecology Group, Wageningen University, Bornsesteeg 69, 6708 PD Wageningen, Netherlands

ULRICH WOTSCHIKOWSKY
Deutingerstraße 15, D 82487 Oberammergau, Germany

1
Introduction

This book deals with the distribution and the management within Europe of wild ungulates, the largest terrestrial mammals occurring in most European countries. Within Europe as a whole, there are some 20 species (and many distinct subspecies). Some distinctive subspecies are very rare and require explicit management efforts for their conservation, but the majority of species are widespread and abundant, often reaching surprisingly high densities. In Austria, for example, in an area of some 85 000 km^2, the estimated number of ungulates is 1.26 million, i.e. nearly 15 animals per km^2. Given that most of these are forest dwelling animals, and that forests cover less than 50% of the land area, local densities may reach even higher high levels. Red deer densities in some parts of Scotland may reach as high as 45 deer per km^2. This, when combined with the potential for high impact on other components of ecological systems means that wild ungulates commonly have a dominant role in the structure and ecological dynamics of both natural and man-made ecosystems (e.g. Putman, 2004).

The fact that many species feed very selectively means that often they select some species and avoid others. They may, in consequence, substantially change the composition and relative abundance of the different components of the vegetation affecting the species composition and species diversity of many plant communities, as well as the age structure and physical structure (e.g. Putman, 1986, 2004).

An obvious outcome of this impact on the vegetation itself is that ungulates may also deeply influence animal communities, especially insects, birds and small rodent faunas (e.g. Hill, 1985; Putman, 1986, 1994; Putman et al., 1989; Petty and Avery, 1990; Feber et al., 2001; Fuller, 2001; Flowerdew and Ellwood, 2001; Suominen and Danell, 2006).

This may in turn have knock-on effects on populations of predators dependent on those animals for prey (Hirons, 1984; Hill, 1985; Putman, 1986, 1994; Petty and

Avery, 1990). In addition, of course, the ungulates themselves represent the main natural prey of larger carnivores that are presently increasing their distribution and numbers in many European countries. In this context, wild ungulates are not only relevant because they are the natural prey of wolves and European lynx and thus represent an essential prey base in conservation measures directed at encouraging the expansion of these species, but they also represent an alternative to predation on livestock (Meriggi and Lovari, 1996), one of the main sources of conflicts between large carnivores and humans (Gazzola et al., 2008).

Whatever their role in the ecological dynamics of natural or semi-natural systems, it is also recognised that the impacts of wild ungulate species can often cause conflict with human land-use objectives (e.g. Eiberle and Nigg, 1983; Putman and Moore, 1998; Putman, 2004; Ammer, 1996). Whereas in the past most reported damage from ungulates occured in agriculture (Gossow, 1983; Putman, 1989, 2004; Doney and Packer, 1998; Packer et al., 1999; Putman and Kjellander, 2002), now damage to forestry through browsing and bark stripping seems to be a major and increasing problem in many European countries (e.g. Mitchell et al., 1977; Mayer and Ott, 1991; Welch et al., 1991, 1992; Gill, 1992a, 1992b; van Hees et al., 1996; Reimoser, 2000). In areas with high densities of ungulates, young trees in particular may be heavily selected for and thus ungulates may also have a significant impact both in commercial plantations and in conservation areas, by reducing the chances of natural regeneration (e.g. Reimoser and Gossow, 1996; van Hees et al., 1996; Gill, 2006; Vera et al., 2006).

There is, in addition, increasing concern over damage to conservation habitats more generally (i.e. other than simply within woodlands) both in America (e.g. McShea et al., 1997; Rooney and Waller, 2003) and Europe (Putman, 2004) – as reflected more generally in the provisions of Directive 92/43/EEC on the Conservation of Natural Habitats.

Collisions of ungulates with motor vehicles (accidents with cars, trains, etc.) are also increasing (Groot Bruinderink and Hazebroek, 1996; Romin and Bissonette, 1996; Putman, 1997; Hedlund, 2003; Putman et al., 2004). Sickness transfer by wild ungulates to domestic animals and humans is also considered a severe problem for some pathologies (e.g. Bouvier, 1963; Delahay et al., 2002; Huitema, 1972, for bovine tuberculosis) even if their role has been reconsidered for others (e.g. Gray et al., 1992; Jaenson and Taalleklint, 1992, for Lyme disease).

Finally, in this brief review of the place that wild ungulates play in our lives – and the range of management issues that they raise – we should also remember that, while the majority of species are expanding in Europe in both range and distribution, some taxa are less favoured and themselves warrant explicit conservation attention, coupled with management measures deliberately designed to safeguard dwindling populations and encourage their recovery. Still other populations, however well-established, are threatened from a genetic point of view, due to repeated introductions of non-native individuals (in misguided attempts to 'improve' their qualities – usually as trophy animals – or bolster up populations perceived to be under threat) or through ongoing hybridisation with alien species (as, for example, hybridisation between red and sika deer in Great Britain, Eire, or the Czech Republic: Harrington, 1973, 1982; Ratcliffe *et al.*, 1992; Abernethy, 1994; Goodman *et al.*, 1999; Pemberton *et al.*, 2006).

For all the reasons outlined above, the need for effective policies for management of ungulate populations and their impacts at both a national and a European scale is abundantly obvious.

At the same time, we must place across this yet another 'strand': ungulate populations, which may build up biomasses exceeding 150 000 kg per 100 km^2, are also a significant economic resource in their own right, through the production of game meat and in recreational hunting (whether for venison or for trophies). Recreational hunting of ungulates is extremely important, both in sociological and in economic terms, and in many countries provides a very significant source of revenue. Ungulate populations thus represent a valuable resource, ecologically, economically and culturally, which should never be overlooked in determining appropriate strategies for management.

For such an important resource, and one with such a potential for a profound influence on the dynamics of both natural and man-made ecosystems, informed and effective management is absolutely crucial: a management based on thorough scientific understanding of the ecology and population dynamics of these species, and the wider systems of which they are a part.

In practice, current approaches to the management of ungulates are extremely diverse among European countries. This is in part due to differences in species present and their relative abundance, differences in the conflicts experienced between wild ungulate populations and other land-use interests and differences, in consequence, of whether or not management is primarily directed towards control, conservation or exploitation (by hunting). In addition, however (and particularly where management is carried out by 'volunteer' hunters), there are enormous variations in the cultural approach to hunting or game management, and strong national traditions in hunting practice.

Once again reflecting this diversity of objective and variety of national tradition, there are also marked differences between countries (often even between close neighbours!) in the legislative framework and regulations affecting hunting and wildlife management, while differences in patterns of land ownership, from mostly private to completely state ownership, have a profound effect on the organisation and integration of management activities. In some cases this may lead to extreme cases of opposite attitudes between bordering countries, resulting in a clear conflict of interest, often with negative consequences for the environment.

It is clear that while some of the differences in management practice and approach reflect differences in the objectives of management (or more usually, differences in priority of objectives) some differences are more 'arbitrary'. It is also apparent that, while some management approaches have been developed in a targeted way in order to tackle particular perceived problems of, say, agricultural or forest damage, in other cases, the problems *themselves* may actually arise as a consequence of inappropriate management practice.

While it is accepted that differences in legislation, differences in cultural tradition, together with differences in species of ungulates and objectives of management, will mean that management systems and management practices will often differ in different places, it is suggested that we should all work towards a more informed management, a management better designed to deliver the objectives sought – and at least learn something from each other's mistakes! Development of effective management in any one country might thus benefit enormously in learning from the experiences of others. Last, but not least, we consider of utmost importance a common approach in the management of populations shared by bordering countries or of taxonomic endangered units that are living in different nations. Taking into account all these factors we may foresee an attempt to reach a European perspective, not necessarily in the means adopted, but in the aims that are the ultimate goal of ungulate management, that is, biodiversity conservation.

For all of these reasons, we think it is time to promote a better knowledge of ungulates and their management within Europe. We believe this may help to reach better national management strategies and to develop a more integrated European management policy that will strengthen the conservation of healthy environments in Europe. We are convinced that only with open and informed comparisons of our different national experience will we be able in the future to avoid the serious mistakes that almost all nations have made in the past. This is especially true now as our environment is undergoing rapid changes. If successful, we will be in the position not only to achieve a more sensitive, and more effective management of ungulates in Europe but also to integrate wild ungulates and their management with the demanding requirements of the Agricultural Policy signed by the European Community and many non-members, and the wider conservation objectives established by the Rio Agreement.

This belief led us to bring together a group of expert scientists with special interest in applied ungulate ecology and specifically in ungulate management systems, at the International Conference Centre in Erice, Italy, in November 2004, to exchange information on the status and management of the ungulates in their respective countries and to discuss common problems and possible solutions. The conference was enormously successful, and we decided to extend upon this initiative by producing a book to review many of these same issues for a somewhat wider audience. At the same time we resolved to offer broader coverage of Europe as a whole. At the conference itself, presentations were received from representatives of some 11 different European countries; for this book we have drawn together contributions describing ungulate populations and their management in 28 different countries (almost all countries of the EU plus Norway, Switzerland and Croatia).

This book thus aims to present an overview of wild ungulate populations throughout Europe: species composition, numbers and distribution, as well as considering current management practices in different countries and problems experienced – either with the impacts of ungulates themselves, or in controlling those impacts. The book is deliberately constructed to highlight similarities and differences, to try to show how successes or failures of management may be correlated with a particular approach to that management, and finally to seek to learn from the successes and failures of others, which management approaches work in which circumstances – and which do not.

The book is targeted at managers themselves, those involved in the actual management of wild ungulate populations on the ground, but also at policymakers, those who create the administrative and legislative framework within which such management activity must be undertaken, since so often this regulatory context affects what management options may be available.

Quite deliberately, no attempt is made within the current volume to offer a detailed synthesis of this diverse body of material. Our main aim was, explicitly, to draw together in one place a convenient single source of reference for the primary information itself – and with the book already extending to some 27 chapters as it is, an equivalent 'weight' of synthesis would render the work so large as to be virtually unusable. In addition, we wished to make the material available to a wider readership as soon as possible. For now, therefore, we must leave readers to make their own contrasts and comparisons, and to draw their own inferences and conclusions.

However, a companion volume is already in preparation which will, in due course, offer a more comprehensive analysis and overview of various topics. Exploring, for example, the variation in hunting seasons in different countries – the apparent mismatch between hunting seasons and biological seasons in most cases – and the implications that this may have for achieving effective management; other constraints on management imposed by national and international law; the impact of ungulates on agriculture, forestry and conservation habitats, and management options; the problems posed by ungulate–vehicle collisions and the mitigation measures available; large carnivores and the impact of predation on populations of wild ungulates; large ungulates as vectors of disease; and the role of diseases in limiting or regulating ungulate populations.

In the meantime, we hope the present volume, as a compendium of information on ungulates and their management in 28 different European countries, will help to stimulate informed debate and improved management of this valuable resource. We truly hope that this will begin a process through which we may be able to improve our future management of this valuable resource into the twenty-first century.

Disclaimer

We live in changing times and, with 28 countries covered within the pages of this book, it is inevitable that something changes somewhere. As one Polish correspondent wryly remarked to the editors: 'In Poland hunters are never bored. The law changes every few years!' Even at the final stages of editing of this book, hunting seasons changed in England and Eire – and more changes are to be anticipated in the shelf-life of such a volume. While every effort has been made to ensure that the information presented in this book is accurate as we go to press, information on legislation and administrative structures must be taken as indicative only and not definitive. We believe the facts to be accurate as we write, but they may nonetheless be subject to future change; anyone requiring up to date information on, for example, hunting seasons, permitted weapons, licensing arrangements, etc., should not rely on details presented in these pages, but should seek independent confirmation of the current situation from the specific country concerned.

Acknowledgements

First of all we would like to thank all the colleagues in 28 European countries that have been involved as authors.

We also thank Ettore Majorana Foundation and Centre for Scientific Culture of Erice and the Director of the School of Ethology, Prof Danilo Mainardi who gave us the apportunity to hold the meeting on ungulate management in Europe in November 2004.

We have received economic support from the Italian Ministry of Environment and the Directorate for Nature Management in Norway.

Chapter layout

The essence of this book is to offer a review of the situation in each of the different European countries in relation to

1. status of wild ungulate populations,
2. administrative and regulatory systems and constraints,

3. current management practices and
4. problems arising from ungulate impacts, or problems with current management systems

Since contributions cover no fewer than 28 different countries, contributing authors were therefore asked to prepare their accounts according to a particular format in order to both ensure that all relevant topics were addressed in each account, and to better facilitate speedy comparison between countries (since the immediately comparable material will be presented in the same subsection for each chapter).

Inevitably, in some cases this 'fixed framework' leads to some stiltedness in presentation, or some repetition within chapters; in other cases, the need to address a particular topic which is not relevant to a particular area may be solved simply by saying that there is no information available, or the topic is not applicable in that particular country, but we felt that such disadvantages were more than outweighed by the advantages offered in terms of ready comparison between different countries.

The reader will thus find that all chapters share this common format, and treat topics according to the following framework:

- **Introduction to the country and the ungulate species present**
    1. **Individual species accounts**

       For each species present: history (native or introduced), history of distribution, current distribution. Where known, genetic status and estimated number of individuals for each species.
    2. **Legislation affecting management**
    3. **Management objectives**

       Is management/hunting primarily directed towards sport/recreation, for control of damage, for venison production/harvest, or for conservation management?
    4. **Management structure**

       Who does the management? Is it largely state-controlled managers/rangers, or is it mostly done by private individuals? Is there any overall (state-managed, or voluntary) coordination of management activities, at local, regional or national level.
    5. **Management organisation**

       Size of management unit, hunting licences cost if applicable, hunting examination, numbers of hunters, numbers of ungulate hunters.
    6. **Actual management and hunting practices**

       Are censuses or shooting plans required by law? Are records kept of hunting bag statistics? Actual hunting practices and general description.
    7. **Census types and methods**
    8. **Ungulate impacts and damage**

       Damage caused by ungulates to agriculture, to forestry or to conservation habitats; road accidents involving ungulates. Estimated value of damage and economic significance.
    9. **Supplementary feeding**

       Species fed, distribution of the practice in the country, aims.

10. **Effectiveness of current management strategies**
    Each chapter ends with a section where the authors were invited to consider problems with current management and suggest possible changes in management approach for the future.

Management of wild ungulate populations: clarification of English language terminology

Clearly, people of different nationalities use technical terms in ways which may show subtle differences of actual meaning. In translating this book into English we have again tried to standardise terminology to current English usage. This may, however, mean that in their usage here some technical terms have a rather different meaning than where used elsewhere. To help readers who may be used to using these terms in a rather different way, we present a short glossary of usages adopted in this book.

Hunting/hunter: In English, these words carry the implication of recreation/pleasure, rather than simply management, and imply that people take pleasure in the killing itself, rather than simply using it as a management tool to control population size. However, in the majority of European countries the two terms are interchangeable, and use of the word 'hunter' simply implies a person who shoots game (for whatever goal).

Culling/to cull: To kill animals during the process of management of the population for control or exploitation. Usually, the implication is killing for control.

Control/controlling: Again a useful word for attempts directed at influencing/affecting the size of an animal population. It implies efforts to reduce numbers or at least to stop them increasing.

Harvest/harvesting: By whatever method (rifle, shotgun, bow, trap, etc.), the implication in the use of this word is *sustainable exploitation* of the population concerned.

Management: The *concept* of 'taking responsibility for' or influencing the dynamics of animal or plant populations, and the *activities* associated with that.

Manager: One who is responsible for, or involved in the management of wildlife populations.

Native/Introduced/Exotic:

Although the words **autochthonous**, or **allochthonous** are used by some continental authors, in English these words are archaic and not in current usage. In this book we use the words.

Native: to imply a population which is considered to have had continuous presence in a given area (= autochthonous).

Introduced: to imply a species which could occur in any geographic region but in practice is not native in that particular country and has been introduced within historic time by humans.

Exotic: to imply a species introduced by humans well outside its natural geographic distribution.

Status: The word status is used to refer to the numerical abundance of a species and whether it is abundant and/or widespread, or whether it is rare or threatened.

Composition: In relation to community or population structure, a more suitable word would be composition. Thus we talk of the 'species composition' of a community, or the age- and sex-composition of a population.

(These two words (status and composition) are thus used throughout this book to replace the usage by some authors of the word '**consistency**' which, in this particular context, is not correct English.)

Provisioning/artificial feeding/foraging: One regular source of confusion that emerged during editing of these chapters was use of the word 'foraging'. In English, 'foraging' is used for natural grazing by the animals themselves, and literally means the activity of searching for and consuming natural foodstuffs. For artificial provision of additional or supplementary foodstuffs at different periods of the year, we would talk about 'artificial feeding' (if it was intended to supply 100% of all needs), or 'supplementary feeding'. Very occasionally one might see the word 'provisioning' (meaning the providing of feed), but this is not usual.

In this book,

Foraging: implies therefore natural grazing by the animals themselves

Provisioning/artificial feeding: implies the provision of artificial feedstuffs to wildlife populations

Supplementary feeding: As above, but here the clear implication is that feeding is in addition to natural feed available, and a supplement only. It does not attempt to provide 100% of nutritional requirements.

Latin binomials

In this book, common names are used through the text except where the latter are used to identify a particular subspecies. Species implied are:

Cervidae:
Chinese muntjac	*Muntiacus reevesi*
Chinese water deer	*Hydropotes inermis*
Moose	*Alces alces*
Reindeer	*Rangifer tarandus*
Roe deer	*Capreolus capreolus*
White-tailed deer	*Odocoileus virginianus*

Red deer	*Cervus elaphus*
Sika deer	*Cervus nippon*
Wapiti	*Cervus canadensis*
Fallow deer	*Dama dama*
Axis (or chital)	*Axis axis*
	and their subspecies

Bovidae/Ovidae:

European bison, or wisent	*Bison bonasus*
Musk ox	*Ovibos moschatus*
Alpine chamois	*Rupicapra rupicapra*
Pyrenean chamois	*Rupicapra pyrenaica*
Barbary sheep	*Ammotragus lervia*
Mouflon	*Ovis orientalis musimon*
Alpine Ibex	*Capra ibex*
Spanish ibex	*Capra pyrenaica*
Wild goat	*Capra aegagrus*
	and their subspecies

Suidae:

Wild boar	*Sus scrofa*

References

Abernethy, K. (1994) The establishment of a hybrid zone between red and sika deer (genus *Cervus*). *Molecular Ecology* **3**, 551–62.

Ammer, C. (1996) Impact of ungulates on structure and dynamics of natural regeneration of mixed mountain forests in the Bavarian Alps. *Forestry Ecology and Management* **88**, 43–53.

Bouvier, G. (1963) Transmision possible de la Tuberculose et de la Brucellose du gibier a l'homme et aux animaux domestiques et sauvages. *Bulletin de l'Office International des Epizooties* **59**, 433–6.

Danell, K., Bergstrøm, R., Duncan, P. and Pastor, J. (2006) Large herbivore ecology, ecosystem dynamics and conservation. Volume 11 of *Series Conservation Biology*. Cambridge, UK: Cambridge University Press.

Delahay, R. J., de Leeuw, A. N. S., Barlow, A. M., Clifton-Hadley, R. S. and Cheeseman, C. L. (2002) The status of *Mycobacterium bovis* infection in UK wild mammals: a review. *The Veterinary Journal* **164**, 90–105.

Doney, J. and Packer, J. (1998) An assessment of the impact of deer on agriculture. In C. R. Goldspink, S. King and R. J. Putman, eds., *Population Ecology, Management and Welfare of Deer*. Manchester, UK: British Deer Society/Universities' Federation for Animal Welfare, pp. 38–43.

Eiberle, K. and Nigg, H. (1983) Über die Folgen des Wildverbisses an Fichte und Weisstanne in montaner. *Lage. Schweizerische. Zeitschrift. Forstwesen.* **134**, 361–72.

Feber, R. E., Brereton, T. M., Warren, M. S. and Oates, M. (2001) The impacts of deer on woodland butterflies: the good, the bad and the complex. *Forestry* **74**, 271–6.

Flowerdew, J. R. and Ellwood, S. A. (2001) Impacts of woodland deer on small mammal ecology. *Forestry* **74**, 277–88.

Fuller, R. J. (2001) Responses of woodland birds to increasing numbers of deer: a review of evidence and mechanisms. *Forestry* **74**, 289–98.

Gazzola, A., Capitani, C., Mattioli, L. and Apollonio, M. (2008) Livestock damage and wolf presence. *Journal of Zoology* **274**, 261–9.

Gill, R. M. A. (1990) *Monitoring the Status of European and North American Cervids.* GEMS Information Series, 8. Nairobi: Global Environment Monitoring Systems, United Nations Environment Programme, 277pp.

Gill, R. M. A. (1992a) A review of damage by mammals in north temperate forests I: deer. *Forestry* **65**, 145–69.

Gill, R. M. A. (1992b) A review of damage by mammals in north temperate forests 3: impact on trees and forests. *Forestry* **65**, 363–88.

Gill, R. (2006) The influence of large herbivores on tree recruitment and forest dynamics. In K. Danell, R. Bergstrøm, P. Duncan and J. Pastor, eds., *Large Herbivore Ecology, Ecosystem Dynamics and Conservation*. Cambridge, UK: Cambridge University Press, pp. 170–202.

Goodman, S., Barton, N., Swanson, G., Abernethy, K. and Pemberton, J. (1999) Introgression through rare hybridization: a genetic study of a hybrid zone betweeen red and sika deer (genus *Cervus*) in Argyll, Scotland. *Genetics* **152**, 355–71.

Gossow, H. (1983) Zur geschichtlichen Entwicklung der Beziehungen zwischen Jagd und Waldwirtschaft. *Cbl. Gesamte Forstwesens* **100**, 191–207.

Gray, J. S., Kahl, O., Janetzki, C., Stein, J. (1992) Studies on the ecology of Lyme disease in a deer forest in County Galway, Ireland. *Journal of Medical Entomology* **29**(66), 915–20.

Jaenson, T. G. T. and Tälleklint, L. (1992) Incompetence of roe deer as reservoirs of the Lyme borreliosis spirochete. *Journal of Medical Entomology* **29**(55), 813–17.

Harrington, R. (1973) Hybridisation among deer and its implications for conservation. *Irish Forestry Journal* **30**, 64–78.

Harrington, R. (1982) The hybridisation of red deer (*Cervus elaphus* L. 1758) and Japanese sika deer (*C. nippon* Temminck, 1838). *International Congress of Game Biologists* **14**, 559–71.

Groot Bruinderink, G. W. T. A. and Hazebroek, E. (1996) Ungulate traffic collisions in Europe. *Conservation Biology* **10**, 1059–67.

Hedlund, J. H., Curtis, G., Williams, A. F. (2003) *Methods to Reduce Traffic Crashes Involving Deer: What Works and What Does Not*. Arlington, VA: Insurance Institute for Highway Safety.

Hill, S. D. (1985) *Influences of Large Herbivores on Small Rodents in the New Forest*. PhD thesis, University of Southampton.

Hirons, G. J. M. (1984) The diet of tawny owls (*Strix aluco*) and kestrels (*Falco tinnunculus*) in the New Forest, Hampshire. *Proceedings of the Hampshire Field Club and Archaeological Society* **40**, 21–6.

Huitema, H. (1972) Tuberculosis in animals other than cattle domesticated and wild: its relation to bovine tuberculosis eradication and its public health significance. *First International Seminar on Bovine TB for the Americas* **258**, 79–88.

Mayer, H. and Ott, E. (1991) *Gebirgswaldbau Schutzwaldpflege*. Stuttgart-New York: Fischer Verlag.

McShea, W. J., Underwood, H. B. and Rappole, J. H. (1997) *The Science of Overabundance: Deer Ecology and Population Management*. Washington D.C.: Smithsonian Institute.

Meriggi, A. and Lovari, S. (1996) A review of wolf predation in Southern Europe: does wolf prefer wild prey to livestock? *Journal of Applied Ecology* **33**, 1561–71.

Mitchell, B., Staines, B. W. and Welch, D. (1977) *Ecology of Red Deer: A Research Review Relevant to their Management*. Cambridge: Institute of Terrestrial Ecology.

Packer, J. J., Doney, J., Mayle, B. A., Palmer, C. F. and Cope, M. (1999) *Field and Desk Studies to Assess Tolerable Damage Levels for Different Habitats and Species of Deer*. Report to the UK Ministry of Agriculture, Fisheries and Foods on contract VC 0315.

Pemberton, J., Swanson, G., Barton, N., Livingstone, S. and Senn, H. (2006) Hybridisation between red and sika deer in Scotland. *Deer* **13**, 22–6.

Petty, S. J. and Avery, M. I. (1990) *Forest Bird Communities*. Occasional Paper 26. Edinburgh: Forestry Commission.

Putman, R. J. (1986) *Grazing in Temperate Ecosystems: Large Herbivores and their Effects on the Ecology of the New Forest*. London: Croom Helm/Chapman and Hall.

Putman, R. J. (1989) *Mammals as Pests*. London: Chapman and Hall.

Putman, R. J. (1994) Effects of grazing and browsing by mammals in woodlands. *British Wildlife* **5**, 205–13.

Putman, R. J. (1996) *Competition and Resource Partitioning in Temperate Ungulate Assemblies*. London: Chapman and Hall.

Putman, R. J. (1997) Deer and road traffic accidents: options for management. *Journal of Environmental Management* **51**, 43–57.

Putman, R. J. (2004) *The Deer Manager's Companion: A Guide to Deer Management in the Wild and in Parks*. Shropshire, UK: Swan Hill Press.

Putman, R. J. and Kjellander, P. (2002) Deer damage to cereals: economic significance and predisposing factors. In F. Tattersall and W. Manly, eds., *Farming and Mammals*. London: Linnaean Society of London Occasional Publications.

Putman, R. J. and Moore, N. P. (1998) Impact of deer in lowland Britain on agriculture, forestry and conservation habitats. *Mammal Review* **28**, 141–64.

Putman, R. J., Edwards, P. J., Mann, J. C. E., How, R. C. and Hill, S. D. (1989) Vegetational and faunal changes in an area of heavily grazed woodland following relief of grazing. *Biological Conservation* **47**, 13–32.

Putman, R. J., Langbein, J. and Staines, B. W. (2004) *Deer and Road Traffic Accidents: A Review of Mitigation Measures. Costs and Cost-effectiveness*. Contract report RP23A. Deer Commission, Inverness, Scotland.

Ratcliffe, P. R., Peace, A. J., Hewison, A. J. M., Hunt, E. J. and Chadwick, A. H. (1992) The origins and characterization of Japanese sika deer populations in Great Britain. In N. Maruyama, ed., *Wildlife Conservation: Present Trends and Perspectives for the 21st Century*. Tokyo Japan: Wildlife Research Center, pp. 185–90.

Reimoser, F. (2000) Income from hunting in mountain forests of the Alps. In M. F. Price and N. Butt, eds., *Forests in Sustainable Mountain Development: A State-of-Knowledge Report for 2000*. IUFRO Research Series 5. New York: CABI Publishing, 346–53.

Reimoser, F. and Gossow, H. (1996) Impact of ungulates on forest vegetation and its dependence on the silvicultural system. *Forest Ecology and Management* **88**, 107–19.

Romin, L. A. and Bissonette, J. A. (1996) Deer-vehicle collisions: status of state monitoring activities and mitigation efforts. *Wildlife Society Bulletin* **24**, 276–83.

Rooney, T. P. and Waller, D. M. (2003) Direct and indirect effects of white-tailed deer in forest ecosystems. *Forest Ecology and Management* **181**, 165–76.

Scottish Natural Heritage/Deer Commission for Scotland (2002) *Wild Deer In Scotland and Damage to the Natural Heritage*.

Smith, B. L. and Roffe, T. (1992) Diseases among elk of the Yellowstone ecosystem. In W. van Hoven, H. Ebedes and A. Conroy, eds., *Wildlife Ranching: A Celebration of Diversity*. Pretoria, South Africa: University of Pretoria Centre for Wildlife Management, pp. 162–6.

Suominen, O. and Danell, K. (2006) Effects of large herbivores on other fauna. In K. Danell, R. Bergstrøm, P. Duncan and J. Pastor, eds., *Large Herbivore Ecology, Ecosystem Dynamics and Conservation*. Cambridge, UK: Cambridge University Press, pp. 383–412.

van Hees, F. M., Kuiters, L. A. T. and Slim, P. A. (1996) Effects of browsing on silver birch, pedunculate oak and beech regeneration. *Forest Ecology and Management* **88**, 55–64.

Vera, F. W. M. (2000) *Grazing Ecology and Forest History*. Wellingford Oxon, UK: CABI Publishing.

Vera, F. W. M, Bakker, E. S. and Olff, H. (2006) Large herbivores; missing partners of western European light-demanding tree and scrub species? In K. Danell, R. Bergstrøm, P. Duncan and J. Pastor, eds., *Large Herbivore Ecology, Ecosystem Dynamics and Conservation*. Cambridge, UK: Cambridge University Press, pp. 203–31.

Welch, D., Staines, B. W., Scott, D., French, D. D. and Catt, D. C. (1991) Leader browsing by red and roe deer on young sitka spruce trees in western Scotland I. Damage rates and the influence of habitat factors. *Forestry* **64**, 61–82.

Welch, D., Staines, B. W., Scott, D. and French, D. D. (1992) Leader browsing by red and roe deer on young sitka spruce trees in Western Scotland. II Effects on growth and tree form. *Forestry* **65**, 309–30.

2

Ungulates and their management in Norway

REIDAR ANDERSEN, ERIK LUND, ERLING JOHAN SOLBERG
AND BERNT-ERIK SÆTHER

2.1 History, present distribution and genetic origin of ungulate species in Norway

There are five different species of ungulates in Norway: moose, red deer, wild reindeer and roe deer which are all native species, and the musk ox which is an introduced species. In addition, wild boar are occasionally sighted in southern Norway, close to the Swedish border, while fallow deer and mouflon are farmed at several localities.

2.1.1 Moose

The oldest fossil record of moose in Norway dates from approximately 8500 BP. One theory is that the moose have followed two different dispersal routes in colonising Norway: one from the south, through Denmark; and the second (a later colonisation event) from the northeast through Finland and northern parts of Sweden (Ryman *et al.*, 1980). This theory has lead to speculations about the existence of two different variants of moose in Scandinavia (Markgren, 1974). Several studies have shown that there is significant variation in life history variables between moose in northern and southern parts of Norway and Sweden. However, this variation has been related to environmental variables (e.g. Sæther and Haagenrud, 1985; Sand, 1996), and not to genetic differences.

The moose has always been an important game species in Norway, and various forms of hunting have led the moose to the brink of local extinction several times. As early as 1274, the use of skis during moose hunting was prohibited, but the first total ban of hunting did not occur until 1818, and was then in effect only for six years. At this time, some hunting pitfall systems were still in use, guns were widely

Fig. 2.1 Present distribution of wild large herbivores in Norway

distributed, and the populations of large ungulates were generally at a minimum on the Scandinavian Peninsula.

Over the last 50 years, the status of moose has changed from being a relatively rare species to becoming a widely distributed and dominant species all over the forested part of Scandinavia (Fig. 2.1). From harvesting approximately 6000 individuals annually in Norway in the start of the 1970s, more than 37 000 (4 moose per 1000 ha forest) were harvested in the most recent years (Fig. 2.2). There are

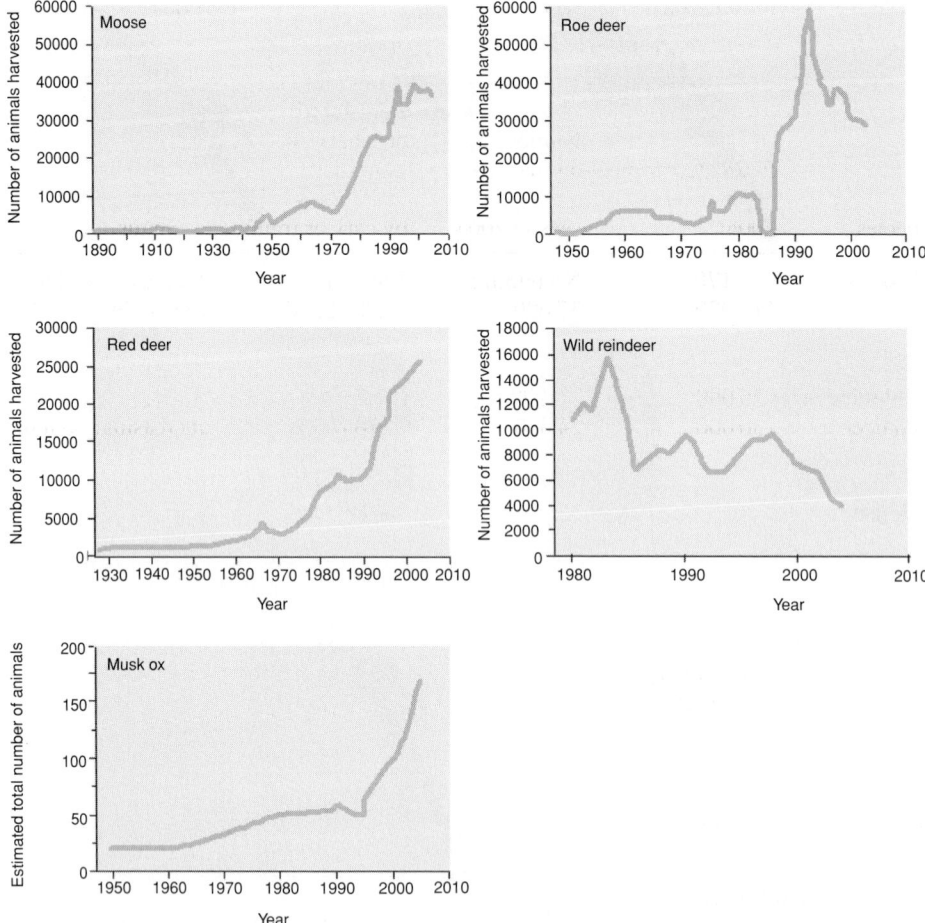

Fig. 2.2 Annual number of harvested cervids (moose, reindeer, red deer and roe deer), and estimated number of musk ox in Norway

no formal census figures available, but this strong increase in harvest presumably reflects some similar increase in population size, and appears to have several causes, with the absence of wolves and bears, changing practices in forestry (increasing frequency of clear cuts) and the introduction of sex- and age-specific harvesting probably being the most important.

2.1.2 Red deer

Europe has six subspecies of red deer. The Norwegian subspecies, *Cervus elaphus atlanticus*, is smaller than red deer in Central and Eastern Europe (*C. e. hippelaphus*), but bigger than its nearest relative, *C. e. scoticus*. The general pattern of a small genetic divergence between subspecies, but a high fraction of

Table 2.1 *Summary of estimated population size, number of animals shot and killed in traffic, and population status of large ungulates in Norway 2004*

Species	Estimated winter population size 2004[1]	Number of animals shot during hunting season 2004	Registered non-harvest mortality 2003/2004 (killed by cars or trains)	Status
Musk ox	170	No hunting	See text	Increasing/stable
Moose	110 000	37 000	3 280 (2200)	Stable, but a slight increase in distribution
Wild reindeer	25 000	6 500	37 (7)	Stable
Red deer	130 000	24 000	970 (640)	Increasing, both in numbers and distribution
Roe deer		30 000	3 990 (3 400)	Variable, but increase in distribution

[1] Musk ox and wild reindeer: based on direct counts from ground and air; red deer and moose: estimated using known population growth rate, number of animals shot and data from the observation inventory system.

the total gene diversity distributed between them, may indicate that founder effects and genetic drift have influenced the recent evolution of the north European red deer (Gyllensten *et al.*, 1983).

Archaeological data show that the animal was present in Norway 4500 BP, and nearly all fossil records are found along the western coast, even north of the present day distribution (Fig. 2.1). Historical data indicate that semi-domesticated red deer were present in some of the northernmost areas in the sixteenth century. In the following centuries, the red deer population went through a steady decrease until 1850, presumably due to predation, human persecution and grazing by livestock. Early in the twentieth century, red deer were only found in seven more or less isolated areas along the west coast of Norway, and several local and regional hunting regulations were established. Since 1971, the red deer population in Norway has increased gradually, except for a slight hiatus in 1985 and 1986. If we may assume that hunting statistics reflect the population trend, a seven-fold increase occurred between 1971 and 2000 (Fig. 2.2). Official hunting statistics can be found back to 1892, where 213 animals were culled. Until World War I, between 84 and 371 animals were culled annually. In 1970, the total red deer population in Norway was estimated at about 20 000 animals, while 34 years later in 2004, the population size before hunting was estimated to be more than 130 000 (Table 2.1).

Several factors are likely to be involved in the strong population increase in red deer. There has been less utilisation of wild land, less competition with livestock, increased availability of winter food, increased mean temperatures and increased height of forest line, which have all improved the food situation. In addition, establishment of conifer tree plantations in western Norway during the 1950s and 1960s has increased access to habitats with excellent cover. However, most important are changes in hunting practice, especially under the old Hunting Act of 1951 (replaced by the Wildlife Act of 1981), which introduced new principles for permits (need to have land), and the introduction of selective harvesting in the 1970s, focusing the culling on young animals and adult males.

2.1.3 Roe deer

Roe deer have been present in northern Europe since the late Preboreal period 9500 BP (Lepiskaar, 1986). Studies of mt-DNA (Vernesi *et al.*, 2002) indicate that three different refugia existed for roe deer, and that the French, Spanish and Norwegian roe deer share much of the same genetic material. Thus, the present roe deer in Norway appear to be descendants from roe deer that survived the last ice age in a refugium on the Iberian Peninsula.

After periods with considerable population fluctuations throughout the Holocene, roe deer nearly went extinct in the seventeenth century, and in Scandinavia, only some 200 individuals survived in the southernmost part of Sweden (Hagström, 1988). From this restricted area, roe deer started their expansion in 1850. After 75 years, roe deer were established in central Norway, 880 km further north; an expansion rate of 11.7 km per year. Heading further northwards in Norway, they expanded more than 500 km in 50 years (10.4 km per year). In contrast, a much lower expansion rate was found in more optimal habitat along the southern coast of the Scandinavian Peninsula. In the first four decades of the twentieth century, expansion rates were less than 1 km per year (Andersen *et al.*, 2004).

Today, roe deer can be found in all 19 counties in Norway (Fig. 2.1). However, in the western parts and in the three northernmost counties, there are only small local populations. The distribution and population size of roe deer in marginal habitats fluctuates according to the winter severity (Grøtan *et al.*, 2005) and lynx predation. However, local extinctions are normally soon followed by re-colonisation from source populations inhabiting better habitats.

In the last parts of the 1980s mild winters and low density of red fox (which is the main predator on roe deer fawns) due to a sarcoptic mange outbreak (Lindstrøm *et al.*, 1994), resulted in a rapid growth in the roe deer populations (Cederlund and Liberg, 1995). The highest number of shot roe deer ever recorded in Norway was 59 600 animals in 1993 (Statistics Norway, 2002; Fig. 2.2). Subsequently, more severe winters with high snow accumulation, increased populations of red fox and lynx, and hunting by humans led to a decrease in population densities (Mysterud and Østbye, 2006), indicated by a yearly culling of *c.* 30 000 animals in the period 2000–2004 (Table 2.1).

2.1.4 Wild reindeer

Reindeer or caribou (*Rangifer tarandus*) are distributed throughout the northern Holarctic, and were probably the key species permitting the human immigration and colonisation of the Arctic and sub-Arctic following the retreat of the ice in the last glacial. Reindeer in Fennoscandia are almost continuously distributed in the mountains and tundra regions and exist both as semi-domestic herds and as wild populations. However, wild reindeer are only distributed in the mountain region in southern Norway; these are at present managed in 23 different management units (Fig. 2.1).

Wild reindeer have been in Norway and the rest of Fennoscandia since the glaciers retreated 9–10 000 years ago. At the start of the eighteenth century wild reindeer could be found in all mountainous areas in Finland, Sweden and Norway. However, increased ranging of semi-domestic reindeer, and heavy hunting pressure in the eighteenth and nineteenth centuries, led to the disappearance of wild reindeer in Finland, Sweden and northern parts of Norway. In 1920 the estimated number of wild reindeer was 2700 animals; numbers have, however, increased since and the present estimated winter population of wild reindeer is of 33 000 animals (excluding the northernmost populations in Spitsbergen, which numbers about 8500 animals (Jordhøy *et al.*, 1996; Fig. 2.2)).

Previous studies with use of protein polymorphism (Røed *et al.*, 1987; Røed, 1998) and more recent analyses using DNA microsatellite loci show significant genetic structuring among Scandinavian reindeer populations, particularly between the wild populations on one hand and the domestic herds on the other. Furthermore, the marked genetic dichotomy between the wild herds inhabiting the southern part of their range (Hardangervidda and Setesdal-Ryfylke) and the northern (Dovre and Rondane), respectively, may suggest a different post-glacial origin of the populations living in these regions (Røed *in prep*). Historical records (Asbjørnsen, 1852; Friis, 1876) also indicate a distribution pattern with no detectable migration between northern and southern populations in the seventeenth to nineteenth centuries.

Recently, Flagstad and Røed (2003) assessed the phylogeography of reindeer, worldwide, as revealed from sequence variability patterns in the DNA mitochondrial control region. Three major haplogroups were detected, presumably representing three separate populations during the last glacial period. The most influential one has contributed to the gene pool of all extant subspecies and seems to represent a large and continuous glacial population extending from Beringia and far into Eurasia. A smaller, more localized refugium was most likely isolated in connection with ice expansion in western Eurasia. A third glacial refugium was presumably located south of the ice sheet in North America, possibly comprising several separate refugial populations.

Although widely distributed in the Arctic/Alpine, *Rangifer* and their habitats are under increasing pressure from natural resources exploitation and anthropogenic activities (UNEP, 2001). Due to habitat fragmentation and increased tourism in both wild and domestic reindeer habitats in Norway and the fact that Norway maintains most of the remaining European wild reindeer, the Norwegian Directorate for Nature Management (DN) has declared wild reindeer as a priority species for national conservation efforts (DN-Report, 1999: 21).

2.1.5 Musk ox

Musk ox (*Ovibos moschatus*) has not occurred naturally in Norway since the last ice age. The first animals were introduced from Greenland as early as 1932, but all animals disappeared during World War II. In the period 1947–53, 27 calves and yearlings from East Greenland were introduced to Dovre Mountains in Central Norway (Fig. 2.1).

By the end of August 1953 probably only 10 individuals were alive (Alendal, 1972). In the next two decades the population reached 40 individuals. In 1971, five animals dispersed eastwards to the border areas between Norway and Sweden, and these animals were the founders of a small population in that region, increasing to 34 animals in 1985 (Lundh, 1992); however only six animals were still alive in 2004 (Rehnfeldt, *pers. obs*). In Norway, the population increased to 51 animals in 1978, but was reduced to 36 animals in 1983 after irregular mortality (avalanches, lightning). Since that time, however, there has been a steady increase to 170 animals before calving in spring 2005 (Asbjørnsen *et al.*, 2005, Fig. 2.2). The main population is still utilising a restricted area close to where they were introduced.

A total of 262 dead animals have been documented in the period 1953–2005 (Gundersen *et al.*, 2005). Of these, 30% were shot for public safety reasons, 26% were killed in vehicle collisions (all but one involving trains), 8% died from disease, while 50 animals (19%) died or were lost from the population from a range of other causes including accidents, trauma, dispersal/translocation, poisoning and anaesthesia. Forty-three animals (16%) died from unknown causes.

The musk ox is treated as an introduced species, but is managed according to the Norwegian Wildlife Act within a defined area in Dovre Mountains, with the County Governor's Office of South Trøndelag as the responsible management agency.

However, it is a general feature of the resolutions in the Wildlife Act (see section 2.2) that they could not be used in development of a routine management policy for musk ox, but only to justify culling under certain conditions.

2.2 Legislation

Norway has been an active participant in the development and implementation of the International Convention on Biological Diversity. In a recent strategic document for the Directorate for Nature Management, it is stated that nature management in Norway should be based on the concept of integrated ecosystem management and the so called Malawi principles that were formulated in a workshop in Lilongwe, Malawi, in January 1998 (Convention of Biological Diversity, 1998).

Some of the most relevant principles are:

- Management objectives are a matter of societal choice
- Management should be decentralised to the lowest appropriate level
- A key feature of the ecosystem approach includes conservation of ecosystem structure and functioning
- The ecosystem approach should seek the appropriate balance between conservation and use of biodiversity

The Wildlife Act of 1981 emphasises that the concept of *sustainable use* should underpin all wildlife management in Norway. The most important principle is that all game species, including their eggs, nests and lairs, are protected unless otherwise stated by law or decisions pursuant to the legislation. The Wildlife Act has been modified several times since its introduction in 1981, due to changes in national policy and for the inclusion of new knowledge. The last change occurred in 2000.

The Directorate for Nature Management prescribes the hunting season for all species and defines also in which areas hunting are permitted (Table 2.2).

No hunting is allowed on any species on specific days during Christmas and Easter. Where serious damage has been caused (or may be anticipated) to timber or crops, or to the natural heritage, the municipality may relax regulations of hunting season, and owners/occupiers or others authorised by them may kill a certain number of animals.

For hunting moose, red deer, wild reindeer and musk ox, only rifles are permitted. This also applies to male roe deer between 10 August and 25 September, although shotguns are permitted for roe bucks at other times, and also for roe does.

For moose, red deer and roe deer, it is forbidden to use semi-automatic rifles with more than three cartridges (two for wild reindeer) in the magazine and one in the chamber. For moose, red deer and reindeer ammunition with expanding bullets weighing a minimum of 9 g is required. For bullets between 9 and 10 g (139 and

Table 2.2 *Hunting season for the ungulate species in Norway*

	Season	Area
Musk ox	No hunting	
Moose	25 Sept–31 Oct	Whole country
Red Deer	10 Sept–11 Nov	All areas where red deer are present in viable populations
Roe Deer	25 Sept–23 Dec	All areas where roe deer are present in viable populations
Males	10 Aug–23 Dec	
Wild Reindeer	20 Aug–30 Sept	All areas where wild reindeer are present in viable populations

154 grains) an impact energy of at least 2700 J (275 kg/m) at a range of 100 m is required (energy at 100 m: E100). Bullets that weigh more than 10 g (154 grains or more) must have impact energy of at least 2200 J (225 kg/m) at a range of 100 m (E100). When hunting roe deer with a rifle, expanding bullets with an impact energy of at least 980 J (100 kg/m) at a range of 100 m (E100) must be used.

Shotguns may be used on roe deer females and young, and for roe bucks outside the period between 10 August and 25 September; there are no specific requirements on calibre or shot size, but only shotguns with up to two cartridges are allowed.

From 1 January 2005, all use of lead shot in shotguns is prohibited, except for slugs.

2.3 Management objectives

The main objective for cervid management in Norway is based upon sport/recreational hunting, but with a focus on venison production. The right of hunting belongs to the landowner, see below, and the gross profit from hunting is for a small number of landowners considerable, exceeding the income from traditional forestry.

Most of the venison is consumed by the hunter and family/friends, and only small amounts are accessible for trade.

In certain areas there may be problems with winter browsing of pine in commercial forests, and in a few areas there are occasional conflicts with red deer causing damage to fruit farms, but these problems are generally localised; in such areas management may be more strongly motivated for damage control.

Populations of all species of cervids in Norway are viable and conservation is not an issue; however, for musk ox, *Pasteurella* bacteria and contagious ecthyma have reduced the population to a worryingly low level.

Table 2.3 *Ungulate management structure in Norway*

Organisations	Role
Ministry of Environment	Superior, responsible for the Wildlife Act
Directorate for Nature Management	Decides hunting periods
	Sets regulations of the Wildlife Act
	Appeal court for decisions made by County Governor
County Governor (18)	Appeal court for decisions made by municipalities
Municipalities (430)	Set hunting quotas
	Set local goals for cervid populations
	Approve local hunting areas
	Approve management plans worked out by landowners
Landowners	Produce management plans
	Not a part of the public management agencies

2.4 Management structure

The right of hunting belongs to the landowner (two-thirds of total land area private, one-third state owned). An increasing emphasis is put upon local population management plans developed by the landowners. However, since the mid 1950s, a *Wildlife Board* within each municipality (approx. 430 in total) sets the quotas for moose, red deer and roe deer (Table 2.3). The role of central authorities like the Directorate for Nature Management is today mostly focused on producing guidelines and transfer of new research based knowledge.

The wildlife agencies mentioned in the law are the public agencies, which are given certain tasks in wildlife management. In addition, non-governmental organisations (NGOs) such as the hunters association and several landowner associations, all play an important role as managers at the local level and as participants in co-operative management groups.

2.5 Management organisation

The required fee for a licence to hunt big game (in 2006) is EUR 40 payable each year to the state. In addition, there is an obligatory fee to the municipality (moose, red deer) or wild reindeer administration unit (reindeer) for each *individual* shot. The fee varies with species and age of the animal shot. Approximately 200 000 hunters pay the hunter's fee each year, generating about EUR 7.5 million for the Wildlife Fund. These monies are spent on management, wildlife research and wildlife monitoring (see Table 2.4 and section 2.7).

Table 2.4 *The income and expenses of the Wildlife Fund in 2007 (budgeted figures in 1 000 NOK (and in 1 000 €))*

	NOK	€
Income		
Income total	**62 112**	**7 450**
Hunting tax	58 605	7 029
Felling taxes on wild reindeer	867	104
Interest	800	96
Sundry income	2 640	317
Expenditure		
Expenditure, total	***64 000**	**7 677**
Subsidies wild-reindeer boards and local game mngmt	6 800	817
Projects, administration, statistics, etc.	20 100	2 416
Cervid management; Efforts and subsidies	10 600	1 274
Miscellaneous subsidies, incl applied science	26 500	3 185

* The difference from income is due to allocation of reserves

2.5.1 The hunters' proficiency test

Anyone who wants to become a hunter must demonstrate a minimum skill in handling firearms, traps, and so forth, and have an adequate knowledge of game species and relevant rules and regulations. All new hunters in Norway must undergo a hunting proficiency test. This involves a mandatory 16-hour course and a theory exam. The courses are organised by various adult education associations, while the municipalities are responsible for holding an appropriate number of theoretical tests.

In addition to the mandatory test to be passed by all new hunters, big game (includes all ungulates) hunting demands a yearly shooting test. This test has two parts: the first part is a mandatory target shooting of at least 30 shots on an approved shooting field, spread over at least two different days, with no qualified hits. The latter is five shots on a reindeer figure at a distance of 100 m. All five shots must hit within the area of vital organs (a 40 cm diameter circle), and the test has to be passed for each of the weapons a hunter plans to use for his/her big game hunting.

2.5.2 Local population management plans and licence system

Although the wildlife boards in each municipality have specific management goals, large landowners or groups of collaborative landowners may be treated as an independent management unit, and be allowed to develop their own population management plans for moose, red deer and roe deer. For moose and red deer such plans have to describe in detail the number and proportion of each sex and age category of animals proposed to be harvested during the planning period, normally spanning 3–5 years. To be approved, the management plan must show that it is adapted to the municipal management goals, e.g. to what extent the local authorities want the moose or red deer density to increase or decrease.

For roe deer, management units formed by landowners covering more than 500 ha of land may be granted an exemption of no limit in numbers. For each of the 23 wild reindeer populations, there is a wild reindeer board that sets the quotas.

Size of management area also varies with species. In consequence, management units vary from less than 100 ha (roe deer) up to more than 9000 km^2 (largest state-owned municipality in Norway).

Since the introduction of new hunting regulations in 2002, hunting areas for moose and red deer with an approved population management plan have been given the complete hunting quota for the planning period at the outset. If the hunting areas significantly deviate from their approved plan and/or the moose or red deer population development is radically changed, the approval may be withdrawn or amended by the municipality.

The general mechanism of regulating number of moose, reindeer and red deer to be harvested is a quota system with licences issued by local or regional authorities. Quotas are specified to sex and age categories (calf, adult female, adult male) or alternatively, may simply define number of individuals to be shot where the hunting area already has an approved population management plan of 3–5 years duration, since this plan is itself supposed to define the yearly cull of each sex and age category. Landowners are free to lease the quota, or part of it, to other hunters; however, it is the responsibility of the landowner to pay the obligatory fee to the municipality for each individual shot.

There is no regular hunting of musk ox. A few animals are shot every year, either because they are far out of their limited range or they are close to settlements and are considered a threat to public safety.

A total of 195 200 persons paid the hunting fee for small game or large game for the hunting year 2005/2006, of whom 23% were women. A total of 65%, or 125 000 of the hunters in 2005/06 were aiming for cervids. In total there are more than 400 000 persons on the official register of hunters, i.e. 10% of the population.

2.6 Actual management and hunting practices

There is strong tradition of recreational hunting, and most deer management is aimed at keeping deer populations highly productive without causing unacceptable damage to agriculture or forestry. For moose, red deer and roe deer, both hunting parties and individuals hunting alone are required to have a trained dog available to

Table 2.5 *Registered non-harvest mortality of cervids caused by car or train collisions in Norway 2000–2005*

	Moose Bag	Moose Car/train	Red deer Bag	Red deer Car/train	Reindeer Bag	Reindeer Car/train	Roe deer Bag	Roe deer Car/train
2000/01	38 300	1968	22 534	461	7631	5	31 300	5747
2001/02	37 300	1945	23 599	611	6976	7	28 900	5922
2002/03	37 892	2602	24 533	540	6117	5	30 600	6727
2003/04	38 564	2244	25 194	629	4417	4	28 500	6247
2004/05	36 770	1762	25 896	700	3895	11	28 900	6226

locate animals that have been shot, but not found. If such a dog is not present while the hunting is in progress, written agreement must be obtained ensuring the access to a trained dog within a reasonable time after the quarry has fallen. The local authority may require documentation showing compliance with these conditions.

Reindeer hunting in Norway is entirely done by individuals on foot. When it comes to the other species, use of high seats is quite frequent, often in combination with game drives, although stalking animals on foot is also common. Traditionally, use of dogs is the most frequent method for moose hunting. In this case, dogs may be restrained on a leash and used for tracking deer or moving them towards hunters already positioned in high seats, or may be run loose by hunters on foot.

A hunting statistics report is issued annually and contains a comprehensive survey on hunting statistics collected by Statistics Norway based on data from hunters, municipalities, counties and the Directorate for Nature Management.

Hunters are obliged to submit records of all animals shot and the report contains statistics on number and sex of hunters, the annual number of cervids and small game harvested, recorded mortality of carnivores and non-harvest mortality of cervids.

Collisions with cars or trains are the most frequent non-harvest mortality caused by humans on ungulates in Norway (Table 2.5). During the hunting year 2003/04, 6250 deer were killed by cars or trains in Norway. This is a decrease by 7% from the previous hunting year. Beyond ordinary hunting, cars and train continue to represent the greatest threat to cervids. Cars account for 5250 (84%) of all game collisions, whereas the remaining 1000 are killed by trains. Roe deer are particularly vulnerable. A total of 3400 roe deer were killed in traffic during the hunting year 2003/04, corresponding to 12% of the number killed during ordinary hunting. The number of moose killed in traffic corresponds to 6% of the number killed during ordinary hunting. In addition, 2030 large ungulates (of these 1030 moose) are recorded dead from other reasons, including having been killed by predators or killed for humane reasons. Mortality caused by predators is not formally recorded, but is considered to be considerable especially for roe deer.

2.7 Census types and methods

For roe deer, there is no regular census method in use, except in some smaller restricted areas where spring counts are performed along roads by local landowners. Musk ox with a restricted distribution in an open mountainous area, are easily counted by the county authority prior to the breeding season, when snow cover is almost continuous. In wild reindeer areas animals are counted from planes in summer.

A national monitoring programme for moose, red deer and wild reindeer was established by the Directorate for Nature Management in 1991, and financed by the Wildlife Fund (i.e. hunting fee). A series of different survey methods is being used in 16 monitoring areas, seven for moose, six for wild reindeer and three for red deer. The hunters are responsible for large parts of the primary data collection (i.e. performing daily observation inventories, and collecting lower jaws, reproductive organs and measuring body weights from shot animals). The Norwegian Institute for Nature Research (NINA) is responsible for analysing the data and maintaining good communication routines with hunters and local managers. Finally, in order to generate systematic and updated information on the health of wild cervids, a national health surveillance programme for wild cervids was established in 1998 (see below).

2.7.1 The observation inventory system for moose and red deer

The system was first established for moose in the eighties, based on positive experience from the Vefsn area in Nordland County where a similar inventory has been conducted since 1968. The observation inventory is best developed for moose, but is currently also implemented in most red deer districts as a management tool (Veiberg *et al.*, 2003). The inventory is a systematic recording and collation of information on sex and age (calf or adult) of all moose and red deer observed by the hunters during the hunting season, from which several indices on population structure and density are calculated. Most important are the 'animals seen per hunter-day' as an index of population density, and 'calves per female' and 'females per male' as indices of recruitment rate and adult sex ratio, respectively. At present, data from the observation inventory are used in more than 80% of the areas where moose and red deer are hunted, and for moose a database of more than 4 million observations is currently available.

Precision of observation inventory parameters

The general experience is that animals seen per hunter-day is a reasonable reflection of the variation in population density (Ericsson and Wallin, 1999; Solberg and Sæther, 1999), although with some deviation caused by varying observation conditions, changing hunting effort and possibly variation in the hunting methods over time. For instance, moose seen per hunter-day tends to overestimate population size when the hunting success is high, indicating that factors influencing hunting success may also affect the probability of detecting moose (Solberg and Sæther, 1999). Despite the crude sampling procedure and a high number of likely confounding variables the observation indices are found to give quite precise information on the temporal development in population size provided that the number of observations is relatively high (Ericsson and Wallin, 1994; Sylvèn, 2000). The recruitment rate (calves per female) and adult sex ratio (e.g. males per females) recorded by the hunters are also closely related to similar rates in the population (e.g. Ericsson and Wallin, 1999; Solberg and Sæther, 1999; Solberg *et al.*, 2002), indicating that hunter observation data may provide useful information about both density and structure of moose and red deer populations.

2.7.2 *National monitoring programme for moose, red deer and reindeer*

The main objective of the programme is to detect the spatial and temporal variation in:

- body condition (through comparisons of age-related body weight, and length of lower jaw).
- reproductive parameters (determining ovulation and pregnancy rates by analysing female reproductive tracts (Langvatn *et al.*, 1994)).
- population density and sex- and age-structure of moose, red deer (by using the Observation Inventory system) and wild reindeer populations (by performing total and structural counts from helicopters or fixed-wing planes).

From the seven monitoring areas for moose, data are being collected from on average 3000 moose each year, or approximately 70% of all moose harvested within the monitoring areas. For red deer, material is collected from nearly 4000 individuals annually in three different regions in western Norway, representing 75% of all shot animals in the monitoring areas, while the wild reindeer monitoring programme takes place in 6 out of 23 different reindeer management areas. On average, approximately 4000 individuals are harvested in the monitoring areas, although the number of animals from which data are collected varies between areas and years.

The present design of the monitoring programme is able to monitor the variation in cervid population condition. The main strength of the programme is that it is

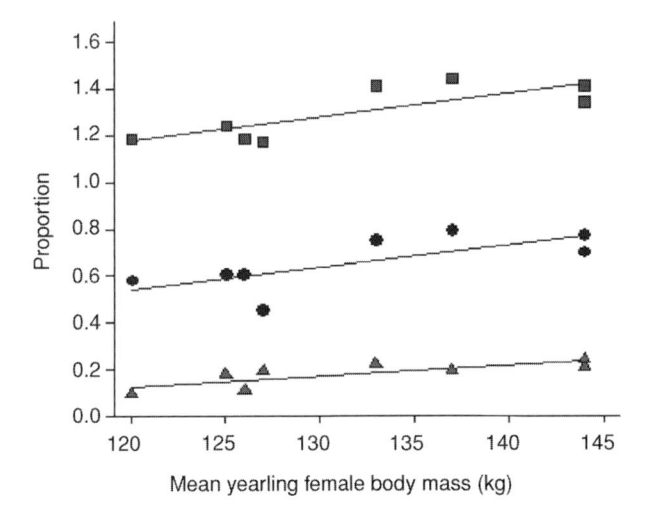

Fig. 2.3 Proportion of reproducing 2 year olds (triangles), proportion of twin-producing 6–14 year old females (circles), and number of calves observed per female with calf at heel (squares) in relation to mean yearling female body mass (carcase mass) in the different monitoring areas

relatively inexpensive, and that it has high credibility among hunters and managers, as the primary data are, to a large extent, collected by hunters themselves. Thus, the programme has been a good 'tool' when evaluating the outcome of management decisions and has contributed to several management improvements.

The main conclusions are:

- *Spatial variation* – large variation exists in physical condition among areas for all involved species, affecting both age of first reproduction and reproductive success in older age groups (see Fig. 2.3 for moose as an example).
- *Temporal variation in physical condition* – Several analyses of the material have established that variation in summer feeding conditions caused by variation in temperature and density-dependent food limitation are the most likely reasons for the pattern observed (Solberg and Sæther, 1994; Solberg et al., 1999). As is often found in large ungulates, however, the effect of density dependence is time delayed, introducing time lags in the population dynamics.
- *Temporal variation in reproduction based on ovary analyses* – As expected there is a close correlation between yearling body mass and probability of ovulation (Solberg et al., 1997). Thus, the variation in physical condition of yearlings seems to be a good index of variation in the general physical condition in the population, and thus of the variation in fecundity among adults.
- *Other aspects* – Age is determined for all animals collected. Although variation in age structure based on harvested animals is notoriously difficult to interpret, these data have proven valuable for retrospective reconstructions of the population development by the

use of cohort analysis (Solberg *et al.*, 1999). Using reproductive data and population structure from the observation inventory system, it is suggested that the proportion of adult males in many Norwegian moose and red deer populations now is too low to ensure timely reproduction in females (e.g. Solberg *et al.*, 2002).

2.7.3 'The Cervid Register'

The Cervid Register is a management and monitoring tool accessible on the world wide web. The register is the main (and in a few years the only) database for collecting and collating data from the observation inventory system. The primary users are the municipalities who can use this tool to handle shooting licences, store data on shot animals and other losses. In addition, there is an open access to anyone who wants to have a closer view into aggregated data in different areas and regions (www.hjortevilt.no).

2.7.4 The national health surveillance programme for wild cervids in Norway

A National Health Surveillance Programme for Wild Cervids (HOP) was also established in 1998. This programme is funded by the Ministry of the Environment and the Ministry of Agriculture, and coordinated by a secretariat located at the National Veterinary Institute (NVI) in Oslo. The main aim of the programme is to generate systematic and updated information on the health of wild cervids for the interest and benefit of the animal health and wildlife management authorities. The programme includes the monitoring and surveillance of infections and other diseases as well as the causes of death in wild moose, red deer, roe deer and reindeer. In 2004 the musk ox was also included. The aim of the programme is to assess the causes of disease in individual animals, in addition to the detection of epizootics or increased mortality in populations during the early phase of an outbreak. Other objectives are the study of infections that might spread between cervids and farm animals and the clarification of the role cervids play as reservoirs of zoonotic agents.

The tools used in the gathering of data in HOP are: (1) systematic registration of diseases and causes of death in cervids from 65 selected municipalities which report quarterly to the HOP-secretariat; (2) systematic sampling of serum and tissue samples during ordinary hunting, for screening purposes; (3) diagnostic work; and (4) research. In cases where the cause of disease or death is unknown, a local veterinary surgeon may perform a field post mortem and, where necessary, submit specimens to the NVI for laboratory examination in order to establish a diagnosis. The NVI offers a free diagnostic service with regard to wild cervids to all municipalities in the country.

2.8 Ungulates impact and damage

There is no state compensation system for damage to forest and agriculture. However, the landowners can apply to the municipality for economic support to prevent damage through specific programmes of action in local areas with high impact.

Winter aggregations of red deer may have an impact on spruce plantations in Western Norway through bark stripping; however, the most serious losses seem to be connected to spring grazing by red deer on grazing fields for livestock (Meisingset, 2003). There are also reports on roe deer damage to strawberry fields caused by browsing on plants and trampling on the plastic ground cover (E. Lund, *pers. obs.*).

In contrast to the locally significant, but regionally moderate, impacts caused by red deer and roe deer, heavy browsing and bark stripping on forest, especially on Scots pine (*Pinus sylvestris*) in wintering areas for moose have attracted much attention in the last two decades. Although, salix (*Salix caprea*), aspen (*Populus tremula*) and rowan (*Sorbus aucuparia*) are the most preferred browsing species, and may be browsed to local extinction in some wintering areas (Hjeljord *et al.*, 1982), Scots pine are the dominant winter browse.

In the 1980s a large number of investigations both in Sweden (summarised in Agerlid, 2000) and Norway (summarised in Sæther *et al.*, 1992), documented intake of browse on both an individual and a population level, calculated intake rates of browse and estimated the economic significance in forestry. The 'average moose' has an estimated daily intake of 11–12 kg of Scots pine shoots during winter (Solbraa, 2002). Moose in Norway stay in their winter grounds between 4 and 5 months a year, which means that the average moose needs between 1.500 and 1.700 kg browse during winter. The impact this browsing has on timber production of Scots pine is in a reduction of the number of trees per area, reduction in growth rate and also in timber quality. It may also result in changes in tree species dominance, as spruce may be planted instead of Scots pine to reduce impact of browsing (Solbraa, 2002). In the last two decades, prices for forestry products have been relatively low, and in most areas land owners have been willing to trade the costs of forest damage for a high density of moose.

As local landowners have the opportunity to develop management plans within a larger management unit, the impact can be dealt with directly by increasing quotas in areas where impact is above a certain level. There is however a problem with this model; in many cases, moose have their wintering areas and summer areas in different management units. In such cases one management unit may cover the cost due to reduced timber production, whereas the other unit receives the income related to harvesting the moose. Certainly, such situations have stimulated to the creation of larger management units, covering the annual distribution area of the specific moose population.

Traffic accidents represent a total loss of 6000 cervids each year including both car and train collisions (Table 2.1). A large effort is put on preventing accidents by transport authorities, wildlife authorities, hunters and landowners associations. Special shooting plans, supplementary feeding, clear cuttings along roads and railroads are some of the actions which have been implemented.

2.9 Supplementary feeding

There is no tradition of supplementary feeding of larger cervid populations in Norway. However, in south-eastern areas with a continental winter climate, supplementary feeding of roe deer occurs regularly. In most cases feeding stations are established by local people, not necessarily hunters, and basically reflect human's innately emotional affiliation to other living organisms – biophilia (*sensu* Wilson, 1993). Only in a few cases management units establish artificial feeding stations specifically in order to reduce winter mortality of roe deer.

As mentioned earlier (section 2.8) the loss of moose in traffic accidents represents not only a serious threat to drivers, but also decreases the potential income to land owners. Consequently, in many areas where roads run through moose wintering grounds, silage is being put out to attract the moose away from roads.

2.10 Effectiveness of current management strategies, and future challenges

2.10.1 When the Malawi principle creates problems

According to the Malawi principle, management should be allocated to the lowest appropriate level, and automatically most managers feels that the municipality is the right level. Despite the support of the Malawi principles by the vast majority of municipalities, we often have a mis-match between management scale and the scale used by the focal resource. As individual wild reindeer use up to 5000 km^2 during a year, covering several municipalities and, in many cases, also several counties, it is evident that the management should be at a regional level, and not at a local level. This is reflected by the existence of one management unit for each of the 23 wild reindeer areas.

But the problem arises when we have seasonally migrating moose and red deer that utilise summer and winter areas often more than 100 km apart. In such cases, certain landowners may bear the cost in terms of damage to forestry, while other landowners get the income from selling hunting licences. That is, we still need more knowledge about space use of the different cervid populations in order to set the appropriate management level.

2.10.2 Lack of knowledge about the long-term consequences of the heavily selective harvesting regimes

Despite the fact that overall population sizes have risen following the introduction of a sex- and age-specific harvesting regime in the early seventies, the proportion of adult males in most Norwegian moose and red deer populations has declined significantly with possible demographic and genetic effects. For instance, a biased sex ratio is likely to strongly influence the rate of genetic drift (Engen et al., 2005) and may lead to rapid loss of genetic variation. Similarly, size selective harvesting or focusing the harvest on certain sex and age groups may reduce the effective population size, and in the long term have both ecological and evolutionary consequences (Engen et al., 2005).

2.10.3 Do high density cervid populations affect biodiversity?

Large mammalian herbivores are known to affect the structure of their habitat in several ways (Pastor et al., 1993; Kielland and Bryant, 1998; Olff and Ritchie, 1998). Thus, there is growing concern that large populations of cervids will have an adverse impact on forest vegetation and simplify vertical structure by selectively browsing on herbs, shrubs and young trees. That is, the concern is related to conservation values, not to the economy in silviculture. It has been shown that moose browsing in taiga leads to lower humidity, lower soil humidity, higher temperature and light intensity at ground layer (Kielland and Bryant, 1998); however, it is not straightforward to predict their effects on biodiversity.

In a study on the role of moose in structuring the Swedish boreal forest ecosystem, indirect effects were found on the invertebrate communities at the ground layer, with a decrease in the number of individuals in most invertebrate groups. The actual diversity of species was, however, higher in browsed areas (Suominen et al., 1999). However, in general it is found that biodiversity is highest at moderate browsing pressure, and that increased browsing pressure alters the structure and composition of woodland vegetation and reduces the abundance of some flowering plants. Such changes are likely to be detrimental to both vertebrate and invertebrate fauna (e.g. Gill, 2000).

Furthermore, as cervid populations in Norway are primarily managed by hunting, an eventual lowered interest in hunting among an increasing urban population may be detrimental for forest biodiversity.

2.10.4 How will a climate change affect our cervid populations?

A rapid climate change will inevitably cause large changes in distribution of large herbivores, and may eventually lead to local extinction. In Norway, we should be most concerned about wild reindeer and musk ox. By the year 2080, Arctic summer temperatures are predicted to increase by 4.0–7.5°C, accompanied by a 10–20% increase in precipitation. Winter temperatures are predicted to increase by 2.5–14.5°C, with a 5–80% increase in precipitation (Anisimov and Fitzharris, 2001). It is well established that winters marked by deep snow and multiple ice-crusting events can extract a significant toll on reindeer and musk ox populations (Klein, 1968; Lee et al., 2000; Solberg et al., 2001; Asbjørnsen et al., 2005). Reindeer retreated from their southern late Pleistocene habitats throughout Europe and North America, and this retreat coincided with the climatically driven extinction of a variety of large herbivores throughout the northern hemisphere (Grayson and Meltzer, 2002). Increased temperatures in areas inhabited by wild reindeer and musk ox may therefore cause heavy mortality, accompanied by a significant retreat of the southern boundary of the distribution of reindeer (Grayson and Delpech, 2005), and extinction of the local musk ox population in Central Norway.

References

Agerlid, G. (2000) Är älgen ett hinder för att nå de skogspolitiska målen? Kungl. Skogs-och Lantbruksakademiens Tidsskrift No 2 (In Swedish).

Alendal, E. (1972) Musk ox at Dovrefjell: population dynamics, social interactions and nutritional ecology. Masters degree thesis, University of Bergen, Norway.

Andersen, R., Herfindal, I., Sæther, B.-E., Linnell, J. D. C., Odden, J. and Liberg, O. (2004) When range expansion rate is faster in marginal habitats. *Oikos* **107**(1), 210–14.

Anisimov, O. and Fitzharris, B. (2001) Polar regions. In J. J. McCarthy, O. E. Canziani, N. A. Leary, D. J. Dokken and K. S. White, eds., *Climate Change 2001: Impacts, Adaptation, and Vulnerability*. Cambridge, UK: Cambridge University Press, pp. 801–41.

Asbjørnsen, E. J., Sæther, B.-E., Linnell, J. D. C. *et al.* (2005) Predicting the growth of a small introduced muskox population using population prediction intervals. *Journal of Animal Ecology* **74**, 612–18.

Asbjørnsen, P. Chr. (1852) Vildrenen. Illustreret Nyhedsblad nr 55. (In Norwegian).

Cederlund, G. and Liberg, O. (1995) Rådjuret. Viltet, ekologin och jakten. *Svenska Jägareförbundet, Solna*. 301 s.

Danielsen, J. (2001) Local community based moose management plans in Norway. *Alces* **37**, 55–60.

Direktoratet for Naturforvaltning (1999) Nasjonal rødliste for truete arter. DN Rapport **99**(3), 162 pp. (In Norwegian).

Engen, S., Lande, R. and Sæther, B.-E. (2005) Effective size of a fluctuating age-structured population. *Genetics* **170**, 941–54.

Ericsson, G. and Wallin, K. (1994) *Antall älgar som ses – bare en fråga om hur många som finns?* Sweden: Swedish University of Agricultural Sciences, Department of Umeå, 30 pp. (In Swedish).

Ericsson, G. and Wallin, K. (1999) Hunter observations as an index of moose *Alces alces* population parameters. *Wildlife Biology* **5**, 177–85.

Flagstad, Ø. and Røed, K. H. (2003) Refugial origins of reindeer (*Rangifer tarandus* L.) inferred from mitochondrial DNA sequences. *Evolution* **57**, 658–70.

Friis, J. A. (1876) *Tilfjelds i Ferierne*. Christiania, Norway. (In Norwegian).

Gill, R. (2000) *The impact of deer on woodland biodiversity*. Information Note August 2000, Edinburgh, UK: Forestry Commission.

Grayson, D. K. and Delpech, F. (2005) Pleistocene reindeer and global warming. *Conservation Biology* **19**, 557–62.

Grayson, D. K. and Meltzer, D. J. (2002) A requiem for North American overkill. *Journal of Archaeological Science* **30**, 585–93.

Grøtan, V., Sæther, B.-E., Engen, S. *et al.* (2005) Spatial synchrony in population fluctuations of a temperate herbivore. *Ecology* **86**, 1472–82.

Gundersen, L. H., Whist, A. C., Bretten, T. *et al.* (2005) Causes of mortality in an introduced muskox (*Ovibos moschatus*) population at Dovre, Norway, 1953–2005. *Norsk Veterinærtidsskrift* **8**, 613–19. (In Norwegian with English abstract).

Gyllensten, U., Ryman, N., Reuterwall, C. and Dratch, P. (1983) Genetic differentiation in four European subspecies of red deer (*Cervus elaphus* L.). *Heredity* **51**, 561–80.

Hagström, T. (1988) *Arkeologi i Västsverige*, Göteborgs arkeologiska museum, Göteborg, Vol. 3.

Hjeljord, O., Sundstøl, F. and Haagenrud, H. (1982) The nutritional value of browse to moose. *Journal of Wildlife Management* **46**, 333–43.

Jordhøy, P., Strand, O., Gaare, E., Skogland, T. and Holmstrøm, F. (1996) Monitoring programme: Wild reindeer, 1991–1995. NINA report 22, 57pp. (In Norwegian with English summary).

Kielland, K. and Bryant, J. P. (1998) Moose herbivory in taiga: effects on biogeochemistry and vegetation dynamics in primary succession. *Oikos* **82**, 377–83.

Klein, D. R. (1968) The introduction, increase and crash of reindeer on St. Matthew Island. *Journal of Wildlife Management* **32**, 350–67.

Langvatn, R., Bakke, Ø. and Engen, S. (1994) Retrospective studies of red deer reproduction, using regressing luteal structures. *Journal of Wildlife Management* **58**, 654–63.

Lee, S. E., Press, M. C., Lee, J. A., Ingold, I. and Kurtttila, T. (2000) Regional effects of climate change on reindeer: a case study of the Muotkatunturi region in Finnish Lapland. *Polar Research* **19**, 99–105.

Lepiskaar, J. (1986) The holocene history of theriofauna in Fennoscandia and Baltic countries. *Striae* **24**, 51–70.

Lindström, E., Andrén, H., Angelstam, P. *et al.* (1994) Disease reveals the predator: sarcoptic mange, red fox predation, and prey populations. *Ecology* **75**, 1042–9.

Lundh, N. G. (1992) Moskus. Trondheim: Fylkesmannen i Sør-Trøndelag (In Norwegian).

Markgren, G. (1974) The moose in Fennoscandia. *Le Naturaliste Canadien* **101**, 185–94.

Meisingset, E. L. (2003) *Hjort og hjortejakt i Norge*. Naturforlaget. (In Norwegian).

Mysterud, A. and Østbye, E. (2006) Effect of climate and density on individual and population growth of roe deer *Capreolus capreolus* at northern latitudes: the Lier Valley, Norway. *Wildlife Biology* **12**, 321–9.

Olff, H. and Ritchie, M. E. (1998) Effects of herbivores on grassland plant diversity. *Trends in Ecology and Evolution* **13**, 261–65.

Pastor, J., Dewey, B., Naiman, R. J., McInnes, P. F. and Cohen, Y. (1993) Moose browsing and soil fertility in the boreal forests of Isle-Royale-National-Park. *Ecology* **74**, 467–80.

Ryman, N., Reuterwall, C., Nygrén, K. and Nygrén, T. (1980) Genetic variation and differentiation in Scandinavian moose (*Alces alces*): are large mammals monomorphic? *Evolution* **34**, 1037–49.

Røed, K. H. (1998) Influence of selection and management on the genetic structure of reindeer populations. *Acta Theriologica* Suppl **5**, 179–86.

Røed, K. H., Mossing, T., Nieminen, M. and Rydberg, A. (1987) Transferrin variation and genetic structure of reindeer populations in Scandinavia. *Rangifer* **7**, 12–21.

Sand, H. (1996) Life history patterns in female moose (*Alces alces*): the relationship between age, body size, fecundity and environmental conditions. *Oecologia* **106**, 212–20.

Solberg, E. J. and Sæther, B.-E. (1994) Male traits as life history variables: annual variation in body mass and antler size in moose (*Alces alces*). *Journal of Mammalogy* **75**, 1069–79.

Solberg, E. J. and Sæther, B.-E. (1999) Hunter observations of moose *Alces alces* as a management tool. *Wildlife Biology* **5**, 43–53.

Solberg, E. J., Heim, M., Sæther, B.-E. and Holmstrøm, F. (1997) Oppsummeringsrapport, Overvåkningsprogram for hjortevilt. NINA Fagrapport 30.

Solberg, E. J., Sæther, B.-E., Strand, O. and Loison, A. (1999) Dynamics of a harvested moose population in a variable environment. *Journal of Animal Ecology* **68**, 186–204.

Solberg, E. J. P., Jordhøy, O., Strand, R. *et al.* (2001) Effects of density-dependence and climate on the dynamics of a Svalbard reindeer population. *Ecography* **24**, 441–51.

Solberg, E. J., Ringsby, T. H., Sæther B.-E. and Heim, M. (2002) Biased adult sex ratio can affect fecundity in primipareous moose. *Wildlife Biology* **8**, 109–20.

Solbraa, K. (2002) Beiteskader av elg. Presentations from University course LP 300 at the Agricultural University, Ås, Norway (In Norwegian).

Statistics Norway (2002) Jaktstatistikk. Statistisk Sentralbyrå, Kongsvinger og Oslo.

Suominen, O., Danell, K. and Bergström, R. (1999) Moose, trees, and ground-living invertebrates: indirect interactions in Swedish pine forests. *Oikos* **84**, 215–26.

Sylvèn, S. (2000) Effects of scale on hunter moose *Alces alces* observation rate. *Wildlife Biology* **6**, 157–65.

Sæther, B.-E. and Haagenrud, H. (1985) Life history of the moose *Alces alces*: relationship between growth and reproduction. *Holarctic Ecology* **8**, 100–6.

Sæther, B.-E., Solbraa, K., Sødal, D. P. and Hjeljord, O. (1992) Sluttrapport Elg-Skog-Samfunn. *NINA Forskningsrapport* **28**, 1–153 (In Norwegian).

UNEP (2001) *Global Methodology for Mapping Human Impacts on the Biosphere*. Environment Information and Assessment Technical Report, UNEP-DEWA.

Veiberg, V., Meisingset, E. L. and Samdal, B. (2003) Evaluering av Sett-hjort og vårteljing som hjelpemiddel for den lokale bestandsforvaltninga av hjort. *Norsk Hjortesenter Fagrapport* **1/03**, 1–48.

Vernesi, C., Pecchioli, E., Caramelli, D. *et al.* (2002) The genetic structure of natural and reintroduced roe deer (*Capreolus capreolus*) populations in the Alps and central Italy, with reference to the mitochondrial DNA phylogeography of Europe. *Molecular Ecology* **11**, 1285–97.

Wilson, E. O. (1993) Biophilia and the conservation ethic. In S. Kellert and E. O. Wilson, eds., *The Biophilia Hypothesis*. Washington, DC: Island Press, pp. 31–41.

3

Ungulates and their management in Sweden

OLOF LIBERG, ROGER BERGSTRÖM,
JONAS KINDBERG AND HANS VON ESSEN

3.1 History, current distribution and genetic origin of Swedish ungulates

There are three native species of ungulates in Sweden that have occurred continuously in the country since they first appeared after the last ice age; moose, red deer and roe deer. The native red deer subspecies (*Cervus e. elaphus*) however occurs only in a very restricted area in the extreme south of the country, while introduced red deer of various origins occur in several subpopulations further north. The native wild boar was exterminated in the seventeenth century, but has been reintroduced through repeated escapes from game farms during the last 25 years. Fallow deer is an exotic species that was introduced on many large estates in southern Sweden in several separate introductions since the sixteenth century, and a small group of musk ox has recently colonised naturally from Norway. Finally, also as a result of escapes, there are a couple of small populations of mouflon with very restricted distribution.

3.1.1 Moose

Moose colonised the Scandinavian peninsula over the land-bridge from Denmark after the last ice age in the Preboreal period, i.e. 10 000–11 000 BP (Brönsted, 1957; Ekman *et al.*, 1992). Speculations on a second, later immigration route from northeast have little support (see Andersen *et al.*, Chapter 2). According to both fossils at Stone Age settlements ('middens') and ancient rock-paintings, moose was an important game species in Sweden from the very beginning of human settlements, and has continued to be so up to present time.

During the Middle Ages, monarchs obtained an increasing hunting monopoly on all cervid game (except wild reindeer). The royal family held this monopoly on deer hunting over the whole country for a long period, although in the seventeenth century aristocrat families were granted rights to hunt moose and other deer on their own estates. Despite this, illegal hunting of moose was common, especially in the vast uninhabited northern parts of the country. Also, moose experienced increasing competition from farmers that allowed their domestic stock to graze freely in the forests during summer, and were cutting winter forage in the form of twigs and shoots from palatable trees and shrubs (Ahlén, 1975). As a consequence, moose were already rather uncommon around 1700. Linneaus for example did not mention moose in any of his famous travel reports from different parts of the country during the 1720s and 30s, including a report on Lapland.

In 1789, the year of the great French Revolution, the Swedish king Gustav III relaxed the restrictions on hunting, by linking hunting rights for all game, including cervids, to ownership of land, independent of the owner's ancestry and social status. As Sweden never had a well developed feudal system, most of the land was owned by a large class of free farmers and peasants. Thus enormous hunting activity ensued and all hoofed game suffered. Especially damaging was the practice of chasing moose on crusted snow in late winter, when hunters on skis could move on top of the snow but the moose broke through the crust (Lloyd, 1854). Moose were reduced to small numbers in a few remote areas in western and northern Sweden.

However, concerned about the fate of the moose in Sweden, a few far-sighted and influential hunters managed, in 1825, to persuade the government to enforce a ten-year hunting ban on moose. The moose responded with expansion both in numbers and distribution. After this moratorium the overexploitation started again, but in 1836 a prohibition of the particularly devastating winter hunting was enforced (Ekman *et al.*, 1992).

During the late 1800s, several factors contributed to a slow, but steady, recovery and expansion of the moose population. Modern hunting legislation was gradually introduced and the large carnivores, especially wolves, were exterminated in southern and central Scandinavia (Lönnberg, 1934). Also important was the growing timber industry that put a stop to the practice of grazing livestock freely in the forests (Bergman, 1960). The recovery of the moose, however, was not a steady, progressive expansion. Periods of hunting bans were followed by periods with overexploitation, but the long-term trend was increase and expansion.

In 1879 the official national harvest was 926 moose, and in 1932 it was 5740 (Ekman *et al.*, 1992). By this time, the moose had regained its former distribution and once more occurred over most of the country.

The introduction of the 1938 Hunting Act encouraged owners of small farms to unite these into larger game management areas, where moose were hunted according to a licence system with bag limits adjusted to the abundance of moose.

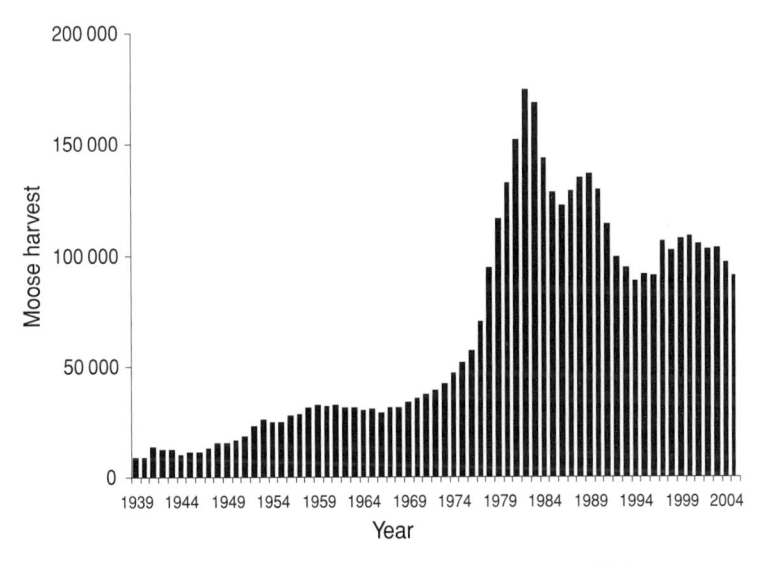

Fig. 3.1 The Swedish moose harvest 1939–2005

In the 1970s most land was included in this system, at the same time the ill-advised regulation prohibiting shooting calves but allowing killing of their mothers was finally abandoned. Now, instead, shooting calves was encouraged.

There were also large-scale changes in the habitat during this period, which were favourable for the moose. The spread of the clear-cutting practice in the forestry, which mimicked forest fires, with a subsequent rich supply of deciduous browse, favoured the moose. During the 1960s and 1970s the rationalisation of agriculture led to large areas of arable land on poor soils becoming abandoned and replaced by forest plantations or natural succession with again, a rich supply of deciduous browse in the early stages (Ahlén, 1975). Moose occurred over practically the whole country, except high alpine habitats and the large island Gothland in the Baltic. In 1966, approximately 30 000 moose were harvested, and in 1982, only 16 years later, this figure peaked at the amazing level of 183 000 harvested moose (Cederlund and Markgren, 1987; Lavsund and Sandegren, 1989) (Fig. 3.1). This is the largest moose harvest on record in a single year for any country in the world.

The other side of the coin was, and still is, increasing damage to forestry, especially young pine, whose top shoots are much sought after by moose during winter. Forestry interests have for a long time lobbied for lower moose populations, and since 1983 the trend has been downward (Fig. 3.1). In 2004 there were around 100 000 moose shot in the country, and assuming that bag size reflects population number, this suggests an overall decline in numbers; despite this, many foresters still regard this reduction as too small. Also, the quality of the moose has deteriorated. Because of selective harvesting of adult males, sex ratios have been heavily biased towards cows, and the age structure is far from natural, especially for bulls, where the mean age is below 2 years. This means there is a shortage of bulls of prime age, and thus of trophy bulls (Lavsund and Sandegren, 1989).

There have also more recently been increasing numbers of reports of problems with disease. During the 1990s a mysterious disease of unknown origin, that at first was believed to affect only old cows in a certain locality ('Älvsborgssjukan'), caused much distress among moose managers. It was finally determined that the main reason for this 'disease' was malnutrition caused by overpopulation and over-browsing (Broman et al., 2002).

Finally, wolves (*Canis lupus*), that were functionally extinct in Scandinavia during 1965–1980, have recently re-colonised the peninsula from Finland (Wabakken et al., 2001). Moose have become the main prey for these re-colonising wolves. In 2005 there were around 150 wolves in the Scandinavian population, the majority of them in Sweden. The challenge to moose managers now is to balance the foresters' demands to reduce moose populations further with the expanding wolf population's increasing consumption of moose and the hunters' desperate efforts to save at least some of their former rich moose harvest.

There are no definite figures on the total number of moose in Sweden, but the harvest level and local censuses indicate that the present (2005) winter population, before the spring breeding pulse, is around 200 000 head. Moose occur all over the country except on the island of Gothland. The densest populations occur in south central Sweden, where they may locally reach 12–15 moose per 1000 ha (10 km^2).

3.1.2 Red deer

Red deer also colonised Scandinavia from the south after the retreat of the ice, but due to different habitat requirements they appeared in Sweden approximately 1000 years later than the moose, i.e. in the Boreal period around 9000 BP, when the climate was milder and oak and other deciduous forests started to form in the south (Ahlén, 1965a). During the late-Boreal period red deer continued to spread northward. However, according both to fossils and sub-fossils as well as later historic records, the red deer never became established further north than an approximate line from northern Dalsland to Östergötland (Fig. 3.2), either during prehistoric or historic periods before the twentieth century.

There are many fossils of red deer found around Mesolithic settlements in Denmark and southern Sweden, indicating that red deer was a very important game species for the Older Stone Age people (Brönsted, 1957). They probably continued to be so all the way up to historic times. However, the combined pressure of hunting and competition with domestic stock probably affected the red deer even more than it did moose, as the red deer did not have access to the refuges in the northern remote areas of Sweden. Already during the sixteenth century, several of

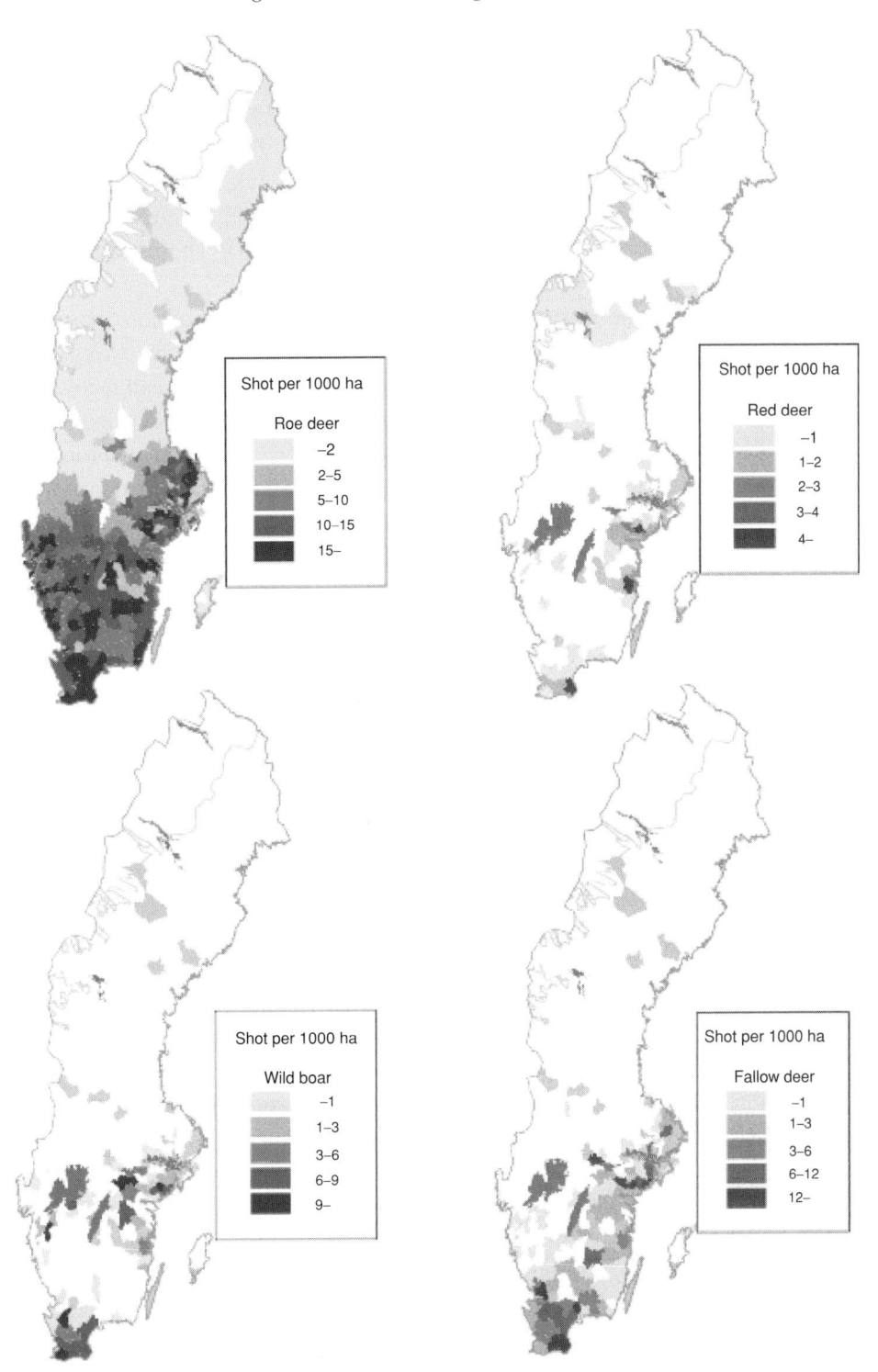

Fig. 3.2 The distribution of roe deer, red deer, wild boar and fallow deer in Sweden according to the harvest 2004

the Swedish kings had to remind their forest keepers of the ban on common men hunting deer, and they also complained that predators like the wolf were allowed to grow in numbers that damaged the deer stock (Kjellberg, 1991).

The end of the ban on hunting of hoofed game by common men in 1789 had an even more devastating effect on red deer than on moose. At the beginning of the nineteenth century, red deer were pressed back to a few large estates in the southernmost province of Scania, where they were protected by the aristocrat estate owners (Ahlén, 1965a).

In contrast to moose, the native red deer did not respond to more protective hunting legislation and relief of the competition with domestic stock by regaining their former range, but have remained restricted to southern Scania all the way up to present. The main reason for this is probably is its bad reputation for damaging forest plantations, especially stripping the bark of the introduced spruce that became very popular among foresters in southern Sweden during the twentieth century (Ahlén, 1965c). Because of this the number of deer has deliberately been kept down, so that the population never managed to bridge the gap between the forests in southern Scania and the large tracts of forests in the provinces further north.

Because native red deer in Scania are the only remaining representatives of the nominate subspecies described by von Linné (*C. e. elaphus* L.), there have been some efforts to encourage the expansion of its range. Several transfers of native red deer from the original Scanian herd to other localities have been performed in Sweden, the first one to the county of Västergötland (Hunneberg) during the 1950s (Ahlén, 1965b). Unfortunately, during the twentieth century, red deer of Danish and continental origin were also introduced into a large number of localities in southern and central Sweden, and thus it is uncertain whether there are any pure bred native red deer anywhere in the country outside of the isolated southern Scania population.

Also, it is likely that a number of deer from game farms have escaped, or in some cases even been deliberately released (which is illegal in Sweden). Most of these new subpopulations have thrived and increased (Figs. 3.2 and 3.3). Today, the annual harvest is almost 3000 animals, and the population in the whole country is estimated to exceed 10 000.

3.1.3 Roe deer

Roe deer appeared in Sweden about the same time as red deer, i.e. in the Boreal period around 9000 BP, colonising from the south, just like the red deer. The northern boundary of its range in Sweden has probably swung back and forth with the various climatic regimes. In historic times its northern limit was probably

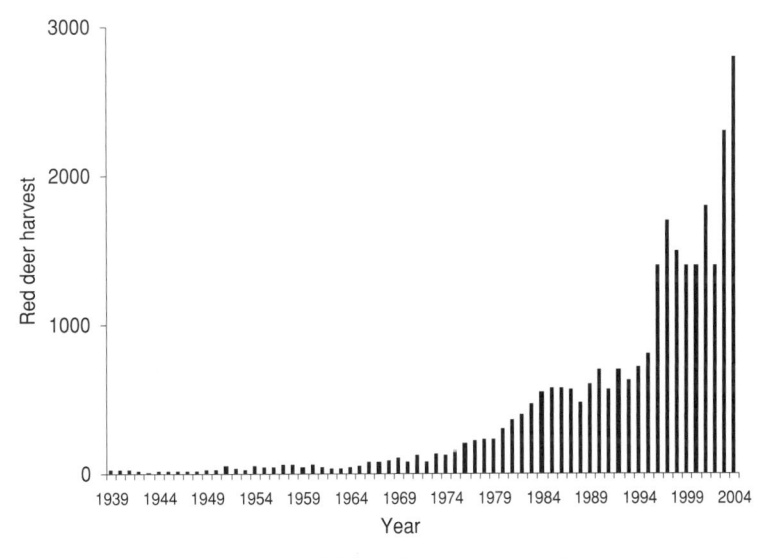

Fig. 3.3 The Swedish red deer harvest 1939–2004

somewhere just north of the 60th latitude. Linneaus commented on a small local occurrence of roe deer during his visit to the county of Dalarna as something special, indicating that was at or near the northern limit. Roe deer suffered as much as moose and red deer from the hunting law reform in 1789 that allowed common men to hunt deer. Around 1820, just 30 years later, they were limited to only one estate in the southernmost province of Scania, where they were protected by its aristocrat owner. When animals from here started to re-colonise neighbouring estates, their owners followed his example.

Like moose, roe deer also expanded during the second half of the nineteenth and most of the twentieth century, and for the same reasons: restrictive hunting laws, removal of domestic competitors from the forest, extermination of the large predators, and improved habitat through changed forest practices and abandonment of marginal agricultural land (Liberg et al., 1994). For roe deer, the spread of the winter feeding practice was also of importance, especially for the expansion during the second half of the twentieth century into northern Sweden, where they had not occurred before in historic time. Around 1990, roe deer occurred over most of the country except for the alpine areas and the extreme north (Fig. 3.2).

The geographical expansion was accompanied also by a tremendous numerical increase (Liberg et al., 1994). When the Swedish Association for Hunting and Wildlife Management started its harvest statistics in 1939 around 10 000 roe were being shot each year in Sweden. This figure was increasing until 1993 when it peaked at 380 000 (Fig. 3.4). The increase was exceptionally fast during the late

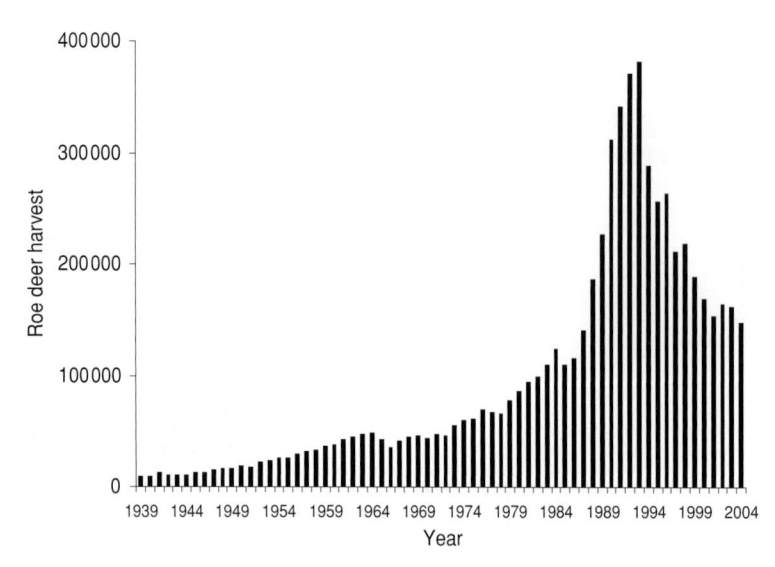

Fig. 3.4 The Swedish roe deer harvest 1939–2004

1980s and early 1990s, coinciding with an outbreak of fox scabies that almost eliminated the red fox over large areas (Lindström et al., 1994; Jarnemo and Liberg, 2005). The global climate change with milder winters also favoured roe deer survival and production. After the fox started recovering in the middle of the 1990s, roe deer harvest figures dropped gradually, reaching around 122 000 in 2007.

The distribution has also decreased in the north and north-west of the country, with the northern limit of the range pushed southwards and towards the Baltic coast. During the 1990s the lynx (*Lynx lynx*) increased rapidly in the north-central parts of the country, probably as a response to the increasing roe deer in these regions. The lynx is an efficient predator on roe deer and is probably a main factor behind the dramatic decrease of roe deer in the more recently colonised areas of the north and north-central regions (Liberg, 1997; Liberg and Andrén, 2006). Now lynx is expanding south, but it is not known how strong an effect this predator will have on roe deer in more productive habitats.

Roe deer are the most numerous of Swedish ungulates. In optimal mixed agricultural/forest habitats in the boreo/nemoral zone in the southern third of the country, densities may reach as high as 10–15 animals per km^2, although average densities over larger areas in this part of the country are 5–10 animals per km^2. In the forested boreal zone, densities are lower and fall with increasing latitude. The annual harvest was around 120 000 animals during the period 2005–2007 (Fig. 3.4). No national censuses have been performed, but, based on the harvest figures, a rough estimate of the total population is 400 000–600 000 head in spring just before the birth season.

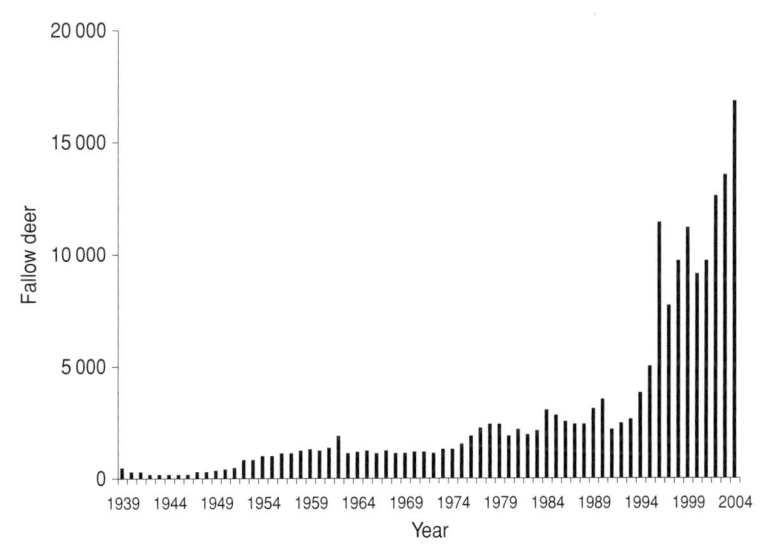

Fig. 3.5 The Swedish fallow deer harvest 1939–2004

3.1.4 Fallow deer

Fallow deer are an exotic species originating in the Mediterranean area and the Middle East. Already during the sixteenth century fallow deer had been imported to fenced hunting grounds ('deer parks') in Sweden by wealthy land owners in the aristocracy, including the royal family, a practice that was common all over Europe. During the nineteenth century, animals that had escaped from these parks, or been deliberately released, started forming wild populations at different localities distributed over the southern third of the country. The fallow deer has thrived and increased in number and distribution (Fig. 3.5). However, due to their innate reluctance to disperse (Liberg and Wahlström, 1995), the geographical expansion has been very slow. Still, today, fallow deer has an extremely fragmented distribution, restricted to the nearest surroundings of each release point, with very high local densities in occupied patches, but virtually no fallow deer in others (Fig. 3.2).

3.1.5 Mouflon

Mouflon are an exotic species in Scandinavia originating in the Mediterranean area. During the last few decades some sheep have escaped (or been released deliberately, but illegally) from game parks and enclosures in southern and south-central Sweden, and formed small, but growing, free-living populations. The authorities have little knowledge and control of the distribution, abundance and development of these populations. They occur primarily in a fragmented distribution in the county of Södermanland just south of Stockholm, but also along the coast and on islands further south along the east coast of the country, as well as some isolated occurrences on the west coast. The mouflon is treated as an exotic species with no hunting regulations, except for a ban on hunting ewes with accompanying lambs. During the last ten years, between 50 and 150 sheep have been reported to have been shot annually. Presumably, the true figure is higher. There has been a slight downward trend in the number of reported animals shot since the year of 2000. It is not known whether this reflects a true trend in the living wild population or not. The total number of free-living mouflon in the country is not known, but an educated guess is that it does not exceed 1000 sheep.

3.1.6 Musk ox

There are no undisputed fossils of musk ox found in Scandinavia from the period after the last ice age, although the species probably occurred here during interglacials. During the period 1947–53 a small number of musk ox were introduced to Norway from Greenland, which founded a new free living population in the Dovre area, close to the Swedish border (see Andersen *et al.*, Chapter 2 in this book). The number of founders probably was not more than 10 animals. This population has later increased considerably (see Andersen *et al.* this volume). In 1971 a small group of five animals, two cows with their respective calves and one young bull, broke away from this population and travelled to the Rogen area in the southern alpine region in Sweden. This group increased to a maximum of just over 30 animals in the mid 1980s. Since then it has again decreased, presumably as a consequence of inbreeding problems (Laikre *et al.*, 1997). In 2005 there were only six animals left. Several attempts have been made to increase the genetic basis of this herd, including failed attempts to release captive born animals. The latest attempt was to capture one of the cows in the wild herd, keeping her together with a captive bull until she conceived, and then release her when pregnant. The release occurred in the winter 2006, she has rejoined the small wild herd, and the birth of the new calf is expected in the summer 2006.

3.1.7 Wild boar

Wild boar (*Sus scrofa*) is an indigenous species, colonising Scandinavia at about the same time as the roe deer. Due to extensive hunting, and also partly to hybridisation with the free ranging herds of domestic pigs, it disappeared from the wild Swedish fauna during the seventeenth century. The wild boar has more recently been reintroduced to various game parks and enclosures. In the 1940s a small

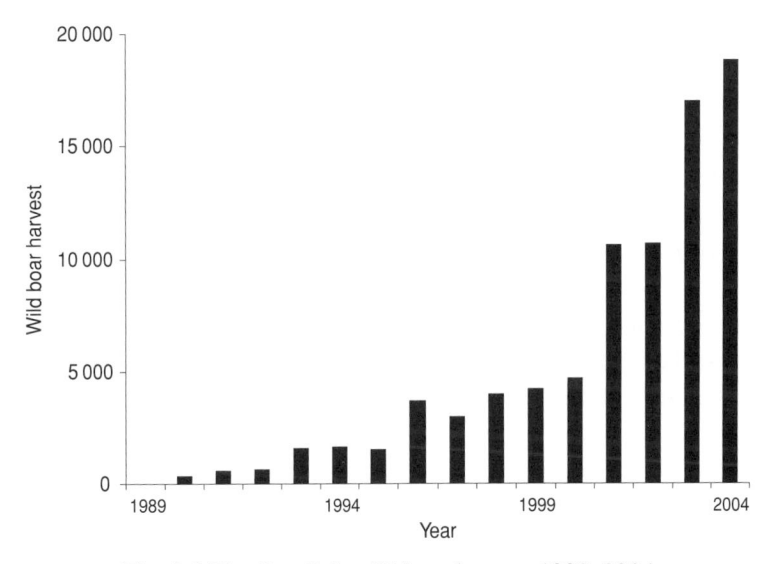

Fig. 3.6 The Swedish wild boar harvest 1990–2004

number escaped from an enclosure in Scania and established a small population there; however, this was intentionally culled after a few years. During the 1970s and 1980s wild boars again escaped (and probably in many cases were illegally released) from enclosures and established several small populations in southern and south-eastern Sweden. A parliamentary decision in 1980 banned them all as a undesirable exotic, declaring that they should be shot out except for a small population in the Trosa-area, 50 km south of Stockholm, which for a time should be kept for research purposes. However, many hunters were reluctant to follow the official recommendation, and both number and distribution of wild boar continued to increase. In 1988, the Parliament changed its former decision, and declared the wild boar as a natural member of the Swedish fauna, and thereby it was granted the same treatment in the hunting regulations as other game species.

The wild boar is now distributed over a large part of southern Sweden, and the expansion continues. The natural spread of the species has been calculated at 3–4 km/year, but the expansion is speeded up by new illegal releases (Truvé and Lemel, 2003). The annual bag has increased steadily since the 1980s and reached almost 20 000 animals in 2004 (Fig. 3.6). The absolute number of boar is not known, but was estimated to be a minimum 40 000 animals in 2004. As the population was founded by animals which had escaped from a large number of enclosures, their genetic origin is very heterogeneous. Most of them are probably descended from German and other central European stock. Some of them have also mixed with domestic stock, which can be seen from a spotted skin colour.

3.2 Legislation

The first national legislation regarding hunting was proclaimed as early as the fourteenth century. Important parts of it regulated the traditional hunting privileges of the aristocracy and the royal family, who were granted the hunting monopoly on all hoofed game. But it also regulated the duties of the common man in the war against large carnivores, including participating in large organised beats, and keeping nets and other equipment for these operations. New versions of these acts appeared during the sixteenth and seventeenth centuries, conserving old traditions and attitudes regarding hunting and ownership of game. An important change came in 1789, when the Swedish king ended the aristocratic monopoly on hoofed game and introduced the principle that the hunting rights on all game belonged to the land owner. This new legislation has been the basic principle for hunting rights ever since.

During the nineteenth century legislation that restricted hunting modes and seasons appeared for the first time. The present hunting legislation has its basis in the 1938 Hunting Act, which reformed most of the former legislation in this area. More recent legislations are just modifications and amendments to this Act.

Sweden has no specific legislation regarding conservation or management of game. All treatment of mammals and birds is regulated in the Hunting Act. The basic principle here is that all mammal and bird species are protected, unless stated otherwise in the hunting regulations.

A special committee appointed by the Swedish Environment Protection Agency (SEPA), with representatives of hunters and conservationists included, lists species that may be hunted each year, together with the opening and closing dates of the hunting season specified for each species. The principle here is that species may only be hunted if there is some practical purpose either in production of food, or of other revenues like pelts, or for protection of other game or property (e.g. crows and magpies to reduce nest predation on game birds) and only if they are present in viable populations.

The open season for a certain species might change from year to year and differ between different parts of the country. Factors considered here are breeding seasons, dependency of young upon their mothers (e.g. seasons open only for antlered animals), and climatic factors that might impose physical restrictions on certain species. The legislation imposes a duty on the landowner, or the person leasing the hunting right from the landowner, to manage the game in such a way that its preservation and welfare is safeguarded, but also to balance the abundance to minimise damage on other economic or welfare interests, like forestry, crop growing, stockholding, fishing and the road traffic.

There are specified requirements on the weapon, depending on the game species. For all hoofed game, except roe deer, rifles are requested, with minimum calibres and ballistics of the bullet specified for different species. Shotguns are allowed for roe deer, and can also be used for wild boar, but only with special cartridges containing a bullet instead of grains ('brenneke'). Hunting with bow and arrows is not allowed in Sweden, but this ban is currently under review. Also, all trapping of wild animals is regulated. Only trap types approved by SEPA are allowed. The use of steel traps is not allowed, nor is poisoning for any species.

The ethics of hunting are also strictly regulated by the Hunting Act. The basic principle is that the hunting should be humane and cause the game as little suffering as possible and the killing should be swift and painless. Stressing, painful or risky hunting methods like par-force chases or deer hunting during dark hours are not allowed. During all hunting of hoofed game the hunter must have access to a dog that can find wounded animals, and promptly investigate the effects of any shot fired and perform a thorough search if wounding has occurred. Hunting from motor vehicles of any kind is not allowed.

3.3 Management objectives

The only general and national objective for the management of game species in Sweden is that they should be preserved in viable populations, but not be allowed to seriously damage other vital interests of society. Within this rather wide frame, it is up to every single landowner, hunting team or management area to make their own management objectives and plans. Generally, it can be said that the objectives for hunting and game management to most hunters are a combination of hunting for sport and venison. Trophies are important, but not to the same degree as in many countries on the continent. Hunting for furs was important in the past, but as a result of falling prices this has completely ceased in Sweden. So far, management plans are common only for moose and red deer management areas. Here, the typical objective is to balance the hunting interests to hold a large stock against the forestry and farming interests to minimise damage to trees and crops. In recent years, there has been a growing interest among hunters in not only maximising the hunting bag, but also in increasing the quality of the stock, e.g. in the form of more mature trophy bulls and bucks. For some large estates in the southern part of the country, this has been an important objective for a longer period. Scientific management plans based on hard data and kept operational through continuous updating, however, are still rare.

3.4 Management structure

As already mentioned, the hunting rights on all game are granted to the landowner. The landowner in turn may lease out the hunting rights to another person or group of persons, and this is common in Sweden. Normally, in these cases, the hunting right is leased for a period of five years or longer, with the rights and obligations of the two parties confirmed in a formal contract. There are many examples of single hunters or small hunting coteries that have leased the same hunting ground for many decades or even generations.

The leasing fee is an important revenue for many landowners, and may be rather high, especially in the more densely populated southern part of the country. Fees amounting to SEK 250 (approx. EUR 30) per hectare and year are not uncommon. The majority of the 300 000 registered hunters in Sweden are hunting on their own hunting ground, either as landowners or on a leased ground, where they are often members of a hunting team or hunting club that leases the ground together. Some larger landowners also lease out hunts on a daily basis, so called day cards, which carefully specify what species and categories of animals you may hunt and bag limits.

The national authority officially responsible for the supervision of hunting and management and conservation of wild species is SEPA (Naturvårdsverket). SEPA prepares directives which control or regulate hunting activities and which regulate modes of hunting, design of traps, determine which species can be hunted and set the hunting seasons. SEPA also maintains the national register of licensed hunters, and collects the annual hunting fee required from each person who wants to hunt (in 2006 it was SEK 200, approx. EUR 25). The money from this fee is devoted to a 'Wildlife Management Fund' ('Viltvårdsfonden', see also Norway, Chapter 2). With 300 000 registered hunters paying EUR 25 each, the fund presently receives around EUR 7.5 million per annum. From this fund, around EUR 2 million are taken annually for financing wildlife research. SEPA has a Wildlife Research Committee that distributes the research funding after evaluating applications from the scientific community.

At the regional level, each county has game officials and a game management committee, consisting of members from different sectors of society with interest in the game (landowners, hunting associations, conservationists, etc.), but with an official from the county as a chairperson. The most important task of these committees is to handle the moose hunting licence systems including registration of moose hunting grounds and treating applications for quotas (see below and Box 3.1). There is no state or regional control over harvests of any ungulate species other than moose. This is left entirely to the landowners or 'Game Management Areas' (GMAs, 'Jaktvårdsområden').

In the 1938 Hunting Act, the Swedish Association for Hunting and Wildlife Management ('Svenska Jägareförbundet', hereafter called 'SJF'), a non-governmental organisation (NGO) that organises around two-thirds of all registered hunters in the country, was given rather wide responsibilities by the government, to organise hunting and take responsibility for the management of the game. For this work a large allowance was granted to the SJF annually from the Wildlife Management

Fund. In recent years some of these official responsibilities have been taken over by SEPA (which did not exist in 1938). The SJF has established a regional game management office in most counties. The tasks of these offices are to educate, advise and support the local hunters and collect information on the status of the local game, and collect hunting statistics. The 1938 Hunting Act also provided the opportunity for landowners to cooperate in collaborative management within GMAs for a more efficient management of the game. An important task of the regional game management offices is to encourage the establishment of such wildlife management areas and support them. The SJF also participates in the annual censuses of large carnivores, and organises the 'moose observation scheme'.

3.5 Management organisation

Firearms in Sweden can only be purchased when a licence for the specific weapon has been issued to the buyer by the police authorities. Since 1985, every person who applies for a firearm licence for hunting purposes first has to pass a standardised 'Hunters' test'. In the test, the applicant is required to answer a large number of written questions on hunting legislation, hunting ethics, biology of the game species, proper preparation of pelts and meat, as well as demonstrating a knowledge of weapons, ballistics and safe handling of firearms. Practical tests of the person's shooting skills are also included. Courses to prepare applicants for the test now are a big commercial enterprise in Sweden.

In 2008 there were 264 000 registered hunters in Sweden, including 14 500 women, paying the annual hunting fee. There is no special register for ungulate hunters, and most of the Swedish hunters combine ungulate and small game hunting. The number of registered hunters has decreased slowly, but steadily, during the last ten years. The majority of the hunters today are urban people that hunt on leased land or with friends, but still a substantial proportion are farmers that hunt on their own land. Hunting was traditionally a male occupation, but in recent years there have been an increasing number of women taking up hunting, and this trend is encouraged by, for example, the Swedish Association for Hunting and Wildlife Management, which organises around 190 000 of the hunters. There is a second, competing, organisation for hunters in Sweden 'The National League for Countryside Hunters' ('Jägarnas Riksförbund – Landsbygdens Jägare'), but with its markedly lower number of members, approximately 15 000 members, it is much less influential.

Approximately 25% of the forested land in Sweden is owned by the state, another 25% by big forest companies, and the remaining 50% by medium sized or small private farmers (10–500 ha), with a few larger private estates in the south (500–10 000 ha). As the hunting rights are tied to the landowner or leaser of the hunting ground, game management in Sweden is a private affair. On most smaller hunting grounds, the management is at best of an informal trial and error type, without any written management plans. Where small hunting grounds have been united into GMAs often covering 5000 ha or more, the management may be a little more formal. Usually hunting statistics are collected annually, and rough shooting plans are issued each year after consideration by the GMA board and based on earlier years' experience and general impressions of game population status. In many of the GMAs, all stakeholders are allowed to personally hunt over the whole area irrespective of the size of his or her own hunting ground. Apart from shooting plans, winter feeding of deer (not moose) is the most common management action performed both by single hunters and GMAs. Today there are almost 2000 GMAs covering 7.5 million ha, i.e. more than 15% of the country. The big forest companies, including the state forests, which often own large areas in different parts of the country, usually operate a similar level of game management. They often divide their land into more manageable hunting units (1000–5000 ha), with teams of employees or outsiders leasing the rights on these units. Normally the companies have one or several persons employed to specifically handle the hunting issues, mainly occupied with organising the communication with their different hunting teams, solving conflicts, collecting fees, receiving and checking annual reports, etc. It is normal that the company demands reports on shooting bags from their hunting teams, and they expect them to perform certain management apart from shooting, like winter feeding. In recent years there has been a growing conflict between several companies and their hunters regarding the desired moose density, which the companies want to push down lower than is desirable for the hunters.

Many of the larger private estates in the south have an even more developed structure for game management, much like the management on similar estates on the European continent. They often employ a professional hunter, responsible for at least some minimal management plans for deer and moose. These plans however rarely build on continuous collection and analysis of data, other than harvest data like body weights, trophy qualities and rough age structure analysis built on inspection of tooth wear, combined with a general impression by the hunter of the status of the game population through their daily work in field. Standardised censuses of densities are almost never performed other than for moose.

3.5.1 The management of moose and red deer

The great exception to this rather loose and informal approach to game management is the treatment of moose and, to a certain extent, red deer. The moose is the most valuable game species in Sweden, and moose hunting has been surrounded by special regulations and management for a long time. Already in the 1938 Hunting

Act provision was made for larger units of land (minimum approximately 1000 ha) to combine to hunt moose on 'licence', a kind of quota, with a specified number of animals that could be taken within a given open season (initially one month, but nowadays up to five months). For those hunting on the 'general system', there was no restriction on number of animals, but the open season was much more restricted: only three or four days. During the 1950s and 1960s more and more hunters united into larger units to be allowed to 'hunt on licence'. In 1975 the so called 'coordinated moose hunting system' was decided by Parliament. Most hunters and land were included in the licence system, and the hunters who chose to stand outside of this system were not only restricted by the short season (maximum five days), but also limited to a maximum of one adult moose and one calf. During the 1990s, moose management became even more organised, with the establishment of 'Moose Management Areas' (MMAs, 'älgskötselområden') where landowners and hunting teams unite (on a voluntary basis) into even larger areas, big enough to make management of this large mobile species more feasible. A rule of thumb is that the areas should be large enough to annually produce at least 25 moose, which in most parts of the country means a minimum of 10 000 ha, although there are examples of areas down to 4 000 ha. The hunting itself may continue to be divided into smaller areas, but the MMA agrees on a communal management plan for the whole area, including harvest quotas based on whatever information they have on moose density and production, and forest damage level. Many of these areas are large enough to afford occasional air censuses used for the preparation of the plans, and they also use data from the 'moose observation scheme'. The MMA management plans, including a proposal of how many moose should be taken, run for three years. The local county authorities check and approve the plans, based on evaluation of how well earlier plans have worked.

The moose management areas today include 11 million ha, which is approximately 25% of the total hunting ground in the country. For those standing outside of the MMAs there are a number of different options available with a rather complicated set of regulations, which is described in detail in Box 3.1. The most common system is the so called A-licence areas, covering about half of the country, where there is a minimum area requirement of approximately 200 ha, and where the hunters apply for a certain quota, and have a rather long open season. For smaller units there are several options, all of them restricted either by length of season or number of animals allowed.

In a similar way red deer management units have been formed on a voluntary basis in most areas where breeding populations of this species occur. Often, the moose and red deer management areas merge. For moose, but not for red deer, a report to the county on number and sex/age of shot animals is mandatory, and a certain fee is paid for each adult moose shot, calves are free.

> **Box 3.1**
> **The different options in the Swedish moose management system**
>
> 1. Moose management areas (MMAs). Large areas (minimum annual production of 25 moose, which means a minimum of 5000–10 000 ha, but most are much larger). Decide their own harvest quota in 3-year management plans, which are based on presumed moose production and tolerable level of damage on forest. The plans are checked and approved by the local county. Minimum 70 days open season, but usually 3 months or more. In 2004, MMAs comprised 11 million ha.
> 2. A-licence areas. Large enough to annually produce at least one moose (min. ≈ 200 ha). Apply annually to the county for a quota. In some counties no restriction on number of calves. Long open season (70 days–3 months). In 2004, A-licence areas comprised 24.6 million ha.
> 3. B-licence areas. Minimum 5 ha. Only one moose allowed (adult or calf is optional). Restricted open season, 1–5 days depending on county. In 2004, B-licence areas comprised included 856 000 ha.
> 4. E-licence areas ('calf-areas'). Minimum 20 ha. One calf only is allowed, but the open season is 70 days. In 2004, E-licence areas comprised 579 000 ha.
> 5. Unregistered land. No minimum area required. Only calves allowed, but no restriction on number. Restricted open season, 1–5 days. Unknown coverage, but in 2004 only 34 moose were shot in this category.

The fees vary between SEK 200 and 400 per moose, dependent on the county. These fees are used by the counties for paying the hunting administration and for some other moose management actions, for example subsidising regional air censuses.

For ungulate species other than moose and red deer, there are no efforts to have coordinated management outside that of the GMAs and single hunting grounds. The need for such effort does not seem to be great at present, as all species of ungulates in Sweden seem to be thriving, with one exception. The only species of ungulate that is really having problems is the musk ox, but that has nothing to do with hunting, as it is a protected species.

3.6 Actual management and hunting practices

3.6.1 Harvest planning

As noted above (section 3.2) shooting or harvest plans are not required by the authorities, other than for the specific moose and red deer management areas. Nonetheless many landowners and hunting teams have tried to establish such plans, with varying degrees of success. Apart from the moose and red deer management areas, the best shooting plans for deer species are probably prepared on the large private estates in southern Sweden where professional hunters are employed and where often hunting of specific trophy animals is sold to wealthy hunters from abroad. But, for the majority of hunting grounds, there are no written harvest plans for any ungulate species.

Maybe the most difficult obstacle to preparing useful harvest plans is lack of information, especially on densities. For a long time the only statistics that have been available are harvest records, and even those are rough since there is no statutory requirement for return of figures other than for moose and larger carnivores. However, recently different census methods for ungulates are developing and coming into broader use (section 3.7).

3.6.2 Harvest statistics

On a national level, the only information available on fluctuations and long-term trends in the different game species populations, except for some game bird species, are the harvest statistics. In Sweden, a statutory return on number of harvested animals is compulsory only for moose and large carnivores. However, since 1939, the Swedish Association for Hunting and Wildlife Management has collected bag records on all game species from its members on a voluntary basis. Response frequencies to the annual requests for bag records vary strongly between areas and periods. In the best counties, up to 80% of the hunting grounds are covered, but in some counties and years it is below 20%. The figures received for each county are extrapolated to give a total figure representative for the whole county, and these are then summed up for the whole country. The graphs in Figures 3.1, and 3.3–3.5 are based on these records. To improve the quality of these statistics, there has been discussion on making reports on bag records compulsory, as they are in Denmark. It is feared, however, that forcing all hunters to come up with harvest figures every year might make them even more unreliable.

3.6.3 National wildlife health investigations

The National Veterinary Institute in Uppsala has, since the 1940s, run a programme for post mortem investigations of wild mammal and bird species (Borg, 1970). The objective is to scan the health status of wildlife. The programme receives an annual grant from the government for financing port mortems of wild animals. Anyone finding a dead wild mammal or bird in the field can send the animal free of charge to the Institute and will get a report of the findings of the post mortem, including cause of death. In this way, the Institute is supplied with several thousand animals each year for their monitoring work. Beside these routine investigations, the Institute also initiates special directed investigations, e.g. during the local presumed epidemic among moose in the Älvsborg county in the 1990s.

3.6.4 The moose hunting team

Most moose hunting is performed in teams. A moose hunting team is a tight group of people, normally consisting of 5–20 persons, all of whom have usually known each other for a long time, and with a composition that changes only slowly and gradually. Each team has its own traditions and sets of rules concerning a lot of aspects of the hunt, from requirements on training, shooting skills and shooting tests each year before the hunt starts, to how meat and trophies are distributed. Safety rules are usually very strict.

There is always a leader of the team, usually appointed through consensus. The team might discuss most matters, but the leader takes the final decision on everything, from distribution of posts to actions when a moose is wounded. It is the duty of the leader to check that all hunters have legal licences for their weapons and paid their hunting fee. Usually the team also has its own rules for which categories of animals are allowed to shoot and how many. These rules might be changed from one day to the next depending on the development of the hunt.

The classical moose hunting method in Scandinavia, and by many regarded as the most interesting, is hunting with a loose dog that operates within the team and is controlled by one person, the 'dog-leader', who knows the dog well, usually its owner. There are a couple of dog breeds specifically bred for this type of hunting. The dog searches for moose, usually upwind, and when it gets contact it tries to catch up with the moose and make it 'stand'. Here, the typical moose defensive behaviour against wolves is exploited. When the dog has managed to get the moose at bay it starts barking in a characteristic monotonous rhythm. It is now the task of the 'dog-leader' to stalk the moose and try to get a shot while the dog continues to bark and hold the moose at bay, which requires a good amount of stalking skill. At the slightest mistake by the hunter, the moose 'breaks loose' from the stand and runs off. When this happens the dog follows silently until again the moose stops and faces the dog. This type of hunting might be performed by the dog-leader alone with his dog, but usually it is done in a team where the rest of the hunters are posted at places known by tradition to be passing points for moving moose. Most moose in this type of hunt are actually killed by the posted hunters, not by the dog-leader. There might be more than one dog team operating simultaneously, but then they divide the operation area between them. A variation of this method is that the dog-leader operates with the dog on leash, either with or without posted hunters.

This latter variety of hunting with dogs is actually a special case of the most common moose hunting method, which basically is a line or wide circle of posted shooters around a certain sector of the hunting ground, from where efforts are made to press the moose present in the sector out of it, by which they hopefully will be exposed to the hunters. Methods for pushing out the moose vary, from a large number of beaters, to a single or a few persons zigzagging through the sector, either with or without dogs.

In southern Sweden, where there is a high density of moose, the sectors usually are not more than a couple of hundred hectares, and a hunting team might manage up to four or five sectors per day. The rapid change of sectors makes the hunt more varied and less boring for the hunters posted to fixed positions around the hunting area. In northern Sweden, however, the sectors might be thousands of hectares, and here it takes much patience to be one of the hunters posted to the periphery.

The simplest form of moose hunting, usually practised on small hunting grounds where the hunters are anxious not to drive out any moose to the neighbours, is a silent sit-and-wait strategy. As this method is usually used on B-licence areas with a short open season, the hunters might sit silently waiting at the same post every day for the whole open season, i.e. for 2–5 days.

Some hunters prefer to operate completely alone and without dogs, often with a combination of stalking and a mobile sit-and-wait strategy.

3.6.5 Hunting methods for smaller ungulates

Red deer, fallow deer and roe deer are hunted either by the method of posting hunters to fixed positions and beating game towards them, described above, or by stalking. Instead of beaters or in combination with them, one or several flushing dogs might be used. On small hunting grounds sit-and-wait, often from some kind of shooting tower, is the most common method for all these species.

A special Scandinavian method, originally developed for hares and foxes, but now also used for roe deer, is using specially trained 'driving dogs'. Only one dog is used, which is let loose to search for fresh roe deer tracks. When the dog has found the deer it slowly pursues ('driving') it while barking, thereby announcing to the hunters the location of the drive. Only slow driving dog breeds with short legs, like dachshunds or dachsbracken are used for this type of hunting. The deer moves away slowly, often waiting for the dog, and not leaving its normal home range, which for a roe deer usually is less than 50 ha. The hunters' job is to try to figure out in advance where the deer will pass, based on earlier experience and the continuous information from the actual drive, and move to such passages and post there.

The most common hunting method for wild boar is sit-and-wait at a bait, which can be composed of fruit, sugar beets, bread or corn, or some other attractive food. Wild boar is the only ungulate species which it is permitted to shoot during the dark hours, so many boar hunters are equipped with special night spotting scopes. Lamps are allowed at baited areas. Boars are also hunted with beaters, or with loose dogs.

3.7 Census methods

Sweden, for a long time, had no systematic nationwide system for the census of any species of ungulates, apart from the harvest statistics. All census efforts were sporadic and local. However, during the 1980s a national system for an index of population size and trend at least for moose was developed by the Swedish Association for Hunting and Wildlife Management, based on observations of moose during the first week of the moose hunting season. The system is simply called 'moose-observation' ('Älg-obs') (Kindeberg *et al.* 2009). In the northern half of the country, the moose hunting season starts the second Monday in September, and in the southern half the second Monday in October. By tradition this has been so since the early 1900s, and these starting dates are the same irrespective of the hunting system. To many hunters, the first 'moose week' is just as important as Christmas, and most save a week of their holiday for this event. Thus, there are an extremely large number of potential moose observers out this week, and this fact is exploited by the 'moose-obs' programme (cf. also Norway).

The 'moose-obs' system does not give absolute figures, just indices. The observation data gathered generate estimates in population trends, reproduction and sex ratio for use in the management of the moose populations. The hunters systematically record number and category of all moose observed during the first 7 days of the moose hunt together with observation effort (hours). The system is in use all over Sweden and logs annually about 4.5 million observation hours on 35 000 submitted standard forms with around half a million moose observations. Since 1998, large carnivores have also been included on the form, and approximately 1000 observations are registered annually of wolf, lynx and brown bear, together.

The harvest statistics and the moose observation programme are the only nationwide ungulate census programme in Sweden. There are, in addition, a number of direct census methods used to produce actual density figures, but these are only applied in particular local areas, and even then, irregularly (not every year). There have never been any official direct censuses of number of ungulates over very large areas to produce total numbers for whole counties or for the whole country.

Air censuses of moose have, so far, been the most common method to census absolute numbers. Such counts started during the 1960s in certain areas. Most censuses have been organised and financed by large forest companies for their own forests, but some counties have also performed air censuses for parts of their territory. For a long time, only fixed wing aircraft were used, but gradually fixed wing aircraft have been replaced by counts from helicopters. Today, only helicopters are used. Two types of censuses are made, total counts over a whole area, and counts in sampling units. A typical sampling unit is 400 ha. Censuses are performed during winter, preferably after a snowstorm when all trees are snow covered, giving better contrast to the dark moose. Tests of accuracy have been performed in areas with marked moose, but this can only be done after expensive marking programmes. Recently a cheaper method of determining accuracy has been developed. Each sampling area is censused twice by two different crews immediately after each other, the position of each sighted moose is determined exactly by GPS techniques, and then the proportion of moose seen by both crews can be used to calculate visibility. In recent years, trials counting red deer from the air also have been performed, and the results seem promising.

One problem with air counts is that in forested landscapes it can be used only for very large ungulates like moose, and possibly red deer. For smaller species like roe deer it is not feasible. However, a possible method here is based on 'pellet counts'. Pellet counts, i.e. a sampling of faecal pellet groups in small plots (10–100 m^2) distributed over the census area, have been a widely used method to census ungulates in North America and elsewhere (Neff, 1968). In Sweden, it has been used within some research projects since the 1970s (Liberg, 1980; Cederlund and Liberg, 1995). Recently, the method has been tested for management purposes in the county of Värmland, coupled with track counts during winter. Evaluations of this trial will determine whether this will become a more widely used method in a national official context.

3.8 Damage and ecosystem impact

The growing ungulate populations in Sweden have caused concern and debate about ungulate impact on forest trees (Lavsund, 1987), agricultural crops (Ministry of Agriculture, 1990), ecosystems (Persson *et al.*, 2000), as well as about ungulate–vehicle collisions (Seiler, 2004). Such concerns affect the ungulate management in a significant way and have initiated an increasing demand for counter-measures.

3.8.1 Forest damage

Most focus has been on moose damage in economically important forest trees, mainly Scots pine (*Pinus sylvestris*). The forest damage is surveyed locally or regionally through a method called ÄBIN ('Moose Browsing Survey'; www.skogsstyrelsen.se). This method has also recently been included in the

Swedish National Forest Inventory. ÄBIN is a package of methods for estimating forest damage, browse abundance and recent (last winter's) accumulated browsing. However, the main aim is to quantify the damage on main stems of Scots pine. Main stems are stems which will form the future stand and damage is defined as a negative impact on stem quality, induced by top shoot browsing, stem breaking and bark stripping. The method does not include estimation of damage in terms of timber production losses (i.e. mediated through needle biomass loss).

The damage level varies between areas, with a range of 1–25% between counties or smaller areas. Data from the Swedish National Forest Inventory 2003–2004 indicate a mean level of 12% for the country, with a range of 9–25% between large regions (National Board of Forestry, 2006). This figure means that on average 12% of the main stems of Scots pine are damaged each winter in young forests (1–4 m tall) and with at least 10% Scots pine. Some parts of the forestry sector, especially forest companies, have, at present, a goal of not more than 2%. The accumulated damage level (all damage irrespective of time of the damage) is 40–50%, i.e. 40–50% of the pine stems have damage caused by moose (National Board of Forestry, 2006).

The damage level is not only related to moose density, but also to the characteristics of the forest (Bergström *et al.*, 1995). This is especially true on a large, e.g. national, scale, on which there is a weak correlation between damage level and moose densities alone. This relationship is strengthened if one also considers forest characteristics, such as amount of young forests (reflecting winter food abundance) and amount of Scots pine in the young forests. The amount of available preferred deciduous trees and shrubs seems to decrease the risk of damage (Bergström *et al.*, 1995). What makes moose start browsing in a pine forest stand in the first place is poorly understood. But, once a stand is being browsed and damaged, the risk for future impact will increase (Bergqvist and Bergström, *unpublished*). Such re-browsing patterns between winters also hold for the tree level, i.e. a tree that is browsed has an increased risk of future browsing (Bergqvist *et al.*, 2003).

The other major concern when it comes to economically important damage to trees by moose (and other ungulates) is the browsing impact on southern deciduous species, such as oak (*Quercus robur*) and ash (*Fraxinus excelsior*). Little information is available on this issue, but recent surveys have indicated roe deer browsing as a factor contributing to failures of oak regeneration in southern oak forests (Götmark *et al.*, 2005).

Measures to reduce forest damage by moose include hunting. Many forest owners also consider the risk of moose browsing during pre-commercial forest thinning and change their way of thinning. There is, however, a lack of knowledge concerning when and how to perform pre-commercial thinning in order to minimise risk of damage to pine. Due to the present decrease in moose harvest and the large predators operating in more areas, habitat management is increasingly discussed. In southern Sweden, where areas are suitable for regeneration with more southern tree species, fencing is used to some extent.

Other types of forest damage related to ungulate browsing are bark-stripping by red deer on Norway spruce (*Picea abies*; Lavsund, 1974) and roe deer browsing on conifer and hardwood seedlings (Bergström and Bergqvist, 1997; Kullberg and Bergström, 2001). A forecasted increase in red deer is believed to increase the future risk of bark stripping. No surveys are specifically done to estimate such damage. The recent decrease in roe deer population densities has resulted in lowered concern about seedling damage. Locally, however, the damage to seedlings is still reported to be high. There is a considerable difference in the risk for various types of tree seedlings of being attacked by large herbivores. Tree species, height and age, seedling type (potted, bare-rooted, self-regenerated) and earlier browsing influence this risk (Bergström and Bergqvist, 1997, 1999; Kullberg and Bergström, 2001). Within a national forest survey ('Polytax') of regeneration success, browsing damage on seedlings is registered.

3.8.2 Damage to agricultural crops

In the past, compensation could be claimed from county authorities for damage caused to agricultural crops by moose, red deer and fallow deer. Damage reported was verified on the ground by inspectors from regional authorities who then agreed on appropriate compensation. Over the 8-year period 1980–7, the total compensation awarded for damage from red deer, fallow deer and moose averaged SEK 8 700 000 (equivalent to about EUR 1 million). Analysis of the severity and distribution of such damage suggested that while damage at a local or farm level might be of real economic significance, with up to a 26% loss of yield in unprotected oat crops when compared against fenced controls (Kjellander, *unpublished data*), the overall area of crops reported as suffering damage (as a proportion of the area grown in any region) never exceeded 5% and is usually lower than 1% (Putman and Kjellander, 2002).

There was also some considerable year-to-year variation in damage levels recorded , a fact that was attributed to variation in time of harvest. Recent analyses indicate that time of sowing and early growth rates of cereal crops are highly correlated to spring temperatures, and that this in turn may influence time of maturity and harvest. Where crops can be harvested early, there is correspondingly less damage from ungulates, since the crops are available for shorter periods and over a period when there is a greater abundance of alternative natural food available (Putman and Kjellander, 2002).

Under new legislation enacted in 1995, it is no longer possible to obtain compensation for damage by ungulates either to agricultural crops or to forest crops. In consequence, few data are available to offer current estimates of the annual value of damage to agricultural crops.

However, given the low overall significance of damage of this sort, this type of damage is generally not ranked high in discussions about ungulate management. On the other hand, the increasing wild boar population may result in more focus on this issue. Although damage on crops may take place the whole year, wild boars visit arable fields mainly in August and feed on a number of crops, such as oat, wheat, peas and barley (Lemel, 1999). The risk that individual fields will be visited by wild boar is dependent on the amount of surrounding natural vegetation (forests). Several counter-measures are discussed and, to some extent, used: set-aside arable land with preferred crops, artificial feeding and electric fences (Lemel, 1999).

3.8.3 Ecosystem effects

In parallel to the general increase in ungulate populations across Europe and increased focus on biodiversity, the interest in the impacts of ungulates on ecosystem dynamics and ecosystem characteristics has increased dramatically (Danell et al., 2006). In Sweden, consideration has mostly been directed towards the impact of moose on preferred tree species, such as aspen (*Populus tremula*), rowan (*Sorbus aucuparia*) and willows (*Salix* spp.) (Ericsson et al., 2001); these species are important, both as living mature trees and dead wood, for many types of organisms, some of which are on the Red List.

Surveys and exclosure experiments have indicated that current levels of ungulate browsing retard height, growth and the development of the trees into adult individuals. However, there is a knowledge gap concerning the impact of ungulates on tree population dynamics and this, together with lack of good historical data, hampers the understanding of the present effects of ungulates on biodiversity mediated through browsing on preferred deciduous tree species.

From an international perspective, Swedish moose densities have been high or very high. Simulation of different moose densities has revealed that densities higher than 1 moose/km^2, a density that is commonly observed in the country, may have considerable effects on ecosystem structure and function (Persson et al., 2000, 2004, 2005). Many of the observed effects of moose activities seem to be mediated through changes in the vegetation (especially in the tree layer) and in quantity and quality of litter fall (Suominen et al., 1999). Such cascading effects are also dependent on habitat productivity and similar moose densities may give reversed effects in poor, compared to productive environments (Suominen *et al.*, unpublished).

In the early 1990s, the roe deer population peaked in Sweden (Fig. 3.4) and a general strong impact of roe deer, together with moose, on the field layer vegetation was observed (Bergqvist, 1998). Studies on clear-cuts of different ages indicated a strong impact on total plant biomass and relative plant abundance, as well as on seed and berry production (Bergquist, 1998).

Rooting by wild boar is a common phenomenon and may encompass 10% of a forested area (Welander, 2000). A 30% increase in the number of vascular plants was observed in rooted areas compared to unrooted ones and more diaspores of more species was found close to, than away from, rubbing trees (Welander, 2000).

3.8.4 Traffic accidents

Ungulate–vehicle collisions are common. In 1982, some 5000 road accidents were recorded in Sweden due to collisions with moose, red deer and roe deer; by 1993, the number of road kills had risen to 55 000, with mortality of roe deer alone in excess of 50 000 (Groot Bruinderink and Hazebroek, 1996). According to figures in a Swedish database (www.sesgruppen.se), the number of reported collisions in 2005 was 4092 (involving moose), 27 761 (roe deer), 580 (red deer and fallow deer) and 987 (wild boar). These figures are underestimates as all collisions are not reported (Seiler *et al.*, 2004).

Analysis of changes in the frequency of vehicle collisions with different species over the years suggests that the number of collisions seems to correlate quite closely with recorded harvests with some time lags (Seiler, 2004). Such a relationship is also reflected in a considerable increase in number of accidents involving wild boar; a species which now is expanding its range and increasing in population size (Truvé and Lemel, 2003). The reported number of wild boar–vehicle collisions per year was around 50 only a few years ago, but has now soared to almost 1000 collisions per year. Mitigation measures for reducing ungulate–vehicle collisions are mainly information to drivers, game-proof fences along the roads and, to some extent, thinning of forests near roads.

3.8.5 Economic costs of ungulate damage

The costs related to the above-reported impact of ungulates are mainly unknown. Some recent calculations indicate that the national losses for the forest owners due to moose impact on pine wood quality will be at least EUR 50 million per year (Glöde *et al.*, 2004; Ingemarsson *et al.*, 2005). No compensation is paid for forest damage caused by ungulates. No recent estimates of costs due to game damage on agricultural crops are available, but as mentioned above, the ungulates caused an annual loss of about EUR 1 million between the years of 1980–1987 (Ministry of Agriculture, 1990). The costs of the moose–vehicle collisions have been estimated in a recent report to be about 2.5 times the economic loss due to forest damage (Ingemarsson *et al.*, 2005).

3.9 Habitat improvement and supplementary feeding

For mobile ungulate species with large area requirements and high food demands, effective habitat improvement can be laborious and difficult. In spite of that, directed habitat improvements for ungulates are performed locally on private initiatives, but often this is not performed as a part of formal wildlife management plans.

Growing crops attractive to ungulates on small fields or along their edges are locally important contributions to food production, especially on hunting grounds and estates where there is a strong desire to hold high densities of deer. Various types of cabbage (*Brassica* spp.) are often used and sometimes fertilisers are applied. Much of the forage is, however, usually consumed before the season of food shortage, and, therefore, fencing is sometimes practised to protect the crop until winter arrives (Cederlund and Liberg, 1995).

Winter supplementary feeding of moose has not been used much in Sweden, although the interest is now increasing. Silage of grass or other crops is put out along low-traffic forest roads in wintertime and this attracts many moose. Along a 2.5 km-long forest road in the county of Värmland, where silage bales had been put out, 100 moose have been seen at the same time (R. Styffe, *pers. comm.*). The primary aim for supplying moose with extra food is to keep high moose densities and at the same time keep forest damage at acceptable levels. As in Norway (Gundersen *et al.*, 2004), there is also a wish to use supplementary feeding to intercept migrating moose before they reach damage-sensitive forests, usually in lowlands. A side-effect of supplementary feeding for moose is that a great number of local people and tourists are visiting the feeding sites to see moose. Alone, or in combination with for example supplementary feeding, presentation of salt blocks for game is very common.

Supplementary winter feeding of roe deer has been a very common management practice all over Sweden, but due to a series of mild winters the extent of supplementary feeding has recently decreased (Cederlund and Liberg, 1995). Without regular and widespread winter feeding, it is doubtful whether there would have been any roe deer populations at all in the interior of northern Sweden. Also northern occurrences of small and discrete red and fallow deer populations are dependent on supplemental winter feeding. Finally, on some estates in the south very high densities of especially fallow deer are made possible through winter feeding.

All feeding is on private initiative; there are no official feeding programmes for game. Natural forage, such as dried deciduous twigs with their leaves still on, and hay (for roe deer: clover hay or other herbs) are recommended (Cederlund and Liberg, 1995), but many people also feed crushed oats or other cereals, and a number of special 'game fodders', e.g. 'Capre'. Usually feeding starts in late autumn, to avoid indigestion problems, which might occur in ruminants if you suddenly supply rich food in the middle of the winter after the animals' metabolism has adjusted to the poor natural winter food.

The wild boars in Sweden rely heavily on food supplied by hunters. Of 57 stomachs inspected from an area in southern mid-Sweden, 91% of the stomachs contained less than 20% of natural food; the rest was food from supplementary feeding sites (Lemel, 1999). The main food supplied is maize, legumes (*Fabaceae* spp.) and cereals. The main objectives for supplementary feeding of wild boars are to enhance shooting and to reduce crop damage.

3.10 Problems with current management and future challenges

The moose hunting system has improved greatly over the years, but is still not perfect. The system where some landowners can continue to take moose annually on very small hunting grounds (in the worst cases, just one or a few ha) is not favouring coordination of the management and a production-based harvest. Many landowners are tempted to stay out of the coordinated moose management or licence areas, where their share annually might be only a few kilogrammes of meat (the harvested meat in united management areas is usually distributed among the hunters based on the size of their respective hunting ground), and instead to gamble for a whole moose on a 'B-licence', even if the extremely short season makes this option more risky. For decades proponents of a more biologically based harvesting system have tried to stop this possibility, and force all hunters into a coordinated moose management, but each time the Parliament has treated the issue, there has been a marginal majority for also keeping a more 'free' option. At present there is a new government committee charged to explore possible further ways to achieve a more complete coordination of the moose management. What is being discussed here is even larger units than the MMAs of today.

Another problem, that has to do with the quality of the moose, is the fact that for a long time maximisation of production of moose has been the first priority. This means that the sex ratio was skewed very strongly towards cows. In the worst areas there were five to six cows for each bull. The mean age of bulls was below two years, competition between the bulls was thus non-existent, and trophy bulls were extremely rare. In recent years an increasing proportion of hunting teams has acknowledged this problem, and made efforts to correct this mismanagement.

There are also visible results of these efforts, mean ages of bulls are increasing, and trophies have improved.

The problem for red deer management units is that there is a lack of sanctions for those breaking the system. The management plans for red deer are completely voluntary, they do not have to be approved by the game officials, there are no limits on the harvest as long as the animals are shot inside the season, and no reports of shot animals to the authorities are required. In other words, the wildlife authorities have left overall control to the hunters and landowners, which to some is too large a temptation. The obvious remedy here is to establish a system like the one for moose, but there is no political majority for such a change today.

At present, at least three or four additional challenges for the future can be identified. The first regards moose management and forest damage. The moose population has been reduced by 50% during the last 20 years, but forestry officials in high positions have recently demanded that another 50% reduction is necessary to get damage down to a tolerable level. The basis for their calculations of damage costs, however, has been strongly questioned, especially by hunters. An optimal solution of this conflict is still a long way away. Research in the area, however, is presently intensive in Sweden, although nothing has yet been published. Recently, locally high densities of the expanding red deer population are creating concern among foresters.

The second field of concern for the future management of ungulates is the rapidly expanding populations of large carnivores (Liberg and Andrén, *in press*; Wabakken *et al.*, 2001). The conflict between foresters and hunters is seriously intensified when wolves are present. At moose densities above 8–10 moose/1000 ha there is little competition between wolves and hunters, but at the low moose densities now demanded by foresters (< 4 moose/1000 ha), the competition between hunters and wolves is likely to be increased (Sand *et al.*, in press). Likewise there is a strong conflict between hunters and lynx (Liberg, 1997). The lynx population has recently increased and expanded, and has depressed roe deer densities over large parts of central Sweden. In the areas where this process has developed furthest, the lynx population is itself also now decreasing, presumably as an effect of prey scarcity (Liberg and Andrén, 2006). Now lynx are expanding into the heartlands of roe deer in southern Sweden, and the worry among hunters is high. Balancing the interests of hunter to have reasonable roe deer densities with the conservationists' demands for a large and viable lynx population will be a difficult task for the future.

The third challenge will be how to manage the wild boar, which is the ungulate species that is growing and expanding most rapidly in Sweden today. This is a relatively new species to Swedish hunters, and, along with its expansion, new hunters are exposed to this game. Farmers are anxious about the impact of this new problem species, and also the rapidly increasing number of road accidents with boars is causing concern for the authorities responsible for road traffic safety. Maybe this challenge can be coupled to a possible fourth, progressing climate change. This is expected to have strong impacts on flora and fauna, and species like wild boar and red deer are presumed to be favoured by these changes. What effect this will have on their productivity, density and range is today completely unknown, and is coupled with the uncertainty for both forestry and agriculture.

References

Ahlén, I. (1965a) Studies on red deer *Cervus elaphus* L. in Scandinavia I: History of distribution. *Swedish Wildlife* **3**, 1–88.

Ahlén, I. (1965b) Studies on red deer *Cervus elaphus* L. in Scandinavia II: Taxonomy and osteology of prehistoric and recent populations. *Swedish Wildlife* **3**, 89–176.

Ahlén, I. (1965c) Studies on red deer *Cervus elaphus* L. in Scandinavia III: Ecological investigations. *Swedish Wildlife* **3**, 177–376.

Ahlén, I. (1975) Winter habitats of moose and deer in relation to land use in Scandinavia. *Swedish Wildlife* **6**, 45–192.

af Sillén, A. W. (1851) *Svenska handelns och näringarnas historia*. Del 1. Uppsala 1851. 142 pp.

Ball, J. P., Danell, K. and Sunesson, P. (2000) Response of a herbivore community to increased food quality and quantity: an experiment with nitrogen fertilizer in a boreal forest. *Journal of Applied Ecology* **37**, 247–55.

Bergman, F. A. (1960) Skånes skogar. *Skånes Naturskyddsförenings Årsskrift* **47**, 199–222.

Bergquist, J. (1998) Influence by ungulates on early plant succession and forest regeneration in south Swedish spruce forests. PhD thesis, Department of Animal Ecology, Swedish University of Agricultural Sciences, Umeå, Sweden.

Bergqvist, G., Bergström, R. and Edenius, L. (2003) Effects of moose (*Alces alces*) rebrowsing on damage development in young stands of Scots pine (*Pinus sylvestris*). *Forest Ecology and Management* **176**, 397–403.

Bergström, R. and Bergqvist, G. (1997) Frequencies and patterns of browsing by large herbivores on conifer seedlings. *Scandinavian Journal of Forest Research* **12**, 288–94.

Bergström, R. and Bergqvist, G. (1999) Large herbivore browsing on conifer seedlings related to seedling morphology. *Scandinavian Journal of Forest Research* **14**, 361–7.

Bergström, R., Jernelid, H., Lavsund, S., Lundberg, K. and Wallin, K. (1995) Älgtäthet – betestryck – fodertillgång – skogstillstånd – skadenivåer – skaderisker. Slutrapport från projektet Balanserad älgstam. [Moose densities: browsing and damage; Final report from the research project, Balanced moose populations]. (In Swedish.)

Borg, K. (1970) On mortality and reproduction of roe deer in Sweden during the period 1948–1969. *Swedish Wildlife* **7**, 121–49.

Broman, E. K., Wallin, K., Steen, M. and Cederlund, G. (2002) A wasting syndrome in Swedish moose (*Alces alces*): background and current hypotheses. *Ambio* **31**, 409–16.

Brönsted, J. (1957) *Danmarks oldtid I*. Copenhagen: Stenalderen.

Cederlund, G. and Liberg, O. (1995) *Rådjuret – Viltet, Ekologin, Jakten*. Svenska Jägareförbundet, Stockholm, 310 pp. (In Swedish.)

Cederlund, G. N. and Markgren, G. (1987). The development of the Swedish moose population. *Swedish Wildlife Research, Suppl* **1**, Part 1, 55–62.

Danell, K., Bergström, R. and Dirke, K. (1983) Moose browsing on juvenile and adult birches (*Betula pendula* and *B. pubescens*): test of a hypothesis on chemical defence. *Proceedings of the International Union of Game Biologists*, Tjeckoslovakien, pp. 400–6.

Danell, K., Bergström, R., Duncan, P. and Pastor, J., eds. (2006) *Large Herbivore Ecology, Ecosystem Dynamics and Conservation*. Cambridge, UK: Cambridge University Press, 506 pp.

Ericsson, G., Edenius, L. and Sundström, D. (2001) Factors affecting browsing by moose (*Alces alces* L.) on European aspen (*Populus tremula* L.) in a managed boreal landscape. *Ecoscience* **8**, 344–9.

Ekman, H., Hermansson, N., Petterson, J.-O. *et al.* (1992) *Älgen-Djuret, skötseln och jakten*. [Moose Biology, Management and Hunting]. Stockholm: Svenska Jagareförbundet. (In Swedish.)

Glöde, D., Bergström, R. and Pettersson F. (2004) Intäktsförluster på grund av älgbetning av tall i Sverige. [Income losses due to moose browsing on Scots pine in Sweden]. Arbetsrapport Nr 570, Skogforsk, Uppsala. (In Swedish.)

Götmark, F., Berglund, Å. and Wiklander, K. (2005) Browsing damage on broadleaved trees in semi-natural temperate forest in Sweden, with a focus on oak regeneration. *Scandinavian Journal of Forest Research* **20**, 223–34.

Groot Bruinderink, G. W. T. A. and Hazebroek, E. (1996). Ungulate traffic collisions in Europe. *Conservation Biology* **10**, 1059–67.

Gundersen, H., Andreassen, H. P. and Storaas, T. (2004) Supplemental feeding of migratory moose *Alces alces*: forest damage at two spatial scales. *Wildlife Biology* **10**, 213–23.

Ingemarsson, F., Thuresson, T. and Claesson, S. (2005) Älg-och rådjursstammarnas kostnader och värden. [The costs and values of moose and roe deer populations]. Preliminary report. National Forestry Board Mimeo. (In Swedish.)

Jarnemo, A. and Liberg, O. (2005) Red fox removal and roe deer fawn survival: a 14 year study. *Journal of Wildlife Management* **69**(3), 1090–8.

Kindberg, J., Ericsson, G. and Swenson, J. E. (2009) Monitoring rare and elusive large mammals using effort-corrected voluntary observers. *Biological Conservation* **142**, 159–65.

Kullberg, Y. and Bergström, R. (2001) Winter browsing by large herbivores on deciduous seedlings in southern Sweden. *Scandinavian Journal of Forest Research* **16**, 371–8.

Laikre, L., Ryman, N. and Lundh, N. G. (1997) Estimated inbreeding in a small wild muskox *Ovibus moschatus* population and its possible effects on population reproduction. *Biological Conservation* **79**, 197–204.

Lavsund, S. (1974) Skadegörelse på tall *Pinus silvestris* L. av kronhjort *Cervus elaphus* L. [Damage to Scots pine *Pinus silvestris* L. from red deer *Cervus elaphus* L.]. Institute of Forest Zoology, Royal College of Forestry, Stockholm. (In Swedish.)

Lavsund, S. (1987). Moose relationships to forestry in Finland, Norway and Sweden. *Swedish Wildlife Research*, Supplement **1**, 229–44.

Lavsund, S. and Sandegren, F. (1989) Swedish moose management and harvest during the period 1964–1989. *Alces* **25**, 58–62.

Lemel, J. (1999) *Populationstillväxt, dynamik och spridning hos vildsvinet*, Sus scrofa, *i mellersta Sverige*. Final report. Uppsala, Sweden: Swedish Association for Hunting and Wildlife Management, 40 pp. (In Swedish.)

Liberg, O. (1980) *Census of herbivores over large areas, based on pellet counts*. Swedish Hunters Association Conference, Nordiska Viltforskarkongressen Uppsala, Sweden.
Liberg, O. (1997) *Lodjuret – Viltet, ekologi och människan*. Uppsala: Svenska Jägareförbundet/Almkvist and Wiksell, 95 pp.
Liberg, O. and Andrén, H. (2006) The lynx population in Sweden 1994–2004. An evaluation of census data and methods. Report from Wildlife Damage Center/Grimsö Swedish University of Agricultural Sciences (in Swedish with English figure texts and abstract).
Liberg, O. and Wahlström, L. K. (1995) Habitat stability and litter size in the Cervidae: a comparative analysis. In K. Wahlström, ed., *Natal Dispersal in Roe Deer*. Ph.D. thesis, Stockholm University, Sweden.
Liberg, O., Cederlund, G. and Kjellander, P. (1994) Population dynamics of roe deer in Sweden: a brief review of past and present. *Proceedings of the 3rd International Congress on the Biology of Deer*, Edinburgh, pp. 96–106.
Lindström, E., Andrén, H., Angelstam, P. *et al.* (1994) Disease reveals the predator: Sarcoptic mange, red fox predation, and prey populations. *Ecology* **75**, 1042–9.
Ligné, D. (2004) *New Technical and Alternative Silvicultural Apporaches to Pre-commercial Thinning*. PhD thesis, Department of Silviculture, Swedish University of Agricultural Sciences, Umeå, Sweden.
Lloyd, L. (1854) *Scandinavian Adventures during a Residence of Upwards of Twenty Years*. Vol. 1, 512 pp.; Vol. 2, 546 pp. R. Bentley, London.
Lönnberg, E. (1934) Bidrag till vargens historia i Sverige. Kungl. *Vetenskapsakademins skrifter i naturskyddsärenden* **26**, 1–33.
Ministry of Agriculture (1990) *Skada av vilt* [Damage by game]. Statens offentliga utredningar 1990. Stockholm. (In Swedish.)
National Board of Forestry (2006) *Swedish Statistical Yearbook of Forestry 2006*. Sweden: Jönköping.
Neff, D. J. (1968) The pellet-group count technique for big game trend, census and distribution: a review. *Journal of Wildlife Management* **32**, 597–614.
Olsson, C. (2004) *Modifierad avverkningsmetod för att öka tillgänglig viltfodermängd vid gallring* [Modified thinning method for increasing the available game fodder quantity]. Honor thesis. School for Forest Engineers, Swedish University of Agricultural Sciences, Skinnskatteberg, Sweden. (In Swedish.)
Persson, I.-L., Danell, K. and Bergström, R. (2000) Disturbance by large herbivores in boreal forests with special reference to moose. *Annales Zoologici Fennici* **37**, 251–63.
Persson, I.-L., Pastor, J., Danell, K. and Bergström, R. (2004) Impact of moose population density on the production and composition of litter in boreal forests. *Oikos* **108**, 297–306.
Persson, I.-L., Danell, K. and Bergström, R. (2005) Different moose densities and accompanied changes in tree morphology and browse production. *Ecological Applications* **15**(4), 1296–305
Putman, R. J. and Kjellander, P. (2002) Deer damage to cereals: economic significance and predisposing factors. In F. Tattersall and W. Manley, eds., *Conservation and conflict: Mammals and farming in Britain*. London: Linnean Society Occasional Publications, pp. 186–97.
Seiler, A. (2004). Trends and spatial patterns in ungulate-vehicle collisions in Sweden. *Wildlife Biology* **10**, 301–13.
Seiler, A., Helldin, J.-O. and Seiler, C. (2004). Road mortality in Swedish mammals: results of drivers' questionnaire. *Wildlife Biology* **10**, 225–33.

Skoglund, M. (2006) *Available forage and utilization by moose* Alces alces *on felled Scots pine* Pinus sylvestris. Honor thesis. Grimsö Wildlife Research Station, Department of Biological Conservation, Swedish University of Agricultural Sciences, Sweden.

Suominen, O., Danell, K. and Bergström, R. (1999) Moose, trees, and ground-living invertebrates: indirect interactions in Swedish pine forests. *Oikos* **84**, 215–26.

Truvé, J. and Lemel, J. (2003) Timing and distance of natal dispersal for wild boar, *Sus scrofa* in Sweden. *Wildlife Biology* **9** (Suppl 1), 51–7.

Wabakken, P., Sand, H., Liberg, O. and Bjärvall, A. (2001) The recovery, distribution and population dynamics of wolves on the Scandinavian Peninsula, 1978–1998. *Canadian Journal of Zoology* **79**, 710–25.

Welander, J. (2000) *Spatial and temporal dynamics of a disturbance regime: wild boar* Sus scrofa *and its effects on plant species diversity*. PhD thesis, Department of Conservation Biology, Swedish University of Agricultural Sciences, Uppsala, Sweden.

4

Ungulates and their management in Denmark

REIDAR ANDERSEN AND VIDAR HOLTHE

This chapter is based on materials in Bregneballe (2003), Bregneballe *et al.* (2003), Asferg *et al.* (2004), databases compiled by Statistics Denmark, www.statbank.dk, Balarin (2004), and www.gamehuntersguide.com/Encyclopedia/Country/Denmark/Statistics.htm, where source is not otherwise quoted.

4.1 History and present distribution of ungulate species in Denmark

Denmark as a country covers 43 000 km^2, and consists of five large islands (Sjaeland and Fyn being the largest) and Jutland which is connected to the northernmost part of Germany (see Fig. 4.1). Only 12% of the land area is covered with forest, while farmland covers 65% of the area. Hunting activities are performed within nearly 90% of the area. At present there are three native ungulate species, red deer, roe deer and wild boar, and three exotic species, fallow deer, sika deer and mouflon in Denmark. Estimated population sizes and annual harvests are summarised in Table 4.1.

4.1.1 Red deer

Until the mid-1970s free-ranging red deer were restricted to eastern, central and western parts of Jutland. Later, red deer spread through natural colonisation into southern and northern parts of Jutland, although the northern population was strengthened with animals released from pens.

In Sjaelland, red deer were exterminated in 1854, but re-established in 1971 after the escape of nine animals from a farm. The present small populations in northern and central Sjaelland have also been 'subsidised' with released animals.

Table 4.1 *Estimated population size, annual hunting bag and status of large ungulates in Denmark*

Species	Estimated population size 2002	Estimated annual hunting bag 2002	Population trend	Conservation status	Effect of hunting
Red deer	12–14 000	3 338	Increasing	Good	Sustainable
Fallow deer	5 800	3 133	Increasing	Good	Sustainable
Sika deer	500	357	Increasing	Good	Sustainable
Roe deer	No info	103 300	Stable	Good	Sustainable
Mouflon	>80	No info	–	–	–
Wild boar	Few	<25	–	–	–

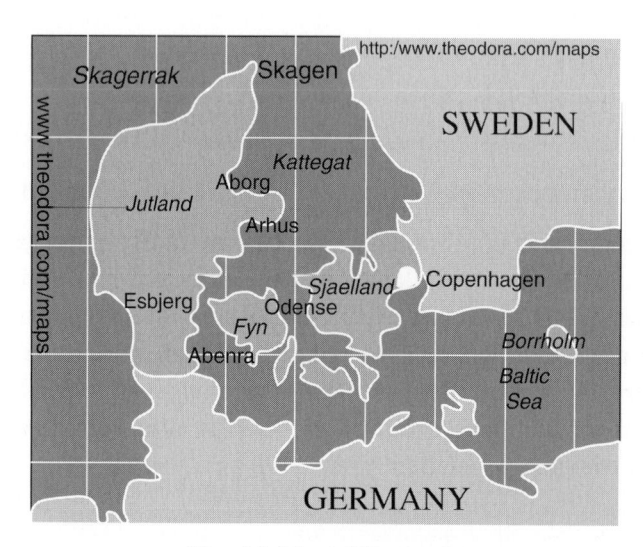

Fig. 4.1 Map of Denmark

There are large regional variations in population densities, and carrying capacity is not reached in any area. However, there are no reliable estimations of numbers. The Forest and Nature Agency, based on culling data, estimated the population to be 12–14 000 animals in 2002.

In the early 1970s annual cull levels were between 500–1000 animals, but increased steadily to 3500 in mid 1990, reflecting the increase in population density and distribution. In the season 2001/2002 the total hunting bag was estimated at 3338 animals. More than 90% of the animals are shot in Jutland, including animals shot inside a large pen (Jægersborg Park).

All populations of red deer are heavily affected by culling, and a reduced hunting pressure will increase both population density and distribution. The shooting is slightly male biased (58.9%, 2 years old and older), giving few prime age males in most populations.

4.1.2 Roe deer

In the late nineteenth century roe deer were exterminated in most parts of the country. However, in the early twentieth century the distribution and numbers again increased, and roe deer can now be found all over the country. A strong population increase occurred between 1970 and 1990, related to increased access to winter green pastures and reduced predation by red fox. The red fox population was significantly affected by sarcoptic mange in Jutland and Bornholm in the mid-1980s, and in Bornholm few, if any, red foxes were left after 1990. The increase in roe deer populations is also caused by a shift in attitudes among hunters, including reduced harvest of adult does.

The annual hunting bag of roe deer has increased from 20 000 animals in the 1940s, to more than 100 000 in recent years. Nearly 50% of the cull is adult bucks, and more than 80% of the bucks are shot with rifles during the summer hunting period, most in May.

4.1.3 Fallow deer

Fallow deer were introduced presumably in the Viking era, and can be found in most parts of the area that is Denmark today. After the end of the 1970s, when fallow deer were restricted to the main islands and eastern part of Jutland, several escapes from established farms in the 1980s led to the establishment of small local populations in western and northern parts of Jutland as well.

In Jutland the overall estimated population has doubled from 500 in 1997 to 1000 in 2002. The total minimum population size in Denmark is estimated to be 5800 animals, although of these, 1600 animals are found inside a large fenced enclosure (Jægersborg Park).

Annual culls increased from around 1500 in the mid-1980s, to more than 4000 animals in the early 1990s, and dropped to an estimated number of 3133 in the season 2001/2002. This clearly indicates that the present population estimate is far below the true number.

4.1.4 Sika deer

Japanese sika deer were introduced to Sjaelland in 1900, and can now be found in most parts of Denmark, although in tiny populations with a total number estimated at only 500 animals. In addition sika deer are kept in several fenced farms. From 1941 onwards, annual culls have been between 200 and 500 animals (estimated to be 357 animals in the season 2001/2002) and hunting is considered to severely restrict both number and distribution of sika deer.

4.1.5 Mouflon

Mouflon were introduced to Denmark around 1950, and have been kept in several private collections, and on some few smaller islands. At present there is only one small population (80 animals) on the small island Vejrø, in addition to some few animals on Aebelø, and in a few parks or zoos. There is no information regarding annual hunting bags for mouflon.

4.1.6 Wild boar

The last native wild boar in Denmark was shot at the start of the nineteenth century. Since then, some few animals have been kept in zoos, from where they occasionally escape. At present three zoos have populations ranging between 25 and 150 animals; in addition, some farmers keep wild boar for interbreeding with domestic pigs. The expected number of free ranging wild boar is low, and in order to prevent transfer of diseases between wild boar and domestic pigs, there is a strategy to prevent the establishment of free ranging populations. It is expected that wild boar from northern parts of Germany may disperse into southern parts of Jutland.

No records are kept regarding annual hunting bags for wild boar, but it is thought that fewer than 25 animals are shot annually.

4.2 Legislation

All hunting and wildlife management is controlled by the regulations of the National Hunting Act – *Lov om jagt og vildtforvaltning* – of 6 May 1993, amended on 28 January 1997. The main purpose of the act is to secure species richness and large populations of wildlife and maintain sustainable management by:

1. protecting the wildlife, especially in the breeding season;
2. maintaining the quantity and quality of wildlife areas through the establishment of nature reserves, and in other ways establish, re-establish and protect wildlife areas;
3. regulating hunting in accordance to ecological and ethical principles, and paying attention to the protection of wildlife, especially to rare and endangered species.

The National Hunting Act also includes basic hunting regulations: open seasons (revised every 3 years), hunting methods, hunting firearms and ammunition, regulation/control, trade, and protected areas. All regulations are national.

Table 4.2 *Danish hunting season for large ungulates 2004/2005, and the species and sex-specific weapon requirement for hunting*

English name *Scientific name*	Gender	Open season	Weapon minimum requirement
Red deer	Stag	01.09–31.01	
Cervus elaphus	Hind and calf	01.10–31.01	
Fallow deer	Buck	01.09–31.01	9 g (139 gr.) E100 > 2700 J
Dama dama	Doe and fawn	01.10–31.01	10 g (154 gr.) E100 > 2000 J
Sika deer	Stag	01.09–31.01	
Cervus nippon	Hind and calf	01.10–31.01	
Roe deer	Buck	16.05–15.07	3.2 g (50 gr.) E100 > 800 J
		01.10–15.01	3.2 g (50 gr.) E100 > 800 J
Capreolus capreolus	Doe and fawn	01.10–15.01	Shotgun gauge 12–20, max. 4 mm shot
Mouflon	Ram	01.09–31.01	
Ovis musimon	Ewe and lamb	01.10–31.01	9 g (139 gr.) E100 > 2700 J
Wild boar	Boar	01.09–31.01	10 g (154 gr.) E100 > 2000 J
Sus scrofa	Sow and squeaker	01.10–31.01	

The following firearms can be used for hunting in Denmark: shotguns with a barrel length not shorter then 55 cm, not bigger then 12 gauge and which hold no more than two shots; and rifles, except automatic rifles, are allowed. Semi-automatic rifles which hold more than two cartridges are not allowed. Shotguns may be used only for hunting roe deer (but not for hunting bucks in summer); the maximum legal shot diameter is 4 mm. Lead shot for shotguns is not allowed in Denmark, and the use of steel shot in forest areas is not allowed. For red, fallow and sika deer, rifles must be used, with bullet weight > 9 g (139 gr)/energy at 100 m (E100) > 2700 J or bullet weight > 10 g (154 gr) or E100 > 2000 J. Where rifles are used for roe deer, bullet weight must be > 3.2 g (50 gr) or E100 > 800 J.

In general, all hunters have to use either a rifle or a shotgun; however, from 1 May 1999 bow hunting has been allowed in Denmark but for roe deer only.

The main hunting seasons are summarised in Table 4.2. Hunting is only allowed between sunrise and sunset.

The Hunting Act states that native fauna and introduced species that have been released or escaped from pens, zoos or farms, and established free ranging, reproductive populations should be given the same protection, unless they traditionally have been treated as domestic animals. Hunting is only allowed for species which have a specific hunting period.

Other legal provisions are the Animal Welfare Act of 6 June 1991, amended 1993, 1996, 1999, the Nature Protection Act of 1 November 1997, amended 1998, 1999 and the Firearms Act of 11 August 1994, amended 1997, 1999.

4.3 Management objectives

The most central political demand is that hunting should be carried out according to the principles of sustainability. This implies that the populations should not decrease due to hunting, and that hunting activities are not forcing the wildlife away from their natural living areas.

There is a growing interest in hunting red deer and roe deer in Denmark, and hunting opportunities on private land may be considered accordingly. Generally, it can be said that the objectives for hunting and game management to most hunters are a combination of hunting for sport and venison. Trophies are important but not to the same degree as in many other countries on the continent.

4.4 Management structure

The hunting right belongs to the landowner, and can be leased to third parties for a maximum of 30 years. The national authority officially responsible for the supervision of hunting, management and conservation of wild species is the Ministry of Environment. The Ministry may set hunting periods for each species with the basic presumption of no hunting at all for any species between 1 February and 31 August. The Danish Forest and Nature Agency, which is part of the Ministry of the Environment, works to promote sustainability in the administration of Denmark's natural and historical heritage in a balance between use and protection. The Danish Forest and Nature Agency includes a central office in Copenhagen with six divisions, 20 state forest districts, the State Forest Tree Improvement Station and the Danish Forestry College.

4.4.1 Community based natural resource management

Public interest in wildlife management and conservation in Denmark is represented by over 325 000 individuals, collectively organised into hunters associations, conservation societies, birdwatchers and outdoor interest groups. Some of these institutions date from as early as the 1880s.

Hunting is regulated by state licences and the hunters associations. Every hunter must undergo training, pass an examination and pay for the rights to use the hunting areas. In Denmark, with over 170 000 registered hunters, state licence fees amount annually to over EUR 10 million in addition to the EUR 8 million paid as membership fee to hunting clubs and as much again paid by conservation society members. When added to state contributions, this amounts to a large investment.

The principle hinges on a tax-based economy (public and private) where the users (i.e. the consumptive and non-consumptive community groups) collectively, or through the state, are able to generate sufficient revenue to finance conservation.

If Community Based Natural Resource Management (CBNRM) is simply defined as 'co-management arrangements between state and user groups jointly treating the environment as economic goods', then Denmark has been practising CBNRM for over a century.

However, for many years the conservation groups (e.g. birdwatchers) and the consumptive user groups (e.g. hunters) and the state were at loggerheads with each other. Each interest group was blaming the other for the decline in wildlife. Game watchers were blamed by hunters for damaging habitat and frightening off breeding animals, especially birds, and vice versa.

The turning point came in 1979 with the establishment of the *National Wildlife Management Council*, which could act as advisors of public interest to the Ministry of Environment. This united lobby group, representing community interests, began to negotiate for improvements to the legislation and the wildlife act. In 1992, they were instrumental in establishing a process that would add an additional 50 new wildlife sites. In all, Denmark now has over 120 'graduated use areas' each of which has a fully protected sanctuary core, surrounded by designated areas for game viewing and areas where hunting is permitted. Most of these sites and their rules were set-up in co-management with community interest groups.

4.5 Management organisation

There are 172 000 hunters in Denmark, which is 3.4% of the total population (5.4 million), which means there are close to 4 hunters per km^2 of land. The recruitment of hunters is good, and 37% of the hunters are between 21 and 39 years old. However, only 4% of the hunters are female. It is estimated that an annual turnover of EUR 400–530 million is generated by hunting in Denmark.

Hunters must pass a mandatory examination, covering species, game biology, firearms, safety, hunting and regulations, and a shooting test for rifle hunting. In addition there is a mandatory firearms course. No one is allowed to hunt unless he/she has the hunting right or has the permission of the person who has the hunting right.

4.5.1 Game hunting licence

Game hunting licences are issued by the National Forest and Nature Agency. To obtain a game hunting licence the applicant must have a permanent address in Denmark, be 16 years old or over and pass the hunting test. The test gives the right to hunt with a shotgun. In order to hunt with a rifle or bow the hunter needs to complete additional tests. Foreigners with no permanent address in Denmark (which includes the Faroe Islands and Greenland) can, by request, get a Danish game hunting licence, if they have a valid game hunting licence from their home country. The Danish game hunting licence is valid from 01.04–31.03, at a price of DKR 515 (approximately EUR 65) for 2004/2005. The price includes third party liability insurance for damage done by firing a weapon.

4.5.2 Shooting test

In order to hunt with a rifle the hunter must have a Danish game hunting licence and needs to pass a shooting test. To pass the rifle shooting test the applicant needs to place five of six shots within a circle, 20 cm in diameter. The distance to the target is 100 m. The applicant also needs to show proper weapon handling. Foreigners (which includes the Faroe Islands and Greenland) with no permanent address in Denmark do not require a shooting test if they have a valid game hunting licence from their home country. If the foreign game hunting licence does not require a test or is not equal to the Danish hunting test, the National Forest and Nature Agency can demand that the applicant has to pass the practical part of the Danish hunting test to prove that the applicant is capable of handling a gun.

4.5.3 Ammunition and calibres

As noted above (Legislation), shotguns may be used for hunting roe deer (but not for shooting bucks in summer), the maximum legal shot diameter is 4 mm. For red, fallow and sika deer, bullets weight > 9 g (139 gr), minimum energy at 100 m (E100) > 2700 J or bullet weight > 10 g (154 gr), E100 > 2000 J. For roe deer, bullet weight is > 3.2 g (50 gr), E100 > 800 J.

4.5.4 Bow hunting

From 1 May 1999 it has also been legal to hunt roe deer with a bow in Denmark. In order to hunt with bows you have to pass a theoretical and practical test. The practical test is administered by the Forestry and Nature Agency and so far only *c.* 500 hunters have passed. In 2005, the bow hunters shot 130 roe deer.

4.5.5 Miscellaneous

For ordinary hunting, persons below the age of 18 years who have a valid hunting certificate may perform hunting if they are accompanied by a person above 18 years who has the legal rights to hunt in the area. A special register of tracker dogs must be called for in case of wounding of hoofed game. About 160 registered dogs are scattered around the country and the hunter can request their assistance free of charge.

4.5.6 Non-governmental organisations (NGOs)

The Danish Hunters' Association has approximately 93 000 members who are organised in some 900 local hunters' clubs spread throughout Denmark. The purpose of the Association is to ensure Danish hunting/shooting interests and game availability, and to promote the reputation of hunters in general. The Danish Hunters' Association is represented in the Wildlife Management Council, the Danish Ministry for the Environment's advisory committee for matters regarding hunting and wildlife. Other organisations represented in the Wildlife Management Council include the Danish Society for the Conservation of Nature (Danish National Trust), the Danish Ornithological Society and various landowner organisations. Through joint effort and mutual understanding, these organisations ensure that future generations in Denmark will be able to enjoy the natural landscape variety and large numbers of species of wildlife, and that hunting/shooting can continue to be a natural feature of Danish cultural activities.

4.6 Actual management and hunting practices

4.6.1 Harvest planning of red deer

In order to strengthen the management of red deer in Denmark, the Forest and Nature Agency decided, in 2000, to establish regional management units. The country was divided into twelve different regions, and at present there are established regional management groups in nine regions (seven in Jutland and two in Sjaeland). Each management group consists of six persons, including representatives from the Danish Hunting Organisation, agricultural and silvicultural organisations, and at least two persons from 'green' NGOs like the Danish Nature Protection organisation. A representative from the regional state forest district is the secretary.

The management groups suggest hunting quotas and report to the Wildlife Management Board administrated by the Ministry of Environment and Energy. In addition, to collect information regarding number of animals within each region (based on questionnaires to hunters), the regional management groups focus on hunting ethics and hunting practice.

It is believed that a focus on hunting ethics will maintain a broad acceptance of hunting in Denmark. Included in this management strategy is a focus on maintaining a natural sex and age structure of the populations, securing of sustainable hunting, which is taken to mean that fewer than one red deer should be shot per 25–50 ha area.

A set of 'rules' for hunting activities related to red deer hunting have also been developed.

- Drive hunts should not be arranged in September when other groups of 'users' have high activity related to the picking of berries and mushrooms.
- Red deer hinds with calves should not be shot in October.
- There should be at least three weeks between drive hunts.
- There should be a maximum of three to four large organised hunts per season in the same hunting area.
- The use of large, fast running dogs should be limited.
- The hunting should be planned with neighbouring hunters.

There is no tradition, or legal provision for management plans or harvest plans for roe deer, sika or fallow deer. The only regulation is through different lengths of the hunting season for males, females and calves. In the ordinary hunting statistics, only the total number harvested is recorded for each species and no breakdown is offered of age and sex structure of that cull.

4.6.2 Hunting practice

The four deer species in Denmark may be found free-ranging or inside pens. The pens could either be a deer farm or a park. A deer farm may have up to 10 red deer hinds or 18 fallow deer does per hectare. Animals inside farms are treated as domestic animals, and should not be hunted, and the number of culled animals should not be included in the national game bag survey. Pens larger than 50 ha having a winter population less than two red deer or four fallow deer per hectare, are treated as a deer park. Hunting may be performed inside parks.

Red deer and sika deer are mainly shot as free-ranging animals. In the season 2001/2002, it is estimated that a total number of 3338 red deer and 357 sika deer were shot. In total, 83.5% of the red deer and 74.4% of the sika deer were shot outside of parks. For fallow deer, 3133 were shot in the season 2001/2002, half of these were shot inside of parks.

There are four different hunting methods that are used: drive hunt and walk-up hunting (many and few hunters in a drive line, respectively), stalking and still hunting (either from high-seats or from the ground). Most red deer are shot during drive hunts (29.3%) and stalking (27.8%); however, the hunting techniques varied with age and sex of the animals hunted, as more than 65% of the stags were shot using stalking. We find the same pattern for fallow deer where nearly 80% of the stags were shot when stalking. Most sika deer hinds were shot using drive hunting (77.8%).

4.6.3 Harvest statistics

The Danish Game Bag Record is a database with information on the number and geographical distribution of wild birds and mammals killed by hunters in Denmark since 1941. For the hunting seasons 1941/1942 and 1979/1980, only average data are available for five-year periods. For the hunting season 1980/1981 and today, data are available for every hunting season as well as averages for five-year periods. Until 2000/2001 the Game Bag Record was published by Statistics Denmark. From 2001/2002 the National Environmental Research Institute (NERI), the Department of Landscape Ecology, Kalø, (Danske Miljøundersøkelser – DMU) receives the basic data, compiles the statistics, writes a report and releases it at the end of the year. This report is a new initiative from the DMU and has resulted in a new policy on the part of Statistics Denmark, which means that the statistics will only be available in S*tatistikbanken*, a database from Statistics Denmark. All persons holding a Danish shooting licence are registered in a central database in the Forest and Nature Agency. When applying for a game licence for the following season, all hunters, about 172 000 per year, are obliged to give information on their personal game bag each year according to species and county. That is, it is the individual hunter who reports their individual hunting bag, not the landowner/hunting area. The deadline for the reporting of the game bag is the end of October.

The overall purpose of the game bag statistics is to monitor developments for different species of animals and to monitor the size and well-being of stocks. The Ministry of Environment and Energy uses the statistics to inform all hunters and sportspeople about the size of the game bag in the hunting season. Unfortunately, all data are on a county level, which means that it is not possible to relate the hunting bag within a specific area to management strategies in the same area. In addition, the accuracy of past data in the database is questioned.

Although all hunters are obliged to report their annual hunting bag, there are no legal actions taken against hunters not reporting. This has prompted a decrease in the proportion of responding hunters from 80–85% in the 1980s to less than 60% at present. In analysis of these statistics, it is assumed that the hunters who did not report through the questionnaire bag the same quantity of game as the hunters who did report through the questionnaire, on average. However, an investigation in 1993–94 showed that this enumeration gave a higher estimate of the total bag of game. The investigation showed that those hunters who did not report through the questionnaire had a bag of game of 5.7 head of game on average (small game included), whereas the hunters who do report through the questionnaire had a bag of game of 17.3 head of game on average. As a consequence, an extrapolation based on an assumption of bags taken by hunters who did not respond to the questionnaire being equal to those of hunters who did report their harvest rates will lead to an overestimation, which was calculated as 14% in 1993–1994 (Asferg, 1996). Although a new correction method applied from the season 2000/2001 is expected to give a more precise estimate of number of animals shot (Asferg and Lindhard, 2003), the increased proportion of non-reporting hunters may jeopardise the intention of getting better temporal and spatial population estimates.

4.6.4 Wildlife health surveys

State forest rangers from the 25 Danish state forest districts collected blood samples from 237 roe deer during the 2002/2003 hunting season (reported by Skarphedinsson et al., 2005). Overall, 36.6% of deer were seropositive for *Borrelia burgdorferi*, while 95.6% were positive for *Anaplasma phagocytophilum*; all animals were negative for *Bartonella quintana* and *B. henselae* by indirect immunofluorescence assay. When a haemagglutination-inhibition test was used, 8.7% of deer were found positive for tickborne encephalitis (TBE)-complex virus. A total of 42.6% were found positive by polymerase chain reaction (PCR) for *A. phagocytophilum* with significant seasonal variation. PCR and sequencing also showed a novel bacterium in roe deer previously only found in ticks. The study showed that the emerging pathogen *A. phagocytophilum* is widely distributed and that a marked shift has occurred in the distribution of TBE-complex virus in Denmark. This finding supports studies that predict alterations in distribution due to climatic changes. Conclusions from Saxmose Nielsen et al. (2000) state that bovine virus diarrhoea virus infection does not occur in roe deer in Denmark. The presence of the antibody in a few red deer from various districts in Jutland probably results from cattle to deer transmission, rather than spread among deer. Hence the possibility of free-living deer as a source of infection for cattle in Denmark seems to be minor.

4.7 Census methods

There are no consistent census methods applied to estimate regional or national deer populations in Denmark. In some cases, hunters are sent questionnaires and asked for their opinion regarding population trends. Estimations of total population size are based on hunting bag and predicted species-specific productivity (cross-referenced to other countries).

4.8 Damage and ecosystem impact

The Ministry of Environment may suggest specific measures for regulating wild game populations to reduce their impact on humans and human health, to reduce the risk of disease transfer, to protect fauna and flora, and to hinder damage to agricultural land and forests.

The Ministry has the option of requiring that individual landowners shall undertake remedial actions to fulfil the above mentioned goals. In case the landowner refuses to do so, the Ministry may perform such remedial actions with costs being paid by the landowner. So far, this regulatory power has not actually been used.

4.8.1 Impact on forest and agricultural crops

Red deer cause damage in agricultural areas and by bark-stripping young spruce and pine forest. There is no compensation for such damage, since the hunting rights for each landowner are treated as a form of compensation. Neither the State/Government, nor the person renting the hunt pays any compensation for game damage. The farmer can apply for a special permit to hunt red deer on his/her agricultural land before sunrise and after sunset, if he/she has severe game damage on unharvested crops. Red deer, fallow deer and sika deer may be shot outside hunting season if they are found inside properly fenced areas and fruit plantations.

In the last decades Denmark has faced a paradigm shift from a largely timber production-oriented approach to a more multifunctional-oriented approach, i.e. a nature-based forestry where emphasis is on increased forest stability, resilience and tolerance to future climatic conditions (Hahn *et al.*, 2004). Danish silviculturists are concerned that deer numbers will jeopardise their goal of restoring more stable, resilient and natural forest ecosystems by causing browsing damage on broadleaved tree species. On the contrary, deer are often greatly appreciated by the forest owners, hunters and people using the woods for recreation. In fact, many forest owners get greater income and pleasure out of the deer than out of the timber production. As a result, a reduced deer population scenario is unrealistic at most places in Denmark (Madsen *et al.*, 2007).

4.8.2 Traffic accidents

There are no reliable figures for the number of deer killed in traffic in Denmark. However, it is estimated that more than 20 000 roe deer are killed every year in traffic. The Ministry of Environment presented an action plan in 2002 in order to reduce the problem.

4.9 Habitat improvement and supplementary feeding

Although supplementary feeding is neither required nor prohibited by law, such feeding is not widely used in Denmark. However, hunting in the vicinity of artificially established feeding sites is not allowed, and hunting towers cannot be established closer than 130 m to a neighbouring hunting area.

4.10 Problems with current management and future challenges

Viewed as one of the most important challenges in the future is the need to develop a national set of laws that are in accordance with international demands specified in the Habitats Directive (European Directive 92/43/EEC on the Conservation of Natural Habitats) and the Birds Directive (European Directive 79/409/EEC on the Conservation of wild Birds). As the Habitat Directive demands that all defined habitats shall be maintained in favourable condition and protected species shall be maintained at secure population levels, there is a further need to have more precise census data regarding the development of the ungulate populations. Until such methods are available some type of precautionary principle must be used in setting hunting quotas.

In addition, there is a need to increase flexibility when establishing the network of reserves, designed to reduce the disturbing effects of hunting and other activities, by taking into consideration the biological status and development of the different species. There is also be a need to develop a set of more specific definitions regarding hunting ethics in accordance to international standards.

There are so far no reports of breeding between sika and red deer. Lack of such hybridisation is expected by some to be due to the fact that the introduced sika deer is a Japanese breed, which is the smallest breed of sika, and the genetically most distant from red deer. This seems very unlikely as UK populations, populations in Eire and elsewhere are all of *Cervus n. nippon*, and hybridisation is widespread. The present strategy is to exterminate sika deer in red deer areas, in order to prevent mixed breeding.

In a number of different years moose have been able to swim across Öresund from Sweden. Ultimately, they have always been killed in traffic. The Ministry of Environment is now evaluating the possibility for an introduction of moose into Denmark.

References

Asferg, T. (1996) *Fejlkilder i den danske vildtutbyttestatistikk*. Faglig rapport fra DMU, nr. 167, 25 pp. (In Danish.)

Asferg, T. and Lindhard, B. J. (2003) *Korrektion for manglende indberetninger til vildtudbyttestatistikken*. Faglig rapport fra DMU, nr. 473, 28 pp. (In Danish.)

Asferg, T., Riis Olesen, C. and Preil Andersen, J. (2004) *Krondyr, dådyr og sika i Danmark*. Faglig rapport fra DMU, nr. 512. (In Danish.)

Balarin, J. D. (2004) *Traditional Hunting?* Denmark and Malawi Civil Society Partnership, www.africanconservation.org.

Bregneballe, T. (ed.) (2003) Vildtarter og jagttider [*Game Species and Hunting Periods*]. København: G. E. C. Gads Forlag.

Bregneballe, T. *et al.* (2003) *Vildtbestande, jag tog jagttider I Danmark 2002*. En biologisk vurdering av jagtens bæredyktighet som grundlag for jagttidsrevisionen 2003. Faglig rapport fra DMU, nr. 428. (In Danish.)

Hahn, K., Emborg, J., Larsen, J. B., Madsen, P. (2004) Forest rehabilitation in Denmark using nature-based forestry. In J. Stanturf and P. Madsen, eds., *Restoration of Boreal and Temperate Forests*. Boca Raton, FL: CRC Press, pp. 299–317.

Madsen, P., Buttenschøn, R. M., Madsen, T. L. and Olesen, C. R. (2007) Restoring a mixed species forest landscape on privately owned land under heavy deer browsing pressure. Paper presented at the Forest Landscape Restoration conference, Seoul, May 2007.

Saxmose Nielsen, S., Roensholt, L. and Bitsch, V. (2000) Bovine virus diarrhea in free-living deer from Denmark. *Journal of Wildlife Diseases* **36**, 584–7.

Skarphedinsson, S., Jensen, P. M. and Kristiansen, K. (2005) Survey of tickborne infections in Denmark. *Emerging Infectious Diseases*, July 2005.

5

Ungulates and their management in Finland

VESA RUUSILA AND ILPO KOJOLA

Finland is a country characterised by large boreal forests and severe winters. Forests are predominantly of pine (*Pinus sylvestris*), spruce (*Picea abies*) and birch (*Betula pendula* and *B. pubescens*). There are seven species of wild ungulates present in Finland; four are true native species, while the others have been more recently introduced.

Over the summer period leaves, grasses and water-plants are widely available as forage, but harsh winter conditions and thick snow cover, particularly in the north, restrict food availability markedly so that during winter ungulate diet consists of twigs and branches and, to a lesser extent, bark.

5.1 Ungulate species and their distribution

The ungulate fauna of Finland is an interesting combination of old and new species. Although close to extinction several times, moose has established itself more strongly in recent times and is currently the most important game species. Wild forest reindeer and roe deer both became extinct in Finland at one time or another; both, however, remained in the neighbouring countries, and after natural dispersion and re-introductions have re-established viable populations. Among alien species, white-tailed deer has a very dense population in the south-western part of the country, while fallow deer and mouflon have relatively small, but stable populations, also in the south. Wild boar in Finland find themselves at the northern edge of their distribution and there is, in consequence, only a relatively small and scattered population, mainly in the south of the country.

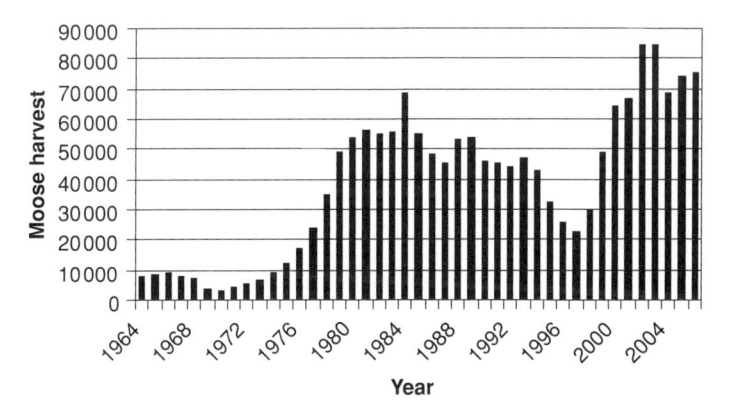

Fig. 5.1 Moose harvest in Finland in 1964–2006 (Hunters Central Organization)

5.1.1 Moose

Moose is a native species in Finland. According to archaeological evidence, it has been important as a species for human exploitation since the Mesolithic Stone Age, 4200 BC–7000 BC. It appears that during the Mesolithic and Comb-Ceramic Ages moose distribution covered the whole area of Finland (Taavitsainen, 1980).

During the eighteenth and nineteenth centuries the moose population of Finland declined to low levels, even coming close to extinction. In 1868 moose were protected by law, and consequently the population soon began to increase; hunting was allowed again in 1906.

After World War I, moose was again protected in 1923–33. After World War II the moose population was low, but recovered without formal protection and increased until the late 1960s. Heavy harvesting decreased the population again and in large parts of the country moose was once more afforded protection for a period between 1969 and 1971 (Nygrén, 1987).

Finnish moose populations (and harvest) started to increase again rapidly during the 1970s until the early 1980s as a result of more selective hunting (e.g. increase in calf harvest) and good foraging conditions (Fig. 5.1). High population density however resulted in increased damage caused by moose and consequently high harvest numbers foreshortened this period of increase. From the mid-1980s to mid-1990s harvest numbers remained relatively stable, but nonetheless appeared to cause a population decline. During mid-1990s harvest was at the lowest level for 20 years, initiating a new phase of rapid increase that continued until early 2000s accompanied by increasing forestry damage and increasing problems with road traffic accidents (Nygrén, 1987; Lavsund et al., 2003).

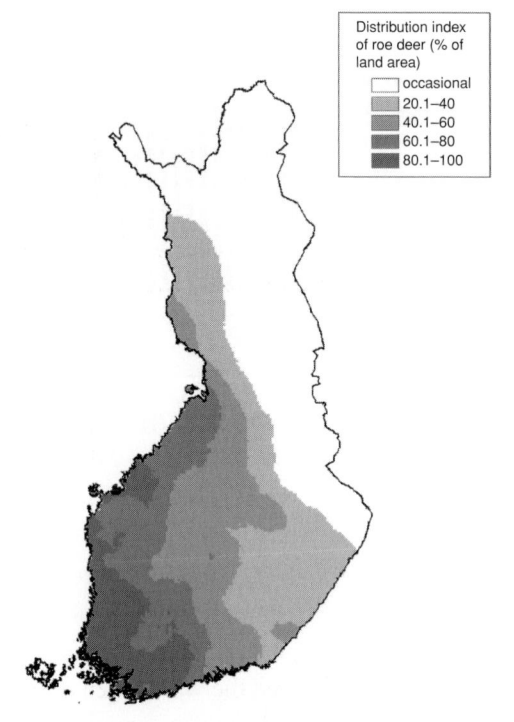

Fig. 5.2 Distribution of roe deer in Finland

An unprecedentedly high level of culling, over 84 000 moose, in two consecutive years (2002–03) caused the population to decline again particularly in southern parts of the country. After the 2006 hunting season, the population size is estimated to be 79 000– 93 000 moose (J. Pusenius *et al.*, unpublished data).

Moose distribution covers the whole area of Finland. The highest densities are in the coastal areas and in the central inland parts of the country.

5.1.2 Roe deer

Roe deer is also a native species in Finland, but translocations greatly influence its present distribution. In the early 1900s it expanded its range naturally into south-eastern Finland from Russia, and during the 1950s to northern Finland from northern Sweden (Helle, 1996). However, in addition, by 1941 roe deer had been introduced into Åland archipelago, south-west of Finland, and subsequently there have been other releases into several locations in south-western Finland (Sormunen and Moilanen, 1979).

The current distribution range covers southern and western Finland (Fig. 5.2). The present population size in continental Finland is at least 15 000–20 000

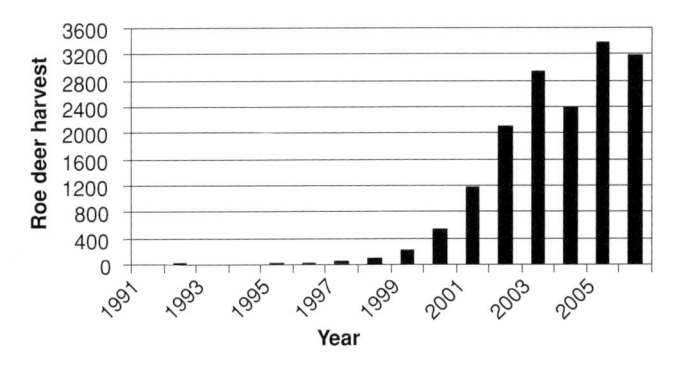

Fig. 5.3 Roe deer harvest in Finland (Hunters Central Organization)

individuals and there are probably about another 10 000 roe deer in the Åland archipelago. In continental Finland, densities are highest in the south-west coastal areas. The annual harvest is about 3000 animals (Fig. 5.3). It would appear that the recent population growth rate has been high in continental Finland because population estimates for 1995 (if accurate) suggested that there were only 2000 deer (Helle, 1996).

5.1.3 Wild forest reindeer

Wild forest reindeer (*Rangifer tarandus fennicus*) were originally distributed all over the boreal forests of Finland, but the distribution reduced gradually during the 1800s and the subspecies became extinct in the early 1900s (Montonen, 1974). The most probable reason was over-harvesting since firearms had become prevalent (Montonen, 1974; Helle, 1981). Legal protection in 1913 came too late to prevent wild forest reindeer from disappearing and they were absent from Finland for about 40 years. However, the species was still common in Russian Karelia and from there it naturally extended its range into Finland in the late 1950s; the first breeding of resident populations was confirmed in the province of Kainuu in the early 1960s (Montonen, 1974).

The number of wild forest reindeer in eastern Finland was about 300 individuals in 1979–80 when some additional reindeer were translocated from Kainuu to Ostrobothnia, western Finland, to be introduced into the area where the last reindeer in the western part of the country were known to have persisted (Nieminen and Laitinen, 1983; Kojola, 1993). The founder population comprised ten females and two males. Over the four first years they were kept in a 15-ha enclosure from which only reindeer that were born in the enclosure were released into the wild. In 1984 all reindeer were released resulting a free-ranging population of 40 animals (Kojola, 1993).

Fig. 5.4 Distribution of wild forest reindeer in Finland

At present the range covered by the two populations in eastern and western Finland is about 17 000 km^2 (Fig. 5.4) and in both areas there are about 1000–1200 reindeer. Population dynamics have been strikingly different in these two areas. In the west, the number of reindeer has increased steadily with an annual population growth rate (λ) of about 1.20 (Kojola *et al.*, 2004).

The eastern population increased with annual growth rate of 1.13 up to 2001, but decreased from 1800 to less than 1000 during 2001–07 (K. Heikura, unpublished data). The reasons for this dramatic decline are partly obscure, but it appears that the increased wolf population has a strong association with decreased calf production.

Wild forest reindeer are the only ungulates in Finland with a conservational status. In the eastern area, strictly limited harvesting was initiated in the early 1990s with harvest rates being 1–3% of the population estimate. Since 2003, when the population decline became evident, no harvesting has been allowed in the east. In the western area, harvesting started in the mid-1990s. During this decade 7–8% of the reindeer have been annually shot in the west (Fig. 5.5). Harvesting in the eastern population has been aiming to be selective against hybrids with semi-domesticated reindeer (*R.t. tarandus*) which occur in the same areas. Hybridisation has been identified as a problem in the northern part of the eastern range that is

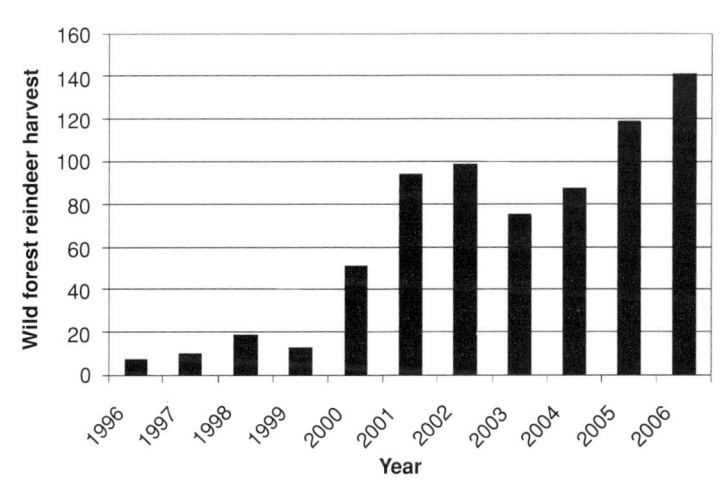

Fig. 5.5 Wild forest reindeer harvest in Finland (Hunters Central Organization)

bordering upon the area of reindeer husbandry. The ranges of wild forest reindeer and semi-domesticated reindeer have been separated from each other with a 80-km fence that involves special bridge constructions at road passes. This fence is not 100% effective in preventing movements between the two areas, but has decreased them substantially (J. Keränen, *pers. comm.*). In the west reindeer are shot on farmland in order to reduce their grazing on agricultural fields (J. Bisi, unpublished report).

5.1.4 White-tailed deer

The Finnish population of white-tailed deer (*Odocoileus virginianus*) has its origins in a founder population of four females and one male that were transported in 1934 from northern Minnesota to a fenced area located in southern Finland. Deer were released into the wild in 1938 when the population consisted of three adult females, one adult male and two male calves (Kairikko and Ruola, 2004). Managers were anxious about the small number of founders and therefore some additional deer were transported from Minnesota again in 1948 when the Finnish population was about 100 deer (Sormunen and Moilanen, 1979; Kairikko and Ruola, 2004). It is unclear how much this additional introduction may have affected the genetic structure of the Finnish white-tailed deer population (Kairikko and Ruola, 2004).

The distribution range has increased gradually with the increase of population size and covers the whole of south-central Finland (Fig. 5.6). Densities are highest in areas surrounding the locations from which animals were released. The present distribution range comprises areas where maximum snow depth is usually below

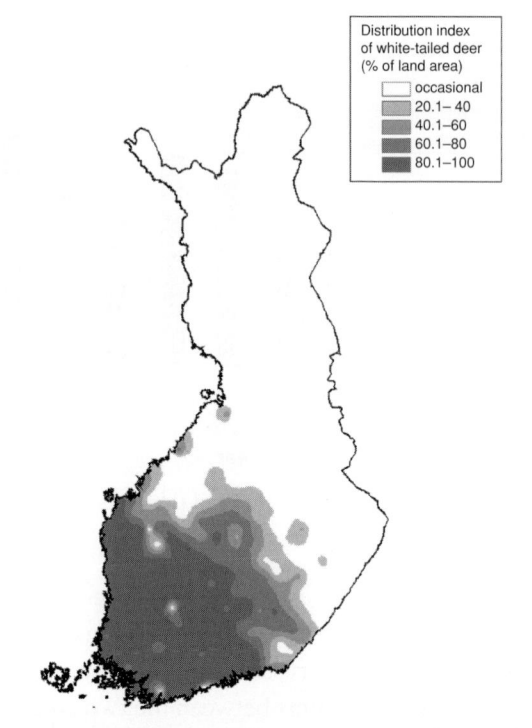

Fig. 5.6 Distribution of white-tailed deer in Finland

50 cm. The present population size, before the hunting season, is estimated at about 55 000 deer.

Harvesting was initiated in 1958. The number of white-tailed deer shot annually has increased to *c.* 20 000 animals (Fig. 5.7). Supplementary feeding is extensive. Ecological effects of browsing by white-tailed deer are not well documented. The presence of this deer in Finland is probably not a big issue in the conservation of natural ecosystems, because it mostly lives in semi-cultural landscapes, and only a few deer move in protected areas (natural parks, strictly protected nature reserves) that are usually located in backcountry wilderness regions. The white-tailed deer is an important prey of Eurasian lynx (*Lynx lynx*) in Finland (Pulliainen *et al.*, 1995).

5.1.5 Fallow deer

The first fallow deer in Finland were brought from Germany to a deer park in 1890. In 1914 the deer were taken to a zoo, from where they were unsuccessfully reintroduced to two locations in 1935. One additional unsuccessful introduction and fencing experiment occurred in the late 1930s. However, introductions from southern Sweden and Denmark (1935 to Hättö and 1953–54 to Hyvinkää) were

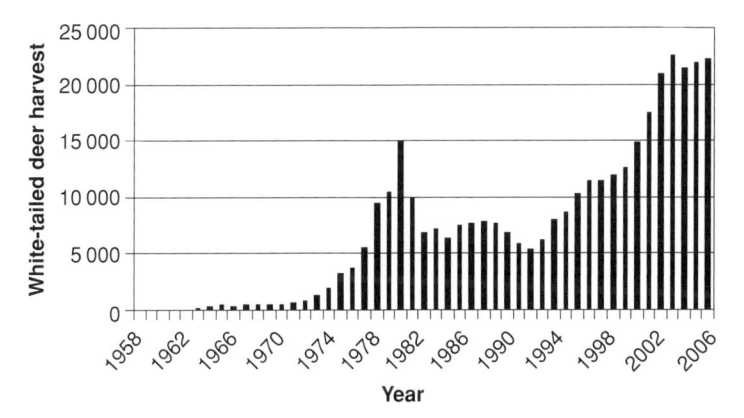

Fig. 5.7 White-tailed deer harvest in Finland (Hunters Central Organization)

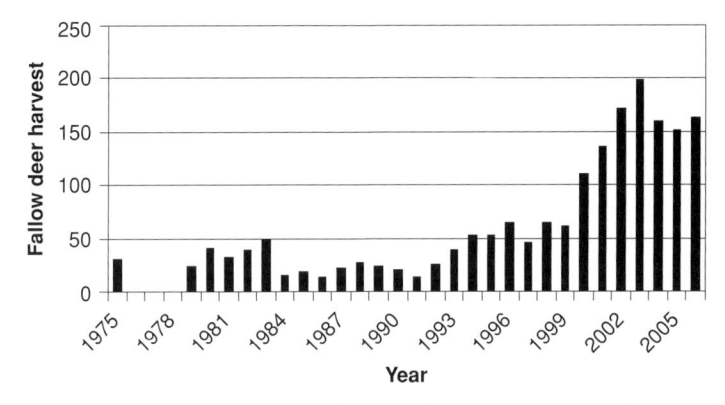

Fig. 5.8 Fallow deer harvest in Finland in 1975–2006 (Hunters Central Organization)

successful enough to produce free ranging populations that still exist in the southern archipelago and the southern inland (Sormunen and Moilanen, 1979).

The inland distribution range and population size have expanded slowly compared to white-tailed deer. Population size is *c.* 600 animals in the areas of three southern Game Management Districts (GMDs) (Fig. 5.8). These deer live almost exclusively in cultivated areas in Finland (Nygrén, 1996a). Practically all Finnish fallow deer use feeding stations in winter, and the main census method is counts carried out at feeding stations where most hunting also takes place. The number of fallow deer shot annually has increased to *c.* 150–200 deer (Fig. 5.8).

5.1.6 Mouflon

Mouflon have been introduced into two islands, one located in the Gulf of Finland, and the other in Bothnian Bay. In the first case, eight mouflon were transported

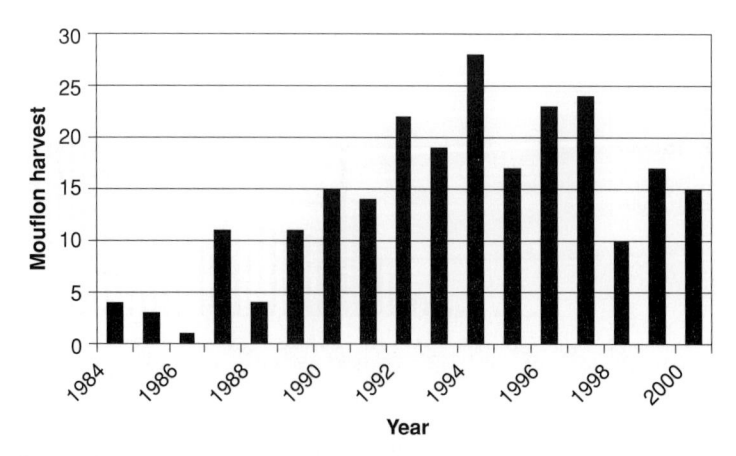

Fig. 5.9 Mouflon harvest in Finland in 1984–2000. Since then, reporting of the harvest has not been compulsory (Hunters Central Organization)

from Helsinki Zoo to a 70-ha island in 1939 and in the second case two females and one male were transported from the first release location to a 150-ha island in 1942 (Nygrén, 1996b). The population on Bothnian Bay island has been supplemented by introducing at least four additional mouflon into the area.

The present distribution is restricted simply to the two islands where they were introduced. The total distribution range is 220 ha and the population size is about 100 animals. Mouflon are supplementally fed and some individuals are shot yearly (Fig. 5.9).

5.1.7 Wild boar

The presence of wild boar in Finland is due entirely to dispersal of individual animals from Russia into south-eastern Finland. The distribution range has been described as covering the whole of southern Finland, but population size is only some hundred animals (Ermala, 1996). Monitoring of population size and distribution is based on sporadic observations that usually concern animals that are feeding on agricultural fields. As a result, population size can only be estimated in orders of magnitude. Some tens of wild boars only are annually killed by hunters, so it is not a significant game species.

5.2 Legislation

According to Finnish legislation, game animals, when alive, are the property of the government. The right to hunt a species is connected to land ownership. The

Table 5.1 *Hunting period and area requirements in ungulate hunting in Finland. For all hunting, permission of the landowner is required*

Species	Hunting period	Minimum hunting area	A licence from GMD required
Moose	25.9*–31.12	1000 ha	Yes
White-tailed deer, wild forest reindeer, fallow deer	25.9*–31.1	500 ha	Yes
Roe deer		–	No
– male	1.9–31.1 and 16.5–5.6		
– female and calf	1.9–31.1		
Wild boar	1.6–29.2 (female with piglet is protected)	–	No
Mouflon	1.9–30.11	–	No

* the last Saturday of September

Table 5.2 *Requirements of weapons used for ungulate hunting in Finland*

species	Minimum bullet wt	Bullet energy at 100 m	Shotgun allowed	Bow hunting
Moose	9 g, no full mantle 10 g, no full mantle	2700 J 2000 J	No	No
Mouflon	3.2 g	800 J	Slug bullet, 10–20 cal.	No
Roe deer	3.2 g	800 J	Yes, 10–20 cal.	Yes, min. power 180 N
White-tailed deer, wild forest reindeer, fallow deer, wild boar	6.0 g, no full mantle 8.0 g, no full mantle	2000 J 1700 J	Slug bullet, 10–20 cal.	No

landowner can transfer all or part of the rights to a second party, e.g. a hunting group, by renting.

All ungulate species can be hunted. Hunting seasons vary according to the species, but most commonly begin in late September and last until December–January. More specific dates are presented in the Table 5.1. Shotgun and bow hunting are only allowed for roe deer, for other ungulates a high power rifle is required (Table 5.2).

5.3 Management objectives

Hunting has long traditions in the Finnish culture as an activity almost everyone can take part in regardless of, for example, wealth or social status. From the total population of 5.2 million in Finland, the number of hunters is about 300 000, and over 100 000 of them participate in moose hunting. Groups hunting moose usually hunt smaller ungulates in their area as well. Particularly in rural areas, the significance of moose hunting is marked in social and recreational ways. For example, private landowners that have rented their area for moose hunting traditionally get some meat or they are offered a moose meat dinner party. Often the majority of members in a hunting club are inhabitants of one rural community (or their close relatives).

It is common that of all members in a hunting club, a proportion form an ungulate hunting group. The average area that any hunting club may rent for moose hunting is about 3500–4000 ha in southern Finland.

The objective of ungulate hunting in Finland is two-fold. Although hunting is classified as a hobby and professional hunters do not exist, particularly in regard to moose hunting, the role of population control to control forestry damage and reduction of deer–vehicle collisions is considered highly important. Even though exercise of a shooting licence is voluntary and there is no specific imposition of quotas, hunters or the hunting organization in any particular area are expected to keep damage at a reasonable level. The role of obtained meat in hunting is very pronounced in Finland, although large antlers are also valued. Meat is very carefully utilised and shared among members of the hunting group. Hides are usually sold to leather industry, although their value has decreased during the last few years because of dear fly *Lipoptena cervi* damage.

5.4/5 Management organisation and structure

As noted above, the right to hunt is connected to land ownership. The landowner can transfer all or part of the rights to a second party, for example a hunting group, by renting. In addition to obtaining hunting rights in a given area, a hunter needs to pass a hunter's exam (including 12 hours of voluntary lectures) to get a personal licence to hunt. The price of the exam is EUR 13 and annual fee for the licence is EUR 24. For moose, white-tailed deer, fallow deer and wild forest reindeer a shooting exam is also required.

Overall control of hunting is vested in the Department of Fisheries and Game at the Ministry of Agriculture and Forestry. Under the governance of the Department, the Hunters' Central Organisation coordinates hunting throughout the country in the 15 GMDs that are each divided into several game management associations, 298 in total. GMDs are provincial, governmental-type organisations having regulatory power, for example, over hunting licences, except on large predators that are hunted with the Ministry permits only. The size of the GMDs varies from 8135 km^2 to 93 003 km^2 land area. The area of game management associations is usually based on communal, administrative boundaries.

The GMDs give necessary licences for ungulate hunting, where the basic unit is one licence. With one licence one adult or two calves may be killed. However, a female followed by a calf is protected. In addition, GMDs can also give recommendations or regulations on the harvest structure, for example in respect of the share of calves in the harvest. Hunting groups or consortiums of several groups may apply for licences from the local game management association, which reports on the application and delivers it further to the GMD for decision-making. The licence fee for hunting ungulates is EUR 22 per application plus a separate fee for every animal shot. For moose the fee is EUR 34 for a calf and EUR 100 for an adult, for smaller ungulates, EUR 8 for a calf and EUR 17 for an adult. For roe deer, mouflon and wild boar there are no such fees.

After the hunting season, each harvested animal has to be reported to the local GMD. This report must include information on the ungulate sex, age (adult/calf), site of the kill and antler tine number. These reports are an important source of information on population density, since every hunting group has to estimate the number of animals left in the area after the hunting season. Wild boar and mouflon kills do not have to be reported.

The main Ministry guideline for hunting is sustainable use of natural resources where hunting does not endanger viability of populations while damage is kept at a reasonable level. Each GMD has an annual meeting with the most important local interest groups related to ungulate populations, for example representatives from forestry, agriculture and traffic organisations. In these meetings, different parties discuss the current status of ungulate populations and the level of ungulate-related damage and set a common goal for the density of ungulate populations. GMDs further discuss with game management associations the number of licences available for the season.

5.6 Hunting practices

Ungulate hunting in Finland is strictly regulated. Except for roe deer, wild boar and mouflon, for every hunting event a designated group leader who has taken a short training course must be appointed; this is required by the law. The leader is responsible for keeping the hunting laws and security. Before the hunting season, the names of the hunting group leaders need to be reported to the local game management association. Every hunter has to wear a red or orange hat and jacket or vest.

A specific shooting plan is not required by the law. However, a fundamental basis in the law is that hunting is not allowed to endanger viability of the populations. Consequently, the number of hunting licences is based on censuses. After the hunting season, the bag has to be reported to the local game management district for the official hunting bag statistics for all except mouflon and wild boar.

Moose are usually hunted in groups with mean size of 18 hunters. The most common practice is hunting with dogs, about 73%. The majority of dogs are Nordic spitz breeds that halt moose by baying. Usually only one dog bays at a time. If the moose is standing still listening to a baying dog, a hunter approaching it can shoot the moose. Usually the rest of the moose-hunting group is waiting in line if the moose escapes the dog or if the dog directs it towards them. In ungulate hunting, use of dogs over 28 cm of height is forbidden. The second most common practice, 26%, is hunting with humans only, i.e. flushing by beaters. Here, part of the hunting group moves forwards in a line in a forest making noise and directing moose towards waiting hunters (Koskela and Nygren, 2002; Ruusila and Pesonen, 2004).

For roe, fallow and white-tailed deer the most common method is to shoot animals at feeding sites and agricultural fields or flushing by beaters. However, hunting with chasing dogs (< 28 cm) is becoming more popular. Wild boars are mainly shot from agricultural fields.

5.7 Census methods

As noted above, an important source of information on population size and distribution of the different ungulate species within Finland derives from the records which must be submitted after each hunting season to the local GMD. After the hunting season, each harvested animal has to be reported to the local GMD and, in addition, every hunting group has to estimate the number of animals left in the area after the hunting season. Methods used to estimate numbers vary somewhat between the species, but are primarily based on records for all species collated during the specific census of moose.

Moose census methods

The most important national census is based on hunters' observations on moose during hunting and their estimate of the remaining population size in the area after the season, together with analysis of cull records also provided. During hunting, daily observations of all moose seen are recorded on a pre-prepared card, as well as the main hunting practice and information on snow cover, number of hunters and dogs, etc. From the moose observation data, estimates of, for example, adult sex ratio and calf production may be derived. The observation card is also used to gather information on the distribution of smaller ungulates and large predators.

Although filling the form is voluntary, coverage of the moose observation card is very good, about 90% (Nygrén and Pesonen, 1993; Lavsund *et al.*, 2003).

In addition to indices which may be derived from the observation card, an estimated minimum population size is also calculated by utilising long-term data on harvest and annual estimates of calf production. In addition to the moose observation card, some GMDs and game management associations have other methods for estimating population density. Most important are aerial surveys (usually from fixed wing aircraft) and snow track counting.

For roe deer and white-tailed deer, wildlife triangle transect line surveys (Lindén *et al.*, 1996): a regional track count scheme where hunters go through their hunting areas during one day in winter) and sightings at feeding stations provide data sources for population trends, although as mentioned, moose hunters also record observations of roe and white-tailed deer within their hunting areas.

Practically all Finnish fallow deer use feeding stations in winter, and the main census method is counts carried out at feeding stations. Census of wild boar is primarily based on sporadic observations of animals that are feeding on agricultural fields.

Population estimates of wild reindeer are based on helicopter surveys in late winter when the animals are gathered into their wintering areas. In these survey flights wintering areas are comprehensively scanned. Counts are usually performed every second or every third year.

5.8 Impact and damage

In general, only moose and white-tailed deer cause significant damage to agricultural or forest crops. In some special cultivations (e.g. strawberry fields) and gardens, roe deer may cause some damage, and wild forest reindeer and wild boar cause some damage to agriculture. Government compensation for agricultural and forest damage is paid to private landowners (not in relation to State-owned forestry, for example), and, in the case of traffic accidents, to persons who do not have private insurance. The primary purpose for the licence fees charged to hunters is to finance this compensation.

Moose cause the most severe problems in relation to traffic accidents and the annual number of accidents is closely related to moose density. During the peak population period in the early 2000s, the number was close to 3000 per year. The number of accidents involving smaller species of deer has varied between 2000 and 2800. Here, the smaller ungulates are not categorised by species, but given relative population sizes we may presume that only a small percentage of the deer accidents are caused by species other than white-tailed deer.

In moose accidents, about 10 persons die and almost 300 are injured annually. In deer accidents, persons are very rarely killed, but *c.* 25 persons are injured annually. The number of traffic accidents for moose in 2006 was 1978, where three persons were killed and 179 were injured. White-tailed deer and roe deer accidents are not separated from each other and their total number was 2799. In these accidents nobody was killed, but 36 persons were injured. In 2003 the total costs of ungulate traffic accidents to society was estimated as EUR 163 million (Rantala and Mänttäri, 2004).

Moose also cause the majority of damage to forestry and agriculture. Forestry damage far exceeds agricultural damage, which is relatively low and does not fluctuate as much as forestry damage. Most forestry damage occurs in young pine plantations where moose aggregate during winter in high densities. Plantations are most vulnerable until trees reach a height of about 4 m, beyond this moose cannot break the main stem, which markedly reduces the future value of timber.

During the period of highest moose density in the 2000s, the compensation paid to forest owners was about EUR 5.4 million, and for agriculture EUR 0.5 million. The total amount of ungulate compensation in 2006 was EUR 3.2 million for forest damage and EUR 0.26 million for agricultural damage.

Wild forest reindeer cause some damage to agricultural fields, although this varies from year to year (for example, in the year 2000 more damage occurred than normal, almost EUR 17 000). Wild forest reindeer wintering areas may differ a lot among years, which makes prediction and protection of damage areas difficult. Collection of lichen for decorations is a secondary occupation in some areas that can be threatened by wintering animals. Such damage is not compensated by the government. The money for the compensation is collected from the licence fees.

5.9 Supplementary feeding

Moose are not supplementally fed, but salt licks are regularly provided to improve mineral availability. In some forest practice guidelines, it is suggested that branches of pine, birch and aspen can be set leaning on, for example, larger stones so they are available as food for moose even after the snow comes. Sometimes aspen are felled in autumn to provide food for moose and snow-shoe hares. Wild forest reindeer are not fed supplementally.

However, for other smaller deer feeding is more regular. Roe deer is assumed to be dependent on artificial supplementation in northern and eastern parts of its present range where snow cover restricts food availability. Supplemental feeding of white-tailed deer is also extensive. There are more than 10 000 feeding stations for deer in Finland and most of them are used by white-tailed deer. For fallow deer, feeding stations in winter are important as well.

Although the main purpose of supplementary feeding is to improve nutrition of the deer, it may also have some negative effects on the species. The lynx population in Finland is increasing and may cause heavy losses during winter by killing deer, and also by keeping deer away from the feeding stations.

5.10 Effectiveness of current management strategies, problems with current management and possible changes in management approaches/structures

Ungulate management in Finland has gone through some changes. Earlier, the Ministry of Agriculture and Forestry gave licences for GMDs. Currently GMDs are more independent in their decision-making and the Ministry only sets guidelines for, for example, moose density (in the south 2–4/1000 ha; in the north 0.5–3/1000 ha). Annually GMDs have an interest group meeting prior to providing the moose hunting licences where representatives from, for example, traffic, forestry and agriculture organisations are heard and common goals for moose density are determined.

The most recent change in ungulate hunting concerns roe deer. Since 2005, a separate hunting licence is not required, but the owner of hunting rights determines whether roe deer can be hunted within the season. Concurrently, forest or agricultural damage caused by roe deer is no longer compensated by the government. Public discussion on ungulates is mainly focused on moose and, particularly, the damage caused by them.

References

Ermala, A. (1996) Villisika. In H. Lindén, M. Hario and M. Wikman, eds., *Riistan jäljille*. Riista-ja kalatalouden tutkimuslaitos. Edita. Helsinki. pp. 94–6. (In Finnish with English summary.)

Helle, P. (1996) Metsäkauris. In H. Lindén, M. Hario and M. Wikman, eds., *Riistan jäljille*. Riista-ja kalatalouden tutkimuslaitos. Edita. Helsinki. pp 100–102. (In Finnish with English summary.)

Helle, T. (1981) Studies on wild forest reindeer (*Rangifer tarandus fennicus* Lönnb.) and semidomestic reindeer (*Rangifer tarandus tarandus* L.) in Finland. *Acta Univsitatis Ouluensis, Series A* **107**, 12, 34 + 83 pp.

Kairikko, J. K. and Ruola, J. (2004) Valkohäntäpeura. Suomen Metsästäjäliitto – Finlands Jägarförbundet ry. Gummerus. Jyväskylä.

Kojola, I. (1993) Peura-ja poroistutusten ekologiaa. *Wildlife in Finland* **39**, 74–84. (In Finnish with English summary.)

Kojola, I., Huitu, O., Toppinen, K., Heikura, K., Heikkinen, S. and Ronkainen, S. (2004) Predation on European wild forest reindeer (*Rangifer tarandus*) by wolves (*Canis lupus*) in Finland. *Journal of Zoology* **263**, 229–35.

Koskela, T. and Nygrén, T. (2002) Moose hunting clubs in Finland 1999. *Wildlife in Finland* **48**, 65–79. (In Finnish with English summary.)

Lavsund, S., Nygrén, T. and Solberg, E. J. (2003) Status of moose populations and challenges to moose management in Fennoscandia. *Alces* **39**, 109–30.

Lindén, H., Helle, E., Helle, P. and Wikman, M. (1996) Wildlife triangle scheme in Finland: methods and aims for monitoring wildlife populations. *Finnish Game Research* **39**, 69–78.

Montonen, M. (1974) *Suomen peura*. WSOY, Porvoo, 111 pp. (In Finnish.)

Nieminen, M. and Laitinen, M. (1983) Metsäpeuran palautusistutus ja stressi. *Wildlife in Finland* **30**, 34–43. (In Finnish with English summary.)

Nygrén, K. (1996a) Kuusipeura. In H. Lindén, M. Hario and M. Wikman, eds., *Riistan jäljille*. Riista-ja kalatalouden tutkimuslaitos. Helsinki: Edita. pp. 97–9. (In Finnish with English summary.)

Nygrén, K. (1996b) Mufloni. In H. Lindén, M. Hario and M. Wikman, eds., *Riistan jäljille*. Riista-ja kalatalouden tutkimuslaitos. Helsinki: Edita. pp. 117–21. (In Finnish with English summary.)

Nygrén, T. (1987) The history of moose in Finland. *Swedish Wildlife Research, Supplement* **1**, 49–54.

Nygrén, T. and Pesonen, M. (1993) The moose population and methods of moose management in Finland, 1975–89. *Finnish Game Research* **48**, 46–53.

Pulliainen, E., Lindgren, E. and Tunkkari, P. S. (1995) Influence of food availability and reproductive status on the diet and body condition of the European lynx in Finland. *Acta Theriologica* **40**, 181–96.

Rantala, H. and Mänttäri, J. (2004) Hirvieläinonnettomuudet yleisillä teillä vuonna 2003. Tiehallinto. (In Finnish.)

Ruusila, V. and Pesonen, M. (2004) Interspecific cooperation in human (*Homo sapiens*) hunting: the benefits of a barking dog. *Annales Zoologica Fennici* **41**, 545–9.

Sormunen, A. and Moilanen, P. (1979) Peurat ja niiden metsästys. In M. Soikkanen, ed., *Tapiola, suuri suomalainen eräkirja*. pp. 216–231. Espoo, Finland: Weilin & Göös. (In Finnish.)

Taavitsainen, J.-P. (1980) Distribution of the moose in Finland in the light of archaeological evidence. *Wildlife in Finland* **28**, 5–14. (In Finnish with English summary.)

6

Ungulates and their management in the Baltics (Estonia, Latvia and Lithuania)

ŽANETE ANDERSONE-LILLEY, LINAS BALČIAUSKAS, JĀNIS OZOLIŅŠ, TIIT RANDVEER AND JURI TÕNISSON

The Baltic countries are situated in the north-east corner of Europe, on the east coast of the Baltic Sea. They are fairly well forested countries with the forest cover being 50% in Estonia, 45% in Latvia and 30% in Lithuania. In addition, up to 10% of each individual country is covered by various wetlands such as raised peat bogs and fens. The total area of these countries is approximately 175 000 km^2, Estonia being the smallest of the three countries ($c.$ 45 000 km^2) while Latvia and Lithuania are roughly the same size, 64 000–65 000 km^2. The Baltics have a temperate climate, which is more continental in the east. Snow cover usually lasts from as early as the end of November up to the end of April in the north-eastern part of the Baltic region but regional and year-to-year variations are very common.

6.1 History, distribution and genetic origin of ungulate species in the Baltics

At present, there are four species of wild ungulates in the Baltics: moose, red deer, roe deer and wild boar. One might also add to the list the European bison, several herds of which are free-ranging in Lithuania. The European bison together with aurochs (*Bos primigenius*) and wild horses (*Equus gmelini sylvaticus*) were a part of the Baltic fauna during the Atlantic and Sub-boreal climatic periods after the last glaciation. In Latvia, the latter two species are believed to have gone extinct about 1000 years ago (Kalniņš, 1943) while European bison in Latvia survived probably until the eighteenth century when it was eradicated by over-hunting (Tauriņš, 1982). However, according to another source, this may not be the case, since the aurochs and the European bison were confused in the historical annals of German feudals' hunting bags (Lange, 1970).

6.1.1 Moose

Moose is the only ungulate species that has always been present in the territory of the Baltic since it first appeared at the end of the last glaciation 8–10 000 years ago. The European subspecies *Alces alces alces* is found in the Baltic (Gripenberg and Nygrén, 1987; Baleišis *et al.*, 2003). Judging by bone excavations, it used to be a very important prey for the ancient humans. Pitfalls, the remains of which can still be found in south-west Estonia, used to be a common hunting technique until less than 100 years ago.

Moose populations withstood the climate cooling in the sixteenth to midnineteenth century (Lõugas and Maldre, 2000) and high predation by wolves much better than wild boar or roe deer that temporarily went extinct or retreated to the south. According to a Polish survey in 1599, a numerous moose population inhabited the Baltic at that time. Moose were abundant in Lithuania until the middle of the nineteenth century (Plater, 1852; Kalniņš, 1943), but the outbreaks of the Siberian plague in the seventeenth to nineteenth centuries caused population crashes in the region (Ivanauskas, 1929; Ling, 1981). However, there were still 2000 moose in Latvia alone by the end of the nineteenth century (Kalniņš, 1943). By the twentieth century the population recovered and A. Martenson (1899) estimated that there were at least about 3000 individuals in Liivi, Kura and Estonia provinces. However, revolutions and World War I in the early twentieth century caused another severe population decline; in 1920, there were estimated to be only 25 moose in Lithuania, in 1924, only 24 moose in Estonia and <100 moose in Latvia at the end of World War I. The population recovered gradually followed by another crash due to World War II.

The species had become abundant again by the 1970s–80s when there were about 20 000 animals in both Estonia and Latvia and at least 9900 animals in Lithuania (Baleišis, 2004) (Fig. 6.1). It should be noted that for Estonia, these figures probably represent a considerable underestimate. At the end of the 1970s, when the moose population was probably at its highest ever, *c.* 9000 individuals were counted annually. According to Tõnisson and Randveer (2005), there were probably twice as many moose at that time, otherwise it would be impossible to harvest on average 4800 moose every hunting season.

A drastic decrease in numbers happened in the early 1990s during the time of political perturbations due to high hunting quotas, considerable levels of poaching and the prevailing idea that the high density of moose was incompatible with good forestry practice. The situation improved by the end of the 1990s and nowadays moose occur throughout the whole of the Baltic including the biggest Estonian islands (Saaremaa, Hiiumaa, Muhu and Vormsi). The density ranges from the average of 1.7 ind./1000 ha of forest in Lithuania to *c.* 5 ind./1000 ha in Estonia. In Latvia and Lithuania (Fig. 6.1), the highest moose density is in the north-east. In

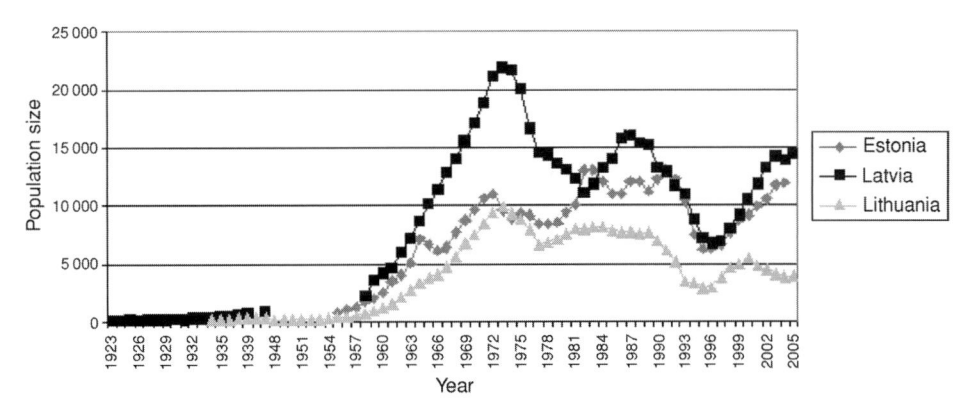

Fig. 6.1 Moose, *Alces alces*, population dynamics in the Baltics 1923–2005 (according to official game statistics)

Lithuania, despite a hunting ban in 2003–05, the population is still declining and modelling has shown that the extent of poaching is about the same as legal hunting (Balčiauskas, 2004b; Baleišis, 2004).

Comparing population structure during the peak phase (1971–5) and during the depression (1996–7), it was found in Estonia, that the sex ratio changed from 1:1.2 to 1:1.8 males to females. The proportion of calves in the population rose from 27.0% to 29.6%, the proportion of all females having calves rose from 48.2% to 54.3%, and the percentage of females having twins changed from 24.3% to 21.0% out of the total number of females with calves. The increased proportion of calves and calved females shows that the population has indeed considerable potential for recovery (Baleišis *et al.*, 1998; Baleišis and Bluzma, 2000; Baleišis, 2004).

The latest monitoring data from Estonia show the excellent state of the Estonian moose population. The share of the calves in the population was 32.9 ± 0.8; the share of calved females, $61.6 \pm 1.4\%$, the twinning rate, $38.3 \pm 1.8\%$ (J. Tõnisson, unpublished data).

Hunting is undoubtedly the main cause of moose mortality in the Baltics. However, the analysis of moose mortality in Estonia has shown that the summer mortality of calves reaches 30–40% (Tõnisson, unpublished). In 2000–04, mortality due to human-caused accidents and wounding due to missed shots constituted two-thirds of mortality. At the same time, poaching decreased to 2% (Tõnisson, unpublished). Predation and so-called undefined causes were responsible for one-fifth of mortality of moose in Estonia.

6.1.2 Red deer

The red deer in the eastern part of the Baltics reached its maximum distribution 5000–6000 years ago during the Boreal-Atlantic period. It is clear, however, that the native population of red deer had become extinct by the tenth century in Latvia (Skriba, 1975) and even earlier in Estonia (Paaver, 1965), although the species survived until the Middle Ages in Lithuania. When the species went extinct there is not exactly known, presumably in the middle of the nineteenth century. In the eighteenth century book the red deer is mentioned as common (Ładowski, 1783), but in 1830 it was already gone (Eichwald, 1830).

The present Baltic population of red deer has been fully reintroduced and the genetic origin of the animals is not always known, as the founders were brought from different countries including Germany, Poland and Russia. It is always presumed that stocks are of the Middle European subspecies of the red deer (*Cervus elaphus hippelaphus*) (Baleišis *et al.*, 2003), but in practice genetic analysis has never been done. Also, in the last few years there have been occasions when captive sika deer escaped from enclosures in Lithuania and possibly formed hybrids with the red deer, especially in central Lithuania and on the coast of west Lithuania where fenced sika deer herds are numerous.

The first reintroduction attempt started in the seventeenth century in Latvia. Animals were brought from Germany by the aristocracy and were kept in fenced areas called 'deer parks'. In the nineteenth century the same practice started in Estonia and Lithuania, where a herd was formed from the animals from Count Naryshkin's enclosures. At the beginning of the twentieth century, some individuals in Latvia escaped and established a population in the wild. Later several animals were released on purpose. Several local micro-populations that were not connected established themselves in western and southern Latvia. The first game survey in the early 1900s in Lithuania showed 18 red deer in the Žagarė forests in north Lithuania, which probably originated from the deer that had dispersed from Latvia.

In Estonia, intentional red deer releases started in 1927 when some animals, a gift from the German consul, were released on the small island of Abruka (close to Saaremaa). A bigger campaign was launched at the beginning of the 1970s, when 28 deer from Voronezh Nature Reserve (Russia) were released in Hiiumaa. Later, some more were brought from Lithuania and Tallinn Zoo. These were of German origin.

At the same time, red deer from Latvia were introduced to the large island of Saaremaa. Also, deer from the neighbouring Abruka Island managed to disperse to Saaremaa.

Some red deer from Latvia were found on the mainland, in south Estonia, in the 1930s, but these were probably largely transients and no resident population was established. A wider dispersal started in the 1980s after red deer from west Latvia were deliberately reintroduced to several areas in north Latvia (near Mazsalaca and Smiltene). Simultaneously, another centre of distribution originated in Ida-Viru county due to red deer escaping from an enclosure.

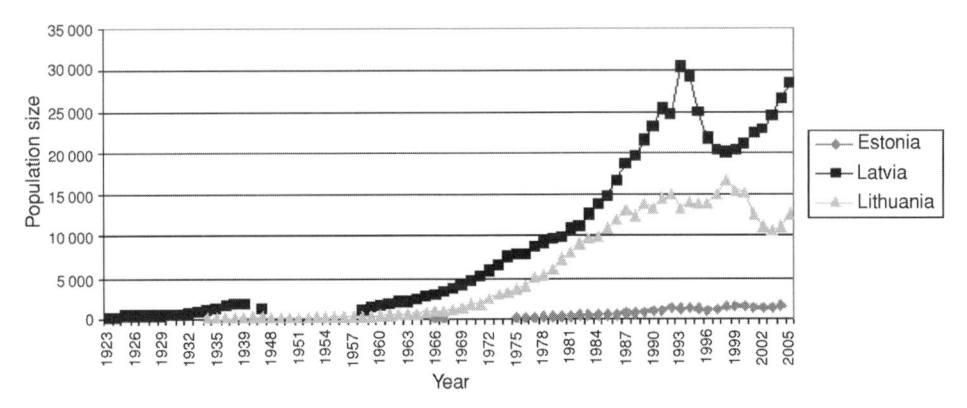

Fig. 6.2 Red deer, *Cervus elaphus*, population dynamics in the Baltics 1923–2005 (according to official game statistics)

The condition of the Estonian population seems to be very good. In the autumn there were >25% of calves in the population and between 0.55 and 0.6 calves per adult hind, similar to ratios reported for red deer in Germany (Briedermann et al., 1988). Almost a quarter of stags at the age of 1.5 years already have forked antlers.

In Lithuania, the intentional reintroductions started in the 1930s. In 1935 and 1939, some red deer were brought from Latvia (two animals each time), in 1956 and 1972 animals were brought from the Voronezh nature reserve in Russia (37 and 14 deer, respectively). Animals from the neighbouring Kaliningrad region dispersed to south Lithuania during World War II or soon afterwards and by 1982 reached 500 individuals. The first red deer from Poland came to Lithuania in 1967 and 1972. By 1984, there were 137 deer of Polish origin in two administrative districts. In 1969 a red deer translocation programme was started within Lithuania itself. By 1987, 1030 red deer were translocated to 29 administrative districts. Some of these animals migrated to Latvia. A total of 38 red deer were transferred to Estonia in 1979, 1980 and 1987 (Baleišis and Škėris, 1984; Baleišis et al., 2003).

At present, red deer are rather evenly distributed across Latvia and Lithuania (Balčiauskas et al., 1999), but in Estonia the species mainly occurs on Saaremaa (c. 800 ind.) and Hiiumaa islands (c. 500 ind.) and in south Estonia (c. 200 ind.). On islands the density reaches 20 ind./1000 ha in some places and the population is still growing on the islands and the mainland. In Lääne-Viru county in north Estonia there is a small population of 40 red deer. Single animals may be encountered almost all over Estonia. The average density of red deer in Lithuania was 6.5 ind./1000 ha of forest in 2001 (with the maximum of 21.4–22.9 in two northern districts). In 2004 the average density reached 7.2 ind./1000 ha of forest. The maximum density was recorded in 1982, 240 ind./1000 ha of forest (north Lithuania). The herd size exceeded 80 animals, especially in winter near feeding stations, in clear-cuts and by farms. Currently, the herd size is much lower, as densities have declined (Fig. 6.2).

This species was clearly benefiting from anthropogenous landscape (Balčiauskas, 1988). At high population densities, up to 90% of red deer may leave forest at night and graze in the agricultural land.

6.1.3 Roe deer

Roe deer is another species that appeared in the territory of the Baltic 8–10 000 years ago, after the last glaciation. The European subspecies *Capreolus capreolus capreolus* occurs in all three countries. Unconfirmed data reveal that in the nineteenth century Siberian roe deer were brought to Saaremaa and may perhaps have left some 'reminder' of their genotype. During the Soviet period, a few individuals of this subspecies were also released in some hunting grounds in Latvia.

In the fifteenth to sixteenth century roe deer were common in the region (Rzączyński, 1721; Ładowski, 1783; Eichwald, 1830), but during the climatic cooling in the seventeenth to eighteenth centuries the species retreated to the south, disappearing from Estonia and Latvia and decreasing in density in Lithuania. A significant increase in wolf numbers at that time may have facilitated the temporary extinction of the species. Natural repopulation started in the nineteenth century, especially in its second part, when the climate became warmer and the number of wolves was significantly reduced (Tauriņš, 1982). Lange (1970) suggested that the population recovery was also helped by intentional release and occasional escapees from deer parks. By the turn of the century, the northern margin of the distribution range once again reached the Gulf of Finland. In the twentieth century, the population size fluctuated depending on the harshness of winters, the intensity of poaching and the number of carnivores (Fig. 6.3). Temporary hunting bans were aimed at increasing the population. A hunting ban in 1935 in Lithuania resulted in an increase in populations to 35 000 roe deer by 1940. The severity of winter conditions is one of the crucial factors to roe deer survival. For example, the cold winter of 1969–70 reduced the Lithuanian roe deer population by almost 35% (Baleišis *et al.*, 2003).

At present, the roe deer is found all over the Baltic countries including most of the Estonian islands and the outskirts of the biggest cities (Balčiauskas *et al.*, 1999; Balčiauskas *et al.*, 2005). The density of the population is highest in less forested regions as the species does not reach high densities in big forest massifs. The average roe deer density in Lithuania was 34.7 (10–88.6) ind./1000 ha of forest in 2001, but decreased to 30 ind./1000 ha by 2004. Densities of roe deer are higher in smaller forest patches (100–500 ha). Small patches and other elements of agricultural landscapes, such as hedgerows, gardens and trees around farms are considered to be very important roe deer habitats. If their area is at least a

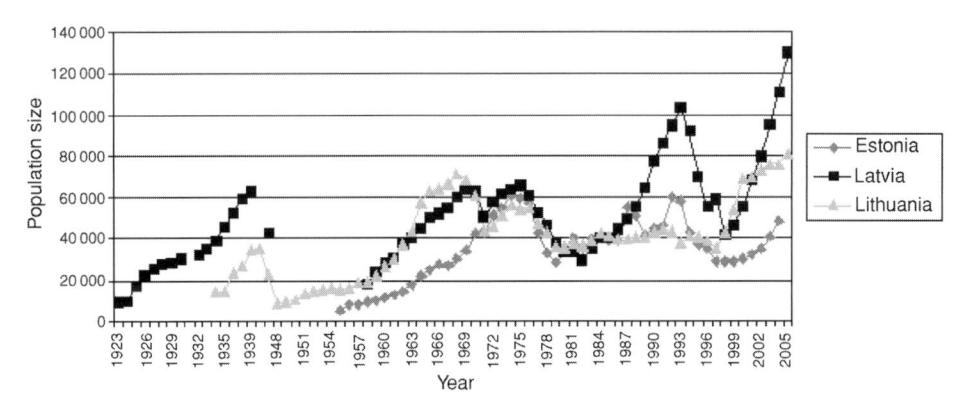

Fig. 6.3 Roe deer, *Capreolus capreolus*, population dynamics in the Baltics 1923–2005 (according to official game statistics)

hectare, roe deer may stay there for a long time. In south Lithuania roe deer became adapted to life in the open agricultural areas. The ecotype of the 'field roe deer' is mainly present in Suvalkija, where roe deer density in the fields may reach 5–15 ind./1000 ha (Baleišis *et al.*, 2003).

6.1.4 Wild boar

The so-called Middle European wild boar *Sus scrofa scrofa* subspecies occurs in the Baltics (Baleišis *et al.*, 2003). Danilkin (2002) specifies wild boar living in Estonia as a mixed type *Sus scrofa indet.*, with $2n = 36-38$ and a distribution from Western Europe to Krasnojarski Krai in Siberia.

The wild boar has been found in the Baltic since the Boreal time (Tauriņš, 1982) until the seventeenth to nineteenth centuries when, due to the climate cooling, high numbers of wolves and, possibly, over-hunting, the species distribution range retreated to the south (Greve, 1909). The period of absence was shortest in Lithuania. By the end of the nineteenth to the beginning of the twentieth century, wild boar started to disperse northwards again until they reached Estonia in the 1930s (Paaver, 1965). By the end of the 1930s wild boar reached northern Estonia (Ling, 1955), but after the cold winters of 1939–40 and the following years, wild boar disappeared again until the end of the 1940s (Fig. 6.4). In the 1960s, the first wild boar reached the islands of Estonia and now the island of Saaremaa has both the highest wild boar density and hunting intensity in Estonia.

At present, wild boar occurs everywhere in the Baltic countries. Wild boar can even be found on the outskirts of Vilnius city (Balčiauskas *et al.*, 1999; Balčiauskas

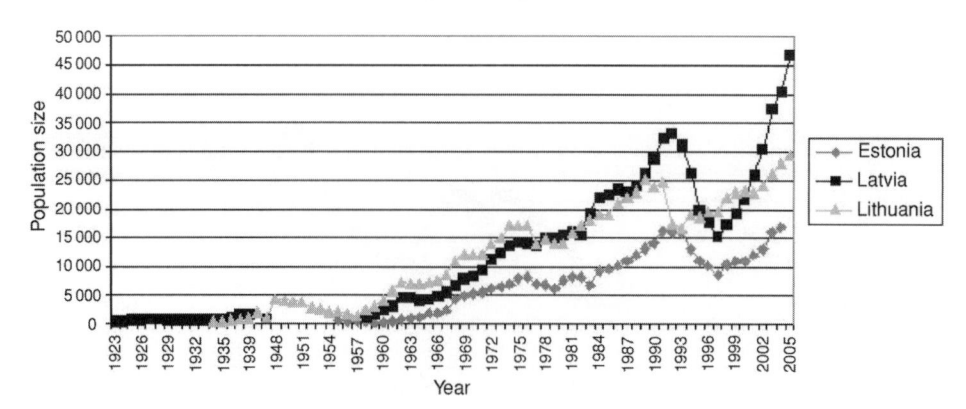

Fig. 6.4 Wild boar, *Sus scrofa*, population dynamics in the Baltics 1923–2005 (according to official game statistics)

et al., 2005). In 2001, the average wild boar density in Lithuania was 11.7 (3.4–25.6) ind./1000 ha of forest (Baleišis *et al.*, 2003).

Due to its broad, generalist diet, a high proportion of the wild boar in the population could be infected with *Trichinella spiralis* (*c*. 3% in Lithuania). Without the appropriate veterinarian control (mostly when the animal is illegally killed) meat can be dangerous to eat and infestation cases occur in humans every year.

6.1.5 European bison

Historically, distribution of the European bison was in the forested zone of West, Central and parts of Southern Europe, on the steppes of the west and south, and in the Caucasus. The northern boundary of its distribution range was slightly to the north of Riga (Geptner *et al.*, 1961).

Formerly found in the Baltic countries was a further form, *Bison priscus* (Paaver, 1965), which disappeared in the Ice Age. What appeared again in the late Holocene was already *Bison bonasus*. These animals were abundant in the territory of Lithuania in the first and second millennium. According the review of forests of the Grand Duchy of Lithuania, in 1559 European bison were present in all areas inspected (Volovič, 1867). The last archaeological remains are dated to the fifteenth to sixteenth centuries; in 1800, bison were present near Narva River, but they were not a part of the fauna of Lithuania at that time (Eichwald, 1830).

From 1923, an international campaign for species restoration from the remaining few captive individuals took place. Lithuania became a part of this initiative from 1969, when two captive herds of lowland bison (two males, eight females) were brought from Russia. In 1973 a free-ranging herd was started in central Lithuania, and it still remains viable. A second attempt targeted at east Lithuania in 1974 failed,

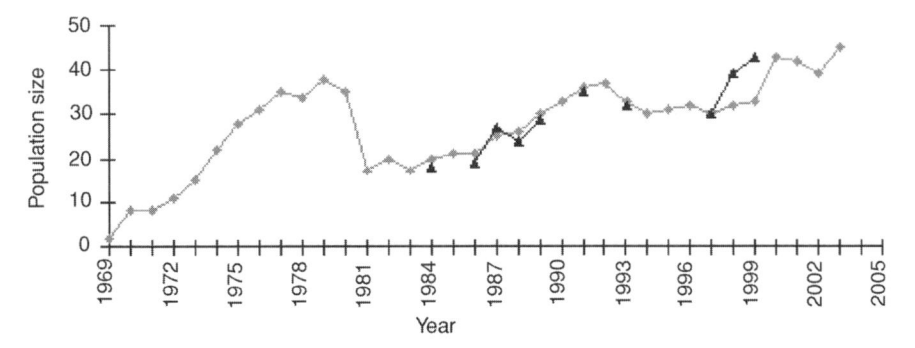

Fig. 6.5 The population dynamics of the European bison in Lithuania (continuous line – official data, broken line – the data of the Bison breeding station and data on migration)

for various reasons the bison did not survive. In 1981, 12 animals were transferred to the Choper Reserve. All bison brought to Lithuania were of the lowland line (*Bison b. bonasus*), so were their offspring up to 2000. Unfortunately, in 1996 a breeding sire, Zwerg, with Caucasian bison blood was brought to Lithuania from the Podkrusnohorsky Zoo Park, Chomutov, in former Czechoslovakia. The presence of his hybrid offspring in the population is undesirable (Pucek, 2004).

Two decades ago sightings of wild bison from Poland and/or Belarus started to occur. Such sightings became more common when two herds were established in Belarus near the border with Lithuania. As both countries breed the lowland line, these visits are welcome from a genetic point of view. In the last two years, a group of strange bison (three individuals) stayed in south Lithuania. Though migrating bulls reached every part of the country and even Latvia (Figs. 6.5 and 6.6), the main part of the free-ranging herd remains in central Lithuania. Currently the herd is split into the main part (*c.* 20 animals) which migrated south from the former area and is near Kėdainiai town, and two smaller bison groups, which have established their territories to the north of the bison breeding station. Several individuals, mainly males, are wandering around. No wild bison are found in Latvia or Estonia.

Bison in Lithuania offer a striking example of the species' adaptation to unusual habitats. Throughout most of its range the European bison is reported to prefer sparse mixed and deciduous forests with luxuriant undergrowth, meadows and glades (Pucek, 2004); forest edges are of great importance. In Lithuania, the preferred habitats are different. In the anthropogenous landscape bison are used to open areas, including agricultural fields, where they find food easily. After two decades of additional feeding in winter, the free-ranging herd now is over-wintering without help by humans. Mosaic landscape is preferred in winter, giving easy access to meadows, fields and small forest patches (Balčiauskas, 1999, 2000a).

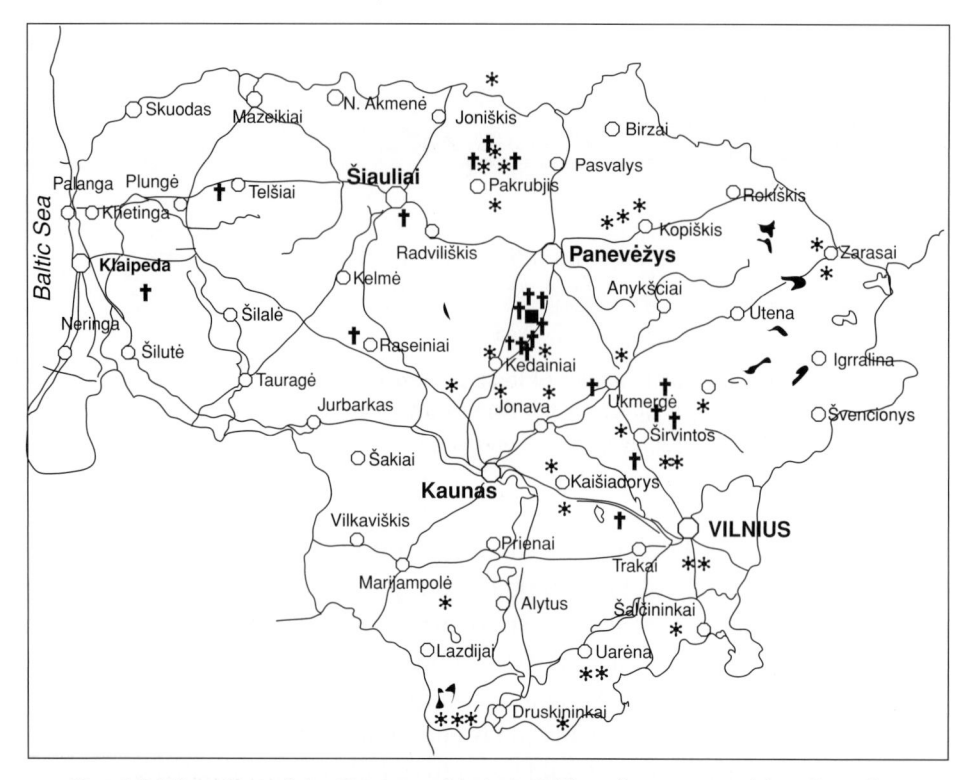

Fig. 6.6 Migration of the European bison in Lithuania: square – bison breeding station, crosses – places of poaching of free-ranging bison, grey marks – migrations of free-ranging animals of Lithuanian origin, light grey marks – migrations of free-ranging animals of presumably Polish or Belarussian origin

Status of protection: EC Habitat Directive, Annex II; Bern convention, Appendix II; IUCN List of Threatened Animals, Endangered (EN A2ce, C2a), priority species of European importance. In Lithuania: Red Data Book, category 5(Rs), restored species.

There is no hunting bag for bison in Lithuania, as it is a protected species. A few animals are culled from time to time, depending on the situation, with a special licence for each from the Ministry of Environment. Mainly these are old non-reproducing cows in the enclosure, or surplus bulls creating problems because of conflicts with the dominant bull.

6.2 Legislation

Hunting in the Baltics is regulated by various legislative acts: the Hunting Act in Estonia (2002), Hunting Law and Hunting Regulations in Latvia (2003), and Hunting Law (2002, Amendments 2005) and Hunting Regulations (2005) in Lithuania.

Table 6.1 *Hunting seasons for wild ungulates in the Baltics*

	Estonia	Latvia	Lithuania
Moose	15 Sept–30 Nov, calves – until 15 Dec	1 Sept–15 Dec	1 Sept–15 Nov (bulls), 1 Oct–15 Nov (cows and calves)
Red deer	1 Sept–30 Nov (hinds), fawns and stags – until 31 January	1 Sept–31 Jan (stags), 15 Aug–31 Dec (hinds and fawns)	15 Aug–15 Oct (stags), 1 Oct–31 Dec (hinds and fawns)
Roe deer	1 June–30 September (bucks), 1 Sept–30 Nov (females and young)	1 June–30 Nov (bucks), 15 Aug–30 Nov (females and young)	1 June–1 Nov (bucks), 1 Oct–31 Dec (females and young)
Wild boar	All year round	1 May–31 Jan	1 May–1 March (piglets, yearlings and older tuskers) (2 Feb–1 March – just from towers), 1 Oct–1 Feb (> 2 years old sows)

Some hunting regulations are also included in the Law on Wildlife in Lithuania. The right to hunt is connected to land ownership, i.e. hunters must rent or own hunting grounds. But the wildlife belongs to the state (or nobody in Latvia and Estonia). After the animal is killed, property rights change, i.e. the dead animal belongs to the user of the hunting grounds, and the trophy to the hunter who made the kill.

In some cases hunting animals beyond the shooting season (Table 6.1) or quota is allowed, e.g. if they cause considerable damage to the forest or agriculture, in which case the State Forest Service issues additional permits. It is often the case with wild boar raiding the crops that hunting clubs choose to eliminate the troublesome animal rather than pay compensation to the farmer which is a legal requirement in relation to damage caused by the game species.

6.3/4 Objectives and management structure

In the Baltic countries ungulate hunting is done primarily for sport/recreation and for damage control. Recreational hunting brings income to local communities as many hunting clubs organise hunts for foreign trophy hunters. Hunting also helps to keep ungulate populations at a level compatible with commercial forestry.

The state, through its governing bodies such as the State Forest Service (Latvia) or the Ministry of Environment (Estonia and Lithuania), controls hunting in each country by determining hunting quotas for each forestry district. For example, in Estonia, hunting is regulated by the chief hunting specialist and a network of 15 hunting specialists in each County Environmental Department, and by the Game Monitoring Department of the Centre of Forest Protection and Silviculture, which was established in 2005. In Lithuania, survey and game regulation is done by the scientific/educational body, in accordance with the management programme, which is approved by the regional department of the Ministry of Environment. In Latvia, the State Forest Service manages nearly 300 forestry units in the country that carry out the annual census of the game species, based on which the central office sets annual quotas for each forestry unit.

All three countries are divided into hunting units within forestry districts. The number of the actual hunting units can exceed 300 in every country, and are further divided into individual hunting clubs. Hunting is undertaken by the public, but regulated by the state (e.g. by the State Forest Service in Latvia and by the Ministry of Environment in Lithuania). Hunting grounds can be both public (State-owned) and private. Hunting rights belong to the owner or user of the land. The landowner can let the rights to anyone else. The owner cannot hunt without any restriction in his/her own lands. He/she needs to have a hunting licence as the major pre-requisite. On his/her own land, he/she can hunt so-called 'unlimited' game species (foxes, racoon dogs, hares, etc.), but even for these he/she needs to buy a (general) licence for each season. For so-called 'limited' game species (including big game such as ungulates) a separate licence is necessary for each animal to be shot.

6.5 Management organisation

In Lithuania, the minimum size of the hunting unit should be 1000 ha or more of uninterrupted hunting grounds. In Estonia, the owner holding a valid hunting certificate may hunt on his/her land provided that the area exceeds 20 ha.

Big game (including ungulates) may only be hunted if the area of hunting grounds is over 5000 ha. In Latvia, four restrictions are set for the minimum size of a hunting ground: 200 ha for hunting roe deer, 1000 ha for wild boar, calves and hinds of red deer, 2000 ha for red deer stags and 2500 ha for moose. Besides, the wild boar, red deer and moose can be harvested only if a hunting ground includes the mentioned amount of woodlands.

Sometimes private owners let the land to hunters on the basis of their membership in the hunting club instead of taking rent for the land. On the State-owned land, hunting clubs pay rent to the state. The rent depends on the area, and the quality of hunting grounds and the share of each hunter is decided by the club itself.

Land or forest owners have a right to forbid hunting on their private land, even if this territory is included in the hunting grounds. This wish should be taken into account when forming hunting grounds. Land and forest owners must be informed about intention to include their private land in hunting grounds no less than one month before the decision is taken. Owners inform the commission at the local government about their decision to forbid hunting. If the owner forbids hunting on the private land, hunters do not compensate wildlife-caused damage.

There are also so-called 'free grounds' (both state and privately owned) for which no rent contracts are made and which can be rented out on an individual basis, for individual hunts. Another category is State Hunting Enterprises where high densities of ungulates are maintained and large carnivores usually severely controlled. In Soviet times, only VIPs could hunt there but now any fee-paying person can hunt in their grounds. The enterprises are commercial bodies and sell licences at a higher price than ordinary hunting clubs. Foreign trophy hunters are typical clients of these enterprises.

A few hunting grounds are devoted to scientific and educational bodies: for game and hunting research, hunters' training, education of game managers, game monitoring, testing of damage prevention measures and other similar purposes.

6.5.1 *The hunter examination and licensing*

To acquire a hunting licence in Latvia a person must be over 18 and pass an examination organised by the State Forest Service. The examination consists of a theoretical test and a shooting test. A training course has been required for each applicant since 2005. Afterwards, the certificate is valid for life.

In Estonia, all candidates for a hunting certificate have to take a 56-hour training course and subsequently to sit an examination including a practical shooting test. A hunter for big game (including wild ungulates) must pass a shooting test using a weapon loaded with bullets. A hunting certificate is valid for 5 years. To renew the certificate, one must pass an 8-hour cycle of lectures covering legislation, hunting, hunting ethics, game biology, current status of game populations in a particular district, etc.

In Lithuania, a person who wants to become a hunter must train in the field for one year, then he/she must attend special courses of hunters' education and later pass a hunter's examination. A hunter's certificate holder must be at least 18 years old, have Lithuanian citizenship or be a permanent resident in the country. Special courses are organised for hunters who wish to obtain a special category of hunter-selectioner (hunter who is qualified to carry out selective hunting in order to improve the quality of the ungulate population) and also to obtain the right to hunt moose, red deer and roe deer males.

There are c. 15 000 hunters in Estonia (c. 1% of the total population), 38 000 hunters in Latvia (1.6%) and over 30 000 in Lithuania (c. 1%). However, in Latvia the bulk of hunters is not active anymore. One way to judge the numbers of active hunters is by the number of season's cards (annual document confirming a state fee) issued and the number of those was 19 000 in 2004. The total number of hunters practically equals the number of ungulate hunters as this type of hunting is the most popular in the Baltics, so the majority of active hunters are involved in ungulate hunting (either as beaters or shooters). One does not have to be a landowner to be able to exercise the right to hunt. All hunters holding a valid hunter's licence can participate in ungulate hunting, but only a holder of the valid shooting test certificate for big game may act as a shooter.

Hunters can either be organised into clubs or hunt on an individual basis. In Lithuania, there are three main hunting societies: Lithuanian Society of Hunters and Fishermen, Lithuanian Hunter Union Gamta and Sūduvos Society of Hunters and Fishermen. These societies have the right to manage the Hunters Register – the newly introduced database on hunters. Commercial hunting is run by some forestry districts and firms. In Estonia, approximately 80% of hunters and the majority of hunters' societies are under the umbrella of the Estonian Hunters Society (Eesti Jahimeeste Selts). In Latvia, the biggest hunters organisation is the Latvian Hunters Association which represents the interests of the Latvian hunters both nationally and internationally. However, a large proportion of hunting clubs in Latvia are independent.

In Estonia, the licence price for ungulates is determined by each hunting society individually with no participation of the State except in hunting grounds managed by the state, i.e. state hunting districts and large nature reserves and national parks where the so-called regulation of population density substitutes hunting in its common sense. Therefore, the price range is very wide: up to several thousand euros for a very big red deer stag. Hunters' societies have to pay an annual fee to the state for the right to use the hunting grounds (the fee is based on the area and the quality of habitats suitable for wild game). The state also issues licences for hunting big game, but it does not determine their cost. Every hunters' society decides itself where to get the money from to pay the state fee. As a rule, the society sets the licence price and collects money from the hunters who shoot the animal. Alternatively, it can set a membership fee and use it to pay the fee to the State. Ungulate hunting may even cost nothing to the members of the hunting club if the club sells a few licences to foreign trophy hunters (e.g. from Norway) which generates enough money to pay the state fee.

Similarly, in Latvia, the state or another landowner grants the hunting right to the hunter clubs. The annual fee is approximately EUR 0.5 per ha of woodland in the state forests; however, the payment may be much less for private land.

Shooting permits are issued according to the annual quotas for big game without particular payment. The hunters' clubs only pay minor administrative costs for printing permits and collecting them back at the end of the season for aggregation of statistics.

6.6 Actual management and hunting practices

The state, through its governing bodies such as the State Forest Service or the Ministry of Environment, is responsible for organising game censuses, setting up annual hunting quotas and issuing licenses.

The state institutions responsible for hunting control carry out the official annual census using a variety of methods (pellet count in spring, hunters' estimations based on the all year round observations, etc.). Sometimes double-counting can occur and that can subsequently cause over-hunting of the population as the quotas are set based on the census numbers. Therefore, if the quota is set based on the over-estimated population size, it is likely to cause a decline in the population size. Large carnivores whose predation rates are not taken into account when setting hunting quotas can add to this effect.

In 2005, the Minister of Environment in Lithuania confirmed what should be required in drawing up management plans for any given hunting unit. The plan must evaluate environmental conditions and carrying capacity of the grounds, game stock and conditions of game use (including minimum and maximum recommended density), biotechnical measures, etc. The management plan must include data on wildlife surveys and population assessment, assessment of cervid pastures, game bags in the last ten years, the assessment of carrying capacity for cervid species, cervid rutting places (mapped), planned measures of additional feeding of game in wintertime, measures for reducing the damage to the forest and for conservation of rare plant species and habitats. Such plans should be renewed every ten years or sooner. Similar principles of drawing up management plans for hunting units are used in Estonia. In Latvia, no management plans exist either for individual ungulate species or for the hunting units. Only border plans of the hunting unit and contracts with land owners are required.

An example of guideline maximum density is shown in Table 6.2.

In Estonia, every year the Centre of Forest Protection and Silviculture draws up the moose management plan for the whole country based on the census data from counties and population observation data: population density, demographic structure, the rate of real increment, juveniles/100 adults, etc. and the situation of habitats in hunting districts, including forest damage. Data for the management plan are collected in all hunting districts (2004: data on 12 100 moose): mandibles for estimating age (2004: 3200 moose), samples of rumen contents for the diet

Table 6.2 *Guideline maximum densities for wild ungulates in Lithuania*

Forest type	No. of individuals per 1000 ha of forest		
	Moose	Red deer	Roe deer
Deciduous and mixed deciduous	4	15	55
Mixed coniferous and deciduous	3	12	45
Mixed coniferous with small amount of deciduous stands	2	12	35
Pure pine stands	1	6	15

Notes:
1. If forests are inhabited by several species of cervids, the given densities may be kept only when density of other species is lowered, with re-calculation of 1 moose equals 3 red deer, and 1 red deer equals 4 roe deer. If red deer are not present, moose and roe deer densities may be kept as shown.
2. If the isolated forests are smaller than 300 ha and the distance from the massif more than 300 m, red deer and moose densities can be neglected.
3. If the forests are smaller than 300 ha the roe deer density may be doubled.

study (2004: over 1000), samples of uteri and ovaries for studying moose cows' fertility (2004: over 350) and antlers (2004: nearly 800 bulls). The plan is based on the assumption that the highest density of moose that is compatible with human economic interests is 5–5.3 ind./1000 ha. The management plan takes into consideration changes of the situation mainly at the county level and suggests the quota with the view of keeping the population stable. Other ungulate species are also monitored in Estonia. Results from the monitoring feed into the population management planning (especially for red deer), but it has a more general character and is less detailed than in the case of moose. No management plans for ungulates exist in Latvia.

Various hunting methods are used in the Baltics: drive hunting (with unlimited number of beaters and/or dogs), still hunting (in a high seat, hide, boat or without hide; callers are allowed), stalking (with a dog for stopping game or just cradling), hunting with dogs (also chasing), hunting in row (in line, in the open area) and circular drive hunts (surrounding open area and moving to the centre). In Lithuania, not only firearms but also bows and cross-bows are legal. Hunting methods may vary from country to country, but drive hunting is one of the most common types of ungulate hunting.

Moose are mainly shot during collective driven hunting. Collective hunting is done in a group by members of a hunting club that rent their hunting grounds either from the state or from a private owner. This involves drive hunting when an area is encircled and beaters with or without dogs walk through the forest driving the animals towards a line of shooters. Sometimes combined hunting is organised by smaller groups of hunters, i.e. when an area is surrounded by hunters who position

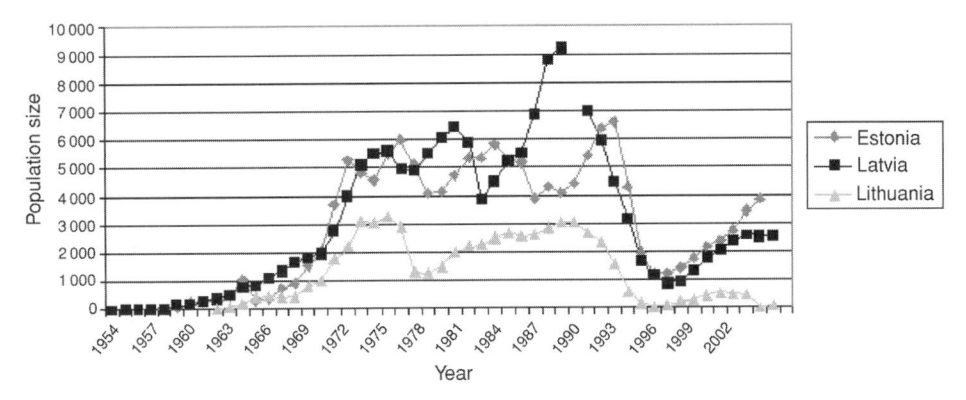

Fig. 6.7 Moose, *Alces alces*, hunting bag in the Baltic 1954–2004 (according to official game statistics)

themselves on possible crossings while one hunter follows a moose trail with a dog. During collective hunting, hunters are obliged to wear a red vest or other brightly coloured overdress. The popularity of dogs in moose hunting has been growing. Mainly Russian and Siberian laikas are used but recently also other breeds appeared such as Norwegian, Finnish and Jämtland moose dogs. Dogs are used to find and stop the game as well as to find a wounded animal by the blood trail. Also, hunting from hides and calling are allowed which enables selective hunting. These methods are used mainly in September during the rutting season.

Hunting bag statistics are shown in Figure 6.7. In Estonia, 4075 moose were shot in 2004, of those 32.4% were calves, the ratio of cows to bulls was 0.71. In Lithuania, the quota for moose for the 2005/2006 hunting season was set as zero.

Red deer are usually hunted in driven hunts (with dogs or a silent beat), stalking or hunting from hides (hunting towers). Stag stalking and calling is practised during the rutting season. In Estonia and Latvia, collective hunting and using dogs is allowed from 1 October. In the season of 2004/2005, 124 red deer were shot in Estonia (Fig. 6.8), of those 41 (33%) were fawns, 31 (25%) hinds and 52 (42%) stags.

For roe deer, calling, stalking and hunting from hides is allowed. Dogs can be used only for searching for wounded game. Driven hunts for roe deer are forbidden (in Estonia), but allowed in Lithuania and Latvia. Shooting bucks without antlers is forbidden. The hunting bag for roe deer is shown in Figure 6.9.

The main hunting methods for wild boar are drive hunts in winter time and waiting on the high seats (towers) on the forest edge where wild boar come out to feed on the agriculture land. This method is also used to reduce the damage caused by wild boar. Over half of the game bag should be piglets. In the last hunting season, the hunting bag in Estonia was composed of 52.1% piglets, 32.8% yearlings and 15.1% adults. The hunting bag dynamic is shown in Figure 6.10.

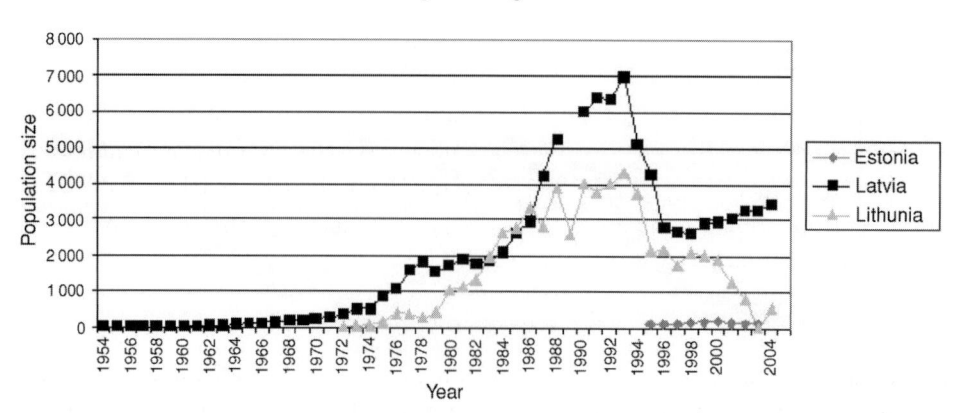

Fig. 6.8 Red deer, *Cervus elaphus*, hunting bag in the Baltic 1954–2004 (according to official game statistics)

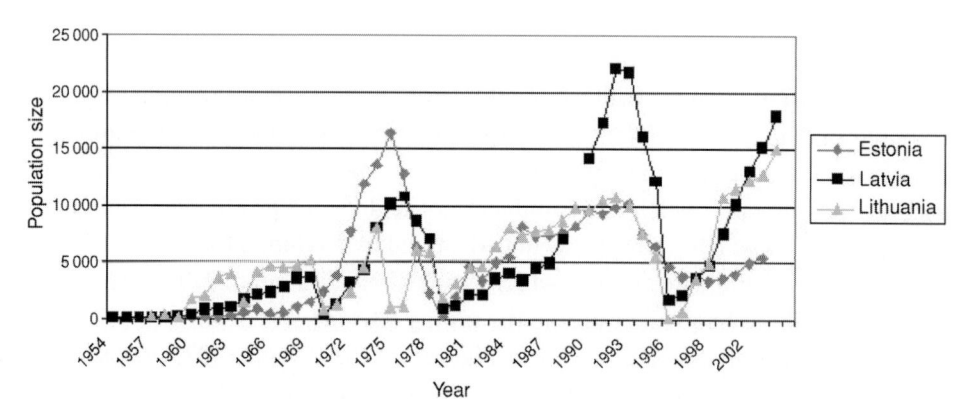

Fig. 6.9 Roe deer, *Capreolus capreolus*, hunting bag in the Baltic 1954–2004 (according to official game statistics)

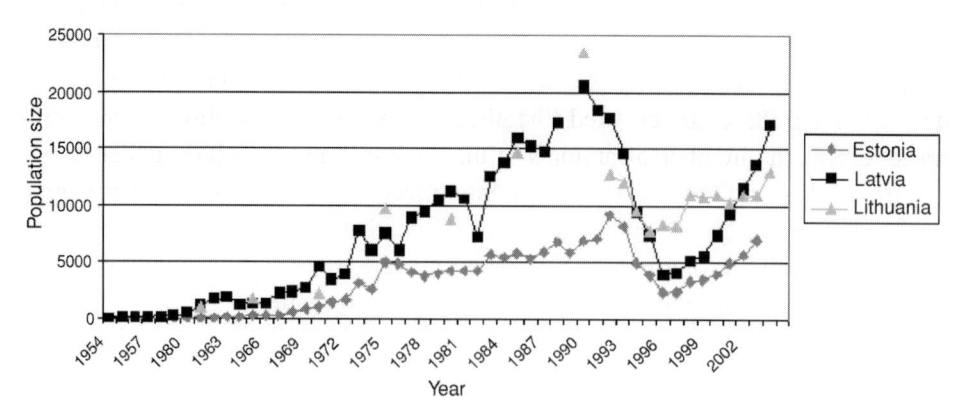

Fig. 6.10 Wild boar, *Sus scrofa*, hunting bag in the Baltic 1954–2004 (according to official game statistics)

The free-ranging bison herd in Lithuania is not managed. Uncontrolled poaching is the main problem. In 2000–01, eight animals were killed illegally. According to the international status of the species, Natura 2000 territory for the free-ranging herd should be established, but the Lithuanian Ministry of Environment avoids doing this and there are plans to move free-ranging animals to enclosures. Such a measure is not compatible with the EU policy in the nature conservation field.

6.7 Census methods

As noted above, the state, through its governing bodies such as the State Forest Service or the Ministry of Environment, is responsible for organising game censuses, setting up annual hunting quotas and issuing licences.

Generally, all-year-round observations by hunters, snow-tracking in winter and spring pellet group counts are used for ungulate censuses in the Baltic countries. In Latvia, the ungulate counting is done on the basis of rough estimates in relatively permanent hunting grounds (which may shift regularly depending on changes in land ownership, which is tied to the hunting rights) while censuses, mainly as a pellet group count, are used irregularly.

6.7.1 Moose, red deer and roe deer

The primary source of official census data is hunters' estimations of population numbers on the basis of long-term experience and observations. When the number of moose is low the estimation error is not big. When it is high, the numbers tend to be underestimated which may aggravate damage to the forestry. In control counts, the methods used are winter track counting and pellet-group counting in spring, and, less frequently, aviation and driven counting and mapping of winter locations.

Surveying of the roe deer in Estonia is done by two main methods: double snow-tracking, where on the first day all tracks are removed and on the second day only fresh tracks are counted (the difference between incoming and outgoing tracks equals the number of animals in the territory) and by winter pellet count. The error in counting roe deer is remarkably greater than in case of other ungulates. The dynamics of roe deer populations are determined more by the variability of natural mortality (which is not easily identifiable and predictable) than by the yearly increment (which is determined during observations). In Estonia, the percentage of fawns in the entire population, which characterises yearly increment, has been growing in the last few years and even exceeded 40% in 2000–02.

Cervid surveys in Lithuania are done by spring pellet group counts according to McCain (1948), Jurgenson (1961) and Padaiga (1970), wintering grounds are assessed by the Aldous method (Aldous, 1944). For moose, red deer and roe deer the number of individuals, density per 1000 ha of forest, sex ratio and age structure (adults : calves) should be presented as well. In Lithuania, survey data were deliberately underestimated in the Soviet times as hunters were not interested in hunting many roe deer, which had to be given to the state. Case studies showed that the real roe deer numbers were 1.3–1.6 times higher than was shown in the official survey. After Lithuania regained its independence all hunting bags belonged to hunters. Therefore, hunters sometimes now deliberately overestimate the population on order to obtain higher hunting quotas.

6.7.2 Wild boar

As wild boar are gregarious, leaving clear activity marks and visiting feeding places, their counting is more accurate than those of other ungulates. The yearly counting includes observations of the size and composition of herds, on the basis of which the increment is estimated.

6.8 Ungulate impacts and damage

All species of large ungulates can cause damage to agriculture and/or forestry. Moose and red deer can in areas of high local densities cause damage to forest plantations, both deciduous and coniferous.

In mixed spruce–deciduous stands moose may completely destroy aspen, oak and ash saplings, thus changing the future composition of forest stands. Red deer can cause a high level of damage by stripping spruce bark in young plantations during winter, while moose tend to damage pine plantations by breaking the tips of young trees while feeding. Red deer can cause lots of damage to ash and heavy browsing on young deciduous shoots (Prieditis, 1996; Prieditis and Prieditis, 1998).

At the time of high moose density in the 1970s–80s, significant damage to pine plantations and later to middle-aged spruce forests was caused in Latvia and Estonia (Õrd and Tõnisson, 1986; Randveer, 1995; Randveer and Heikkilä, 1996).

The biggest economic impact of moose-caused damage is the damage to pine plantations and middle-aged spruce forests. For example, in 1991 according to the inventory by the Estonian Forest Protection Service, moose damage was found in 2424 ha of young pine plantations, 13 541 ha of pine plantations, and 12 778 of middle-aged spruce forest (unpublished data). At present, when the moose population has almost doubled after the very low density in the mid-1990s, hundreds of hectares of damaged plantations are found again. The solution is to keep the density of the moose population at a lower level, since other methods of forest protection (such as fencing or the use of repellent chemicals) are not widely used, as yet, in the Baltics. Using salt licks can help the problem to some extent and natural regeneration in clear-cuts can help to diminish damage.

Seasonal migrations of moose may reach 30–50 km (Baleišis, 1977) and that can have implications for the damage to forestry, therefore further studies on the subject are required.

In Lithuania, red deer cause the most damage to agriculture after wild boar. They target rye, wheat, oats, corn, white beets and potato fields. Clover is preferred in improved meadows. In Estonia, the red deer density is very low and no significant damage is done to forestry or agriculture. In Latvia, red deer cause less damage than moose and roe deer. Damage is mainly observed in forest plantations, but it is not registered centrally as forest owners are more interested in quick profits from forest logging and less concerned about reforestation. Also, the forested area is constantly increasing due to reforestation of former agricultural lands which is paid for, therefore the overall damage becomes negligible.

Roe deer usually do not cause significant damage to forestry or agriculture. In deciduous stands, their selective browsing on saplings of oak, ash and maple can decrease their value and make them unsuitable for timber production while in young pine and spruce plantations they browse on leader shoots of young trees. By targeting broad-leaved species, roe deer may actively encourage re-growth of such species as birch and alder.

Wild boar can cause significant damage to agriculture, raiding potato fields and other crops (oats, wheat, corn, peas and white sugar beets). The extent of the damage is directly related to the density of wild boar: if there are $c.$ 100 animals per 1000 ha of forest, they visit 23.3–51.6% of agricultural fields around the forest; if there are only 6 animals per 1000 ha of forest, only 2.6% of agricultural fields (Baleišis *et al.*, 2003). The damage is aggravated by trampling. In protected areas (e.g. in Viidumäe nature reserve in Estonia), wild boar can destroy orchids and their habitats. The species can cause damage to ground-nesting birds such as *Galliformes*, but there is not enough research on the subject. Wild boar can also damage oak monocultures and uproot other forest stands. For example, in Lithuania wild boar root up $c.$ 0.4% of pure pine stands, 2.9% mixed stands, 0.9% mixed spruce–deciduous stands and 2.4% deciduous stands every year. At the same time, their digging activity is favourable for diversifying forest stands and increasing small-scale biodiversity.

Bison damage to forest stands is concentrated in the limited wintering area where bison feed on branches and peel bark from trees. In other forest areas damage is not significant compared to that by red deer or moose (Baleišis *et al.*, 2003; Balčiauskas, 2000b, 2004). Damage to agriculture by bison costs from several hundred to several thousand Euro per year. Since the species is protected, the law requires the damage to be compensated, but no data on the amount of compensation paid are available. Currently, white sugar beet crops in central Lithuania cause the main point of conflict.

Damage caused to agriculture or forestry by game species should be compensated by the users of the hunting rights in that specific area. It is a legal responsibility for hunters to pay for the damage caused by the game species. In practice, instead of direct compensation, hunters often choose to eliminate troublesome individuals or reduce the density of a particular species that causes damage.

All four species of ungulates are occasionally a cause of traffic accidents, however statistics on the extent of the problem are not available. Wild boar rarely cause traffic accidents because they are rather careful animals and active late at night when there is little traffic. About 200–300 moose per year are involved in traffic accidents in Estonia. Spring and autumn have the highest number of traffic accidents, partly due to salting of roads, which attracts moose.

6.9 Supplementary feeding

Supplementary feeding is provided throughout all three countries in order to increase the numbers of ungulates and the quality of trophies in any given hunting unit and is done on a voluntary basis by the hunting clubs. The target species for supplementary feeding are wild boar and red deer. Hunters invest in wild boar feeding more than in supplementary feeding of other species. Also, special feeding fields are created in order to keep animals away from agricultural land and to facilitate counting and harvesting of animals.

6.10 Future challenges

In the future hunting quotas should be set in a way that takes account of the carnivore predation rate so that the double hunting pressure (from human hunters and from large carnivores) does not have a negative effect on populations. In Lithuania, it is crucial to re-establish a state-wide survey of game species.

As each country has a slightly different situation with ungulate populations, future recommendations may differ for different species and different regions.

6.10.1 Moose

In Estonia and Latvia, the species should be managed in order to keep economically acceptable density when the level of damage to the forestry can be tolerated, while in Lithuania, where the species is declining due to over-harvesting and poaching, the priorities are the following:

- Ban on moose hunting in the forests with moose density below 2 ind./1000 ha;
- Strict and immediate poaching control;
- Re-establishment of the state-wide survey together with initiating scientific research on the species and modelling hunting bag based on the existing demographic structure of the population.

6.10.2 Red deer

Selective hunting of certain age groups (young and old animals) is recommended in order to achieve a favourable age structure of the population in Lithuania (Baleišis *et al.*, 2003). Until then, hunting in the forests with red deer density below 3 ind./1000 ha should be stopped. In Estonia, red deer are a relatively new game and training of hunters is required in order to enable them to carry out selective hunting based on a proper assessment of the age and quality of deer, thus avoiding depletion of the future trophy pool.

6.10.3 Roe deer

Population planning and management to keep high both species density and hunting bag is a priority for the future. It is particularly important since research has shown that roe deer is an important food item for large carnivores in the Baltic (Andersone, 1998; Andersone and Ozoliņš, 2004; Valdmann *et al.*, 2005). Therefore, keeping a high density of roe deer will help to safeguard large carnivore populations in the region. According to Bluzma (2004), roe deer densities can be improved by biotechnical measures of game management to take into account densities of other ungulate species.

6.10.4 Wild boar

The prevention of damage to agriculture by this species is a priority in all three countries. This can be done by way of luring animals into special feeding sites/fields away from the agricultural land. Also, hunting should ensure that the favourable demographic structure is maintained, for example, by applying a heavy hunting pressure on piglets and yearlings, and avoiding harvesting sows (Baleišis *et al.*, 2003).

6.10.5 Bison

The future management of European bison in Lithuania should implement several measures (Balčiauskas, 2004):

- Free ranging herd translocation to south and north-west Lithuania, creating areas for metapopulation, along with Belarus and Poland, and solving conflict with the EU requirements on nature protection;
- Poaching control measures;
- Elimination of hybrid animals from the population;
- Confirmation of origin for fenced animals through genetic analysis;
- Elaboration and adoption of the population management plan in accordance with the EU requirements and Species Action Plan (SAP).
- Enlarging living area for the fenced herd and improving their veterinary care.

References

Aldous, Ch. (1944) A deer browse survey method. *Journal of Mammalogy* **25**(2), 130–6.

Andersone, Ž. (1998) Summer nutrition of the wolf (*Canis lupus*) in the Slītere Nature Reserve, Latvia. *Proceedings of the Latvian Academy of Sciences Section B* **52**(1/2), 79–80.

Andersone, Ž. and Ozoliņš, J. (2004) Food habits of wolves *Canis lupus* in Latvia. *Acta Theriologica* **49**(3), 357–67.

Balčiauskas, L. P. (1988) [Anthropogeneity of the landscape of Lithuania as a factor for high densities of ungulates]. *Vesci AN BSSR* (Proceedings of the Belorussian Academy of Science), *Ser. Biol.*, **2**, 105–7. (In Russian.)

Balčiauskas, L. (1999) European bison (*Bison bonasus*) in Lithuania: status and possibilities of range extension. *Acta Zoologica Lituanica* **9**(3), 3–18.

Balčiauskas, L. (2000a) Restoration of European bison in Lithuania: achievements and problems. In *Proceedings of International Symposium "European bison: yesterday, today and tomorrow"*. 9–10 December 2000, Šiauliai, Lithuania. Šiauliai, 8–15.

Balčiauskas, L. (2000b) Possibilities of range extension of European bison in Lithuania. In *Proceedings of International Symposium "European bison: yesterday, today and tomorrow"*. 9–10 December 2000, Šiauliai, Lithuania. Šiauliai, pp. 16–20.

Balčiauskas, L. (2004a) Situation of European bison in Lithuania. In M. Krasinska and K. Daleszczyk, eds., *Proceedings of the Conference "European Bison Conservation"*. MRI PAS, European Union's Centre of Excellence BIOTER, pp. 14–18.

Balčiauskas, L. (2004b) Game survey as a mean of sustainable population management. *Proceedings of the International Symposium "Rational Management of Cervids in Forest Habitats"*. Šiauliai, pp. 40–9.

Balčiauskas, L., Trakimas, G., Juškaitis, R., Ulevičius, A. and Balčiauskienė, L. (1999) [*Atlas of Lithuanian mammals, amphibians and reptiles*]. 2nd edn. Vilnius, Lithuania. 120 pp. (In Lithuanian.)

Balčiauskas, L., Mažeikytė, R. and Baranauskas, K. (2005) Diversity of mammals in Vilnius city. *Acta Biologica Universitatis Daugavpiliensis* **5**(1): 55–66.

Baleišis, R. (1977) *Briedis*. Vilnius, Lithuania. 68 pp.

Baleišis, R. (2004) [Moose and red deer in Lithuania: population status and exploitation.] *Proceedings of the International Symposium "Rational Management of Cervids in Forest Habitats"*. Šiauliai, pp. 33–5. (In Russian.)

Baleišis, R. and Bluzma, P. (2000) The structure of the moose population in Lithuania. *Folia Theriologica Estonica* **5**, 27–9.

Baleišis, R., Bluzma, P., Ornicans, A. and Tonisson, J. (1998) The history of moose in the Baltic countries. *Alces* **34**(2), 339–45.

Baleišis, R. M. and Škėrys, I. I. (1984) [Introduction, translocations and tagging of red deer in Lithuania.]. *Proceedings of the Academy of Science of the Lithuanian SSR, Serija B* **3**(87): 89–96. (In Russian.)

Baleišis, R., Bluzma, P. and Balčiauskas, L. (2003) [*Hoofed animals of Lithuania*]. Vilnius, Lithuania: Akstis, 216 pp. (In Lithuanian.)

Bluzma, P. (2004) [European roe deer (*Capreolus capreolus*) in Lithuania: population status and management]. *Proceedings of the international symposium "Rational management of cervids in forest habitats"*. Šiauliai: pp. 92–9. (In Russian.)

Briedermann, L., Dittrich, G., Lockow, K. W. (1988) Rotwild *Cervus elaphus* L. In H. Stubbe, ed., *Buch der Hege: B. 1, Haarwild*. Berlin: VEB Deutscher Landwirtschaftsverlag, S. pp. 2–56.

Danilkin, A. A. (2002) Suidae. In *Mammals of Russia and the Neighbouring Countries*. Moscow: Geos, 309 pp. (In Russian.)

Eichwald, E. (1830) *Naturhistorische Skizze von Lithauen, Volhynien und Podolien*. Wilna.

Geptner, V. G., Nasimovič, A. A. and Bannikov, A. G. (1961) *Mammals of the Soviet Union*. Moscow, Vol. 1. (In Russian.)

Greve, K. (1909) *Säugetiere Kur-, Liv-, Estlands*. Riga, Latvia: W. Mellin u. Co. pp. 1–183.

Gripenberg, U. and Nygrén, T. (1987) Methods in chromosome studies in the Scandinavian moose (*Alces alces*). In *Procedings of the Second International Moose Symposium*, Supplement **1**. Part 2, 749–52.

Ivanauskas, T. (1929) [Moose] *Medžiotojas* **6**, 1–12. (In Lithuanian.)

Jurgenson, P. B. (1961) [Survey of moose and their winter activity in the forests of the mid-latitude zone using spring pellet count method]. *Proceedings of the Priokso-Terrasy State Reserve* **3**, 19–28. (In Russian.)

Kalniņš, A. (1943) [Huntsmanship]. Latvju gramata, Riga. pp. 1–704. (In Latvian.)

Ładowski, S. (1783) *Natural History of the Polish Kingdom*. Kraków. (In Polish.)

Lange, W. L. (1970) *Wild und Jagd in Lettland*. Hannover-Döhren: Harro von Hirscheydt Vrlg., pp. 1–280.

Ling, H. (1981) [Changes of distribution of wild boar (*Sus Scrofa* L.) in the Baltic states during last centuries]. *Yearbook of Estonian Naturalist's Society* **48**. Tallin, Estonia: ERK. (In Estonian.)

Lõugas, L. and Maldre, L. (2000) The history of theriofauna in the Eastern Baltic region. *Folia Theriologica Estonica* **5**, 86–100.

Martenson, A. (1899) *Wald, Wild und Jagd in den russischen Ostseeprovinzen*. Neudamm 131 S.

McCain, R. (1948) A method for measuring deer range use. *Transactions of the 13th North American Wildlife Conference,* Washington.

Örd, A. and Tõnisson, J. (1986) Elk damage to young pine stands in the Estonian S.S.R.: Possibilities of decreasing this damage. *Metsanduslikud Uurimused.* **XXI**, 7–25. (In Russian.)

Paaver, K. (1965) Formation of the theriofauna and variability of mammals of the Baltic in the holocene. *Tartu. AN Est SSR*. 494 pp. (In Russian.)

Padaiga, V. I. (1970) Methods of the cervids control in the intensive forestry. *Kaunas* 1–32. In Russian.

Plater, A. (1852) List of local mammals, birds and fishes. *Wilno*. (In Polish.)

Priedītis, A. (1996) Browsing on woody plants and the living conditions of cervid populations. *Proceedings 22nd IUGB Congress*, Sofia, Moscow, St. Petersburg: Pensoft publishers, pp. 239–44.

Priedītis, A. and Priedītis, A. (1998) The use of woody plants by cervids during the vegetation period and winter. *Proceedings of the Latvian Academy of Sciences, Section B* **52**(1/2) (594/595), 58–62.

Pucek, Z. (ed.) (2004) *Status Survey and Conservation Action Plan: European Bison*.

Randveer, T. (1995) Spruce damage caused by moose: a serious problem in Estonian forestry. *Ekologija* **2**, 84–5.

Randveer, T. and Heikkilä, R. (1996) Damage caused by moose (*Alces alces*) by bark stripping of *Picea abies*. *Scandinavian Journal of Forest Research* **11**, 153–8.

Rzączyński, G. (1721) *Historia naturalis curiosa Regni Poloniae, Magni ducatus Lithvaniae*.

Skriba, G. (1975) History and results of reacclimatization of red deer in Latvian SSR. *Proceedings of the Latvian Academy of Agriculture* **83**, 29–40. (In Russian.)

Tauriņš, E. (1982) *Mammals of Latvia*. Zvaigzne, Riga. pp. 1–256. (In Latvian.)

Timm, U., Pilāts, V. and Balčiauskas, L. (1998) Mammals of the East Baltic. *Proceedings of the Latvian Academy of Sciences Section B* **52** No. 1/2 (594/595), 1–9.

Tõnisson, J. and Randveer, T. (2005) Monitoring of moose: forest interactions in Estonia as a tool for game management decisions. *Alces* **39**, 255–62.

Valdmann, H., Andersone-Lilley, Ž., Koppa, O., Ozoliņš, J. and Bagrade, G. (2005) Winter diets of wolf and lynx in Estonia and Latvia: implications for predator-prey management. *Acta Theriologica* **50**, 521–7.

Volovič, G. B. (1867) Revision of forests and paths of game animals in the Grand Duchy of Lithuania with enclosed writings and privileges on entering the forest and the land. *Vilna*. (In Russian.)

7

Ungulates and their management in Great Britain and Ireland

RORY PUTMAN

When one considers the relatively small land area involved, deer management within the British Isles seems to have become remarkably complicated. Within the British Isles as a whole, there are six different species of deer (red deer, roe deer, fallow, sika, muntjac and Chinese water deer) – although muntjac and Chinese water deer have not yet become established in Scotland or Ireland, and roe deer also are absent from Ireland.

There are also populations of wild (feral) goats and sheep, and, in the south of England, a small number of local populations of wild boar established much more recently by escapes from farms.

Dependent on the local density and local objectives (often affecting very local areas indeed, of perhaps a few hundred hectares) these ungulates may be managed primarily for sport, for control of damage to agriculture, forestry or conservation habitats – or not managed at all. There is certainly no *national* pattern and there is considerable freedom of decision, as to what to manage for, and how to manage. Management is mainly at the (largely unregulated) discretion of individual landowners.

To make things more complicated, Scotland, the Republic of Ireland, Northern Ireland, England and Wales have completely independent administrative and legal systems – and the laws affecting deer and their management are significantly different in the different countries. To attempt any review here, therefore, is certainly complex!

Finally, on a note of semantics, the British Isles includes five countries: Scotland, England, Wales, Northern Ireland and the separate Republic of Ireland (Eire). The expression 'Great Britain' is used to describe Scotland, England and Wales; 'United Kingdom' refers to Great Britain and Northern Ireland, while 'the British Isles' embraces all these countries and the Republic of Ireland.

7.1 Ungulate species and their distribution

Six species of deer are currently found in the wild state in the British Isles. Only two of these (red deer and roe) may be regarded as truly native – and the distribution and genetics even of these have been influenced by introduction and re-introduction. Populations of all other species (fallow deer, sika, Chinese muntjac and Chinese water deer) derive from ancient or more recent introductions. Deer of one or more species now occur in over 60% of all 10 × 10 km grid squares of Britain.

In Scotland, the most abundant and widespread species are red deer, roe and sika, although there are small, essentially local, populations of fallow deer in the south. By biogeographical history, roe deer have never been present in Ireland (and have never been introduced); here the main species are fallow and sika, with one significant population of red deer present in Killarney in southern Ireland (and other smaller populations in Co. Donegal and Co. Wicklow).

Wales also has a restricted number of species present, with only fallow deer of widespread distribution; however, both roe deer and Chinese muntjac are currently expanding their distribution into Wales.

All six species of deer occur in England; although again the species may be considered in a number of distinct groups: (1) species of rather restricted distribution and abundance (sika deer and Chinese water deer, which both occur in a few localised areas in the lowlands, in a number of discrete and separate populations); (2) those of restricted distribution, but of local significance (red deer); (3) species of widespread distribution currently increasing in numbers within their existing range but not showing significant expansion of geographical distribution (fallow deer); (4) species expanding both in distribution and abundance (roe and muntjac deer).

In addition to these six deer species, there are also established populations of feral sheep (*Ovis aries*; Jewell and Bullock, 1991) and goats (*Capra hircus*; Bullock, 2008, for further details) and a few very local populations of wild boar (*Sus scrofa*), much more recently established by escapes from farms.

7.1.1 Red deer

Red deer are native to Britain and were originally widespread throughout the British Isles. The present day distribution within the Great Britain (Scotland, England, Wales) is largely confined to Scotland, north of the central industrial belt, south-west Scotland (Galloway) and a number of established, but essentially local populations, in England (notably those in Cumbria, East Anglia, Hampshire and south-west England (Devon and Somerset) (Fig. 7.1). Red deer do not occur widely in Wales, and are restricted in Ireland to Eire (the Republic of Ireland).

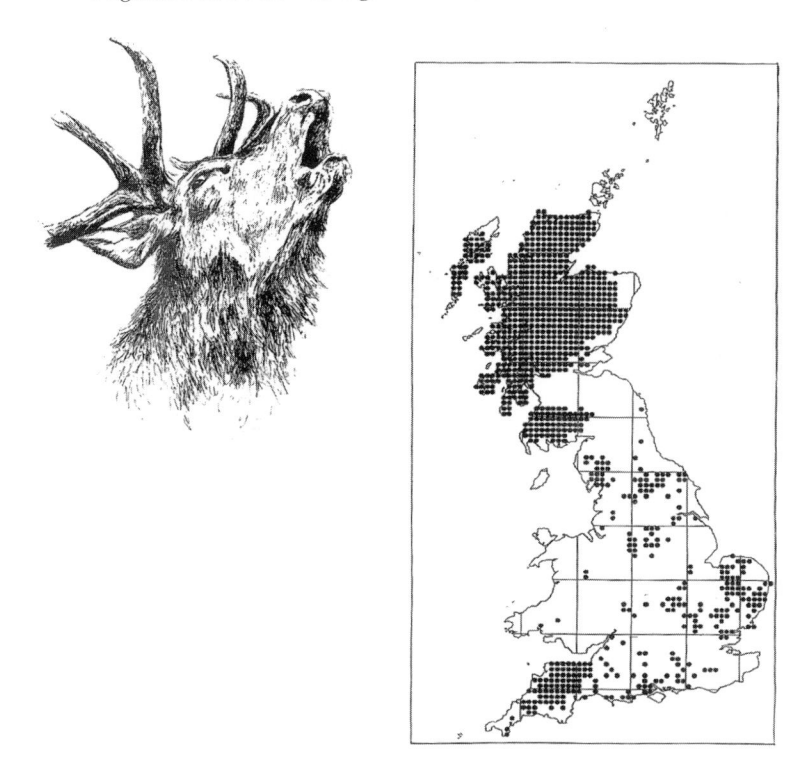

Fig. 7.1 Red deer distribution. Drawing by C. Putman

Although historically a woodland species, red deer are now found in a variety of habitats – on open moorland as well as in coniferous and deciduous forest; densities vary with quality and structure of the habitat. Densities of 5–40 per km^2 occur in forestry plantations and densities of between 12 and 20 per km^2 are typical for open moorland habitats (Ratcliffe, 1984; Stewart and Hester, 1998).

Estimates of total population size within Britain were offered by Harris *et al.* (1995) at around 360 000 (Scotland 347 000, England 12 500). Alternative estimates offered by Ward (2007) suggest total populations may be of the order of 400 000 (range 376 000–426 000). Ward's figures suggest a total population between 360 000 and 400 000 red deer in Scotland alone, with estimates for England between 16 000 and 20 000. Differences in estimates should not be taken as indicative of actual trend in population number, but more probably reflect differences in methods used to estimate population size. Numbers of red deer are currently believed to be stable or declining, except in the south-west of England where they are increasing in both numbers and range (Ward, 2005).

As noted, few red deer are recorded in Wales: Harris *et al.* (1995) estimated numbers at < 50; Ward's more recent estimates also suggest relatively low populations at between 100–400. Numbers in Ireland are estimated at between 3000 and 4000 with < 2000 in Co. Donegal and < 2000 in Co. Kerry (T. Burkitt, *pers. comm.*)

Deer of original native stock are only confirmed in parts of Ireland, Scotland and north-west England (Lowe and Gardiner, 1974); all other populations are introduced (e.g. Galloway, New Forest) or even where native stocks existed, have suffered introductions of English Park stock (mostly of European origin, possibly in some cases including some wapiti blood (*Cervus canadensis*)) in questionable attempts to increase antler quality. Many populations are currently suffering from hybridisation with the more recently introduced sika deer (*Cervus nippon*; Harrington, 1973, 1982; Lowe and Gardiner, 1975; Ratcliffe *et al.* 1992; Abernethy, 1994, 1998; Goodman *et al.*, 1999; Pemberton *et al.*, 2006; Diaz *et al.*, 2006). For a recent review, see Perez-Espona *et al.* (2009).

7.1.2 Roe deer

Roe deer, like red deer, are indigenous to Britain (although they do not occur in Ireland). Due to habitat loss and severe hunting pressure, however, they became extinct throughout much of the country in the Middle Ages; by the beginning of the eighteenth century they are believed to have disappeared from England and Wales and to survive in Scotland only in a few relict populations in the north and west (Ritchie, 1920; Prior, 1968). An increase in woodlands during the eighteenth century led to a range expansion in Scotland, but populations in England stem largely from local introductions of stock translocated from Scotland, or imported from continental Europe.

Roe of unknown origin were reintroduced to Milton Abbas, Dorset, in 1800 and by the early 1900s numbers were estimated in Dorset at 300–400. There were also populations in the New Forest, Surrey and Sussex. The roe population of East Anglia is believed to originate from an introduction of German deer to the area between Brandon and Thetford in 1884 (Chapman *et al.*, 1985); and the roe deer in the Lake District are thought to be of Austrian origin (Staines and Ratcliffe, 1991). From these centres, roe deer have spread throughout much of eastern, northern and southern England during the course of this century. Distributions have continued to expand both within England and Scotland, with an average expansion in distribution from 1972–2002 of 2.3% per year (Ward, 2007).

Hewison (1997) examined the differences between 15 populations from different parts of the UK using a combination of techniques: cranial morphometrics and starch gel electrophoresis of liver, kidney and muscle proteins. Three distinct groups of genetically similar populations were identified, characteristic at least within our samples of Scottish populations (Spadeadam and Craigellachie), and two subsets within England: Thetford, Pickering (Yorkshire), Ringwood and Stanford forests; Alice Holt Forest, Salisbury and Lulworth.

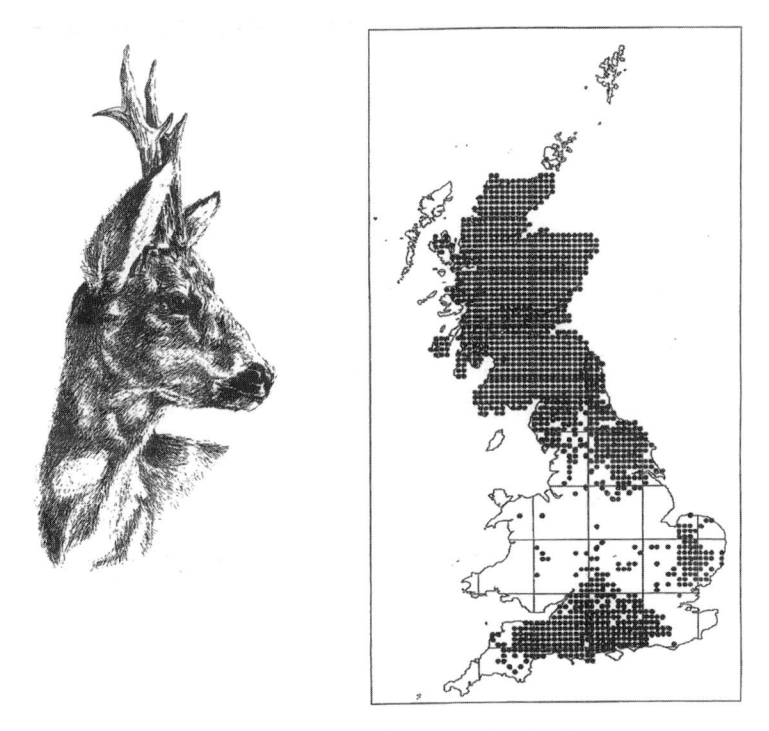

Fig. 7.2 Roe deer distribution. Drawing by C. Putman

Variations in skull morphology (as a descriptor of each 'type') were significantly correlated with differences in reproductive performance between populations, in particular maximum potential litter size, even when variation in environmental factors had been accounted for by redundancy analysis. Population characteristic/ skull morphological type accounted for 21% of the observed variation in fecundity between these populations (Hewison, 1997), with populations of Germanic origin tending to have generally higher fecundity (see also Hartl *et al.*, 1998).

By the mid-1970s, the total roe deer population in Britain was estimated to be 200 000 (Gibbs *et al.*, 1975) although no details are given as to how this figure was obtained. Currently roe are found throughout Scotland and northern England, and in a broad band across southern England and East Anglia, with scattered records from the English Borders and Wales (Fig. 7.2). Estimates of densities in woodland (based on dung group counts at 20 sites in Scotland; J. Latham) vary from 0.5 to 24.8 per km^2. Locally, densities of 75 deer per km^2 have been recorded in isolated woods in southern England but such estimates may in practice have included only part of the animals' ranges. Estimates for actual overall population size are more difficult to assess. Harris *et al.* (1995) offer estimates for roe in England and Wales at 150 000 with an additional 350 000 estimated to occur in Scotland. More recent estimates by

Ward (2007) suggest total populations of around 300 000 (range 275 000–320 000) with perhaps 95 000 in England, 200 000 in Scotland and between 2500 and 4700 in Wales. As noted for red deer however, differences in estimates should not be taken as indicative of actual trend in population number, but more probably reflect differences in methods used to estimate population size. Roe deer do not occur in Ireland.

7.1.3 Sika deer

Native to the Japanese islands and adjacent mainland of Asia, sika deer (*Cervus nippon*) were introduced to the UK at around the turn of the twentieth century: with the first recorded introduction dated around 1860 and numerous further introductions documented up until the 1930s. From parks and private collections sika deer escaped or were deliberately released and established successful feral populations in various parts of England, Scotland and Eire.

Ratcliffe (1987) offers a detailed review of the history of introduction and the subsequent spread of the species through Great Britain. Estimates of range expansion of sika between 1972 and 2002 within mainland Britain are at some 5.3% per year (Ward, 2007).

Numbers in Britain (Scotland, England and Wales) were estimated in 1995 at 11 500 (Harris *et al.*, 1995); Ward's more recent estimates suggest numbers may be as high as 26 600 (Scotland plus England). Numbers are separately estimated in Eire (the Republic of Ireland) at 20 000–25 000 (Hayden and Harrington, 2000).

As a historical consequence of where the majority of introductions happened to be concentrated, sika have reached their highest densities in Scotland (perhaps 25 000) and Eire (20 000–25 000); the damage caused in woodlands is now causing serious concern in commercial coniferous plantations (Ratcliffe, 1989; Gill, 1992; see also Larner, 1977) (Fig. 7.3). Additional cause for concern stems from the discovery that sika deer are able to hybridise with native red deer stocks and that thus, as they expand their range, they pose a serious threat to the genetic integrity of native red deer (Harrington, 1973, 1982; Lowe and Gardiner, 1975; Ratcliffe *et al.*, 1992; Putman and Hunt, 1994; Abernethy, 1994, 1998; Goodman *et al.*, 1999; Pemberton *et al.*, 2006).

The taxonomy of sika deer has been revised many times but there is a general consensus that we may recognise two distinct types: the smaller sika deer of the Japanese islands (*C. n. nippon* and related forms) and the mainland Asiatic sika (*C. n. hortulorum* and its allies) consisting of the larger Manchurian and Formosan forms (Ratcliffe, 1987). Animals of both taxonomic types have been introduced into Britain (in the first introduction of 1860 for example, the Zoological Society of London was presented with specimens reported as *C. n. nippon* and

Fig. 7.3 Sika deer distribution. Drawing by C. Putman

C. n. hortulorum and further introductions of both putative subspecies have been documented since). It is believed however that most of the sika introduced into British parks or collections were of the island form and certainly the small Japanese sika is the only type known to have become established in the wild (Lowe and Gardiner, 1975).

7.1.4 Fallow deer

Although widespread throughout Europe some hundred thousand years ago, fallow deer probably became extinct in Britain sometime during the last glaciation. Fallow deer were subsequently reintroduced to the UK in the eleventh century by the Normans (Chapman and Chapman, 1975; Langbein and Chapman, 2003) and established within deer parks; their early history in Britain is described by Whitehead (1964) while a history of the deer parks and their changing status is provided by Cantor (1989).

Populations in the wild state have become established through regular escapes from such enclosed park populations, or by release when parks were abandoned or broken up. However, as also noted by Liberg *et al.* (chapter 3), dispersion from

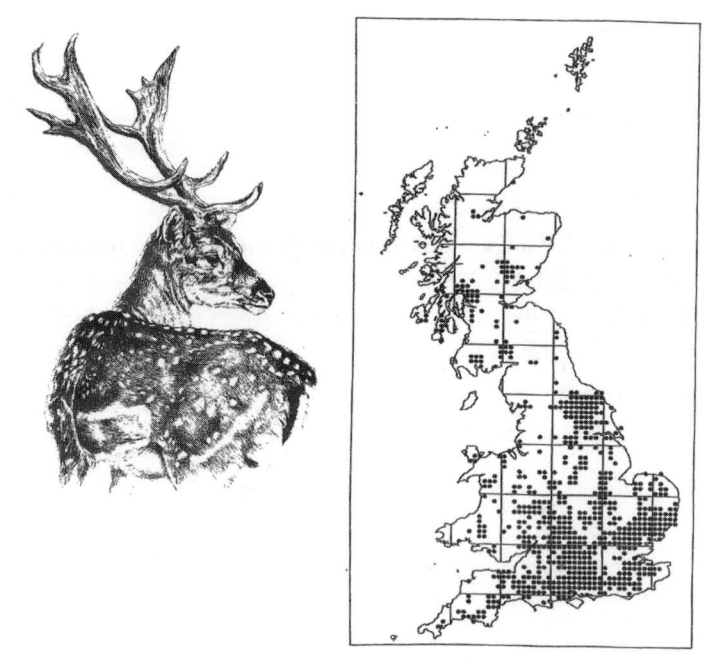

Fig. 7.4 Fallow deer distribution. Drawing by C. Putman

original sites of release is notably slow. As a result their current distribution in the UK still owes much to this history of establishment around the sites of past or present deer parks. Fallow now occur in 29% of all recorded 10 km squares in England and Wales and locally in Scotland and in southern Ireland (Fig. 7.4).

There are few reliable population estimates available; calculated densities may range from between 18 and 43 fallow per km^2 (Harris *et al.*, 1995). Even where accurate counts are available, it is rarely possible to relate these counts to the areas covered by the deer. In agricultural landscapes, densities are particularly hard to estimate, since they can vary tremendously with no apparent environmental cause, although levels of human disturbance and intensity of culling may be more important here than environmental quality per se. Further, populations are often heavily managed, so that density is maintained at a level that is not related to the carrying capacity of that particular habitat type.

Harris *et al.* (1995) estimated overall population number in the region of 100 000, although they noted that such estimates were not particularly robust. Using different methodologies, Ward (2007) estimates numbers of fallow deer at between 144 000 and 184 000, with the bulk of the population occurring in England (127 500–156 500). Although not increasing substantially in overall range, numbers within the established range would appear to be rising. About 2000 fallow deer are shot per annum in the Republic of Ireland although no estimates are available of the actual population size (Hayden and Harrington, 2000).

7.1.5 Muntjac deer

Both Chinese (*Muntiacus reevesi*) and Indian muntjac (*M. muntjac*) have been introduced to the UK at various times, but only the Chinese muntjac is believed to have become established in the wild. Following the original introduction to a private collection in 1894, Chinese muntjac are now established in most of southern England as far north as Derbyshire, Lincolnshire and Nottinghamshire, including some urban areas. In addition, there are scattered records outside this range, including Cheshire, Cumbria, Northumberland and South Yorkshire and in parts of North Wales and most of the counties adjoining the south Wales coast (Chapman *et al.*, 1994; cited in Harris *et al.*, 1995). There are also occasional reports of muntjac in Scotland, although these sightings have yet to be confirmed and the species is not established as a resident part of the fauna. Whilst muntjac are widely recorded in Wales, most of these records are from scattered individuals, and the population is unlikely to exceed 250 adult animals; muntjac do not occur in Ireland.

Despite their wide occurrence in England (Fig. 7.5), their distribution is very clumped. A survey, in the early 1990s, in which large numbers of records were collected from members of the public, found that 50% of the reports came from just five counties i.e. Berkshire, Buckinghamshire, Hertfordshire, Oxfordshire and Warwickshire (Chapman *et al.*, 1994). Elsewhere numbers were low and/or populations were scattered, either due to recent colonisation, or deliberate or accidental releases outside the main areas of distribution. Harris *et al.* (1995) estimated a total population size in England of about 40 000 with current numbers in Wales < 250. Numbers are however still increasing; Ward's (2007) estimate for the number of muntjac in England and Wales was of some 100 000 (range 91 600–116 700) and Ward (2005) estimated an annual rate of expansion of distribution at around 8.2%.

7.1.6 Chinese water deer

Chinese water deer were introduced to two private collections in southern England around the turn of the twentieth century. From these populations, animals were sent to a number of parks around England and Wales, including two in Hampshire, one in Montgomery, one in Norfolk, two in Shropshire and one in Yorkshire. Escapes from these collections led to the establishment of free-living populations and the early history of these is summarised in Whitehead (1964) and Lever (1977). The populations established around the New Forest in Hampshire died

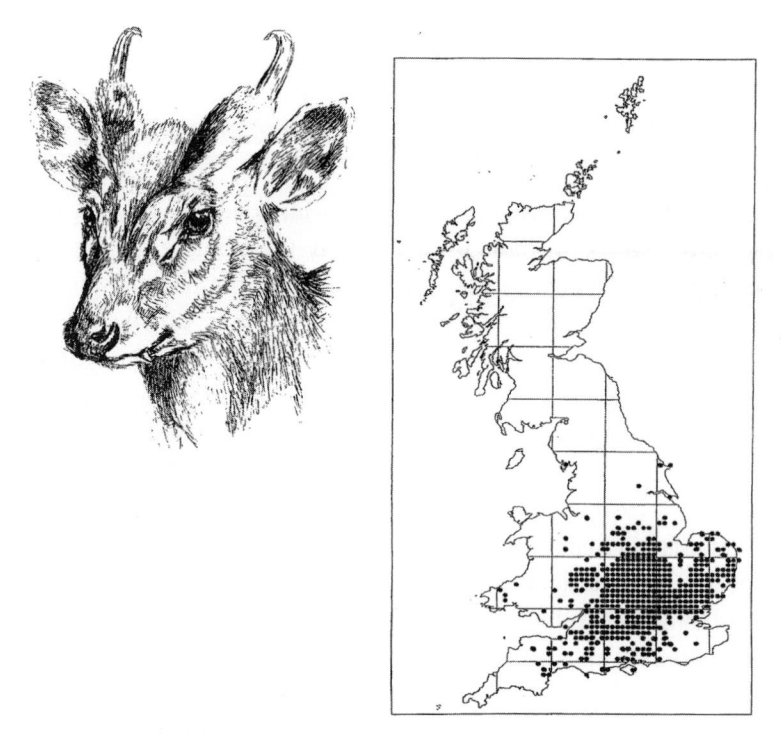

Fig. 7.5 Muntjac deer distribution. Drawing by C. Putman

out by 1963, and those in Northants and Shropshire also appear to have died out. Currently free-living populations persist in Bedfordshire/Hertfordshire, Berkshire, Cambridgeshire, Norfolk and Suffolk (Fig. 7.6).

The low numbers and impermanence of many feral populations suggest that conditions are not ideal for the establishment of this species, and that numbers are likely to remain low (Harris *et al.*, 1995). Free-living populations are estimated by Ward (2007) to number some 1500 animals.

7.1.7 Feral sheep

Two forms of feral sheep (*Ovis aries*), the Soay and the Boreray, occur in Great Britain, each named from islands of St Kilda group. The Soay is the most primitive domestic sheep, resembling wild sheep in its brown coat, relatively long legs, short tail and narrow body. Soays are smallest of all sheep, wild or domestic, about 50 cm at the shoulder (Ryder, 1984). The Boreray is a primitive form of Scottish Blackface, but smaller and variable in colour, ranging from cream–white to blackish.

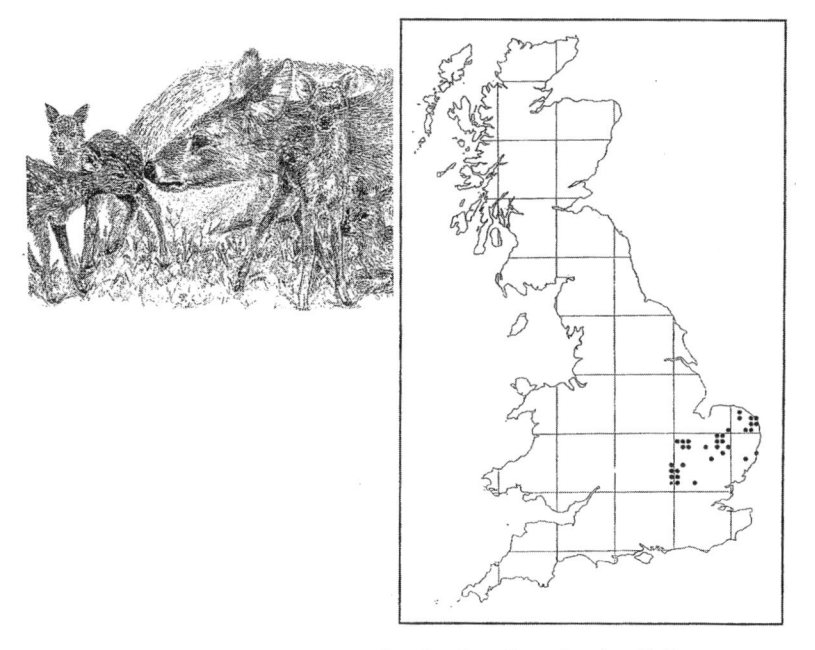

Fig. 7.6 Chinese water deer distribution. Drawing by C. Putman

Both types are restricted to the islands – and are largely within Scotland. Soay sheep were originally confined to islands of the St Kilda group (Soay and Hirta); more recently, populations have been introduced to various other offshore islands: Lundy, Cardigan Island (Wales), Holy Isle (Arran) and Sheep Island (Sanda Islands, Kintyre). A mainland feral population became established in the Cheddar Gorge in Somerset and now numbers over 130. The Boreray is confined to the island of Boreray, St Kilda.

Present policy of management for Soay and Boreray sheep on St Kilda is for minimal interference, whilst at the same time watching for serious damage to the ecosystem. Both races are classified by the Rare Breeds Survival Trust as 'Rare Breeds'. Many consider the St Kildan sheep a valuable heritage and the animals may also have genetic and historical importance; feral sheep share with 'wild mouflon' on Cyprus, Corsica, Sardinia an ancestry which dates from earliest Neolithic sheep (Groves, 1989). The Soay, in particular, is regarded as an important link with the sheep type that was first introduced to Britain in prehistoric times (Boyd and Jewell, 1974).

7.1.8 Feral goat

Feral goat populations (*Capra hircus*) are more widely distributed throughout the British Isles although restricted for the most part to mainly hilly and mountainous

Table 7.1 Approximate numbers of each of the six deer species in Britain, in Scotland, England and Wales Numbers modified/updated from Ward (2007) and Hayden and Harrington (2000)

	C. elaphus	C. nippon	Capreolus	Dama dama	Muntiacus reevesi	Hydropotes
Scotland	360 000–400 000	25 000	200 000–350 000	Uncertain: < 2000?	0	0
England	16 000–20 000	1500–2000	100 000	130 000–150 000 including Wales	80 000–110 000	1500
Wales	100–400	0	<100		4000–8000	0
Eire	<4000	20 000–25 000	0	8000–10 000?	0	0

areas of Scotland, Wales, Ireland and northern England. Populations are often small and discrete rather than scattered over a wide area of apparently suitable ground (Bullock, 2008).

In Britain and Ireland, the total population is 5000–10 000 (estimates from 1990–9), higher than the previous decade (Bullock, 1995). Detailed estimates for different individual populations are summarised by Bullock, 2008.

7.1.9 Wild boar

Wild boar were present in Britain in prehistoric times; they are not recorded from the Late Glacial, but arrived in Britain and Ireland early in the Mesolithic (Yalden, 1999). Boar were apparently extinct in Ireland by the Neolithic, although the archaeological record is everywhere obscured by the arrival of domestic pigs. In England, there is documentary evidence to suggest that wild boar survived certainly to about 1300; its status after that is somewhat doubtful in both England and Scotland. Between the seventeenth century and the 1980s, when wild boar farming began, only a handful of captive wild boar, imported from the continent as exhibits in zoos and wildlife collections, were present in Britain. Thus until very recently, no free-living wild boar had been present in Britain for about 300 years.

In the 1990s sightings of wild boar outside captivity increased and escapes from captivity have been recorded 23 times involving at least 198 animals (Goulding *et al.*, 1998). By 1998 two viable populations existed, one in Dorset, the second in Kent/East Sussex (Goulding *et al.*, 1998). By 2005, several other substantial escapes had been reported and a third population recognised, in Herefordshire (Goulding *et al.*, 2008). The origin of the animals is uncertain, although the increase in escapes of wild boar coincided with the increase in the number of farms rearing wild boar for meat. Some wild boar farmers mate domestic pig sows with male wild boar to give increased litter sizes whilst retaining some of the flavour of wild boar meat; hybrids have the typical appearance of wild boar. Thus, it is unclear whether feral pigs in Britain are pure-bred wild boar.

The actual number of animals in free-living populations is uncertain. In 2004, there was estimated to be 200 animals in Kent and East Sussex, up to 30 in Dorset and a 'significant number' in Herefordshire (Wilson, 2005). Numbers are predicted to increase as wild boar have a high reproductive potential and no natural predators in Britain (Moore and Wilson, 2005). Additions to the free-living populations from further escapes from captivity are also likely. Because the species has established in the wild relatively recently, no formal policies have yet been developed as to future management, although the options are discussed by Moore and Wilson (2005).

Boar could be regarded as a species with high biodiversity value, forming an integral part of woodland ecology, and a sporting quarry providing flavoursome meat; conversely, they could be an undesirable agricultural pest, a danger to the public (a licence issued under the Dangerous Wild Animals Act 1976 is required by all those keeping wild boar) and a route for transmitting disease to domestic pigs.

7.2 Legislation

No one within the the British Isles may purchase or possess a shotgun or firearm without a valid shotgun licence or firearm certificate issued by the police. No formal examination is necessary to obtain such licence/certificate, but adequate reasons must be given for the wish to possess a firearm, and letters of support from appropriately qualified persons are required.

The management and culling of deer is covered under various different pieces of legislation in the UK and the Republic of Ireland. The main implications of these instruments are to define who has the right to take or kill deer, to limit the type of weapons which may be employed (calibre and muzzle velocity/energy) and also restrict the periods of the year when deer may be killed; but the legislation also covers other issues, such as welfare, live capture or movement of deer.

Details vary from country to country (particularly in relation to prohibited seasons), but in essence, these different Acts prohibit the use of smooth bore guns (shotguns) for killing deer except under very specific conditions. They also specify the minimum rifle which may be used, either in terms of calibre and muzzle energy (England and Wales) or by bullet weight, muzzle velocity and muzzle energy (Scotland and Northern Ireland). These laws also prohibit the use of any airgun, air rifle or pistol, cross-bows and other similar weapons as well as the use of drugs in the taking or killing of deer.

Finally, they make clear definition of those who have the legal right to take or kill deer, usually as the owner of the land, his/her legal tenant or others having the *written consent and authority* of the landowner or occupier.

A brief summary of the regulations current in each country is provided below. It should be emphasised however, that such brief overview presents a summary only, and for the purposes of this presentation focuses in the main on differences in the permitted seasons of the year when deer may be shot in each country. We should note in addition that legislation controlling the shooting of deer (in relation to permitted firearms and again in relation to the permitted shooting seasons) are currently under review in England, Wales and Northern Ireland, and (separately) in Scotland.

Table 7.2 *Permitted seasons in which deer may be killed in England/Wales/ Northern Ireland, and Scotland*

Species	Sex	England, Wales Northern Ireland	Scotland
Red Deer	Male	1 August–30 April	1 July–20 October
	Female	1 November–31 March	21 October–15 February
Sika Deer	Male	1 August–30 April	1 July–20 October
	Female	1 November–31 March	21 October–15 February
Red × Sika hybrids	Male	1 August–30 April	1 July–20 October
	Female	1 November–31 March	21 October–15 February
Fallow Deer	Male	1 August–30 April	1 August–30 April
	Female	1 November–31 March	21 October–15 February
		England Wales	**Scotland**
Roe Deer	Male	1 April–31 October	1 April–20 October
	Female	1 November–31 March	21 October–31 March
Chinese Water Deer	Male	1 November–31 March	
	Female	1 November–31 March	
Muntjac		There are at present no statutory close seasons for either sex of this non-seasonal breeder	Do not occur in Scotland

7.2.1 England, Wales and Northern Ireland

At the present time

- Only the following firearms are allowed:
  (1) any rifle with a calibre of, or greater than, .240 inches, and muzzle energy equal to or greater than 1700 footpounds (2305 J); (2) *for muntjac and Chinese water deer only*, any rifle with a calibre of or greater than .220 inches and muzzle energy greater than or equal to 1000 footpounds (1356 J); (3) *For use only by authorised persons who can show that the deer are causing damage to agricultural crops, growing timber or other property*, 12 bore shotguns may be used but only if using cartridges containing shot .203 inches in diameter ('AAA'), or loaded with rifled slugs weighing 350 grains (22.68 g) or more.
- Deer may only legally be killed by the owner or occupier of the land on which they are shot, or with the written consent of the owner or occupier.
- Seasons in which deer may currently be shot legally are summarised in Table 7.2. Note that these have changed recently under a new Regulatory Reform Order in October 2007.
- For the prevention of suffering to injured or diseased deer the law provides certain general exemptions to provisions of the legislation affecting close seasons, prohibited weapons and night shooting. Landowners or occupiers who can demonstrate significant damage being caused to agricultural crops, forestry or other property are permitted to shoot marauding deer during the close seasons and a shotgun may be used under certain circumstances, but only where of appropriate calibre and charge.

- Where significant damage can be demonstrated in this way, landowners or occupiers may also apply to Defra (Department for Environment, Food and Rural Affairs) for licences to permit shooting at night under the Agriculture Act (1947).

7.2.2 Scotland

A major part of the Deer (Scotland) Act (1996) is concerned with establishing the Deer Commission for Scotland (the Government's Statutory Agency for overseeing and coordinating the management of deer populations within Scotland) and laying down its powers and responsibilities.[1]

Regulations controlling the actual management of deer are essentially similar to those operating in England and Wales, with the main variations being:

- Permitted weapons are defined as rifles of a muzzle energy not less than 1750 foot pounds (2373 J) with a muzzle velocity of not less than 2450 feet per second (746.78 m/sec); these must deliver a single bullet, designed to deform in a predictable manner (i.e. soft-nosed or hollow-nosed) and with a weight of not less than 100 grain (6.48 g). However for smaller species such as roe, it is currently permissible to use a bullet of not less than 50 grain (3.24 g) from a rifle with a muzzle energy of not less than 1000 foot pounds (1356 J) and muzzle velocity as above of 2450 feet per second.
- Once again, where serious damage has been caused (or may be anticipated) to timber or crops, or to the natural heritage, regulations may be relaxed and owners/occupiers or others authorised by them may use a shotgun (of not less than 12 bore) loaded with either
    (1) a single slug weighing not less than 380 grain (24.62 g); or
    (2) a cartridge containing not less than 550 grain (35.64 g) of SSG shot none of which is less than 0.268 inches (6.81 mm) in diameter;
    (3) *for roe deer only*: a cartridge containing not less than 450 grain (29.16 g) none of which is less than 0.203 inches (5.16 mm) in diameter (AAA).
- Permitted seasons are summarised in Table 7.2.
- Deer may be shot out of season by the owner of the land where it can be shown they are causing significant damage to agriculture, forestry or the natural heritage. The Deer Commission for Scotland can also issue specific authorisations to persons other than the landowner (his/her tenant, or employee), for shooting out of season, or shooting at night where similar damage may be demonstrated.

7.2.3 Sale of venison and the legal requirement for Trained Hunter Status

Beside these main provisions, both in Scotland and England, Wales and Northern Ireland the Deer Acts or other pieces of relevant legislation include a number of

---

[1] It has just been announced as this goes to press that the Deer Commission for Scotland is to be merged with the national conservation agency: Scottish Natural Heritage

other detailed restrictions and exemptions – as for example in relation to the sale or distribution of venison, in response to the various EU Directives on Game Meat. In practice, this means that venison may not be sold through a game dealer (Approved Game Handling Establishment (AGHE)) unless inspected by a 'trained hunter'.

In establishing who shall be considered to hold such 'trained hunter' status, the statutory bodies have come to recognise and endorse a series of qualifications provided within the industry itself. Although provided by the voluntary sector and not mandatory, there are nationally accredited qualifications (Deer Management Qualification, Level 1 and Level 2) administered by an independent body with representation from all the main hunting associations (British Association for Shooting and Conservation, British Deer Society, Scottish Gamekeepers' Association, etc.).

In consequence, even though there is no legal requirement for some specific level of training, or need for any formal qualification before anyone is permitted to *shoot* deer or other game, because of the legal restrictions which apply, separately, to the handling and sale of game meat, an increasing number of amateur and professional game managers will in fact have passed some basic qualification in deer management and carcase hygiene to achieve 'trained hunter' status. The main exception would be those who shoot only occasionally for purely domestic consumption, where carcasses need not pass through a game dealer, or occasional stalkers accompanied, when shooting, by a professional hunter (in this case, while the shooter requires no such qualification, the accompanying professional hunter will usually hold the appropriate qualification, simply to dispose of the venison).

It is also a legal requirement in all countries of the UK for carcases sold through an AGHE to be tagged and accompanied by details of where and when shot. In practice, this means that carcase tagging is increasingly widespread although not universal.

7.2.4 The Republic of Ireland

Regulations first make clear a definition of who may or may not take deer. The situation here is rather different from that within the UK in that, in the Republic of Ireland, those authorised to kill deer are required to have a Hunting Certificate (not required within the UK) and a valid Firearms Certificate relevant to the firearms restrictions for deer. A Firearms Certificate cannot be issued unless the applicant has a Hunting Certificate. Hunting Certificates, valid for the year 1 August–31 July, are issued by the National Parks and Wildlife Service. No one may take or kill deer without a valid Hunting Certificate and Firearms Certificate, including landowners, even if they have deer on their lands.

Table 7.3 *Permitted seasons in which deer may be killed in the Republic of Ireland*

Species	Sex	Counties other than Kerry	Co. Kerry
Red Deer	Male	1 September–31 December	Shooting red stags not permitted at any time
	Female	1 November–28 February	1 November–28 February
Sika Deer	Male	1 September–31 December	1 September–31 December
	Female	1 November–28 February	1 November–28 February
Red × Sika hybrids	Male	not specified in any statutory order defining seasons	
	Female		
Fallow Deer	Male	1 September–31 December	1 September–31 December
	Female	1 November–28 February	1 November–28 February
Roe Deer, Muntjac, Chinese Water Deer		Do not occur in the Republic of Ireland	

- Permitted firearms are:
    any rifle with a calibre of, or greater than, .22/250 with a muzzle energy of or greater than 1600 foot pounds (2170 J), up to a maximum calibre of .270 and muzzle energy of 2700 footpounds (3661 J)
- Statutory Close Seasons differ in different parts of the Republic. These are summarised in Table 7.3.

7.3 Deer management practice and objectives

Because there are marked differences in the species present, in their distribution and local densities, and because, in addition, there are marked cultural differences in attitude in the different countries, management aims and practices vary widely between the different countries. This partly reflects patterns of land ownership, and also reflects changes in the relative importance of other land-use interests, such as arable or livestock agriculture, or forestry, in different areas.

Within southern Ireland (red, sika, fallow) there is no strong tradition of recreational hunting, and most deer management is aimed at reduction of damage to agriculture or forestry.

By marked contrast, in the north of Scotland, in particular, there has become established a very strong tradition of recreational stalking – especially of red deer on the open moorland, where land is often unsuited to any other form of management or exploitation (e.g. forestry or agriculture). The lease of such stalking provides important revenue to private landowners and an important source of employment within local communities, since many private estates will employ a full-time or part-time 'stalker' with responsibility for management of the deer and their habitat, and responsibility for accompanying paying clients. Such recreational stalking is thus equally, if not more, important, over very large areas of the country, than shooting carried out to control damage. However, the maintenance of high population densities in support of sporting interests may lead to conflict with other, private or state-controlled landowners in the same neighbourhood, whose objectives may be more concerned with reducing impacts to forestry, agriculture or natural heritage interests.

In southern Scotland, Northern Ireland, England and Wales, patterns of land ownership tend to be rather different. Private land-holdings are smaller, and do not present the very large units of land found in northern Scotland (where individual holdings can be as much as 40 000 ha). These smaller private holdings are also more commonly interspersed with areas controlled by the state for forestry or conservation management, and there is an increasing emphasis on arable agriculture (virtually absent from north-west Scotland). The landscape thus presents more of a complex mosaic of smaller land-holdings, and with a patchwork of agricultural and woodland areas. Here, deer management (where present at all) tends to be more focused on attempts to reduce damage to agriculture or forestry. Recreational hunting is still important in some areas, but tends primarily to involve woodland stalking of roe and fallow deer.

7.4/5 Management structure and coordination

Under British legislation, deer are wild animals and belong to no one. The right to shoot them, however, belongs to the owner of the land on which they occur, or any person authorised by him or her to shoot on their land. Within the United Kingdom (Scotland, England, Wales and Northern Ireland) there is no state ownership of deer, nor state control of hunting (the situation, as above, is slightly different in Eire). Thus hunting is not centrally controlled, or carried out under licence; nor is there any central control over numbers to be shot.

The right to take deer, within the permitted seasons, is simply conferred by ownership of land and licences are only required where application is made to take deer out of season, or at night. While there are a number of deer management courses now available, leading to proper, accredited qualifications, and those wishing to shoot deer are strongly encouraged by the hunting organisations (British Deer Society, British Association for Shooting and Conservation) to obtain such qualifications, there is, at the present time, no legal requirement to hold such qualifications in order to shoot deer. All that is otherwise required is possession of a current valid firearms licence.

Note, however, (see section 7.2) that venison offered for sale through a game dealer (AGHE) must, under the EU Game Meat Directive have been inspected by someone of 'trained hunter' status, and (although there are other routes to such accreditation), the simplest route to achieving such accreditation is through passing one of the Deer Management Qualifications offered and administered by an independent body established by the hunting organisations themselves. Thus, while no formal qualification is legally required to shoot deer, the vast majority of professional deer managers, together with others who regularly who shoot deer unaccompanied, or those who regularly accompany paying clients, will have at least DMQ Level 1.

Within publicly owned land (areas owned and managed, for example, by the State Forestry Commission, or areas owned and managed by statutory organisations for natural conservation), culling for management may be undertaken by retained stalker/managers paid from the public purse. But, for the vast majority of land area, management is carried out by, or on behalf of, the individual owner for whatever objectives he or she may determine. This leads to an enormous variation in management practices and intensity in different areas, with significant areas receiving no formal management at all. This is acknowledged as potentially problematic, in that there is in effect no control or coordination of deer population size or management; there is no formal structure for resolving conflicts in management (where one landowner wishes to maintain high deer densities in support of recreational or commercial hunting, while his/her neighbour wishes to reduce deer numbers to minimum presence to control impacts on agriculture or forestry interests). Further, in general, there is no statutory requirement to undertake any management at all, nor any overall mechanism for controlling expanding numbers.

It is acknowledged both in England and in Scotland, that numbers of deer of a number of species are showing significant increase; more to the point, in specific areas, local concentrations of one or other species lead to very high local densities – at levels at which they are perhaps causing significant economic or ecological damage. Yet, apart from Scotland, there is at present no formal provision for state intervention, or coordination of management effort.

In Scotland, in fact, the situation is slightly different. Management of deer in particular areas is to some extent coordinated by discussion/agreement of neighbouring landowners within a framework of voluntary Deer Management Groups. Neighbouring landowners and other interest groups, such as the Forestry Commission, or the state nature conservation organisation (Scottish Natural Heritage, SNH) meet together on a regular basis to discuss management issues affecting their local area, cooperate to undertake regular census of deer numbers within their management area and agree cull targets. At present, something like 90% of the entire land-area of Scotland is covered within one or other of over 50 of these voluntary Deer Management Groups.

Further, there is in Scotland a statutory (governmental) organisation charged with coordination of deer management issues – and with actual legal powers to intervene in situations where it may be demonstrated that deer are causing damage to agriculture, forestry or natural heritage interests, or pose a threat to public safety. Under the 1996 Deer Act (Scotland) this organisation (the Deer Commission for Scotland) has wide-ranging powers, and while up until the present it has attempted to resolve apparent conflicts by encouraging the various local deer management groups to take appropriate and effective action, it does indeed have considerable statutory power to intervene if the problem cannot be resolved by such voluntary agreement.[2]

No such system exists elsewhere within the UK. Although there are a number of local deer management groups, which attempt to coordinate deer management within their local area, these are relatively few in number, and coverage of the country as a whole is poor (less than 10%). In both England and Wales, a number of organisations which are all independently concerned with deer management issues in one context or another (highways authorities, animal welfare organisations, state Forestry Commission, state conservation organisations, etc.) have cooperated to establish a joint controlling agency charged with trying to coordinate deer management over larger areas (the Deer Initiative and the Deer Initiative, Wales).

These relatively new bodies, however, have no statutory powers. While they may help by coordinating efforts of their member organisations in addressing deer issues (and ensuring that these different management organisations work together with common objectives), they have no powers to impose on management within the private sector. At most they may they may try to educate and encourage formation of collaborative Deer Management Groups, but this is not a formal requirement, and deer management in England, Wales and Northern Ireland continues, for the most part, to be undertaken by individual landowners, independently of others around them.

7.6 Management practices

Because of this, there is thus no legal structure (in any country) requiring census of deer stocks or presentation of any formal management plan. Increasingly, however, there is pressure on individual landowners, or deer management groups, to

---

[2] It has just been announced as this goes to press that the Deer Commission for Scotland is to be merged with the national conservation agency: Scottish Natural Heritage

voluntarily undertake more formal census and to prepare management plans and this voluntary preparation of formal management plans is increasing, particularly within Scotland.

While much management is by direct population control, it is important to emphasise that management may not depend entirely (or even at all) on shooting. Often management of deer populations (and especially, management of their impact) may be through use of other methods: such as fencing, chemical repellents, habitat manipulations, diversionary feeding, etc. and in many situations management of impacts by such methods has proved more effective than management by attempts at population reduction (Putman, 2004).

Whether in relation to reducing the risk of deer–vehicle collisions (DVCs), or in reducing impacts of deer on agriculture, forestry or conservation habitats, reduction of deer numbers is only one of a variety of alternative options available. Indeed, within the context of DVCs, where local reductions in deer populations have been carried out in an attempt to reduce the risk or frequency of traffic collisions, while we may cite a number of instances where population reductions would appear to have been accompanied by reductions in the frequency of deer–vehicle accidents (Jones and Witham, 1993; Jenks *et al.*, 2002; Rondeau and Conrad, 2003), there is an almost equal number of studies where no such relationship has been established (e.g. Waring *et al.*, 1991; Doerr *et al.*, 2001). In the same way there is little evidence to suggest that damage by deer to agriculture or forestry shows any simple relationship with deer density. Attempts to control impacts by reductions in deer populations alone are thus unlikely to prove wholly effective (Putman, 2004). Since the severity of damage caused by deer is in fact only relatively weakly related to the actual density of deer, in consequence, even where culling efforts have genuinely achieved a real reduction in deer densities, this has not necessarily been rewarded by an equivalent reduction in perceived impact – (unless the deer have been reduced to a minimal presence).

I myself advocate that management strategies should be developed quite separately for

1. management of deer populations themselves,
2. management of damaging impacts.

While the regulation of numbers of deer within any area may contribute partially to regulation of impact, it is perhaps best seen as directed primarily to regulating the numbers of the deer themselves in relation to the land's capacity to support healthy stocks or in terms of managing a sporting/recreational resource. Quite distinct consideration may need to be given to other, complementary, strategies which will help to control the impact of grazing and browsing on conservation, forestry or agricultural interests utilising measures such as fencing, habitat manipulation or the use of repellents/deterrents (Putman, 2004).

7.6.1 Culling

Considering simply the management of deer populations themselves through culling, the majority of imposed mortality on deer populations in Britain is by shooting with high velocity rifles. There was until recently a small tradition of pursuing deer with dogs (hunting to hounds). This practice was restricted to a few areas in the south of England (in the New Forest in Hampshire, and in Devon and Somerset. For details, see Langbein and Putman, 1996; Macdonald *et al.*, 2000).

Pursuit of any animals with dogs is now prohibited within the UK.

Management, or recreational hunting in woodlands, or shooting of deer to prevent damage to agricultural land, is commonly undertaken from high seats (shooting platforms) although occasionally animals are stalked on foot.

In the open moorland conditions of the Highlands of Scotland, red deer are usually stalked on foot and here it is common for estates to employ professional managers (stalkers) to control numbers of hinds and to accompany those clients who may pay to come to shoot stags in season. (Some shooting of hinds is now also, increasingly, leased.)

There are within Britain no standardised methods of calculating what should be the size of cull taken in any year/any situation. Because there is no central organisation responsible for managing the countries' deer populations, and culling is the responsibility of the individual landowner on whose land the deer may occur, there can, by definition, be no centralised calculation or control of cull targets, as might be the case in countries where all culling is under state licence. It is entirely up to the individual owner to determine objectives of management and to determine the cull that he or she may wish to take. There is no central coordination.

Only in Scotland may the DCS (or its successor body) intervene if they have reason to believe (and can produce supporting evidence to demonstrate) that deer populations are causing damage to agriculture, forestry or natural heritage interests, or pose a threat to public safety.

On state-owned lands (forestry or conservation), culls may be more formally determined by using simple population models, so that culls may be determined for maintenance of existing numbers or to engineer some specified reduction. Some private owners or professional managers also undertake careful census of populations of deer on the ground for which they have responsibility, and apply rigorous methods to determine appropriate cull levels – once again usually directed towards maintenance. A few more enterprising individuals who are managing properties specifically for the production of trophy males for stalking may even try to influence overall population age- and sex-structure, but such examples are relatively few. Once again, we may perhaps make an exception of the north of Scotland, where the majority of deer herds on privately owned land are managed for sporting interests. Here age- and sex-structure of the population are generally carefully engineered to sustain a given annual harvest of trophy males, and annual cull levels are equally carefully calculated to maintain steady populations (e.g. Clutton-Brock and Lonergan, 1994; Buckland *et al.*, 1996).

7.7 Censuses

Because, as noted above, there is no formal coordination of deer management effort outside Scotland, there is likewise no formal structure for population census. Counts of open-moorland red deer are undertaken by the vast majority of voluntary deer management groups in Scotland on an annual or biennial basis, but not all groups undertake such counts as regularly.

In the past, the Deer Commission for Scotland attempted to undertake counts of most management areas every five years or so, but due to limited resources available this practice has been discontinued, and counts are now undertaken only as part of monitoring programmes where deer populations are actually causing concern, through damage to agriculture, forestry or conservation areas, or where they pose a threat to public safety (perhaps through involvement in road traffic accidents). Regular estimates of deer numbers or densities are carried out within the majority of state-controlled, Forestry Commission woodlands – but again not necessarily all are counted on a regular basis. Otherwise, deer numbers on their own ground may be censused on an informal basis by private landowners, or voluntary deer management groups established in parts of England, Wales and Northern Ireland; inevitably, of course, this does not offer complete coverage.

A more formal attempt to estimate total numbers of deer of each species within the United Kingdom (excluding Ireland) was made by Harris *et al.*, 1995, providing the figures quoted earlier, here. An attempt to provide an update on this was presented by Ward to a recent conference of the (English) Deer Initiative (March 2007) from which data are drawn for the present chapter (Ward, 2007).

Methods used are not coordinated, nor consistent. Population numbers of red deer on the open hill in Scotland are estimated by direct count (ground or helicopter); numbers of other species, or deer in more concealing habitats such as woodland, are variously estimated by driven census, vantage point counts or dung pellet surveys (Mayle and Staines, 1998; or Mayle *et al.*, 1999; for review).

7.8 Deer impacts: ecological and economic damage

Where they are present at high density, deer populations may have a significant impact upon native range vegetation or cultivated agricultural or forest crops. They may also pose risks to human life, or cause economic damage through involvement in traffic accidents. Before embarking on this assessment of negative impact, however, it is perhaps worth noting by way of introduction that we should be cautious of over-reaction. Damage caused by grazers or browsers, whether to commercial or conservational interests, merely represents the extreme expression of a perfectly natural set of impacts of herbivory on the environment. We consider it 'damage' when the consequences are extreme and more importantly, where they happen to come into conflict with human interests or management objectives. Damage is in a very real sense in the eye of the beholder: impacts are impacts and nothing more – damage implies a subjective value judgement that recorded impacts conflict with alternative (and human-centred) management objectives. We should always remember that grazing and browsing by deer have many positive, facilitative effects, as well as a *potential* for causing damage – and reduction of population levels in response to perceived damage may itself result in even greater disturbance to the system in other ways (Putman, 2004).

7.8.1 Damage to agriculture and forestry

Within Great Britain, as within Europe as a whole, negative impacts of deer on agriculture, forestry or conservation interests tend to be of only local, rather than national significance. Because of a public perception of increasing deer numbers generally – and a presumption that this must be accompanied by an increase in damage – there has in fact been a great deal of recent work within the UK to offer a more formal assessment of actual damage levels (e.g. Doney and Packer, 1998; Putman and Moore, 1998; Putman, 2004; Wilson, 2003).

Despite the fact that individual farms, or individual crops, may on occasion suffer serious damage causing real losses to individual farmers in that year, over the country as a whole, at a national level, economic losses to agriculture due to deer are small (Putman, 2004; Wilson, 2003). All available data would suggest (e.g. Doney and Packer, 1998; Putman and Moore, 1998; see also Putman and Kjellander, 2003), that damage to agricultural crops tends to be of very local significance (at the level of individual farms, or even individual fields) and shows high temporal and spatial variation, such that while one farm or field may suffer serious damage in one year, losses may not be significant in neighbouring fields, or in subsequent years.

Total costs of damage to agriculture (in England only) are estimated by (Wilson, 2003) at around GBP 4.37m, within the range GBP 1.11m–5.56m (EUR 6.56m; range EUR 1.66m–8.34m).

Damage to commercial forestry is similarly 'patchy'. Although there is perhaps a larger impact overall (Gill, 1992) and I could cite an impressive list of publications recording high damage levels in individual instances, damage still tends to be localised and concentrated in certain areas/crop stages. In a recent survey of Forestry Commission conifer plantings between three months and three years of age, covering the whole of the UK, except Northern Ireland, damage due to deer was only found to be a significant problem in Scotland, while in England and Wales damage from rabbits was between three and ten times as high as that caused by deer (Wray, 1994). This study concluded that damage due specifically to deer in (coniferous) plantations in England and Wales rarely exceeded 5–10% (see Wray, 1994; Putman, 2004).

There is within Britain no established system for paying compensation to those suffering damage to agricultural or forest crops.

7.8.2 Damage to conservation habitats

Once again, there are many published examples of individual instances where deer grazing/browsing, or trampling pressure may cause serious damage to amenity woodlands or conservation habitats (and no one would dispute that in such cases, there is a need for effective management).

Such cases, however well-publicised (e.g. Tabor, 1993; Cooke, 1994; Cooke and Farrell, 2001; Fuller and Gill, 2001) are far from representative, and for most parts of the UK in general problems are extremely local. In a recent survey of national nature reserves (NNRs) conducted on behalf of English Nature (Putman, 1996), questionnaires were sent to managers of 162 sites designated as NNRs in England. Managers were asked to provide information on the general distribution of deer across NNRs (species present, estimated numbers and patterns of use of the reserve) and were also invited to comment on the extent of damage caused by deer presence within a site and whether or not this adversely affected their ability to meet the management objectives of the site.

Questionnaires were distributed to 162 sites, with a total of 155 returns received; follow-up site visits were undertaken to a sample of those sites reporting significant damage (Putman, 1996, 1998). Not all sites had deer present; of those site managers recording deer visiting or resident within the reserve, 45% (50/112) recorded a measurable impact at some level (browsing damage to coppice, lack of regeneration, impact on ground flora). Only 18% of reserve managers however considered that damage sustained was sufficient to cause difficulty in meeting management objectives for the site; all of these considered that current management measures (culling, fencing of vulnerable areas) was adequate at present to reduce damage to tolerable levels.

What was, however, highly significant was that, at least in England, all those sites which reported damage from deer at any level were, without exception, woodland reserves – managers of 'open sites' (grasslands, meadows, heathland or fenland sites), generally regarded the presence of deer as neutral or positively advantageous in suppressing encroachment by scrub.

Perhaps the exception to this more general rule is within Scotland, where locally high densities of red deer (in places exceeding 30 deer per 100 ha) are more regularly implicated in damage to protected habitats – dry *Calluna* heathland; *Eriophorum* mires and blanket bogs – protected under the EU Habitats Directive legislation (Directive 92/43/EEC on the Conservation of Natural Habitats), or in suppression of regeneration of native birchwoods or Caledonian pine, *Pinus sylvestris var. scotica* (e.g. Callander and Mackenzie, 1991; Milne *et al.*, 1998; Stewart and Hester, 1998; Hunt, 2003). Indeed it is notable that most cases of active intervention by the Deer Commission for Scotland have involved situations where deer pressure has been considered to be causing actual damage to natural heritage interests.

7.8.3 Deer–vehicle collisions

One final area of conflict concerns the involvement of deer in collisions with motor vehicles. Road traffic accidents involving deer have presented a major problem in the UK for many years. From such limited data as are presently available, it is estimated that there are at least 30 000, and perhaps as many as 50 000, deer–vehicle collisions each year, with an additional (unknown) number of accidents resulting from drivers swerving to avoid deer in the roadway. Over the past five years alone such deer–vehicle collisions in the UK have resulted in some 1500 cases of injury to drivers and passengers, over 50 human fatalities, as well as resulting in the death or serious injury of some 150 000 or more deer (Langbein and Putman, 2006; Langbein, 2007). With recent reported increases in both the numbers and distribution of several deer species in Britain, as well as significant rises in traffic volume and speed, it seems likely that this problem will continue to get worse.

By contrast with the situation in many other European countries, until now there has been no system for central collection of data on road traffic accidents involving deer in Britain, and previous attempts to build a picture of the full extent and geographical distribution of deer-related road traffic accidents have been hampered by the need to rely on retrospective analysis of such patchy data as happened to be available – none of which had been specifically collected to address the questions now being asked of it (SGS, 1998; Staines *et al.*, 2001). A survey commissioned by the Highways Agency during 1997 estimated that the toll of deer injured or killed annually in traffic collisions within the UK was likely to lie between 30 000 and 50 000 (SGS Environment, 1998), but firm statistics on the true scale of the problem in this country remained unavailable.

The lack of accurate recording of such incidents was highlighted in separate studies commissioned by the Highways Agency in England and Wales (SGS Environment, 1998) and the Deer Commission for Scotland in 2000 (Staines et al., 2001), and poses a major handicap to development of effective management. The authors of both the above studies strongly recommended a national system for recording deer–vehicle collisions to assess the true scale and geographical distribution of the problem, and research on key factors influencing accident risk, in order better to target most effective mitigation measures in the future. From that basis a national 'Deer–Vehicle Collisions Project' was launched early in January 2003 in order to develop a national register for deer-related traffic accidents throughout mainland UK (England, Wales and Scotland, but not including either Northern Ireland or the Irish Republic) and to undertake research into preventative measures at the roadside. Full information on this project and its findings are available on the project website at www.deercollisions.co.uk, and summarised in Langbein and Putman (2006); Langbein (2007).

The total number of deer collisons within mainland UK (England, Scotland and Wales) is are estimated at between 37 000 and 55 000 per year (Langbein and Putman, 2006), confirming earlier estimates (SGS, 1998). The annual cost of car repairs, over and above human injury costs, is estimated to exceed GBP 11 million.

7.8.4 Benefits from deer

Against these potentially negative impacts of deer, we should balance the positive benefits. Deer are an important part of our wider biodiversity; light or moderate levels of deer grazing pressure can be actively beneficial (even essential) to management of open-ground communities of high conservation value and in the prevention of scrub-encroachment, and the 'deer industry' itself provides very significant social and economic benefits through the provision of employment, sales of guns and ammunition, clothing, vehicles, etc. While much recreational stalking is enjoyed by owners and occupiers of land, a number have developed significant commercial enterprises based on deer stalking, by 'letting' stalking opportunities to others.

Thus the letting of stalking of red deer or roe on the 'open hill' in Scotland, or of woodland stalking of roe and fallow deer in lowland areas within the UK may provide a significant and important revenue to landowners or management companies.

7.9 Winter feeding

While some form of winter feeding may be provided for deer maintained by fences in deer parks, in general no regular feeding is provided for wild deer in England, Wales, Ireland or southern Scotland. Provision of supplementary forage over winter is more commonplace in northern Scotland where it is targeted specifically at red deer. There is no statutory or legal presumption for or against such feeding; the decision to feed or not to feed is entirely at the discretion of the individual landowner.

In an attempt to assess the current status and distribution of supplementary winter feeding of red deer in Scotland, a questionnaire was prepared for circulation to individual estates and land-holdings throughout Scotland (Putman and Staines, 2003). Of the 122 estates/land-holdings responding to the questionnaire, 84% offered some form of supplementary feeding; 16% did not offer winter feed. Of the 100 estates considered by us as primarily sporting estates, 64 offered supplementary winter feeding while 36 did not do so. Of those estates which did offer some supplementary food overwinter, 41% offered feed to stags only; the remaining 59% fed both stags and hinds. A few estates maintained separate feeding stations for stags and hinds.

The main reasons offered for providing feed were (in rank order) that owners considered it necessary in order to sustain high densities of deer over winter and that it helped reduce dispersal of stags; that it was considered that supplementary feeding helped improve condition and antler quality of stags; that it helped improve condition and fecundity of hinds; as a diversionary tactic to draw animals away from areas sensitive to heavy browsing impact such as forestry blocks, areas set aside for natural regeneration, or areas of high nature conservation interest.

Those who do not feed offered a number of reasons. A number were estates or holdings managed primarily for conservation or for forestry, who did not seek to sustain high numbers of deer on the ground – who indeed sought to reduce deer populations rather than to encourage them. Others, smaller estates or those with low stocking rates, argued that numbers or densities of deer on their ground were not sufficient to require supplementary feeding; even some with quite high resident deer populations felt that their estate offered good natural forage and shelter so that supplementation was not necessary.

Putman and Staines (2004) offer a wider review of winter feeding practice throughout Europe and North America, considering feeding practice, the reasons given for winter feeding, and reviewing the actual scientific evidence as to the true effectiveness of feeding in (1) increasing antler size or body weight of stags, (2) increasing body weight or fecundity of hinds, (3) increasing overwinter survival. This paper also considers in some detail the problems associated with provision of supplementary food in this way: such as (1) actual loss of body weight/condition,

(2) increased competition between animals for food provided resulting in damage or loss of body condition, (3) local environmental damage due to poaching/trampling around feed sites; (4) increased damage to adjacent forestry blocks, (5) increased risk of disease transmission.

7.10 Evaluation of current management policies, and management for the future

Against such background we should note that populations of most species of deer continue to increase in number and distribution throughout the British Isles as elsewhere in Europe (Gill, 1990; Harris *et al.*, 1995; Putman, 1995; Ward, 2005). Current management techniques are clearly failing to control numbers or contain damage beyond providing very short-term or temporary alleviation of the problem in very local areas where culling effort is high.

A number of contributing factors have been suggested for this failure to achieve more general control. These may be loosely divided into (1) actual logistical problems; (2) problems due to lack of knowledge or lack of proper planning of a management programme; and (3) purely biological problems of achieving and sustaining a reduction in population size of animals which respond to any reduction of density by increased recruitment.

7.10.1 Logistical problems: coordination of management effort

Many organisations concerned with deer and deer management within Britain (such as the British Deer Society or British Association for Shooting and Conservation) argue that the failure to exercise adequate control over expanding deer populations stems at least in part from the difficulty of killing sufficient animals under the restrictions imposed by current legislation.

These bodies have thus been pressing for changes to 'close' seasons to extend the legal cull period, as well as changes in the legislation to permit night shooting and permit the use of smaller calibre weapons. It is partly in response to this that legislation in both Scotland and England, Wales and Northern Ireland, is currently under review (e.g. Defra, 2003) and permitted seasons for females of all species have recently been extended to the end of March in England and Wales (section 7.2).

These same organisations and others also argue that some part of the problem in exercising control over deer populations comes through lack of coordination of management effort over a sufficiently large area. Implications of this are apparent at two distinct levels. At present, outside the area of the Highlands of Scotland, where control of red and sika deer has until now been closely coordinated by the Deer

Commission, most culling effort is patchily distributed, undertaken by individual stalkers over a small patch of ground. Within England, Wales and Northern Ireland, only a small area is subject to any such management at all, although the recently constituted Deer Initiative is working to increase awareness and to encourage the formation of cooperative deer management groups in such areas.

Because of the past and current lack of wider coordination, the overall impact of any management effort on deer numbers at a national, or even regional level is insignificant. Even at the local level, each management block is commonly surrounded by huge areas of land where no management may be undertaken at all, clearly reducing any individual manager's chances of achieving any measurable reduction in numbers. For effective management, culling effort must be coordinated over the entire population range – currently the exception rather than the rule, with most managers forced to attempt to control deer populations solely within the boundaries of their own properties in isolation. How we may achieve such coordination in southern Scotland, England, Wales and Ireland remains to be seen.

7.10.2 Definition of management objectives

Even where prophylactic management of deer populations is attempted on a continuous basis, management is commonly ill-directed through lack of consistency, due in turn to an imprecise definition of management objectives. Effective management of any deer population requires clear definition of objectives, some common policy of purpose and a management strategy directed towards satisfaction of those defined objectives. But it should be noted that the final management 'package' adopted will differ markedly in different situations and will depend very heavily on the objectives of that management (Putman, 2004).

On the positive side, high deer numbers enhance the chances of visitors to the countryside seeing wild deer. A reasonably high deer density is also desirable from the point of view of those landowners who aim to maximise income from venison revenue. On the other hand, damage to local agricultural, woodland or conservation vegetation may become unacceptable at densities far below those that might be suggested by such considerations. Those responsible for management must therefore define very clearly from the outset the objectives of management; only once those objectives are recognised can effective management policy be determined.

7.10.3 Control of damage

Finally, I would reiterate that, where success or failure of deer management policies are based on control of damage, lack of apparent success may be due simply to the fact that damage levels are not in any case closely linked to deer densities, so that control of deer numbers alone may not be particularly effective in reducing damage. All available evidence would suggest that damage levels do not appear to be related in any straightforward way to simple density, but are affected by a complex interplay of various different factors such as forage quality, habitat structure and climate. Since the severity of damage caused by deer is, in fact, only relatively weakly related to the actual density of deer, even where culling efforts have genuinely achieved a real reduction in deer densities, this has not necessarily been rewarded by an equivalent reduction in perceived impact (unless the deer have been reduced to a minimal presence).

Despite the current focus of attention, management of the actual impact of deer cannot therefore be addressed solely (or even primarily?) by improving control of deer populations, but must also embrace a variety of other methods: physical, chemical or cultural, to reduce damage caused. Unless populations are reduced to very low levels indeed management efforts based exclusively on attempted reduction of deer numbers in an area may not have any significant impact in reducing damage levels.

References

Abernethy, K. (1994) The establishment of a hybrid zone between red and sika deer (genus *Cervus*). *Molecular Ecology* **3**, 551–62.

Abernethy, K. (1998) *Sika Deer in Scotland*. Scotland: Deer Commission, Scotland/The Stationery Office.

Boyd, J. M. and Jewell, P. A. (1974) The Soay sheep and their environment: a synthesis. In P. A. Jewell, C. Milner and J. Morton Boyd, eds., *Island Survivors: The Ecology of the Soay Sheep of St Kilda*. London: Athlone Press, pp. 360–73.

Buckland, S. T., Ahmadi, S., Staines, B. W., Gordon, I. J. and Youngson, R. W. (1996) Estimating the minimum population size that allows a given annual number of mature red stags to be culled sustainably. *Journal of Applied Ecology* **33**, 118–30.

Bullock, D. J. (1995) The feral goat: conservation and management. *British Wildlife* **6**, 152–9.

Bullock, D. J. (2008) Feral goat. In S. Harris and D. W. Yalden, eds., *The Handbook of British Mammals*, 4th edn. UK: The Mammal Society, pp. 628–33.

Callander, R. F. and Mackenzie, N. A. (1991) *The Management of Wild Red Deer in Scotland*. Perth: Scottish Rural Forum.

Cantor, L. (1989) English Deer Parks: an historical background. In M. Baxter-Brown and C. R. Goldspink, eds., *Management, Conservation and Interpretation of Park Deer*. UK: British Deer Society, pp. 1–5.

Chapman, D. I. and Chapman, N. G. (1975) *Fallow Deer: Their History, Distribution and Biology*. Lavenham, UK: Terence Dalton, 271 pp.

Chapman, N. G., Claydon, K., Claydon, M. and Harris, S. (1985) Distribution and habitat selection by muntjac and other species of deer in a coniferous forest. *Acta Theriologica* **30**, 287–303.

Chapman, N. G., Harris, S. and Stanford, A. (1994) Reeves' muntjac *Muntiacus reevesi* in Britain: their history, spread, habitat selection and the role of human intervention in accelerating their dispersal. *Mammal Review* **24**, 113–60.

Clutton-Brock, T. H. and Lonergan, M. E. (1994) Culling regimes and sex ratio biases in Highland red deer. *Journal of Animal Ecology* **31**, 521–27.

Cooke, A. S. (1994) Colonisation by muntjac deer *Muntiacus reevesi* and their impact on vegetation. In M. S. Massey and R. C. Welch, eds., *Monks Wood National Nature Reserve, the Experience of 40 Years 1953–93*. Peterborough, UK: English Nature, 45–61.

Cooke, A. S. and Farrell, L. (2001) Impact of muntjac deer (*Muntiacus reevesi*) at Monk's Wood National Nature Reserve, Cambridgeshire, eastern England. *Forestry* **74**, 241–50.

Defra (2003) *Achieving the Sustainable Management of Wild Deer in England*. Consultation Paper, The Department for Environment, Food and Rural Affairs.

Diaz, A., Hughes, S., Putman, R. J., Mogg, R. and Bond, J. M. (2006) A genetic study of sika dear (*Cervus nippon*) in the New Forest and in the Purbeck region of southern England: is there evidence of recent or past hybridization with red deer (*Cervus elaphus*)? *Journal of Zoology* **207**, 227–35.

Doerr, M. L., McAninch, J. B. and Wiggers, E. P. (2001) Comparison of four methods to reduce white-tailed deer abundance in an urban community. *Wildlife Society Bulletin* **29**, 1105–13.

Doney, J. and Packer, J. (1998) An assessment of the impact of deer on agriculture. In C. R. Goldspink, S. King and R. J. Putman, eds., *Population Ecology, Management and Welfare of Deer*. UK: British Deer Society/Universities' Federation for Animal Welfare, pp. 38–43.

Fuller, R. J. and Gill, R. M. A. (2001) Ecological impacts of increasing numbers of deer in British woodland. *Forestry* **74**, 193–9.

Gibbs, E. P. J., Herniman, K. A. J., Lawman, M. J. P. and Sellers, R. F. (1975) Foot-and-mouth disease in British deer: transmission of the virus to cattle, sheep and deer. *Veterinary Record* **96**, 558–63.

Gill, R. M. A. (1990) Monitoring the Status of European and North American Cervids. *GEMS Information Series* 8, Nairobi: Global Environment Monitoring Systems, United Nations Environment Programme, 277 pp.

Gill, R. M. A. (1992) A review of damage by mammals in north temperate forests. I. Deer *Forestry* **65**, 145–69.

Goodman, S. J., Barton, N. H., Swanson, G., Abernethy, K. and Pemberton, J. M. (1999) Introgression through rare hybridization: a genetic study of a hybrid zone between red and sika deer (Genus *Cervus*) in Argyll, Scotland. *Genetics* **152**, 355–71.

Goulding, M. J., Smith, G. and Baker, S. J. (1998) *Current Status and Potential Impact of Wild Boar (Sus scrofa) in the English Countryside: A Risk Assessment*. Central Science Laboratory report to the Ministry of Agriculture, Fisheries and Food, UK.

Goulding, M. J., Kitchener, A. C. and Yalden, D. W. (2008) Wild boar. In S. Harris and D. W. Yalden, eds., *The Handbook of British Mammals*, 4th edn. UK: The Mammal Society.

Groves, C. P. (1989) Feral mammals of the Mediterranean islands. In J. Clutton-Brock, eds., *The Walking Larder*. London: Unwin Hyman, pp. 46–57.

Harrington, R. (1973) Hybridisation among deer and its implications for conservation. *Irish Forestry Journal* **30**, 64–78.

Harrington, R. (1982) The hybridisation of red deer (*Cervus elaphus* L. 1758) and Japanese sika deer (*C. nippon* Temminck, 1838). *International Congress of Game Biologists* **14**, 559–71.

Harris, S., Morris, P., Wray, S. and Yalden, D. W. (1995) *A Review of British Mammals: Population Estimates and Conservation Status of British Mammals Other than Cetaceans*. Peterborough, UK: Joint Nature Conservation Committee, 168 pp.

Hartl, G. B., Hewison, A. J. M., Apollonio, M., Kurt, F. and Wiehler, J. (1998) Genetics of European roe deer. In R. Andersen, P. Duncan and J. D. C. Linnell, *The European Roe Deer: The Biology of Success*. Oslo, Norway: Scandinavian University Press, pp. 71–90.

Hayden, T. and Harrington, R. (2000) *Exploring Irish Mammals*. Dublin: Duchas – The Heritage Service.

Hewison, A. J. M. (1997) Evidence for a genetic component of female fecundity in British roe deer from studies of cranial morphometrics. *Functional Ecology* **11**, 508–17.

Hunt, J. F. (2003) *Impacts of Wild Red Deer in Scotland: how fares the public interest?* Report for World Wide Fund for Nature, Scotland and the Royal Society for the Protection of Birds, Scotland.

Jenks, J. A., Smith, W. P. and DePerno, C. S. (2002) Maximum sustained yield harvest *versus* trophy management. *Journal of Wildlife Management* **66**, 528–35.

Jewell, P. A. and Bullock, D. J. (1991) Feral sheep. In G. B. Corbet and S. Harris, eds., *The Handbook of British Mammals*, 3rd edn. Oxford, UK: Blackwell Scientific Publications, pp. 547–52.

Jones, J. M. and Witham, J. H. (1993) Urban Deer "Problem-Solving" in Northeast Illinois: an overview. In the *Proceedings of the 55th Midwest Fish and Wildlife Conference. Urban Deer: A Manageable Resource*, St. Louis, MO, pp. 58–65.

Langbein, J. and Chapman, N. G. (2003) *Fallow Deer*. UK: The Mammal Society/British Deer Society.

Langbein, J. and Putman, R. J. (1996) Studies of English red deer populations subject to hunting-to-hounds. In V. Taylor and N. Dunstone, eds., *The Exploitation of Mammal Populations: Principles and Problems in Sustainable Use*. London: Chapman and Hall, pp. 208–25.

Langbein, J. and Putman, R. J. (2006) *National Deer-Vehicle Collisions Project, Scotland (2003–2005)*. Report to the Scottish Executive, June 2006.

Langbein, J. (2007) *National Deer-Vehicle Collisions Project, England (2003–2005)*. Report to the Deer Initiative/Highways Agency, November 2007.

Larner, J. B. (1977) Sika deer damage to mature woodlands of southwestern Ireland. *Proceedings of the International Congress of Game Biologists* **13**, 192–202.

Lever, C. (1977) *Naturalised Animals of the British Isles*. London: Hutchison, 600 pp.

Lowe, V. P. W. and Gardiner, A. S. (1974) A re-examination of the subspecies of red deer (*Cervus elaphus*) with particular reference to the stocks in Britain. *Journal of Zoology, London* **174**, 185–201.

Lowe, V. P. W. and Gardiner, A. S. (1975) Hybridisation between red deer and sika deer, with reference to stocks in north-west England. *Journal of Zoology (London)* **177**, 553–66.

Macdonald, D. W., Tattersall, F. H., Johnson, P. J. *et al*. (2000) *Managing British Mammals: Case Studies from the Hunting Debate*. Oxford, UK: Wildlife Conservation Research Unit, University of Oxford.

Mayle, B. A. and Staines, B. W. (1998) An overview of methods used for estimating the size of deer populations in Great Britain. In C. R. Goldspink, S. King and R. J. Putman, eds., *Population Ecology, Management and Welfare of Deer*. UK: British Deer Society/Universities' Federation for Animal Welfare, pp. 19–31.

Mayle, B. A., Peace, A. J. and Gill, R. M. A. (1999) *How Many Deer? A Field Guide to Estimating Deer Population Size*. Forestry Commission Field Book 18. London: HMSO.

Milne, J. A. et al. (1998) The impact of vertebrate herbivores on the natural heritage of the Scottish uplands: a review. *Scottish Natural Heritage Review No.* **95**.

Moore, N. P. and Wilson, C. J. (2005) *Feral Wild Boar in England: Implications of future management options*. Report on behalf of Defra European Wildlife Division. July 2005. UK: The Department for Environment, Food and Rural Affairs.

Pemberton, J., Swanson, G., Barton, N., Livingstone, S. and Senn, H. (2006) Hybridisation between red and sika deer in Scotland. *Deer* **13**, 22–6.

Perez-Espona, S., Pemberton, J. M. and Putman, R. J. (2009) Red and sika deer in the British Isles, current management issues and management policy. *Mammalian Biology* **74**, 247–62.

Prior, R. (1968) *The Roe Deer of Cranborne Chase*. Oxford, UK: Oxford University Press.

Putman, R. J. (1995) *Status and Impact of Deer in the Lowlands and Options for Management*. Technical review, contract VC0316, MAFF, London.

Putman, R. J. (1996) Deer on national nature reserves: problems and practices. *English Nature Research Reports* **173**, 1–50.

Putman, R. J. (1998) Deer impact on conservation vegetationin England and Wales. In C. R. Goldspink, S. King and R. J. Putman, eds., *Population Ecology, Management and Welfare of Deer*. UK: British Deer Society/Universities' Federation for Animal Welfare, pp. 61–66.

Putman, R. J. (2004) *The Deer Manager's Companion: A Guide to Deer Management in the Wild and in Parks*. Shrewsbury, UK: Swan Hill Press, 180 pp.

Putman, R. J. and Hunt, E. (1994) Hybridisation between red and sika deer in Britain. *Deer* **9**, 104–10.

Putman, R. J. and Kjellander, P. (2003) Deer damage to cereals:economic significance and predisposing factors. In F. Tattersall and W. Manly, eds., *Farming and Mammals*. London: Linnaean Society of London Occasional Publications.

Putman, R. J. and Moore, N. P. (1998) Impact of deer in lowland Britain on agriculture, forestry and conservation habitats. *Mammal Review* **28**, 141–64.

Putman, R. J. and Staines, B. W. (2003) *Supplementary Feeding of Deer in Scotland: A Review of the Extent and Geographical Patterns of Supplementary Feeding of Wild Deer in Scotland; Reasons for Feeding and an Analysis of the Balance of Advantage/Disadvantage*. Report to the Deer Commission, UK.

Putman, R. J. and Staines, B. W. (2004) Supplementary winter feeding of wild red deer *Cervus elaphus* in Europe and North America: justifications, feeding practice and effectiveness. *Mammal Review* **34**, 285–306.

Ratcliffe, P. R. (1984) Population dynamics of red deer (*Cervus elaphus* L.) in Scottish commercial forests. *Proceedings of the Royal Society of Edinburgh B* **82**, 291–302.

Ratcliffe, P. R. (1987) Distribution and current status of sika deer (*Cervus nippon*) in Great Britain. *Mammal Review* **17**, 37–58.

Ratcliffe, P. R. (1989) The control of red and sika deer populations in commercial forests. In R. J. Putman, ed., *Mammals as Pests*. London: Chapman and Hall, 98–115.

Ratcliffe, P. R., Peace, A. J., Hewison, A. J. M., Hunt, E. J. and Chadwick, A. H. (1992) The origins and characterization of Japanese sika deer populations in Great Britain. In N. Maruyama, B. Bobek, Y. Ono et al., eds., *Wildlife Conservation: Present Trends and Perspectives for the 21st Century*. Tokyo, pp. 185–90.

Ritchie, J. (1920) *The Influence of Man on Animal Life in Scotland: A Study in Faunal Evolution*. Cambridge, UK: Cambridge University Press.

Rondeau, D. and Conrad, J. M. (2003) Managing urban deer. *American Journal of Agricultural Economics* **85**, 266–81.

Ryder, M. L. (1984) Sheep. In I. L. Mason, ed., *Evolution of Domesticated Animals*. London: Longman, pp. 622–8.

SGS Environment (1998) *The Prevention of Wildlife Casualties on Roads Through the Use of Deterrents: Prevention of Casualties Among Deer Populations*. Report to UK Highways Agency SW335/V3/11–98.

Staines, B. W. and Ratcliffe, P. R. (1991) Roe deer. In G. B. Corbet and S. Harris, eds., *The Handbook of British Mammals*, 3rd edn. Oxford, UK: Blackwell Scientific Publications, pp. 518–25.

Staines, B. W., Langbein, J. and Putman, R. J. (2001) *Road Traffic Accidents and Deer in Scotland*. Report to the Deer Commission, Scotland.

Stewart, F. and Hester, A. (1998) Impact of red deer on woodland and heathland dynamics in Scotland. In C. R. Goldspink, S. King and R. J. Putman, eds., *Population Ecology, Management and Welfare of Deer*. UK: British Deer Society/Universities' Federation for Animal Welfare, pp. 54–60.

Tabor, R. C. (1993) Control of deer in a managed coppice. *Quarterly Journal of Forestry* **87**, 308–13.

Ward, A. I. (2005) Expanding ranges of wild and feral deer in Great Britain. *Mammal Review* **35**, 165–73.

Ward, A. I. (2007) Trends in deer distribution and abundance within the UK. Presentation to *Deer, Habitats and Impacts*, the Deer Initiative Conference, Buxton, UK, 23rd March 2007.

Waring, G. H., Griffis, J. L. and Vaughn, M. E. (1991) White-tailed deer roadside behavior, wildlife warning reflectors and highway mortality. *Applied Animal Behaviour Science* **29**, 215–23.

Whitehead, G. K. (1964) *The Deer of Great Britain and Ireland: An Account of their History, Status and Distribution*. London: Routledge and Kegan Paul.

Wilson, C. J. (2003) *A Preliminary Estimate of the Cost of Damage Caused by Deer to Agriculture in England*. Consultation Paper, the Department for Environment, Food and Rural Affairs, UK.

Wilson, C. J. (2005) *Feral Wild Boar in England: Status, Impact and Management*. A report on behalf of Defra European Wildlife Division. July 2005. UK: The Department for Environment, Food and Rural Affairs.

Wray, S. (1994) Competition between muntjac and other herbivores in a commercial coniferous forest. *Deer* **9**, 237–42.

Yalden, D. W. (1999) *The History of British Mammals*. London: T. & A.D. Poyser, 305 pp.

8

Ungulates and their management in the Netherlands

SIPKE E. VAN WIEREN AND GEERT W. T. A. GROOT BRUINDERINK

8.1 Ungulate species and their current distribution

Eight species of ungulates in the wild or semi-wild state can be found in the Netherlands: red deer, roe deer, wild boar, fallow deer, muntjac, mouflon, cattle and horses. Except for roe deer, which has a country wide distribution, the greatest number of animals of the other species can be found in the Veluwe, a forest-heathland area of *c.* 100 000 ha in the central Netherlands (Provincie Gelderland, 2000).

8.1.1 Red deer

Although red deer were widespread throughout the country in the early Middle Ages, their main stronghold had always been along the major rivers. Over the years their numbers and distribution gradually decreased and around 1800, red deer were only present in the forested areas in the Veluwe in central Netherlands where they were protected and cared for by the royalty and the nobility. During the next 150 years numbers remained low but populations became increasingly fragmented as more and more areas were fenced.

Outside the fenced areas conditions worsened through land reclamation and further degradation of the heathlands. In World War II numbers were decimated and hunting pressure remained high till into the 1950s. However, at the same time the condition of the fences deteriorated and the number of red deer living outside the fenced areas increased. In the 1950s better protection and regulatory measures resulted in increasing numbers (Litjens, 1991; Broekhuizen *et al.*, 1992). The increase in numbers continued till the present time when current numbers are estimated at a spring number of 2135, while also the shift of focus of the population

Fig. 8.1 Distribution of red deer in the Netherlands

from being primarily within fenced areas towards non-fenced areas has become more pronounced (Lensink and Spek, 2004; Oerlemans and Van Wieren, 2005).

Legally speaking, there are no fenced areas left on the Veluwe: in all cases the animals can move in and out through openings in the fence. Nevertheless we cannot (yet) speak of one population because of a further increase in barriers of various kinds: fences, highways, secondary and local motorways, human occupation and recreational pressure (De Boer *et al.*, 2004; Van Wieren and Worm, 2001).

The red deer in the Veluwe are of a quite mixed origin. Before 1940, red deer were introduced here from various parts of Europe: Scotland, the Carpathians, Mecklenburg and Rominten.

In 1992, red deer were introduced in the Oostvaardersplassen, a newly created wetland of 5500 ha in one of the new Polders in the province of Flevoland. Their numbers increased fast and at present there are about 1600. Like those of the Veluwe, these red deer are also of mixed origin, coming in part from Scotland, Hungary and the Veluwe (Ministerie van LNV, 2000).

In addition, since spring 2005 the Netherlands shares a small, cross border population (spring number 80) with Germany near the city of Nijmegen (Groot Bruinderink *et al.*, 2003) (Fig. 8.1).

In total there are about 2735 red deer in the Netherlands (spring population), divided over 11 (sub) populations of which four inhabit fenced areas with openings.

8.1.2 Roe deer

In the Middle Ages the species was common throughout the country; after this time numbers declined steadily to reach a low around 1900 and the species was only to be found in the forests in the central parts of the country. After World War II, roe deer re-colonised parts of the country, in part coming from Germany. In the second half of the last century, roe deer also started to colonise the dunes and open landscapes of the western and northern part of the country, including the newly created polders. Around 1980 almost the complete country was occupied, including two Wadden Islands. Also local densities increased and, at present, total numbers are estimated to be about 60 000 (Broekhuizen *et al.*, 1992).

8.1.3 Fallow deer

In the past centuries, fallow deer have been introduced in a number of fenced areas, notably in a few dune areas along the west coast and in the Veluwe (Litjens and Pelzers, 1988; Broekhuizen *et al.*, 1992). Escapees, sometimes together with other deliberately introduced animals, also formed small populations outside the fenced areas. As a result, fallow deer have established at present in at least six areas. The largest populations (*c*. 400–500 animals and still growing) are found in a dune area and in the Veluwe (Fig. 8.2). The total number of fallow deer in the country comprises about 1150 (Oerlemans and Van Wieren, 2005).

8.1.4 Muntjac

In the past years regular sightings of Chinese muntjac in the central and eastern Netherlands are reported. To what extent a population is building up is not known at present. A guesstimate would be between 50 and 100 animals in total.

8.1.5 Mouflon

In the twentieth century a number of fenced areas were stocked with moufflon for hunting purposes. At the present time moufflon are only found in four fenced areas. Total numbers are *c*. 300.

8.1.6 Wild boar

From being a resident in large parts of the Netherlands in historical times, the distribution of the wild boar has shrunk tremendously in succeeding periods, due to changes in land use and heavy persecution. By around 1830, wild boar were

Fig. 8.2 Distribution of fallow deer in the Netherlands

virtually extinct in the country. In the early twentieth century wild boar were introduced, for hunting purposes, in a number of fenced areas on the Veluwe. The animals originated from Eastern Europe. Regular escapees, together with the few resident animals still present, formed a new population which showed steady growth despite heavy hunting pressure shortly after the war (Broekhuizen *et al.*, 1992). Despite serious attempts to keep the spring population at a constant level, the wild boar population has kept growing, and seems to have done so especially in the past decade (cf. Fig. 8.5, Oerlemans and Van Wieren, 2005).

Some 2160 animals are currently estimated to occur within the Veluwe; in addition, a smaller, cross border population is present along the south eastern border with Germany. In the past decade more and more individuals are being observed all along the eastern border with Germany (Fig. 8.3).

In total about 2300 wild boar (spring population) are believed to be present in the Netherlands, divided over 13 (sub) populations of which four live in those areas of the Veluwe to which they were originally introduced. These areas remain fenced, but fences are porous.

Fig. 8.3 Distribution of wild boar in the Netherlands. Dots are incidental sightings

8.1.7 Free-ranging cattle and horses

In the past 25 years there has been much debate in the Netherlands about various different approaches to the restoration of natural ecosystems including consideration of what may have been the former role of large grazing animals like cattle and horses as part of the natural community of ungulates in western Europe (Vera, 2000; Hodder *et al.*, 2005). As a result of this discussion, grazing by cattle and horses is increasingly being adopted as a method for vegetation management in protected areas: a total of 500 smaller and larger nature reserves are being grazed part of the year by cattle and/or horses. In two areas in particular, completely free-ranging and otherwise unmanaged populations of cattle and also horses have been (re)introduced as replacements of the extinct aurochs and tarpan to play the roles they had in the past. Currently their status is considered somewhere in between wild and domesticated.

In a part of the Veluwe about 150 feral Scottish Highland cattle are managed in this way, while in the Oostvaardersplassen about 700 Heck cattle and 900 Konik horses roam freely, together with 1550 red deer and about 50 roe deer (spring numbers) (Ministerie van LNV, 2000).

8.2 Legislation

After a long period of preparation, a new Flora and Fauna Act came into force on 1 April 2002. This act was meant to replace a number of existing laws and to bring all legislation regarding wildlife under one coherent system. The main starting point of the act is that all wild (mammal) species are protected (except brown rat, black rat and house mouse) (Ministerie van LNV, 2002).

Interestingly, within this new law only six species of animals are officially defined as game and can, as such, be hunted without a specific reason, i.e. sports hunting. These species are: wood pigeon, rabbit, hare, partridge, pheasant and wild duck. At the moment partridge have a closed hunting season.

The Flora and Fauna Act provides a general framework only; actual detailed prescriptions are provided by other legislative orders and ministerial decisions. Within the law, dispensation from protection can be given for a variety of reasons, after which the species can be controlled or managed; and, importantly, a great part of the execution of the law has been delegated to the provincial level. Provinces receive the requests for dispensation and may grant dispensation and hand out the permits for control and management. In practice, therefore, management of wildlife is not the same throughout the country.

Roe deer, red deer, wild boar and fallow deer are fully protected and can only be culled when one or more of the following applies:

- for reasons of public health and public safety;
- in the interest of safety of air traffic;
- to prevent damage to crops, cattle, forests, fishery and waters;
- to prevent damage to flora and fauna or
- other reasons, to be defined by specific order in Council.

These are potential reasons but before shooting is allowed two more conditions need to be fulfilled:

1. Other possible solutions should be tried first.
2. Damage should be *considerable*.

Other relevant conditions of the law regarding ungulate management are:

1. Supplementary feeding is forbidden, exceptional (severe winter) conditions excluded.
2. Should any management be necessary, it should be based on the population level and to ensure this, the minimum area on which ungulate management can take place is 5000 ha. This implies that ungulates kept in fenced areas smaller than 5000 ha should be managed as 'kept animals' and their numbers cannot be controlled by hunting under the Flora and Fauna Act.

Table 8.1 *Periods in which culling of ungulates is allowed*

Species	Period
Red deer	1 August–15 February
Wild boar	1 July–31 January
Fallow deer	1 September–15 February
Roe deer (male)	1 May–15 March
Roe deer (female)	1 January–15 March

3. Techniques permitted:
   - For red deer, fallow deer and wild boar, guns of minimal gauge 6.5 mm are required with an impact of 2200 J at 100 m distance.
   - For roe deer, a minimum impact of 980 J at 100 m distance is required.
   - Drive hunts are not allowed; only in the case of wild boar one beater per hunter may disturb the animals with the intention of bringing them within the shooting range of a hunter. He or she is not permitted to use a dog.
4. The culling periods are given in Table 8.1.

The muntjac is considered an exotic species and has therefore been put on the list of unwanted species that preferably should be eradicated.

The policy regarding the free ranging cattle and horses is covered by the *Large Grazers Guidelines* of the Ministry of Agriculture, Nature and Food Quality from 2000 (Ministerie van LNV, 2000). The *Guidelines* give the limits of the degree of 'naturalness' to which the large grazers may be subjected. The well-being of the animals should be monitored closely and not exceed some defined lower limit. The *Guidelines* also contain paragraphs on veterinary aspects, supplementary feeding and what to do with dead animals.

Finally, it must be noted that in the areas where ungulates are living under the law mentioned above, both the EU Habitat Directive and the EU Bird Directive are in force.

Until recently, wild boar, red deer and fallow deer were on the Dutch Red List of Indigenous Threatened Mammals. In particular, fallow deer benefitted from this status and numbers on the Veluwe could increase significantly, the species enjoying special protection. At present only fallow are a Red List species.

8.3 Management objectives

As noted above, under Dutch law, all ungulate species are actually offered full protection and can only be culled if this can be shown to be necessary for reasons of public health and public safety; in the interest of safety of air traffic; to prevent damage to crops, cattle, forests, fishery and waters; to prevent damage to flora and fauna (or other reasons, to be defined by specific order in Council).

In consequence, there is an increasing number of areas where ungulate populations (roe deer in particular) are not subjected to any form of explicit management. This is increasingly adopted as specific policy, particularly in view of changing perceptions and policies regarding conservation at large and an increasing shift amongst management and conservation organisations towards a rather 'hands-off', non-interventional, approach to ecosystem management (see below; section 8.6).

Even where wildlife management policies do include some form of active population control, we should remember that this can only legally be undertaken if it is demonstrated as necessary for the prevention of damage, prevention of traffic accidents, etc. (above) and thus 'formally' these must be regarded as the main objectives of management. In practice, these justifications are rarely supported with objective evidence, and part of the motivation for culling remains a desire of individuals to hunt.

8.4/5 Management structure and management organisation

In principle, anyone in the Netherlands is entitled to hunt. However, there is a minimum requirement of a hunting area of ≥ 40 ha, a recognised hunting examination and a requirement to possess a licence. The last needs to be renewed every year and costs EUR 80. Hunting rights for a given area belong to the user of the land who may in practice give permission for hunting and/or counteracting game damage to other persons, i.e. licensed hunters.

The law also obliges licensed hunters to organise themselves into Fauna Management Units (FMUs). An FMU is a cooperation of landowners and licensed hunters and is responsible for the management, including damage prevention and control, in a certain area. The lease period for a certain hunting area is generally six years. The area covered by an FMU should be at least 5000 ha and at present almost all of the country is 'covered' by a total of about 500 FMUs. These FMUs have to make Fauna Management Plans (FMPs) on a five yearly basis (Ministerie van LNV, 2002).

The FMPs are important because they need to contain all the information necessary to justify any management measure for which the province needs to give permission.

An FMP should at least contain information on the following:

- the size of the managed area
- a map of the area

- quantitive data on size of populations
- reasoning why measures are needed (how interests have been harmed)
- description of the degree by which interests have been harmed in the past five years
- the desired population density (with reasons given)
- for ungulates: food availability, the relationship between food availability and density including carrying capacity of the area
- the expected effects of proposed measures.

In two areas the *Large Grazers Guidelines* are in force and here the landowner (= the conservation organisation responsible for the management) carries out the measures.

8.6 Actual management and hunting practices

In the Netherlands, three kinds of ungulate management practices can be distinguished: no management, management according to the *Large Grazers Guidelines* for domestic cattle and horses, and culling of wild ungulates based on a Fauna Management Plan.

8.6.1 No management

As we have noted, more and more areas appear where ungulates are no longer actively managed. This development needs to be viewed against the background of changing perceptions and policies regarding conservation at large.

Since the mid-1970s the idea of 'let nature run its own course, where the right conditions exist' has increasingly influenced conservation thinking in the Netherlands. One of the spin-offs of this new wilderness concept has been a change in attitude of many conservation managers towards a management more based on natural processes and less on human interference (Provincie Gelderland, 2000; Bureau Waardenburg, 2004). Because of this, the necessity of interfering with ungulate populations has been radically reviewed in a number of the larger conservation organisations (both private and state) and, primarily directed at roe deer, the first experiments of zero culling started 15 years ago. At present in most of the areas owned and managed by the larger conservation bodies roe deer are not culled any more. In one of the larger dune areas (the Amsterdam Water Supply Dunes), the fallow deer are also not managed and at present this population is still growing rapidly (De Boer *et al.*, 2004).

In the Veluwe a few smaller areas have been set apart as hunting free zones for red deer, fallow and wild boar but these zones are still part of a larger management unit (Van Wieren and Worm, 2001). In one area of *c.* 1000 ha an experiment has started in 2001 whereby in addition to roe deer the culling of red deer and fallow deer has stopped. Wild boar are still culled annually as a concession to neighbouring landowners (Bureau Waardenburg, 2004).

8.6.2 Management according to the Large Grazers Guidelines

This practice is executed in two reserves: the National Park Veluwezoom (the southeastern part of the Veluwe, 11 000 ha) and the Oostvaardersplassen, a wetland in the western part of the country (5200 ha). In the Veluwezoom the focus is on a herd of Scottish Highland cattle (*c.* 150) while in the Oostvaardersplassen about 700 Heck cattle and 900 Konik horses are subject to this kind of management.

In this latter area, numbers of red deer and roe deer are also, technically, not controlled by humans, although they do not fall under the *Guidelines*. The only constraint on this is that the manager still has an obligation to take care of the well-being of the animals and ensure that they are not allowed to die from natural causes in the field (Ministerie van LNV, 2002). In practice, the condition of the animals is monitored on a regular basis and when the condition has reached level 1 (on a scale from 1 to 5), the animal is shot and taken out of the system. This management can be seen as a (political and societal) compromise between the 'wild' and the 'domestic' status of the Heck cattle and Konik horses.

In the Oostvaardersplassen, the density of ungulates is very high while the area is both fenced and, although very productive, small. In practice, therefore, despite the theoretical concept of non-intervention, this situation has led to high levels of culling, especially in the winter of 2004–2005. In total 231 cattle, 126 koniks and 340 red deer were culled in that winter. This type of management is intensely debated in the country, including the Dutch Parliament. In December 2005, an international committee was formed to answer the question of whether it is possible to maintain a resilient, self-sustaining ecosystem including large herbivores in the Oostvaardersplassen reserve, which is acceptable in terms of animal welfare. Although the committee acknowledged that a management strategy involving no intervention is a feasible one, it was of the opinion that some form of intervention is necessary to fulfill animal welfare standards. A reactive culling strategy involving the culling of all animals whose physical condition has declined to a set level by established welfare criteria best fits the overall management strategy (ICMO, 2006).

8.6.3 Management with a reason

In all areas where the above management types do not apply, ungulates are managed according to an approved Fauna Management Plan (FMP) as described in section 8.4/5. For roe deer, this is the case in the greater part of the country, while for fallow deer, red deer and wild boar the main management area is in the 100 000 ha Veluwe area in the central Netherlands.

The Fauna Management Plans have to be made by the Fauna Management Units in a five year cycle (Ministerie van LNV, 2002).

It should be clear that for management to be permitted for any population at all one of the justifications, as mentioned in the law, needs to apply. Here, a serious problem is encountered because in most cases a thorough justification of proposed measures is lacking (Bureau Waardenburg, 2004). For roe deer, some of the following reasons are given: to prevent damage, to prevent traffic accidents, to prevent the population to exceed carrying capacity, to preserve the well-being of the animals, keep them in good health, etc., but this is rarely supported with objective evidence. For the ungulates on the Veluwe it is even more difficult to find the reasons for population control. In summary: valid reasons within the framework of the law are rarely given and this is acknowledged by all parties involved (FMUs, provinces, state; Bureau Waardenburg 2004).

We can only conclude that for all Fauna Management Plans a necessity for some kind of population control is stated and accepted by the provinces, which consequently hand out the requested permits.

For a treatment of how measures are executed in practice, we therefore have to take as a starting point that the numbers always need to be controlled and set to some desired level (it will be obvious that no good arguments are given why a certain level is desired). Part of the objective is that numbers should be kept at a minimum viable population level (set at 100–150 animals). Apart from a set number, there are also objectives regarding population structure, e.g. sex ratio, percentage of recruits and 1-year olds. The management cycle starts with a yearly census in spring. In almost every FMU, ungulates are counted during two or three consecutive evenings at the end of April or early May.

Based on certain population parameters and expected natural mortality, an expected population size with a certain structure for the next year is calculated and on the basis of this and the desired level, the estimated number per age class that need to be culled is estimated.

Most of the shooting is done from fixed places where also some supplementary feeding is given. All animals shot are labelled and carefully recorded. Sometimes, when the required cull has not been achieved, extra time is allotted after the official period has elapsed to allow completion of cull plans.

About 30% of the estimated spring population of roe deer and red deer and 30–50% of the wild boar are culled each year.

8.7 Census types and methods

Population estimates have to be given by the Fauna Management Units in their management plans. Therefore, yearly counts are organised by the FMUs where ungulates are counted during two or three consecutive evenings at the end of April or early May.

For red deer and fallow deer, sub-areas are counted by small teams of counters, both by means of traversing the area by car (driven transects) or by sitting at specific places which are favoured by the animals (vantage point counts) (Oerlemans and Van Wieren, 2005). Wild boar are counted slightly differently. Six weeks before counting begins, food is supplied to attract wild boar to certain places. On two evenings in May, the boar are counted on these feeding places. Double countings are removed and minimum spring densities are thus calculated.

8.8 Impact of large ungulates/damage

The FMUs have an obligation to prevent damage in their areas (and also outside these if the species responsible for the damage falls under their responsibility). In principle, they also have to pay for the damage. Damage compensation at the state level is possible when damage is inflicted by a protected species and if it is unreasonable that the damage should be charged solely to the party concerned.

In this context, we should reiterate that in the Netherlands, all ungulate species fall within that list of protected species. Requests for damage compensation are considered by the Fauna Fund and this fund can pay for the damage. The Fund is part of the Ministry of Agriculture, Nature and Food Quality and the funds are provided both by the ministry and the provinces (whose contribution comes in part from the money being paid by the hunters for their hunting permit). The total amount paid for damage compensation by the Fauna Fund for all species was EUR 6 177 274 and EUR 4 239 434 in 2003 and 2004, respectively. The major share of this money was for damage by geese (Bureau Waardenburg, 2004).

Damage by ungulates is only taken into account when this has occurred outside their permitted area of habitation. Most of the damage then is on crops on adjacent agricultural lands, e.g. maize (wild boar, red deer), grassland, grain (wild boar, red deer, roe deer), or bulbs (roe deer, fallow deer). Actual damage compensated is very little on a yearly basis (Table 8.2).

As it is acknowledged that, especially for red deer, the nutrient rich agricultural fields in the central Netherlands could (and should) play a significant role in the forage supply in an otherwise rather poor habitat, policies are being developed to allow red deer more and more as joint-users on these lands.

At present the Fauna Fund has made agreements with 50 landowners in which they provide opportunities for red deer to use their land for a certain period of the year. As compensation they receive EUR 50 per year. In total this scheme amounts to EUR 35 000 per year. These agreements are part of a separate scheme and are in addition to the figures given in Table 8.2.

Table 8.2 *Total compensation payed by the Fauna Fund for ungulate damage in the period 2001–2004; in Euros*

	2001	2002	2003	2004
Red deer	4 800	12 700	30 000	3 200
Fallow deer	9 400	10 700	4 200	9 200
Wild boar	7 400	12 300	1 300	8 900
Roe deer	2 900	6 600	17 600	17 700
Total	24 500	42 300	53 100	39 000

Table 8.3 *Number of traffic accidents with red deer and wild boar in the central Netherlands (Veluwe) in the period 1995–2002*

Year	Red deer	Wild boar
1995	18	142
1996	21	212
1997	32	124
1998	14	124
1999	27	216
2000	21	159
2001	32	257
2002	39	239
2003	40	320
2004	31	100

8.8.1 Traffic accidents

For a densely populated country such as the Netherlands it is not surprising that many accidents happen especially with roe deer, a species that is found in almost all of the country. On a national level an estimated 5–10% of the roe deer, red deer and wild boar die in collisions with traffic (Groot Bruinderink and Hazebroek, 1996).

Forty per cent of the accidents with roe deer occur in April, May and June, a period coinciding with an increased movement of males searching for a territory.

The number of accidents with red deer and wild boar in recent years in the central Netherlands is given in Table 8.3 (Groot Bruinderink *et al.*, 2003). It is clear that many more accidents happen with wild boar while further it can be noticed that for both species the number of traffic accidents is on the rise. As with roe deer, the accidents are not equally distributed across the year. For both red deer and

Table 8.4 *Results of the monitoring of the health status of ungulates in the National Park Veluwezoom (part of the Veluwe) and the Oostvaardersplassen (from Groot Bruinderink and Lammertsma, 2006)*

Area	N.P. Veluwezoom	Oostvaardersplassen
Cattle	Not demonstrated: TBC, para-TBC, brucellosis, IBR, leptospirosis and BVD	Not demonstrated: TBC, brucellosis, leptospirosis and BVD Demonstrated: para-TBC and IBR
Red deer	No data	Not demonstrated: TBC, brucellosis, BVD, leptospirosis Demonstrated: Para-TBC, IBR

wild boar, 40% of the accidents happen in September, October and November, a clear association with an increase in movements related to the reproductive season.

8.8.2 Disease

Cattle and red deer populations are continuously screened for Category I diseases, like the highly contagious classical swine fever or foot and mouth disease. This monitoring is undertaken and organised by the landowner and samples are collected by the hunters during the regular cull or, when necessary, by veterinarians. Populations of free-ranging cattle and horses are also screened. A few results are shown in Table 8.4. Checks on wild boar for classical swine fever during the last outbreak in 1997–8 were all negative. Also checks on roe deer, red deer and wild boar for foot and mouth disease during the outbreak in 2000–2001 were negative.

8.9 Supplementary feeding

As already noted, provision of supplementary feed is prohibited by law, since the whole Dutch management philosophy is to leave things as natural as possible.

8.10 Ungulate management in the Netherlands: crucial points for the future

In the past 25 years much has changed in ungulate management in the Netherlands. From a more sectoral approach (forestry versus game), in many forest areas a much more integrative management has been adopted with less focus on timber production and more on the development of biodiversity, recreational use and some timber production. In many areas the production option has been discarded altogether. Ungulates thus have become less seen as a nuisance or a trophy, but more as part of the system in their own right.

This gradual development has led to a number of changes, including:

- no supplementary feeding
- no maintenance of game meadows and the like
- the cessation of hunting of roe deer in many areas
- more attention to attaining normal population structures (less focus on trophies)
- enlargement of habitat through removal of fences and adding nutrient rich (former) agricultural areas
- increased connectivity through the creation of wildlife overpasses
- more culled animals are left in the field (in some areas 100% of the red deer and wild boar).

In the light of the changed views in conservation management in which also the new Flora and Fauna Act can be placed, all these developments are positive.

Nevertheless much can be improved upon as exemplified by the following two points.

1. Good reasons to intervene in populations are seldom given. It is too easily taken for granted, by all parties involved, that control of populations is necessary and from that all the rest follows automatically. Managers need to find out if damage is taking place, if that damage is substantial, if there are no alternatives to counteract the problem, if the proposed actions are effective, etc. Possible reasons why this is not happening are, on one hand, that old habits do not die easily and that in many ways present management is simply a continuation of the old management. And, on the other, that for a real assessment of damage (or for what other cause) proper research is needed and maybe long-term studies. Further, it is quite clear that in many cases, after close scrutiny, the supposed reasons to intervene would crumble like biscuits under a tank and this notion is not in the interest of some parties. We have to conclude that at present no scientific basis underlies the larger part of the management actions taken.
2. If one finds it important that the desired population levels are maintained, it can be expected that the efforts are geared towards that end. In practice, this does not seems to be so easy to accomplish. Figures 8.4 and 8.5 give the proposed spring numbers and actual spring population level for red deer and wild boar in the central Netherlands. For red deer, the proposed population size at steady-state has increased over the years from 800 to 900. It is noted, first, that desired numbers are quite fixed (no room for any dynamism in numbers) and, second, that for both species numbers have actually increased significantly in the past decade(s). There are many reasons for this mismatch, but one is certainly that the proposed yearly cull is seldomly achieved. For red deer,

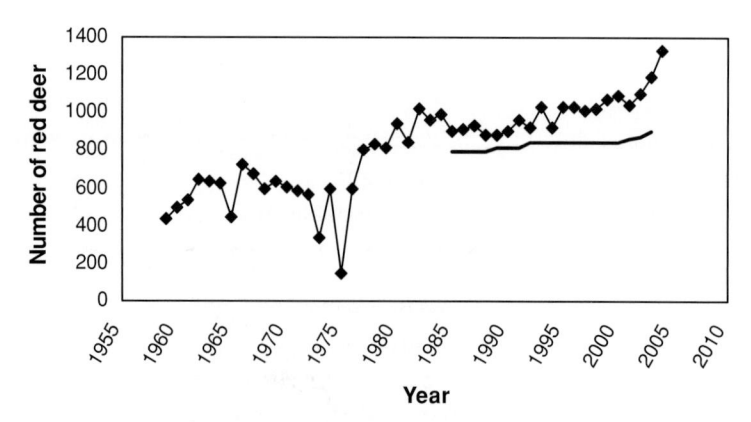

Fig. 8.4 Spring levels (line with dots) and desired abundance (approximately straight line) of red deer on the Veluwe ($R^2 = 0.73$)

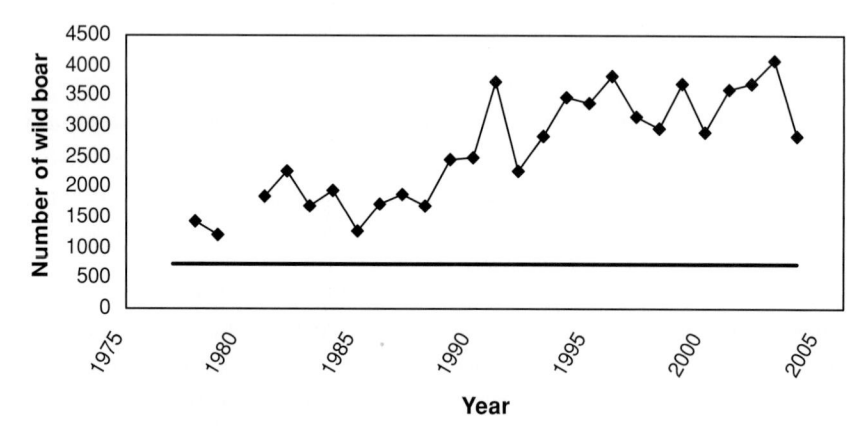

Fig. 8.5 Spring levels (line with dots) and desired abundance (straight line) of wild boar on the Veluwe ($R^2 = 0.71$)

the percentage of animals that should have been culled but have not, ranges from 10–35%, while for wild boar this ranges from 5–35%. This is still a long way from proper adaptive management and, apparently, little is learned from the yearly experiences. Probably this is also part of the reason why in a recent report on the future management new spring densities have been proposed which are about twice as high as the ones from Figures 8.4 and 8.5.

Contrary to objectives, the actual adult sex ratio of adult wild boar is very skewed at 1:4.2. Improvement is also needed here.

8.10.1 Future developments

Pressure by society for proper science-based ungulate management is increasing and frequently debated in the Dutch parliament. We do not really know much

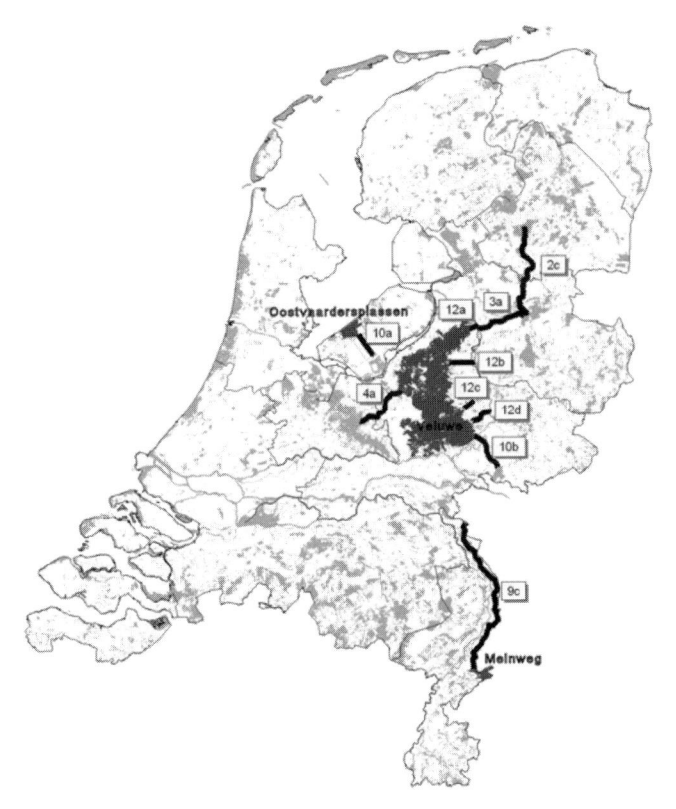

Fig. 8.6 Core areas for red deer and wild boar in the Netherlands and the ecological corridors that will, in future, connect them (source: H. Kuipers, Alterra)

about the actual damage inflicted by ungulates. We still seek solutions for wildlife collisions but, thus far, without much success. From a veterinary point of view the contamination risk from livestock farms towards ungulates in the wild is far greater than the other way around. Defragmentation of the current ungulate habitat is a major financial effort but knowledge about their design and management is lacking to a large extent.

Nature in northwestern Europe is the most fragmented of the world (Groot Bruinderink *et al.*, 2003). Defragmentation of the ungulate habitat is in many ways a major effort and we are just at the beginning of implementing ecological networks. This raises the question of the right design of this type of ecological corridor. Robust connections, i.e. connections on the ecosystem level, imply that many target species for these ecosystems should profit from the expansion of their habitat.

For the red deer this concerns five main corridors (Fig. 8.6). Based on the advice of an international committee of scientists, one of the first corridors to be realised will be the OostvaardersWold between the Oostvaardersplassen and the Horsterwold to the south (ICMO, 2006; corridor 10a in Fig. 8.6).

Farmers in the corridors will be given the opportunity to continue their farms elsewhere or will be bought out. Much of the agricultural land will be transformed into 'new-nature'.

It is clear from Figure 8.6 (corridor 10b and 9c) that realisation of an ecological network for large mammals implies an international effort by the Netherlands, Germany and Belgium.

References

Broekhuizen, S., Hoekstra, B., Van Laar, V., Smeenk, C. and Thissen, J. B. M. (1992) *Atlas van de Nederlandse zoogdieren*. Utrecht: Stichting Uitgeverij KNNV. (In Dutch.)

De Boer, H. Y., Van Breukelen, L., Hootsmans, M. J. M. and Van Wieren, S. E. (2004) Flight distance in roe deer *Capreolus capreolus* and fallow deer *Dama dama* as related to hunting and other factors. *Wildlife Biology* 10(1), 35–41.

Bureau Waardenburg (2004) *Faunabeheerplan Veluwe*. 241 pp. (In Dutch.)

Groot Bruinderink, G. W. T. A. and Hazebroek, E. (1996) Ungulate-traffic collisons in Europe. *Conservation Biology* 10(4), 1059–67.

Groot Bruinderink, G. W. T. A. and Lammertsma, D. R. (2006) Besmettingsrisico's tussen vrijlevende en gehouden dieren. *De Levende Natuur* 107(1), 4–7. (In Dutch with English summary.)

Groot Bruinderink, G. W. T. A., van der Sluis, T., Lammertsma, D. R., Opdam, P. F. M. and Pouwels, R. (2003) Designing a coherent ecological network for large mammals in northwestern Europe. *Conservation Biology* 17(2), 549–57.

Hodder, K. H., Bullock, J. M., Buckland, P. C. and Kirby, K. J. (2005) *Large Herbivores in the Wildwood and Modern Naturalistic Grazing Systems*. English Nature Research Reports No. 648. Peterborough, UK: English Nature.

ICMO (2006) *Reconciling Nature and Human Interests*. Report of the International Committee on the Management of large herbivores in the Oostvaardersplassen (ICMO). The Hague/Wageningen, Netherlands. Wageningen UR-WING rapport t018. 2006. ISBN 9032703528.

Lensink, R. and Spek, G. J. (2004) *Ruimte voor grofwild op een Eindeloze Veluwe*. Culemborg: Bureau Waardenburg BV. (In Dutch.)

Litjens, B. E. J. (1991) *Roodwildbeheer in de vrije wildbaan van de Veluwe*. Het Edelhert, extra uitgave, 1–32. (In Dutch.)

Litjens, B. E. J. and Pelzers, E. (1988) Het damhert *Cervus dama* in Nederland. *Lutra* 31, 132–144. (In Dutch.)

Ministerie van LNV (2000) *Leidraad Grote Grazers*. Den Haag. (In Dutch.)

Ministerie van LNV (2002) *Flora- en Faunawet. Koninklijke Vermande*. Den Haag. (In Dutch.)

Oerlemans, M. and Van Wieren, S. E. (2005) *Population dynamics of red deer (*Cervus elaphus*), fallow deer (*Dama dama*) and wild boar (*Sus scrofa*) on the Veluwe, The Netherlands*. Report, Wageningen University, Wageningen.

Postma, E., Van Hooft, W. F., Van Wieren, S. E. and Van Breukelen, L. (2001) Microsatellite variation in Dutch roe deer (*Capreolus capreolus*) populations. *Netherlands Journal of Zoology* 51(1), 85–95.

Provincie Gelderland (2000) *Veluwe 2010, een kwaliteitsimpuls!* Rapport, Gedeputeerde Staten Gelderland, Arnhem. In Dutch.

Van Wieren, S. E. and Worm, P. B. (2001) The use of a motorway wildlife overpass by large mammals. *Netherlands Journal of Zoology* **51**(1), 97–105.

Vera, F. W. M. (2000) *Grazing Ecology and Forest History*. Wallingford, UK: CAB International.

9

Ungulates and their management in Belgium

JIM CASAER AND ALAIN LICOPPE

When describing the distribution and management of ungulates in Belgium a clear distinction should be made between the north, the Flemish region (Flanders) and the south, the Walloon region (Wallonia). Where the Flemish region has a human population density of approximately 442 inhabitants per square kilometre, the density in the southern region is only about 200 inhabitants per square kilometre. Barely 10% of the Flemish region is forested, whereas more than 30% of the Walloon region is covered by forest.

With the exception of a few fallow deer, red deer and wild boar established as escapes, the only wild ungulate species in Flanders is roe deer. By contrast, in the Walloon region populations of red deer, wild boar and roe deer are widely distributed. The distribution of mouflon is limited to the valley of the Semois. Here and there, fallow deer and muntjac, all descendants of escaped individuals, can be found in both the Flemish and Walloon region, but thus far no viable, wild, populations occur.

Since 1980 hunting is a regional responsibility and consequently both regions have their own hunting organisations, laws and open seasons. There is no longer a national overarching hunting legislation. Nevertheless, given the fact that until 25 years ago both regions shared the same hunting legislation, many similarities between the laws of the two regions still remain.

9.1 Species, history and present distribution

Until the end of the eighteenth century red deer, wild boar, roe deer and even fallow deer occurred in high densities all over the country in the larger forested areas such as in the Ardenne, around Leuven and south of Brussels. At the end of the eighteenth century, Joseph II ordered capture or killing of the overabundant populations of wild boar in order to reduce the excessive crop damage in fields and forests. The various revolutions and wars which followed in later years further reduced the populations of ungulates in the Belgian forests. People were hungry, armies swarmed over the country and there were no authorities to control poaching. Where wild boar and roe deer still commonly occurred, be it at low densities, the occurrence of red deer populations became restricted to two relict areas, one around Saint-Hubert, and the other close to the border with Germany.

When Belgium became independent (1830), attempts were made to restore the once abundant wildlife populations. A new national hunting law was introduced and red deer, fallow deer and roe deer were reintroduced at several places during the second half of the nineteenth century. This led to an increase of both numbers and the area occupied by the different species. In 1936, mouflon was introduced in the Valley of Semois, for the first time. More important introductions occurred in the same area (Herbeumont) in 1954.

The two successive world wars in the beginning of the twentieth century again led to a drastic reduction of both the forested area and the ungulate populations. Both the German soldiers and the local inhabitants overexploited forests to secure wood and meat. After World War II the populations of roe deer and red deer were only a fraction of what they had been at the beginning of the twentieth century (Haÿez, 1999). But, following the end of WWII populations of red deer, roe deer and wild boar in the Walloon region and populations of roe deer in the Flemish region boomed. Both numbers and range increased at a rate never before witnessed in recent history. Current levels probably are the highest seen since the end of the seventeenth century.

9.1.1 Flanders

Though in Flanders wild boar occurs, at very low densities, in one region (Voeren, province of Limburg, separated from the rest of Flanders by the river Meuse), and occasionally individual red deer are observed, roe deer are the only ungulate species considered to be a self-sustaining population. For Flanders Table 9.1 therefore only mentions the estimated roe deer population.

The enormous increase in population abundance of roe deer in Flanders over the last few decades has not only resulted in local roe deer populations reaching very high densities, exceeding 30 animals per 100 ha of forested area, but also led to an increase in the geographical distribution of the roe deer population. Where the geographical distribution in the 1960s was limited to the north of the provinces of Limburg and Antwerpen and some relict populations were found around Leuven and Brussels, roe deer now occupy almost all forest patches of

Table 9.1 *Estimations of ungulate population in Belgium in 2006 (source: Casaer et al., 2003; DGRNE, 2004)*

Species	Region	Min.Estimated pop (*)	Estimated population change since 1980	Introduced/native
Roe deer	Flanders	20 000	500%	Native
	Wallonia	40 000	80%	Native
Red deer	Wallonia	10 000	75%	Native
Wild boar	Wallonia	21 000	150%	Native
Mouflon	Wallonia	400	0%	Introduced (20th century)
Fallow deer	Belgium	Escaped indiv. 200		Introduced

* population estimation after the hunting season, before births.

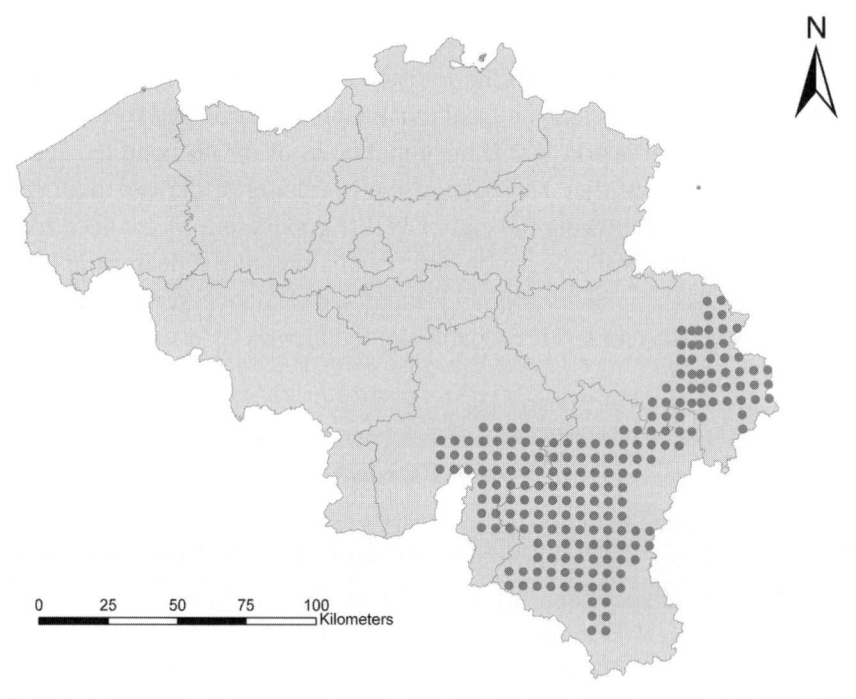

Fig. 9.1 Geographical presentation of the distribution of roe deer in Belgium. The lines indicate the borders of the different provinces (sources: own data; Verkem et al., 2003; Libois, 2006)

the provinces of Limburg, Antwerpen and Vlaams-Brabant (Casaer *et al.*, 2003; Figure 9.1). Even in Oost- and West-Vlaanderen, where roe deer has been absent for many decades, roe deer populations are starting to reappear (sometimes with some human help).

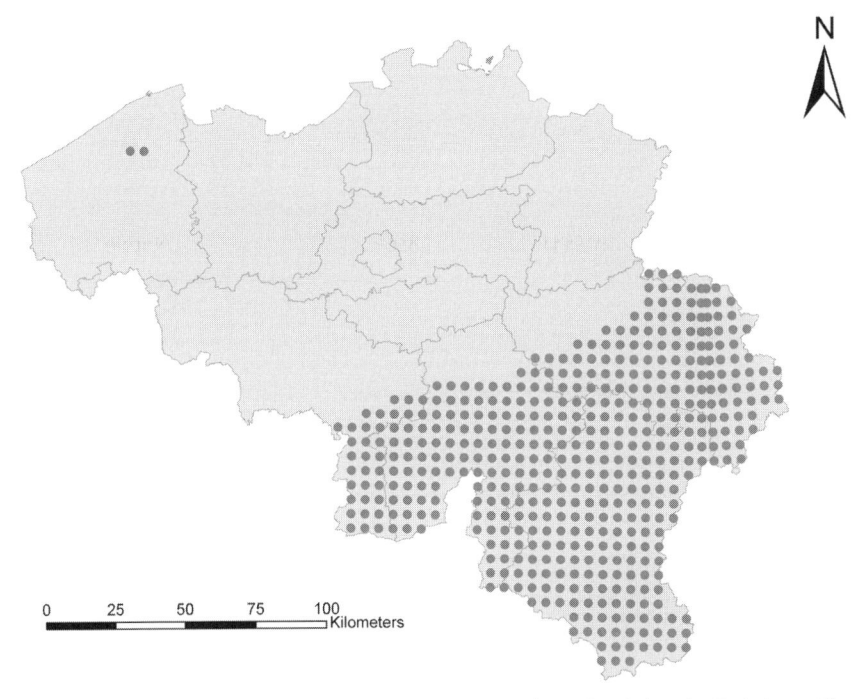

Fig. 9.2 Geographical presentation of the distribution of red deer in Belgium. The lines indicate the borders of the different provinces (sources: own data; Verkem et al., 2003; Libois, 2006)

9.1.2 Wallonia

Population densities of red deer and wild boar have increased since the end of the thirteenth century to more than two red deer and more than four wild boar per 100 ha forest. Often the abundance of both species increased together as well as densities of roe deer in one and the same area. The core areas for red deer in Wallonia (Fig. 9.2) are the region around the nature park 'Hautes Fagnes', the Plateau des Tailles, the Thiérache, the Famenne, the valleys of the Semois and the Haute-Lesse and the region around Saint-Hubert (de Crombrugghe, 1999). Distribution of roe deer is included in Figure 9.1; that of wild boar is shown in Figure 9.3.

Fallow deer and mouflon have a much more restricted distribution. Only one population of free ranging fallow lives in Famenne around Ciergnon. Mouflons range around the town of Herbeumont in the Valley of Semois.

9.2 Legislation

9.2.1 Flanders

Belgian law stipulates that the hunting rights belong to the landowner, being a private person or a national, regional or local public authority. The landowner can

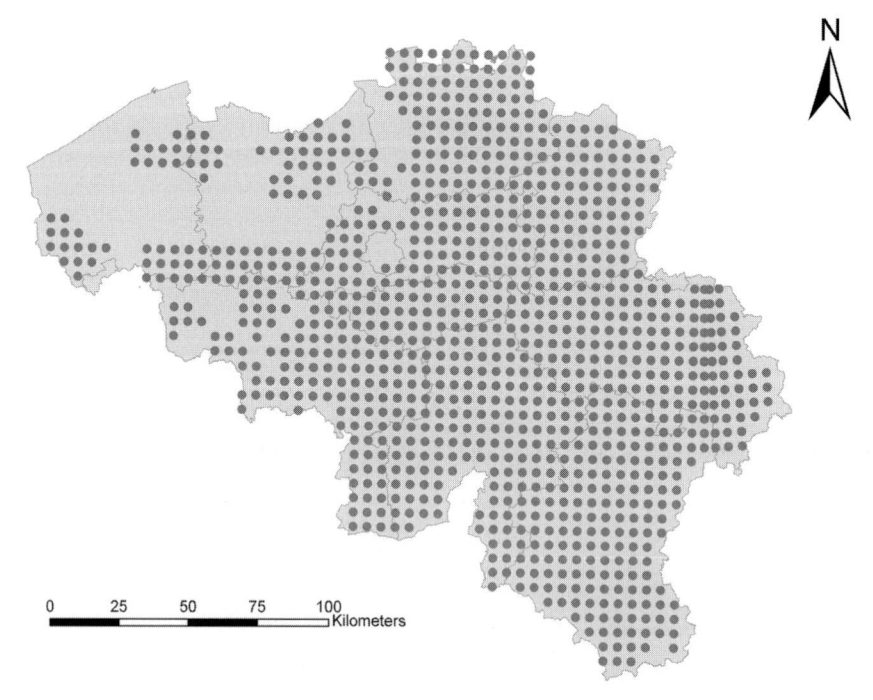

Fig. 9.3 Geographical presentation of the distribution of wild boar in Belgium. The lines indicate the borders of the different provinces (sources: own data; Verkem et al., 2003; Libois, 2006)

decide to exercise his/her right by hunting himself or he/she can lease the right to hunt on his property to a third party. The landowner can also decide not to hunt nor to allow hunting on his or her property. Whoever wants to hunt with a rifle or shotgun needs to have the hunting rights on a minimal unbroken area of at least 40 ha. Moreover, since 2003, the hunting territory has to be at least 1000 ha, or to contain a minimum 250 ha of forested patches before any roe deer hunting is allowed.

In Flanders, only the use of rifles with bullets of a minimum diameter of 5.6 mm (0.222 inches) and an energy equal to or greater than 980 J at 100 m from the muzzle can be used for shooting wild ungulate species. There are no differences in the type of rifles that can be used for recreational hunting or for damage control. Roe deer can only be shot from high seats or by stalking. Any form of drive hunting of roe deer is forbidden.

Permitted seasons for roe deer are divided into an open season for roe fawns (both sexes) and adult females (15 January–15 March) and an open season for adult and yearling bucks (15 May–15 September). Although there are no established populations of wild boar, red deer, fallow deer or mouflon, open seasons exist for these species in the Flemish region. These seasons coincide with the open seasons

Table 9.2 *Open seasons for the different ungulate species in Belgium*

Species	Region	Sex/age	From	To
Roe deer	Flanders	Adult male	15 May	15 September
		Adult female and fawns	15 January	15 March
Roe deer	Wallonia	Adult male – high seats and stalking	1 May and 1 August	15 May 30 September
		Both sexes and all ages – all hunting methods	1 October	30 November
Red deer	Belgium	All sexes and ages – all hunting methods	1 October	31 December
	Wallonia	Large adult male* – high seats and stalking	21 September	30 September
Wild boar	Wallonia	All sexes and ages** – every hunting method	1 October	31 December
	Wallonia	All sexes and ages – high seats and stalking	1 January	31 December
	Flanders	All sexes and ages – high seats and stalking	1 October	31 December
Mouflon	Belgium	All sexes and ages – all hunting method	1 October	31 December
Fallow deer	Belgium	All sexes and ages – all hunting method	1 October	31 December

* Adult males are defined on the description of their antlers. 'Large adult males' develop antlers with 1 crown on each beam.
** In agriculture areas, drives are allowed from 1 August to 31 December

in the Walloon region. This apparently strange regulation is related to the fact that selling fresh game meat in Flanders is only allowed from the first day of the opening season until ten days after the last day of the open season.

Hunting of wild ungulate species is only permitted after submission of a shooting plan that has to be approved by the forestry administration. For roe deer the law stipulates the form and content of this shooting plan.

Any form of (re)introduction of ungulate species for hunting purposes is prohibited by law in Flanders.

9.2.2 Wallonia

Only rifles with bullets of a minimum diameter of 6.5 mm and a energy equal to at least 2200 J at 100 m can be used to shoot ungulates, except for roe deer where the same specifications as in Flanders are applied. All forms of hunting can be used according to the time of the year.

Open seasons (see Table 9.2) for red deer and wild boar are from 1 October to 31 December, using any hunting method. Wild boar can be shot all year from high seats or by stalking. Roe deer bucks may be hunted from 1 August to 30 September by sitting or stalking, and both sexes are open from 1 October to 30 September by any form of hunting. Red deer is the only species for which an actual shooting plan has been required since 1990.

9.3 Management objectives
9.3.1 Flanders

For roe deer, the regional administration based its management aims on the conclusions of a scientific advisory report (Wauters, 1995). The general aim is to maintain or develop natural roe deer populations wherever possible and at such densities that (1) the animals are in a good condition (2) the animals do not provoke unacceptable levels of damage to forestry, agriculture or human health (traffic accidents).

With the exception of the small wild boar population in Voeren, the general objective for the management of the other ungulate species is to eradicate them wherever they occur outside enclosures. This regional policy is based on the consideration that the establishment of a viable population of any of these species is impossible or at least undesirable in Flanders given the high human population density and the high fragmentation of the region due to the network of highways, canals, railroads and other infrastructure. The potential for, and desirability of, the establishment of a red deer population in the north of the province of Limburg (bordering the Netherlands) was analysed and initially judged positively in preliminary research conducted in 2003 (Kurstjens *et al.*, 2003). However, advisory bodies on hunting and nature conservation advised against such an introduction as a result of which the minister decided not to grant a permit to release red deer in Flanders.

9.3.2 Wallonia

The general aim is to maintain viable populations of ungulates, allowing for the possibility of hunting, but at the same time to reduce, as much as possible, the high damage levels sustained in forestry schemes.

Damage is often triggered as the result of an apparent disequilibrium between artificially raised ungulate populations and man-made forests or a disequilibrium between a forest's provision of cover (thermal cover and protection) and the availability of food resources (Reimoser and Gossow, 1996). Therefore, the forestry administration aims on the one hand to maintain somewhat reduced densities of red deer and wild boar but at the same time aims to try and increase availability of non-crop food resources, so that there are ample alternative foraging opportunities for those populations which do remain, so that browsing on forest crops by such ungulates is correspondingly reduced.

Ungulate populations are kept as natural as possible and any reintroduction is prohibited. A new biodiversity service order suggests guidelines for sustainable management of ungulate species by reducing artificial practices such as supplementary feeding or the creation of game pastures in the forest.

All these guidelines fit within the Natura 2000 recommendations.

Alien species such as fallow deer or mouflon are not the subject of eradication at this moment.

9.4 Management structure and coordination

9.4.1 Flanders

Professional managers or rangers, employed by the state, with responsibility for culling of roe deer do not at present exist in the Flemish region. To achieve the management objectives outlined above, the Flemish authorities fully rely on private hunters. In an effort to improve management the Flemish government recently (1998) introduced a system of game management units. Game management units are associations of private hunters with adjoining hunting territories that total up to at least 1000 ha. At present, 70% of the Flemish area, where almost all roe deer are shot, is under the control of game management units (Casaer *et al.*, 2005). These units are assisted by the authorities in order to achieve sustainable hunting. The rest of the area is either not hunted, or hunted by hunters not belonging to any management unit at all.

Shooting plans (see also section 9.5) are submitted by the hunters or by the game management units to the forest administration. Based on the information supplied in the shooting plan, such as population estimations, habitat information and the number of animals shot during the previous three years, the forest district inspector evaluates the requested cull. He or she approves the shooting plan, imposes slightly different quotas or declines the shooting plan. A decision frame of desirable densities, as a function of the biotope, and of the required culling percentages to achieve certain management goals (stabilising, increasing or decreasing the current roe deer densities) is used as a guideline for this purpose (Wauters, 1995).

9.4.2 Wallonia

Ungulate management, in general, focuses mainly on red deer because of the legal requirement for a shooting plan for this species (section 9.2). The actual policy is to give a maximum responsibility to the hunters through the game management units.

In Wallonia, to hunt red deer stags, hunters have to belong to a game management unit (covering at least 5000 ha of wooded areas). As far the actual number of red deer to be shot is concerned, the game management unit suggests quotas of deer to the forestry administration, which can accept or decline. If the culling plan is not approved, it must be revised by the game management unit. If no agreement occurs, there is a possible resort to a commission of appeal made up out of hunters and foresters.

In addition to agreement over numbers to be harvested, game management units have to respect some general guidelines enacted by the administration concerning the sex- and age-ratios of the requested quota. When these guidelines are not taken into account, the game unit may lose all its responsibilities resulting in the suspension of hunting stags. Whatever the legal responsibilities, some game management units also adopt more restrictive rules over and above those legal requirements.

No other species of ungulates are subject to the requirement for a shooting plan, except in some areas, in a voluntary way (e.g. roe deer in Elsenborn).

9.5/6 Management organisation and practice

9.5/6.1 Flanders

In accordance with the legislation of 1995 the shooting plan for roe deer in the Flemish region has to mention the size of the hunting territory, the forested area in the hunting territory, the estimated population on the 15 September (after the hunting season) and the number of roe deer to be shot in order to realise the management goals. Both the population estimation as well as the requested cull have to be subdivided in adult male (> 1 year), adult female (> 1 year) and fawns (disregarding the sexes). The number of roe deer shot in the previous three years also has to be reported. Based on this information, and when required, after advice of the local forester, a maximum and/or minimum number to be culled of each of the three classes is set.

An equal number of uniquely numbered labels (see Fig. 9.4) is given to the hunters or to the game management unit. Each animal shot has to be labelled, and the date must be cut out of the label, before any transport of the dead animal on public roads is allowed. Whenever a roe deer is shot the local forester has to be informed. The place where the animal will be kept available for inspection for the next 24 h has to be reported to the forester. Only a very small proportion of the total number of roe deer shot is inspected by local staff of the forestry administration.

For each roe deer that has been culled, a form has to be filled out and sent to the forestry administration. On these forms, the following information must be filled out: date and place where the animal was shot, person who shot the animal,

Table 9.3 *Total cull of the different ungulate species in Belgium in 2003*

Species	Region	Annual cull (2003)	Adult male	Adult female	Fawns
Roe deer	Flanders	3 480	1110	950	1420
	Wallonia	16 989	7900	9098	
Red deer	Wallonia	3 184	990	993	1201
Wild boar	Wallonia	14 368			
Mouflon	Wallonia		65		
Fallow deer	Belgium	Escaped indiv.			

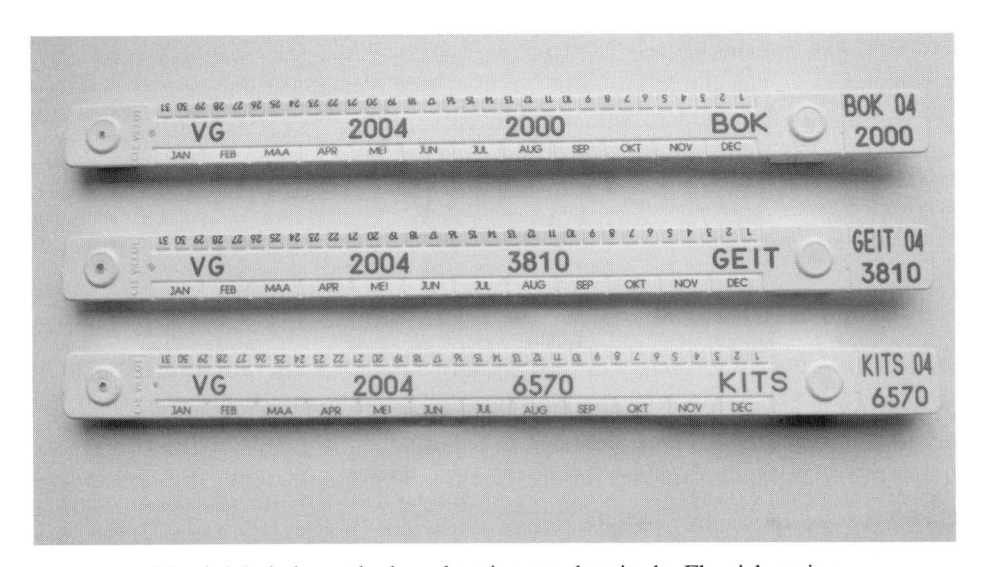

Fig. 9.4 Labels used when shooting roe deer in the Flemish region

sex and age class of the animal and eviscerated weight of the roe deer. Facultative information such as the jaw length, number of embryos, kidney fat index, and information on the antlers can be added. This information is stored in a central database for further analyses by the Research Institute for Nature and Forest. The actual cull for 2003 was 3450 roe deer (see Table 9.3).

9.5/6.2 Wallonia

Each red deer culled in Wallonia is recorded by the forestry administration and once again identified by a numbered plastic label fixed to the thigh of the culled animal. The colour of the label depends on the animal (calf, hind or stag category). A datasheet is filled in by the local forester with obligatory and facultative information.

Among obligatory ones are: date and location of shooting and hunting type; among the voluntary ones: age and weight, antler length and development.

The number of labels delivered by the forestry administration to the game unit depends on the culling plan. To ensure the required distribution among sex-classes, the administration roughly gives two-thirds of white labels (hinds and calves) and one-third red labels (stags). Some game units also demand that their members collect the mandible of each culled animal, in order to avoid any cheating and to allow the ageing of deer. At present, 60% of the mandibles are aged in the Research Institute of the Walloon region.

For other ungulates, since 2001, each animal culled has also to be labelled. The colour of the label will depend on the species (e.g. yellow = roe deer, blue = mouflon, black = fallow deer and green = wild boar). This procedure was first developed to reduce the possibilities of poaching by identifying each culled animal during the transport of venison. Moreover, this procedure will improve the reliability in the future of the culling statistics for these four species

9.7 Census types and methods

9.7.1 Flanders

On top of the specific obligation to give an estimate of the roe deer population present when handling in the shooting plan, all game management units have the general obligation to report annually the estimated spring populations and bag statistics for all hunted species. However, no guidelines or rules exist concerning methods to estimate these populations.

During the last five years the possibility of imposing kilometre indexes (Vincent *et al.*, 1991) as a standardised method was tested. Although results are promising, many roe deer hunters are reluctant to apply this kilometre index method and often restore to their own traditional, often not standardised, guesswork. The most widely used methods thereby are individual counts from high seats during the hunting season or counts from cars driven through the hunting territory.

9.7.2 Wallonia

Hunters have no legal obligation to count red deer but have to suggest a culling plan. The forestry administration has undertaken its own estimates of the densities of each ungulate species since 1924. The reliability of the census method cannot be tested and therefore the results can only be used to estimate the trends in ungulate species over the years. Some management units or large territories have applied existing methods or developed their own census method, to supplement these forestry administration estimates, mainly for red deer. The most popular census method is to combine observations from high seats and stalking observations on small sectors of forest (de Crombrugghe, 1970) which is applied in more than 20% of the red deer distribution area. Night counts are also used, but the procedure changes according to the hunting territory. Some pilot territories (Hunts of the Crown) apply all the existing methods and take part in the development or validation of new ones, for red, as well as roe deer and wild boar. For this purpose, a network of fenced and unfenced squares has been constructed to evaluate the impact of ungulates on some plant species over several years (e.g. *Vaccinium* height).

9.8 Impacts and damage

9.8.1 Flanders

Information on the damage caused by roe deer on forestry, agriculture, or nature or physical damage as a result of road accidents is not centralised in Flanders. This information – if present – is scattered over a multitude of governmental and non-governmental organisations and is basically unavailable for analyses.

An exception was the number of traffic accidents, which used to be recorded more centrally. Until the beginning of the 1990s people involved in a car accident with roe deer could apply for damage repayment by the national insurance fund (Openbaar motorwaarborg fonds). As the number of accidents increased, the fund no longer paid for damage, but opted for the installation of warning signs. As a result, information on the number of traffic accidents is no longer centralised.

No hard data on the impact of roe deer on forests in Flanders exist. However, fencing is nowadays required whenever foresters want to convert previous monocultures of pine forest (*Pinus corsicanus* and/or *Pinus sylvestris*) into mixed or deciduous forest stands. In many areas even in mixed or deciduous forest stands, natural regeneration of deciduous tree species can only be ensured by fencing regeneration areas. Figures on the actual costs of fencing and replanting trees as a consequence of the presence of roe deer populations are not available.

By law, compensation for damage to forestry or agriculture is theoretically payable by those having the hunting rights. The only exception are those cases where proof exists that the wild ungulates causing the damage originate from an nature reserve, in which the regional authorities have prohibited any form of killing or capturing of animals. Under these circumstances damage compensation would be paid by the Flemish authorities. However, thus far, no damage compensation has ever been paid due to damage caused by wild ungulate populations originating from nature reserves.

9.8.2 Wallonia

The information about road accidents with ungulates is very scarce for Wallonia. Recently, a monitoring network of the game health has been developed at Liege University, so that each dead animal can be brought to Liege for an autopsy.

The impact of ungulates on vegetation varies between the subregions of Wallonia, depending mainly on the quality and availability of the food resources. The highest deer populations are concentrated in the poorest wooded areas (low timber productivity) of Haute and Moyenne Ardenne, where the human settlement pressure is the lowest. The cold climate and acidic soils of these forests are the main factors of low diversity in plants and trees. *Picea abies* and *Fagus sylvatica* are almost the only species able to regenerate by themselves and damage occurs mostly on these species. *Quercus* spp. or *Pseudotsuga menziesii* have to be fenced after planting in this part of Belgium.

In order to evaluate the loss of profit due to bark stripping on *Picea abies*, the forestry administration, together with the University of Gembloux, developed a monitoring network of bark stripping damage (Lejeune *et al.*, 2002). The study should last many years and covers 22 forest districts of Wallonia (public areas on the entire distribution area of red deer). The cumulative bark stripping rate (corresponding to the amount of trees stripped according to the amount of monitored trees) may reach 95% in some places, and annual bark stripping rate is usually higher than 2% of the trees. Depending on the owner, the hunters who have the hunting rights over a particular area may be asked to protect young plantations against browsing (by fencing) or bark stripping (by notching).[1]

The main damage to agriculture is caused by wild boar (corn fields and pastures). As in Flanders, costs of damage must be paid by the hunters or by a group of hunters adjoining the damaged fields. The most common solutions to avoid damage by wild boar are electric fences and supplementary feeding.

The monitoring of the impact of ungulates on natural biodiversity will be an important aim of the next decade. An interesting analysis in this regard is to be undertaken by the St Hubert Game Management Unit, through a LIFE project exploring peat bog restoration (Jadoul, 2004).

9.9 Supplementary feeding

9.9.1 Flanders

Given the availability of abundant natural food resources, the mild winters and the strong interspersion of agriculture and forested areas, there is rarely any ecological

---

[1] Notching of the bark artificially with an appropriate tool may be used to stimulate the tree's natural defences against future damage; the technique is mainly used on Norway Spruce.

need for supplementary feeding in the Flemish region. However, in order to keep roe deer within the forested areas and away from dangerous roads where they could provoke traffic accidents, supplementary feeding could be a useful tool in exceptional cases. Private hunters mainly supply extra food, hoping to keep roe deer within their hunting territories and/or hoping to achieve higher roe deer densities, and consequently higher annual game bags, by doing so.

By law feeding of wild ungulates is not forbidden, nor obligatory in the Flemish region. However, the use of supplementary feeding as bait to facilitate the shooting of any game species is illegal in Flanders.

9.9.2 Wallonia

According to the law, one should distinguish between supplementary and diversionary feeding. On the one hand, supplementary feeding is designed for red deer during winter when food resources are supposed to be scarce (January until April). Feeding is roughly defined as any food that can be found in the natural environment of the animal: this excludes mainly industrial preparations. This kind of feeding may only occur at the beginning of January when hunting season is closed. This feeding practice was relevant when hunting territories were separated by high fences, which is now forbidden by law. At present, animals are theoretically able to range freely outside of the forest in winter. However, maintaining such a practice could be justified in order to reduce the occurrence of crop damage.

On the other hand, diversionary feeding is designed to keep wild boar in the forest to avoid any damage to agricultural crops. Diversionary feeding is composed of barley, corn and peas and must be issued all year long. In reality, diversionary feeding is seldom used in accordance with its original function, but used to keep wild boar and red deer within a certain territory and to increase wild boar fertility.

For both kinds of supplementary feeding, the forestry administration is allowed to control the practices in the field, even on private grounds.

9.10 Effectiveness of current management strategies, and problems

9.10.1 Flanders

One of the main problems of the current management of roe deer populations by game management units is the fact that affiliation to a game management unit is a voluntary act of a private hunter. As a result the units were formed based on personal contacts between neighbouring hunters, rather than on the ground of game management considerations. This often results in different game management units operating in what could be considered as a biologically valid 'roe deer management region', without any collaboration between them. On the other hand, one game management unit can contain an amalgam of different ecozones not forming a logical biological management unit.

A second problem, is the reluctance of hunters to shoot adult females, resulting in a sex-biased cull and population structures, although some progress in resolving this has been made more recently. This reluctance is partly due to the 'ethical objection' against shooting female animals in gestation, and partly also due to the conviction that by not shooting female roe and only harvesting antlered males roe deer population densities will further increase and as such will the annual harvest.

A possible solution for the first problem would be the creation of 'roe deer management units' superimposing existing game management units. These 'roe deer management units' should be based on infrastructural barriers such as highways and canals and should apply common management strategies that aim at common roe deer management objectives.

Solving the second problem will require a further shift in the way hunters perceive the management of roe deer populations and possibly setting fines for not reaching a minimum cull. Demonstrating the relation between roe deer densities and the physical condition of roe deer and the number of offspring, will be one of the tools to achieve this goal, but will require even more bio-indicators to be collected and to be analysed over longer periods.

Given the difficulties in counting roe deer and of predicting the influence of culling a certain number of animals on the population dynamics, the forest administration searches an alternative for the currently used guidelines. The feasibility of using population bioindicators (such as fawn weight, kidney fat index and number of embryos) within the frame of a three year shooting plan is being tested in eight game management units (Casaer, 2006).

The eight pilot game management units represented, in 2004, 20% of the total roe deer cull in the region. For each of them the minimum and maximum number of roe deer to be shot annually was fixed for the period of three years (to 2007). Information on the number of embryos, kidney fat index, jaw length, etc. is collected for each animal shot. The collected information will be used to judge the need to alter the population densities in order to achieve a healthy population, not causing unacceptable damage. Based on the number of animals effectively shot during the three year period, the minimum number of animals to be shot in each age and sex class will be fixed again for a period of three years (cf. Guibert, 1999).

Assuming a positive evaluation of the current feasibility study, the application of this working procedure for all the shooting plans will move us away from a roe deer management based on unreliable population estimates towards a management based on the physical condition of the roe deer populations present. The latter is supposed to be an indicator of the equilibrium, or disequilibrium, between the ecological carrying capacity of the hunting territory and the number of animals present. Moreover the administrative burden of requesting and approving shooting plans will be three times less given the fact that the shooting plans will only be adjusted every three years rather than annually.

9.10.2 Wallonia

The legal requirement to produce a culling plan for red deer combined with the efforts of some game management units has been partly successful in helping to restore a better balance of sex- and age-classes of the population. Limiting shooting of stags has allowed them to get older and it starts to be common to have stags > 10 years old in bag statistics. From a quantitative point of view, one of the consequences is an overall increase of deer densities. This could be explained by the lack of coordination in shooting effort between territories (since a quota is established, the neighbour will not necessary kill 'my hinds') and by a probable underestimation by the current counting methods, which should be improved and standardised in the next years.

The use of a label together with a datasheet for each culled animal has allowed a better control of the culled population and very relevant bag statistics on red deer. Even if no culling plan is at present needed for the other ungulates, the use of labels (which could be combined with a datasheet to complete the information) is very useful to improve bag statistics.

To hunt red deer stags, hunters must be associated in game management units. These associations are thus representative for the red deer hunters in Wallonia. The government gives them important management responsibilities but no financial means to achieve their missions.

Since it probably influences fertility, we believe that artificial feeding should be stopped, especially diversionary feeding for wild boar which is unwisely used and far from the philosophy of sustainable management.

As in many places in Europe, hunting rights are very expensive. In some sub-regions showing high red deer density, renting a hunting territory can cost from EUR 50 to 300 per ha. When spending such a huge amount of money annually, hunters will logically not accept stopping feeding as a measure to achieve higher game densities. The challenge will be to convince the owners (public or private) to have a long-term reflection on the other functions that the forest has to fit and to better balance game, timber, nature and tourism.

References

Casaer, J., Neukermans, A. and Baert, P. (2003) Ree (*Capreolus capreolus*, L). In S. Verkem, J. De Maeseneer, B. Vandendriessche, G. Verbeylen and S. Yskout, eds.,

Zoogdieren in Vlaanderen, Ecologie en verspreiding 1987–2002. Mechelen & Gent: Natuurpunt studie & JNM- Zoogdierengroep, pp. 383–8.

Casaer, J., Quataert, P. and De Bruyn, L. (2005) Jacht. In M. Dumortier, L. De Bruyn, M. Hens *et al.*, eds., *Natuurrapport 2005*. Toestand van de natuur in Vlaanderen: cijfers voor het beleid. Brussels: Mededeling van het Instituut voor Natuurbehoud nr. 24.

Casaer, J. (2006) Use of bioindicators as a tool for roe deer management, a pilot study. http://www.inbo.be/docupload/2896.pdf. (In Flemish.)

de Crombrugghe, S. A. (1970) Modes de recensement du Cerf en Belgique et portée pratique. *International Congress of Game Biology* **9**, 298–306.

de Crombruggehe, S. A. (1999) Palmarès de trophées d'Ongulés-gibier récoltés en Belgique au cours de la période 1989–1998. In *Exposition Nationale de Trophées de Grands Gibier*. Laveaux-Sainte-Anne, Belgique, pp. 61–2.

DGRNE (2004) Etat de l'Environnement wallon. http://mrw.wallonie.be/dgrne/eew/.

Guibert, B. (1999) Les conséquences des derniers acquis de la recherche sur la gestion future du chevreuil. *Bulletin Mensuelle de l' ONC* **244**, 120–5.

Haÿez, F. (1999) Le grand gibier en Belgique. In *Exposition Nationale de Trophées de Grands Gibier*. Laveaux-Sainte-Anne, Belgique, pp. 25–34.

Jadoul, G. (2004) Un projet européen LIFE–Nature: la restauration des milieux tourbeux du plateau de Saint–Hubert confiée à un Conseil cynégétique. *Chasse et Nature* **2**, 23–6.

Kurstjens, G.,Van Braeckel, A. and Peeters, B. (2003) *Kansen voor grote hoefdieren in het Kempen-Broek e omgeving*. Stichting Ark & Instituut voor Natuurbehoud. p. 103

Lejeune, P., Rotheudt, H. and Verrue, V. (2002) Proposition d'une méthode d'inventaire de dégâts de cervidés applicable en Région wallonne. *Forêt Wallonne* **60**, 4–11.

Libois, R. (2006) Les mammifères non-volants de la Région Wallone: tendance des populations. *Etat de l'environnement Wallon*. p. 127.

Reimoser, F. and Gossow. H. (1996) Impact of ungulates of forest vegetation and its dependence on the silvicultural system. *Forest Ecology and Management* **88**, 107–19.

Verkem, S., De Maeseneer, J., Vandendriessche, B., Verbeylen, G. and Yskout, S. (2003) *Zoogdieren in Vlaanderen. Ecologie en verspreiding van 1987 tot 2002*. Mechelen, Belgium: Natuurpunt Studie & JNM-Zoogdierenwerkgroep, p. 440.

Vincent, J. P., Gaillard, J. M. and Bideau, E. (1991) Kilometric index as biological indicator for monitoring forest roe deer populations. *Acta Theriologica* **36** (3–4), 315–28.

Wauters, L. (1995) *Beschermingsplan voor het Reewild*. Criteria voor een verantwoord afschotplan. Antwerpen: U.I.

10

Ungulates and their management in Germany

ULRICH WOTSCHIKOWSKY

Germany is known world wide for its abundance of game. With over 82 million people, the country is one of the most densely populated in the world with a human density of 230 people per km^2. There are 340 000 hunters, which is 0.3% of the German population. On average, about 1.7 million ungulates are harvested every year, amounting to five ungulates for the average hunter. Since World War II, bags of all wild ungulates have increased considerably, despite severe losses of available habitat through settlement, industrialisation, traffic, and agriculture. At present, about 1 km^2 of natural habitat is being lost to such processes every day.

About 160 years ago the situation was different. As a consequence of the revolution of 1848, the rights to hunt were given to German landowners who were mainly farmers. Having suffered from overabundant ungulate populations for centuries when the nobles and clergymen exclusively owned the hunting rights, the farmers nearly wiped out the ungulate populations within a few years. At the end of the nineteenth century a growing number of people interested in hunting and wildlife invented the *Hege* (game wardening) in order to restore ungulate populations. Game management in those times included reintroduction (mainly red deer), control of poaching and general enforcement of the law, introduction of winter feeding, and predator control (however, as wolves and lynx had long since been exterminated, this was no longer an issue).

The concept was quickly adopted by nobles who owned large forests, and also by foresters. In 1931, shortly after the Nazi regime had come to power, a new hunting law called the *Reichsjagdgesetz* was set into practice. With respect to ungulate management the main points of this law were the following:

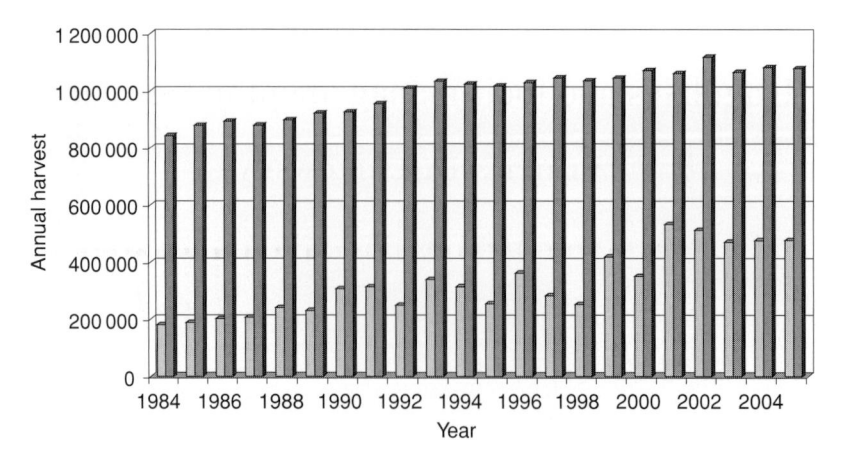

Fig. 10.1 Harvests of roe deer (dark grey) and wild boar (light grey). Roe deer form the staple quarry of German hunters. However, wild boar is rapidly catching up (Deutscher Jagdschutzverband, 2006)

1. The hunting right belongs to the landowner. However, hunting itself was only allowed in a *revier*, a hunting ground with a minimum size of 75 ha and of suitable shape. Landowners with areas too small to form a revier were obliged to join a *Jagdgenossenschaft,* wherein a sufficient number of individual grounds were united to a revier which had to be at least 250 ha in size.
2. Landowners could hunt themselves or lease the right. All hunters had to pass an examination.
3. For the hunting of all ungulate species except wild boar, which was regarded as a pest, an annual shooting plan was required. The plan had to be based on a census, or count of the animals being hunted.
4. All ungulates except wild boar were to be harvested selectively. Selection was by sex and age classes, in order to build up and maintain an even sex ratio and a high percentage of prime age animals. Even within given age- and sex-classes individual animals had to be selected according to their performance and quality. Although, after the end of World War II a new law was established, it did not differ very much from the former *Reichsjagdgesetz*.

10.1 Distribution and status of species present

10.1.1 Roe deer

For the German hunter, roe deer is the staple quarry. In recent years more than one million have been shot each year. According to bag records the number of harvested deer increased markedly from about 567 000 each year in the 1960s to 1.2 million in 2004. Roe deer are found throughout the country up to the upper forest line at 1800 m elevation in the Alps (Fig. 10.1).

These small deer are highly adaptable living in forests, on agricultural land without any trees, close to settlements and even in gardens or parks within cities. The

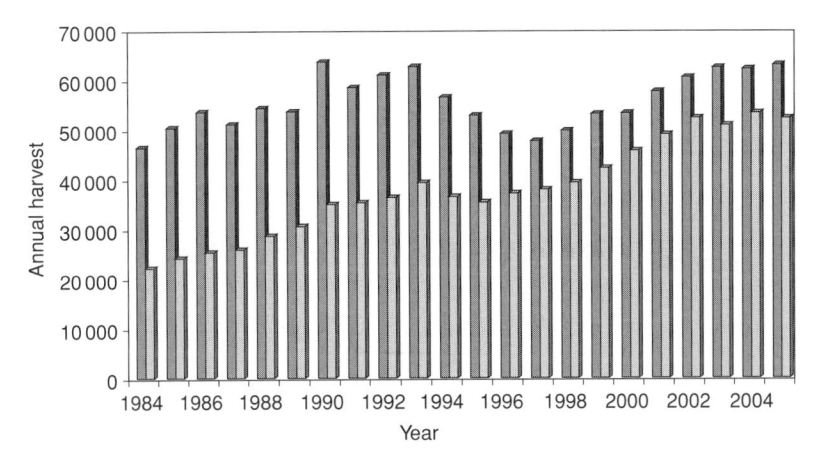

Fig. 10.2 Harvests of red and fallow deer. Overall, the red deer harvests appear to have been stable for the last 20 years. The peak in the early 1990s was caused by efforts to reduce very high populations in the Eastern states of the former German Democratic Republic. Fallow deer populations, on the other hand, are expanding, which is reflected by an increase in harvests (Deutscher Jagdschutzverband, 2006)

highest densities are to be found in areas consisting of a mosaic of forest and meadows. In such habitats, sustainable bags of more than 10 deer per km^2 are common.

Actually estimating the true population size within the country has proven an impossible task. We can only estimate the number of deer by using hunting records and population growth rates. Assuming a net growth rate of only 50% at least 2.2 million roe deer might be living in the country in spring before the hunting season starts.

Little is known about natural mortality. Fawn mortality may be high due to early mowing for silage. Fox numbers are currently high which could also contribute considerably to fawn mortality. Further, perhaps 15% of the annual hunting bag are killed by traffic accidents (Deutscher Jagdschutzverband (DJV), 2006). It is difficult to estimate traffic mortality accurately because an unknown number of deer hit are never found or reported.

10.1.2 Red deer

Since the 1960s, annual red deer harvests increased from about 25 000 to over 50 000. The annual spring population of red deer is estimated to be about 150 000 animals. Red deer are not evenly distributed over the country. Only about 23% of available land is inhabited by red deer (Wotschikowsky and Kern, 2004) and indeed the species is actively confined to specific red deer areas (*Rotwildgebiete*) by law. With a few exceptions deer showing up outside these areas have to be shot. Most of these red deer areas are situated in large forests, mainly owned by the state (Figs. 10.2 and 10.3).

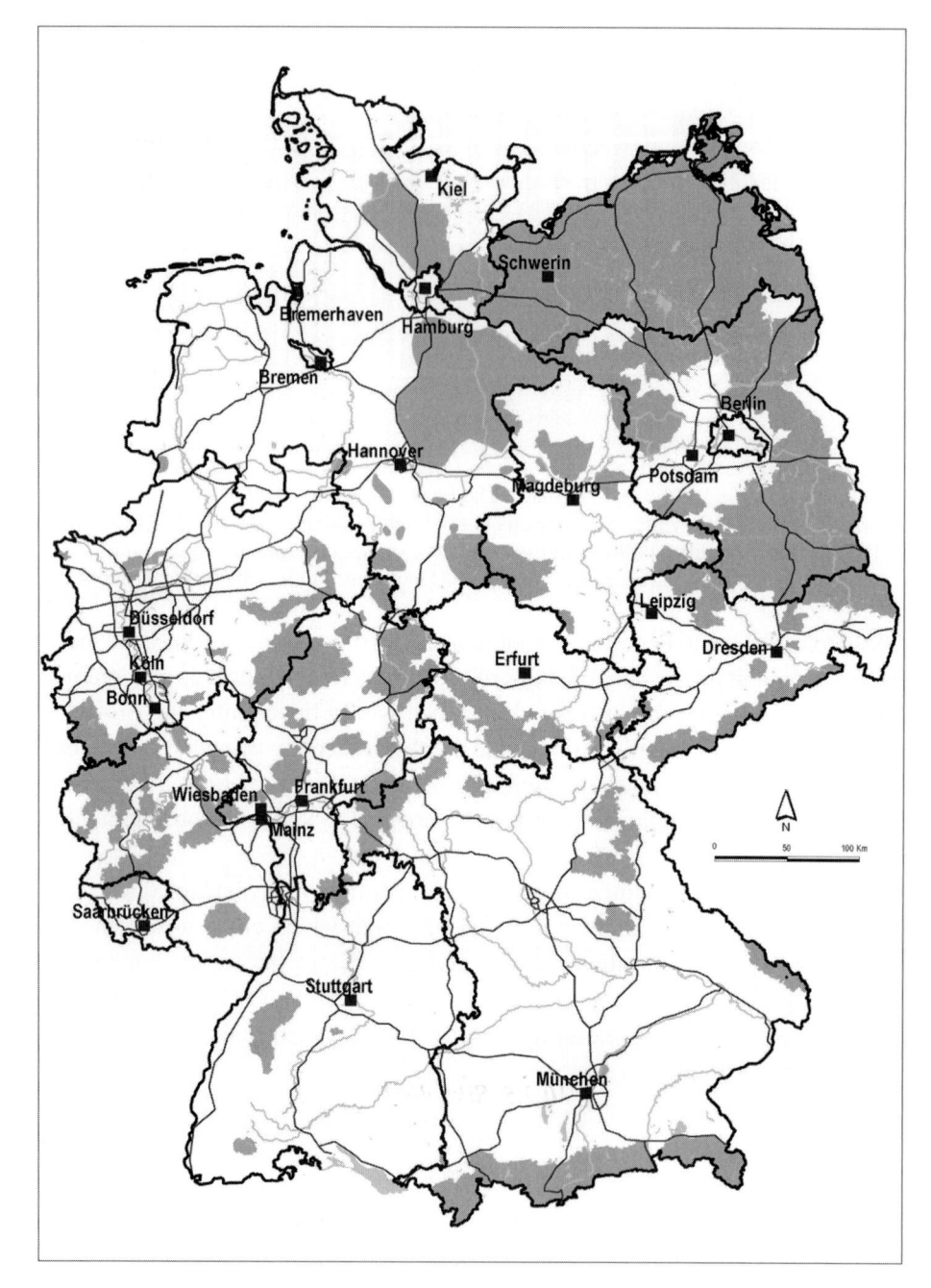

Fig. 10.3 Distribution of red deer. Red deer are restricted to about 23% of Germany. The pattern of distribution shows a large contiguous population in the north-east, while in the southern states, large gaps are showing up in the deer distribution (Wotschikowsky and Kern, 2004)

Natural mortality among red deer is insignificant and calf production is stable at about one calf per hind. Population densities differ considerably from place to place. Estimates based on harvest data show high densities (5–10 deer per km^2) in the western-most states where wealthy leasers pay large amounts for a revier, and in East German areas, where over-abundant populations have not yet been successfully reduced. Lowest densities are around one deer per km^2.

10.1.3 Fallow deer

Native to Turkey, fallow deer were brought to Italy by the Phoenicians long before Christ, and afterwards introduced by the Romans to other European countries. The animals were kept in enclosures and found their way out into the wild where they built up great populations. Today fallow deer is a significant game species mainly in the less-forested land of northern and eastern Germany. About 50 000 fallow deer are harvested annually in the country. Forty years ago, the annual harvests were as low as 6400 animals. Although no distribution maps are available, some idea of actual distribution may be obtained from a map of relative harvest numbers in different states (Figs. 10.2 and 10.4).

10.1.4 Moose

A small number of moose live in the north-east of Germany, connected to a larger population in Poland. There is no open season for the species. The size of the population is unknown, but certainly numbers fewer than 20 animals. In recent years, a few animals from the Czech Republic entered Bavaria. Most of these moose were killed in traffic accidents.

10.1.5 Sika deer

Sika deer (approximately 2500) are not native to Germany. This species is confined to seven small populations, only three of which number more than 100 individuals. The hunting bag amounts to about 1200 deer per year, of a spring population of about 3000 (Deutscher Jagdschutzverband, 2006). As elsewhere within their geographic range, sika interbreed with red deer. Because some sika populations are established close to, or even inside, red deer areas it seems that further hybridisation will be inevitable. However, at least within Germany, the problem is apparently being completely ignored by both hunters and authorities (Wotschikowsky, 2005) (see Fig. 10.5).

Fig. 10.4 Relative density of fallow deer. Increasing shading indicates none, < 10, approximately 20, and approximately 50 animals harvested annually per 10 000 ha, respectively

10.1.6 Wild boar

The wild boar population in Germany is a most striking story of population increase. Although considered a pest animal only 50 years ago and persecuted with the support of bounties into the late 1950s, the annual harvests of today amount to record-high levels. Due to irregular mast years and hard winters, bag records vary a lot, but in the 1960s, the annual harvest was as low as 23 000, and did not exceed 52 000 ten years later. Present-day harvests are now consistently around 500 000

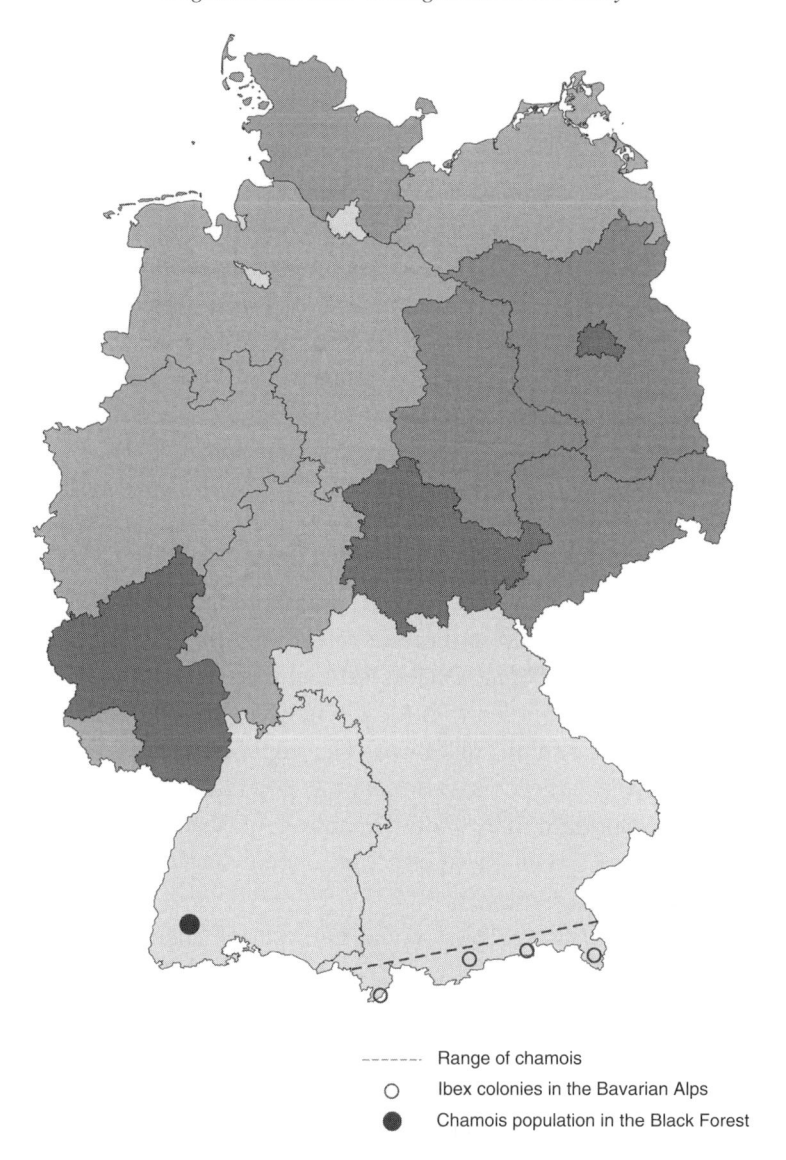

------- Range of chamois
○ Ibex colonies in the Bavarian Alps
● Chamois population in the Black Forest

Fig. 10.5 Mouflon, chamois and ibex. Increasing shading indicates 1–2, 3–5, and 6–8 mouflon harvested annually per 10 000 ha, respectively. The line indicates the range of chamois, the dark spot indicates the isolated Black Forest chamois population. Open dots indicate four ibex populations

animals, annually. A number of factors have been suggested as contributing to this rapid increase, among them winters with little snow, an increasing number and size of corn fields, more frequent mast years, irregular mating patterns, lack of hunting ability, lack of good boar management, and artificial feeding.

Due to the enormous variation of annual growth rates, no estimate can be given for the overall population size in Germany (Fig. 10.1).

In earlier days, wild boar were mainly restricted to large deciduous forests where they were first welcomed by foresters. In areas where agriculture was dominant, however, the species was hunted heavily. Hunters were not required to submit shooting plans and they could hunt boar both day and night, nearly year-round. In the 1980s, wild boar began to spread into poorer habitats like spruce forests and towards Bavaria and Baden-Wurttemberg in Southern Germany, states known for snowy winters. Since the turn of the century, wild boar are even found in the German Alps, as in neighbouring alpine countries of Austria, Switzerland, Italy and France. Today, the species occupies all of Germany, except the alpine region in the South.

10.1.7 Chamois

Chamois is a true alpine ungulate. They are found mainly in the Bavarian Alps. A small population, introduced in the years 1935–40 and numbering about 1200 animals, lives in the Black Forest, Baden-Wurttemberg. A third population, introduced in Saxony near the border with the Czech Republic, no longer exists. The causes of its disappearance are unknown. The population in the Bavarian Alps is connected with the large contiguous alpine population of Austria, Switzerland, France and Northern Italy. After a period of severe reduction in order to prevent damage to mountain forests, the annual harvest today amounts to 4000 animals.

As with other ungulate species, annual harvests of chamois have increased considerably, with fewer than 2000 animals bagged in the 1960s. Assuming a net growth rate of 20% (Knaus and Schröder, 1975), the population size in Bavaria of today may be estimated at about 20 000 animals. As is the case for fallow deer (above) there are no distribution maps available for chamois. However, Figure 10.5 summarises the relative harvest numbers in different states for chamois, ibex and mouflon.

The natural habitat for chamois is the high alpine up to the mountain tops which in Bavaria rarely reach 2500 m a.s.l. Chamois range also includes the forest belt between 1000 and 1800 m.

As a consequence of low harvest in the time after World War II, chamois even occupied the rock-free hills north of the alpine chain and built up high numbers. Since more recent efforts to reduce populations were started, the species has more or less disappeared from these lower elevations. In the Eastern Alps, chamois has repeatedly been subject to sarcoptic mange. Still, the River Inn seems to be an efficient barrier keeping mange from spreading westward (Fig. 10.5).

10.1.8 Ibex

The present ibex in Germany were introduced by hunters and it is questionable whether they ever lived in the Northern Alps. There are four ibex populations in the Bavarian Alps, two of them shared with Tyrol (Austria). They vary greatly in size and, over the long term, numbers appear to be stable at approximately 400 animals. Hunting is generally not permitted. Only recently, one or two single males were allowed to be harvested in order to reduce the local density (Plochmann, *pers. comm.*) (see Fig. 10.5).

10.1.9 Mouflon

Mouflon (13 000) is not a native species in Germany and the present individuals were introduced by hunters or escaped from damaged enclosures. Mouflon are a longstanding matter of concern. Not well adapted to most of the habitats where they have been released, many animals are suffering from problems with their hooves (foot rot, hoof overgrowth; Piegert and Uloth, 2000). Further, mouflon seem to be highly vulnerable to wild predators. Where lynx or wolves have appeared – a recent phenomenon in Germany – mouflon numbers have decreased rapidly, or have even been wiped out (Kluth, *pers. comm.*; Wölfl, unpubl.). For relative densities see Figure 10.5.

10.2 Legislation

As far as the management of wild ungulates is concerned, the basic legislation has not changed much since the *Reichsjagdgesetz* was put into practice in 1931. A major difference to former times, however, may be seen in the fact that within the frame of the federal hunting law, the 16 states of Germany (*Bundesländer*) can have different regulations concerning the length of the hunting seasons, the minimum size for a revier, the formation of larger units of hunting grounds in order to achieve better management (*Hegegemeinschaften*), and more. The main points are as follows:

1. As long as it is alive, game is *res nullius*: it has no owner. As soon as it is dead, it is the property of the person who has exercised the hunting right (not the landowner). Hunting rights belong to the owner of the land, but may be leased to other individuals.
2. Hunting is only allowed in a revier, the minimum size of which differs slightly between the states, but is around 75–80 ha for an area belonging to just one owner, and 250 ha for a group of landowners (*Jagdgenossenschaft*). In the Alps the minimum size is 500 ha.
3. Hunting grounds may be leased. The lease period is 12 years for hunting grounds where red deer are common. The period is 9 years for areas without this species.

Table 10.1 *Hunting seasons for hoofed game in Germany*

Species	Sex/Age	Month
Red deer Sika deer	females ad. female yearlings calves males ad. male yearlings	
Fallow deer	females ad. female yearlings calves males ad. male yearlings	
Roe deer	females ad. female yearlings fawns males yearlings, ad.	15.
Mouflon	all	
Chamois	all	15.
Wild boar	all	16.

Note: The hunting year starts 1 April, which is the point of turnover in the age classes.

4. For all wild ungulates except wild boar an annual harvest plan has to be made which has to be signed by the authorities. The plan has to be fulfilled (see Management objectives).
5. Closed and open seasons are slightly different between states. The main open season lasts through May or June for yearlings of all species, August (red and fallow deer, chamois) and September (roe deer) for females (including their offspring-of-the-year), and for stags from August to the end of January depending on the area (Table 10.1).
6. It is forbidden to hunt during the night (except wild boar), from a vehicle, closer than 200 m to a feeding station, or with the aid of artificial light. Shotguns are not allowed for ungulates.

Due mainly to the rapid expansion of wild boar, some states have introduced special regulations concerning the baiting of game. In some states, winter feeding of all species is strictly forbidden.

10.3 Management objectives

The dominant objective for ungulate management in Germany is the efficient control of population densities in order to prevent intolerable damage to crops and forests. The priority of damage prevention is clearly stated in the federal hunting law: 'Hunting has to be carried out in a way that the demands of agriculture and forestry are not injured' (transl. by the author). Clearly, the interests of farmers and foresters have priority over hunters' interests. Therefore, the question of what population densities are tolerable is a permanent issue of debate among hunters and landowners.

Within this frame, hunters try to ensure high and sustainable harvests of game with a particular emphasis on good trophies. Winter feeding is common, habitat improvement is widespread, and selective culling is obligatory, particularly for red deer.

Further, landowners are eager to make revenue through the leasing of their hunting grounds to hunters. On the other hand, the interests of the general public in seeing or experiencing wildlife are practically non-existent. Wild ungulates, therefore, are not an issue among nature conservation groups like the BUND or the NABU, the two leading conservation institutions. Also, the anti-hunting movement is not strongly active in Germany. The interest groups dealing with wild ungulates may therefore be clearly defined: foresters, farmers, hunters and landowners.

10.4/5 Management structure and organisation

The management of ungulates – planning, harvesting, distribution of venison, and reporting to the authorities – is the duty of the owner or lessor of a given hunting ground or revier. The smallest unit for ungulate management is the individual revier, the size of which may be from 75 to several thousands of hectares, but on average is between 250–350 ha (Wotschikowsky, unpubl.). In practice, in order to achieve effective management of a population of animals in the larger, more mobile species, a number of hunting grounds are organised into a *Hegegemeinschaft* (HG). Depending on the ungulate species a HG may cover 20 000 to 50 000 ha or more. An average size HG for red deer in Germany is about 30 000 ha (Wotschikowsky and Kern, 2004).

In these HGs, shooting plans are discussed and negotiated between all landowners concerned in order to meet the needs of managing widely ranging species. In a few cases other management activities like winter feeding, food improvement, or hunting-free areas may be planned and set into practice. Increasingly, harvest plans are being made at the level of the HG, and then the planned quotas are being distributed among the individual Reviers.

These annual harvest plans (whether at the level of the individual Revier, or the Hegegemeinschaft) must be approved by the regional authorities who also collect from the Revier holders harvest reports. An annual shooting plan is required for all ungulate species, except wild boar. The plan has to be based on the status of the forest vegetation and on a fair estimate of the population size and composition. Because selective hunting is required the numbers of game to be shot have to be planned separately for the different age and sex classes. The plans are discussed among the hunters of the HG and finally approved by the local authority (*Untere Jagdbehörde*). At the end of the hunting season, the total number of game harvested is to be reported to the authority.

We might note, however, that in practice there is no real mechanism for enforcement of this requirement for a shooting plan or harvest report.

10.4/5.1 Qualification for hunting

Any person wishing to hunt has to go through a hunting course lasting about 120 hours and additional practice with rifle and shotgun, after which he/she must take a hunting examination. This entitles him/her to buy a hunting licence, including insurance (app. 60 EURO per year), which may be compared to a car driver's licence in that it simply certifies that he/she is eligible to shoot game. Actually to go out hunting on any hunting ground, he/she must then have the permission of the holder of the revier (or hunting concession). He/she himself is only qualified to lease a hunting ground (revier) in his/her own right after three years of hunting practice.

10.4/5.2 Costs and prices for hunting

Leasing prices for a revier differ widely according to regions, states and wildlife species being hunted. Highest prices are to be found in the densely inhabited western states like Rhineland-Palatinat, Northrhine-Westfalia and Hessen, especially when red deer are abundant. Average prices per year and hectare amount to EUR 20 (Renneke, 2004). In some extreme cases, a leaser may pay as much as EUR 50–100. This amount will not cover all costs. The leaser also has to pay for damage by deer and wild boar to crops and forest, which itself may amount to a similar sum of money. In the eastern German states, however, with low human population density, lower income, and not as well developed infrastructure, leasing prices may be as low as EUR 3–5.

Only a relatively small percentage of German hunters actually lease their own revier. Most hunters get a chance of hunting for free or for moderate prices from a friend who is a leaser. Or they buy a permit in a state forest close by where they may hunt on a certain piece of land and where they have a quota of game to harvest. Prices vary widely, but are affordable for any hunter with average income.

10.6 Actual management practices

In Germany, the hunting of wild ungulates is carried out by many different methods. Hunting from a high seat (*Ansitzjagd*) is the preferred one. In winter, it is often combined with baiting the immediate area around the high seat (*Kirrung*), particularly for wild boar, but increasingly for red and roe deer as well. Stalking of game (*Pirschjagd*) has become less common. It is the preferred method for hunting chamois in the mountains. Combined with simulated roaring it is also successfully practised while hunting red deer stags during the rut.

Later in the season different types of drive hunts are used. In former times only a small number of beaters and only few hounds were used. The number of hounds has markedly increased because of the high costs of beaters during the last years, particularly in large forests, where the control of deer with high seat hunting has become increasingly inefficient. These hunts demand good planning and organisation on large areas. There are often as many as 50–80 hunters, 20–40 hounds and fewer than five beaters. These drive hunts are only feasible after the leaves have fallen by mid-October, and they can only be carried out in sufficiently large forested grounds with no or low traffic. On such grounds, up to 50% of the annual bag may be killed using drive hunts. On small private hunting grounds, however, close to 100% of the game may be harvested via high seat hunting.

10.6.1 Selective hunting

In order to build up and maintain populations with even sex ratios and a high average age, German hunters pay great attention to selective hunting. Populations with such a composition will allow for a high number of prime animals with good trophies to be harvested. In former times, hunters believed also that they could improve the genetic status of a population through selective hunting. This concept was invented and in practice during the Third Reich, but has long since been abandoned. However, it is still in the mind of quite a number of hunters and has even left its mark in current legislation.

10.6.2 Introduction, reintroduction and restocking

All mouflon and sika populations in Germany originate from introductions. Introduction of mouflon was particularly common in the former communist part of Germany but ended after the re-union (Piegert and Uloth, 2000). Further, two chamois populations were founded by introduction (see section on chamois).

Because all native ungulate species except red deer are still abundant and widespread, reintroduction or restocking is not an issue at this time. Red deer have lost more than 70% of their former range in Germany. The species would readily occupy all suitable habitats if the hunting rules were changed to dispersal. However, authorities stick to the concept of red deer areas and red deer free areas preventing deer from enlarging their present distribution. There is only one red deer reintroduction currently happening in Germany, in the Isarauen north of Munich (Fischer and Wotschikowsky, 2004).

Red deer are a special case from a genetic point of view. Because red deer were close to disappearing in Germany 150 years ago, they were introduced from different areas to build up stocks again. Other red deer were introduced specifically to improve quality of trophies (Kleymann, 1976). Today, the red deer in Germany are a mixture of different genetic strains from a variety of different sources.

10.7 Census and monitoring

10.7.1 Census

Counting ungulates in the field has long since been proven impracticable. However, it took quite a time for authorities and hunters to accept this fact. Because game today is abundant all over Germany and the danger of overhunting is practically non-existent, there is no need for accurate censusing of ungulate populations. Therefore, no attempts are made within Germany to census game directly today. Shooting plans are based on recent harvest records and on the amount of damage to forest regrowth and forest stands.

For red deer one may calculate the population size by multiplying the annual harvest by a factor 2.5. This procedure is based on the assumption that a population with a sex ratio slightly skewed in favour of females (which is normal) and with a normal age distribution will produce about 40% offspring, and further, that natural mortality in red deer in Germany is close to zero. If the annual harvest remained stable for a number of years and the bag records are correct, the results may be sufficient for planning purposes.

The same procedure, however seldom set into practice, may be useful for fallow deer and sika deer, because population parameters are similar. For chamois, a factor of 5 is used, assuming high natural winter mortality. All species named above have little variation in offspring rates (just one offspring per adult female), which is a great advantage for such estimations. For roe deer and wild boar, the procedure cannot be recommended.

10.7.2 Hunting bag records

As mentioned earlier, all hoofed game harvested has to be reported to the hunting authorities (*Untere Jagdbehörde*). On a state basis, the German Hunting Association (*Deutscher Jagdschutzverband, DJV*) publishes the results every year. For smaller units, however, statistics are seldom published. Further, because even those reports which are submitted are not being checked, their validity remains questionable.

Leasing prices are influenced by the number of game harvested, so the leaser may be reluctant to report high bags. On the other hand, some leasers avoid harvesting females (however, report bags), in order to maintain (as they believe) a more productive population.

10.8 Damage and damage prevention

All ruminant ungulates may cause considerable damage to forest plants by bark stripping and browsing. Wild boar, red and fallow deer may also cause damage to crops. In a country as intensively cultivated and densely inhabited by humans, it is easy to see why damage prevention plays a significant role in wildlife management in Germany, where there are almost no large predators.

10.8.1 Damage to crops

Wild boar cause by far the most damage to crops. The main damage is to cornfields and meadows, and to a lesser degree potato or oat crops. The increasing size of cornfields is a particular problem. Wild boar can hide in these large fields for months, making it impossible to hunt or even disturb them. In some parts of the country landowners are finding it more and more difficult to lease their hunting grounds because the required compensation for damage caused by wild boar exceeds the price for the lease.

Although red and fallow deer can also cause great damage to crops, these deer are far less involved. Occasionally large herds can destroy oats, corn, rape and other fields. However, they are much easier to drive away using appropriate measures.

Damage caused by hoofed game has to be compensated for by the *Jagdgenossenschaft* (the community of the landowners of a revier), but usually, the compensation is regulated in the lease contract, with the result that the leaser will have to pay. In the case that landowner and leaser cannot agree on the amount of damage, they may call an official damage estimator *(Wildschadensschätzer)*. No compensation is paid for landowners who execute the hunting themselves.

10.8.2 Bark stripping

The primary problem of today's red deer management is damage caused by bark stripping. Although foresters claim that this is mainly due to too many deer more factors are involved. Bark stripping over winter is said to have decreased considerably, but at the same time appears to have increased during early summer. The decrease in winter may be caused through a considerable reduction of densities and through improved feeding methods, especially avoiding fodder rich in energy and protein (see for example Ueckermann, 1983; Pheiffer & Hartfiel, 1984). In the Alps, the practice of luring deer into enclosures over winter, where food may be provided, has undoubtedly led to a significant decline in damage.

In summer both increasing tourism and high hunting pressure are being blamed for increased damage to bark. Foresters argue that deer do not longer dare to leave the forest during daylight and therefore have to feed inside.

10.8.3 Browsing damage

All ruminating game may cause damage to young forest stands by browsing. Over the country as a whole, browsing pressure is considered generally high according to most foresters. In 1986, a programme of forest damage monitoring was initiated in the state of Bavaria, followed by all states in the years thereafter. Every three years the amount of browsing is measured. Methods differ between states and therefore it is impossible to compare the amount of damage between them. In most cases, the number of bitten topshoots is counted and calculated as a percentage of the entire sample. Because this method does not indicate how many plants are on a given area altogether, the further development of the forest cannot be predicted. In red deer areas, an inventory of bark stripping may also (however, not necessarily) be carried out. For details, see Moog (2008). However, no discrimination is made in terms of which species are causing the damage. In Bavaria the highest browsing pressure is in areas known for their high roe deer densities, and only rarely in red deer areas. Overall, browsing damage is significantly higher in private hunting grounds than in state forests (Bayerische Forstverwaltung, 2006).

10.8.4 Prevention of damage

In the past, a number of measures to prevent ungulates from browsing and bark stripping have been practised. Most widespread was fencing. However, this is no longer feasible, because of the high costs for labour. Further, it is required by law that natural re-growth is not seriously hindered by wildlife. Therefore, the only means of damage prevention is adjusting the density of ungulates to the demands of the landowners.

10.8.5 Road traffic accidents

According to statistics from insurance companies, 96–98% of accidents involve hoofed game and 2–4% involve the police, road traffic accidents have increased four-fold during the past 30 years, from about 59 000 in 1975 to about 227 000 in 2005. However, the number of fatally injured people remained stable at around

20 per year. Ungulate species involved are approximately 180 000 roe deer, 13 700 wild boar, 3000 fallow deer, and 2000 red deer (Kerzel, 2005). The economic value of accidents caused by wildlife amounts to EUR 447 000 annually (DJV, 2007).

In recent years, people have become increasingly concerned about the fragmentation of wildlife habitats through highways. The discussion increased shortly after the reunion, when road constructions were planned through the former German Democratic Republic towards Eastern Europe. However, while great efforts have been undertaken to help amphibians to cross roads and fish to migrate upstream, hardly anything has been done to support large mammals. Just 23 green bridges exist on approximately 12 000 km of highway (DJV, 2007). At present, the focus is on isolated red deer populations, but also the small growing populations of lynx and wolves have attracted attention in this aspect. Both the hunters' association and the NABU, in a rare case of action side-by-side, are claiming that highways should be made passable for wildlife through construction of green bridges and/or underpasses (Georgii *et al.*, 2007).

10.9 Supplementary feeding and habitat improvement

Supplementary winter feeding of deer – both red and roe deer, but not chamois and wild boar – has been a tradition in Germany for more than a century. It is subject to a permanent debate among hunters, foresters and naturalists, although not among wildlife biologists! Although the usefulness of supplementary feeding has repeatedly been either supported or questioned (Arnold, 2002; Putman and Staines, 2004), the federal hunting law still claims that 'prevention of fatigue' is an essential part of game wardening. As a consequence, most state hunting laws specifically require the provision of winter feed, including feeding stations, during times of fatigue (*'Notzeit'*). The reasons behind this tradition of feeding deer in the wintertime are manifold. Feeding was developed in red deer management more than one hundred years ago, when revier holders began feeding primarily in order to prevent deer leaving their hunting ground and being shot elsewhere. Within its large hunting grounds in the Alps the royal family of Bavaria played a significant role in the initiation and development of this management tool. Soon, feeding became a kind of a status symbol of revier holders who demonstrated that they were first wardens of wildlife, and not shooters.

Later, wildlife managers claimed that feeding is essential to prevent deer from causing damage to forests. Among hunters, this is the dominating opinion still today. However, feeding was, and still is, very often accompanied by high densities of deer, and at the same time accompanied by severe damage by bark stripping.

A closer look at habitat quality and deer species may give a variety of answers to whether or not winter feeding is appropriate:

Red deer in the Alps, and also in some mountainous areas elsewhere, have lost virtually all their winter habitat to settlement, agriculture and traffic. Forests along the Alpine rivers were the preferred winter habitats in the past. These natural forests have disappeared or have been changed to even-aged spruce forests or fields. Red deer migration is no longer possible. Therefore, winter feeding is regarded as a substitute for lost winter habitat. Without the supplementary feeding of red deer in winter, there would be intolerable damage to the forests or deer would have to be reduced to very low densities.

Despite supplementary feeding red deer have caused a lot of forest damage around feeding stations. It became obvious that the critical time is the 'brown' period – between the white (with snow cover, during which the deer have a reduced demand for food and are easily kept close to the feeding stations) and the green (when vegetation starts to grow and the deer's food intake increases rapidly; Arnold, 2002).

In order to prevent damage to the forest during this critical period, winter enclosures for red deer have become a widespread tool in the Alps. The deer are held there throughout the winter, and they are not allowed to leave before the onset of new green vegetation.

Winter feeding was recently forbidden by law in some states. In many state-owned hunting grounds elsewhere, winter feeding has been abandoned particularly where roe deer are abundant. Hunters on private lands, on the other hand, still feed deer intensively. However, during the feeding period, hunting is not allowed within 200 m around a feeding station.

Besides winter feeding, there is also summer feeding of wild boar, in order to attract the animals to forest sites and distract them from agricultural crops. Although not obligatory, it is common practice not to hunt close to such places; however, baiting at high seats is increasingly being used to attract and shoot game of all species.

10.9.1 Baiting

Besides winter feeding, baiting (*kirrung*) of deer and wild boar is playing an increasingly important role in the hunting of ungulates. This has strongly been enhanced by the spread of wild boar. Hunting of this species and baiting, including hunting during night, have long since been tightly connected to each over. In recent years, however, baiting has increasingly been abused, as great amounts of feed have been laid out in order to attract boar; this practice has more and more influenced the management of red deer as well. Biologists argue that the great input of feed into the system is supporting the fertility of boar and therefore is becoming part of the problem (too high wild boar densities). Indeed, the amount of feed for baiting is tremendous, often exceeding 100 kg per boar bagged (Elliger *et al.*, 2001). People concerned about the management of red deer in turn argue that increasing night hunting of deer is causing lots of trouble with this species (Wotschikowsky *et al.*, 2005). As a result, some states (e.g. Rhineland-Palatinat) have restricted the amount of feed and the number of baiting places. Revier holders have now to report the baiting places to the authorities.

10.9.2 Habitat improvements

Many German hunters believe that deer lack natural food in today's forests. Improvement of food conditions is a permanent issue, particularly in red deer management. Therefore, some hunters may spend a lot of effort to improve meadows by mowing and fertilisation, or by leasing agricultural land for the use of wildlife. However, keeping in mind the home range sizes of red deer, such attempts are only useful on large hunting grounds, and are therefore mainly undertaken by the few leasers who command such grounds. In the state forests, which command by far the largest red deer areas, habitat improvement for deer is considered counter-productive to the present forest policy, which is not in favour of sustaining or supporting deer by any means.

It is, in any case, perhaps questionable if Germany's landscape is poor in food for deer. Due to intensive agriculture, short harvest cycles of timber, and input of nitrogen from industrial emission, the land is offering abundant food for all herbivores. The record-high hunting bags seem to suggest that food is abundant.

10.10 Ungulate management in Germany: crucial points for the future

Germany is a country rich in wildlife, and despite high human population density with a lot of negative consequences for wildlife and hunting, many hunters regard it as near paradise. Nevertheless, there are a number of issues that need discussion and solutions. However, one has to be aware that, right now, wild ungulates are not being ranked high in the mind of German society. Therefore, ideas on how to improve the management of these species are not given priority.

10.10.1 The permanent conflict between forest and deer

As long as foresters and hunters have different objectives this conflict will persist. In the author's view, the foresters have failed to explain what a natural forest (experiencing 'normal' pressures from 'acceptable' populations of browsing herbivores) should look like, in terms of numbers and dimensions of trees in reach of deer.

Therefore, the monitoring system should be improved, in order not only to demonstrate the amount of damage, but also in order to show the expected development of the forest stands in question (Moog, 2008).

10.10.2 Hunting bag monitoring

The current bag records are highly questionable. For example, red deer stags are being shot in excess, but not reported, resulting in skewed sex ratios in favour of females. Red deer females are not being harvested sufficiently, with the same result, and additionally in an increase of population density. Authorities are failing in their efforts to reduce over-abundant game populations, because they do not execute any control of the game harvested. There is an urgent need to develop efficient methods to check whether the reports are reliable, e.g. through the use (and control) of tags. Control is necessary for sound management of wildlife, including the quality of statistical data. The current lack of control makes it easy for leasers to cheat the local authorities, landowners, leasers of neighbouring hunting grounds, and, last but not least, the public.

10.10.3 Management of red deer

Initially, the concept of 'red deer areas' and 'red deer-free areas' was developed in order to protect red deer-free areas from the damage which might be caused by deer. From hindsight, it is difficult to understand why some landowners should bear the burden of keeping red deer, and others not. Seen from a viewpoint of species conservation, the idea of red deer-free areas cannot be justified at all. Further, the concept has not improved the situation of red deer in Germany. Instead, the idea has been abused to declare former red deer areas as red deer-free, as soon as overhunting had led to the local extermination of stock. Neither has this concept solved any problem with deer in forests. It should be abandoned.

Red deer should be managed under the authority of *Hegegemeinschaften*, which means in greater units than single hunting grounds with the help of professionals, and with all interest groups involved in the decision-making process (Wotschikowsky *et al.*, 2005). It should exclusively be harvested on the basis of harvest plans. Control by authorities should be intensified, as explained above.

10.10.4 Management of wild boar

Most hunting of wild boar is carried out during the night at bait stations. Given recent recorded increases in populations, it is questionable whether this method is efficient enough. Night hunting should be restricted as much as possible, in favour of hunting boar in large areas with well organised hunts. Feeding and even baiting should be kept at a minimum.

10.10.5 Hunting methods, seasons and practices

Because of prolonged hunting seasons, night hunting, and overall high hunting pressure, all hoofed game species have become unusually shy. The non-hunting public hardly has a chance to see wildlife, and hunting itself has become more and more difficult, resulting in increased damage. There is an urgent need to develop hunting methods and practices which involve less disturbance to the wildlife. This includes shorter open seasons, more efficient hunting methods, adjustment of seasons (e.g. equal seasons for all age and sex classes found in the same locality), and abandonment of some traditional restrictions due to trophy hunting. An example is a closed season for roe bucks from 16 October onwards, while females and fawns are being hunted until the end of January.

10.10.6 Winter feeding

Most of the justifications of winter feeding offered in Section 9 no longer hold in present times. Winter feeding may seriously alter spacing behaviour, local densities, hunting opportunities, and damage to forest and agricultural crops by red deer, fallow deer, wild boar, and, to a lesser degree even roe deer. Winter feeding of all hoofed game should therefore be reconsidered. In any case, it should be based on a plan of the *Hegegemeinschaft*, in order to prevent abuse by individual revier holders. A thorough analysis of winter enclosures is urgently needed, in order to solve increasing conflicts with deer entering the enclosures early, and also to prevent leaseholders keeping high red deer densities.

10.10.7 Ungulates in nature reserves

Although quite a number of large nature reserves and national parks have been established in recent years, there are no plans or concepts about how to handle ungulates in these areas. Such concepts should be developed on a federal basis in agreement with international rules for nature reserves.

10.10.8 Ungulates and large carnivores

Slowly but surely, large carnivores like wolf and lynx are making their way back to Germany. Future management of ungulates needs to take into account predators in order to minimise the inevitable conflicts with hunters and landowners.

Acknowledgements

I thank Bob Hayes for valuable comments and for improving the language, and Kerstin Guggemoos for providing data.

References

Arnold, W. (2002) Der verborgene Winterschlaf des Rotwildes. *Der Anblick* **2**, 2002, Graz.
Bayerische Forstverwaltung (2006) www.forst.bayern.de/jagd_in_bayern/ verbissgutachten.
DJV (Deutscher Jagdschutzverband) (2006) *DJV Handbuch*. Bonn.
DJV (Deutscher Jagdschutzverband) (2007) *DJV Handbuch*. Bonn.
Elliger, A., Linderoth, P., Pegel, M., and Seitler, S. (2001) *Ergebnisse einer landesweiten Befragung zur Schwarzwildbewirtschaftung*. Wildforschungsstelle des Landes Baden-Württemberg, Nr. 4/2001.
Fischer, A. and Wotschikowsky, U. (2004) *Wald und Schalenwild in den Isarauen*. Forstliche Forschungsberichte München Nr. 197.
Georgii, B., Peters-Ostenberg, E., Henneberg, M., et al. (2007) *Nutzung von Grünbrücken und anderen Querungsbauwerken durch Säugetiere*. Bundesministerium für Verkehr, Bau und Stadtentwicklung Bonn, Heft 971.
Kerzel, H. (2005) *Wildunfälle: Zur Notwendigkeit von Verkehrsschutzzäunen und Grünbrücken*. In *Grünbrücken für den Biotopverbund*. Schriftenreihe des Landesjagdverbandes Bayern e. V., Band **14**. ISBN: 978-3-00-020669-6.
Kleymann, M. (1976) Beiträge zur Kenntnis der Infrastrukturen beim Rotwild, I. Zur Entwicklung und gegenwärtigen Situation der Rotwildbestände in der Bundesrepublik Deutschland. III. Zur genetischen Struktur von Rotwildpopulationen anhand von Blutgruppenvergleichsuntersuchungen. *Zeitschrift fur Jagdwissenschaf.* **22**. Hamburg, Germany: Parey.
Knaus, W. and Schröder, W. (1975) *Das Gamswild*. 2. Hamburg, Germany: Parey.
Moog, M. (2008) *Bewertung von Wildschäden im Wald*. Germany: Neumann-Neudamm Verlag.
Pheiffer, V. and Hartfiel, W. (1984) Beziehungen zwischen der Winterfutterung und dem Schälverhalten des Rotwildes in der Eifel. *Zeitschrift für Jagdwissenschaft* **30**, 243–55.
Piegert, H. and Uloth, W. (2000) *Der Europäische Mufflon*. Hamburg, Germany: Nature Life.
Putman, R. J. and Staines, B. W. (2004) Supplementary winter feeding of wild red deer *Cervus elaphus* in Europe and North America: justifications, feeding practice and effectiveness. *Mammal Review* **34**, 285–306.
Renneke, R. M. (2004) *Die Determinanten des Jagdpachtpreises*. Melsunger, Germany: Melsungen Neumann-Neudamm.
Ueckermann, E. (1983) The effects of various feed components on the extent of bark-stripping by red deer. *Zeitschrift für Jagdwissenschaft* **29**, 31–47.
Wotschikowsky, U. (2005) *Wildtiermanagement im Forstamt Arnsberg*. Report, unpublished.
Wotschikowsky, U. and Kern, M. (2004) *Rotwildverbreitung in Deutschland*. Hamburg, Germany: Deutsche Wildtier Stiftung.
Wotschikowsky, U., Simon, O., Herzog, S. and Elmauer, K. (2005) *Ein Leitbild für das Rotwild in Deutschland*. Hamburg, Germany: Deutsche Wildtier Stiftung.

11

Ungulates and their management in Poland

PIOTR WAWRZYNIAK, WŁODZIMIERZ JĘDRZEJEWSKI,
BOGUMIŁA JĘDRZEJEWSKA AND TOMASZ BOROWIK

Poland lies in the zone of temperate deciduous and mixed (nemoral and hemiboreal) forests that in historical times harboured the richest European community of wild ungulates. The country's topography is mainly of low-lying plains with 91% of the territory below 300 m a.s.l. Uplands (300–500 m a.s.l.) cover 6% and mountains (501–2499 m a.s.l.) 3% of the country. Open landscapes under various forms of agriculture dominate (altogether 60%, mostly arable fields with smaller shares of meadows, pastures and orchards). The mean density of human population is 124 inhabitants/km^2 (Statistical Yearbook of the Republic of Poland, 2002).

Forests cover 29% of the land area (Fig. 11.1). Most of the forests are state-owned, with a smaller fraction of private woods (17% of all forest area). Long-term promotion of Scots pine (*Pinus silvestris*) by forestry has led to a strong overrepresentation of that species in Polish forests; pine-dominated stands grow on 69% of all forests' area. Other species cover, respectively, spruce (*Picea abies*) 5%, beech (*Fagus sylvatica*) 5%, birch (*Betula verrucosa* and *B. pubescens*) 6%, black alder (*Alnus glutinosa*) 4%, oak (*Quercus robur*) and ash (*Fraxinus excelsior*) combined 7% (Leśnictwo, 2005). The average age of tree stands is about 50 yrs, with a high share of young age classes (0–20 yrs, 11% of all forests; 21–40 yrs, 18%). A total of 23 national parks (from 21.5 to 592.2 km^2) cover 1% of the country.

Apart from forest cover and structure, the most important natural variables affecting ungulate populations in Poland are climate and presence or absence of large predators. The country is located in the zone of temperate climate, transitional between Atlantic and continental types, with mean temperatures in January ranging from 0–1°C along the Baltic coast and in the western part of the country, to −5.5°C in the north-east and −7°C in the mountains (the Carpathians and Sudety Mts in the south). Mean temperature in July ranges from 10°C in the mountains, to

Fig. 11.1 Distribution of forests in Poland. Forests cover 29% of the country's area. Map courtesy of the General Directorate of State Forests, Warsaw

16.5°C at the coast and 19°C in the south-west. Mean annual precipitation averages 500–650 mm.

Three species of large carnivores occur in Poland (all with the status of protected species): the brown bear *Ursus arctos* in the Carpathian Mountains (southern verge of the country), and wolf *Canis lupus* and Eurasian lynx *Lynx lynx* largely in eastern and southeastern Poland (Jakubiec and Buchalczyk, 1987; Jędrzejewski *et al.*, 2002a, 2004; Niedziałkowska *et al.*, 2006).

Traditions of ungulate hunting regulated by the hunting legislation date back to the twelfth century, when ungulates, *animalia superiora*, used to be subjects of *venatio magna*, the royal and ducal hunts (Samsonowicz, 1991). Legislation regarding strict protection of megaherbivores, the auroch *Bos primigenius* and European bison *Bison bonasus*, was issued in the sixteenth century (Samojlik, 2005). Indeed, the last wild-living populations of those two species survived in Poland: the aurochs survived until 1627 in Jaktorów Forest, central Poland, and the bison until 1919 in Białowieża Forest (Heymanowski, 1972; Pucek, 2004; Vuure, 2005).

Table 11.1 *Official statistics on population numbers (N, in thousands) and annual hunting bag (bag, in thousands) of five species of the most common game ungulates in Poland in 1975–2005. Sources of data: Forestry statistical yearbooks, 1975–2005*

Year	Red deer N	Red deer Bag	Roe deer N	Roe deer Bag	Wild boar N	Wild boar Bag	Moose N	Moose Bag	Fallow deer N	Fallow deer Bag
1975	44	10	300	47	50	40	3.3	0.6	2.6	0.3
1980	73	19	400	54	85	80	5.8	1.1	4.0	0.4
1985	74	39	480	128	57	77	4.4	1.3	4.1	1.1
1990	92	54	550	167	80	122	5.4	1.5	5.4	1.7
1995	100	49	515	151	81	76	3.1	0.5	7.5	2.5
2000	117	41	597	155	118	92	2.1	0.3	9.1	1.8
2005	141	39	692	151	173	136	3.9	0	13.1	3.0

Currently, six indigenous species (European bison, moose, red deer, roe deer, wild boar and chamois) live in Poland in the wild as well as three non-native species of ungulates (fallow deer, sika deer and mouflon). The large-scale habitat features of the country (lowland temperate forests, woodland–agriculture mosaic) mean that the three species, roe deer, wild boar and red deer, are by far the most numerous in both estimated populations and the hunting harvest (Table 11.1).

11.1 Ungulate species present, their distribution and abundance

11.1.1 Moose

In Poland, moose reaches the south-western border of its geographical range (Fig. 11.2). Archaeological data showed that during the Holocene, until medieval times, moose occurred in the whole territory of contemporary Poland, and its range began to shrink in the late Middle Ages (Wyrost, 1989, see also Schmölcke and Zachos, 2005). The lowest numbers of moose were recorded in the 1930s: within the current boundaries of Poland there were only eight animals surviving in the basin of Biebrza River (Korsak, 1934). In 1950, 18 animals lived in Poland. In 1951, five moose were brought from the Soviet Union (Belarus) to the Kampinos National Park (central Poland). In the following decades, spontaneous immigration of moose from Lithuania, Belarus and Ukraine was recorded (Dzięciołowski and Pielowski, 1993). In Poland, the continuous growth of moose population took place till the 1980s, when about 5000 moose were counted (Table 11.1). However, overharvesting of the population caused its rapid decline to a minimum of about 2000 individuals recorded in 2000. A temporary ban on hunting, introduced in 2001, resulted in a slow recovery of moose population.

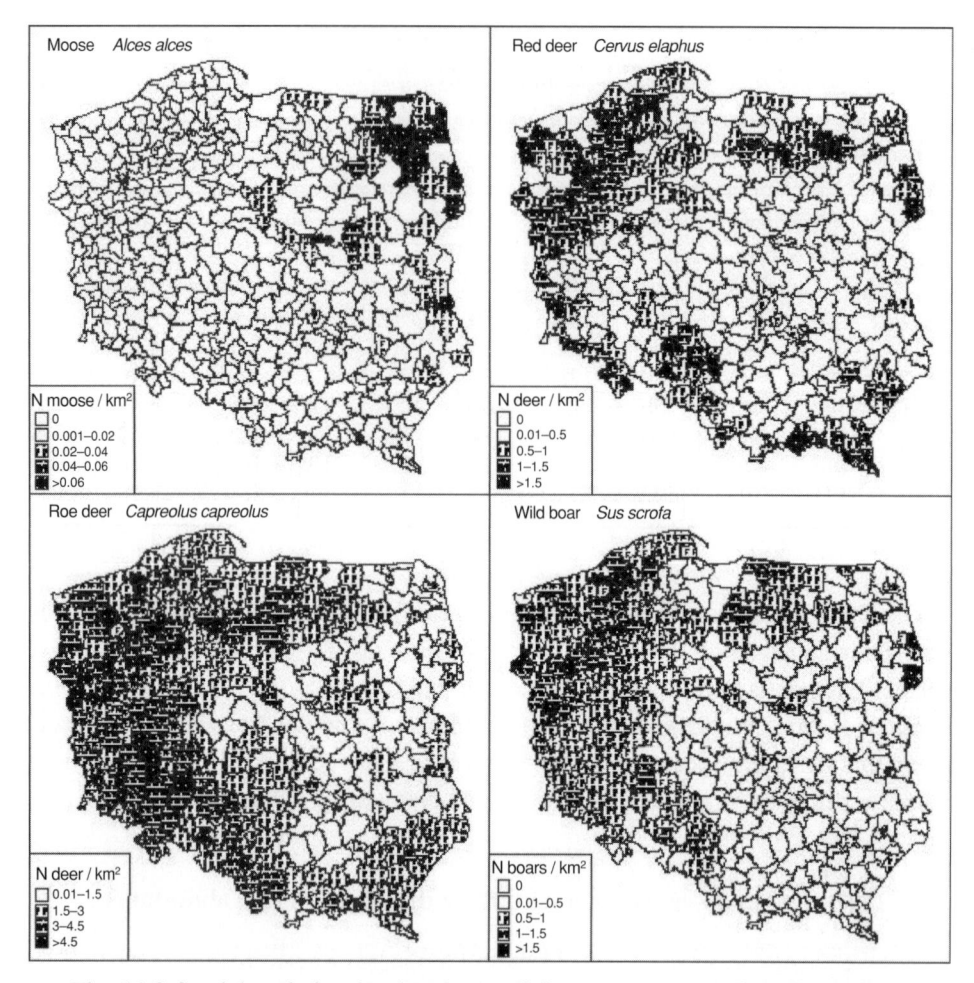

Fig. 11.2 Spatial variation in abundance of four common species of ungulates (red deer *Cervus elaphus*, roe deer *Capreolus capreolus*, wild boar *Sus scrofa*, and moose *Alces alces*) in Poland. Units are districts of Polish state forests (440) and national parks (23). Numbers of ungulates are based on game inventories conducted in 1998–2004; they are relative indices of abundance and not the absolute densities. From W. Jędrzejewski and T. Borowik, unpublished, based on data provided by the Administration of Forest Districts and National Parks

Typical habitats of moose are wet, river-side forests, open marshes, and adjacent pine forests. In Poland, the best habitats for the species are found in the Biebrza National Park and Poleski National Park, where they reach the highest densities of 1–2 individuals/km^2 (Sieńko, 2004; Piasecki, 2004). Since wolves, which in Poland have easy access to their preferred prey – the red deer – take moose as secondary prey, only (Jędrzejewski and Kowalczyk, 2005), the major factor affecting moose population is the hunting harvest by humans. In recent years, it has also been proposed that interspecific competition with other ungulates, in particular, the increasing population of red deer, may be detrimental to moose (Jędrzejewska *et al.*, 1997; Gębczyńska and Raczyński, 2005).

11.1.2 Red deer

Red deer have been present in the area which is now Poland since Mesolithic times (Wyrost, 1989). However, the Little Ice Age (significant cooling of climate with a minimum in the seventeenth and early eighteenth century; Luterbacher *et al.*, 2001) caused a decline and, in many north-eastern regions of Poland, eventually a disappearance of this species (e.g. Brincken, 1826). The contemporary Polish population is a result of many reintroductions conducted throughout the late nineteenth and twentieth centuries (Karcov, 1903; Dzięgielewski, 1970). Generally, the most important sources of relocations were from Germany, Bohemia, Silesia and Pomerania to central and eastern Poland.

The Carpathian Mountains may harbour the only remaining indigenous population of red deer (comp. Feulner *et al.*, 2004). In the twentieth century, red deer suffered from heavy poaching during the times of wars (Jędrzejewska *et al.*, 1997).

Currently, the red deer occurs in the whole of Poland except for the region around Warsaw (Fig. 11.2). Its abundance, however, greatly varies and is positively correlated with percentage forest cover: deer are more numerous in densely wooded regions of the Carpathian Mountains, north-east, north-west and south-west regions of the country than in central Poland with little forest cover (see Fig. 11.1). The official statistics on game populations, though hardly reliable as regards the absolute numbers of deer, correctly reflect the trend of growing population numbers in the last decades (Table 11.1). Red deer is the third most important large game species in Poland after roe deer and wild boar in terms of both estimated numbers and harvest quotas (Table 11.1).

Local, late winter densities of red deer assessed by more rigorous censuses (driving counts) varied from 0.6 to 12.7 deer/km^2 (Pucek *et al.*, 1975; Jędrzejewska *et al.*, 1994; Dzięciołowski *et al.*, 1995). Local densities are positively correlated with the proportion of deciduous tree stands in the forest, which has been interpreted as reflecting the higher supply of food, especially the preferred deciduous browse (Bobek *et al.*, 1984; Jędrzejewska *et al.*, 1994). In eastern Poland, wolf and lynx are major factors of red deer mortality (Okarma *et al.*, 1997; Jędrzejewska and Jędrzejewski, 1998; Jędrzejewski *et al.*, 2000, 2002b).

11.1.3 Roe deer

The most abundant and common ungulate species in Poland, roe deer, occupies various ecosystems from fields to forests and different areas from lowlands to mountains (Pielowski, 1988). The present-day Polish population of roe deer is largely indigenous and has been present throughout the Holocene (Wyrost, 1989). The species is more numerous in western than in central and eastern Poland (Fig. 11.2) and its numbers have increased over the last decades (Table 11.1). In terms of numbers of animals shot by hunters, the roe deer is the most important game species in Poland, with over 150 000 animals harvested annually since 1995 (Table 11.1).

Actual local densities of roe deer are extremely variable, from 2 to over 20 individuals/km^2 (Pucek *et al.*, 1975; Fruziński *et al.*, 1983; Jędrzejewska *et al.*, 1994). In the woodlands of eastern Poland, predation by Eurasian lynx (and, less so, by wolves) exerts a strong limiting effect on roe deer densities (Okarma *et al.*, 1997; Jędrzejewska and Jędrzejewski, 1998).

11.1.4 Fallow deer

Fallow deer are documented to have been bred in wildlife parks in Poland since at least the eighteenth century. White-coloured deer (rare in contemporary Polish populations) were especially valued and common in such parks. One of the largest enclosed populations (600 fallow deer) occurred in the Prince Radziwiłł Wildlife Park near Biała Podlaska, eastern Poland (Kurowski, 1865). During the nineteenth and twentieth centuries many free-living populations were initiated by introductions, but some of them perished during the times of wars (eg. in Białowieża Primeval Forest; Jędrzejewska *et al.*, 1997).

Nowadays, fallow deer occur in mid-west Poland (Fig. 11.3) and since the 1970s the continuous growth of their numbers has been observed (Table 11.1). The annual hunting bag reached 3000 animals in 2005.

11.1.5 Sika deer

Introduced to the area occupied by contemporary Poland twice, in 1895 to the southern and in 1911 to the northern part of the country (Pielowski *et al.*, 1993), sika deer have survived until now in both populations (Fig. 11.3). Throughout the last century the population fluctuated sometimes reaching a critical level of only a few individuals. Nowadays the population numbers over 100 animals with an annual hunting bag of 20–30 animals.

11.1.6 Chamois

In Poland, chamois (subspecies *Rupicapra rupicapra tatrica* Blahout, 1971) is a critically endangered species, protected since 1868 (Gąsienica Byrcyn, 2002).

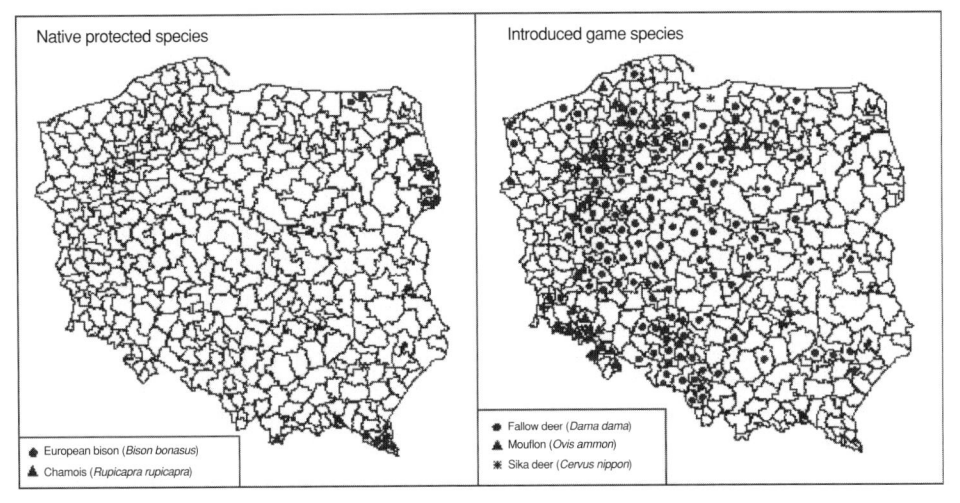

Fig. 11.3 Occurrence and distribution of rare species of native ungulates (European bison *Bison bonasus* and chamois *Rupicapra rupicapra*) and non-native ones (fallow deer *Dama dama*, sika deer *Cervus nippon*, and mouflon *Ovis ammon*) in Polish forest districts and national parks. Symbols mark the occurrence (but not numbers) of the free-living animals of a given species in 1998–2004. From W. Jędrzejewski and T. Borowik, unpublished, data provided by the Administration of Forest Districts and National Parks

Polish chamois belong to the northernmost population of the species. They occur only in the Tatra Mountains (Tatra National Park; Fig. 11.3) and number about 80 animals. In the past, the major threats to chamois living in the Tatra Mts were poaching and excessive numbers of sheep grazing in the alpine meadows. Currently, poaching (though less intense than in the past) and predation by wolves and lynx contribute to its mortality (Gąsienica Byrcyn, 2002).

11.1.7 Mouflon

Mouflon (Fig. 11.3) were brought to south-western regions of the contemporary Polish territory in 1901 from Slovakia (Pielowski *et al.*, 1993). By World War II the population had reached 300 animals. After the war numbers significantly rose up to 750 (1968), but declined to 300 individuals in the following years. After that, the population fluctuated from several hundreds to over a thousand animals. Attempts to introduce the species into other regions were unsuccessful. In the last few decades, further introductions of animals originating from Czech Republic, Slovakia and Hungary have been carried out in the Świętokrzyskie Mountains. Hunting bag is on the level of 200–300 individuals per year.

11.1.8 European bison

European bison occurred in the area occupied by contemporary Poland throughout the Holocene until the Middle Ages (Wyrost, 1989). Later, despite legal protection as royal game (Samojlik, 2005), the distribution of bison shrank and by the late eighteenth century the only remaining free-living population inhabited Białowieża Primeval Forest, East Poland (Pucek, 2004). That population survived until the early twentieth century, and was exterminated by uncontrolled poaching during and soon after World War I (the last animal perished in 1919). The population was re-established from a few individuals collected from European zoological gardens and private parks, and bison were released to the wild in 1952 in Białowieża Primeval Forest (Pucek, 2004). Nowadays, five free-ranging populations live in Poland (Fig. 11.3), with altogether a total of about 650 individuals (data for 2002; Krasińska and Krasiński, 2004). The largest population (350 individuals) inhabits Białowieża Forest. European bison is a protected species, with a status of endangered animal (Pucek and Głowaciński, 2002). However, the largest free-living populations (in Białowieża and Borki Forests, and Bieszczady Mts) are culled annually to halt population growth (annual cull at a level of about 10% of population numbers; Krasińska and Krasiński, 2004). In two of them (Borki and Knyszyn Forest in north-east Poland), culling takes the form of commercial, though strictly regulated hunts (Krasińska and Krasiński, 2004).

11.1.9 Wild boar

Wild boar occurs widely in the whole of Poland (Fig. 11.2) except for the highest altitudes in the mountains (Fruziński, 1992). They are sensitive to severe winters, which may cause mass mortality of local populations (Caboń, 1958; Okarma *et al.*, 1995). This is the main reason for generally higher abundance of boar in western Poland, where winters are milder, than in the eastern part of the country (Fig. 11.2). The Polish population of wild boar is an indigenous one, with the first archaeological records of the species dating back to Mesolithic times (Wyrost, 1989).

Populations of wild boar, a species with a very high reproductive potential, are characterised by great fluctuations in numbers between years. In Poland, the major factors causing those fluctuations are varying crops of acorns (oak seeds) and harsh winters (Jędrzejewska and Jędrzejewski, 1998). Generally, however, the Polish population of wild boar has been increasing in recent decades, as shown by official game statistics (Table 11.1). It is also obvious that official numbers of wild boar are indeed serious underestimates: in some years the hunting bag almost equalled or even surpassed the estimated numbers. Regarding both the numbers and hunting quotas, wild boar is the second most important large game species in

Table 11.2 *Hunting seasons for game species of ungulates in Poland. Moose: seasons effective before 2001, when temporary ban on hunting was introduced*

Species	Males	Females	Juveniles
Red deer	21 Aug–28 Feb	1 Oct–15 Jan	1 Oct–28 Feb
Roe deer	11 May–30 Sept	1 Oct–15 Jan	1 Oct–15 Jan
Wild boar	1 Apr–28 Feb	15 Aug–15 Jan	1 Apr–28 Feb
Moose	1 Sept–30 Nov	1 Oct–31 Dec	1 Oct–31 Dec
Fallow deer	1 Oct–31 Jan	1 Oct–15 Jan	1 Oct–15 Jan
Sika deer	1 Oct–15 Jan	1 Oct–15 Jan	1 Oct–15 Jan
Mouflon	1 Oct–28 Feb	1 Oct–15 Jan	1 Oct–15 Jan

Poland, and if calculated in terms of venison obtained – the most important one (Table 11.1).

Local late-winter densities in various regions and habitats varied from 0.1 to 17.9 individuals/km^2 and were positively correlated with the proportion of deciduous and mixed tree stands in the forests (Pucek *et al.*, 1975; Jędrzejewska *et al.*, 1994).

11.2 Legislation

Ungulate management in Poland is based on two acts: the Hunting Law (October, 1995) in the case of game species and the Act on Nature Conservation (2004) in the case of protected species. In addition, the Forest Act (1991) has some influence on the habitat of ungulates. The Hunting Law states that the free-living game animals are the property of the State. The chief organ of state administration as regards hunting is the Minister of the Environment.

Hunts may take place on state-owned as well as private land such as forests, fields, meadows, and pastures. The only restriction is not to hunt within 100 m of buildings. Both individual and group hunts are allowed but most game is harvested by individual hunts. Hunting seasons generally cover autumn and early winter (Table 11.2). The exceptions are red deer males that are hunted before and during the rutting season in late summer and autumn, roe deer males that can be harvested in late spring and summer (including the rut), and wild boar males and juveniles that are shot in all months but March (Table 11.2).

Hunting of big game (with the exception of wild boar) is allowed during daylight (from one hour before sunrise till one hour after sunset). Wild boar can be hunted during both day and night. Ungulates are hunted with rifles of calibre ≥ 5.6 mm and cartridges with soft point bullet (all species) or shotguns with the hunting bullets (all species except for moose and red deer stags). Bullet energy (at 100 m from a muzzle) must be at least 1000 J for hunting boar piglets, 2000 J for deer, wild boar and mouflon, and 2500 J for moose. Hunts using artificial light, shooting at supplementary feeding places and salt licks, and shooting from vehicles are not allowed.

All hunters (c. 100 500 persons) are members of the Polish Hunting Association. They belong to over 2500 local hunting clubs. A person who intends to be a hunter has to pass the relevant examination and conduct a one-year training in a hunting club. He or she is then allowed to hunt all game except for male deer. The permission to hunt male deer demands at least three year's experience in hunting and passing an additional examination in the biology of large game, trophy evaluation and selective shooting.

11.3 Management objectives

According to the explicit statements in the Hunting Law (1995), the objectives of game management in Poland are: conservation of species diversity of game, conservation of the natural environment towards improvement of the living conditions of game, maintenance of proper population size of game (ensuring balance between game numbers and their environment), achievement of the high quality trophies and physical condition of game, and – finally – maintaining the tradition, culture, ethics and social values of hunting. In practice, the maintenance of so-called proper population size of game (to control damage in tree stands and crops) seems to play the most essential role in game management. Ungulates are hunted not only in commercial forests, but also in the majority of Polish national parks, where the hunts are interpreted as 'reduction of game' for nature conservation objectives. For example, in 2000, a total of 558 wild boar, 441 roe deer and 435 red deer were shot in 17 national parks (data from Ministry of Environment, Warsaw). From a social point of view, hunting is an engaging hobby, a valued social recreation, and a way to cultivate corporate traditions.

11.4 Management structure

The whole area of Poland is divided into 5112 hunting districts, each covering at least 3000 hectares. Hunting districts are leaseheld by hunting clubs of the Polish Hunting Association (93%) or managed by State Forests (SF) and other institutions (7%) for a period not shorter than 10 years. In the hunting districts, game management is done by the leaseholders (hunting clubs) or managers (SF) according to the annual management plans approved by forest district officers (see section 11.5). The leaseholder or manager is also obliged to remunerate damage done by wild boar, moose and deer in agricultural crops but not in forests.

11.5 Management organisation

11.5.1 Management units and cull plan

The Hunting Law states that the management of game should be conducted in accordance to the ecological principles, rational protection and sustainable use. However, the hunting districts are too small to manage ungulate populations effectively. Therefore, larger units called game management regions (each comprising, on average, 15–25 hunting districts) are established and their coordinators are recruited from the State Forests personnel. The coordinators are responsible for organisation of annual censuses and preparation of game management plans. There are two types of plans:

1. Long-term (10-year) game management plans are developed for each game management region by directors of the Regional Directorates of State Forests, in cooperation with regional (voivodship) authorities and councils, and the Polish Hunters' Association. The plans outline the objectives of game management, and determine the desired numbers of ungulates that could be reconciled with the goals of forestry.
2. Annual hunting plans are developed by leaseholders or managers of hunting districts, then consulted with community council, Polish Hunting Association and finally approved by forest district officer or the director of the Regional Directorate of State Forests. The annual hunting plans must conform to the objective of the long-term plan. As regards ungulate game, they report on the number of harvested animals in year n, their sex and age (juvenile or adult, age classes of males), and cases of natural mortality observed in the field in year n. The annual plans set the hunting quotas for year $n+1$ (year is April 1–March 31).

Planning of annual quotas is based on: (1) annual inventory of game conducted in late winter, (2) general indicators of desired population structure, and (3) objectives of the long-term management plan. Methods of counting ungulates are described in section 11.7. The general rules and indices regarding the desired population structure, expected annual increment due to reproduction, and average carrying capacity of Polish forests for ungulates are listed in Table 11.3. Hunting quotas are planned in the form of a number of adult males (in three age classes), adult females, and juveniles of each species. Moreover, the general rules of selective shooting of male deer are observed with the aim to cull out the weakest individuals from the population and improve the quality of trophies, although the effectiveness of such selective shooting has been questioned (Pielowski, 1989).

Table 11.3 *Frame indices of desired population structure and average carrying capacity of Polish habitats for ungulates recommended by the Polish Hunters' Association for developing annual hunting plans*

Species	Assumed annual increment due to reproduction (as per cent of late winter numbers)	Desired sex ratio of adults (males:females)	Assumed average carrying capacity of habitats in Poland
Red deer	10–30	1:1–1.5	1.5–3.5 inds/km^2 of forests
Roe deer	10–30	1:1.5–2.5	3–10 inds/km^2
Wild boar	30–150	1:1	Depends on damage caused by boars in agricultural crops, 0.5 ind/km^2 of forests and marshes
Moose	20–35	1:1–1.5	
Fallow deer	25–30	1:1.5	3–3.5 inds/km^2 of forests
Mouflon	20–30	1:1	3–6 inds/km^2 of forests

11.5.2 Cull recording

At the end of the hunting season, managers of each hunting district are obliged to report to the regional administration on the numbers (by age and sex) of all species harvested, as well as animals found dead from other causes (traffic or other accident, predation, disease). Records are first submitted to the headquarters of local forest districts (*c.* 400 districts in Poland), and subsequently to regional and central headquarters of the Polish Hunting Association. Finally, the data are gathered by the General Forest Directorate (the central headquarters of the State Forests); however, at the national level they only retain the overall numbers culled.

11.6 Actual management practices

Ungulates are harvested during group and individual hunts. Individual hunts are usually carried out by stalking or lying in wait, using high seats or blinds. Their vicinities are often baited with corn and other fodder to attract wild boar. However, in the case of deer such practice is not allowed. During the rutting season, deer-calls (imitating roaring bulls) are quite often used.

Group hunts are performed as drive hunts. This method, very effective for shooting wild boar, involves two or more hunters, the accompanying beaters, and – very often – dogs, which find and flush game. Terriers, laikas, dachshunds and other small and middle-sized breeds of hunting dogs are predominantly used as flushers. In the case of deer, only 'silent drives' are allowed. Two or more beaters (but no dogs) walk slowly and silently to raise game and push them towards a line of hunters. Various types of hounds are used as trackers to find shot or wounded animals during individual and group hunts.

11.7 Census methods

In Poland, the traditional method of censusing ungulates (applied throughout the nineteenth and twentieth centuries; Jędrzejewska *et al.*, 1997) was based on snow-tracking after new snowfall. Observers walked the sample grid, counted all tracks of ungulates, and mapped their direction. The difference between number of tracks entering and leaving a grid cell (usually a forest compartment) gave the number of animals present in that cell (Pucek *et al.*, 1975; Jędrzejewska *et al.*, 1997). In the 1960s and 1970s, the reliability of snowtracking surveys was tested by comparison with driving censuses, i.e. driving the animals out of a grid cell by a dense 'battue' line of people. Each censused cell was surrounded by stationed observers who counted the escaping animals (details in Jędrzejewska *et al.*, 1994). Drive censuses revealed 1.1 to 3.5 times as many animals as did snowtracking surveys. Thus, it became clear that traditional methods of game inventory yielded serious under-estimates of ungulate numbers. Since then, researchers tested various methods of censusing large game: counts of moose from aircraft (Gębczyńska and Raczyński, 1989), modified snowtracking on transects (Dzięciołowski, 1976a), counts of the roaring red deer stags during the rut (Bobek *et al.*, 1986), ear-tagging wild boar and estimating the fraction of tagged animals in the population by visual observations (Andrzejewski and Jezierski, 1978), estimation of roe deer numbers by counts of their faecal groups (Dzięciołowski, 1976b), and decay rate of their faeces (Aulak and Babińska-Werka, 1990).

Except for the driving census, none of those methods turned out to be applicable to regular annual inventories of game in forest districts. In the 1990s, a method based on combination of snowtracking and counts of animals observed on censused plots was elaborated (Bobek *et al.*, 2001), and tested or preliminarily implemented in over 60 forest districts in Poland. However, the reliability of that method also remains unknown.

All in all, at the present time there is no 'single' census method employed consistently in all areas and the official data on ungulate numbers in Poland derive from a combination of various methods of censuses and common-sense guesses done in forest districts and national parks. Driving counts have been conducted in some districts either on an annual basis or at several-year intervals, as the method has been criticised for being too laborious (at least 10% of the total area must be

Table 11.4 *Recorded damage done by ungulates in the youngest classes (1–20 years old) of replanted tree stands managed by State Forests (cold season 2002/2003). Classes of damage: slight <20% of area damaged by ungulates, moderate 20–50%, and heavy >50% of area damaged. Sources of data: State Forests' report on activities in 2003, and Leśnictwo (2005)*

Group	Young forests (1–20 yrs) in Poland	
	Area (thousands hectares)	Percentage
All young forests in Poland	789.5	100%
Slightly damaged	133.2	17%
Moderately damaged	45.9	6%
Heavily damaged	10.9	1%

driven on 1–2 days, so it demands a great number of people). Snow tracking is done during winters with good snow cover. However, most often inventory is based on so-called year-round observations gathered by forest personnel and hunters. As a result, the official statistics are most probably reliable as far as they document, where and when a given species of ungulate is absent, rare, moderately common or very abundant, but they do not show actual numbers of game. Indeed, the numbers of small and medium-sized species (roe deer, wild boar) are most likely seriously underestimated, whereas the official numbers of large species such as moose and particularly so the European bison can be treated as a proxy of their true densities.

11.8 Damage by ungulates in forests and agricultural crops

Any browsing, debarking and trampling by ungulates (mainly red deer, roe deer and moose) in commercial replantations managed by State Forests is automatically regarded as damage. Such damage is recorded in regular (annual) surveys carried out by the State Forest Service.

Most of the damage (88%) is recorded in young tree stands (1–40 years old). Forest services classify the following signs of animal activities as damage: removal of the main shoot, debarking on more than one-third of tree circumference, and trampling of young trees. Damage is classified as slight (affected trees on <20% of the tree stand area), moderate (20–50%), and heavy (>50% of the stand area). In the hunting season of 2002/2003 damage by ungulates (mainly red and roe deer) was noted in 24% of all young forests managed by State Forests (Table 11.4). However, most of the recorded damage (17%) was graded as slight. No such data are available for the private forests (17% of the Polish forest cover).

In 2003, protection of young stands against damage was applied on an area of 109.4 thousand hectares. Most of those stands were treated with various chemical and mechanical repellents, while 14 600 hectares of new replantations were fenced. The costs of protecting forest plantations against ungulates are covered by State Forests. In the whole of Poland, those costs exceeded EUR 11 million in 2002 and EUR 15 million in 2003.

There are no recent data on damage caused by ungulates in agricultural crops. Kałuziński (1982) reported that, despite high densities of roe deer in agricultural areas in western Poland, consumption of vegetative parts of cereal crops outside the growing season was <1% and would not significantly influence yield. Later damage, involving direct removal of ripening ears, caused measurable and irrecoverable loss, yet it was an insignificant proportion of the crop as a whole (Kałuziński, 1982).

Damage in crops caused by protected species (European bison) is compensated by state budget (voivodships). Hunting clubs and managers are obliged to pay remuneration for damage caused by game species. In the hunting season 2002/2003, hunting clubs paid compensation to the owners of 13 200 hectares of crops destroyed mainly by red deer and wild boar.

11.9 Supplementary feeding of ungulates

Traditionally, supplementary feeding of ungulates was one of the main paradigms of game management, widely practised in the late nineteenth and the twentieth centuries, and – in exceptional cases such as European bison population in Białowieża Primeval Forest – as early as in the eighteenth century (Samojlik, 2005). The current Hunting Law states that leaseholders and managers of hunting districts are obliged to feed game, particularly during periods of deficiency of natural food resources or when supplementary feeding could reduce damage caused by game both in plantations and farm crops, as well as in forests.

Supplementary feeding of game has two main forms: (1) provision of fodder (usually hay, dried offshoots with leaves of deciduous trees and shrubs, grain, freshly cut aspen trees as sources of bark and phloem) in winter that is aimed at diminishing winter mortality of ungulates and preventing the decline in their physical condition, and (2) improvement of forest habitat for game e.g. by creating meadows and small fields with attractive fodder plants, planting fruit trees and other species of trees and shrubs favoured by ungulates (Fruziński, 1989). Summer feeding of wild boar has been fairly common: in some places in the forest grain are mixed with soil to attract wild boar in order to diminish damage caused by them in agricultural crops near the forest.

In practice, however, the increase in ungulate numbers observed in the recent decades (see Table 11.1) and indeed overabundance of ungulates in many regions have made supplementary feeding superfluous and even counterproductive. Though in many localities leaseholders and managers of hunting districts still adhere to that tradition, it has been gradually changing its purpose. Nowadays, winter fodder is more and more often used to attract the ungulates to shooting spots convenient for hunters, and is placed along forest roads or near the hunting towers. It is only the European bison populations that are still regularly provided with abundant winter fodder for conservation concerns (Pucek, 2004).

11.10 Effectiveness and problems of current management strategies

One of the major weaknesses of ungulate management in Poland is the lack of modern research in wildlife biology and ecology, and the implementation of research findings in informing or determining management systems. During the late 1960s and the 1970s there was a dramatic development of a number of research programmes in game biology, including studies on methodology of ungulate censuses, population ecology and diet preferences of ungulates as well as their roles in forest and agricultural ecosystems. Unfortunately, Polish studies on game biology and management hardly kept pace with the recent developments of field and laboratory techniques such as radio-tracking, ecological modelling, GIS methods and population genetics. Thus, the practical rules of game management are based on relatively outdated knowledge and rationale, they suffer from schematic attitudes, and lack of monitoring of effects of hunting harvest on game populations. For example, selective shooting criteria in deer populations have been used for decades but without any visible effect on improving deer quality. Commonly, younger age classes are overrepresented in populations.

Hunting male deer during the rutting season, a practice that may be destructive for the population structure and was abandoned in some countries in Europe, is still operative in Poland. It seems that one of the greatest current needs of the Polish system of hunting management is high-quality studies on game population with applied approach, the results of which could be used in managing game populations, planning sustainable harvest, and – when necessary – planning the protection of wildlife and their habitats. As already mentioned, elaboration and implementation of cost-effective, relatively simple and reliable enough methods of monitoring ungulate abundance in the whole country is badly needed.

Although three services (Forest Wardens, Hunting Guards and the police) are legally entitled to check hunters' activities, in practice there is lack of appropriate control over the hunting practices and hunters in the field. Moreover, there is no effective control of game management carried out by leaseholders of the hunting districts.

Generally, however, Poland is one of those European countries that retained a great biodiversity of large mammals. Undoubtedly, modern game management, more conservation-oriented and based on high-quality scientific research, could play an essential role in preserving that biodiversity for future generations.

References

Andrzejewski, R. and Jezierski, W. (1978) Management of a wild boar population and its effects on commercial land. *Acta Theriologica* **23**, 309–39.

Aulak, W. and Babińska-Werka, J. (1990) Estimation of roe deer density based on the abundance and rate of disappearance of their faeces from the forest. *Acta Theriologica* **35**, 111–20.

Bobek, B., Boyce, M. S. and Kosobucka, M. (1984) Factors affecting red deer (*Cervus elaphus*) population density in southeastern Poland. *Journal of Applied Ecology* **21**, 881–90.

Bobek, B., Perzanowski, K. and Zieliński, J. (1986) Red deer population census in mountains: Testing of an alternative method. *Acta Theriologica* **31**, 423–31.

Bobek, B., Merta, D., Widera, E. *et al.* (2001) Nowa metoda inwentaryzacji zwierzyny grubej [A new method of censusing large game]. *Łowiec Polski* **1**, 17–21. (In Polish.)

Brincken, J. (1826) *Memoire descriptif sur la Forest Imperiale de Białowieża en Lithuanie.* Varsovier, Poland: N. Glucksberg. Reprinted in 2004, Paris: Editions Epigraf, 144 pp.

Caboń, K. (1958) Das massensterben von wildschweinen im Naturstaatpark von Bialowieza im winter 1955/56. *Acta Theriologica* **2**, 71–82.

Dzięciołowski, R. (1976a) Estimating ungulate numbers in a forest by track counts. *Acta Theriologica* **21**, 217–22.

Dzięciołowski, R. (1976b) Roe deer census by pellet-group counts. *Acta Theriologica* **21**, 351–8.

Dzięciołowski, R. and Pielowski, Z. (1993) *Łoś* [Moose]. Warszawa, Poland: Anton-5, 208 pp. (In Polish.)

Dzięciołowski, R., Goszczyński, J., Wasilewski, M. and Babińska-Werka, J. (1995) Numbers of red deer in the Słowiński National Park, Poland. *Acta Theriologica* **40**, 45–51.

Dzięgielewski, S. (1970) *Jeleń: Monografia przyrodniczo-łowiecka* [Red deer: Game Biology and Natural History Monograph]. Warszawa, Poland: Państwowe Wydawnictwo Rolnicze i Leśne, 296 pp. (In Polish.)

Feulner, P. G. D., Bielfeldt, W., Zachos, F. E. *et al.* (2004) Mitochondrial DNA and microsatellite analyses of the genetic status of the presumed subspecies *Cervus elaphus montanus* (Carpathian red deer). *Heredity* **93**, 299–306.

Fruziński, B. (1989) Dokarmianie [Supplementary feeding]. In J. Krupka, R. Dzięciołowski, B. Fruziński *et al.*, eds., *Łowiectwo* [Game Management]. Warszawa, Poland: Państwowe Wydawnictwo Rolnicze i Leśne, pp. 387–94. (In Polish.)

Fruziński, B. (1992) *Dzik* [Wild Boar]. Warszawa, Poland: Cedrus, 247 pp. (In Polish.)

Fruziński, B., Łabudzki, L. and Wlazełko, M. (1983) Habitat, density and spatial structure of the forest roe deer population. *Acta Theriologica* **28**, 243–58.

Gąsienica Byrcyn, W. (2002) *Rupicapra rupicapra* (Linne, 1758) Chamois. In Z. Głowaciński, ed. *Polish Red Data Book of Animals: Vertebrates*. Warszawa, Poland: Państwowe Wydawnictwo Rolnicze i Leśne, pp. 106–108. (In Polish with English summary.)

Gębczyńska, Z. and Raczyński J. (1989) Distribution, population structure, and social organization of moose in the Biebrza Valley, Poland. *Acta Theriologica* **34**, 195–217.

Gębczyńska, Z. and Raczyński, J. (2005) The moose: a typical inhabitant of the Biebrza valley. In A. Dyrcz and C. Werpachowski, eds., *Przyroda Biebrzańskiego Parku Narodowego: Monografia* [Nature of Biebrza National Park: A Monograph]. Biebrza National Park, Osowiec-Twierdza, pp. 167–83. (In Polish with English summary.)

Heymanowski, K. (1972) The last mainstay of aurochs and the organization of their protection in the light of contemporary documents. *Sylwan* **116**(9), 9–28. (In Polish with English summary.)

Jakubiec, Z. and Buchalczyk, T. (1987) The brown bear in Poland: its history and present numbers. *Acta Theriologica* **32**, 289–306.

Jędrzejewski, W. and Kowalczyk, R. (2005) Predatory mammals. In A. Dyrcz and C. Werpachowski, eds., *Przyroda Biebrzańskiego Parku Narodowego: Monografia* ([Nature of Biebrza National Park: A Monograph]. Biebrza National Park, Osowiec-Twierdza, pp. 185–200. (In Polish with English summary.)

Jędrzejewska, B. and Jędrzejewski, W. (1998) *Predation in Vertebrate Communities: The Białowieża Primeval Forest as a Case Study*. Berlin: Springer Verlag, 450 pp.

Jędrzejewska, B., Okarma, H., Jędrzejewski, W. and Miłkowski, L. (1994). Effects of exploitation and protection on forest structure, ungulate density and wolf predation in Białowieża Primeval Forest, Poland. *Journal of Applied Ecology* **31**, 664–76.

Jędrzejewska, B., Jędrzejewski, W., Bunevich, A. N., Miłkowski, L. and Krasiński, Z. A. (1997) Factors shaping population densities and increase rates of ungulates in Białowieża Primeval Forest (Poland and Belarus) in the 19th and 20th centuries. *Acta Theriologica* **42**, 399–451.

Jędrzejewski, W., Jędrzejewska, B., Okarma, H. *et al.* (2000) Prey selection and predation by wolves in Białowieża Primeval Forest, Poland. *Journal of Mammalogy* **81**, 197–212.

Jędrzejewski, W., Nowak, S., Schmidt, K. and Jędrzejewska B. (2002a) The wolf and the lynx in Poland: results of a census conducted in 2001. *Kosmos* **51**, 491–9. (In Polish with English summary.)

Jędrzejewski, W., Schmidt, K., Theuerkauf, J. *et al.* (2002b) Kill rates and predation by wolves on ungulate populations in Białowieża Primeval Forest (Poland). *Ecology* **83**, 1341–56.

Jędrzejewski, W., Niedziałkowska, M., Nowak, S. and Jędrzejewska, B. (2004) Habitat variables associated with wolf (*Canis lupus*) distribution and abundance in northern Poland. *Diversity and Distributions* **10**, 225–33.

Kałuziński, J. (1982) Composition of the food of roe deer living in the field and the effects of their feeding on plant production. *Acta Theriologica* **27**, 457–70.

Karcov, G. (1903) *Belovezhskaya Pushcha: Eya istoricheskii ocherk, sovremennoe okhotniche khozaistvo i Vysochaishiya okhoty v Pushche* [Belovezha Primeval Forest: Historical Description, Contemporary Game Management and Monarchial Hunts in the Forest]. St. Petersburg: A. Marks, 414 pp. (In Russian.)

Korsak, W. (1934) *The Elk in Poland*. Warszawa, Poland: Państwowa Rada Ochrony Przyrody, pp. 1–47. (In Polish with English summary.)

Krasińska, M. and Krasiński, Z. A. (2004) *Żubr: Monografia przyrodnicza* [European Bison: Natural History Monograph]. Warszawa, Poland: SFP Hajstra, 312 pp. (In Polish.)

Kurowski, W. (1865) *Myśliwstwo w Polsce i Litwie* [Hunting in Poland and Lithuania]. Poznań, Poland: Księgarnia, J. K., Żupańskiego, 231 pp. (In Polish.)

Leśnictwo [Forestry] (2005) *Główny Urząd Statystyczny*. Warszawa, Poland, 260 pp. (In Polish.)

Luterbacher, J., Rickli, R., Xoplaki, E. *et al.* (2001) The late Maunder Minimum (1675–1715): a key period for studying decadal scale climatic change in Europe. *Climatic Change* **49**, 441–62.

Okarma, H., Jędrzejewska, B., Jędrzejewski, W., Krasiński, Z. A. and Miłkowski, L. (1995) The roles of predation, snow cover, acorn crop, and man-related factors on ungulate mortality in Białowieża Primeval Forest, Poland. *Acta Theriologica* **42**, 203–24.

Okarma, H., Jędrzejewski, W., Schmidt, K., Kowalczyk, R. and Jędrzejewska, B. (1997) Predation of Eurasian lynx on roe deer and red deer in Białowieża Primeval Forest, Poland. *Acta Theriologica* **42**, 203–24.

Piasecki, D. (2004) Sytuacja populacji łosia w Poleskim Parku Narodowym [The situation of moose population in Poleski National Park]. In *Sytuacja populacji łosia w Polsce* [The Situation of Moose Population in Poland]. Biebrza National Park, Osowiec-Twierdza, pp. 29–32. (In Polish.)

Pielowski, Z. (1988) *Sarna, wyd. III* [Roe Deer, 3rd ed.]. Warszawa, Poland: Państwowe Wydawnictwo Rolnicze i Leśne, 293 pp. (In Polish.)

Pielowski, Z. (1989) Użytkowanie łowieckie [Hunting harvest]. In J. Krupka, R. Dzięciołowski, B. Fruziński *et al.*, eds., *Łowiectwo* [Game Management]. Warszawa, Poland: Państwowe Wydawnictwo Rolnicze i Leśne, pp. 364–72. (In Polish.)

Pielowski, Z., Kamieniarz, R. and Panek, M. (1993) *Report on Game Animals in Poland*. Biblioteka Monitoringu Środowiska Państwowej Inspekcji Ochrony Środowiska. Elwoj-Trio, Warszawa, 38 pp. (In Polish with English summary.)

Pucek, Z. (2004). European bison: history of a flagship species. In B. Jędrzejewska, J. M. Wójcik, eds., *Essays on Mammals of Białowieża Forest*. Białowieża, Poland: Mammal Research Institute PAS, pp. 25–34.

Pucek, Z. and Głowaciński, Z. (2002) *Bison bonasus* (Linne, 1758) European bison (wisent). In Z. Głowaciński, ed., *Polish Red Data Book of Animals: Vertebrates*. Warszawa, Poland: Państwowe Wydawnictwo Rolnicze i Leśne, pp. 100–105. (In Polish with English summary.)

Pucek, Z., Bobek, B., Łabudzki, L. *et al.* (1975) Estimates of density and number of ungulates. *Polish Ecological Studies* **1**, 121–36.

Samojlik, T. (2005) *Conservation and Hunting: Białowieża Forest in the Time of Kings*. Białowieża, Poland: Mammal Research Institute, Polish Academy of Sciences, 90 pp.

Samsonowicz, A. (1991) Hunting in Poland of the Piasts and Jagellons. *Studia i Materiały z Historii Kultury Materialnej* **62**, 1–410. (In Polish with English summary.)

Schmölcke, U. and Zachos, F. E. (2005) Holocene distribution and extinction of the moose (*Alces alces*, Cervidae) in Central Europe. *Mammalian Biology* **70**, 329–44.

Sieńko, A. (2004) Aktualna sytuacja populacji łosia na terenie Biebrzańskiego Parku Narodowego [The current situation of the moose population in the Biebrza National

Park]. In *Sytuacja populacji łosia w Polsce* [The situation of moose population in Poland]. Biebrza National Park, Osowiec-Twierdza, pp. 21–27. (In Polish.)

Statistical Yearbook of the Republic of Poland (2002) Warsaw: Central Statistical Office. (In Polish and English.)

Vuure, C. van (2005) *Retracing the Aurochs: History, Morphology and Ecology of an Extinct Wild Ox*. Moscow: Pensoft, 431 pp.

Wyrost, P. (1989) Fauna Polski w Holocenie w świetle badań archeozoologicznych [Fauna of Poland in the Holocene based on archaeozoological studies]. *Folia Quaternaria* 59–60, 219–246. (In Polish.)

12

Ungulates and their management in the Czech Republic

LUDĚK BARTOŠ, RADIM KOTRBA AND JAN PINTÍŘ

12.1 Historical and present distribution of ungulate species in the Czech Republic

Until perhaps the tenth century the distribution of ungulate fauna in what is now the Czech Republic had been almost uniform due to dense forests and low human population in the area. Hunting would have been practised mostly for food. In the centuries that followed, hunting became largely the privilege of the aristocracy and was carried out mostly for recreation (Fig. 12.1). The aristocracy have built castles for hunting and management of game and appointed one person (chief hunter) to organise a collective hunt and provide venison since the tenth century (Kholová, 2003). This person was responsible for forest and game quality, their protection against poachers and predators. Hunting was regulated only by landowners during that time.

In spite of this, numbers of game showed a general decrease in both distribution and abundance, largely as a result of intensive poaching during years of instability (wars) and because of heavy deforestation. This also led to extermination of the moose and wild boar and to rapid decrease of red and roe deer populations. In response to this, from the fourteenth century onwards the aristocracy established game parks and tried to increase game numbers by releasing them from these sites (Kholová, 2003).

Over recent years there has been a total of 11 ungulate species in the Czech Republic. These are (in order of abundance in 2005): roe deer, wild boar, red deer, fallow deer, sika deer, mouflon, white-tailed deer, chamois, moose, Barbary sheep and wild goat. While the roe deer, red deer, moose and wild boar are native to the Czech Republic, other species have been either introduced or accidentally escaped from captivity mostly during the nineteenth and twentieth centuries (Fig. 12.2).

- Hunting for food
- Right for everybody to hunt

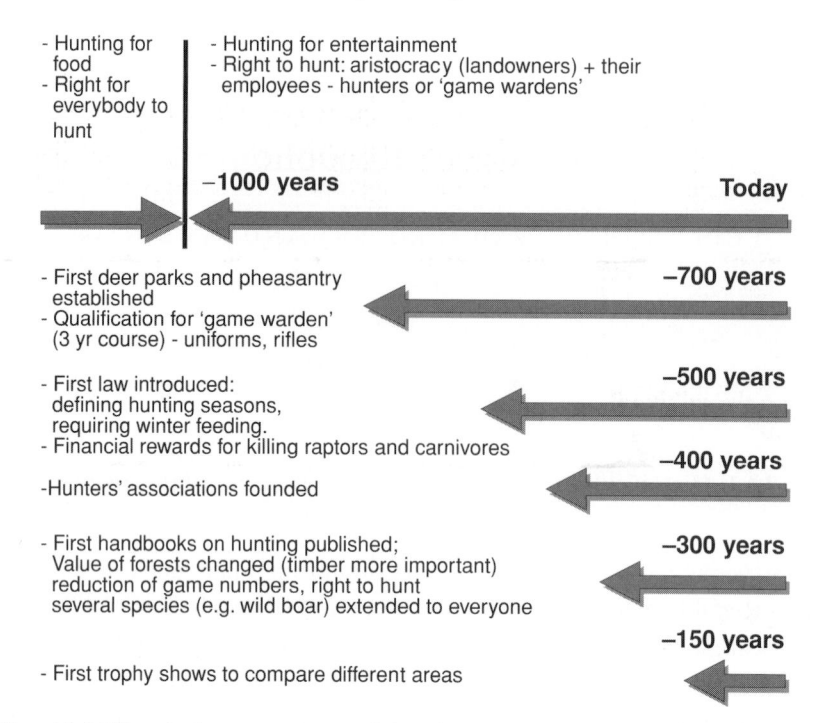

- Hunting for entertainment
- Right to hunt: aristocracy (landowners) + their employees - hunters or 'game wardens'

−1000 years   Today

- First deer parks and pheasantry established   −700 years
- Qualification for 'game warden' (3 yr course) - uniforms, rifles

- First law introduced: defining hunting seasons, requiring winter feeding.   −500 years
- Financial rewards for killing raptors and carnivores

-Hunters' associations founded   −400 years

- First handbooks on hunting published;   −300 years
  Value of forests changed (timber more important)
  reduction of game numbers, right to hunt
  several species (e.g. wild boar) extended to everyone

                                                                   −150 years
- First trophy shows to compare different areas

Fig. 12.1 Historical cornerstones of hunting on the territory of recent Czech Republic

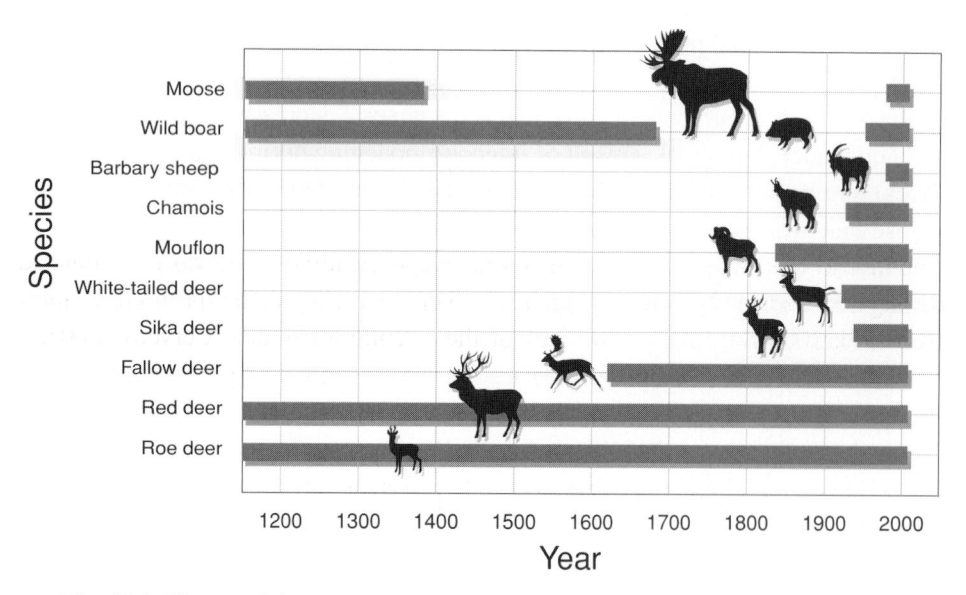

Fig. 12.2 History of the main ungulate species occurrences in the Czech Republic

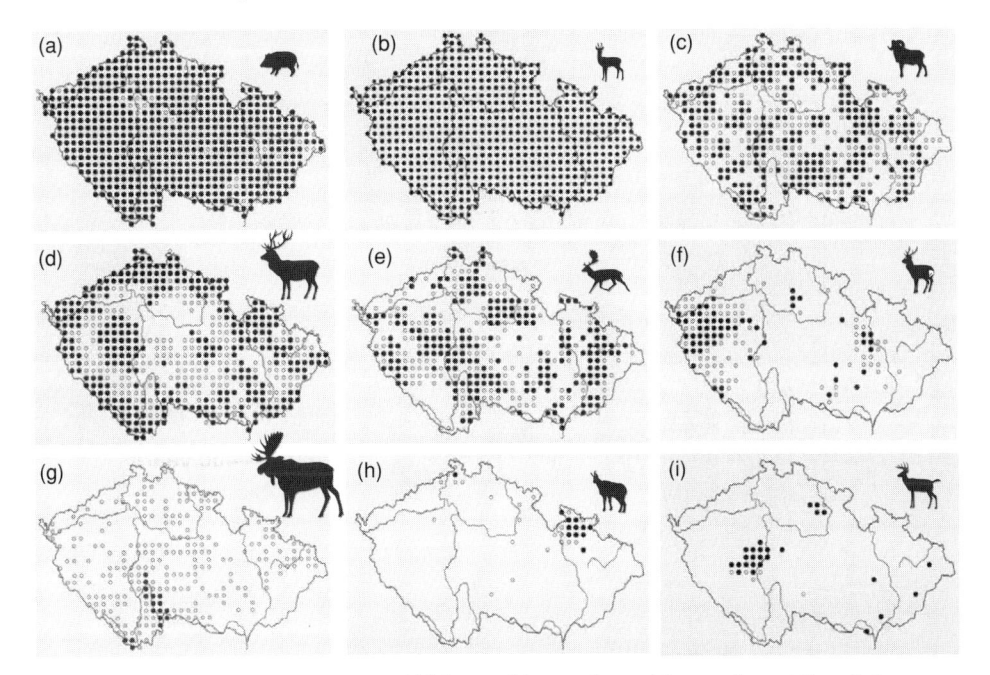

Fig. 12.3 Distribution of (a) wild boar, (b) roe deer, (c) mouflon, (d) red deer, (e) fallow deer, (f) sika deer, (g) moose, (h) chamois, and (i) white-tailed deer. All adapted from Červený (2003b). Open circle represents occasional occurrence, filled circle represents animal's permanent presence

A total area of 66 910 km² (84.8% of total area) is delimited for hunting in the Czech Republic (Czech Statistical Office, 2005). This more or less equates to the total area occupied by wild ungulates. Suitable habitats are mostly fragmented; forests cover 25% of the total area and another 41% is under agriculture.

12.1.1 Moose

The moose is a species native to the Czech Republic although it was exterminated during the fourteenth century (Fig. 12.2). They naturally recolonised the country from Poland during the second half of the twentieth century (Červený, 2003a). Although territory of the Czech Republic is usually just a transit area for them, a stable and regularly reproducing population has established naturally in lowland bordering a lake area in the south Bohemia (Fig. 12.3g). The population is counted up to 32 individuals (Czech Statistical Office, 2005). The moose is not a huntable species, being protected as endangered species.

12.1.2 Red deer

The most popular trophy ungulate species in the Czech Republic is the red deer. During the seventeenth and nineteenth centuries the increase of poaching together

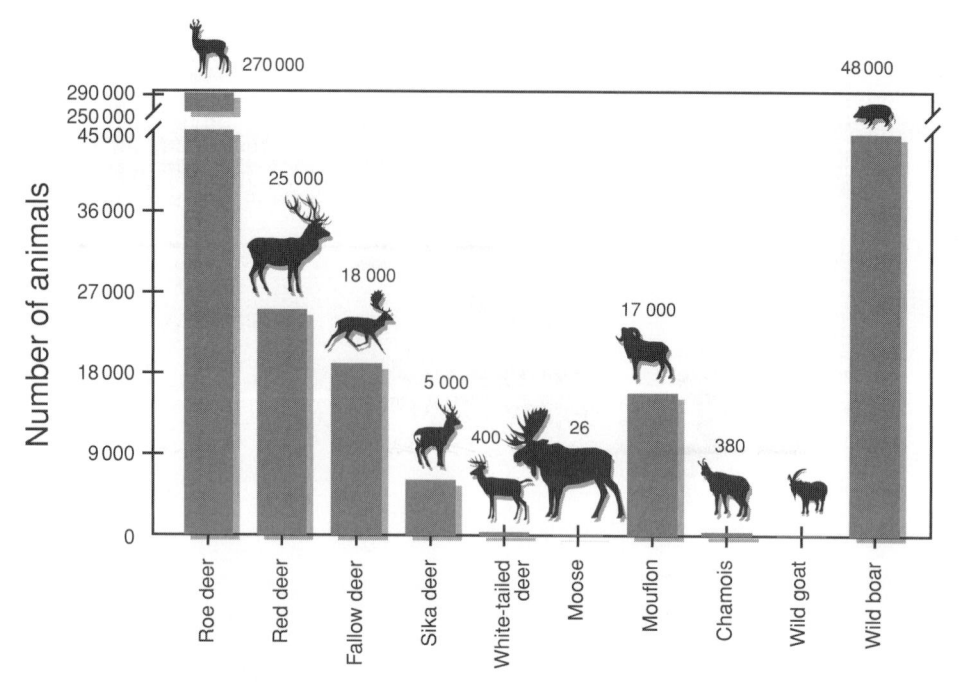

Fig. 12.4 Census of recent (2004) ungulate numbers (except territories of National Parks)

with an intensive deforestation led almost to the extinction of this species (Červený, 2003a). In order to maintain populations some captive red deer (of uncertain genetic provenance) were released from deer parks. In addition, in an attempt to increase trophy quality, maral (*Cervus elaphus maral*), wapiti (*Cervus e. canadensis*) and an alleged subspecies, Carpathian red deer (*Cervus e. montanus*), were also introduced into the Czech Republic (ibid.). In this case, it is likely these introductions resulted in interbreeding with native populations (Kučera, 1977).

These factors, together with presence of the sika deer in the same areas as occupied by red deer (see section 1.5) and known problems of hybridisation where the two species do co-occur (Bartoš *et al.*, 1981; Bartoš and Žirovnický, 1981, 1982; Bartoš & Vítek, 1993), mean that we can not be confident that the red deer population are pure red deer.

Our red deer occur mainly in mountainous dense forested areas close to the state borders (Fig. 12.3d). Their population is slightly increasing (Fig. 12.6) and estimated as up to 23 300 individuals (Fig. 12.4). During 2004 there were harvested 18 503 red deer in the Czech Republic (Czech Statistical Office, 2005).

12.1.3 Roe deer

The most numerous and most widely distributed ungulate species in the Czech Republic is the European roe deer (Fig. 12.3b). This species occurs in all biotopes

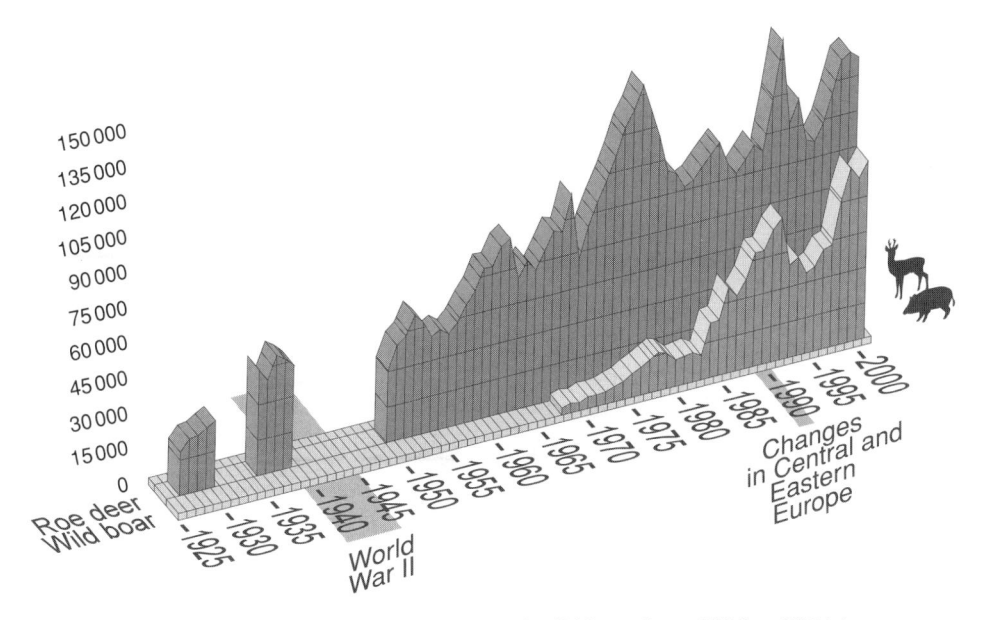

Fig. 12.5 Number of harvested roe deer and wild boar from 1925 to 2004 (except territories of National Parks)

and their distribution has never been seriously affected by increasing human land use (agriculture, forestry, industry). Their distribution covers the entire country and roe are present in both the open agricultural land and the forested areas (Červený, 2003a).

The population is more or less of indigenous origin even though there have been isolated attempts to increase the antler size by the introduction and crossbreeding with Siberian roe deer (*Capreolus pygargus*). Such introductions failed, however (Nebeský, 1956). Nowadays, the European roe deer is the most important huntable ungulate species in the Czech Republic (Figs. 12.2, 12.4 and 12.5). In 2004, almost 121 000 animals were culled from a population censused as approximately 292 800 individuals (Czech Statistical Office, 2005).

12.1.4 Fallow deer

The fallow deer was first introduced into a fenced park during the fifteenth century (Fig. 12.2). At the beginning of the seventeenth century they were released also into the wild (Červený, 2003a). The free living population (estimated around 19 000 animals in 2004) is distributed mainly in deciduous forests up to 500 m a.s.l. (Fig. 12.3e). They are a very popular species for hunting (Fig. 12.6) with overall bag exceeding 9000 animals in 2004 (Czech Statistical Office, 2005).

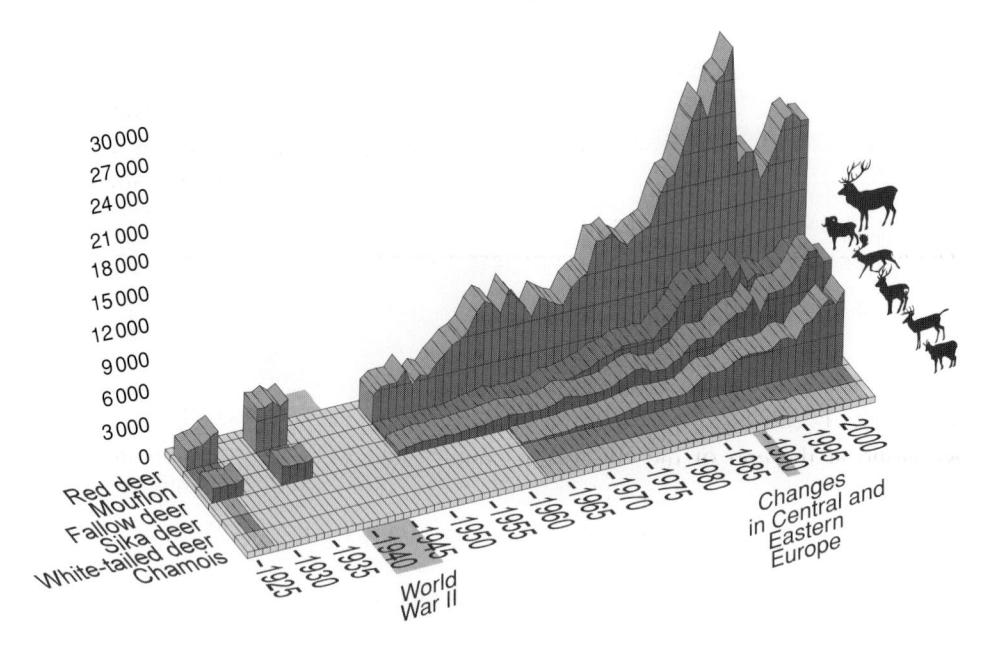

Fig. 12.6 Number of harvested red deer, mouflon, fallow deer, sika deer, white-tailed deer and chamois from 1925 to 2003 (except territories of National Parks)

12.1.5 Sika deer

The introduction of sika deer to deer parks took place during the second half of the nineteenth century (Fig. 12.2, Kokeš, 1970; Wolf and Vavruněk, 1975–1976; Vavruněk and Wolf, 1977). Forty years later, some of these animals were deliberately released into the wild and we have now two large free ranging populations. One is in the west and one in the north-east of the country (Fig. 12.3f). This species is very adaptable and highly competitive with other deer species. We can thus expect wide expansion in both numbers and distribution. Moreover where the two species co-occur, sika is freely crossbreeding with red deer (Bartoš et al., 1981; Bartoš and Žirovnický, 1981, 1982; Bartoš and Vítek, 1993). It is not surprising that their population is quickly increasing and reached approximately 6000 animals during spring count in 2004. The hunting bag in the same year reached 6818 animals (Czech Statistical Office, 2005).

Interestingly, we have two hunting periods for this species. One for the smaller *Cervus n. nippon* and one for the bigger *Cervus n. dybowskii*, despite the fact that distributional ranges overlap and there is no easy cue to distinguish them.

12.1.6 White-tailed deer

The last cervid and also an introduced species is the white-tailed deer (Fig. 12.2). They were firstly released into an enclosure in the nineteenth century (Kraus, 1910;

Kotrlý, 1970). They accidentally escaped and have subsequently established a local population of around 300 individuals in a forested area 50 km south of Prague (Fig. 12.3i). This population supposedly belongs to *Odocoleus v. virginianus* subspecies (Bojovic and Halls, 1984). In 1985, a second population was set up in Moravia by reintroduction of animals from Finland as *Odocoleus v. borealis* subspecies (Červený, 2003a). This population is smaller and of less significance (Fig. 12.3i). The hunting bag is low reaching every year only a few dozen animals.

12.1.7 Wild boar

Wild boar became extinct in the wild in the area now occupied by the Czech Republic at the end of the eighteenth century and were only present in enclosures (Fig. 12.2, Červený, 2003a). They recolonised naturally however, initially spreading from the south (probably from Hungary). Since 1950 it has gradually become the most rapidly expanding ungulate (Fig. 12.5) and in recent years populations have expanded to cover practically the whole territory of the state (Fig. 12.3a).

It is clear that the population estimate of spring 2004, of approximately 44 000 individuals, is a considerable underestimate because the planned hunting bag of 38 391 animals was, in practice, surpassed three times, with over 121 000 animals harvested during 2004 (Czech Statistical Office, 2005). The rise in their population causes a lot of damage to crops every year. Recently, the number of harvested wild boars reached that of roe deer.

12.1.8 Mouflon

The presence of mouflon dates from the middle of the nineteenth century (Fig. 12.2, Červený, 2003a). In the past they were held only in game preserves, but are now widespread across the Czech Republic (Fig. 12.3c). They are equally distributed in lowland areas where deciduous forest and agricultural land is present. According to the spring count in 2004 the population is around 16 000 animals with a hunting bag in the same year of 6309 animals (Czech Statistical Office, 2005).

12.1.9 Wild goat

Another species introduced in the twentieth century (1953; Fig. 12.2) is the wild goat (*Capra aegagrus*) (Červený, 2003a). The small free ranging population which was established in Moravia was transferred to the game park Vřísek located near to Česká Lípa, north of Prague, a few years ago. Only 28 animals were counted in 2004 (Czech Statistical Office, 2005). Although according to the Red List Data

Book of IUCN the wild goat is a vulnerable species, this species may be hunted in the Czech Republic.

12.1.10 Barbary sheep

The Barbary sheep (*Ammotragus lervia*), a completely exotic species occurs in a small area around the city of Plzeň (Pilsen) in the west part of the Czech Republic. The population was established after a one-off escape of a few individuals from the Plzeň zoological garden in 1976 (Červený, 2003a). Their population numbers a few dozen. The Barbary sheep is listed by IUCN as vulnerable and the species is not hunted in the Czech Republic.

12.1.11 Chamois

Although the chamois (*Rupicapra rupicapra*) was probably native to mountainous regions in the past, the present population is not indigenous and was introduced from several Alpine regions during first half of the twentieth century (Fig. 12.2; Červený, 2003a). The population reached approximately 350 animals in 2004. This species is not an important hunted species in the Czech Republic (Fig. 12.3h) and the hunting bag was 28 animals in 2004 (Czech Statistical Office, 2005).

12.1.12 European bison

A recent (August 2005) occurrence of three European bison (*Bison bonasus*) individuals in total (bull and cow with calf) has been reported by the media from two places in Jizerské Mountains. Those animals probably wandered from neighbouring Poland and cannot be regarded as established. According to the Red List Data Book of IUCN, the European bison is an endangered species and is not huntable species in the Czech Republic.

12.1.13 Status and population trends

Populations of wild boar, roe, red, fallow and sika deer have shown a steady increase in both numbers and geographical distribution during the last 40 years (based on harvest statistics regression of harvested numbers across years: wild boar $R^2 = 0.859$, $P < 0.001$, roe deer $R^2 = 0.304$, $P < 0.001$, red deer $R^2 = 0.639$, $P < 0.001$, fallow deer $R^2 = 0.887$, $P < 0.001$, mouflon $R^2 = 0.847$, $P < 0.001$, sika deer $R^2 = 0.876$, $P < 0.001$; Fig. 12.7). Presumably this has happened mainly in response to changes in agriculture, forestry and hunting practices.

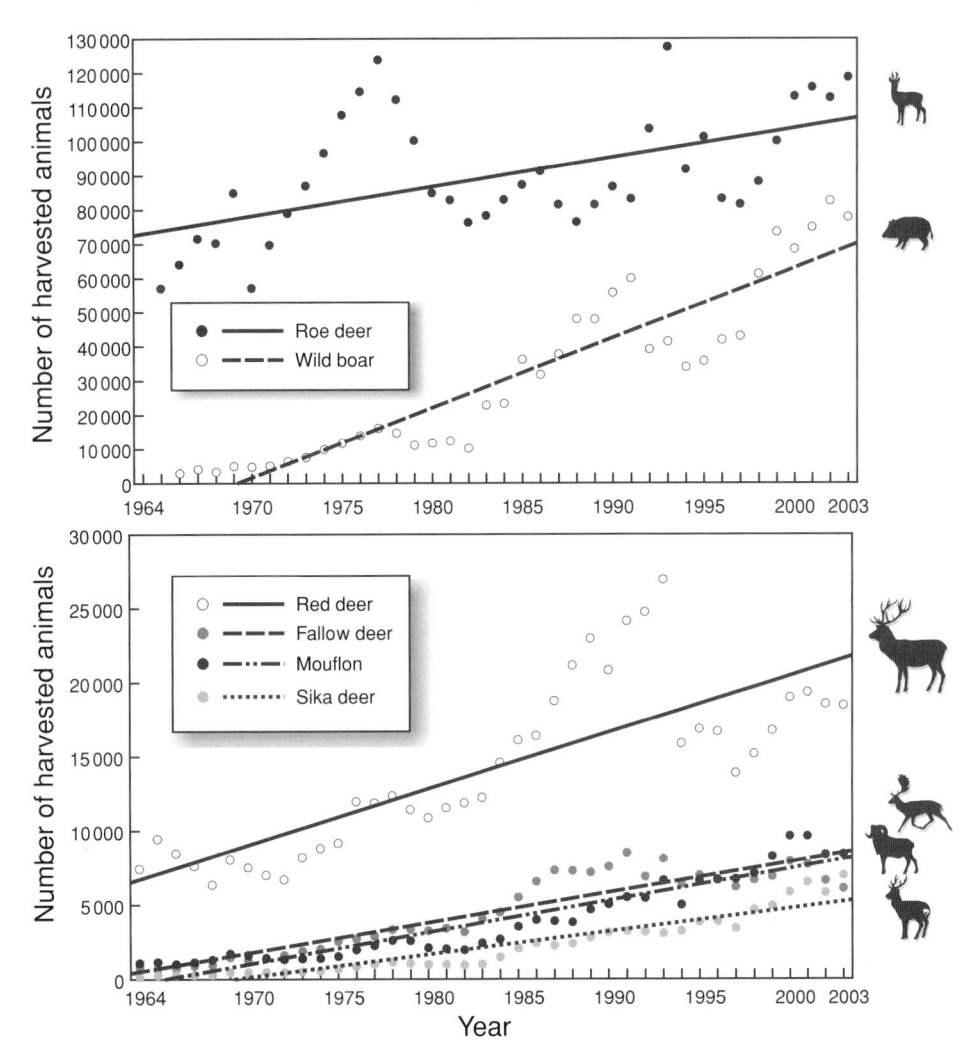

Fig. 12.7 Regression lines showing an increasing trend of harvested roe deer and wild boar (top) and red deer, fallow deer, mouflon and sika deer (bottom) since 1964 (except territories of National Parks)

12.2 Legislation

The first legislation on game management was the Hunting Directive announced in 1568 by Emperor Maxmillian followed by the Directive of Rudolf II in 1599. These directives restricted the hunting of game and any activities likely to cause disturbance, as well as any extensive logging and burning of forest areas (Červený, 2003b). Grazing of domestic stock in forests was also prohibited. These directives were effective for the three following centuries (Fig. 12.1).

In more recent times, the Game Management Act has been the major judicial document determining game management practices. It has been modified more than ten times since its introduction in 1962. The last changes occurred in 2003. This Act states that: game management should be seen as an activity that supports sustainable use of wildlife in the context of protection of national heritage and hunting traditions. The Act then makes explicit definitions of who, how, where, what and when can be hunted.

12.2.1 What species can be hunted?

The game species that may be hunted are the fallow deer, the red deer, white-tailed deer, the chamois, wild goat, the mouflon, the wild boar, the Dybowski sika deer, the Japanese sika deer and the roe deer.

12.2.2 What are the permitted weapons?

It is not permitted:

1. to shoot game with firearms other than hunting firearms (rifle or shotgun or combined firearm designed for hunting purposes),
2. to shoot game with banned firearms (shotgun with total length shorter than 900 mm or with barrel shorter than 450 mm, self exploder firearm trap, non-metal firearms and self-modified firearms), their attachments (firearms with silencer, laser gunsight, night vision gunsight and light gunsight) and any non-standard ammunition (army, self-modified, and with chemical or biological content),
3. to shoot roe deer with firearms other than with the rifle with a muzzle energy lower than 1000 J and other hoofed game with muzzle energy lower than 1500 J; this shall not apply to the shooting of piglets and hoggets of wild boar that may be shot with the shotgun with a single slug during beat, drive hunt and silent beat,
4. to shoot the game with semi-automatic or automatic firearms with the magazine for more than two cartridges.

Hunting seasons (prescribed by the Decree of the Ministry of Agriculture no. 245/2002) are shown in Table 12.1.

It is illegal to catch game with snares, on bird-lime, in steel-traps or with dead-fall traps and contact traps and by means of hooks; to hunt game by any method causing unnecessary suffering; to poison game or to kill it with gas; to catch game with nets unless it is caught for the purposes of restocking; to chase roe deer with pointers or any other hoofed game with dogs with a height at withers more than 55 cm.

Table 12.1 *Hunting seasons according to Decree of the Ministry of Agriculture no. 245/2002*

Species	Category	Hunting season
Fallow deer	buck, doe and fawn	from 16 August to 31 December
Red deer	stag, hind and calf	from 1 August to 15 January
White-tailed deer	buck, doe, fawn	from 1 September to 31 December
Dybowski's sika deer	stag, hind and calf	from 16 August to 31 December
Sika deer	stag, hind and calf	from 1 August to 15 January
Roe deer	buck	from 16 May to 30 September
	doe and fawn	from 1 September to 31 December
Chamois	adult and kid	from 1 October to 30 November
Wild (bezoar) goat	goat and kid	from 1 September to 31 December
Mouflon	ram, ewe and lamb	from 1 August to 31 December
Wild boar	boar and sow	from 1 August to 31 December
	piglet and yearling (hogget)	from 1 January to 31 December

Only young of the year and yearling wild boar may be hunted all year round. Game species in game preserves may be hunted all year round.

Ungulates are primarily hunted by individual hunters (see section 12.6). However, in pursuit of other game, hunters may occasionally organise collective hunts. During these collective hunts it is illegal to shoot ungulates, except hinds and calves of red deer and sika deer, mouflon ewes and lambs, piglets and yearlings of wild boar. In addition to this the Game Management Act also lays down prescriptions on how to protect and breed game, how to establish hunting guilds and grounds, how to control populations and who will cover the cost of damages.

A number of other laws (such as the veterinary law, the environmental and nature conservancy law, etc.) are incorporated in the Game Management Act and affect the wider management of wildlife.

12.3 Management objectives

According to the Game Management Act (2003) one of the major objectives is: 'game management should be taken to mean those activities carried out on wild land, directed towards managing wild game as a part of the ecosystem, and the activities of those associations whose objectives are the maintenance and development of hunting traditions and customs as a part of the Czech national cultural heritage'.

The Act defines major objectives of the game management on the state level, for example the maintenance of sustainable numbers of game based on carrying capacity of a certain area, prevention of damage, maintenance of game quality and genetic purity, etc. In reality, every person who is active in hunting management or in hunting has his or her own motivation. This is mainly based on long-established tradition.

12.4 Management structure

The state administration of game management is at three levels in the Czech Republic (Game Management Act, 2003). The central organ of state is the Ministry of Agriculture (Department for Fisheries, Hunting and Beekeeping), which has authority over the whole country except territories of national parks. The Ministry of Environment is the central organ of the state administration in the territories of national parks.

Much of the actual practical administration is delegated to the regional authority within each of the fourteen individual administrative districts into which the country is divided (section for Game Management within each regional office). Finally, the administration of individual municipalities of each territory serves as the local authority for game management.

Game management may be carried out only within recognised hunting areas which are determined by the local authority for game management. Within these hunting areas, landowners (state or private) may create a hunting guild with a minimum acreage of 500 ha of continuous ground (or at least 50 ha in fenced game reserves) to establish hunting ground (5674 hunting guilds in total were registered in the Czech Republic, 2004).

The hunting guild can exercise the hunting right by themselves or rent the right to hunt to another user. There are currently 4978 rented hunting grounds across the country (Ministry of Agriculture of the Czech Republic, 2005).

The users of any given hunting ground should propose to the state organ of game management the appointment of one game-keeper (or game-warden) for each 500 ha of continuous hunting ground for the term of ten years, and in addition must also appoint a game manager. The game-warden should ask any persons encountered within the hunting ground with a firearm to see a firearms licence, firearms certificate, hunting licence, hunting permits and compulsory insurance. Moreover, he or she can stop and examine any vehicles including transported luggage in the hunting ground or detain any person who may be caught in the hunting ground carrying out an illegal hunt. The game manager is responsible for developing the game management plan for the ground and compiling statistical reports on the game populations and hunting bag in each hunting ground. It is also usually he or she who leads any collective hunt and is also responsible for the shot game and its tags (persons hunting individually have to attach a tag onto the shot game immediately after the kill.) He or she can shoot stray dogs, cats and other animals harmful to game and also any feral domestic animals.

Each of the hunting guilds also elects their hunting mayor. The hunting mayor represents the hunting guild to the public. The hunting mayor may conclude, amend or terminate the contract on the hunting ground lease only with the previous approval of a competent organ of the hunting guild. Ultimately, as above, overall management of hunting in all the territories is controlled by state administration of game management.

12.5 Management organisation

Anyone wishing to hunt game has to have a hunting licence, hunting permit and certificate of compulsory insurance with them at the time of the hunt; for any hunt involving use of firearms they must also have a firearms licence and firearms certificate, and for the hunt with a hunting bird of prey, its registration card (Game Management Act, 2003).

Hunting licences are issued by the local state administration of game management to a person who can demonstrate that he or she is older than 16 years, who has taken a hunting and game management course completed by passing an examination, 'is honest' and is adequately insured. This licence is for life, which is the passport into the hunters register. The cost of course followed by examination ranges between EUR 100 and 200.

According to the Statistical Report of the Ministry of Agriculture (Ministry of Agriculture of the Czech Republic, 2005) a total of 94 529 people currently hold hunting licences related to permanent hunting grounds in the Czech Republic.

According to the Decree of the Ministry of Agriculture no. 244 released in 2002 the actual hunting examination includes answering questions on these subjects: Group I (the history of hunting and blood sports and hunting associations' activities; the significance of hunting, hunting culture and hunting ethics; a hunter's personality, hunting terms, hunting customs and traditions), Group II (the legal regulation on hunting, on firearms and ammunition, on nature and landscape protection, veterinary regulations, regulations on the prevention of cruelty to animals, the European Union legal regulations and international agreements concerning hunting; hunting administration; plans for hunting husbandry and hunting statistics), Group III (game zoology and biology for hunting, knowledge of the main identification features of the game and how it lives), Group IV (game management including artificial game breeding and the basic technology; game care including feeding, constructing and maintaining hunting facilities; ecology and nature protection, animal protection and improving the game's environment, preventing damage caused by game, the relation to other free-living wildlife, ethology and its

Table 12.2 *History of the voluntary and professional hunting associations in the Czech Republic*

Association	Founded
The Order of St. Hubert (founded by Count Spork)	1695
Association of Hunters "The hunter's brotherhood"	1699
Hobby Hunter Association "The Prague Forestry Club Hubertus"	1868
The "Moravian Club for Hunt Protection" in Brno. (One year later this club became the first national hunters' association)	1881
A number of various hunting clubs and associations merged into the only association 'Czechoslovak Hunting Association' (After World War II membership in the 'Czechoslovak Hunting Association' was required by law for all hunters)	1923
The 'Czechoslovakian Hunting Association' split into 'Czech Hunting Association' and 'Slovak Hunting Association'	1968
The Order of St. Hubert has restored activities	1978
The 'Czech Hunting Association' renamed to the 'Czech and Moravian Hunting Association' and became a voluntary based organisation	1992
Czech Branch of the Safari Club	1992
The Association of Professional Hunters	1995

usage in hunting practices, animal welfare), Group V (hunting dogs and their use – knowledge of the breeds and groups of hunting dogs, proper breeding, raising and training, handling and using hunting dogs; hunting dog illnesses; game illnesses), Group VI (hunting firearms, ammunition, aids and equipment, the rules for their usage and safety measures; basic first aid for injuries acquired when carrying out the right to hunt), Group VII (game hunting methods including catching game and hunting rules; tracking; treating wild animals, arranging and appraising hunting trophies).

The voluntary and professional hunting associations (Table 12.2) have had a long-lasting history dating back to the seventeenth century (Červený, 2003c).

12.6 Actual management and hunting

Management and hunting practices are based on annual harvest plans and on principles of selective hunting, i.e. culling predominantly old and sick animals, underdeveloped young animals and harvesting prime trophy animals. The holder of any hunting ground and, in the case of its lease, the leaseholder of hunting ground (hunting ground user), is responsible for maintaining game populations in the hunting ground in the numerical range between minimum viable population size and the maximum population sustainable by available resources – as laid down by the decision of the state organ of game management.

The prescribed game stock is usually that spring stock of current species that corresponds to maintenance of the quality of the living environment of species and the carrying capacity of hunting ground. The local Game Management Authority will also indicate the required sex ratio and age structure of given species and the expected recruitment rate (Game Management Act, 2003).

The hunting ground user is then responsible for carrying out a census of game numbers in the hunting ground every year on a date fixed by the state authorities and notifying the result to those authorities. The hunting ground user must also develop an annual management plan for the hunting ground, which is agreed and controlled by the state authorities.

In order to monitor the quality of the game and to inform future management decisions, the state authorities also require a display of trophies each year.

The hunts are performed as individual hunts (legal for all huntable ungulates) or as a collective hunt. The methods used for individual hunts are the static watch, usually from a high seat (wild boar, deer species) and stalking (deer species, mouflon). Stalking is commonly undertaken accompanied by dogs which seek out game and drive it towards the hunter. Collective hunts for general game-shooting are undertaken by local hunters and their guests. This type of hunt is performed together with hounds and beaters and requires careful organisation. Therefore, the leader or leaders distribute hunters and give them directions for shooting to increase the safety of beaters and those working dogs. The methods of collective hunt are crawling, drive, dog drive and snooping (Kamler, 2003).

In hunting, dogs are commonly used, which have been specifically trained in locating, tracking and fetching small game and/or ungulates that have been killed, shot or injured. According to the Statistical Report of the Ministry of Agriculture (Ministry of Agriculture of the Czech Republic, 2005) there were 9078 licensed dogs used for ungulate hunting in 2004. These dogs are kept under licence and may only be used for the activity or quarry species for which they have been licensed

12.7 Census types and methods

According the Game Management Act (2003) the person who exercises the right to hunt over any piece of ground has to conduct a census every year of numbers of all game species present and develop a harvest plan for that hunting ground. An annual census is generally carried out by visual survey during a fixed period in spring. This figure is then used to plan the following year's harvest (without any control for the accuracy of the census figure produced, nor any real consideration given as to whether the proposed harvest may be effective in maintaining steady population size or achieving an agreed increase or decrease in population). Cull statistics are based on compulsory reports of every culled animal (species, sex, age and weight).

12.8 Impact of large ungulates/damage

Except for a few studies (Bartoš and Mikeš, 1995; Heroldová *et al.*, 2003; Homolka and Heroldová, 2003), there is no real scientific monitoring of wildlife impact on environment (natural forest regeneration, forest and crop damage, etc.).

According to the Game Management Act (2003), the hunting ground user is responsible for controlling the game numbers. As such it is technically the responsibility of the hunting ground user to compensate for the damage that is caused in the hunting ground to standing field crops, grapevine or forest stands by actual hunting activities and in addition to compensate for any damage that is caused in the hunting ground directly by the game animals themselves. If the hunting right is exercised by an association, its members are jointly liable for the damage compensation.

In reality, financial compensation for the damage caused to forest and crop production by the hunting ground users is relatively low. According to the Report on Management in Forestry submitted by of the Ministry of Agriculture (Ministry of Agriculture of the Czech Republic, 2005) the compensation reached more than EUR 2 million in 2002, but only EUR 1 million in 2003. The report mentioned that overpopulation of ungulates caused the most damage to forestry. In fact, the total damage to forest stands (under control of the State Forest Company) caused by ungulates has been estimated to reach up to an astronomical EUR 1.5 million every year (unpublished data).

12.8.1 Income from hunting

There is no real income for the Government from hunting. Administrative charges are gathered only once, when hunting and firearms licences are issued. The fees for these are, respectively EUR 30 and 16. The hunting ground users pay yearly income tax only if hunting is the subject of business or if they sell a game meat. Nevertheless, this means no real income, because most of the harvested game is used by the hunters. On the other hand, the Government and the State Forest Company manage 62% of all forests in the country (Czech Statistical Office, 2005) and financially support little research on wildlife. There is no monitoring of wildlife impact on environment (natural forest regeneration, forest and crop damage, etc.). The overpopulated ungulate species suppress natural forest regeneration and forest companies must invest in protection of seedlings.

12.9 Supplementary feeding

Despite critical discussion on this issue in scientific literature (e.g. Putman and Staines, 2004), winter feeding continues to be obligatory by the law. This is mainly because it has been like that for about 500 years (Fig. 12.1) and is based more on tradition than actual biological need. According to the Game Management Act (2003), the user of the hunting ground is supposed to take care of cribs, feed troughs, salt licks and watering places, and to 'feed the game appropriately at the time of famine'. Numbers and capacities of these facilities should be indicated in the plan of game management and in the annual statistical report on the total hunting areas. According to the Statistical Report of the Ministry of Agriculture (Ministry of Agriculture of the Czech Republic, 2005) there were 83 367 feed troughs, 94 254 salt licks and 8868 watering places in the Czech Republic in 2004 (except territories of National Parks). The Game Management Act from 2003 even states: 'If the state organ of game management finds that game suffers from starvation and if, at the call of the state organ of game management, the user of hunting ground does not rectify the situation immediately, this organ shall decide on game feeding at the user's cost'.

Recently, this has caused considerable controversy and debate among hunters. Still, it is justified by most of the hunters, because of significant changes in environment and of alleged possibility of keeping a higher density of wildlife.

12.10 Ungulate management in the Czech Republic: crucial points for the future

An annual census of free-ranging species of wildlife in Czech Republic is actually required under the Game Management Act (2003). However no one scientific institution is responsible for the development of improved census methods (or for advising the Government on implementation of these improved methods); neither is there any real mechanism allowing for any progress in background biological knowledge to be incorporated into practical management. It is clear that the methods currently prescribed by the law are entirely ineffective. As a result, it happens frequently that the hunting bag recorded for various species exceeds in number the previous census. This is a good example that not only the system of censusing is failing, but also that numbers shot are clearly insufficient to control populations of some species or prevent their rapid growth.

Compensation is rarely claimed for damage caused by game species despite the provision so to do under the Game Management Act (2003). Therefore, in various areas there is no real pressure on hunters to exercise appropriate control of ungulate numbers. Indeed, despite real problems, such as increasing damage over the last few decades due to a population explosion of wild boar, the traditional approach to hunting inhibits the adoption of more appropriate methods which could effectively control the numbers and reproduction (even though the Game Management Act 2003 does allow various innovations).

A separate problem is caused by the fact that the hunting period for all game ungulate species coincides with the rutting season of those same species. Together with selective harvesting (as practised by traditional hunters), with heavy emphasis on trophy males, this management disturbs natural mate selection and may affect stability of the population social structure.

In summary, the need for appropriate wildlife management in the Czech Republic has been underestimated by the authorities for a long time. Management is currently very hunter-dominated and very traditional, while improvement of the coordination of management effort is handicapped by the lack of any scientific institution which would deal with systematic monitoring of the local game populations.

Similarly, there is lack of a modern education system of wildlife management. The institutionalised education of wildlife management for hunters and wildlife managers is limited to a few selected subjects related to hunting rather than management. It is taught at secondary schools level and two forestry faculties. The problem is, that these educational programmes are not associated with deeper knowledge, if any, of general disciplines such as animal genetics, morphology and physiology, nutrition, ethology, population dynamics monitoring, etc. Wildlife management taught by conventional means (i.e. schools of forestry) is not respected in practice due to traditional prejudices. Despite several recent attempts to establish a more sophisticated way of such an education within forestry faculties, modern wildlife management training as practised in North America is still missing in the country.

The hunting organisations, such as the Czech and Moravian Hunting Association, which currently act as substitute educational and advisory establishments are heavily biased in the direction of traditionalism. Basically, the system where each hunter has to pass an examination is a good one and is very well organised. The problem is, however, that training for this examination is old-fashioned, lacking fresh scientific information. This is because the lecturers got their own qualifications mostly through this system itself having little link, if any, to external sources of information such as universities, scientific institutions and so forth. We believe that scientific supervision of the whole system and support for establishing specialised education would improve tremendously the current status of wildlife management.

References

Bartoš, L. and Žirovnický, J. (1981) Hybridization between red and sika deer. II. Phenotype analysis. *Zoologischer Anzeiger* **207**, 271–87.
Bartoš, L., Hyánek, J. and Žirovnický, J. (1981) Hybridization between red and sika deer. I. Craniological analysis. *Zoologischer Anzeiger* **207**, 260–70.

Bartoš, L. and Žirovnický, J. (1982) Hybridization between red and sika deer. III. Interspecific behaviour. *Zoologischer Anzeiger* **208**, 20–36.

Bartoš, L. and Vítek, M. (1993) Cluster analysis of red and sika deer phenotypes. In N. Ohtaishi, & H.-I. Sheng, eds., *Deer of China: Biology and Management*. Amsterdam: Elsevier, pp. 15–21.

Bartoš, L. and Mikeš, J. (1995) Damage to forests by sika deer in Czechia. In E. Eick, R. König and J. Willett, eds., *Sika,* Cervus nippon *Temminck, 1838. Volume II.* 2nd edn. Möhnesee, Germany: International Sika Society, pp. 63.1–63.8.

Bojovic, D. and Halls, L. K. (1984) Central Europe. In L. K. Halls, ed., *White-tailed Deer: Ecology and Management*. Harrisburg, Pennsylvania: Stackpole Books, pp. 557–60.

Červený, J. (2003a) Biologie zvěře srstnaté. In J. Červený, J. Kamler, H. Kholová, P. Koubek and N. Martínková, eds., *Encyklopedie myslivosti*. Prague: Ottovo nakladatelství, pp. 249–345.

Červený, J. (2003b) Legislativa. In J. Červený, J. Kamler, H. Kholová, P. Koubek and N. Martínková, eds., *Encyklopedie myslivosti*. Prague: Ottovo nakladatelství, 61–73.

Červený, J. (2003c) Vznik mysliveckých a ochranářských organizací. In J. Červený, J. Kamler, H. Kholová, P. Koubek, & N. Martínková, eds., *Encyklopedie myslivosti*, Prague: Ottovo nakladatelství, pp. 54–5.

Czech Statistical Office (2005) http://www.czso.cz/csu/edicniplan.nsf/p/2201–05.

Heroldová, M., Homolka, M. and Kamler, J. (2003) Breakage of rowan caused by red deer: an important factor for Sorbeto-Piceetum stand regeneration? *Forest Ecology and Management* **181**, 131–8.

Homolka, M. and Heroldová, M. (2003) Impact of large herbivores on mountain forest stands in the Beskydy Mountains. *Forest Ecology and Management* **181**, 119–29.

Kamler, J. (2003) Lov zvěře. In J. Červený, J. Kamler, H. Kholová, P. Koubek and N. Martínková, eds., *Encyklopedie myslivosti*. Prague: Ottovo nakladatelství, pp. 440–59.

Kholová, H. (2003) Historie lovu a ochrany zvěře. In J. Červený, J. Kamler, H. Kholová, P. Koubek and N. Martínková, eds., *Encyklopedie myslivosti*. Prague: Ottovo nakladatelství, pp. 36–45.

Kokeš, O. (1970) Asijští jeleni na území Československa. *Ochrana Fauny* **4**, 158–61.

Kotrlý, A. (1970) *Zhodnocení současného stavu početního i chovatelského jelence viržinského* Odocoileus virginianus. Praha: Studie MZVŽ.

Kraus, J. (1910) Jelen viržinský (*Cervus virginianus*). *Les a Lov, Písek* **3**, 143–4.

Kučera, J. (1977) *Zvyšování chovné kvality srnčí a jelení zvěře*. Studijní informace. Řada lesnictví. Ústav vědeckotechnických informací pro zemědělství: Praha.

Ministry of Agriculture of the Czech Republic (2005) http://www.mze.cz/attachments/MZe7040_statistika/Tab1_2004M.htm.

Nebeský, L. (1956) *Posuzoηní srnčí zvěře*. Praha: SZN.

Putman, R. J. and Staines, B. W. (2004) Supplementary winter feeding of wild red deer *Cervus elaphus* in Europe and North America: justifications, feeding practice and effectiveness. *Mammal Review* **34**, 285–306.

Vavruněk, J. and Wolf, R. (1977) Chov jelení zvěře v Západočeském kraji. *Sborník Vědeckého Lesnického Ústavu VŠZ v Praze* **20**, 97–115.

Wolf, R. and Vavruněk, J. (1975–1976) Sika východní *Cervus nippon* Temm v Západních Čechách. *Sborník Vědeckého Lesnického Ústavu VŠZ v Praze* **18–19**, 185–99.

13

Ungulates and their management in Slovakia

SLAVOMÍR FIND'O AND MICHAELA SKUBAN

13.1 Historical and present distribution of ungulate species

Slovakia is a country with an area of about 49 036 km² and a population of 5.4 million. To the west it borders Austria and the Czech Republic/Moravia, to the north Poland, the east Ukraine and to the south Hungary. It has been an independent sovereign state since the peaceful break up of the former Czechoslovakia in 1993. Slovakia has a great degree of landscape diversity from the Carpathian Mountains in the north to the Danube flood plains in the south. A total of 41% of the country is forested, and forestry remains an important part of the Slovak economy. Whilst many countries have faced problems of deforestation in the last few decades, Slovakia's forest cover has actually increased. Some 40–45% of the forests are comprised of semi-natural stands, which differ only slightly in species composition from the original forests. About 50% of the land is used for agriculture. Ploughed arable land is concentrated in the lowlands and in the lower parts of the main river valleys. Vineyards, hop fields, fruit orchards and gardens cover small areas and are interspersed throughout the country representing islands of higher biodiversity in the intensively used land. However, the most valuable areas for biodiversity are the meadows and pastures, which constitute one-third of the agricultural land. Most of these have developed as a result of traditional land use practices in the past, and feature distinctive species diversity. At present, over 22% of the country is covered by a network of protected areas, including nine National Parks and 16 Protected Landscape Areas. The impact of the current development of motorways and dual carriageways on wildlife in Slovakia has not been seriously considered. Many wildlife species, ungulates and large carnivores are now especially vulnerable to the increasing development of traffic infrastructure and mitigation measures, which protect the wildlife migration corridors across roads, have only recently been implemented in some areas.

At present eight species of ungulates thrive in Slovakia including: roe deer (*Capreolus capreolus*), red deer (*Cervus elaphus*), fallow deer (*Dama dama*), European elk (*Alces alces*), mouflon (*Ovis orientalis musimon*), chamois (*Rupicapra rupicapra spp. rupicapra* and *tatrica*), wisent (*Bison bonasus*) and wild boar (*Sus scrofa*). Fallow deer, mouflon and Alpine chamois are not indigenous to Slovakia. Aurochs (*Bos primigenius*), wisent and European elk were exterminated in the Middle Ages, probably due to over-hunting. In the twentieth century, however, wisent and European elk were successfuly reintroduced.

The breakdown of communism in 1989 has meant a slow and difficult transition to a more capitalistic economy. Political changes brought about chaos in hunting management accompanied by poaching. Over a period of several years hunting management was effectively reorganised and stabilised. In the latter part of the 1990s the numbers of ungulates dropped, to minimum levels in 1997. To prevent further population decline, shooting plans for 1997 were officially reduced by the county administration bodies responsible for hunting to about 30% for each hunting ground across the country. This step and the introduction of effective antipoaching measures facilitated a population increase of deer, mouflon and wild boar (see population trends in sections 13.1.1–13.1.8).

13.1.1 Roe deer

Roe deer in Slovakia is a native species that belongs to the originally designated subspecies (*Capreolus capreolus capreolus* L. 1758) (Hartl *et al.*, 1993). Roe deer remains have been found in numerous archaeological sites. Near the village of Ondrochov the antlers and lower jaw of a yearling were discovered in a grave dating back to the Roman period. The length of the first antlers after the knobs reached 190 mm and the height of the burrs was more than 20 mm. These antlers document a more robust physical make-up of roes in the past than at the present time. Wide distribution in earlier times is also documented by some of the geographical names derived from 'srnec', which means roe deer. In the Middle Ages, roe deer were not as highly valued by hunters as the other big game species, which included brown bear, European bison, red deer, wild cattle and wild boar. The serfs had a duty to hand over to the landowners fish, birds and pelts of predators rather than venison of roe deer. Historical documents written in Latin refer to the roe deer as Dama or Damma, a name which is currently used for fallow deer (Hell, 1979).

In the past the extensive woodland areas, which covered most of the country, were a less suitable habitat for roe deer than the present farmland interspersed by hedgerows, scattered trees and patches of woodland. The fragmentation of these more continuous woodlands for farming together with various factors such

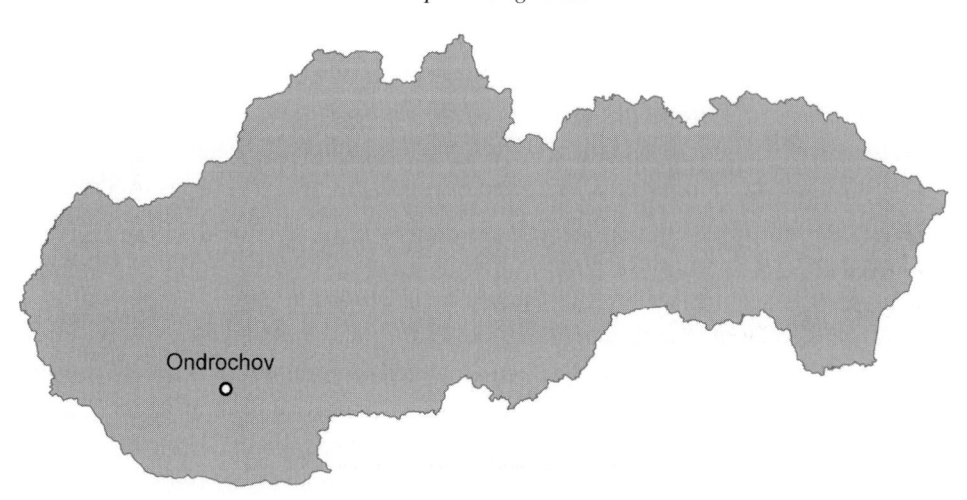

Fig. 13.1 Roe deer distribution encompasses the whole territory of Slovakia (grey area)

as persecution of large carnivores, the protection of ungulates and supplementary winter feeding subsequently contributed to a notable increase of roe deer population density. This higher population density has resulted in a general decrease of body mass.

Today roe deer are widely distributed across the country, inhabiting woodlands, farmlands and even parklands close to human settlements (Fig. 13.1). They permanently occupy almost all types of habitat from lowland up to the timberline (1400 m a.s.l.) and occasionally use high alpine meadows during the summer period.

Based on behavioural features and preferred habitat type, it is possible to distinguish between the *forest* and *field* eco-form (Hell, 1979). The development of the field eco-form dates back to the 1960s when part of the population in the lowlands became habituated to semi-open landscape, especially farmland interspersed with shrubbery and trees.

The population density is highest (on average 46 individuals per 10 km^2) in landscape of this type such as southwestern and central Slovakia. The lowest density (on average 9 individuals per 10 km^2) is recorded in the foothills and mountains of the Western Carpathians, which is especially due to predation by large carnivores and harsh climate conditions. Recent numbers of roe deer were estimated as up to 80 000–85 000 individuals while the annual hunting bag ranges from 17 000 to 18 000 individuals (Fig 13.2).

Roe deer is a game species included in the Act No 23/1963 and Decree No 172/1975 (see section 13.2). The open season is from 16 May to the 30 September.

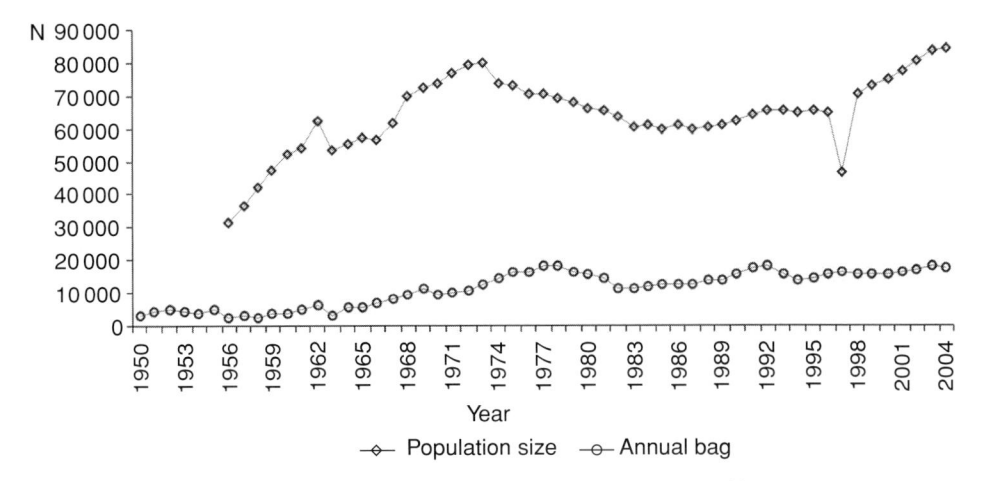

Fig. 13.2 Roe deer population estimate and annual bag

13.1.2 Red deer

In Slovakia, few palaeontological remains of red deer have been documented. During excavations near the village of Dolné Krškany, the remains of *Cervus elaphus priscus* Soerg. were discovered. From the last Ice Period of Würm, antlers similar to those present in Asian and North American deer have been preserved (Bališ, 1980). There is also evidence that the Mesolithic people commonly hunted large deer.

During the Holocene epoch and later, red deer inhabited woodland areas, however at a lower density than at present. They occupied preferentially woodlands and forest-steppes, but ascended to the alpine meadows during the summer months. Some red deer trophies still in velvet dating back to the seventeenth to nineteenth centuries came from the alpine habitat. In the Middle Ages red deer were widely hunted throughout the year by drive-hunts with dogs, or caught in nets and subsequently killed. Large enclosures were built across the country for this purpose.

From the tenth century onward the distribution and numbers of red deer declined with this trend continuing right up until the nineteenth century. The process of red deer elimination was hastened by the development and wider use of firearms. By the first half of the nineteenth century red deer were on the verge of extinction with the remains of a native Carpathian population thriving only in remote mountain areas.

Due to the dramatic population decline, landowners on numerous estates established game enclosures for red deer breeding and later reintroduction into the wild. Red deer of various origins were reintroduced and used for breeding. The establishment of enclosures, either for hunting or population reinforcement, was already known about in the fifteenth century, however the first captive herd was well documented in 1666. This herd originated from animals introduced from Germany, Eastern Carpathians (Marmaros region in the Ukraine) and the Altai mountains (Altai Maral, *Cervus elaphus sibiricus*). Later smaller acclimation pens were established across the country. Since the middle of the nineteenth century efforts were made to introduce red deer of good body and antler conformation.

Thus herds were composed of three subspecies of red deer including *Cervus elaphus hippelaphus* (112 individuals from Bohemia), *C. elaphus sibiricus* (Altai Maral) and *C. canadensis* (Wapiti). All races have subsequently interbred freely, with the typical phenotypic features of Asian and American subspecies diminishing and being overlapped by those of *hippelaphus*. Red deer in Slovakia are often described as belonging to the subspecies *C. elaphus hippelaphus*, therefore, thus present day populations are in practice rather a mongrel mixture of genotypes.

A distinct subspecies *C. elaphus montanus* (Botezat, 1903) has been suggested for the Carpathians. This subspecies was, however, only accepted by the authors of the former Czechoslovakia, for example Bališ (1980) and Lochman (1985). A recent genetic study has not confirmed this as a separate or distinct subspecies (Hartl *et al.*, 1995).

Due to the dramatic decline of red deer numbers in the middle of the nineteenth century, landowners started a large-scale reintroduction to strengthen the remains of the native population. Red deer of various origins were introduced, bred in enclosures and acclimation pens and then released into the wild. Basically, three subspecies of red deer were hybridised: *Cervus elaphus hippelaphus*, *C. elaphus sibiricus* and *C. elaphus canadensis*.

Despite such efforts at reintroduction, the population decline still persisted and in 1924 the population size and annual bag were estimated as up to 4500 and 1273 individuals, respectively (Čech *et al.*, 1935). Indeed, at the turn of the nineteenth century, in many areas of Slovakia currently inhabited by red deer, local people were not even aware of this species. In 1933–6, the average annual bag of red deer was 2369 individuals (Lochman, 1985).

During World War II this increase in population slowed down, but after 1945 continued rapidly (Fig. 13.3). The annual bag in 1970 reached 7650 individuals and peaked in 1991, when 21 793 red deer were hunted.

The size of red deer population in hunting statistics was always underestimated. At present, the population is estimated as up to 38 000 individuals (38 264 in 2004).

Red deer preferentially inhabit forested areas from the foothills up to the alpine meadows above the timberline (e.g. in Tatry, Nízke Tatry, Malá and Vel'ká Fatra mountains) and avoid the open farmland of south-western and eastern parts of the country (Fig. 13.4).

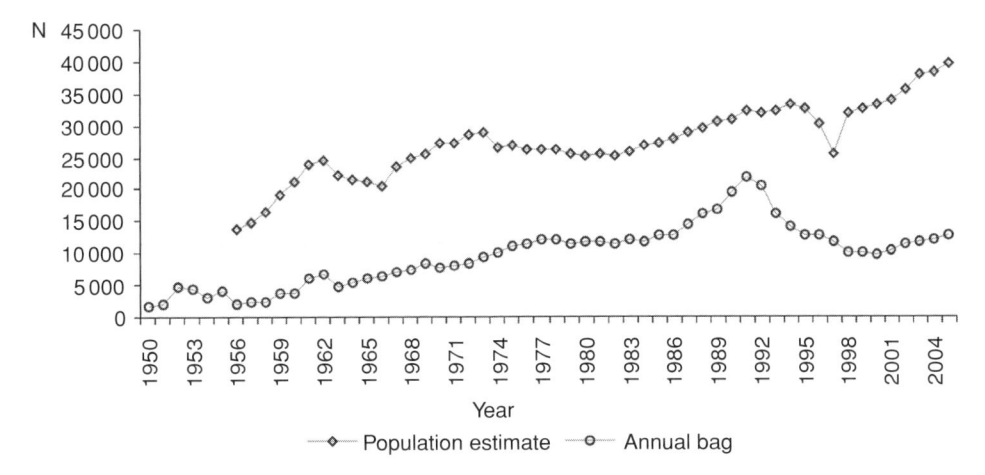

Fig. 13.3 Red deer population estimate and annual bag

Fig. 13.4 Red deer distribution in Slovakia (grey area)

In the high mountains from May to November, part of the population ascends to the alpine habitat. Some stags overwinter at the upper timberline often together with chamois. Red deer currently occupy 39 054 km^2, or 80% of the country.

Red deer is a game species listed in the Hunting Act No 23/1963 and Decree No 172/1975. Open season is from 1 August to 31 December.

13.1.3 Fallow deer

Bones of fallow deer excavated in the caves of prehistoric humans date back to the last interglacial period (Bárta, 1965). The last glacial period initiated the retreat of

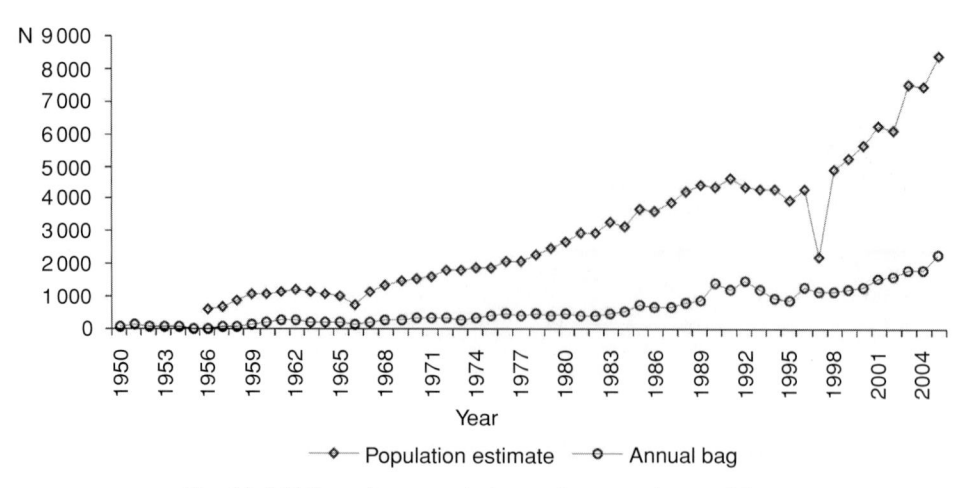

Fig. 13.5 Fallow deer population estimate and annual bag

the fallow deer to the Mediterranean area. Since the last stage of glaciations, there has been no evidence of fallow deer occurrence in Slovakia, hence this species is not considered indigenous. Throughout the past, it was the Romans, in particular, who contributed to the reintroduction of the fallow deer into Europe (Macko, 1985; Bäumler et al., 1986).

The first unconfirmed references of fallow deer breeding in captivity date back to 1586 and 1618, while small free-living herds were mentioned in 1735 (Feriancová-Masárová and Hanák, 1965; Macko, 1985). No doubt, at the beginning of the nineteenth century fallow deer were released into the wild from many estates across the country. Despite this, even much later, the species had little importance in terms of hunting management as documented by the small numbers of hunted animals (average 126 individuals in 1926–9). Until 1936 the annual bag increased to 360 individuals but heavy poaching after World War II resulted in population decline as only 72 fallow deer were hunted in 1952 (Bakoš et al., 1995).

The sluggish population growth until 1966 later hastened, apparently due to the strengthening of existing captive breeds and wild populations by the introduction of animals from Bohemia (the Czech Republic), see Fig. 13.5. Essentially, the trophy quality and numbers of existing herds had also been improved by the introduction of animals from the area of Gyulay in Hungary famous for good trophy stags.

Principal political changes after 1989, and the onset of the market economy, caused the disorganisation of hunting management, accompanied by poaching and a temporary population decline. In 1992 there were 26 small isolated populations in the wild and many captive herds (Hell and Pataky, 1992).

From 1998 onward, the population again increased rapidly up to approximately 7500 individuals and fallow deer are now more numerous than ever in Slovakia. At

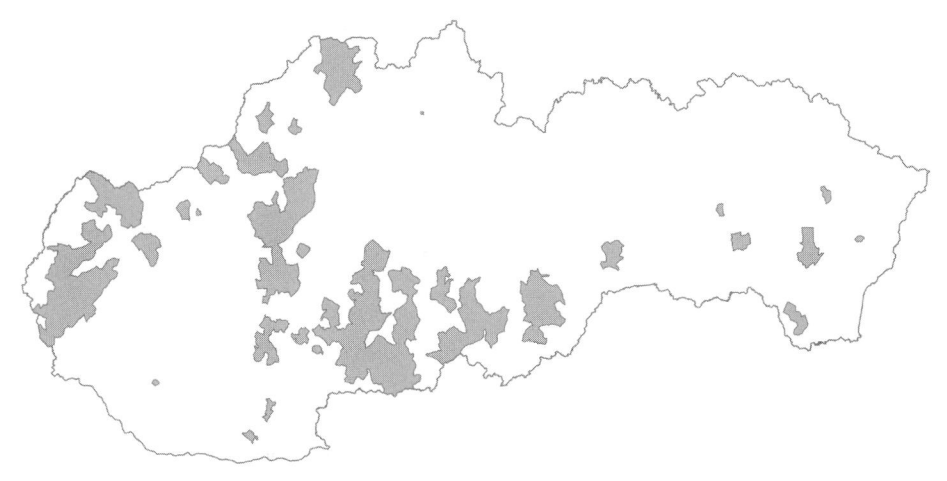

Fig. 13.6 Fallow deer distribution in Slovakia (grey area)

present the fallow deer range encompasses 5613 km^2 or 12.6% of the total hunting area of the country (see Fig. 13.6; Hell *et al.*, 1999). The fallow deer has not been genetically studied in Slovakia.

13.1.4 European elk (moose)

European elk is indigenous to Slovakia and belongs to the originally described subspecies (*Alces alces alces*, Linnaeus 1758). The occurrence of elk in the past was documented by many archaeological findings and historical documents (Melichar, 1928; Schmidt, 1967; Čaplovič, 1987; Kocian *et al.*, 1998). Due to overhunting the elk was exterminated in the second half of the sixteenth century (Gyimesi, 1971). The last occurrence of elk in the Middle Ages was confirmed by the finding of an antler, which was dated by the radiocarbon method to the period between 1535 and 1605. The oldest finding of an elk antler was dated by the same method to 8980 ± 80 years BC (Kocian, *et al.*, 1998).

After a long period of extermination the elk reappeared in Slovakia at the beginning of the 1960s, through natural recolonisation. For the first time in the twentieth century the elk was observed on 10 April 1961 (Chudík and Sládek, 1962). However, a carcase of an adult male had already been found on 4 September 1960 (Karč, 1979). Until 1985, the first dispersals, probably from Poland, were single subadult males. They roamed widely across the country for a short time and then vanished often without trace. Since 1980, elk observations were more frequent alongside the Slovak/Polish border within the area of the Orava district and these sightings peaked between 1989 and 90. An average of six elk were observed yearly throughout the period of 1985–8.

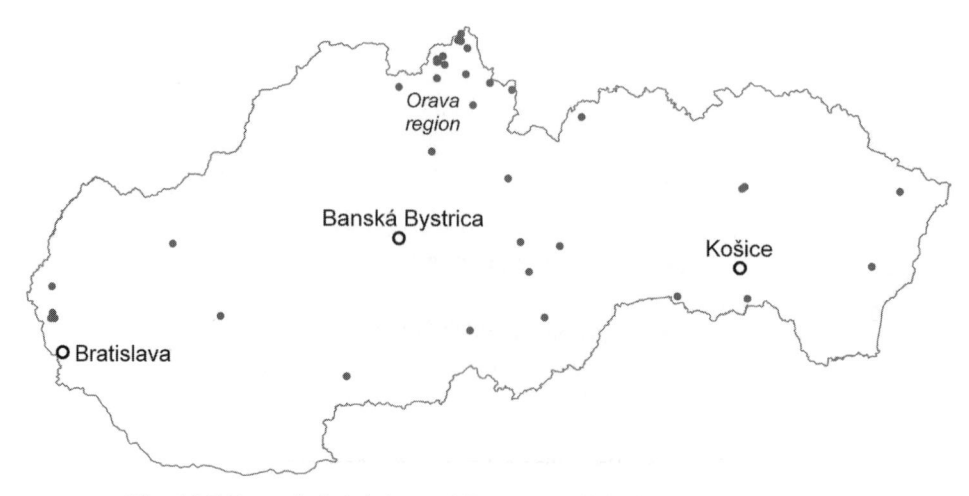

Fig. 13.7 Recorded sightings of European elk in Slovakia 1960–2005

In the Orava region females with newborn young have been observed since 1986. The presence of elk in the Orava region is also documented by other findings such as tracks, cast antlers and skulls of dead females.

From the first occurences in the 1960s, the elk have not been able to establish a viable metapopulation. Most migratory specimens temporarily visited various parts of Slovakia but later disapeared without trace. In some cases migratory elk have been poached or hit by vehicles. Elk observations peaked during the rutting season between August and October.

Currently the elk population is about 10–15 individuals (Fig. 13.7). According to IUCN classification elk is listed as EN endangered species (also Bern 3).

13.1.5 Mouflon

Mouflon (*Ovis orientalis musimon* Pallas 1811) is not indigenous to Slovakia and was initially introduced by Karol Forgách in 1868–9 from the Zoological Gardens in Frankfurt am Main (Germany) and Brussels (Belgium). In total, nine animals were placed in an acclimation pen near the village of Jelenec within the area of the Tríbeč Mountains. From 1883 onward the animals produced in this pen were used to the stock the surrounding hunting grounds. Forgách continued to restock his estate and imported mouflon from the Company of Hagenbeck (Zoo Lainz Wienna, Austria) and also from Corsica. Before World War I, Hagenbeck purchased mouflon from Slovakia and exported them abroad. In 1879 Gyula Edelsheim imported mouflon from Sardinia to the Tríbeč Mountains. A short time later, in 1890, mouflon from

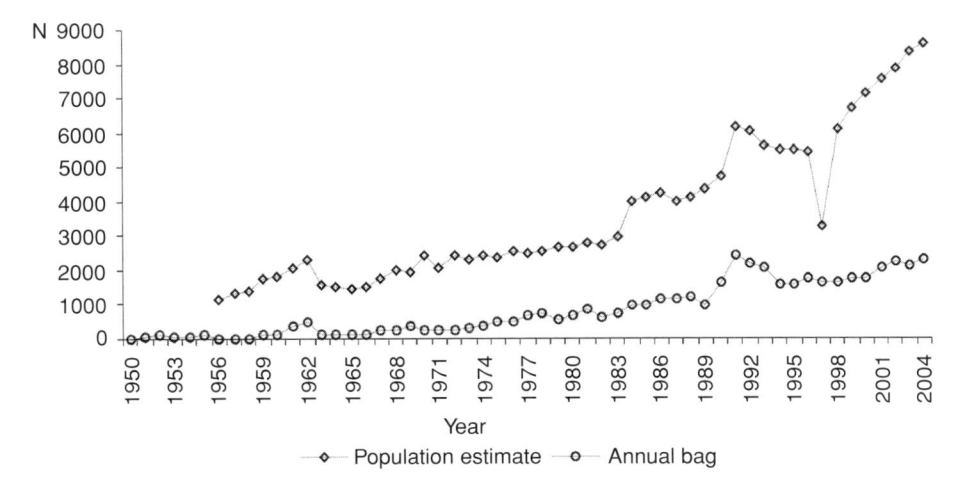

Fig. 13.8 Mouflon population estimate and annual bag

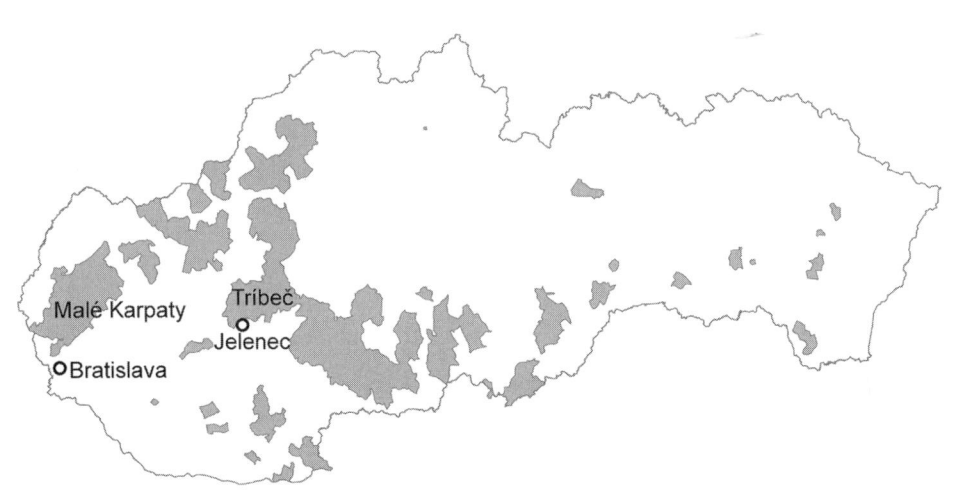

Fig. 13.9 Mouflon distribution in Slovakia (grey area)

Corsica and some other areas of Slovakia were released in the Malé Karpaty Mountains near the city of Bratislava.

The replenishing of stock continued intermittently between 1897 and 1930 with mouflon from Corsica, Austria, Romania and more from established populations in Slovakia. In the mid 1930s around 75 mouflon were hunted annually (Sabadoš, 1976).

After World War II, the numbers and hunting bag gradually increased. Thus, in 1979 the size of population was 2433 and the annual bag 223 individuals.

As mentioned in the introduction, chaos after the political changes in 1989 brought about heavy poaching and temporary population decline for most game

Fig. 13.10 Tatra chamois female in September (photo by Slavomír Find'o)

species including mouflon. Since 1998, the population has been increasing rapidly and in 2003 exceeded 8000 individuals (see Fig. 13.8; Hunting Statistics, 1968–2005).

At present mouflon are considered to be overpopulated. The population size is at least 100% higher than recommended from the point of view of forest and agricultural damage. The mouflon inhabits woodland areas in lower altitudes and its discontinuous range encompasses about 3080 km^2 (Fig. 13.9).

13.1.6 Chamois

Remnants of chamois are sparsely documented from the last interglacial period Ris-Würm about 115 000 years ago. A fragment of skull discovered in the Tatry Mountains was radiocarbon dated back to 10 610 ± 110 years BC (Schaefer, 1975). In 1517, the municipality of Levoča town donated chamois to the king and chamois was also carved in a wooden coat of arms in 1559.

The chamois is indigenous only in the Tatry Mountains and is endemic to the Carpathians. In 1971, it was described as a separate subspecies *Rupicapra rupicapra tatrica* (Blahout, 1972a).

In the past, the Tatra chamois was considered a rare game species, thus the size of the population was thoroughly estimated by the landowners and hunters. At present the cenusus is carried out by the national park staff. In comparison with forest-dwelling ungulates, the estimation of chamois numbers is easier and more accurate to predict. The Tatra chamois throughout the year inhabits open and semi-open high alpine habitat (alpine meadows, cliffs, boulder fields and dwarf pine). The use of alpine habitat above the timberline is a distinctive behavioural feature of Tatra chamois. These chamois had never been observed in forest habitats (Blahout, 1976). Since 1932, chamois numbers are regularly estimated every year by use

Table 13.1 *The numbers of Tatra chamois in 1890–1947*

Year	1890	1922	1932	1934	1936	1937	1938	1943	1946	1947
N	1000	300	1200	1250	1300	1170	1200	1211	280	300

of a standardised method. The tally is carried out during two consecutive days in November (rutting season), usually under good weather and snow conditions. Good visibility, contiguous snow cover and high activity of animals provide advantageous conditions for chamois observation. The whole area of the chamois range is split into sectors with two watchers responsible for each sector. During the day they survey the whole area, record numbers of animals, age–sex composition of observed herds, time of observation and direction of movement at the bordeline of the sectors (double counts are exluded). The results from each day are separately summarised and compared.

The oldest record of chamois numbers dates back to 1873, when 650 individuals were estimated in the whole area of Tatry mountains (Jamnický, 2000). Later on the numbers were notably influenced by wars and in 1922 plummeted to 300 individuals. Then the population steadily recovered until 1943, but by the end of World War II had crashed again to 280 individuals (Table 13.1; Blahout, 1972b; Chovancová and Gömöry, 1999).

At the time of the designation of the Tatry National Park in 1949, the population size was estimated at only 235 individuals. During the growth of the National Park, the population peaked in 1961 and from this point onwards has been gradually decreasing with only 189 chamois being recorded in the year 2000. Due to intensive anti-poaching measures the chamois population again increased in 2005 to 335 individuals (Hunting Statistics, 1968–2005).

Between 1969 and 76 chamois were reintroduced from the Tatry to the Nízke Tatry when 30 animals were used to re-establish the population. Based on recent population estimates the numbers of this metapopulation fluctuate around 100 individuals. Further increase of chamois numbers in Nízke Tatry is not expected due to insufficient size of suitable habitat (rocky terrain) and predation (lynx, wolf and golden eagle).

Besides the native subspecies, there are two small isolated free living populations of alpine chamois (*Rupicapra rupicapra rupicapra*, Linnaeus, 1758). In 1956, chamois were introduced from the Czech Republic to the Vel'ká Fatra mountains. Between 1956 and 60, in total 20 individuals including six males, eleven females and three kids were placed in a small acclimation pen (6.6 ha). From the 17 individuals freed in 1960 the numbers increased to 47 in 1970 and in 2005 the population size was about 52 individuals.

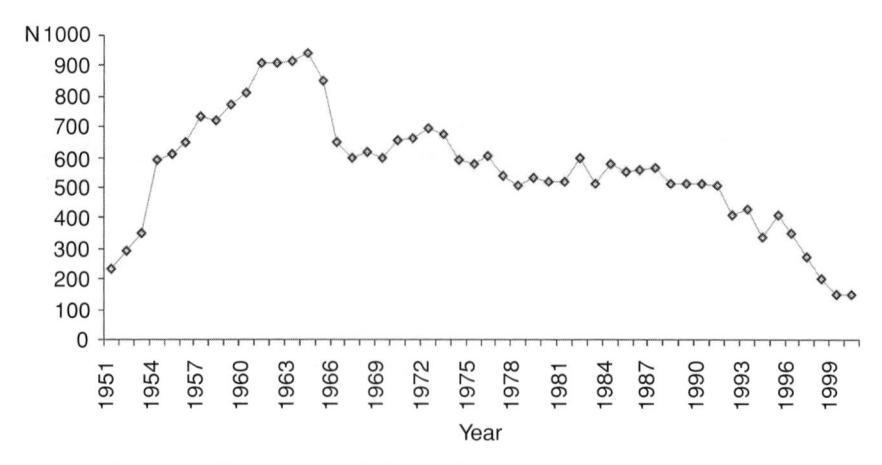

Fig. 13.11 Chamois population estimate in the Tatry National Park

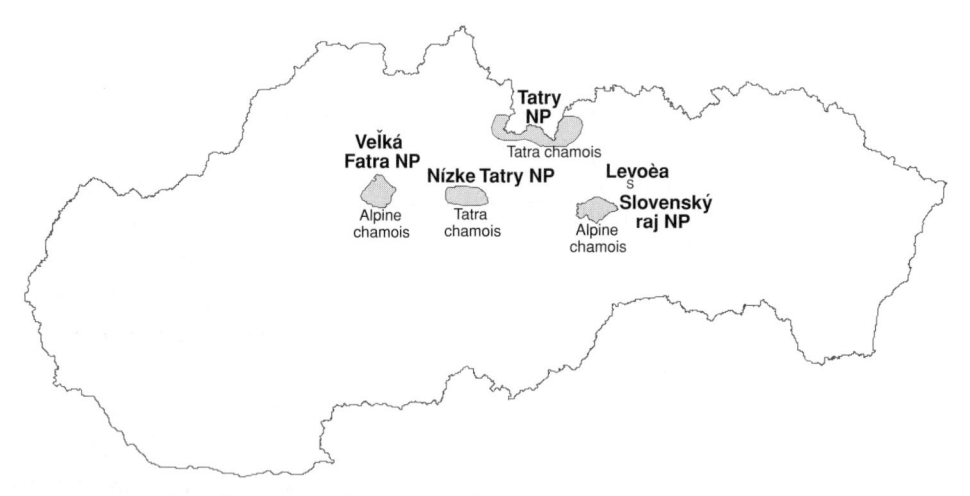

Fig. 13.12 Tatra and Alpine chamois distribution in Slovakia (grey areas)

In 1962, six more alpine chamois (four females and two males) from the Czech Republic were released into the wild within the area of the Slovenský raj. Some of the released chamois dispersed up to a distance of 11–49 km, but later returned to the area of their release.

The growth of this population can be documented by the following numbers of chamois: 11 in 1969, 72 in 1992 and 122 in 2005 (see Fig. 13.11; Hunting Statistics, 1968–2005). The area of Slovenský raj was designated a National Park in 1988 (Fig. 13.12). Due to the serious damage caused by chamois to the native vegetation of the park, a cull of this population has been proposed.

The efforts to protect the Tatra chamois date back to the nineteenth century, when a closed season from 15 December to 1 August was introduced by Hunting

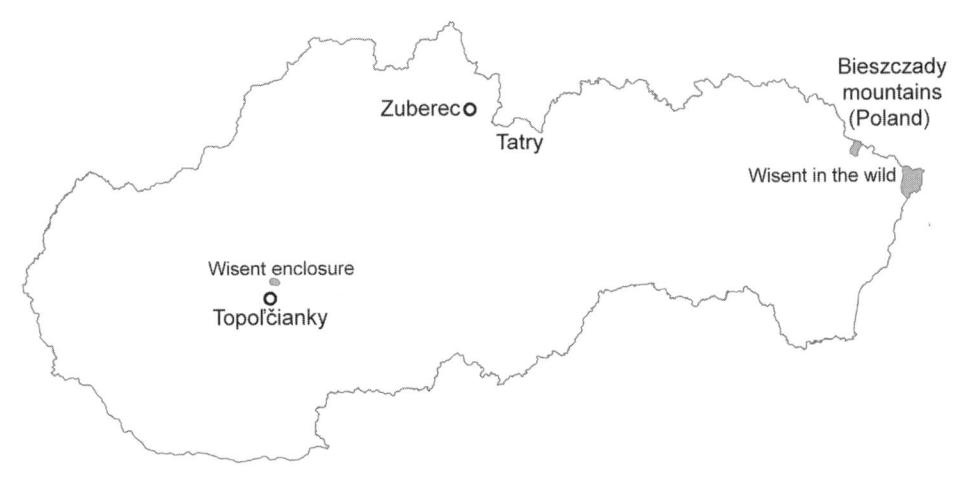

Fig. 13.13 Wisent distribution in Slovakia (grey areas)

law n XX/1883. From 1923 onward, the Tatra chamois has been protected all year in the Slovak and Polish parts of the Tatry mountains.
IUCN status:
Tatra chamois: CR, critically endangered, Bern 3, HD 5
Alpine chamois: NE not evaluated

13.1.7 Wisent or European bison

The extermination and archaeological findings of the wisent (*Bison bonasus*, Linnaeus 1758) have not been well documented. The wisent became extinct as a wild animal around 1730 (Bethlenfalvy, 1937). Some geographical names, for example the village of Zuberec ('zubor' in Slovak means European bison), remind us of the past occurrence of this species.

The International Society for Wisent Protection was established in 1923 in Frankfurt am Main (Germany) and this society embraced 16 member countries. The remaining free-ranging and captive animals were used for the establishment of a breeding stock. Up to 1952 the wisent had been reared in captivity in various zoos and enclosures across Europe and after 1952 free-ranging herds were established in many areas. In the Białowieza Primeval Forest (Poland) the first animals were freed in 1952. There were 24 metapopulations in Poland until 1984.

Between 1957 and 83 the wisent was reintroduced to Slovakia. In 1957, two mated animals from Poland were placed in a small acclimation pen within the area of Tatry Mountains. The first she-calf was born on 1 July 1957. Another pair of animals originated from the former USSR and, in 1958, these animals were located in a 27 ha acclimation pen within the Forest District Topol'čianky. In 1963, all the animals from Tatry were translocated to Topol'čianky and later on another male from Poland was added to this herd.

By the end of 1983 this herd numbered 21 animals consisting of six males, seven females and eight calves. Unfortunately, none of these animals was released into the wild. Furthermore, due to insufficient evidence of the geographical background of all the animals, the breeding herd was recently excluded from the international wisent studbook.

The occurrence of free-living wisent in Slovakia was always dependent on the metapopulations established alongside the Slovak/Polish and the Slovak/Ukrainian border areas (Fig. 13.13). The wisent became extinct in the Ukraine between 1919 and 26 and was successfully reintroduced in 1965. The wisent was released in four areas of the Ukrainian Carpathians and in seven lowland areas. In 2001, the Ukraine harboured about 489 animals in 11 localities while the size of the herds ranged from 3 to 148 individuals (Akimov *et al.*, 2001). There were 48 free-ranging wisents in the Bieszczady Mountains (Poland) near the Slovak/Polish border area in 1971 and, in 1986, the herd numbered up to 162 individuals. In this area, throughout the period 1971–86, up to 173 animals were hunted (112 males and 61 females). Despite the population increase on the Polish side, over a period of 40 years, the wisent was unable to establish a viable metapopulation in the neighbouring area of Slovakia. Thus only three (in 2000) and seven (in 2005) free-living individuals were recorded in the Eastern Carpathians (north-east Slovakia). There were around 10 animals in captivity during 2000–5.

IUCN classification: NE, not evaluated. The government compensates damage caused by wisent (Decree No 24/2003).

13.1.8 Wild boar

Wild boar (*Sus scrofa scrofa*, Linnaeus 1758) is native species and has always existed in Slovakia. The oldest skeletons date back to the early stages of Pleistocene. The wild boar was part of the diet of Mesolithic hunters (Molnár *et al.*, 1984).

In the Middle Ages, wild boar were a common species inhabiting woodland areas in high numbers and causing heavy damage to the crops of serfs (e.g. The Hungarian Act No 18/1504; Ascády, 1955).

The population trend from the end of the nineteenth century can be clearly seen from the size of annual cull as the number of boars taken reflects stock density (Figs. 13.14 and 13.15). Since the turn of the twentieth century up until 1967, the annual bag fluctuated around approximately 2000 individuals. From the late 1960s until the present, both the population size as well as the numbers of hunted animals have been increasing rapidly. The highest population size ever recorded was in 2003 when the numbers were estimated as up to 28 780 individuals (Hunting Statistics, 1968–2005).

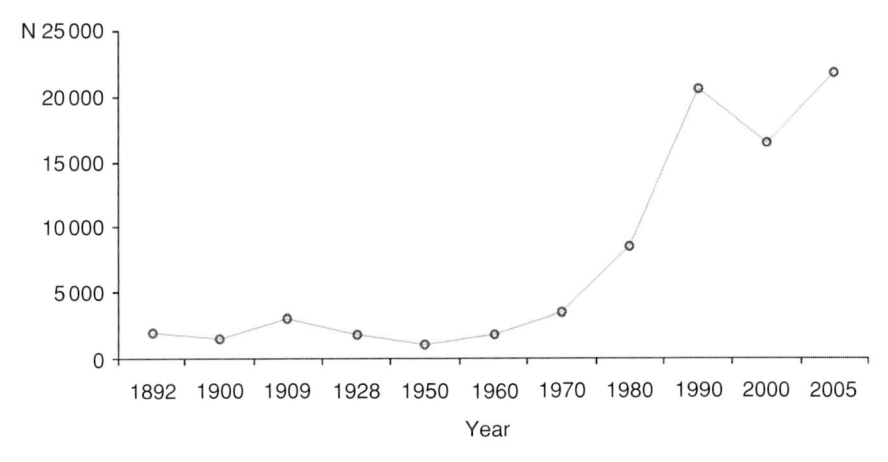

Fig. 13.14 Annual bag of wild boar 1892–2005

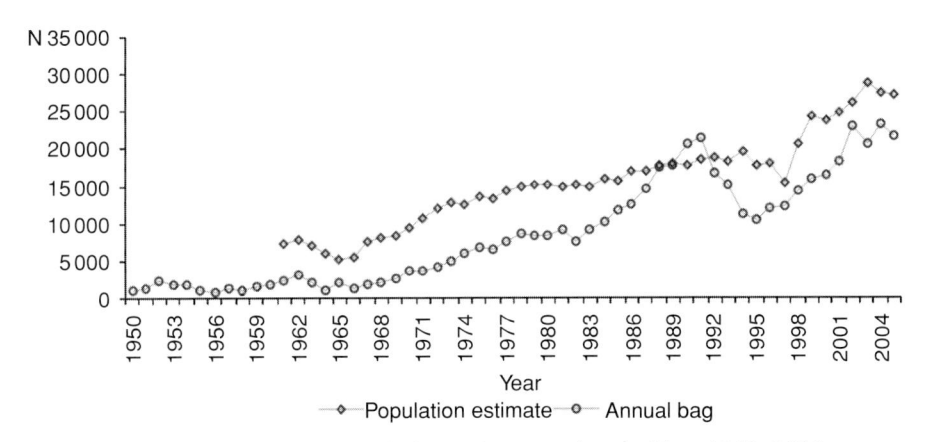

Fig. 13.15 Wild boar population estimate and annual bag 1950–2005

Fig. 13.16 Wild boar distribution in Slovakia (grey areas)

At present wild boar are distributed across the whole country including the open farmland areas in south-western and south-eastern Slovakia. Primary habitats of wild boar are oak and beech forests. The pine forests in south-western Slovakia and lowland poplar forests alongside the river Danube also harbour abundant wild boar populations. Population densities in woodland areas dominated by spruce tend to be substantially lower.

Agricultural areas free of trees, shrubbery and reeds are used by boar only on a seasonal basis, through the period of active vegetative growth (Hell *et al.*, 1984).

13.2 Legislation

The legislation covering management and protection of ungulates in Slovakia is outlined below. The information is current at the time of writing.

Act No 23/1962 of the Legal Codes on Hunting as amended by Act No 99/1993 of the Legal Codes.
Decree No 172/1975 of the Legal Codes on Game Protection, Open seasons and Hunting Methods.
Decree No 171/1975 of the Legal Codes on List of Game Species as amended by Decree No 222/2001 of the Legal Codes.
Act No 543/2002 of the Legal Codes on Nature and Landscape Protection
Decree No 24/2003 of the Legal Codes on Nature and Landscape Protection
Act No 326/2005 of the Legal Codes on Forests

All free ranging ungulates are listed as game species. However, rare species such as European elk, wisent and Tatra chamois are protected all year round. Furthermore, these species are listed in the international agreements signed by Slovakia, e.g. the Bern Convention, and are also included in the Red List of Plants and Animals of Slovakia (Baláž *et al.*, 2001).

A statutory open season was designated for roe deer, red deer, fallow deer, mouflon and wild boar (Table 13.2). Deer and mouflon can be stalked only with rifles while wild boar is also allowed to be killed by a shotgun using rifle slugs. It is legal to organise a drive hunt on wild boars in autumn with dogs less than 50 cm at the shoulder. There is a legal duty to trace wounded animals with utility dogs (bloodhounds or other breeds).

13.3 Management objectives

The management objectives are defined by the Hunting Act No 23/1962 amended in 1993. The purpose of hunting management is to support the conservation and rational use of game species that are designated as national heritage of the Slovak

Table 13.2 *Statutory open seasons for ungulates in Slovakia*

Species	Sex–Age	Open season
Roe deer	Bucks	16 May–30 Sept.
	Does + Kids	1 Sept.–30 Nov.
Red deer	Stags	1 Aug.–31 Dec.
	Hinds + Fawns	
Fallow deer	Bucks	1 Sept.–31 Dec.
	Does	
Mouflon	Rams	1 Sept.–31 Dec.[1]
	Ewes	
Wild boar	Males, Females, Yearlings	16 July–31 Dec.[2]
	Piglets	16 July–31 Jan.
Wisent	Bulls	Protected
	Cows	
European elk	Bulls	Protected
	Cows	
Tatra chamois	Males	Protected
	Females	
Alpine chamois	Males	Hunted on exception[3]
	Females	

Notes:
[1] In game enclosures, 1 Aug.–31 Jan.
[2] For control of swine fever disease, piglets and yearlings are commonly hunted throughout the year.
[3] No open season. Hunted in two areas in small numbers usually in autumn.

Republic. Hunting has also been defined as a part of conservation and proper use of a renewable resource, whether for venison production or production of hunting trophies. Major conflicts between hunting management on one side and the forestry and farming industry on the other side are not acceptable. Other aims thus include control of damage to forest and farm crops.

13.4/5 Management structure and organisation

In total, the hunting area of Slovakia encompasses up to 44 365 km^2. Hunting rights belong to the landowner. The hunting areas belong to various owners such as the government 45%, farm communities 15%, private landowners 14%, associations of the former co-owners called 'Komposesorát' and 'Urbár'[1] 12%, municipalities 9%, church 2%, and others 3%.

---

[1] Kompossesorát: Slovak variation of Latin word meaning indivisible owning of land by the family members. Urbár : Part of aristocratic land given to the serfs for use. The principles of both forms of landowning are still valid in Slovakia.

In 2005, 1806 hunting grounds were designated (average size 2457 ha) including 23 game enclosures and 16 pheasantries. These designated hunting grounds are determined for a period of 10 years by the county government administration body responsible for forestry and game management (there are 40 offices in Slovakia). The designation of a hunting ground requires the following process. One or more landowners have to apply to the county administration body for the designation of a hunting ground on their own land. The applicants suggest the size and the shape of a contiguous hunting ground. Besides this, several other criteria must be fulfilled. Within the hunting management zones where red deer is the main game species, the minimum area of the hunting ground has to be 2000 ha. In the case of management zones predominated by roe deer the smallest size of the hunting ground is 1000 ha. Allocation of a hunting ground imposes responsibilities on the owners of such designated hunting areas as well as the right to stalk game and retain venison and trophies and the right to collect cast antlers.

After the designation of a hunting ground, the owners can either keep the hunting right for themselves or rent it to a third party. The process of designation of a hunting ground is the same on governmental as well as non-governmental land.

Having passed a course on hunting management (either a special course or part of the study at secondary school or university), an person over 18 years can become the holder of a hunting licence, which is issued by the government county administration body. The holder of a hunting licence can apply to the police for a gun licence (either shotgun or rifle). Every firearm is registered by the police. Furthermore, every hunter must be a member of the Slovak Hunting Association, which is a non-governmental organisation associating hunters in various clubs and covering activities such as dog breeding, trials and exhibitions of the dogs, falconry, sport shooting, hunting exhibitions, etc. In 2005 there were 36 581 hunters registered within rented hunting grounds while the number of hunters in non-rented hunting grounds was unknown. Most of the Slovakian hunters stalk free-ranging ungulates (outside enclosures) such as roe deer, wild boar and red deer, and occasionally fallow deer and mouflon.

13.6 Actual management and hunting practices

Within every hunting ground, hunting of ungulates has to be undertaken according to an approved plan. Preparation of such a managment plan is a legal requirement. The main determinant of such a plan is a requirement to keep population densities at a level slightly below that of the carrying capacity. Estimates of the tolerable numbers of each species, which should be maintained in the hunting ground, are derived from an assessment of the amount of winter food supply and the daily food requirements of the particular species. Thus winter food supply for ungulates is decisive for the classification of the carrying capacity of a hunting ground.

Winter food resources for wild ungulates were surveyed in the most important communities of forest types across Slovakia (e.g. Katreniak, 1992). There are five site classes for red deer and roe deer, four for wild boar, three for mouflon and two for fallow deer. For each site class the range of standard (tolerable) numbers of a particular species per 1000 ha of hunting area (forest plus farmland) is prescribed. For example, within a hunting ground classified as the best (site class I) for red deer, prescribed numbers range from 21 to 25 animals per 1000 ha. The population size for all game species is estimated by the end of March every year. The hunters within the hunting ground estimate the numbers. Ungulates are normally counted around feeding stations throughout winter. In addition to this, hunters estimate numbers based on the field survey carried out during two consecutive days in March (see section 13.7).

By the end of March, the observed numbers of animals are summarised. No other methods are used for the population estimate. Based on the estimated numbers of adult females in the stock, the recruitment for a particular year is estimated. The following percentages of females producing offspring (coefficients of recruitment) in the stock are considered: red deer 60–80%, roe deer 70–100%, fallow deer and mouflon 60–80% and wild boar 70–130%. These coefficients are derived either by post mortem examination of the fertility of red deer females culled after rutting season (Hell et al., 1987) or by an estimation of the adult females/offspring ratio in free living species of other ungulates (Lochman et al., 1979; Nečas, 1975; Wolf and Rakušan, 1977; Husák et al., 1986). The timing of the shooting plan's approval (before 1 May) is decisive for the use of coefficients of recruitment as the parturition period of most ungulate species living in Slovakia begins in mid-May.

Culling is an activity aimed primarily at the control of numbers in total, and by sex, so that a suitable number of males, females and young are retained. The task of a shooting plan is to adjust observed spring numbers plus expected recruits to standardise the numbers of animals for each sex and age category within the hunting ground.

Detailed selection principles for culling have been developed for stags. There are exact criteria regarding the stags that can be shot, which take into consideration age and trophy quality. Mature stags with superior heads can be culled at the age of trophy culmination (e.g. 11–13 years in red deer). Females and young are selected according to age and condition.

The Ministry of Agriculture is in charge of coordinating hunting management at national level. Currently there are 40 governmental regional forestry offices responsible for forestry and hunting management. These offices are in charge of gathering and approving hunting management plans for each hunting ground within their territories for the current year, as well as statistical forms on the numbers and culled animals from the previous year.

The leader of the hunting ground is required to complete a statistical form about estimated numbers and the numbers of culled animals from the previous year and to submit it to a regional forestry office by 10 February of the current year. After approval, this form is submitted by 15 February to the National Forest Centre, which summarises the data for the whole territory of Slovakia and produces the Annual Report on Hunting Statistics. Hunting statistics have been compiled annually since 1968.

The leader of the hunting ground is also required to complete a special form called a 'Breeding and shooting plan' for the current year. This plan must be submitted to the regional forestry and hunting management body for approval by 15 April of the current year. After approval, a new hunting season can commence. A shooting plan considers the numbers of game species counted by 31 March.

13.6.1 Hunting methods

There are differences in the hunting methods of wild boar and other ungulate species. Stalking and shooting from high seats by rifle are legal methods of deer (red, roe and fallow) and mouflon hunting. High seats are commonly located at the edge of woodland and a field or meadow. Shooting at night with the use of artificial light and driven hunts are strictly prohibited.

Wild boar can be culled by rifle and/or a shotgun using rifle slugs. Stalking and shooting from a high seat are common throughout the open season while driven hunts take place usually from September to January. Various breeds of dogs including hounds, terriers and spaniels are used for wild boar chasing. For this purpose only breeds smaller than 50 cm at shoulder can be used in order to prevent a long pursuit and killing of the game by the dogs. The dogs are specially trained for wild boar hunts. Driven hunts are subject to the annual managemant plan of a hunting ground and the same hunting area can only be used twice per open season. It is legal to shoot boars from a high seat at night without the use of artificial light three days before and after the full moon.

Tracing of wounded game is a legal duty. Specially trained dogs of almost all hunting breeds are used for this purpose. Within the hunting grounds where the stalking of ungulates takes place, a particular number of utility dogs for tracing wounded animals is prescribed depending on the size of the area and expected numbers of culled ungulates.

13.7 Census types and methods

As mentioned in the previous section, the count of ungulates and other game species is part of the preparation of a shooting plan. Counting of ungulates takes place during the latter part of winter in early March usually on two consecutive days. Game-keepers and hunters responsible for a particular hunting ground carry out the census. The whole area of a hunting ground is split into sectors (transects) with two or more hunters responsible for each sector. The tally is done simultaneously within the whole territory of the hunting ground. A widely used method is to count ungulates around feeding stations, or salt licks during mornings and evenings preferably in good weather. In the lower altitudes free from snow in March, common practice is to tally ungulates coming out to feed in the fields, glades and meadows early mornings and late evenings, either from high seats or by surveying the area on foot.

Where game-keepers are employed, the counting is done by keen observation of ungulates, and by noting their movements, thus establishing an approximate total. Experienced keepers are able, after a month's observation, to arrive at a figure with an acceptable margin of error. This method is commonly used within the area of the government's forestry organisations, which encompasses about 40% of the forestland of the country.

13.8 Damage to forest and farm crops

Wild ruminants and occasionally wild boar cause damage to forestry. The most important damage to forests is imposed by red deer and to a lesser extent by roe deer, mouflon and fallow deer (Fig. 13.17). In the Slovenský raj National Park the introduced Alpine chamois causes harm to native plant species. Wild boar locally root out freshly planted seedlings in newly established forest plantations but this damage is not compensated. The damage imposed by wild ruminants is not distinguished by species.

Browsing of young economically important trees is the usual type of damage followed by bark peeling in thickets. Trees that are highly susceptible to browsing are silver fir (*Abies alba*), Scots pine (*Pinus silvestris*), oaks (*Quercus* spp.), ash (*Fraxinus excelsior*), sycamore (*Acer pseudoplatanus*), elm (*Ulmus montanus*) and poplars (*Populus* spp.)

Red deer cause serious damage to poplar plantations alongside the River Danube by browsing and breaking seedlings shortly after planting. As poplars are the main trees in this vast area, the damage severely disrupts forestry management aims. Widely distributed trees like spruce (*Picea abies*) and beech (*Fagus silvatica*) are also locally affected by browsing, but these species show good resilience and soon regenerate. Larch (*Larix decidua*) is essentially liable to fraying imposed by roe and red deer. Within protected areas some rare plants are damaged or even locally exterminated, e.g. English yew (*Taxus baccata*) (Find'o, 1998).

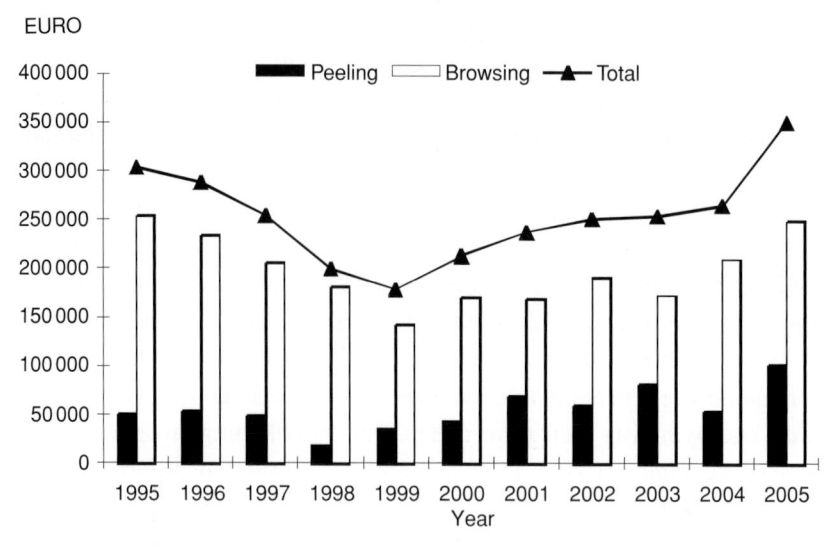

Fig. 13.17 Damage caused by peeling and browsing

Bark peeling is primarily harmful to coniferous trees as wood-decaying fungi frequently infect the fresh wounds on trunks. Winter peeling of spruce is economically unacceptable especially around red deer feeding stations. Other species such as silver fir, pine, larch, ash and alder are also susceptible to peeling.

There is a legal duty for hunters to compensate for damage to forest trees and farm crops (Hunting Act No 23/1963 amended by Act No 99/1993), although the government compensates for damage caused by protected species such as wisent and European elk (Nature and Landscape Protection Act No 543/2002).

From 1960 onward, the damage caused by wild ruminants to forests is annually investigated and assessed. Damage assessment is coordinated on a national level by the Ministry of Agriculture and is carried out according to the uniform national methodology (Find'o et al., 1998). All forest owners have a duty to report past damage on their own land (reporting period is from 1 July to 30 June of the following year) and send a completed statistical form to the National Forest Centre. Additionally the statistical form includes data on mitigation measures carried out by the forest owner. Individual protection of trees by repellents and mechanical scaring devices are widely used methods across the country. Deer-proof fencing is still in use on a smaller scale. There is a legal duty for forest owners to protect trees against damage caused by game (Forest Act No 326/2005). On average about 20 000 ha of forest stands are annually protected while the cost exceeds EUR 1 429 000.

The owners and users of hunting grounds have a legal duty to compensate for damage caused by ungulates to agricultural crops and vineyards. If the harvest is delayed the damage is not compensated. To prevent extensive damage, farmers (landowners) have a duty to carry out adequate preventative measures that do not cause harm to game (e.g. electric fencing, fencing, deterrents). If protective measures have not been taken the damage is not fully compensated. Damage to unfenced gardens, orchards, hedgerows and solitary trees is not accepted.

Records of compensated damage to agriculture are kept annually within the national hunting statistics (see section 13.6). There is no official methodology for investigation and assessment of damage to farm crops. However, experts usually consult and use research results (Hell and Plesník, 1989). Thus damage is evaluated based on expert opinion. The first step is to identify the size of the damaged area. For a final decision, it is recommended to wait until the harvest and compare the yield of damaged and undamaged areas. Average annual damage reported over the period of 2001–2003 to farm crops was EUR 129 630, while in 2005 this increased to EUR 319 190 (Hunting Statistics, 1968–2005).

The legal procedure for making a claim for ungulate damage to forestry and agriculture is included in hunting law (no. 23/1962 amended in 1993). The regional governmental forestry offices responsible for forestry and hunting (see section 13.6) have a legal duty to establish an independent commission for the assessment of damage caused by game. Members of the commission are made up of representatives from the govermental forestry office, local municipality body and the Slovak Hunting Association (NGO). The landowner/user must make a claim for game damage through this commision. The farmers must make a claim within 14 days of the damage being discovered. In the case of forest damage, the claim must be made by the end of July of a current year for the preceeding year (from 31 July to 30 June). Thus three parties are involved in the process of damage assessment and compensation: an independent commission, the injured party and the hunters. It is possible for an agreement to be made between the injured party and hunters about the size and method of compensation (monetary or otherwise). In this case, the size of damage can be assessed and agreed by all parties involved, or they can ask for an expert opinion. If the size and method of compensation is not agreed between the injured party and hunters, the case will go to court. The court normally asks for at least two independent expert opinions.

Of all ungulates, wild boar and red deer inflict the most harm to agricultural crops. Eating, digging and trampling usually damage the crops. Both ungulate species can damage various cultivated plants including maize (*Zea mays*, grain), wheat (*Triticum aestivum*, grain), oats (*Avena sativa*, grain), barley (*Hordeum vulgare*, grain), potatoes (*Solanum tuberosum*, tubers) and turnip rape (*Brassica rapa var. oleifera*). Wild boars root out freshly sown seeds of maize in spring. Deer can seriously damage turnip rape and winter wheat fields during the winter period by browsing and trampling. Damage caused by rare species such as wisent and European elk is so far negligible.

13.9 Supplementary feeding

Supplementary feeding of ungulates during the shortage of natural food recourses in winter is a legal duty and common practice across the country (Hunting Act No 23/1963 as amended by Act No 99/1993). In fact, all species of ungulates besides Tatra chamois inhabiting areas above the timberline are more or less affected by the supplementary winter feeding. The fodder is provided either in specially built feeding stations or often just placed on the ground. To prepare a sufficient amount of food for the winter season is part of the breeding and shooting plan for the current year.

Winter supplementation is targeted specifically on:

- Prevention of winter starvation
- Increased density of trophy males, antler points and weights
- Prevention of agricultural and forest damage

In all cases, feeding is associated with the desire to maintain artificially high densities of ungulates to support hunting interests. Animals are permanently offered hay. Other bulk feeds commonly provided include silage made from whole plants and fruit-husks, root crops (turnips, carrots, potatoes, etc.) or maize. A variety of commercial pelleted rations are available based on alfalfa, lucerne, maize or other cereals.

There is no scientific proof of the positive effects of winter-feeding programmes on targeted aims. On the contrary, many disadvantages have been observed (see also Putman and Staines, 2004).

Poor quality food has often caused gastrointestinal disorders. As a rule, when red deer, mouflon and fallow deer aggregate around feeding stations they seriously debark trees up to a distance of 300 m from the food resource. Spruce forest stands aged 20–60 years are usually heavily peeled, probably as a result of intraspecific competion. Large predators such as wolf, lynx and brown bear commonly visit areas around feeding stations as the concentrated prey attracts them (Find'o and Chovancová, 2004). Moreover bears regularly feed on food provided for wild ungulates. Large predators in Slovakia inhabit about 45% of the country and are sympatric with all ungulate species. At feeding stations, regular access to supplementary food by ungulates is commonly disrupted by predation, even for several days. Thus a regular intake of supplementary food provided to ungulates is commonly denied.

To secure regular access and intake of food by ungulates is basically the most important requirement of proper winter feeding. To avoid forest damage to forest stands that are liable to browsing and peeling, it is recommended not to feed wild ruminants within their vicinity.

13.10 Effectiveness and problems of current management strategies

There are several limitations of the existing system of hunting management. Probably the most important problem is the ineffective system of creating shooting plans. As mentioned above, spring numbers of ungulates counted in March within a hunting ground are essential for the formation of a shooting plan. This early date for counting ungulates, however, neglects the beginning of spring migrations of red deer to their summer ranges that normally start in the second half of April (Find'o, 2002; Find'o et al., 2006). Thus disproportion between spring and autumn numbers can seriously bias the shooting plan. Furthermore, inaccurate methods of census and constant underestimation of real numbers results in a gradual increase of the deer, mouflon and wild boar populations. At present, in some areas of Slovakia the numbers of these species are well above carrying capacity. Consequently the damage to forestry and agriculture is increasing. Moreover, it is absolutely necessary to reduce the wild boar population in order to control swine fever disease.

There is an attempt to introduce large-scale planning to mitigate the existing problems. This means that the essential area required for making a plan would be a larger hunting management unit instead of the smaller hunting grounds. Such a large management unit would encompass several neighbouring hunting grounds. Unfortunately, the main objection to the introduction of this new system of planning is the fact that hunting right belongs to the landowner. Thus hunting ground owners are not interested in the proposed system of planning.

References

Akimov, I., Kozak, I., Kryzanovskij, V. and Perzanowski, K. (2001) Long-term population records: a crucial factor for the success of the re-establishment of European bison (*Bison bonasus*) population in Ukraine. *Ekológia* **20** Supplement 2, 57–62.

Ascády, I. (1955) *Dejiny poddanstva v Uhorsku*. (The history of Serfdom in Hungary). Bratislava: Vydavatel'stvo SAV, 445 pages. (In Slovak.)

Bakoš, A., Hell, P. *et al.* (1995) *Pol'ovníctvo na Slovensku 1920–1995*. (Hunting in Slovakia in 1920–1995). Bratislava: Parpress, 265 pp. (In Slovak.)

Baláž, D., Marhold, K. and Urban, P. (2001) *Červený zoznam rastlín a živočíchov Slovenska*. (Red list of plants and animals in Slovakia) Ochrana prírody, Štátna ochrana prírody, Supplement 20, Banská Bystrica, 160 pp. (In Slovak.)

Bališ, M. (1980) *Jelenia zver*. (The red deer). Bratislava: Príroda. 335 pp. (In Slovak.)

Bárta, J. (1965) *Slovensko v staršej a strednej dobe kamennej*. (Slovakia in Palaeolithic and Mesolithic periods). Bratislava: Vydavatel'stvo SAV. 305 pp. (In Slovak.)

Bäumler, W., Postner, M. and Ueckermann, E. (1986) Die Forstschädlinge Europas. (Forest pests of Europe). *Band 5, Wirbeltiere.* Hamburg and Berlin: Paul Parey, 300 pp. (In German.)

Bethlenfalvy, E. (1937) *Die Tierwelt der Hohen Tatra.* (Wildlife of the Tatry Mountains). Spišské Podhradie: Edmund Schustek, 115 pp. (In German.)

Blahout, M. (1972a) Zur Taxonomie der Population von *Rupicapra rupicapra* (Linnaeus 1758) in der Hohen Tatra. (The contribution to taxonomy of *Rupicapra rupicapra* (Linnaeus 1758) in the Tatry mountains). *Zoologické listy* **2**, 115–32. (In German.)

Blahout, M. (1972b) Súčasný stav a perspektívy rozvoja chovu kamzíkov v TNP. (Current status and future of chamois management in the Tatry National Park). *Lesnícky časopis* **18**, 401–407. (In Slovak.)

Blahout, M. (1976) *Kamzíčia zver.* (The chamois). Bratislava: Príroda. 171 pp. (In Slovak.)

Čaplovič, P. (1987) *Orava v praveku a včasnej dobe dejinnej a na začiatku stredoveku.* (The Orava county in prehistoric times, early historical period and in the beginning of the Middle Ages). Martin: Osveta, 264 pp. (In Slovak.)

Čech, C., Vodička, F. and Záborský, D. (1935) *Naša zverina.* (Our wildlife). Bratsilava: Academia. 559 pp. (In Slovak.)

Chovancová, B. and Gömöry, D. (1999) Vplyv prírodných činiteľov na populáciu kamzíka vrchovského tatranského (*Rupicapra rupicapra tatrica* Bl. 1971) v Tatranskom národnom púartku. (The influence of natural factors on the population of the Tatra chamois (*Rupicapra rupicapra tatrica* Bl. 1971) in the Tatry National Park). *Folia venatoria* **28+29**, 85–97. (In Slovak.)

Chudík, I. and Sládek, J. (1962) Los veľký (*Alces alces* L.) na Slovensku. (European elk (*Alces alces* L.) in Slovakia). *Biológia* **8**, 616–20. (In Slovak.)

Feriancová-Masárová, Z., Hanák, V. (1965) *Stavovce Slovenska IV: Cicavce.* (The vertebrates of Slovakia IV: Mammals). Bratislava: Vydavateľstvo SAV. 336 pp. (In Slovak.)

Findʼo, S. (1998) The influence of red deer browsing on forest regeneration in the Poľana Biosphere Reserve. In Z. Zomborszky, ed., *Advances in Deer Biology. Proceedings of the 4th International Deer Biology Congress,* Kaposvár, Hungary, pp. 226–9.

Findʼo, S. (2002) Domovské okrsky, migrácie a denná aktivita jelenej zveri v horských lesoch. (Home ranges, migrations and daily activity pattern in mountain red deer). *Folia venatoria* **32**, 7–14. (In Slovak.)

Findʼo, S. and Chovancová, B. (2004) Home ranges of two wolf packs in the Slovak Carpathians. *Folia Zoologica* **53**, 17–26.

Findʼo, S., Petráš, R. and Paulenka, J. (1998) Metodický postup pre výpočet náhrad za poškodzovanie lesných porastov zverou. (Damage inventory and assessment caused by game to forest stands). *Lesnícky výskumný ústav Zvolen. Odborná lesnícka aktualita* **1**, 17 pp. (In Slovak.)

Findʼo, S., Bučko, J. and Steyaert, S. (2006) Seasonal migration pattern of red deer (*Cervus elaphus* L.) in the central Slovakian mountains. In L. Bartoš, A. Dušek, R. Kotrba and J. Bartošová-Víchová, eds., *Advances in Deer Biology. Proceedings of the 6th International Deer Biology Congress,* p. 222.

Gyimesi, J. (1971) Imigrácie losa mokraďového západného (*Alces alces alces* L. 1758) do ČSSR. (Immigration of moose (*Alces alces alces* L. 1758) to the former Czechoslovakia). *Folia venatoria* **1**, 217–224. (In Slovak.)

Hartl, G. B., Markov, G., Rubin, A. *et al.* (1993) Allozyme diversity within and among populations of three ungulate species (*Cervus elaphus, Capreolus capreolus, Sus*

scrofa) of Southeastern and Central Europe. *Zeitschrift für Säugetierkunde* **58**, 352–61.
Hartl, G. B., Nadlinger, K., Apollonio, M. *et al.* (1995) Extensive mitochondrial-DNA differentiation among European red deer (*Cevus elaphus*) populations: implications. *Zeitschrift für Säugetierkunde* **60**, 41–52.
Hell, P. (1979) *Srnčia zver*. (The roe deer). Bratislava: Príroda, 310 pp. (In Slovak.)
Hell, P. and Pataky, T. (1992) Súčasné rozšírenie a zhodnotenie mikropopulácií danielej zveri na Slovensku. (Present distribution and assessment of fallow deer micropopulations in Slovakia). *Folia venatoria* **22**, 23–45. (In Slovak.)
Hell, P. and Plesník, J. (1989) *Škody spôsobené zverou v pol'nohospodárstve a ochrana proti nim*. (Damage Caused by Game to Agriculture and Mitigation Measures). Praha: Federal Ministry of Agriculture, 44 pp. (In Slovak.)
Hell, P., Hrnčiar, M. and Šimiak, M. (1984) Rozšírenie a rajonizácia svine divej (*Sus scrofa* L.) na Slovensku. (Distribution and zoning of wild boar (*Sus scrofa* L.) in Slovakia). *Folia venatoria* **14**, 71–88. (In Slovak.)
Hell, P., Farkaš, J., Komárek, V. and Pataky, T. (1987) Fertilita a prenatálny vývoj jelenej zveri v prírodných podmienkach Slovenska. (Fertility and embryogenetic development of free living red deer in Slovakia). *Folia venatoria* **17**, 17–41. (In Slovak.)
Hell, P., Lehocký, M., Sabadoš, K. and Farkaš, J. (1999) Súčasná situácia a perspektívy chovu danielej zveri na Slovensku. (Present situation and outline of fallow deer management in Slovakia). *Folia venatoria* **28+29**, 37–44. (In Slovak.)
Hunting Statistics (1968–2005) *Hunting Statistics*. Bratislava: Ministry of Agriculture of the Slovak Republic.
Husák, F., Wolf, R. and Lochman, J. (1986) *Daněk, sika, jelenec*. (Fallow deer, sika deer and whitetailed deer). Praha: Státní zemědelské nakladatelství, 320 pp. (In Czech.)
Jamnický, J. (2000) Otázniky nad kamzíkmi. (Questionmarks over the chamois). *Tatry* **5**, 8–9. (In Slovak.)
Karč, P. (1979) Los mokrad'ový (*Alces alces* L. 1758) v Liptove. (The European elk (*Alces alces* L. 1758) in the Liptov county). *Zborník Liptov* **5**, 251–4. (In Slovak.)
Katreniak, J. (1992) Zásoba potravy pre prežúvavú zver v zimnom období v I. až IV. lesnom vegetačnom stupni. (Winter food resources for wild ruminants from I-IV forest vegetative belt). *Folia venatoria* **22**, 1–11. (In Slovak.)
Kocian, L., Halák, K. and Žiak, D. (1998) Radiometric dating of occurrence of European elk (*Alces alces*) in Slovakia using the radiocarbon technique. *Folia Zoologica* **47**, 155–7.
Lochman, J. (1985) *Jelení zvěř*. (The red deer). Praha: Státní zemědelské nakladatekství, 351 pp. (In Czech.)
Lochman, J., Kotlý, A. and Hromas, J. (1979) Dutorohá zvěř. (Wild sheep and goats). Praha: Státní zemědelské nakladatelství, 384 pp. (In Czech.)
Macko, Š. (1985) Príspevok k histórii daniela škvrnitého (*Dama dama* L.). (Contribution to the history of European fallow deer (*Dama dama* L.)). *Folia venatoria* **15**, 191–203. (In Slovak.)
Melichar, J. (1928) Fosilní a recentní kopitníci na Orave. (Fossil and present ungulates of the Orava county). *Věda přírodní* **IX**, 3–5. (In Slovak.)
Molnár, L., Teren, Š. *et al.* (1984) *Naše pol'ovníctvo*. (Our hunting). Bratislava: Obzor, 400 pp. (In Slovak.)
Nečas, J. (1975) *Srnčí zvěř*. (The roe deer). Praha: Státní zemědelské nakladatelství, 304 pp. (In Czech.)

Putman, R. J. and Staines, B. W. (2004) Supplementary winter feeding of wild red deer *Cervus elaphus* in Europe and North America: justifications, feeding practice and effectiveness. *Mammal Review* **34**, 285–306.

Sabadoš, K. (1976) História a perspektívy chovu muflónej zveri na Slovensku. (The history and outlook of moufflon management in Slovakia). *Folia venatoria* **5+6**, 94–104. (In Slovak.)

Schaefer, H. (1975) Holozäne Kleinsäuger und Vögel aus der Hohen Tatra (Muran II). (Holocene small mammals and birds of the Tatry Mountains). *Decheniana* **127**, 105–14. (In German.)

Schmidt, Z. (1967) *Cestami miliónročí po Slovensku*. (Routes across Slovakia over millions of years). Bratislava: Príroda. (In Slovak.)

Wolf, R. and Rakušan, C. (1977) *Černá zvěř*. (The wild boar). Praha: Státní zemědelské nakladatelství, 204 pp. (In Czech.)

14

Ungulates and their management in Hungary

SÁNDOR CSÁNYI AND RÓBERT LEHOCZKI

14.1 Ungulate species and their distribution

In old chronicles, the Carpathian Basin was always mentioned as an area abundant in game. When the Hungarians settled in 896, the landscape was quite different: 40–50% of the current territory of Hungary was woodland. The decline of forests started in the thirteenth century as forested areas were converted into agricultural lands or used for animal husbandry (Keresztesi, 1991).

Over the centuries, Hungary was regarded as the most plentiful European country in game, which was attributed to the interactions of fertile soils, mild climate and the rich flora. The general abundance of wildlife was accompanied by the excellent trophy quality of deer and in the World Hunting Exhibition held in Berlin (1937) Hungarian red, fallow, and roe deer trophies won lots of medals and the majority of the major prizes (Nemeskéri *et al.*, 1942).

Five species of ungulates form free-living populations in Hungary: red deer, fallow deer, roe deer, mouflon and wild boar. Of these species red deer, roe deer and wild boar are native species, while fallow deer and mouflon were both introduced at different periods of time. A sixth ungulate species, sika deer (Japanese sika, *Cervus nippon nippon* and Dybowski sika deer, *Cervus nippon hortulorum*) can also be found in Hungary but it is restricted to a single game park, and it does not have any management importance.

14.1.1 Red deer

Red deer is a native species within the Carpathian Basin. According to archaeological studies red deer or very similar species were continuously inhabiting it (at least 100 000 years BP) and were important protein resources for people living here (Szunyoghy, 1963). During the last millennium red deer was the most important

Table 14.1 *Reported spring population size and annual harvest for five ungulate species in Hungary*

Year	Red deer Population	Red deer Harvest	Fallow deer Population	Fallow deer Harvest	Roe deer Population	Roe deer Harvest	Mouflon Population	Mouflon Harvest	Wild boar Population	Wild boar Harvest
1960	16 733	3 800	900	100	68 800	3 700	1 400	200	8 300	3 900
1961	10 200	4 700	300	..	71 575	4 700	1 200	..	8 909	4 200
1962	16 350	5 400	400	380	75 100	5 300	1 200	220	9 543	5 212
1963	17 483	5 431	1 590	..	68 450	9 442	1 360	..	8 959	5 602
1964	20 871	5 394	1 814	468	76 780	7 668	1 140	..	9 674	4 707
1965	21 000	6 500	1 820	500	88 380	7 931	1 030	100	9 422	5 192
1966	20 800	6 700	1 550	..	96 500	9 400	1 530	..	10 300	5 800
1967	21 800	5 600	1 580	350	107 570	12 060	1 740	200	12 220	7 100
1968	24 980	6 804	1 920	400	118 620	14 980	2 680	250	13 287	8 203
1969	29 605	8 135	2 275	395	135 963	18 206	2 598	297	13 969	7 342
1970	32 590	9 061	2 443	659	141 280	19 613	2 319	166	15 669	8 992
1971	36 039	11 869	2 628	470	148 868	25 910	2 396	130	16 473	12 076
1972	38 489	14 429	3 094	758	163 345	29 434	2 730	138	16 926	13 945
1973	39 227	15 993	3 140	1 185	173 118	45 122	3 174	328	17 419	14 288
1974	37 801	15 410	3 370	958	172 499	40 794	3 748	391	16 979	12 895
1975	38 665	16 642	4 232	1 420	177 784	54 337	4 293	583	16 569	14 050
1976	37 557	18 020	4 690	1 375	184 417	59 720	4 308	664	18 096	17 150
1977	38 225	19 157	4 554	2 143	185 464	62 424	4 917	1 043	18 672	18 906
1978	39 183	19 072	4 554	2 591	194 575	61 341	5 025	818	18 697	19 018
1979	39 416	22 710	5 713	2 221	194 899	72 251	5 575	1 119	20 354	20 729
1980	36 955	19 617	5 696	1 585	184 923	51 143	5 238	960	20 397	20 241
1981	41 262	19 216	5 822	1 326	188 439	46 171	5 362	886	23 000	23 242
1982	42 836	19 769	6 379	1 169	196 931	42 649	6 171	896	24 411	24 620
1983	45 032	22 275	7 774	1 683	206 002	43 672	7 008	854	26 261	33 780
1984	47 475	23 268	9 765	2 380	219 568	41 302	7 100	1 179	31 279	34 101
1985	52 249	29 831	11 502	3 394	225 499	41 535	7 904	1 469	31 751	35 774
1986	54 640	31 268	13 739	3 555	226 953	38 653	8 609	1 500	33 074	35 751

Year									
1987	51 557	27 186	12 787	2 880	216 202	34 000	9 280	1 654	31 688	34 675
1988	50 725	27 422	12 811	2 455	213 534	33 367	9 496	1 915	33 813	40 219
1989	51 310	30 515	13 804	3 367	228 559	36 313	9 631	2 353	37 060	40 908
1990	55 125	35 240	14 259	4 621	236 239	41 494	10 679	2 976	38 826	46 672
1991	58 367	36 749	18 019	6 205	246 793	44 005	10 519	2 812	43 531	43 768
1992	53 813	32 787	16 536	6 463	241 036	42 512	9 166	2 408	42 055	42 895
1993	54 313	29 959	18 870	7 456	225 196	37 606	9 435	2 568	44 008	42 851
1994	51 689	23 943	16 877	6 493	235 927	38 801	8 457	1 803	42 329	33 451
1995	50 063	21 825	15 975	5 462	233 367	37 890	8 502	2 344	39 389	34 979
1996	54 388	20 428	16 069	4 389	245 599	35 423	9 398	2 080	43 104	35 053
1997	71 685	19 692	14 126	4 722	237 573	34 481	10 661	1 464	58 900	38 126
1998	74 053	20 105	20 637	5 460	269 060	37 894	9 961	2 002	65 621	48 481
1999	74 503	24 184	20 259	5 480	274 149	44 437	9 570	2 615	68 680	58 368
2000	77 758	28 912	20 645	5 976	293 754	52 754	10 493	2 332	76 054	67 745
2001	82 592	34 048	20 943	6 652	307 807	61 851	9 938	2 674	82 433	88 297
2002	82 572	41 702	22 107	9 004	319 553	72 452	9 577	3 723	91 071	93 962
2003	82 623	43 224	20 933	8 437	324 414	76 854	9 337	2 936	86 637	81 468
2004	78 542	41 216	20 577	9 113	320 859	85 939	7 875	2 829	77 773	86 770
2005	74 130	36 679	21 620	8 903	316 157	89 920	8 288	2 781	78 143	79 519

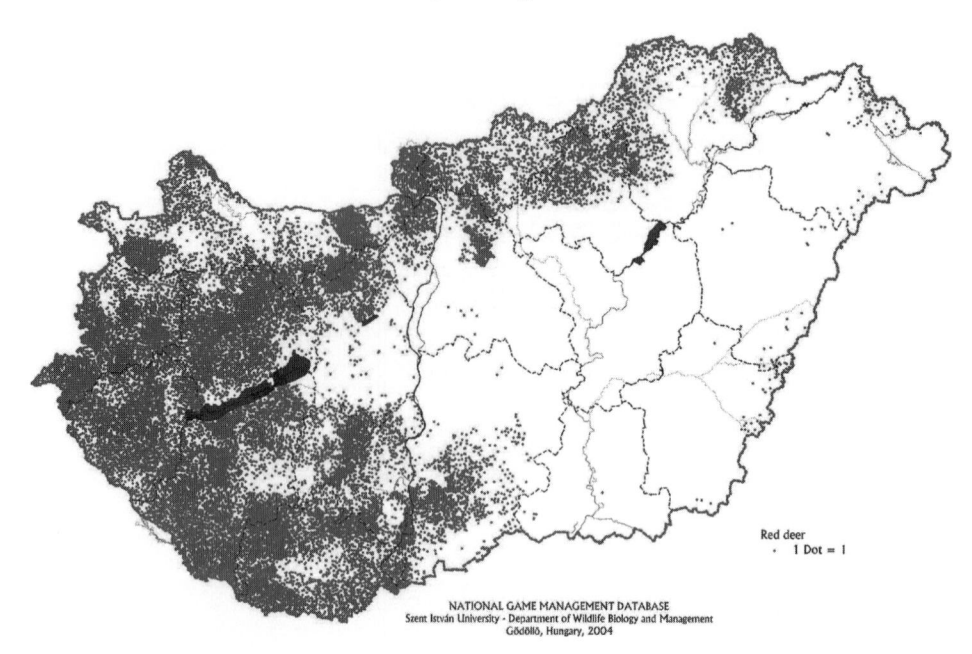

Fig. 14.1 Distribution of red deer in Hungary based on harvest reports for the 2003/2004 hunting year

big game species, and was considered as a 'royal game' (Csöre, 1996). From the end of the nineteenth century until World War II, red deer were introduced into several game parks or released into the wild in order establish new stocks or to improve local populations (Szederjei, 1961).

Over the last 50 years the abundance and range of red deer has increased further. Between 1960 and 2005 the reported red deer population showed a fivefold increase and the harvest increased from 3800 to 43 000 (Table 14.1). Red deer had spread into newly afforested areas in agricultural landscapes (Csányi, 1999a; Tóth and Szemethy, 2000) and also their density has increased in traditional areas (Fig. 14.1). Genetic studies have indicated high polymorphism in Hungarian red deer populations (Ernhaft et al., 1994; Hartl and Köller, 1989), but the variation discovered did not conform with the genetic differences expected on the basis of typical antler shapes and size (Szederjei, 1965; Szederjei and Szederjei, 1971b). Red deer is a highly regarded trophy species and during the last century four of the CIC world records were taken in Hungary (Szidnai et al., 1989). Shooting trophy stags in Hungary is popular among foreign hunters and 45–70% of stags were shot by Western hunters in the last 15 years (Table 14.2). About 6% of the red deer population can be found in game parks (fenced hunting gardens) and 5% of the annual harvest is taken in these areas (Table 14.3).

Table 14.2 The number and proportions of ungulate trophies taken by foreign hunters and Hungarian hunters between 1990 and 2005 in Hungary (Source: National Game Management Database)

	Ungulate		1990	1991	1992	1993	1994	1995	1996	1997	1998	1999	2000	2001	2002	2003	2004	2005
Foreign hunters	Red deer	no.	4 930	5 055	5 480	4 942	4 953	4 354	3 874	3 416	4 040	4 267	5 025	4 951	5 188	5 210	4 266	5 120
		%	51.61	55.24	58.06	65.31	68.72	70.00	71.57	67.59	69.48	63.94	61.39	56.88	53.15	50.75	46.90	52.70
	Fallow deer	no.	580	816	804	745	872	869	578	510	551	608	645	671	743	690	633	699
		%	62.17	67.38	71.34	68.66	70.27	75.17	70.40	70.54	58.68	51.83	49.46	44.79	42.05	40.09	36.30	37.10
	Roe deer	no.	10 240	11 717	12 965	11 920	11 012	10 587	10 299	10 221	10 798	11 201	13 178	14 685	15 415	15 960	13 841	17 796
		%	54.84	59.96	65.62	67.75	68.94	67.62	67.56	73.10	67.27	65.13	62.88	62.70	56.93	54.09	49.50	53.60
	Mouflon	no.	738	777	678	657	526	563	374	339	380	458	395	355	440	423	390	402
		%	75.54	81.28	79.48	82.23	82.57	80.89	76.48	77.22	77.55	68.46	65.94	60.07	51.34	53.34	47.00	47.30
	Wild boar	no.	1 748	1 799	1 692	1 796	1 869	1 803	2 399	1 882	1 954	2 207	2 469	2 751	2 983	3 332	2 849	2 843
		%	60.15	62.01	59.00	63.85	70.18	70.90	81.71	75.61	70.98	71.59	65.06	63.05	64.54	70.24	68.40	70.00
Domestic hunters	Red deer	no.	4 622	4 096	3 958	2 625	2 255	1 866	1 539	1 638	1 775	2 406	3 161	3 753	4 573	5 055	4 831	4 596
		%	48.39	44.76	41.94	34.69	31.28	30.00	28.43	32.41	30.52	36.06	38.61	43.12	46.85	49.25	53.10	47.30
	Fallow deer	no.	353	395	323	340	369	287	243	213	388	565	659	827	1 024	1 031	1 109	1 185
		%	37.83	32.62	28.66	31.34	29.73	24.83	29.60	29.46	41.32	48.17	50.54	55.21	57.95	59.91	63.70	62.90
	Roe deer	no.	8 433	7 825	6 792	5 673	4 962	5 069	4 945	3 761	5 253	5 996	7 778	8 737	11 663	13 549	14 110	15 418
		%	45.16	40.04	34.38	32.25	31.06	32.38	32.44	26.90	32.73	34.87	37.12	37.30	43.07	45.91	50.50	46.60
	Mouflon	no.	239	179	175	142	111	133	115	100	110	211	204	236	417	370	439	448
		%	24.46	18.72	20.52	17.77	17.43	19.11	23.52	22.78	22.45	31.54	34.06	39.93	48.66	46.66	53.00	52.70
	Wild boar	no.	1 158	1 102	1 176	1 017	794	740	537	607	799	876	1 326	1 612	1 639	1 412	1 314	1 220
		%	39.85	37.99	41.00	36.15	29.82	29.10	18.29	24.39	29.02	28.41	34.94	36.95	35.46	29.76	31.60	30.00

Table 14.3 *The numbers and proportions of ungulates kept in game parks compared to the spring population and the harvest in game parks*

Year	Reported spring population Total	Park	Ratio	Harvest Total	Park	Ratio
Red deer						
1997	71 658	4 515	6.3%	19 692	1 090	5.5%
1998	74 053	3 612	4.9%	20 105	567	2.8%
1999	74 503	4 437	6.0%	24 184	1 021	4.2%
2000	77 758	4 153	5.3%	28 912	1 035	3.6%
2001	82 592	4 128	5.0%	34 048	1 489	4.4%
2002	82 572	4 728	5.7%	41 708	1 277	3.1%
2003	82 623	4 964	6.0%	43 224	1 584	3.7%
2004	78 542	5 083	6.5%	41 216	2 121	5.2%
2005	74 130	5 202	7.0%	36 697	1 519	4.1%
Fallow deer						
1997	14 126	4 328	30.6%	4 722	1 051	22.3%
1998	20 637	5 477	26.5%	5 460	1 126	20.6%
1999	20 259	5 790	28.6%	5 480	1 196	21.8%
2000	20 645	6 213	30.1%	5 976	1 605	26.9%
2001	20 943	5 918	28.3%	6 652	1 747	26.3%
2002	22 107	6 108	27.6%	9 004	2 204	24.5%
2003	20 933	6 585	31.5%	8 437	1 884	22.3%
2004	20 577	5 517	26.8%	9 113	1 550	17.0%
2005	21 620	5 398	25.0%	8 903	1 651	18.5%
Mouflon						
1997	10 661	1 013	9.5%	1 464	70	4.8%
1998	9 961	1 244	12.5%	2 002	132	6.6%
1999	9 570	1 439	15.0%	2 615	206	7.9%
2000	10 493	1 316	12.5%	2 332	141	6.0%
2001	9 938	1 983	20.0%	2 647	380	14.4%
2002	9 577	2 427	25.3%	3 723	495	13.3%
2003	9 337	2 379	25.5%	2 936	400	13.6%
2004	7 875	1 990	25.3%	2 829	341	12.1%
2005	8 288	1 964	23.7%	2 781	404	14.5%
Wild boar						
1997	58 900	5 446	9.2%	38 126	2 963	7.8%
1998	65 621	6 038	9.2%	48 481	4 696	9.7%
1999	68 680	7 661	11.2%	58 368	5 235	9.0%
2000	76 054	8 043	10.6%	67 745	5 833	8.6%
2001	82 433	9 738	11.8%	88 297	9 029	10.2%
2002	91 071	12 776	14.0%	93 964	8 974	9.6%
2003	86 637	13 145	15.2%	81 468	9 359	11.5%
2004	77 773	13 900	17.9%	86 770	9 563	11.0%
2005	78 143	14 585	18.7%	79 519	9 194	11.6%

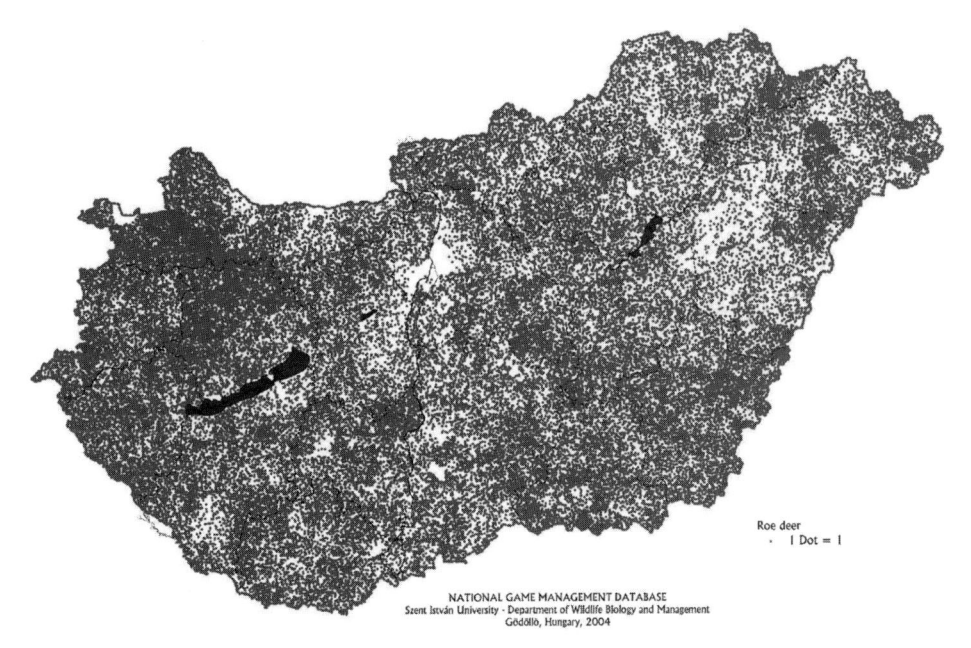

Fig. 14.2 Distribution of roe deer in Hungary based on harvest reports for the 2003/2004 hunting year

14.1.2 Roe deer

Roe deer are the most widespread and most numerous big game species in Hungary. Traditionally roe deer were considered a forest dwelling animal; they also occurred in open, agricultural landscapes, but in low numbers. Roe deer took over the agricultural flatlands of Hungary during the 1960s (Farkas and Csányi, 1990; Csányi, 1991a). Since then the population distribution shows a rather uniform picture (Fig. 14.2). Between 1960 and 2005, the reported roe deer population increased five-fold; harvests increased until 1979, but declined in the following decades (Table 14.1). Roe deer antlers are heavier in the more productive agricultural areas of the country (Szidnai *et al.*, 1989). In the Great Plain (central and eastern part of Hungary) roe deer is the most important big game species and very popular among foreign hunters (Table 14.2). Genetic studies revealed high polymorphism in roe deer in Hungary (Hartl *et al.*, 1991).

14.1.3 Fallow deer

Fallow deer is an introduced species in the Carpathian Basin. In the Hungarian game management literature there are two theories regarding the time of introduction (Nagy, 1985). According to the first, fallow deer were brought into Pannonia (now

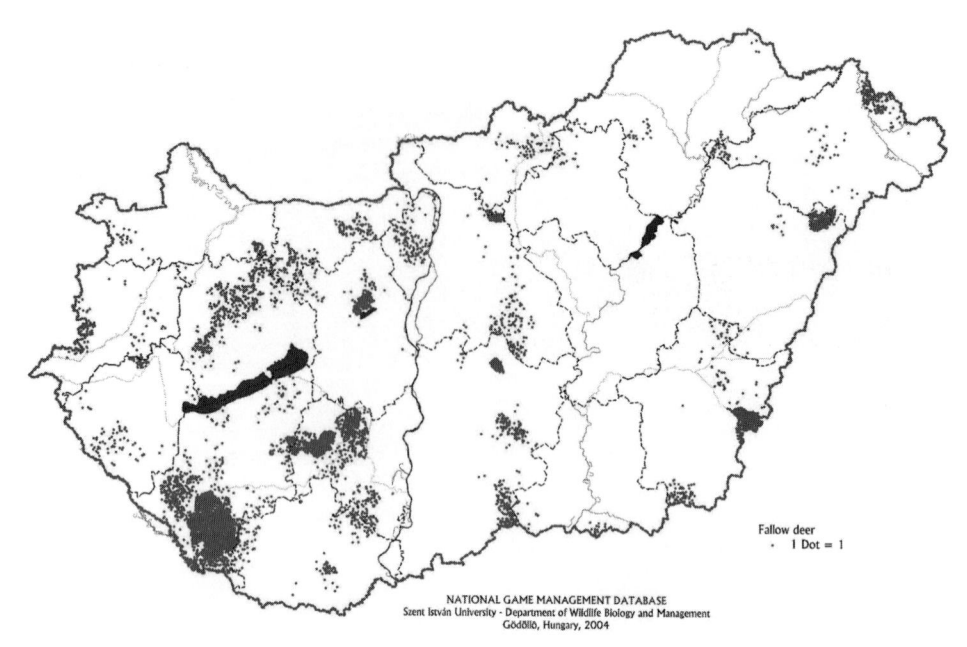

Fig. 14.3 Distribution of fallow deer in Hungary based on harvest reports for the 2003/2004 hunting year

Transdanubia, the western part of Hungary) by the Romans. The second theory assumes that fallow deer were introduced by one of the Hungarian kings during the middle ages, between the twelfth and fifteenth century, not later than 1500 AD. The latter one seems more likely as several of the Hungarian kings were keen hunters and famous for their deer parks (Csöre, 1996, 1997). Until the 1970s, fallow deer distribution was restricted and their numbers were only a few thousand deer. By 2005 reported numbers had increased to 24 times the estimated population in 1960; the harvests were raised from 100 to 9000 (Table 14.1). In the 1970s and 1980s fallow deer were introduced into several new areas resulting in the current, more widespread distribution of this species (Fig. 14.3).

Based on protein polymorphism studies, similar to other European findings, no genetic heterozygosity could be found in fallow deer in Hungary (Pemberton and Smith, 1985; Hartl et al., 1986; Ernhaft et al., 1994).

Fallow deer is a locally important trophy species and all of the CIC world records were taken in Hungary (Szidnai et al., 1989). Shooting trophy males is an important source of income in areas where fallow deer are abundant and foreign hunters take between 40% and 70% of all bucks (Table 14.2).

One-third of the population can be found in game parks (fenced hunting gardens) and some 25% of the annual harvest is taken in these areas (Table 14.3).

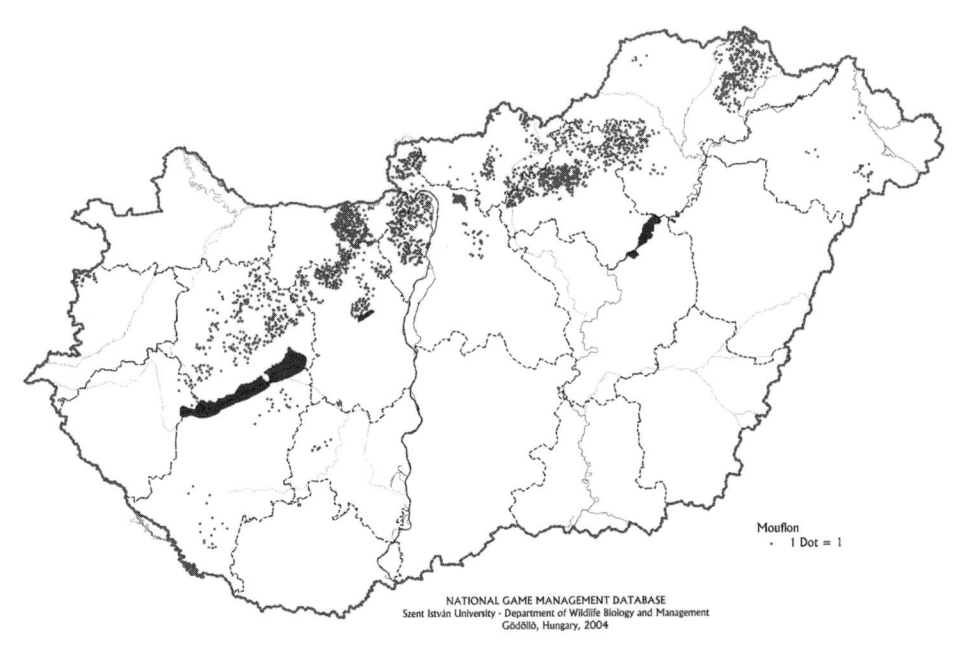

Fig. 14.4 Distribution of mouflon in Hungary based on harvest reports for the 2003/2004 hunting year

14.1.4 Mouflon

Mouflon is an introduced species in Hungary and its history is well documented (Mátrai, 1980). The first mouflon were brought into Ghymes (now Slovakia) and the population within present day Hungary was established in the Márta Mountains in 1903. Normally, mouflon introductions were done in the mountains, but some occurred in hilly woodlands (Náhlik, 1996, 2005).

Between 1960 and 2005 the reported spring mouflon population increased gradually from 1400 to 10 000; the harvests were raised from 200 to 2500–3000 (Table 14.1). About 25% of the population can be found in game parks (fenced hunting gardens) and 12–14% of the annual harvest is taken in these areas (Table 14.3).

Because of its discontinuous distribution and low population numbers (Fig. 14.4) mouflon has a low game management importance.

However, even though mouflon hunting, in itself, is not too popular among foreign hunters > 50% of rams were shot by them in the last 15 years (Table 14.2).

14.1.5 Wild boar

Wild boar is a native species in the Carpathian Basin. As in other parts of Europe (Sáez-Royuela and Tellería, 1986) their range and numbers have increased

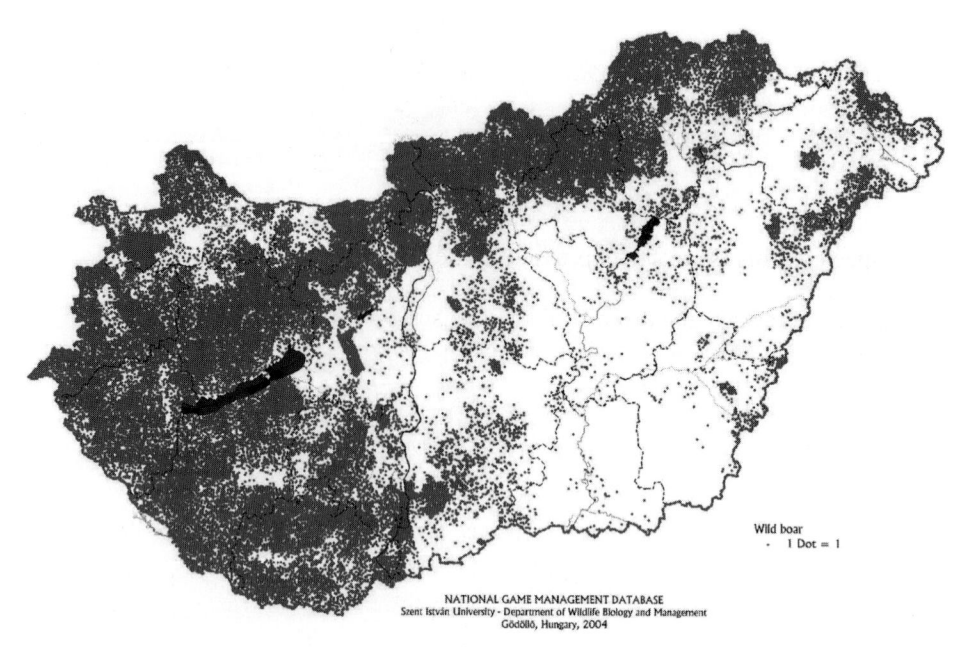

Fig. 14.5 Distribution of wild boar in Hungary based on harvest reports for the 2003/2004 hunting year

dramatically during the last half century in Hungary (Páll, 2001). Historically, wild boar was considered as a forest dwelling animal and it was considered as a pest species in agricultural lands. Consequently, it could be hunted during the whole year until the last decade. Wild boar started to appear more frequently in agricultural areas in parallel with the afforestation of low productivity arable lands (Csányi, 1989).

The actual range of wild boar is much larger and it can be found almost everywhere in Hungary (Fig. 14.5). Between 1960 and 2005 reported wild boar population increased gradually from 8300 to > 90 000; harvests were steadily increasing from 3900 to > 89 000 (Table 14.1). Although the harvest is very high, it does not reach the 110–150% harvest rates on pre-reproductive population size necessary to decrease the population (Csányi, 1989, 2004).

Shooting wild boar is an important source of income, especially driven shoots in game parks. About 15% of the population can be found in fenced hunting gardens and around 10% of the annual harvest is taken in these areas (Table 14.3). Foreign hunters took 65–80% of trophy males in the last 15 years (Table 14.2).

14.2 Legislation

Act LV/1996 on game conservation, game management and hunting (hereinafter: Game Act) regulates game management in Hungary. The Game Act consists of the basic principles and fundamental provisions, while the details of application are regulated by the Decree 79/2004 of the Minister for Agriculture and Rural Development. Some game management and hunting related provisions can be found in the Act LIV/1996 on forestry and Act LIII/1996 on the protection of nature.

The Game Act balances the interests of the conservation and sustainable use of game species. This is clearly expressed in the preamble of the act:

The Parliament recognizing that all wild animal species form an irreplaceable part of the renewable natural resources of Earth and of ecosystems, being aware that wild animals carry aesthetic, scientific, cultural, economical and genetic values, and therefore – as a treasure of humankind as a whole and of our nation – they should be conserved in their natural state for the future generations also, creates the following act in the interest of conserving nature and rationally utilizing the populations of game species.

Game animals are state property (in sense of *res communis*) and the hunting rights belong to the landed property. In order to use these rights a landowner (including the Hungarian State as an owner of lands) should have at least 3000 ha continuous land suitable for game management purposes. In all other cases, landowners should join to use their hunting rights and form a game management unit. The owner of the hunting rights – either a single legal entity or as a joint group of landowners – can decide on the form of use. Actually, 1200 game management units are registered; about 30% of these use the hunting rights themselves and in 70% the hunting rights are leased to hunting clubs.

According to the Game Act, game management units are responsible for the *conservation of game and their habitats:* the party exercising the hunting right may not endanger the survival of non-game animal species, cannot endanger other living organisms, and is responsible for holding the determined minimum density of game. It is forbidden to disturb (apart from legal hunting) hiding cover, feeding, nesting and breeding places of game; forbidden to destroy, damage or disturb nests of birds by means of hunting. Torturing game is prohibited and there is an obligation to kill wounded or seriously ill game.

All activities 'related to the conservation of game populations and their habitats – including also the *biocenosis* – and to the control of game populations qualify as game management' (section 40 of Game Act). In order to achieve these goals, planned game management should be carried out in the interest of

- the conservation of game and its habitat,
- ensuring its long-term survival,
- creating a balance among the economic interest and activities related to different land uses conducted on the hunting-grounds (including game management as a land use),
- implementing nature conservation objectives in nature conservation areas,
- furthermore of professionally exercising and utilising the hunting rights (section 41).

Table 14.4 *Open seasons for ungulates according to age/sex classes in Hungary*

Red deer	
Prime age stags:	01.09–31.10
Young and low quality stags and old hinds:	01.09–31.01
Yearling hinds and calves:	01.09–28.02
Fallow deer	
Prime age bucks:	01.10–31.12
Young and low quality bucks:	01.10–31.01
Adult and yearling does and fawns:	01.10–28.02
Roe deer	
Bucks:	15.04–30.09
Adult and yearling does and fawns:	01.10–28.02
Mouflon	
The open seasons for all age and sex classes of mouflons are between 01.09 and 31.12.	
Wild boar	
Boar yearling and piglet:	All year
Mature sow:	01.05–31.12

In accordance with international conventions and EU directives the Game Act lists the forbidden tools and methods of hunting. Hunters must not use automatic and semi-automatic rifles; semi-automatic shotguns bearing > 3 cartridges at the same time; poisoned or explosive arrows; crossbows; silenced guns; electronic optical devices (e.g. infra-red); electronic acoustic devices (e.g. tape recorders); artificial scent materials (e.g. sex pheromones); mutilated live decoys, spotlights (except for red fox and wild boar with permission).

The following hunting methods can be used for all species: stalking on foot or by horse cart, high seats. For roe and red, deer may also be 'lured' by calling at the rut and (for wild boar only) by winter tracking in snow (although this is rarely used). Females and calves can be shot in drives (red, roe and fallow deer, mouflon), but dogs are not allowed to drive deer and roe may only be shot in drives with the special permission of the Hunting Inspectorates. Dogs may be used on drives of wild boar and boar may also be shot at specific luring sites where artificial feed is provided.

A rifle of muzzle energy > 1000 J may be used to kill roe deer while for all other species a rifle with muzzle energy > 2500 J must be used. For wild boar, the use of shotgun bullets (rifled slug) is also allowed and, with the permission of Hunting Inspectorates, night hunting (spotlight lamping) of boar is also allowed for the control of agricultural damage.

Bow hunting with appropriate arrows is also permitted for all species.

Open seasons for all ungulate species are given in Table 14.4.

14.3 Management objectives

Red deer populations are managed to satisfy two goals: management of the quality of trophy stags with selective shooting of stags (Szederjei and Szederjei, 1971b) and the management of quantity to keep population numbers at acceptable and damage at tolerable levels (Csányi, 1991b; Csányi et al., 2005). Fallow deer populations are maintained primarily for recreational hunting and are also managed for trophy quality with selective shooting, as well as to keep population numbers at reasonable levels and reduce levels of damage. Roe deer populations are managed to improve the quality with selective shooting of bucks (Szederjei and Szederjei, 1971a). Damage caused by roe deer is considered negligible. During the last five years, in recognition that there had been a long period where populations were under-culled, the harvest quotas were systematically increased and hunters encouraged to shoot more females and young (Csányi et al., 2005).

Mouflon populations are managed to achieve better quality with selective shooting of rams and to maintain control of population numbers (Mátrai, 1980; Náhlik, 1989). In some protected areas where there is argued to be some conflict between mouflon and conservation objectives, conservation authorities have even proposed local eradication. The real importance of conservation damage is not well documented however and seems to be overemphasised (Náhlik, 2005). During the last years, the harvest quotas were systematically increased and free-living mouflon populations started to decline (Csányi et al., 2005).

Wild boar populations are generally managed to to keep population numbers as low as possible or at least to decrease them in order to reduce agricultural damage (Csányi, 1989, 2004). Management for trophy quality is also proposed but inevitably conflicts with the need to control numbers to minimise damage (Köhalmy et al., 1987). Only in game parks can males realistically be left to reach the older ages necessary to have large tusks. During the last years the harvest quotas were systematically increased and free-living wild boar populations started to decline (Csányi et al., 2005).

The idea of management planning has a century-long tradition in Hungary (Csányi, 2000b). The long-term plans of game management units (GMUs) and the annual game management plans were first introduced in a very similar form > 35 years ago (OVA, 1997).

To achieve the above general goals of game management a three-level system of planning was introduced (Csányi, 1998, 1999b):

1. *Regional game management plan* for 24 game management regions; their purpose is to provide ecologically sound frameworks for game management.
2. *Long-term game management plan* of the GMUs; the plans are followed for 10 years and contain the framework of activities in accordance with the regional plan.

3. *Annual game management plan* of the GMUs; contains data on the proposed harvest for the given year, planned game damage protection measures; developments planned on the area of GMU (e.g. feeding sites, salt licks, game fields, high seats). The purpose of the annual plan is the control and coordination of game management activities. The annual game management plans are approved by the locally responsible Game Management Inspectorates.

The National Game Management Database (OVA) was established to collect data on game management and hunting, and to monitor changes of game populations and their habitats.

14.4 Management structure

At the governmental level game management and hunting is the responsibility of the Ministry of Agriculture and Rural Development. This ministry exercises the overall national control and coordination of management activities within the Department of Game Management, Fishery and Waters. At Ministry level there is interaction between the Ministry of Agriculture and Rural Development and Nature Conservation Authority (Ministry of Environment and Water Management). Nature conservation bodies have several legislative entitlements in natural resource management issues (forestry, game management, hunting, fisheries, etc.).

Within this overall structure, in the Hungarian system of administration the actual managing authority of first instance is at the level of the counties (19). Accordingly, in each county's Office for Agriculture a Hunting and Fishery Inspectorate is responsible for game management and hunting issues. At the county level, the inspectorates have a wide range of mandates: to supervise hunts, issue hunting licences for foreign hunters, approve game management plans, approve local hunting regulations, keep a register of game-keepers, keep a register of legal entities possessing hunting rights, hunting and game management data collection, and participate in hunters' examination.

The staff of the 19 Hunting and Fishery Authorities is around 60–70 civil servants. At the level of counties the National Park Directorates interact with relevant Hunting and Fishery Inspectorates. With much more limited powers overall the State Forest Service also has a restricted mandate in issues related to game management (e.g. planning, forest damage).

14.5 Management organisation

14.5.1 Game management organisation

In the Hungarian system, the game management unit (GMU) is the basic functional unit. The GMUs are responsible for all game management and hunting activities in accordance with the provisions of the Game Act. To exercise these rights and activities the GMU should have an approved long-term management plan as well as an approved annual game management plan. According to the law, each GMU should employ one professional game-keeper for each 3000 ha of hunting area.

The GMUs can be classified according to three characteristics determined by the law:

- According to the *ownership of lands* forming the GMU (section 4): (1) it is exclusively owned by a single person – also including the State of Hungary – this person shall be entitled to the hunting rights independently (independent hunting rights), or (2) it is owned by several persons – also including the State of Hungary – the owners of the hunting ground shall be entitled to the hunting rights jointly (joint hunting right). In both cases the person or the joint group can decide to use the hunting rights or to lease them out.
- According to their *function* (section 21) the GMU may serve ordinary game management, or special functions (special functions can be determined as (1) those necessitated by the preservation of the genetic stock of game; (2) those necessary for the purpose of education and research; and (3) those necessary in order to assert the interests of nature conservation).
- According to their *form*, the following parties may be the leaseholder of hunting rights on a game management unit (section 16): (1) an association consisting of members having a hunting licence (hereinafter: hunting club); (2) an organisation of hunting associations representing hunting interests; (3) business associations, quasi public companies, cooperatives registered in the agricultural or sylvicultural sector and forest-owners' associations, all being in local ownership exclusively, provided that they use more than half of the hunting-ground for conducting agricultural, sylvicultural or nature conservation related business activities.

The average GMU has an area of 7708.9 ha (OVA, unpublished data).

Most GMUs are managed by hunting clubs meaning that game management is primarily based on non-professionals. As expected the most important motivation of club members is sport shooting and not management. Consequently, in the Hungarian legislation and management system goals related to resource management, economics and sporting interests are intermingled. This means that it is difficult to find clear borders between different parts of game management as a professional action and shooting as form of recreation.

14.5.2 Requirements to be allowed to hunt

Over the last decades the number of domestic hunters has been slowly increasing. In the last few years their numbers ranged between 50 000 and 51 000 individuals. Of these 47 000 persons were sportspeople and 3600 game-keepers (OVA, unpublished). Domestic hunters have to pass a hunters' examination to be eligible for a hunting licence. The theoretical part of the examination consist of a written test and oral examination covering the basic theoretical knowledge of game ecology, hunted and protected species, game management, hunting law, use of weapons, etc. The practical part consists of a shooting proficiency test and knowledge of safety rules.

In Hungary, hunting tourism has a century old tradition and before World War II on large estates fee hunting could be an important source of income. 'Hunting tourism' and game trading were regarded as competitive source of hard currencies on a national level (Nemeskéri et al., 1942). During the last decade the number of foreign hunters varied between 22 000 and 25 000 persons, being stable or slightly increasing.

Traditionally, Austrian, German and Italian hunters were the most important consumers, but in the last decade the share of Spanish and Belgian hunters showed a considerable increase (OVA, unpublished). In spite of the considerable interest of foreign hunters in hunting in Hungary, the proportion of income originating from their hunting fees is declining. This is a consequence of the strong price competition among the central-eastern European countries (depressed prices) as well as the relatively strong Hungarian currency making hunting in Hungary quite expensive.

14.6 Actual management and hunting practices

As above, the following hunting methods may be used for all species: stalking on foot or by horse cart or shooting from high seats. For roe and red, deer may also be 'lured' by calling at the rut and indeed there are regional and national 'roaring' competitions. Females and calves can be shot in drives (red, roe and fallow deer; mouflon), but dogs are not allowed to drive deer and roe may only be shot in drives with the special permission of the Hunting Inspectorates. Dogs may be used on drives of wild boar and boar are also often shot from high seats overlooking specific luring sites where artificial feed is provided.

It is compulsory for GMUs to report the spring population size of all ungulates occurring on their area. The data contain sex and age information (adults by sex and young, for example, in case of red deer: number of adult stags, number of adult hinds, and the total number of calves). The deadline for reporting is 15 February each year. The most important problem of spring population reports is that timing and methods are not standardised, and no methods for population evaluation (counting or estimation) are given. These shortcomings result in the fact that neither precision nor bias can be evaluated, and the quality of this information is regularly debated. Spring population numbers can carefully be treated as educated guesses or guesstimates. In parallel to the spring population reports, GMUs also have to submit the proposed number of animals planned for sporting or management cull (five big game and two small game species: brown hare and ring-necked pheasant). In the case of big game, the plans must offer detail according to age/sex groups similar to the categories described in the spring reports.

Finally, GMUs have to report game bags (shootings) as well as live captures at the end of the hunting year (1 March–28/29 February). Harvest reports include all small and big game species. In the case of ungulates, harvest reports require detailed breakdown by sex and age (mature, subadult or young of the year) and actual age-class of males harvested. Additionally, the number of animals captured live should be provided, and the information is also divided by the number of animals taken in open areas and hunting parks. GMUs report the venison sold and used locally. Hunting reports are generally considered more reliable than spring population reports, but they can be biased by non-reporting of some animals taken, or misreporting when sex/age data are manipulated. Information on poaching is also missing, but can be significant depending on game species (e.g. because of its smaller size roe deer is more suitable for poaching than red deer).

14.6.1 Data collection

Collection of game management data (hunting bags) started in the last decades of the nineteenth century (Csöre, 1996). A continuous database has been available since 1960 for all important game species. The Game Act established (section 48) the National Game Management Database (OVA) with the purpose to keep records of all important information.

These data include the following reports from GMUs: spring population reports, annual management/harvest reports, annual management plans, and trophy scoring data.

The OVA also collates the data of monitoring programmes (e.g. non-hunting mortality, hunted and protected predators) and research programmes (e.g. ungulates, predators) financially supported by the Ministry of Agriculture and Rural Development.

The large databases covered by OVA offer opportunities for statistical analyses, modelling of population changes, development of decision-making studies. As the digitised maps of GMUs are also available, a wide spectrum of spatial analyses (GIS) can be done (Csányi and Ritter, 1999; Ritter and Csányi, 1999; Lehoczki and Csányi, 2001). The OVA publishes the annual statistical yearbook of game management and maintains a web site (www.vvt.gau.hu/adattar.html).

14.6.2 Trophy scoring

Since 1970 has been it compulsory to present each antler (cervids) and horns (mouflon) of ungulates taken for a trophy evaluation (scoring) by independent persons authorised by the state authorities. In case of wild boar tusks longer than 15 cm should be presented for evaluation. The trophy evaluation is done according to the CIC rules of trophy measurements.

The purpose of compulsory trophy evaluation is to keep a record of quality changes of ungulate populations, monitor the effects and efficiency of big game management, as well as to give basis for management decisions. In addition (as above), statutory returns of animals harvested require, for males, the actual number shot in each year-class; the evaluation of trophies by regional or national authorities offers a cross-check of the accuracy of such cull returns.

14.7 Census types and methods

As noted above, it is compulsory for GMUs to report the spring population size of all ungulates occurring on their area. The data contain sex and age information (adults by sex and young, for example, in the case of red deer: number of adult stags, number of adult hinds, and the total number of calves). However, as already mentioned, timing and methods are not standardised. Counting on vantage points, counting on feeding sites and roadside counting are the most common methods.

These shortcomings result in the fact that neither precision nor bias can be evaluated, and the quality of this information is regularly debated. Spring population numbers can be carefully treated as educated guesses or guesstimates.

In spite of the fact that methods are not standardised and neither precision nor bias can be evaluated, these figures are nonetheless useful indicators of long-term trends and regional differences. Modelling and population reconstruction proved this in the case of several ungulate species in Hungary (Csányi, 1991b, 1992, 2000a, 2002; Csányi and Tóth, 2000).

Compulsory submission of bag returns also provides an independent method for assessing the population trend.

14.8 Impact of large ungulates

Damage caused by game to forestry and agriculture is the most sensitive issue of game management (Csöre, 1996; Tóth, 2005). The amount and level of forest damage had always been an evergreen issue, and agricultural damage received less attention. This does not mean that agricultural damage had less importance, but its measurement and compensation was easier than in case of forest damage. This was a consequence of the former Forestry and Game Management Act (1961) that determined the responsibilities and rules for compensation of agricultural damage, but does not include similar regulations for forest damage (Csányi, 1994). Increasing game numbers resulted in rise of agricultural and forest damage and the latter became a never-ending problem.

According to the Game Act the party exercising the hunting right is responsible for damage caused by game, and damage related to hunting activities. Responsibilities can involve the compensation of damage and also the contribution to prevention measures (e.g. payments for fencing). According to the law 95% of damage should be compensated.

The Hungarian terminology distinguishes two forms of forest damage:

- In case of *quantitative damage* to the plantation, the afforestation is fully destroyed and it should be replanted
- In case of *qualitative damage* some proportion of saplings or young trees is damaged but they can recover.

The amount of damage is determined by Forest Service personnel when overseeing (controlling) the status of forest plantations. Even though this information serves mostly as the basis for compensation claims, it is not recognised as being official. The methods of measurement are not standardised, being especially problematic in the case of qualitative damage (a plantation can either be damaged by 15% or 75% without distinction).

According to Forest Service data between 1989 and 2004 both forms of forest damage were declining and have been rather stable in the last years (Table 14.5). Except for the declining period of the early 1990s, no association of ungulate numbers and forest damage could be found. Instead of a linear dependence, they may occur when density reaches a threshold (Putman, 2004).

About 3.36% of quantitative forest damage and 66.24% of qualitative damage could be attributed to game in 2003.

Deer species cause most of both kinds of damage (Table 14.6).

Additional information can be taken from the game management statistics because GMUs report the amounts paid (nominal values) for the compensation of agricultural and forest damage (Table 14.7). According to this information, the compensation paid for forest damage was fairly stable, while agricultural damage compensation was steadily increasing. Based on nominal values, a strong positive correlation between big game numbers and agricultural damage can be proposed. A more careful analysis reveals that the association of agricultural damage and red deer/wild boar numbers is much more complex and, at least, the following points must be considered (Table 14.8; Csányi, 2004):

- In the early 1990s the inflation was very high and it has been gradually declining to under 5% per year. Consequently, if the effect of inflation is filtered out, the steep increase of nominal values disappears and no association of damage and game numbers can be found. After removing the effect of inflation, the changes of agricultural damage compensation show some fluctuation.
- The year-to-year changes of agricultural damage compensation seem to be depending on the changes of the stockmarket prices of the most important cultivated plants (wheat,

Table 14.5 *Registered forest damage between 1985 and 2004 (Source: Forest Service statistical reports)*

Year	Quantitative damage (ha)	Qualitative damage (ha)
1985	1 305	7 951
1986	953	8 327
1987	1 417	9 482
1988	1 156	10 577
1989	1 270	11 805
1990	1 024	10 951
1991	1 354	13 526
1992	664	10 196
1993	575	9 267
1994	445	7 159
1995	509	6 024
1996	504	6 461
1997	356	5 422
1998	354	5 708
1999	226	4 987
2000	316	4 840
2001	715	5 219
2002	475	5 943
2003	427	6 470
2004	610	5 565

Table 14.6 *Damage registered in forest plantations in 2003 (Source: Forest Service unpublished report)*

Name	Quantitative damage (ha)	Qualitative damage (ha)
Sum of registered damage	12725.3	9767.6
Of which game damage	427.4	6470.4
Proportion of game damage	3.36%	66.24%
Game damage according to species		
Red deer	190.7	3281.1
Roe deer	79.8	2662.3
Wild boar	92.4	35.5
Mouflon	4.3	55.1
Fallow deer	13.4	137.2
Brown hare	46.8	298.2
Other game	0.0	1.0

Table 14.7 *Compensation paid for agricultural and forest damage between 1994 and 2004 in nominal values and values corrected for the effect of inflation (Sources: National Game Management Database (OVA) annual publications)*

Year	Nominal value HUF 1000 Agriculture	Forestry	Corrected for inflation HUF 1000 Agriculture	Forestry
1994	389 114	109 410	389 114	109 410
1995	568 571	124 100	443 503	96 802
1996	858 898	112 623	542 045	71 076
1997	708 930	81 933	378 192	43 709
1998	730 805	78 135	341 086	36 468
1999	929 238	124 752	394 273	52 932
2000	1 367 889	140 534	528 589	54 306
2001	1 375 833	180 815	486 867	63 985
2002	1 618 354	181 653	543 864	61 046
2003	1 507 275	195 688	483 796	62 811
2004	1 478 623	183 392	444 382	55 116
2005	1 259 638	161 387	365 413	46 817

corn, and sunflower). When the stockmarket prices increase the damage compensation mirrors the price increase and not only the change in the amount of damage (in area and/or in amount of product). This is important as the agricultural damage compensation is based on the amount of lost product and the actual price of the product.

- Though it cannot be proved on the basis of the available information, it can be supposed that the damage tolerance of farmers is also dependent on price conditions. Lower damage tolerance and higher prices can lead to situations where, in spite of declining big game numbers and decreasing damaged area, the claims for compensation may be still rising.

14.9 Supplementary feeding

As in other Central European countries, winter feeding of game, especially big game, is a traditional and common practice in Hungary. The aims of feeding are: providing supplemental feed for the period when food is less available, improvement of condition and survival of over-wintering game, reduction of damage by provision of more easily available food (Bencze, 1979; Kölüs, 1986; Putman and Staines, 2004). Diversionary feeding is also an increasing practice in order to keep game away from vulnerable areas (forest plantations, agricultural crops). Feeding of game and the cultivation of game crops (crop fields, food planting) is a typical activity of GMUs and is also a part of management planning. The area of game fields and the amounts of food stuffs used are greater in counties where big game

Table 14.8 Distribution of ungulates harvested and agricultural and forest damage compensated in 2004 (Source: National Game Management Database OVA)

County	Share from harvested numbers of ungulates					Share from damage compensation		
	Red deer	Fallow deer	Roe deer	Mouflon		Wild boar	Agriculture	Forest
Baranya	11.9%	2.6%	4.8%	0.0%		8.3%	12.9%	2.7%
Bács-Kiskun	3.4%	4.1%	7.6%	0.0%		2.8%	1.2%	1.1%
Békés	0.2%	10.5%	6.9%	0.0%		0.4%	0.4%	1.2%
Borsod-Abaúj-Zemplén	3.6%	0.3%	5.3%	16.4%		10.7%	2.6%	2.2%
Csongrád	0.1%	0.3%	5.1%	0.0%		0.3%	0.2%	0.2%
Fejér	4.1%	3.3%	4.2%	9.0%		4.5%	2.5%	3.7%
Győr-Moson-Sopron	5.7%	1.0%	8.2%	0.0%		5.8%	2.7%	11.2%
Hajdú-Bihar	0.0%	3.7%	4.1%	0.0%		1.3%	0.6%	0.3%
Heves	2.9%	0.3%	3.3%	25.2%		6.1%	0.4%	0.5%
Komárom-Esztergom	4.5%	2.2%	1.9%	11.9%		4.1%	3.0%	6.4%
Nógrád	2.7%	0.9%	2.4%	5.1%		7.5%	2.7%	5.8%
Pest	4.5%	3.8%	7.1%	16.9%		7.8%	1.3%	5.0%
Somogy	18.4%	42.0%	6.2%	2.3%		11.1%	31.4%	29.2%
Szabolcs-Szatmár-Bereg	0.4%	2.2%	7.1%	0.6%		1.7%	0.6%	1.2%
Jász-Nagykun-Szolnok	0.0%	0.0%	5.6%	0.0%		0.2%	0.7%	0.3%
Tolna	5.5%	15.6%	4.1%	0.0%		5.7%	3.8%	1.0%
Vas	10.4%	1.4%	5.3%	0.8%		5.9%	9.4%	13.6%
Veszprém	12.6%	5.1%	5.9%	11.5%		9.1%	8.7%	8.8%
Zala	9.0%	0.8%	5.0%	0.4%		6.9%	15.1%	5.5%

Table 14.9 *The area of cultivated game fields and feed stuffs in the 2004/2005 hunting year*

Counties	Cultivated area (ha) Food planting	Crop field	Hay	Feed stuffs used (tons) Grains	Silage	Pellets
Baranya	1 276	1 618	615	6 475	2 613	38
Bács-Kiskun	1 590	1 364	643	2 997	3 713	156
Békés	1 433	1 084	831	3 146	293	467
Borsod-Abaúj-Zemplén	1 804	2 533	832	4 446	3 559	245
Csongrád	1 142	631	436	2 199	246	140
Fejér	1 466	1 483	886	4 828	3 313	475
Györ-Moson-Sopron	2 055	705	300	4 718	6 848	186
Hajdú-Bihar	1 289	599	497	4 050	943	273
Heves	1 266	1 992	1 976	3 607	2 642	115
Komárom-Esztergom	1 323	749	1 008	1 821	1 462	57
Nógrád	1 177	1 464	362	2 218	1 758	39
Pest	1 897	1 672	1 336	6 625	4 900	444
Somogy	4 194	2 001	872	8 022	6 285	138
Szabolcs-Szatmár-Bereg	1 112	1 550	479	3 094	3 830	274
Jász-Nagykun-Szolnok	2 037	720	620	2 185	213	802
Tolna	1 292	1 383	513	4 412	4 194	363
Vas	1 538	854	206	2 441	3 122	17
Veszprém	2 512	1 386	1 084	3 923	4 203	197
Zala	1 842	1 478	994	2 861	1 862	19
Total	**32 245**	**25 266**	**14 490**	**74 068**	**55 999**	**4 445**

densities are higher (Table 14.9). In spite of the large areas and the amounts used, the effectiveness of feeding is less well investigated (Hopp, 2001; Náhlik et al., 2002). GMUs generally use the most easily available crops for game fields (corn, wheat, oat, rye, barley), do not consider the requirements of the given game, and the areas are in a few large blocks instead of more smaller patches.

14.10 Ungulate management in Hungary: Crucial points for the future

1. Damage caused by game ungulates in forests and agricultural areas is generally a local problem and needs local action (Csányi et al., 2005). Treatment of game damage cannot be simply solved by the reduction of ungulate populations. As the relationships of ungulate abundance and damage are not linear, finding tolerable population densities is a complex task. Understanding problems and development of proactive management of damage need reliable methods for damage measurement.
2. To reduce big game damage in south-west Hungary red deer and wild boar populations should be decreased. Past reduction programmes show that after achievement of lower

abundance greater hunting pressure should be kept to avoid the return to high population numbers (Csányi, 1991b; Csányi *et al.*, 2005). Agricultural damage is a serious problem for the long-term prosperity of game management. Compensation paid for it can reach 20–30% of the income of game management (Csányi, 2004), and this takes the financial resources necessary for investments, development, employment and better salaries, etc. In the last few years, game management has shown a deficit in the counties with the largest numbers of red deer, fallow deer and wild boar (Csányi *et al.*, 2005). At the same time, the distribution and amounts of damage show that damage is not a countrywide problem but can be managed locally.

3. Management of forest and agricultural damage is a key issue for game management authorities. Consequently, the closed season shooting of damaging animals is regularly permitted by hunting inspectorates. The new quota system of big game management planning was initiated to achieve higher harvests in order to stop the increase of big game populations, as well as to reduce these populations where overabundance and damage seem to be closely connected. These actions contain many political elements displaying good will to foresters and farmers (Putman, 2004).

4. It is necessary to clarify the status of fallow deer and mouflon. Although they are introduced neither of them is an invasive species and negative effects attributed to them are the results of extraordinarily high densities and not of their specific characteristics (Náhlik, 2005).

5. Habitat management and changes in land use practices can ease the above problems. Forests are as much habitats of wildlife as sites of timber production. Not all actions related to forests are ecological or conserving nature: sylvicultural practices neglecting the needs of game/wildlife in forests and increasing the risk of game damage should be decreased or minimized (Szemethy *et al.*, 2001; Mátrai *et al.*, 2003; Náhlik *et al.*, 2003).

6. The future of ungulate management depends on two contrasting conditions: the stability of the legislative environment and the ability to change the philosophy of management. The stability of the game management system is a key element of long-term successes (Csányi, 1994; 1997). Different interest groups are using failures of game management as tools to influence political decision-making processes. Independent of political system, forest and agricultural damages had been widely used by different groups against hunting, or to argue for the changes of the game management system.

The Hungarian game management system is based on hunting clubs, meaning that game management is primarily done by non-professionals. The most important motivation of hunting club members is sport shooting and the average sport hunter is not professionally educated. Most hunters show low levels of cooperation or refuse changes because of unknown risks. To reach professionally sound goals, sport hunters have to be convinced, motivated and directed to accept and follow new directions and solutions. Most GMUs are managed by hunting clubs meaning that game management is primarily based on non-professionals. As expected, the most important motivation of club members is sport shooting and not management. Consequently, in the Hungarian legislation

and management system goals related to resource management, economics, and sporting interests are intermingled. This means that it is difficult to find clear borders between different parts of game management as a professional action and shooting as form of recreation. A tapestry of controversies can be seen from the following examples:
- game management and hunting are regarded as a form of land use done mostly by non-professional sportspeople;
- game management and hunting are expected to be profitable and in accordance with another land uses, with particular reference to keep agricultural damage at tolerable levels;
- objectives of game management and hunting should be in accordance with nature conservation objectives normally not quantified or accountable.

To mitigate these controversial objectives, game management and hunting tend to be over-regulated, and administrative rules are regularly changing in minor details. In hunting clubs, the main reason for management is to provide the basis for Hungarian hunters and enough incomes for the survival of hunting clubs. Typically, a hunting club is interested in a zero-trade-off budget where incomes cover management costs and damage compensation, as well as the hunters satisfying their sporting needs. The system is very sensitive to shooting incomes (market prices and number of foreign hunters) and gives a weak basis for true economic thinking, long-term investments, and employment of educated/quality labour. This is a fragile balance of sporting interest, long-term existence, and control of damage. As game management and hunting is secondary compared to other land uses and/or nature conservation, it is easily influenced by stronger interest groups (e.g. dark greens, animal rights activists, ornitho-chauvinists).

7. The most important failure of the traditional game management paradigm is the assumption that carrying capacity (or a tolerable population density) can be rigorously determined, population size and parameters can be measured exactly, and management decisions can be based on simple calculations. This is an overcomplicated approach in trying to impose excessive refinements on a system which is, in any case, subject to variations outside any manager's control (Putman, 2004). This kind of information is not available in normal game management conditions and the cost necessary to collect them cannot be covered.

8. Adaptive management of renewable natural resources is a learning process (Boyce and Haney, 1997) and to improve game management efficiency a more flexible planning system should be targeted. This requires the use of more reliable data on populations and habitats, as well as improved feedback. Use of bio-indicators can replace the old paradigm, where relatively easily measured parameters can be used to describe the status of the individual–population–environment system (Groupe Chevreuil, 1996; Anonymous, 1999). The advantage of this system is that most relationships can easily be interpreted and understood, and the collection of data is less expensive and/or incorporated into normal management activities. In order to assist this process, the planning system ought to allow for voluntary use of these methods, they must be promoted by guidelines describing their use.

The stability of the management system will also depend on the size of management units, the long-term existence of the planning system, and the use of relevant data in decision-making and administration. The monitoring programmes and long-term research programmes supported by the Ministry of Agriculture and Rural Development provide vital information for the control and development of Hungarian ungulate management.

References

Anonymous (1999) *Actes du colloque "Suivi des populations de chevreuils"*. Lyon: France, 140 pp.

Bencze, L. (1979) *A vadállomány fenntartásának lehetõségei*. A vadászati ökológia alapjai. Budapest: Akadémiai Kiadó, 250 pp.

Boyce, M. S. and Haney, A., eds. (1997) *Ecosystem management. Applications for sustainable forest and wildlife resources.* New Haven and London: Yale University Press, 361 pp.

Csányi, S. (1989) A hazai vaddisznóállomány dinamikája 1960–1986 között. *Nimród Fórum*, **109** (Április), 13–19.

Csányi, S. (1991a) A hazai özpopuláció dinamikája, hasznosítása és a környezet változásai közötti kapcsolatok Kandidátusi értekezés. *Gödöllöi Agrártudományi Egyetem*. Gödöllö, 112 pp.

Csányi, S. (1991b) Red deer population dynamics in Hungary: management statistics versus modeling. In R. D. Brown, ed., *The Biology of Deer*. New York: Springer Verlag, pp. 37–42.

Csányi, S. (1992) Large-scale modelling of the roe deer population dynamics in Hungary: statistical data *vs.* simulated results. In B. Bobek, K. Perzanowski and W. L. Regelin, eds., *Global Trends in Wildlife Management.* Transactions of the 18th IUGB Congress, Jagiellonian University Kraków, Poland; August 1987, pp. 537–40.

Csányi, S. (1994) Moving toward coordinated management of timber and other resource uses in Hungarian forests. *Forestry Chronicle* **70**, 555–61.

Csányi, S. (1997) Challenges of wildlife management in a transforming society: examples from Hungary. *Wildlife Society Bulletin* **25**, 33–7.

Csányi, S. (1998) Game management regions and three-level planning in Hungary. *Hungarian Agricultural Research* **7**, 12–14.

Csányi, S. (1999a) A gímszarvasállomány terjeszkedése az Alföldön. *Vadbiológia* **6**, 43–8.

Csányi, S. (1999b) Regional game management system in Hungary. *Gibier Faune Sauvage* **15**, 929–36.

Csányi, S. (2000a) The effect of hand-reared pheasants on the wild population in Hungary: a modelling approach. *Magyar Apróvad Közlemények* **5**, 71–82.

Csányi, S. (2000b) A megörzés és a fenntarthatóság eszméje a magyar vadgazdálkodásban. In S. Oroszi, ed., *A magyar vadászat ezer éve – Millenniumi emlékülés, Magyar Tudományos Akadémia, Budapest, 2000. január 20.* Budapest: Millenniumi Vadászati Bizottság, pp. 53–64.

Csányi, S. (2002) Populáció-rekonstrukció alkalmazása a muflonállomány létszámának meghatározására. *Vadbiológia* **9**, 54–65.

Csányi, S. (2004) Miért és hol kell csökkenteni a gímszarvas és a vaddisznó létszámát? *A Vadgazda* **3** (Július), 26–31.

Csányi, S. and Ritter, D. (1999) A fenntartható nagyvadlétszám meghatározása az állomány területi eloszlása alapján térinformatikai eszközökkel. *Vadbiológia* **6**, 23–32.
Csányi, S. and Tóth, P. (2000) Populáció-rekonstrukció alkalmazása a hazai gímszarvas állomány létszámának meghatározására. *Vadbiológia* **7**, 27–37.
Csányi, S., Lehoczki, R., Sonkoly, K. and Bognár, G. (2005) *Vadgazdálkodási Adattár 2004/2005.* vadászati év. Országos Vadgazdálkodási Adattár, *Gödöllö*, 68 pp.
Csöre, P. (1996) *A magyar vadászat története.* Budapest: Mezögazda Kiadó: 310 pp.
Csöre, P. (1997) *Vadaskertek a régi Magyarországon.* Budapest: Mezögazda Kiadó, 140 pp.
Ernhaft, J., Hartl, B. G., Kabai, P., Köller, J. and Nikodémusz, E. (1994) Az európai gímszarvas populációgenetikai vizsgálata. *Vadbiológia* **4**, 27–40.
Farkas, D. and Csányi, S. (1990). Current problems of the roe deer (*Capreolus capreolus*) management in Hungary. *Folia Zoologica (Brno)* **38**, 37–46.
Groupe Chevreuil (1996) *Les bio-indicateurs: Futurs outils de gestion des populations des chevreuils?* Bulletin mensuel, 209 Fiche No. 90, Office National de la Chasse, Paris (Mars 1996), 2 pp.
Hartl, G. B. and Köller, J. (1989) A magyar gímszarvas biokémiai-genetikai elkülönültsége és agancsjellemzöi. *Vadbiológia* **3**, 38–48.
Hartl, G. B., Schleger, A. and Slowak, M. (1986) Genetic variability in fallow deer, *Dama dama* L. *Animal Genetics* **17**, 335–41.
Hartl, G. B., Reimoser, F., Willing, R. and Köller, J. (1991) Genetic variability and differentiation in roe deer (*Capreolus capreolus* L) of Central Europe. *Genetics Selection Evolution* **23**, 281–99.
Hopp, T. (2001) Az etetés hatása az özre, élöhelyjavítás etetéssel. *Magyar Apróvad Közlemények* **6**, 59–78.
Keresztesi, B. (1991) *Forestry in Hungary 1920–1985.* Budapest: Akadémiai Kiadó, 350 pp.
Köhalmy, T., Iváncsics, L. and Rakk, T. (1987) Vaddisznóállományunk kezelésének idöszerû kérdései. *Nimród Fórum* (1987. július), 11–17.
Kölüs, G. (1986) *Vadgondozás, élöhely-gazdálkodás.* Budapest: Mezõgazdasági Kiadó, 126 pp.
Lehoczki, R. and Csányi, S. (2001) Földrajzi információs rendszerek alkalmazása az élöhelyfejlesztésben. *Vadbiológia* **8**, 93–103.
Mátrai, G. (1980) *A muflon és vadászata.* Budapest: Mezögazdasági Kiadó.
Mátrai, K., Szemethy, L., Tóth, P., Katona, K. and Székely, J. (2003) A vegetáció jellemzöi és a szarvas területhasználata közötti összefüggések egy alföldi erdöségben. *Vadbiológia* **10**, 26–35.
Nagy, D. I. (1985) A dám Magyarországon. *Nimród Fórum* (1985, június), 13–18.
Náhlik, A. (1989) A Dunántúli-középhegység néhány újabb muflontelepítésének értékelése a trófeák adatai alapján. *Vadbiológia* **3**, 102–115.
Náhlik, A. (1996) Faults in Hungarian mouflon management and their consequences. In E. Hadjisterkotis, ed., *The Mediterranean Mouflon: Management, Genetics and Conservation.* Proccedings of the Second International Symposium on Mediterranean Mouflon. Game Fund, Ministry of the Interior, Cyprus, Nicosia, Cyprus, pp. 37–45.
Náhlik, A. (2005) A muflongazdálkodás élôhelyi és természetvédelmi megítélése. *Heves Megyei Vadász* **7**, 19–23.

Náhlik, A., Nagy-Balázs, A., Hopp, T., Nacsa, J. and Sándor, G. (2002) A célzott takarmányozás hatása az özállomány testi fejlödésére és szaporodási teljesítményére. *Vadbiológia* **9**, 46–53.

Náhlik, A., Tari, T. and Nacsa, J. (2003). A gímszarvas és öz téli erdösítéshasználatának jellemzöi. *Vadbiológia* **10**, 15–25.

Nemeskéri K. G., Félix, E. and Glóser, D. (1942) *A hivatásos vadász I. "Pátria"*. Budapest: Irodalmi Vállalat és Nyomdai Rt, 375 pp.

OVA (1997) *Utmutató a vadgazdálkodási üzemtervek készítéséhez és vezetéséhez*. Gödöllő: Országos Vadgazdálkodási Adattár, 18 pp.

Páll, E. (2001) *A vaddisznó*. Nimród Vadászakadémia 8. Nimród Budapest: Alapítvány, 61 pp.

Pemberton, J. M. and Smith, R. H. (1985) Lack of biochemical polymorphism in British fallow deer. *Heredity* **55**, 199–207.

Putman, R. J. (2004) *The Deer Manager's Companion: A Guide to the Management of Deer in the Wild and in Parks*. Shrewsbury, UK: Swan Hill Press, 180 pp.

Putman, R. J. and Staines, B. W. (2004) Supplementary winter feeding of wild red deer *Cervus elaphus* in Europe and North America: justifications, feeding practice and effectiveness. *Mammal Review* **34**, 285–306.

Ritter, D. and Csányi, S. (1999) Földrajzi információs rendszerek alkalmazása az Országos Vadgazdálkodási Adattár fejlesztésében. *Vadbiológia* **6**, 33–42.

Sáez-Royuela, C. and Tellería, J. L. (1986) The increased population of wild boar (*Sus scrofa* L.) in Europe. *Mammal Review* **16**, 97–101.

Szederjei, Á. (1961) Adatok a hazai szarvaspopulációink kialakulásának vizsgálatához. *Erdészeti Kutatások*, 111–33.

Szederjei, Á. (1965) Szarvas. Budapest: Mezögazdasági Kiadó, 211 pp.

Szederjei, Á. and Szederjei, M. (1971a) *Geheimnis des Weltrekordes. Das Reh*. Terra, Budapest, 403 pp.

Szederjei, Á. and Szederjei, M. (1971b). Geheimnis des Weltrekordes. *Der Hirsch*. Terra, Budapest, 449 pp.

Szemethy, L., Mátrai, K., Katona, K. and Orosz, S. (2001) A forrás-felhasználás dinamikája a területváltó gímszarvasnál egy erdö-mezögazdaság komplexben. *Vadbiológia* **8**, 9–20.

Szidnai, L., Bognár, G. and Huszár, T. (1989) *Magyarország aranyérmes trófeái*. Budapest: Superpress Kft., 560 pp.

Szunyoghy, J. (1963) *A magyarországi szarvas Kandidátusi értekezés*. Budapest: Természettudományi Múzeum, 193 pp.

Tóth, P. and Szemethy, L. (2000) A gímszarvas elterjedési területének változása Magyarországon. *Vadbiológia* **7**, 19–26.

Tóth, S. (2005) *A hírnév kötelez. Vadászat és vadgazdálkodás Magyarországon 1945–1990*. Budapest: Nimród Alapítvány, 359 pp.

15

Ungulates and their management in Romania

ION MICU, ANDRÁS NÁHLIK, ŞERBAN NEGUŞ, ILIE MIHALACHE AND ISTVÁN SZABÓ

Romania is situated in south-east Europe; it is bordered by the Black Sea in the south-east, the river Danube in the south, the Pannonian Plain in the west and the Northern Carpathian Mountains to the north.

The highest elevation above sea-level is 2548 m, namely the Moldoveanu peak in the Fogaras Alps, and the different topographical types of mountain, plateau or lowland plain each cover about one-third of the land area. The climate of Romania is continental and strongly affected by terrain and location. In the western part of the country the continental effects become less pronounced, because of the impact of the Pannonian Plain and a more sub-mediterranean influence. In the south-west there are also pronounced sub-mediterranean effects and in the south-east of the country there is a strong influence from the Black Sea. Summers are very hot and dry; winters are very cold with chill winds bringing regular snowstorms and snowdrifts although these more extreme winters are particularly apparent in the Moldova region and in the southern part of the country, between the southern Carpathians and the river Danube.

The annual average temperature is 7–8°C, but once again varies somewhat in different areas In the east it is 8–9°C, in the south 9–10°C, in Transylvania 7.5–8.5°C, in the high peaks 2–3°C and in the western part 9.5–10.5°C. The amount of precipitation also depends on the geographical zones. This means in the east and south it is only between 350 and 600 mm, in the central part of the country between 650 and 950 mm and even higher in the mountains and in the north-west.

The Pannonian plain is exclusively an agricultural area, with cereal crops the main focus, although maize is also grown and there are some fruit orchards. Livestock husbandry is mostly carried out at farming complexes. In this region the forested area is about 10%, but forests are like islands here occurring in isolated blocks. These may be from some few hectares to 100 even 1000 ha, although larger

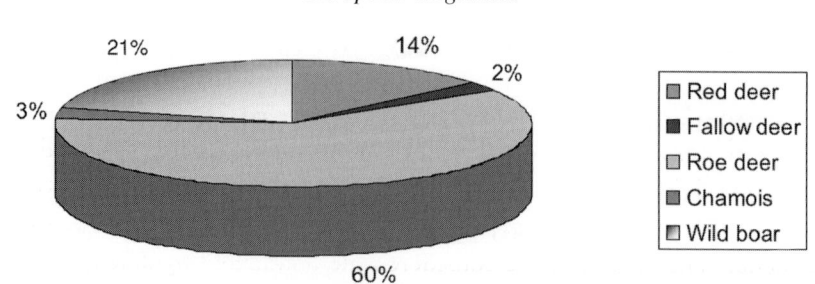

Fig. 15.1 Ratio of different ungulate species in 2006

blocks may contain some agricultural areas within the overall area. Some areas of disused agricultural land are also present.

On the plateau, once again, the primary pattern of land-use is arable agriculture; however animal husbandry and fruit-growing once more are of significance. On hilly or low plateau parts there are mainly forested areas, 30% of which can be seen on lower and 50% on higher parts.

On the mountains, forests predominate, but these surround fields and grassy areas, and there are also meadows, used for summer grazing of sheep and cattle, or for production of hay and other dry feed for winter. There arc few agricultural areas and these are primarily restricted to subsistence crops.

In total, forests cover 27% of the entire landmass of 237 000 km^2, which is about 62 000 km^2 (6.2 million ha). For each inhabitant this means 0.30 ha of forest since the population of the country is 20 million. Conifers (predominantly spruce) and beech each comprise approximately 31% of forest cover. Oak and Turkey oak stands mainly occur on hilly sites especially on lower hills where, with other species, they form mixed forests.

In the country there are 16 national parks, which cover 60 000 km^2 and this equals 2.5% of the country's total territory.

Of significance to ungulate populations, three big predators can be found within Romania: brown bear, wolf and lynx. The brown bear mostly occurs in the mountains but may also be sometimes found in orchards, broadleaved forests and beech-stands. Wolf and lynx can also be found in mountainous forests and on hilly sites, although both species tend to be restricted mostly to higher elevations.

Romania's native ungulates include the red deer, the roe deer, the wild boar and the chamois. Other species have also naturalised and these include fallow deer at certain places (particularly in the western part of the country, where the climate is warmer) and also mouflon in small game-reserves of Dobrudia, in the south-east of the country and around Bucharest (see Fig. 15.1 for relative proportions of the different species overall).

15.1 Ungulate species present, their distribution and abundance

15.1.1 Red deer

As a result of increasing human populations and modification of habitat, the native 'Carpathian red deer', as they are generally referred to in Romania, have tended to become displaced from plains and hilly sites to the mountains, where they have found shelter. They may now be considered the dominant ungulate species in the mountains.

Thus, over the course of time the distribution has changed markedly. In some regions they have vanished completely (Western Carpathians), but in some of these areas they have later become re-established (e.g. Tara Barsei in the surroundings of Brasov), by natural recolonisation or through deliberate reintroduction, especially in the western regions. This was mainly carried out through the introduction of animals from Austria in the nineteenth and early twentieth centuries. Nowadays red deer are not only present in the mountains but also on hills and plains, for example in the western regions where they are of Austrian, German and Hungarian origin. We can also encounter red deer on flat lands near Bucharest, in Dobrudia and other territories (ICAS, 1997).

Currently red deer can be found over an area of 4 million ha, but its density varies in different geographical regions. Areas with rich deer population are the Eastern Carpathians, and the Southern and Western Carpathians. Within these large regions some smaller areas with high population numbers can be found like the Fagaras Alps, Cindrel, Sebes in the Southern Carpathians and some low population areas in the northern mountains of Oltenia.

The genetics of current red deer populations are, however, somewhat mixed. Red deer from Austria were introduced into Transylvania in the western part of the country; they had antlers of much smaller size but which were characterised by a multi-tine crown. These introduced animals were quickly absorbed into the wider population. In general, professional hunters refer to individuals with many tines (20 and above) as 'Austrian deer', and apply the name 'Carpathian deer' to those individuals that count 12 or fewer tines (Comşia, 1961). The situation is very similar in other areas of the country with red deer populations (ICAS, 1997).

Nowadays, the typical antlers in the Carphathians are characterised by 12 or 14 tines (dependent on whether or not the bay tine is present). Increasingly, the majority take after the ancestors introduced from Austria (with short antlers and thin beams). However there is a proportion of individuals which seem to have inherited big robust main beams from their indigenous parents, but an increased number of tines inherited from their Austrian forebears. There are only a few stags culled that have more than 18 tines (approximately 1% of the bagged individuals

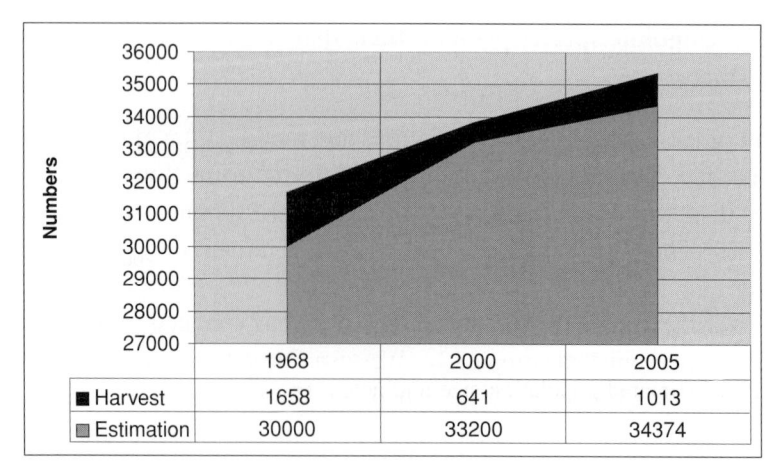

	1968	2000	2005
■ Harvest	1658	641	1013
▨ Estimation	30000	33200	34374

Fig. 15.2 Estimated population size and actual harvest rates for red deer 1968–2005

according to the results of a survey over 23 years; Comşia, 1961). However these 'mixture' deer are in considerable demand from sport-hunters because of their beauty and high CIC scores.

Available data over the past decades offer estimates of the Romanian red deer population as follows: In March 1968 the population of red deer was estimated at about 30 000, out of which 1450 were harvested by culling, hinds and calves included. In 2000, the estimated number reached 33 200, but the harvest was restricted to only 670 specimens. In 2006, the population was estimated at about 36 100, out of which 18 200 individuals were reported by state forestries, 17 900 by hunting societies (Fig. 15.2).

Counties with the highest populations are Suceava with 11.5% (4120 specimens), Harghita with 9% (3220 specimens), Mures with 9%, Covasna and Sibiu 6% each. Counties with the smallest population are Dolj, Vaslui with about 0.12%, Tulcea with 0.20% and Ialomita with 0.25% (MAPDR, 2006).

As an average of the past seven years (1999/2000–2005/2006) licences have been granted for approximately 4.5% of the population (1640 specimens) to be culled, although in practice only 50% (825 specimens) of the approved cull was taken representing about 2.3% of the total population (MAPDR, 2006).

Death from natural causes (disease, accident, predation) must not however be overlooked. The main cause of death (other than from hunting) in the case of red deer is from predation by wolves and lynx; the contribution made by brown bear may be considered negligible (ICAS, 1988).

The total natural mortality probably accounts for 10% of the population. The proportion is higher on the mountains (15–20%) and on areas of poor resource

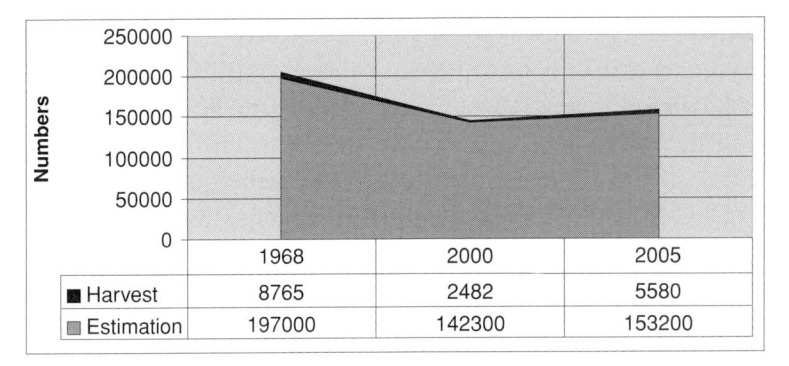

	1968	2000	2005
■ Harvest	8765	2482	5580
▨ Estimation	197000	142300	153200

Fig. 15.3 Estimated population size and actual harvest rates for roe deer 1968–2005

quality, and it is lower on the hill-country and lands of good quality where the proportion is between about 5 and 10% (ICAS, 1988). Natural mortality due to disease is low and does not exceed 1–3% of the population.

15.1.2 Roe deer

Roe deer are the most numerous ungulates in the whole country, and besides hare and wild boar they are also the most hunted species. They are present in all the regions of the country, even in mountainous forests and open areas with no forest cover, albeit at reduced density (Almăşan, 1967). We can find them in highest density on agricultural areas interspersed with small forest blocks from 50 to 100 ha. Roe deer can also be found on higher or lower hill-country. In general there is no significant difference between the population of the areas of the country either in the east, south, central or the west. Population size/density relates more closely to land-use patterns and human activities.

Estimates of actual numbers of roe deer in Romania over recent decades suggest values as follows. In March 1968, the population of roe deer was estimated at about 197 000, out of which 8765 were harvested by culling, does and kids included. In 2000, the estimated number reached 142 300, but only some 500 individuals were harvested. In 2006, the population was estimated about 159 000, out of which 45 600 individuals were counted within state forests and 113 400 on areas managed by hunting societies (Fig. 15.3).

Lowest numbers were recorded in the counties of Constanta and Ilfov (0.7%), Braila and Gorj (1.2%). Highest numbers were recorded in the counties of Timis with 5.5%, Caras with 4.7%, Mures with 4.6%, and Hunedoara with 4.5% (MAPDR, 2006).

Recruitment rates are high at about 50%, but on areas of good quality habitat it can be between 65 and 70%, or on lower quality areas 20% of the total population (ICAS, 1988). (Recruitment rates are estimated by the Forest Research Institute, by means of the observation of roe deer does with fawns. This was mostly in the winter season when females and young ones gather in groups. These studies were undertaken in several habitat types of different quality. The method was also applied to other ungulate game species).

Natural mortality is relatively high in the first months (about 50% of roe kids). The main reason for this is weather conditions but attacks by predators, mostly foxes and stray dogs, etc., also contribute significantly to mortality. In the case of adult roe deer natural mortality is assessed at between 20 and 30% per annum, out of which 3–5% is caused by different diseases or parasites (lung-worms) (ICAS, 1988).

Roe deer are an important quarry species. As an average of the past seven years culling licences have been allowed for some 5770 specimens (3.6% of the 2006 population). In point of fact, only some 4300 individuals were culled (75% of the full allocation), which is 2.7% of the total population (MAPDR, 2006).

15.1.3 Fallow deer

Fallow deer are not native to Romania but are an introduced species. Hunters do not show much interest in them. Fallow deer were introduced into the Banat and the Cris river regions, the western part of the country, at the end of the nineteenth century (Cotta *et al.*, 2001). Good documentary evidence dates back to 1904 when the 'Sarlota game reserve' was founded in Banat. The species introduced here were taken from Central Europe (Austria, the Czech Republic and other Central European countries) (Bodea *et al.*, 1964).

Fallow deer are now naturalised as free-ranging populations in the western part of the country bordering with Hungary (in Banloc and Sochodov, Timiş county; Balc, Bihor county) and nearby Bucharest in 'Malul Roşu' forest, and also occur in a number of enclosures (Sarlota, Valea Lunga, Hateg). In March 1968, the total fallow deer population was estimated at 4030 individuals, of which 3130 were free-living and the rest in game reserves and enclosures. By 2000, the estimated number reached 6000 with some 500 individuals harvested. In 2006, the size of the population was 5900 and 934 individuals were harvested (Fig. 15.4; MAPDR, 2006).

15.1.4 Chamois

In March 1968, the chamois population was estimated at about 7800, of which 187 specimens were harvested by culling. In 2000, the estimated number of the species reached 7900 but only 185 were harvested.

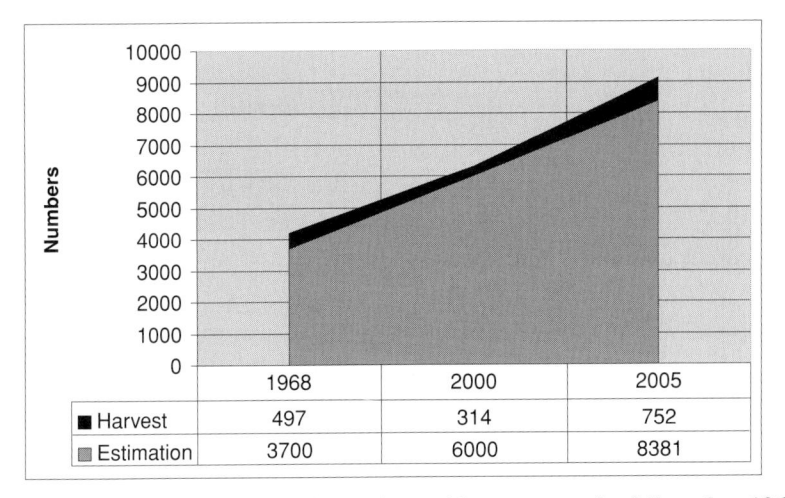

	1968	2000	2005
Harvest	497	314	752
Estimation	3700	6000	8381

Fig. 15.4 Estimated population size and actual harvest rates for fallow deer 1968–2005

In 2006 the chamois population in Romania was estimated at 6800 individuals on 221 000 ha (MAPDR, 2006).

Chamois live in the alpine ridges of the Carpathians ranging from the northern parts of the country to the south-west. The largest population is to be found in the Fagaras Alps and in the Retezat mountains. Lower densities are found in the Buzau mountain range, Vrancea and Hasmasu Mare mountains.

The Carpathian chamois is the largest subspecies both from the point of view of morphology and the size of the horn. Trophies originating from the Carpathians are in the first 10–15 places on the world-list. The world record of the species is a 1937 specimen with its 141.4 CIC points (Berlin exhibition).

Recruitment rates of chamois in the Carpathians are estimated at about 30% of all females although this varies considerably from year to year depending on weather conditions in the breeding season (May–June). Other factors affecting mortality of both kids and adults are lynx and also sheepdogs, once sheep flocks are returned to the high-ground pastures later in the summer. The most negative impact to the population is human beings themselves, particularly poachers and shepherds, who may threaten the total population of a certain area. The seasonal grazing of sheep on alpine pastures also provides significant competition for food; because of this, chamois tend to select meadow areas that are hard for sheep to get to, but these tend to be of inferior quality.

As an average of the past seven years, approval has been given to cull 340 specimens each year (some 5% of the estimated total population). In practice only about 203 have been culled, representing 3% of the estimated total population (Fig. 15.5; MAPDR, 2006).

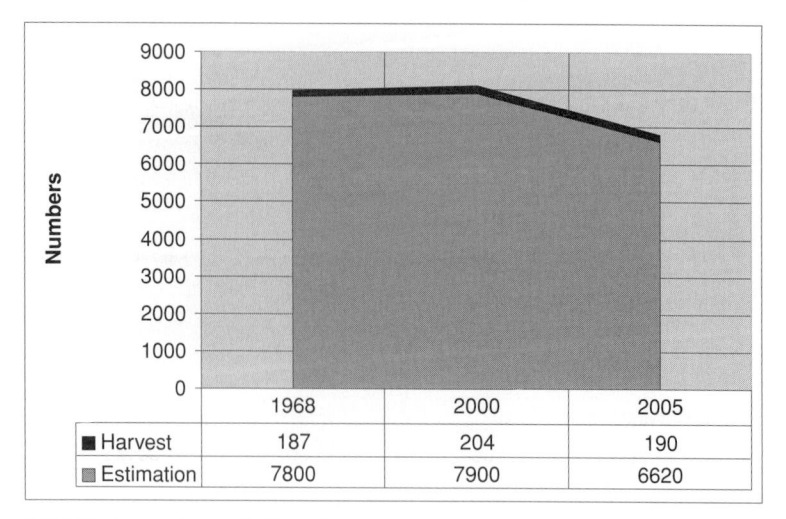

	1968	2000	2005
■ Harvest	187	204	190
■ Estimation	7800	7900	6620

Fig. 15.5 Estimated population size and actual harvest rates for chamois 1968–2005

Natural mortality accounts for between 3% and 5% of the population and the highest loss occurs in the winter season. Much of this results following weight loss of chamois males during the breeding season and there is a clear difference in mortality rates between sexes. Avalanches also cause occasional mortality, although snow depths are much less than those for example in the Alps. Keratoconjunctivitis and sarcoptic mange nowadays cause minimal mortality.

15.1.5 Mouflon

Mouflon were introduced to the 'Balc' game reserve, Bihor county, during World War II. Around 1900, they also tried to introduce them in the Retezat mountains, but populations failed because of the thick snow and predators. In 1966 and 1967, 37 individuals were set free in Dobrudia (next to the Black Sea). These formed the basis of the Dobrudia mouflon tock and they were observed until 1990 and then they disappeared for undetermined reasons (but probably due to poaching) (Cotta et al., 2001). In consequence, there are no longer free-ranging populations and all mouflon in Romania are confined within game reserves.

15.1.6 Wild boar

Wild boar is to be found on the whole territory of the country from the Danube delta, where they often interbreed with boars raised by the inhabitants, to the mountainous mixed forests; they can also be found in pure spruce coniferous forests.

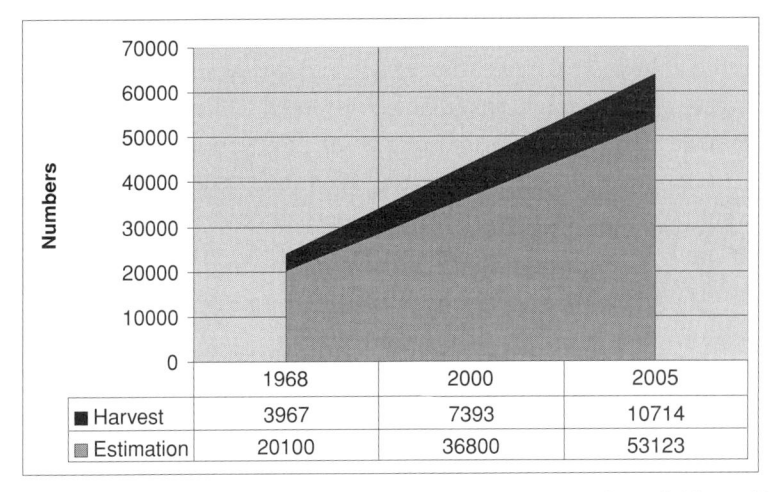

	1968	2000	2005
Harvest	3967	7393	10714
Estimation	20100	36800	53123

Fig. 15.6 Estimated population size and actual harvest rates for wild boar 1968–2005

They are particularly numerous on hillsides in oak, Turkey oak and beech stands or in a mixture of these. Wild boar can find suitable living conditions here, especially if these stands are surrounded by agricultural areas used for cultivation. They also occur even in open plains or in agricultural lands interspersed with smaller forest blocks of 100–500 ha.

The size of the wild boar population varies, however, between regions. It is rather low in the east of the country (Moldova and Dobrudia), but pretty high in Transylvania. Counties with high wild boar population are as follows: Arad with 6.6%, Harghita with 5.3%, Caras, Mures, Sibiu, Suceava with 4.7% each. The smallest population is in Braila with 0.6%, and Ilfov, Giurgiu and Dambovita with 0.9% each.

During the past decades the wild boar population in Romania showed values as follows. In March 1968 the wild boar population was estimated overall at about 20 100, out of which 3967 were harvested by culling, females and offspring included. In 2000, the estimated number reached 36 800, but only some 6400 specimens were culled. In 2006, the population was estimated at 56 730 in the whole country (Fig. 15.6; MAPDR, 2006).

Recruitment of offspring is 100%, on average, although recruitment rates may vary from place to place in response to differences in habitat conditions. So recruitment may be as high as 110–120% in good quality habitats, but only about 80% (of the total boar population) in the case of habitats of lower quality.

As an average, over the past seven years, approval has been given to cull 12 580 specimens a year, which is 22% of the 2006 population. In practice the actual number of wild boar culled was only 16% of the population (MAPDR, 2006).

Natural mortality tends to be primarily concentrated in young of the year particularly in the cold and rainy weather of the late spring season. Indeed this factor of unfavourable weather might result, in some years, in the total loss of youngsters born in February and March. In the mountains mortality remains high even after this period, when brown bears, wolves and lynx may cause a significant decrease in the population regarding the offspring. The total observed mortality may be of the order of 50% of the total population (ICAS, 1988). Swine fever has not been particularly notable in recent years (ICAS, 1988).

15.2 Legislation

Management of species and organisation of hunting were, until recently, both regulated according to the law 103/1996, which has been altered several times in the years since its first enactment in 1996. In November 2006, law 407 came into force, which is the law protecting hunting and game populations. We must also take account of the 1996 forest law when talking about hunting activities and managing huntable species, because this effectively controls the environment of the most important huntable species and this is not negligible in the management of game species.

According to paragraph 2, section 1 of the Act 407: 'Game stock is a continuously renewable natural source, a national and international public property . . . Hunting activity assures the ecological balance, improves the quality of hunting. Furthermore it serves interests on science, education and sport.' The new law also connects the right for hunting to land ownership.

The law for hunting and game stock protection forbids the usage of semi-automatic shotguns with more than two cartridges. It also forbids the usage of guns with a calibre not authorised for a certain hunting activity or game species. This is to say big game must not be hunted with a shotgun and small game must not be hunted with a rifle.

Both the older law 103/1996 and the newer one 407/2006 divide the game population into two parts:

- game species the hunting of which is permitted
- game species the hunting of which is forbidden

Strictly protected species that are subject to internationally approved agreements (brown bear, wolf, wild cat) belong to the second group. Animal species introduced not long ago such as beaver and other endangered species also belong to this group.

Table 15.1 *The regulation on hunting ungulates in Romania, Law No. 407/2006*

Chamois	
– hunting of game with a trophy	15 October–15 December
– culling	1 September–15 December
Roe deer	
– buck	15 May–15 October
– doe	1 September–15 February
Red deer	
– stag	10 September–15 November
– cull stag	1 September–15 December
– hind + calf	1 September–15 February
Fallow deer	
– buck	10 October–1 December
– cull buck	1 September–15 December
– doe + fawn	1 September–15 February
Wild boar	1 August–15 February

The hunting season is usually in the autumn and winter, however there might be some exceptions because of biological peculiarities, for example capercaillie cock or roe deer can be hunted between May and October (Table 15.1).

The law prohibits hunters from exceeding or under-utilising the quantity permitted for culling. It also regulates the measures needed for the protection of game stock. In accordance with the law the authorised hunters must guarantee the sustainable use of game stock on the basis of management plans which are carried out by registered experts. Authorised hunters must provide one game warden within one hunting unit who is responsible for the protection of the game stock. Management plans must contain the size of the actual game stock, which should be stated on the occasion of the game census each year. The hunting law forbids the authorised hunter to provide false information concerning evaluation of the size of the game stock.

15.3 Management objectives

The aim of managing hunting is to keep the ecological balance between animal and plant species. This takes place in the interest of preserving biodiversity and for the prevention of damage to farmland and forests.

According to the hunting law, leisure time sport-hunting takes place in the interests of keeping the ecological balance and for the improvement of game stock.

Game and venison is a secondary product which results from hunting activity as means of keeping the ecological balance. Getting game and venison is not an aim itself. The most important thing is the conservation of biodiversity and maintaining the ecological balance.

15.4 Management structure

Responsibility for game managment rests with the Central Public Authority responsible for forestry (currently this is the Ministry of Agriculture, Forest and Rural Development). This authority arranges management of property and approves rights and liabilities. An authorised party is a Romanian legal entity entitled by law and is allowed to manage the game stock of a certain hunting territory. The authority assures the right for hunting (1) for those natural or legal entities who own at least 51% of the hunting area, (2) for the state in case the area is minimum 51% state-owned, (3) for the owner, individual or a society if they own less than 51% of the hunting area in case points (1) and (2) cannot be validated. Supposing the right to hunt cannot be awarded to either party, the hunting right is kept for bidding. The party for hunting enters into a 10 year contract with the authorities, and pays a fee twice a year for administration.

According to the law the guidance of game management falls within the competence of the authorities. The utilisation of the game may be by professional hunters or hunters with hunting exams if they have permission from the authorities approving hunting activities.

According to the regulations of the law, the Central Public Authority responsible for forestry gives the authorised party the administration of the hunting area and controls the management carried out on the basis of the plans. The authority approves the number of species to be shot, and controls the implementation of the plan. As noted above, authorised hunters must provide one game warden within one hunting unit who is responsible for the protection of the game stock. Management plans must contain the size of the actual game stock, which should be stated on the occasion of the game census each year.

Managing contracts are made between the Central Public Authority and the authorised party for hunting. The latter could be a forest holder, a joint tenure, a hunting society, a state forest manager or an institution providing education and research for hunting. The contracts are for 10 years, but in some cases they can be terminated (if, for example, it is seen that there is some reduction of the population over the permissible rate, that the authorised hunting authority is considered to be overstepping the approved harvest ratio or if they are failing to supply the supplementary food determined by the contract, etc.)

15.5 Management organisation

Game management and hunting takes place within units of game management. Hunting areas were created on the basis of the hunting law 407/2006. At the moment there are 2151 hunting areas in Romania. Their size is more or less similar but there are different legal minimum areas in the case of plains, hill-countries and mountains. Thus, minimum hunting unit size is 5000 ha on plains areas and in the Danube delta, 7000 ha on hill-countries and 10 000 ha in the mountains.

The minimal territory for one hunter is 150 ha on plains, 250 ha on hill-countries and 350 ha in the mountains.

In Romania every sport hunter (about 55 000, 50% of them hunting ungulates) is compulsorily the member of a hunting society which joins a hunter association (General Association of Romanian Hunters and Professional Anglers; AGVPS). AGVPS is subordinated to the Central Public Authority (Ministry) and does its job in relation to the administration of managing the game stock. The managing of the game stock is carried out by the authorised party for hunting (hunting society, state forestry, etc.).

The hunting society performing game management can be divided into separate hunting groups in terms of areas of the hunting territory. These smaller groups deal with the protection and hunting of their game stock. A hunting society is allowed to operate officially with minimum of three members. The foundation of the hunting society must be approved by a court decision. After the lawful foundation of the society it can have the legal rights to handle the hunting area according to the legal regulations.

To achieve the legally required hunters' qualification an examination must be taken. The recommendation of an established hunter who has already had a minimum of five years experience is also required, plus in the period of the first, probationary, year of the licence different activities of hunting and management must be fulfilled under supervision.

Any natural entity has the right to hunt, if he or she practices hunting in accordance with the law. In hunting areas which were given to hunting societies on the basis of land ownership the members are allowed to hunt. In hunting areas given out to state managing, only forestry staff employed by the state are allowed to hunt or natural entities with permission who asked for and received hunting permits issued by the manager of the land (state forestry).

Hunting of permitted species can be done individually, in smaller or in larger groups. In every case an individual or group permission is needed referring to the hunted species and given out by the leadership hunting society. To hunt fallow deer, red deer, roe deer and chamois only individual permits are issued because these species are not hunted from drives or during other group hunting. Both individual and group permits are approved for hunting wild boar.

The membership fee is defined by the hunting society managing the hunting area. The price of the permits to be issued is defined by the Central Public Authority. These permits are valid for hunting areas they manage on the basis of the contract made with the central authority.

15.6 Actual management and hunting practices

Harvest by hunting is regulated by annual hunting plans that are issued separately for each game species in accordance with the population of the hunted game, the agreed optimum population number for sustainability, the loss and the weather of the current and the previous year (harsh, cold winters, rainy springs might result in the loss of small animals, poaching, etc.).

The trustee of the hunting territory proposes the huntable number of game species, and this is further analysed by the administration representative of the area. Then they send the proposal to the central authorities who declare the shootable number of population referring to species, sex, age, and possible trophies. After approval these become mandatory conditions.

Statistical data on hunting and game animals are stated and verified by the Central Public Authority responsible for forestry.

To hunt big game, they use individual hunting methods, like hunting from high seats or stalking. For small game animals, they use a drive. Dogs are mostly used during group hunting, when they take part in the drive together with the drivers. Hunting dogs (like bloodhounds) are rarely used for individual hunting.

15.7 Census methods

The census is coordinated by the Central Public Authority responsible for forestry. Until now methods used for assessment have varied from species to species but in general census is based on a visual assessment or by the counting of certain signs. Big game animals are observed during the whole of the year, especially during mating season and in the winter when they gather together in herds. In winter they record the tracks left in the snow, and in spring they check the remaining stock. Chamois are assessed twice: once during autumn in the mating season and again in spring after the snow melts.

From 2007 a new regulation will be introduced in the assessment of game species. This will include the need for managers to undertake a number of different estimation methods in the case of every game species and will require that methods include counts of footprints left in the snow.

This method is based on the calculation of footprints in and out of the hunting area. For the sake of the ease of this activity and the increase of accuracy, the hunting areas are divided into districts and sub-districts according to natural and artificial boundaries, so that the distances can be covered within a single day. This method has not been used in the country yet for ungulates, but has been used for estimation of large carnivore populations since 2005.

Results of this one method are not used on their own, but taken in combination with other specific methods characteristic of the certain species. Some examples are the counting of grouped deer in the winter season, recording at feeding places, etc.

These various complementary methods are needed because we cannot get unambiguous information concerning sex, age or health condition due to the errors implicit in direct counts (double records or under-recording of numbers of individuals in more closed areas). In the case of some hunted species the only assessment method is visual recording because of their way of life and habitat. This method can give us a real picture about the area, just like in the case of chamois.

For other species, like roe deer, the recording of number of tracks is practically impossible due to the winter gathering and the significant change of place. This is why the census of roe deer stock is based on visual assessment during the mating season, the counting of individuals during winter and spring when they enter the fields and the counts at the feeding stations.

The stock of wild boar may also be estimated on the basis of the tracks left in the snow. Where there are feeding stations they must be taken into consideration so that the structures of boar groupings can be assessed and the population of the defined area can be evaluated properly (ICAS, 2006).

15.8 Impact and damage

Until the 407/2006 law came into force, damage caused by game species had been settled by the party adversely affected and the manager of the hunting area. According to the new law, damage caused by protected species (wolf, lynx, bear, wild cat) is the responsibility of the Central Public Authority dealing with environment, while compensation for damage caused by game ungulates remains the responsibility of the hunting authority operational in that game management area. According to the law, technical and judicial experts estimate the kind and amount of damage; thereafter, depending on the damage done, the party adversely affected has the right to demand compensation.

We do not have exact data concerning damage caused by game since there has not been scientific research on the topic. There is no centralised system for assessing damage and in consequence there are no formal quantitative data available. Further, game damage in plantations or in naturally regenerating areas cannot be estimated properly because damage caused by pasturing cannot be separated from damage caused by game.

The level of damage done in forests is probably relatively small owing to the low density of ungulates. Such damage as does occur is mostly concentrated in artificial and natural regenerations. Compensation is rarely given by the authorities responsible for forestries and only in those cases where it can be shown that all preventive measures have been taken. Most of the game damage is done by red deer and wild boar and the least by roe deer and chamois.

The most important damage of the red deer is browsing, while bark stripping is less important. Roe deer cause less damage, which is only significant in the case of roe deer groups. Wild boar cause the most damage in artificial and natural regenerations, where they pick up a number of nuts by rooting and destroy seedlings.

In the case of agricultural crops the most damage is done by wild boars, particularly in cornfields or potato patches close to forests. Because of high costs of prevention, many of the agricultural property owners whose property is close to hunting areas do not defend against game or other damage. In general, the property owners try to protect their lands by cracking or with petards, fire and guard dogs.

At the moment, data concerning the problems due to involvement of game animals in traffic accidents are not available.

15.9 Supplementary feeding

In Romania, supplementary feeding of wild ungulates is obligatory, by law, both on plains and on the hill-country between 1 November and 31 March and in the mountains between 16 October and 30 April. Although in the case of chamois, the earlier opinion of the authorities was that they do not require supplementary feeding, since they are capable of getting the required nourishment needed to survive, a new regulation of 2002 has now prescribed obligatory supplementary feeding over winter for this species also, in the hopes that winter losses may be decreased and the animals might be in better condition by the end of the winter.

As mentioned earlier adequate provision of supplementary feeding is part of contract conditions for hunting leases and the lack of its execution may lead to the cancellation of the contract. The actual amount of supplementary feeding required varies for each ungulate species according to the quantity and the altitude level of habitats. Among the requirements may also be provision of salt, depending on the altitude and the habitat.

15.10 Effectiveness and problems of current management strategies

Management and forward-planning for ungulates is currently insufficient within the country. Although an action plan was prepared in 2002 for large carnivores, red deer and capercaillie, which included recognition of a need for better record-keeping, the improvement of habitat conditions, etc., the prescriptions made have never been implemented.

It is notable that numbers of animals culled over the last 7 years (for all species of ungulates) have been consistently less than the number authorised. There are probably two main reasons for this. First, the original application for quota from the authorised hunters may deliberately seek a higher quota than that which may be achieved. Under our existing administrative system, applications for quota are submitted to the Central Public Authority in charge of forestry for approval. If the authority thinks that the number of animals is too high it has the right to decrease that number, and by doing so the manager of the stock will have fewer chances to hunt. To achieve higher quotas many hunters therefore suggest a higher quota than is actually appropriate so that if the suggested number is decreased later on by the authorities, they may still get the desired number anyway. To reach their original goal of the number of animals they want to shoot, the hunters overestimate the number of animals in the area, knowing that the authorities will reduce whatever number they are given.

The problem might originate from the inaccuracy of game census. Unfortunately there are no exact methods for determining the number of game stock. This is, at present, simply based on the observations of the staff at the certain territory. Thus, not only may aspiring hunters deliberately overestimate game numbers in a given area, actual censuses may not have been particularly accurate in the first place. The numbering of tracks at the beginning of spring is also important when game assessment is started nationwide.

Besides this deliberate 'overestimation' of what is an achievable quota, numbers actually shot may still be lower than an appropriate harvest rate, given the true number of animals in a given area. Hunting conditions are often difficult on hilly terrain, yet here we can find the most ungulate game species. Further, there are, in Romania, a number of predators (bear, wolf, lynx), which make the behaviour of herbivorous game species rather unpredictable. Wolves usually attack in packs of six or more and they chase prey animals from their normal range. The prey return to the given area only after several days or weeks. If this period coincides with the hunting season, hunting will be unsuccessful.

Some other factors are worth taking into consideration. First of all, large predators in hilly areas have a strong impact on the growth of the population. Most of the ungulate game species can be found in such places. We must add the mortality rate caused by harsh winters of the continental climate. Due to this predators are able to regulate the ungulate game populations of lowered density and this may well have as significant an affect on game populations as does human hunting pressure. Poaching may also have a significant impact on game numbers in certain areas.

For all these reasons, we can assume that the allocated quotas of animals which may be hunted in different areas are not really related to any preplanned wildlife management objectives. The consequence is that for some species, such as wild boar, the stock must continuously grow (as is apparent from both data on population number and the increasing incidence of game damage).

An additional problem in effective management relates to the lack of any suitable system to evaluate such damage. That is why we cannot value the amount of game damage, and an effective managing method for game damage cannot be worked out.

Central recording and the unification of estimating game damage is required both in agriculture and in forestry. The knowledge of the amount of damage and its distribution would not only be a useful statistic in terms of assessing ungulate impacts, but might also offer a clearer picture of the size of the game stock and the effectiveness of its management.

However, in evaluating successes and shortcomings of current wildlife management systems in Romania, it is only fair to note that much of what is described here was under the old operating system which has now, theoretically, been set aside by the new hunting law at the end of 2006, and we should perhaps wait to see what will be the effectiveness of this new system. In practice, the old contracts for managing hunting areas are still valid, which were made on the basis of the 103/1996 law.

In our opinion it is essential that a strategy and management plan must be worked out which will make proper recommendations for future management of each ungulate species and each carnivore species countrywide. The basis of such action plans should be much greater objectivity in management and decision-making, based on better systems of record-keeping

Proper evaluation needs to be undertaken of actual rates of population increase (and range expansion) for each of the different species and a stricter monitoring undertaken of mortality rates. Poaching should also be taken into account and consideration of all these factors used in determination of true rates of recruitment.

Similarly, we must devote proper consideration to the management of habitats, and the effects this may have on ungulate populations and their impacts. This in itself can only be based on improved research into the selection of habitats by the different ungulate species and the factors affecting habitat utilisation, patterns of distribution and movement, etc.

More effective measures need to be taken for the supervision of pasturing and, in some cases, this must be forbidden. The prevention of poaching is also an important activity, which is, besides pasturing, the main reason for the decrease in the population of huntable ungulates. We must create the interest of the trustee of the area by raising the payment of the rangers.

Last, but not least, we must note that Romania is a country where a wide range of natural biodiversity still exists (native forests, habitats not influenced by humans, game species that have disappeared from other parts of Europe or are on the edge of extinction). This must be preserved and extinct or near-extinct species must be protected and re-established.

As new members of the wider European Union, it is critical that a proper action plan should be developed, to preserve biodiversity and to address problems concerned with the environment (pollution, education, awareness, etc.) giving proper attention to up-to-date methods of game population management. Within such a plan, individual consideration should be given to all the different species irrespective of whether the given species is significant in terms of hunting or not, since there is a close correlation among all the elements of the ecosystem.

References

Almăsan, H. (1967) *Capriotul*. Bucureşti: Editura A.G.V.P.S., 293 pp.
Bodea, M., Comşia, A. M., Cotta, V. et al. (1964) *Vânat şi vânătoare*. Bucureşti: Editura A.G.V.P.S., 462 pp.
Comşia, A. M. (1961) *Biologia şi principiile culturii vânatului*. Bucureşti: Editura Academiei, 587 pp.
Cotta, V., Bodea, M., Micu, I. (2001) *Vânatul şi Vânătoarea în România*. Bucureşti: Editura CERES, 786 pp.
ICAS (1988) *Bonitatea fondurilor de vânătoare şi efectivele optime la principalele specii de vânat din România*. Bucureşti, 1988.
ICAS (1997) *Cercetări privind renaturarea vânatului crescut în captivitate*. Bucureşti, 1997.
ICAS (2002) *Refacerea cheilor de bonitate fondurilor de vânătoare şi a efectivelor optime la principalele specii de vânat*. Bucureşti, 2002.
ICAS (2006) *Norme de estimarea efectivelor la principalele specii de interes cinegetic, bazate pe cercetări efectuate anterior*. Bucureşti, 2006, 100 pp.
MAPDR (2006) *Situaţia cotelor de recoltă şi a realizărilor la principalele specii de vânat în perioada 1999–2006*. Bucureşti, 2006.

16

Ungulates and their management in Austria

FRIEDRICH REIMOSER AND SUSANNE REIMOSER

Austria covers an area of 84 000 km^2 with altitudes up to 3800 m and a wide range of different landscapes. The proportion of ground covered by forest is 47% and this forest area is increasing about 2000 ha per year. At the same time about 7000 ha of grassland and arable land are lost to concrete and asphalt areas for roads, settlements and industry. So grassland and arable land in total decrease about 9000 ha per year.

About 8 million inhabitants give a mean density overall of 97 people per square kilometre. Tourism is a very important economic factor (7.6% of GDP) and also a major disturbance factor for wildlife. All forms of mass recreation (such as hiking, mountain biking, paragliding, skiing) show increasing popularity. Approximately 120 million overnight stays per year are registered. That equals 15 stays per inhabitant. About 118 000 hunters are responsible for ungulate management.

Large predators (as a potential habitat factor for wild ungulates) play a very little role in Austria. At present, we have about 15 brown bears (*Ursus arctos*) and 30 lynx (*Lynx lynx*) in all Austria. The wolf (*Canis lupus*) is recorded occasionally simply as a transient; there are none permanently resident in Austria. All these large predators were exterminated during the nineteenth century and reappeared about 50–100 years later. Now they are under protection.

16.1 Ungulate species

Nine ungulate species are present in Austria. The most common ungulate is roe deer (*Capreolus capreolus*). Its habitat covers about 90% of the country area. The maximum population density reaches about 40 per km^2. The yearly hunting bag in 2005 was about 280 000 head. Further abundant ungulate species are red deer (*Cervus elaphus*), chamois (*Rupicapra rupicapra*) and wild boar (*Sus scrofa*)

(Table 16.1). The other ungulates, mouflon (*Ovis musimon*), sika deer (*Cervus nippon*), ibex (*Capra ibex*) and fallow deer (*Dama dama*) are restricted to small areas. A few moose (*Alces alces*) have reappeared near the border with the Czech Republic during the last few years.

16.1.1 History of ungulates in Austria

Among the native species (Table 16.1) the red deer has suffered greatest genetic admixture as the result of numerous introduced animals being brought in from Asia, America and, particularly, Carpathian countries. Roe deer, chamois and wild boar show little genetic impact from introduced animals. Fallow deer and mouflon were introduced in the fifteenth and sixteenth centuries. At first they were held in enclosures and then released. Sika deer was released in 1907. Ibex was exterminated in the eighteenth century and was reintroduced in 1924. The moose is a native species in Austria. It disappeared in the tenth century (probably due to climate and human impacts) and reappeared from about 1964 having re-colonised naturally from the north-east (Poland, Czech Republic).

16.1.2 Population size, development of hunting bags

Population sizes of wild ungulates are not systematically recorded. Simply the results from the yearly recorded hunting-bag lists, given by the chief hunters of each hunting-district, are collected within the official Austrian hunting statistics and used as an indicator of population-size changes. These statistics are recorded separately for 'culled', 'killed by traffic' and 'death due to other reasons' with registration of sex-, age-class (3–4 classes), and body weight. Trophy measurements by hunters are not registered in the official record.

This systematic record for the whole of Austria started in the year 1948 and the recorded mortality divided into animals culled by hunters, animals found dead by traffic or other reasons and in total is shown in Figure 16.1. If we accept these figures as reflecting trends in actual population size, we see that numbers of red deer showed a significant increase up to the 1970s and then have maintained a more or less stable number. Roe deer 'bag' has shown a more or less linear increase and has a particularly high share of animals found dead for reasons other than hunting (mainly traffic kills). Sika and fallow deer show a stronger increase on a lower culling level. The recorded numbers of chamois that were killed or found dead were highest in the 1980s and have been slightly decreasing during the last decade. Ibex and wild boar show a very strong increasing culling rate, presumably once again reflecting an actual increase in population number. Other mortality is low, but there are more and more problems with wild-boar traffic kills and accidents on roads.

Table 16.1 *History, habitat area, maximum population density, and recorded mortality of ungulate species 2005*

Species	History	Habitat (% of country area)	Max. pop. density/10 km^2	Recorded mortality (2005) Culled	Traffic	Other
Roe deer	native	90	400	280 474	38 543	31 631
Red deer	native	50	100	49 615	587	1 786
Chamois	native	25	300	22 708	15	2 706
Wild boar	native	20	400	27 223	408	332
Mouflon	not native	2	100	2 402	15	99
Sika deer	not native	0.2	100	835	26	2
Ibex	native	2	100	460	0	84
Fallow deer	not native	0.1	100	551	29	9
Moose (not hunted)	native	0.001	3	0	0	0
Total	–	95	500	384 268	39 623	36 649

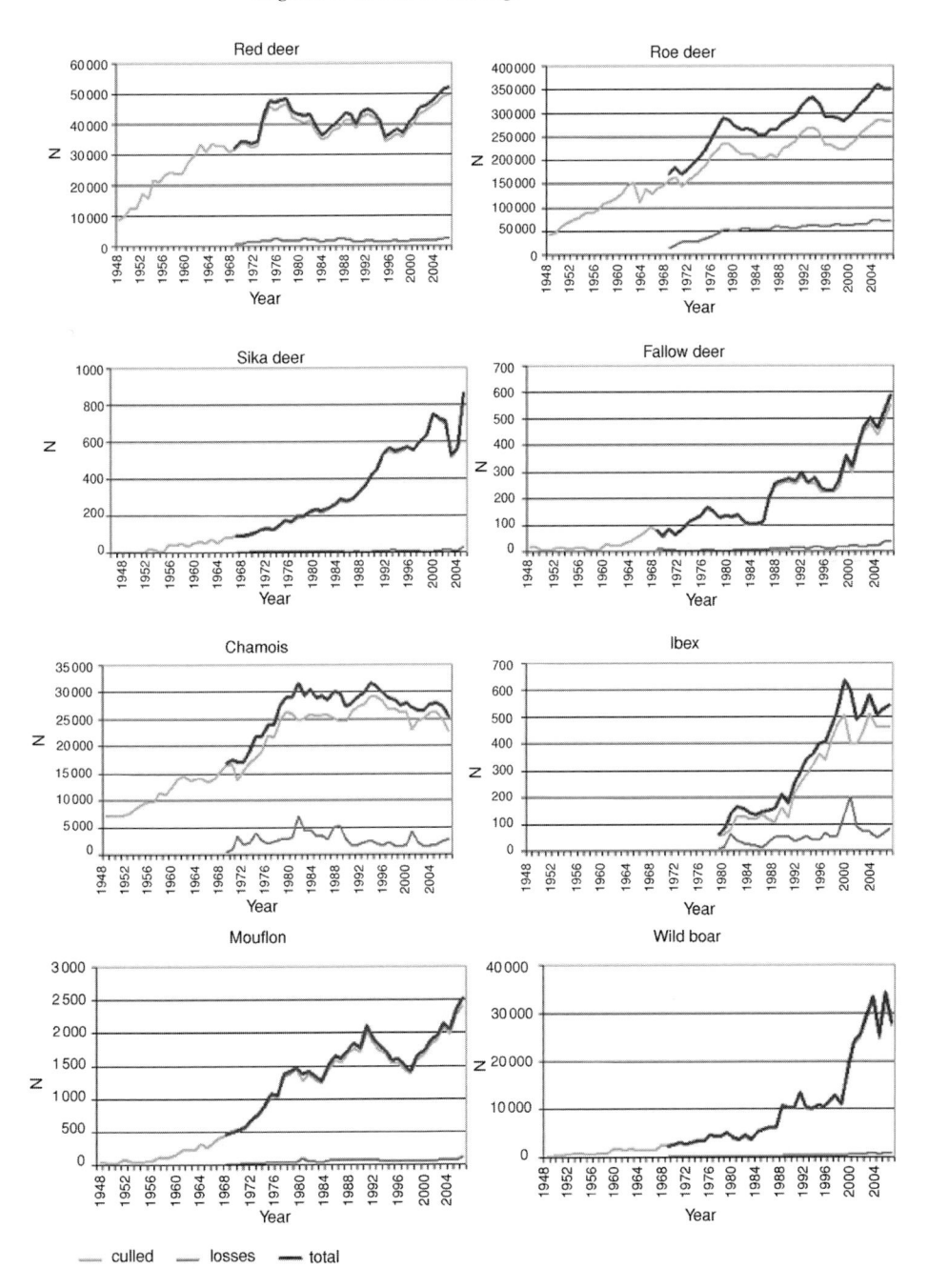

Fig. 16.1 Recorded mortality of wild ungulate species in Austria 1948–2005 (head per year)

If we concentrate on the animal numbers culled by the hunters, it is noticeable that the proportion of juveniles culled has increased since the 1960s, whereas the ratio of male and female adults is more or less constant. This is true for red deer as well as roe deer (Fig. 16.2). But while this ratio has remained constant over time, the actual proportion of males and females culled for the two species differs: in red deer more adult females than males are culled, while for roe deer, the adult males comprise the majority of the hunting bag over all years. For chamois and ibex, both so-called high mountain species, the share of culled juveniles is less because the winter has a stronger impact on their mortality. For wild boar the sex and age classes have not been recorded up to now.

Maps are presented to show the changes in cull figures in each of the 99 public administration units of Austria, for each species, in three sample years beginning in 1961, then 1982 and finally 2003 (Fig. 16.3). For roe deer, in 1961, the highest culling density existed in the hilly areas of Austria, less in the plains and in the high mountains. Two decades later (1982) cull numbers (and thus presumably population density) had increased, particularly in the plains of eastern Austria and also in the mountain regions. A further 20 years later (2003), this tendency of increasing culling rates continued.

Red deer, with a somewhat lower culling level overall, shows a similar tendency, but populations remain concentrated on the forested mountain regions. For chamois, which lives mainly in the high mountains, mostly above the timberline, the highest culling rates were reached in the 1980s. Culling of ibex was not yet permitted in the 1960s; at the present time low culling rates are recorded widely scattered in the Austrian alps. Wild boar in 1961 was concentrated in the eastern lowlands. In 1982 the map shows a similar situation. But during the last two decades a dramatic increase of the distribution area and culling rates for wild boar was registered. Distribution development of the introduced species fallow deer, sika deer and mouflon is also included in Figure 16.3.

16.1.3 Current population trends

More intensive methods of estimating population size (for instance pellet and track counts, infra-red photography by helicopter) are only locally used. Direct data about the number of ungulates living in Austria do not exist. Only the records of numbers culled are more or less reliable (hunters and culling can be controlled by hunting authorities and the public administration). Estimates of actual numbers can thus be assessed only indirectly, based on hunting bags. A simple calculation may be based on the assumptions of (1) sex ratio, (2) population growth rate, and (3) that the total recorded mortality (number of animals culled plus animals found dead due to traffic or other reasons) is about as high as the

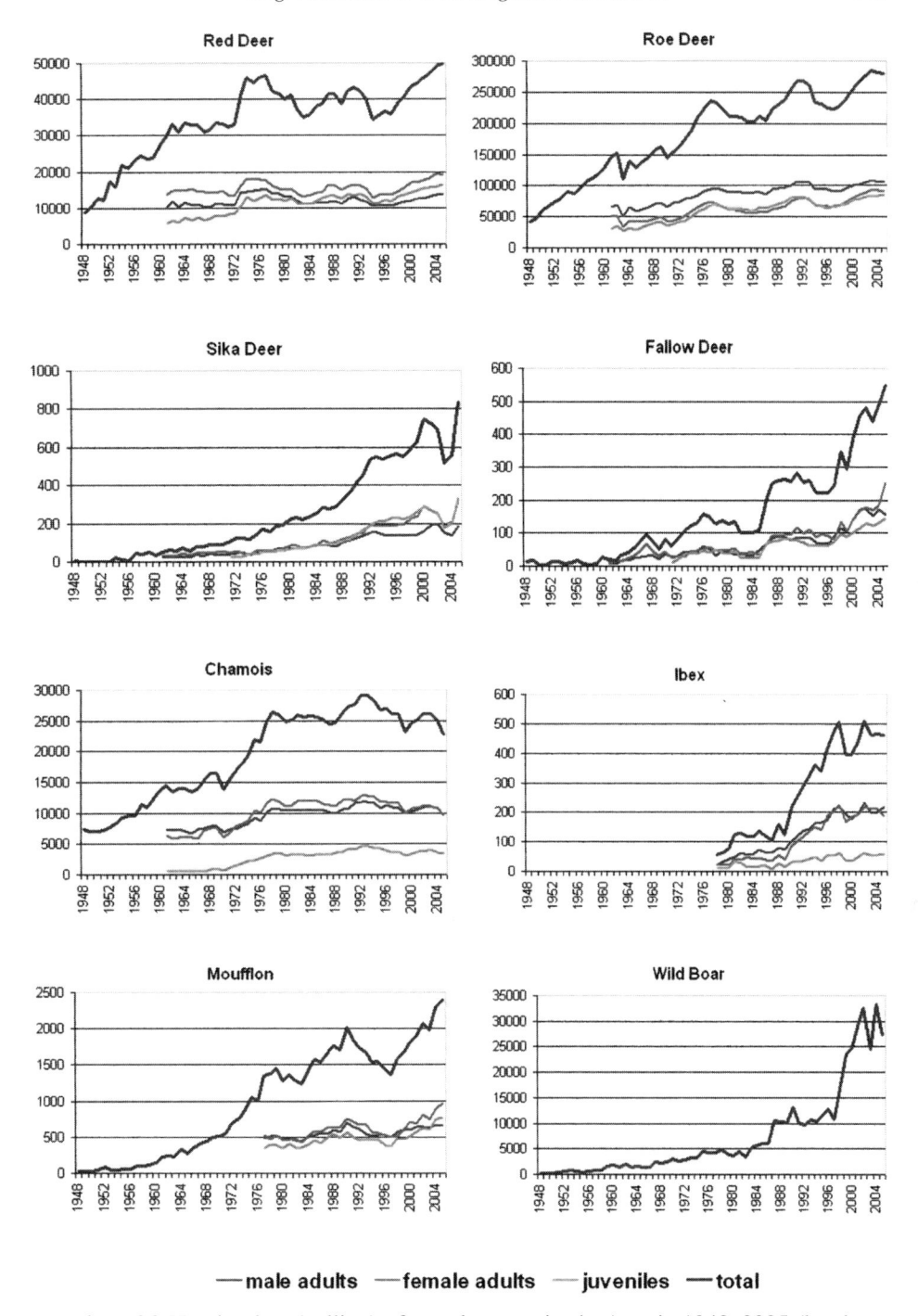

Fig. 16.2 Hunting bag (culling) of ungulate species in Austria 1948–2005 (head per year)

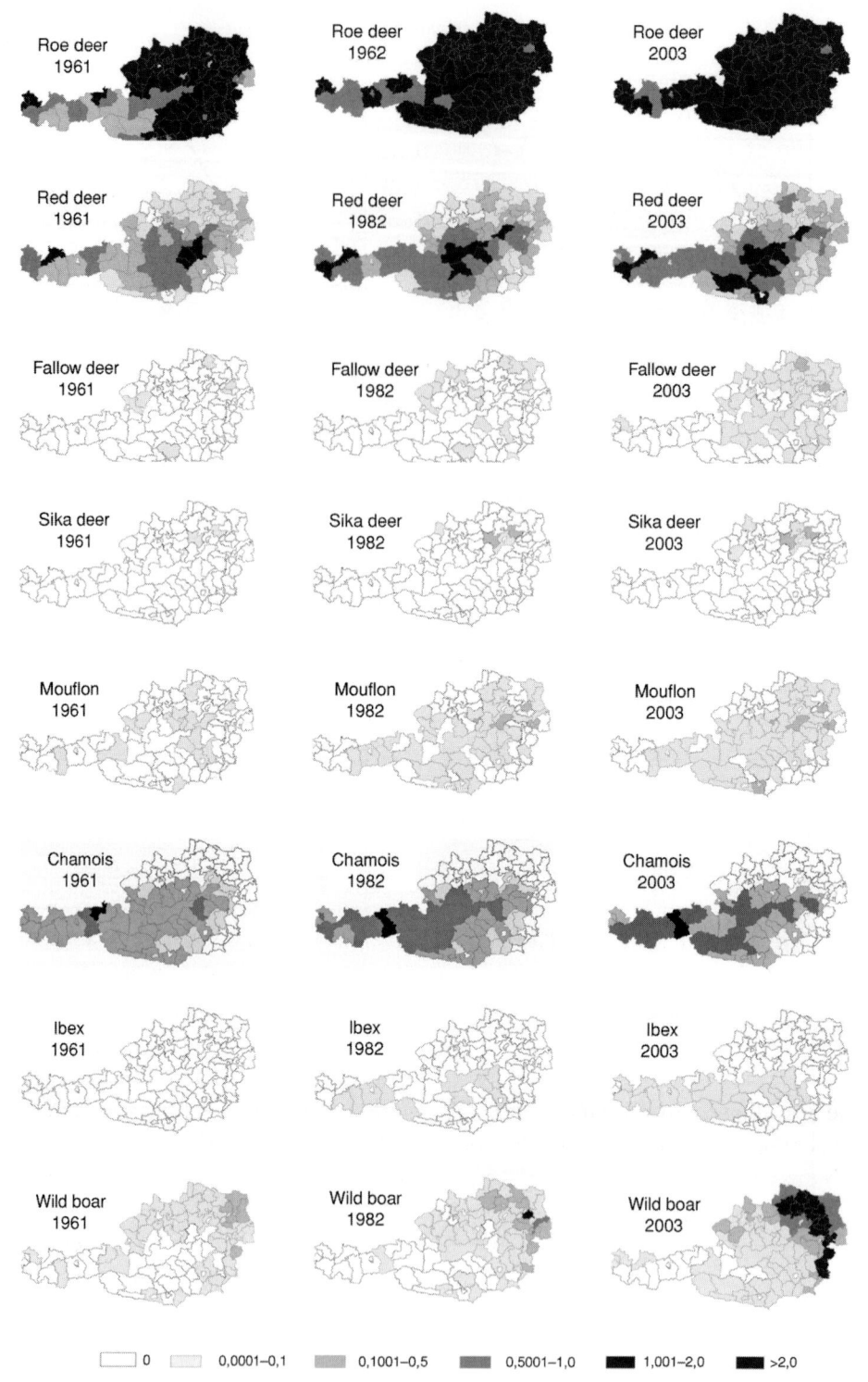

Fig. 16.3 Development of culling density of ungulate species in the 99 Austrian administration units (head per km^2 and year) for 1961, 1982 and 2003 (also used as an index of ungulate species distribution over time)

yearly recruitment rate of the species. Management usually tries to achieve a sex ratio close to 1:1 for all ungulate species. For instance, if red deer has a sex ratio of 1:1 and an assumed growth rate of average 75 calves per 100 adult females (of all ages) living in spring, then a mortality for Austria of about 52 000 head (2005, Table 16.1) would imply a minimum population (April) of approximately 140 000 head (multiplication factor 2.66) and a maximum after birth of juveniles (June) of about 190 000 head (for method and growth rates see also section 16.7).

Similar calculations for roe deer, using an estimated average growth rate of 100% and a registered mortality of 351 000 head (2005, Table 16.1) suggest a minimum population of 700 000 head (factor 2.0) and a maximum of 1 050 000 head for the country as a whole. The same calculation for chamois (with 40% growth) leads to 130 000 head minimum (factor 5.0) and 150 000 head maximum population.

Based on such estimates, trends for the last five years for chamois indicate a slight decrease in population number, whereas all other ungulate species are increasing (particularly wild boar and ibex) or at least remaining stable. Large predators as a habitat factor for ungulates are mostly stable or slightly increasing (lynx). The number of human hunters is also increasing.

16.2 Legislation

Austria is subdivided into nine provinces. Each province has a separate hunting law that sets the general regulations for ungulate management. In contrast to Germany there is no overall law for the whole of Austria. A coordination bureau of the hunting authorities (which are self-organisations of the hunters defined in the hunting laws) ensures some level of consistency between the different provinces and helps to ensure that wildlife management is in keeping with EU directives. The hunting rights are strictly connected to the landowner.

Essential contents of the nine hunting laws are the definition of the wildlife species allowed to be hunted (max. 16 mammal species, 17 bird species), the procedure of wildlife-damage compensation (in forest and agriculture), permitted shooting seasons (that differ between the species and their sexes), and the possibility of creating habitat-protection areas (only few provinces).

Official aims in all hunting laws are (1) high diversity of wildlife species, (2) protection of wildlife populations, (3) avoidance of damage by wildlife to vegetation, and (4) sustainable use of wildlife species. A weak point is the protection of habitats, which is expressed in the laws of only a few provinces.

Permitted hunting seasons differ somewhat between the provinces and are detailed in section 16.4.

16.3 Management objectives

For the landowner the right to hunt is often an important part of his/her income (selling ungulates particularly trophy game for shooting, leasing out small land areas or whole hunting districts to hunters). The main objectives for individual hunters are mainly for recreation, sport and sustainable harvest but they have also learned (more or less) to feel responsible for controlling population size and helping to prevent unacceptable ungulate damage in forestry and agriculture. Most of the hunters do not like to be called a 'manager'. They argue that 'hunting' (in German 'Jagd'), particularly in their 'own' hunting district, is more than just 'management' because they feel more emotion, pleasure, idealism and are, therefore, more closely connected to wildlife and its habitat than 'managers' usually want to be.

Venison production usually is no more a main objective, because of the very low venison prices. Poaching is not a severe problem.

16.4 Management structure

Each of the nine Austrian provinces has a separate hunting law that establishes the legal framework for ungulate management. Within all provinces hunting is organised in hunting districts. This district-hunting system consists of about 12 000 hunting districts (wildlife-management units) in Austria with a minimum district size of 1.15 km^2 and a mean size of 7 km^2 per district. Landowners with at least 1.15 km^2 continuous area are able to decide whether to hunt themselves (if they have the qualification for hunting), to sell some or all ungulates to hunters, or to lease out one or more of their hunting districts to hunters. Landowners with less than 1.15 km^2 area hold the hunting right but they are not allowed to use it themselves. They have to connect their area with areas of other small landowners and to lease out the total area to hunters, or to connect and lease out the area to a neighbour district that is large enough to use the right to hunt.

The hunting laws regulate wildlife management. That means that the hunters are responsible for the management of wildlife. The ultimate control over whether or not hunters respect the law is the public administration. It is supported by game wardens: for each hunting district the hunters must appoint a special qualified game warden with an advanced hunting education and public responsibility to prevent illegal hunting activities; a few of them are full-time professional hunters (employees of hunt leasers or landowners).

16.5 Management organisation

16.5.1 Preconditions for practical ungulate management (hunting)

Each hunter must first pass a hunting examination; then is allowed to buy an official hunting licence for about EUR 50 to 100 per year (depending on the province), and finally he or she needs a hunting permit (or lease) for a certain hunting district. Hunters who own at least 115 ha continuous land area have this permit automatically.

16.5.2 Shooting plans

Hunters must provide shooting plans for all ungulate species (except wild boar). They have to be created in spring before the hunt starts, yearly or in 3-year intervals (depending on the province). The plan must include a minimum and maximum number to be culled, or only a minimum determined in relation to the observed level of ungulate impact on vegetation (which is more flexible for the hunters). Cull figures have to be determined separately for each species, sex and age class. Injured and sick animals are mostly allowed to be shot in addition to the numbers planned.

16.6 Management practices

In general a rifle must be used for hunting ungulates (shotguns are allowed for roe deer in one province, but are not practically used there). The practice is mostly hunting from high seats, or stalking (creeping), and more rarely driving, which is nowadays increasing. Hunting dogs working singly or in small groups (no large packs) for driving (mobilising) ungulates are allowed in most provinces.

16.6.1 Hunting seasons

The shooting times differ between the species, age and sex class (Table 16.3) and are also slightly different between the provinces. The earliest start for roe deer is May; the latest end is December. For red deer, earliest is May and latest January. For sika and fallow deer, the season is between August and January. The season for chamois starts in the middle of May and runs until December, for ibex August until January, and mouflon May until January. Wild boar may be hunted all year, except sows when they have piglets. More than 20 years ago sows were also hunted all the year. Perhaps the protection of mother animals now is one of the reasons for the exploding population. Wild boar is the only ungulate species that may be hunted during the night.

16.6.2 Hunting statistics

A total of 98% of the country area is officially declared as hunting area. Around 1.4% of the Austrian inhabitants are hunters, one of the highest proportions compared to the other Central European countries. An average 4.7 ungulates are culled

Table 16.2 *Number of hunters, culled ungulates (all species), and culled ungulates per hunter from 1960 to 2005*

Year	Hunters (licences)	Culled ungulates total	Ungulates/hunter
1960	68 000	174 000	2.6
1970	84 000	195 000	2.3
1980	104 000	281 000	2.7
1990	109 000	341 000	3.1
2000	115 000	353 000	3.1
2005	118 000	384 000	3.3

Table 16.3 *Hunting seasons in Austria (differences between provinces)*

Species	social class	earliest start	latest end
Roe deer	buck	1 May	31 October
	doe-yearling	1 May	31 December
	doe and fawn	1 August	31 December
Red deer	stag	1 August	31 December
	hind (no calf)	16 May	15 January
	hind and calf	1 July	15 January
	calf	1 June	15 January
Sika deer, fallow deer	stag	1 August	31 December
	hind and calf	1 August	15 January
Chamois	buck	1 June	31 December
	yearlings	16 May	31 December
	female and kid	16 July	31 December
Ibex	all classes	1 August	31 January
Mouflon	ram	1 May	15 January
	female and lamb	1 May	31 December
Wild boar	male, juvenile		all year
	female		all year, except mothers

per km^2 (of hunting area). In Central Europe, only Germany has a slightly higher culling density. The average density of hunters per km^2 is 1.4, which is a figure somewhere around the middle for Central Europe. The average number of ungulates culled per hunter in the year 2005 reached 3.3 animals.

The development of ungulates culled per hunter in 10-year steps from 1960 is shown in Table 16.2. Because hunters as well as ungulates increased during this period, the number of ungulates culled per hunter shows only a relatively slight increase. It seems that more hunters need more ungulates to be sustainable in hunting success. This would be another aspect of sustainability that in practice we rarely consider.

16.6.3 Ungulate management in national parks (IUCN, Cat. II)

In national parks the management is called 'ungulate regulation', and is reduced in area and time. In parts of the park ungulates are regulated (shot) in short periods of the year. Only ungulate species are regulated, not the small game. Supplemental winter feeding of red deer may be allowed if there are no natural winter habitats available. Ungulate populations inside the park are mostly regulated by rangers (not by common hunters), and outside, when animals leave the park, by the hunters.

16.7 Census methods

As already noted, there is no scientific or systematic monitoring of ungulate populations installed by public administration. Ungulate stocks are simply estimated by the hunters in their districts every year as a basis for their management and culling plan.

Once in a while, regional minimum stocks based on hunting bags are calculated. As in the calculations above (section 16.1) this is based on the assumptions of (1) sex ratio, (2) population growth rate (surviving offspring when shooting season starts in summer/autumn), and (3) that the total recorded mortality (number of animals culled plus animals found dead by other reasons) is about as high as the yearly offspring number of the species. In Austria, practitioners use the following growth rates related to all females in spring (before birth of calves): red deer 70–75%, roe deer 80–120%, chamois about 30–50%, wild boar 200–400% and ibex 20–40%. Concerning these percentages (originally investigated in different Austrian regions): the growth rates of roe deer, red deer and wild boar are relatively high because of supplementary winter feeding of these species in many regions. In addition, many of the offspring of these three species are usually shot already in the year of birth or in the following spring (high growth rates due to the reduced share of young females without offspring within the populations).

Other methods of estimating population size, e.g. pellet and track counts or infrared photography by helicopter are only locally used. In general, the most important information taken into account when planning the hunting bag of ruminant ungulates is the browsing and debarking intensity in forests, which is systematically monitored in the whole country by the public forest administration (sampling, partly in addition to exclosures).

16.8 Impacts on vegetation, damage and benefit

16.8.1 Agriculture

There are no formal estimates of the amount of damage caused by ungulates to agriculture, but damage to arable land and meadows is strongly increasing due to the increasing number of rooting wild boar. From the viewpoint of the landowners and hunters, this wild boar problem is now one of the most significant problems in ungulate management. Hunters mostly do not know how to stop the increasing wild boar populations.

16.8.2 Forestry

The economic costs of damage to forests by browsing, fraying and bark stripping was calculated some years ago (Reimoser, 2000) and estimated at about EUR 218 million per year (between 1990 and 1999), which implies on average EUR 218/ha with at least 10 000 km^2 of forest area damaged per year. In principle, because they are responsible for ungulate management within their hunting district, the hunters have to pay for ungulate damage that occurs within their district, independent of the cause of the damage, but in actual practice only about 20–30% of this damage is compensated for to the forest owners (the owner has to report new browsing, fraying, or debarking damage within one year, first to the hunter and then – if there is no agreement possible on the amount of damage – to the public administration). To put these figures in fuller context, we may note that this estimated cost of total ungulate damage in forests was about 50% of the economic value of hunting in Austria within the same period.

The bulk of the damage (about 70%) is due to heavy browsing of top twigs (leader shoots) of young trees by roe deer, red deer and chamois that are living in forests.

An established monitoring system (non-monetary) clearly illustrates the damage trends: Since 1961, all important characteristics concerning the structure and development of the Austrian forests have been registered on statistical basis in the *National Forest Inventory* (NFI) (http://bfw.ac.at, forest inventory). Record is made of: type of enterprise and property; forest area; amount of wood stocked; increment and utilisation; ratio of tree species; damage; care measures; ecological characteristics; and habitat structure. This forest inventory is updated and reported every five years. The regular inventory of the entire Austrian forest is an important instrument for monitoring the forest industry and forest owners with a view to ensuring sustainability, and for advising of any measures needing to be taken on the part of authorities.

One part of the NFI is a comprehensive forest damage observation system that includes ungulate impacts on forest trees (intensity of twig browsing, fraying, bark stripping).

Over the last five years the following trends were observed:

- The negative impact of forest browsing and fraying was slightly decreasing primarily due to the change of the forest system to fewer clear-cuts and more natural regeneration (surplus of young trees, less edge effect) (Schodterer, 2004);
- Debarking damage was increasing because of the increased area of dense spruce pole stands which are very susceptible to bark stripping (Völk, 1998; Reimoser, 2004).

In the last monitoring period of NFI (2000/02) bark stripping was registered on 8% of forest trees that have more than 5 cm breast height diameter (that is in total 280 million trees) (Büchsenmeister and Gugganig, 2004). The highest levels of damage (debarking and browsing) are found in forests with clear-cut system and spruce afforestation particularly when clear-cuts are small (< 2 ha).

For sustainability (recruitment to replace rates of harvest), regeneration (trees up to 1.3 m height) was considered to be needed at a level of 35% of total forest area but grew only on 15%.

Factors considered significant in inhibiting such regeneration (and their proportional contribution) include browsing by wild ungulates (24%), livestock (13%) and other site factors (63%). A total of 36% of sample areas with regeneration were classified as damaged by wild ungulates, based on comparisons of site-dependent regeneration targets and thresholds (minimum density of undamaged trees required, tree species, maximum browsing intensity) with the current status (Schodterer, 2004).

Selective browsing of preferred tree and shrub species partly changes the diversity of woody plants. More importantly, about 30% of Austrian forests have a specific function to stabilise slopes and reduce risk of avalanches, rock falls, land slips, erosion, etc. In these so-called protective forests of the Alps heavy browsing of the forest regeneration weakens the stability of these forests so that expensive artificial measures become necessary to prevent such natural impacts on human settlements, roads, etc.

The main reasons for increasing forest damage by ungulates on landscape scale during the last five decades are thought to be: (1) the obstruction and fragmentation of ungulate habitat, and harassment of ungulates (for instance caused by human settlements, highways, fences, tourism and hunting pressure); (2) the disadvantageous ungulate distribution (refuge areas in steep protective forests and in dense pole stands that are particularly susceptible to ungulate damage); (3) the so-called 'overabundance' of wild ungulates – caused by poor culling and too attractive habitats (high ungulate settling stimulus by attractive edge effects, increased thermal and hiding cover, with this 'attractiveness' not adequately balanced by availability of palatable forages), and incorrect winter feeding; and (4) the existence of forests with a high predisposition to ungulate damage (e.g. strip-clearcut systems with spruce afforestation) (Reimoser and Gossow, 1996; Reimoser, 2003).

One the other hand, we should also emphasise that ungulates may have beneficial effects within forests and perhaps the possible beneficial impacts of ungulates on forest vegetation and on the achievement of silvicultural targets (Reimoser and Reimoser, 1997) have not until now been fully appreciated. Beneficial effects can result from increasing diversity and improved economic value by ungulates selectively browsing unwanted plant species and by improving germination conditions (seed dispersal, impact of hooves and droppings).

16.8.3 Conservation habitats

The authorities of the seven Austrian wilderness areas and national parks (IUCN Cat. I and II) follow the philosophy that plant communities and animals have the same significance within the ecosystem, but there is a danger of unnatural ungulate 'overpopulations' in cultivated landscapes. Therefore, managers developed the so-called 50:50 rule: On a maximum 50% area of each plant community the ungulates are allowed to shape their habitat as they want (more or less browsing, fraying, bark stripping, trampling, etc.), and an area of at least 50% of these 'natural' plant communities (particularly forest communities) is allowed to regenerate and grow up without significant change by ungulate impact.

The parks have mapped the plant communities and installed a monitoring system with a net of browsing exclosures each with a comparable patch outside (6×6 m each) as well as thresholds for the local tolerable ungulate impact for every plant community (Reimoser, 2002). In a 3-year observation interval this monitoring system shows whether the samples reach the 50% limit or not. If a threshold is exceeded for a couple of years the park managers have to react with a regulation of the number or/and distribution of the ungulate populations (in most cases in cooperation with the hunters of the neighbouring hunting districts).

16.8.4 Vehicle collisions

The number of ungulates found killed by collisions with motor vehicles has been yearly registered since 1974. In 2005, almost 40 000 ungulates were killed through vehicle collisions (97% of them roe deer, Table 16.1); that is 9% of total mortality registered. In 1974, the number was 17 000 (98% roe deer), 6% of total registered mortality were vehicle collisions. Monetary damage figures are not regularly monitored (no data available).

16.8.5 Sickness transmission (to domestic animals, humans)

Classical swine fever and brucellosis of wild boar are a problem in some parts of Austria. The last cases of swine fever were registered in 2002. Tuberculosis and paratuberculosis are currently at a low level, but are increasing, particularly in red deer, as well as in roe deer and ibex. The giant liver fluke (*Fascioloides magna*), an alien species from America, was first registered in Austria in the year 2000. During the last few years it has become an increasing problem in eastern parts of Austria (close to the river Danube). Particularly, roe deer have died through the impact of this parasite (and there is danger of transmission to domestic animals). Countrywide monitoring exists only for epidemic diseases such as swine fever and brucellosis.

16.9 Supplementary feeding and luring

For red deer, roe deer and mouflon supplementary feeding over winter is the norm in many districts, beginning in October/November and ending in April/May. In some Austrian provinces, supplementary feeding of red deer and roe deer is legally required during 'emergency time' (usually in winter), in other provinces it is only allowed if necessary to avoid game damage to vegetation.

Chamois and ibex are normally not fed. Usually shooting ungulates close to the feeding station is not allowed. Luring (to attract animals for easier culling with small quantities of palatable food) is only allowed for wild boar, but not for ruminants. Luring wild boar with corn all the year round is a widespread practice.

For red deer in some provinces, in addition to supplementary winter feeding, so-called winter enclosures with fences around feeding stations exist (Sackl, 1992). They are 10–50 ha with 40 to 200 animals inside for about a half-year. The aim of the enclosures is to prevent red-deer damage to forests outside and disturbance by tourism inside the fence (during winter and spring periods).

Supplementary feeding of red deer results in a marked change in their avoidance and habitat-use strategies (less true for roe deer). Such feeding as an overwintering strategy is an important steering instrument in alpine red-deer management, but it is not equally efficient everywhere and at all times (e.g. Schmidt and Gossow, 1991). Judged by the effectiveness in preventing browsing and bark-peeling, poorly situated feeding sites have often been found to be counterproductive (Leitner and Reimoser, 2000). Advantages as well as disadvantages of supplementary feeding are possible (see reviews and analyses of Putman and Staines, 2004; and Peek *et al.*, 2002).

16.10 Main management problems and consequences

The dominating, and most obvious concern associated with the management of ungulates in Austria is the damage caused to forestry and agriculture. Underlying this, however, there are other problems and significant factors hindering effective management, such as

1. In most provinces there is a complete lack of integrative large-scale management strategies for populations and habitats.
2. Many of the ungulate populations have become extremely shy as a result of long hunting seasons and high hunting pressure, recreation activities and tourism, so that the culling goals (shooting plans) are often not fulfilled.
3. The monitoring of ungulate populations needs to be improved and made much more objective/quantitative. In Austria, monitoring of habitats is carried out by the National Forest and Landscape Inventory and is generally very good, but the monitoring of ungulate populations is unsatisfactory.
4. The price of venison has become very low; there is no motivation to shoot more.
5. Increasing traffic kills and more and more barriers by roads. Motorways are often fenced on both sides of the carriageway; such traffic infrastructures are often barriers for wild ungulates. The density of motorways in Austria is average for Europe, but fast increasing because of the opening to the new EU countries.

The main requirement to solve these problems is a better *integrative large-scale habitat management* both for conservation and sustainable use of ungulate populations as well as ungulate damage avoidance. If that could be achieved, then the regulation of ungulate populations and small-scale habitat management by foresters would be more effective. Up to now ungulate management has mainly focused on the stocks of one or a few hunting districts and does not consider the entire biological population range of the species concerned and the whole range of human impacts which may affect that larger area.

Achievement of such integrated management means particularly *better co-operation of the different land users*. We believe that an effective instrument to coordinate and develop cooperation among the different interests in the intensely multiple-used landscape on large-scales is the so-called WESP (Wildlife Ecological Spatial Planning), and its integration into regional planning, landscape and traffic planning. Up to now WESP has been used successfully only in relatively few countries (for instance parts of Austria and Switzerland). WESP is developed interactively with the local interest groups and focuses on population areas as seen from the wildlife species of interest, often across national borders (Reimoser, 2003).

The first step in creating the WESP is to define the true, biological, population range of a given species-population (which may well cross purely administrative borders. Once this is identified, then any very large population area can be subdivided into wildlife regions. So three administrative layers emerge (population area, wildlife region, hunting district). The next step is to define within each area so-called wildlife management zones (core, border and free zones) areas with different management priorities within each population area. Further steps can be a detailed planning for instance protected areas with little disturbance for ungulates.

A further important consequence for the future is to *define sustainable use of natural resources clearly*. We need an operational system to measure the sustainability more objectively. During the course of the last four years an assessment system called 'criteria and indicators for sustainable hunting' has been developed in Austria based on international obligations.

Ecological, economic, as well as sociocultural principles, criteria and indicators have been defined. The results are published as a book (Forstner *et al.*, 2006) and are also available via the Internet (www.biodiv.at/chm/jagd).

16.10.1 Towards a holistic management strategy

Wildlife management in Austria is considered as involving three interconnected component systems comprising habitat, wildlife and damage-tolerance factors. These components require adjustment if society's demands and needs are to be met. Human impact, in terms of landscape management, has a profound and direct influence on two of these components – habitat (attraction for wildlife, susceptibility to damage, conditions for hunting) and damage-tolerance level (related to vegetation). Direct human impact on the wildlife component results primarily from hunting and different kinds of anthropogenic disturbance to wildlife populations.

There are three main goals: (1) minimising conflicts between different interest groups (stakeholders) related to ungulate damage; (2) protecting biodiversity and related natural ecological interactions; and (3) protecting economic values by seeking sustainable use of plant and wildlife resources.

The principles of the proposed integration strategy to manage for an acceptable (tolerable) level of ungulate damage require: definition of land-use aims for various areas; coordination of habitat and ungulate management (regarding composition, area and seasonality); inclusion of ungulate species as a site factor in land-use planning; and the planning of hunting programmes, ensuring that the local vegetation has the capacity to support the intended ungulate density with tolerable impact. Key actions needed to support such a strategy are: (1) promotion of a flexible, integrated pattern of wildlife and landscape management (advanced Wildlife Ecological Spatial Planning – WESP), (2) objective measures for ungulate-damage assessment and population control, (3) optimised hunting strategies, (4) improved ungulate management in winter, and (5) establishment of protected areas (see Reimoser, 2003).

References

Büchsenmeister, R. and Gugganig, H. (2004) Stammschäden im Österreichischen Wald. *Bundesamt und Forschungszentrum für Wald, Wien, BFW-Praxisinformationen* **3**, 12–14.

Forstner, M., Reimoser, F., Lexer, W., Heckl, F. and Hackl, J. (2006) Sustainability of hunting: principles, criteria and indicators. Agrarverlag, Vienna: avBUCH, 126 pp.

Leitner, H. and Reimoser, F. (2000) Grundsätze der Winterfütterung. *Österreichs Weidwerk* **9**, 8–12.

Peek, J. M. et al. (2002) Supplemental feeding and farming of elk. In D. E. Toweill and J. W. Thomas, eds., *Elk of North America: Ecology and Management*, 2nd edition, Washington D.C.: Smithsonian Institute Press.

Putman, R. J. and Staines, B. W. (2004) Supplementary winter feeding of wild red deer *Cervus elaphus* in Europe and North America: justifications, feeding practice and effectiveness. *Mammal Review* **34**(4), 285–306.

Reimoser, F. (2000) Income from hunting in mountain forests of the Alps. In M. F. Price and N. Butt, eds., *Forests in Sustainable Mountain Development: A State-of-Knowledge Report for 2000*. IUFRO Research Series, No. 5, New York: CABI Publishing, pp. 346–53.

Reimoser, F. (2002) Schutz des Waldes und Wildtiermanagement in Naturschutzgebieten. *Revue de Geographie Alpine* **90**(2), 73–85.

Reimoser, F. (2003) Steering the impacts of ungulates on temperate forests. *Journal for Nature Conservation* **10**(4), 243–52.

Reimoser, F. (2004) Waldinventur 2000/02: Wildökologische Schlussfolgerungen. *Forstzeitung* (Vienna) **115**(4): 36–7.

Reimoser, F. and Gossow, H. (1996) Impact of ungulates on forest vegetation and its dependence on the silvicultural system. *Forest Ecology and Management* **88**, 107–19.

Reimoser, F. and Reimoser, S. (1997) Wildschaden und Wildnutzen: Objektive Beurteilung des Einflusses von Schalenwild auf die Waldvegetation. *Zeitschrift für Jagdwissenschaft* **43**, 186–96.

Sackl, K. (1992) Erfahrungen mit der Kommissionierung von Rotwildfütterungen und Rotwildwintergattern. Diploma Thesis, Agricultural University of Vienna.

Schmidt, K. and Gossow, H. (1991) *Winter ecology of alpine red deer with and without supplemental feeding: management implications*. Trans. XXth IUGB-Congr. Game Biology, Gödöllö (Hungary), pp. 180–5.

Schodterer, H. (2004) Die Verjüngung des Österreichischen Waldes. *Bundesamt und Forschungszentrum für Wald, Wien, BFW-Praxisinformationen* **3**, 17–20.

Völk F. (1998) *Schälschäden und Rotwildmanagement in Relation zu Jagdgesetz und Waldaufbau in Österreich*. Berlin: Beiträge zur Umweltgestaltung A141, Erich Schmidt Verlag.

17

Ungulates and their management in Switzerland

NICOLE IMESCH-BEBIÉ, HANS GANDER AND
REINHARD SCHNIDRIG-PETRIG

Switzerland is a small country in central Europe, with an area of 41 285 km². To a large extent the landscape is dominated by mountains and constitutes a suitable habitat for most ungulates. Between the Jura Mountains in the north (10.5% of total area) and the Alps in the south (62.5%) there is only a small area of plains (27%), the Central Plateau, which runs from west to east and reaches 50–100 km in width. The majority of the 7.4 million inhabitants live on the Central Plateau. Of the total area of Switzerland, forest covers 30.8%, and agricultural land uses 36.9%, while the non-productive area comprises 25.5%. However, in the Central Plateau the percentage of land used for agriculture is declining due to increasing urban sprawl, increasing traffic infrastructure and decreasing profitability of agriculture. Urban sprawl has reached a high degree; currently an area of 2987 km² (397 m² per inhabitant) is occupied by buildings. On the other hand, forest is increasing in the mountainous regions, because traditional non-intensive cultivation of small areas is increasingly being given up (BFS, 2001). These changes have an important influence on ungulate populations, but they are of even greater concern to more vulnerable species, especially many birds, reptiles and amphibians (BUWAL, 1994).

Modern Switzerland with an authoritative constitution has existed since 1848. The political system gives a great deal of sovereignty to its 26 cantons (federal states). In relation to ungulate management, the Confederation sets the directives for the protection of animals and habitats (e.g. protected periods for each huntable species), but it is left to the cantons to decide how to achieve the goals of management. Therefore every canton has its own hunting law and forest policy.

17.1 Ungulate species in Switzerland: status and distribution

Currently seven ungulate species are present in Switzerland; roe deer, chamois, red deer, ibex, wild boar, sika deer and mouflon. Three further species were present in the recent past: moose, wisent (or European bison) and aurochs, which all disappeared during the Middle Ages, mainly because of increasing human land use (Schibler and Lüps, 2005).

All native ungulates were exterminated in the nineteenth century except the Alpine chamois, which survived in very low numbers in some remote mountain areas, and perhaps the roe deer. There are several reasons for this drastic decline of ungulate numbers during that period. After the Napoleonic wars, the people were suffering from starvation, and uncontrolled hunting, improved arms, overexploitation of forests (browsing by cattle, firewood), and competition by high numbers of cattle browsing on alpine pastures increased pressure on ungulate populations (Schnidrig-Petrig, 2005). Subsequent re-establishment has been by a mixture of reintroduction and natural re-colonisation.

17.1.1 Red deer

The red deer disappeared from Switzerland around 1850, but towards the end of the nineteenth century, the species reappeared in Switzerland as a result of natural immigration from Austria and releases in different regions. Over a few years, a considerable population re-established itself in the Canton of Graubünden in the south-east of Switzerland. A genetic study (Haller, 2002) showed that in Graubünden the ancient native red deer population, the immigrated population and the present population are genetically very close. Additionally, this study showed that this present population is genetically very close to Austrian Alpine populations. In the Canton of Valais in the south-west of Switzerland red deer from the Carpathians have been released in addition to the already existing population.

Today the species is present in Switzerland mainly in the eastern and southern Alps, spreading from east to west and from south to north into the lowlands and from France into the Jura Mountains. The current population is around 25 000 (BAFU 2006, Table 17.1), of which 13 000 are living in the Canton of Graubünden (figures are approximate estimates only since there are no formal censuses; see section 17.7). Several cantons have produced action plans to enhance the spreading of red deer into regions with suitable habitats.

17.1.2 Roe deer

Around 1800, roe deer had disappeared from Switzerland, or they had been reduced to a couple of individuals. A hundred years later, roe reappeared naturally in

Table 17.1 *Population estimates and recorded death of main ungulate species in 2004 (culled and deceased)*

Species	Population estimates	Number	Culled % of population	Number	Deceased main causes of death	% of deceased
Roe deer	133 575	42 449	32	15 260	road traffic	53.28
					undefined	10.87
					age and disease	10.21
Chamois	89 324	15 463	17	1 817	age and disease	47.00
					undefined	18.49
					natural accidents	17.17
Red deer	25 647	7 135	28	1 151	road traffic	29.45
					age and disease	21.55
					natural accidents	18.85
Ibex	13 388	935	7	455	natural accidents	41.32
					age and disease	35.82
Wild boar	–*	5 810	–*	635	road traffic	64.25
Sika deer	239	144	60	11	no specification	
Mouflon	237**	—***	—***		—***	

*: No official estimate of wild boar population. Mouflon: population estimates 2002 (**), death numbers not communicated (***).

Switzerland by immigration from neighbouring countries to the north and east. Within a few decades, the animals had spread from the north-east of Switzerland through the Central Plateau and then into the Alps (Kurt, 1991). Additionally, deliberate releases of roe deer of unknown origin were carried out at the end of the nineteenth century, particularly in the southern parts of Switzerland. A genetic study (Hartl *et al.*, 1991) showed that although genetic variability in roe deer is high, the genetic diversification between Austrian and Swiss roe deer populations is not considerable.

The roe deer is the most common ungulate species nowadays in Switzerland, and occupies almost any suitable habitat from the lowlands up to an altitude of 2000 m. Since 1980 the population has been stable at around 130 000 (BAFU, 2006, Table 17.1).

17.1.3 Sika deer

The sika deer is a relatively recent addition to the Swiss fauna. Swiss populations became established as natural immigrants after a number of animals were released from an enclosure at Bayern München in Germany, near the Swiss border, in 1941. Soon a small free-ranging population established itself at the extreme north of

Switzerland, in the Canton of Schaffhausen (Righetti, 1995). It reached a maximum of 500 in 2002, and the current number is estimated at around 250 (BAFU, 2006; Table 17.1). A few isolated observations in neighbouring cantons indicate the animals' tendency to spread, but migrants are strictly culled. Therefore, it seems that no other populations exist in the country up to now.

17.1.4 Chamois

The chamois never disappeared totally from Switzerland. After the first federal hunting law was enacted in 1875, its populations recovered rapidly, spreading not only through the Alps, but also towards the Prealps and many steep, rocky habitats in hilly regions (Schnidrig-Petrig, 2005). From 1950 to 1962 several releases of individuals of the Swiss Alpine population into the Jura Mountains took place and a population established itself thereafter in the Jura Mountains (Salzmann, 1977). Archaeological data show that the animal formerly lived in any steep, rocky place, including forest habitats, all over the country (Baumann, 2005). Current population estimates are around 90 000 (BAFU, 2006, Table 17.1).

17.1.5 Ibex

The ibex had already become extinct in Switzerland by 1809. In addition to the more general reasons for declines in ungulate populations mentioned above, ibex products were said to have medicinal effects. The only region in the world where alpine ibex survived was in the Gran Paradiso, a Royal Italian hunting ground. An official request for reintroduction to Switzerland having been refused by the Italian authorities, smugglers brought some young animals to Switzerland in 1906. In 1909, reproduction was successful in a Swiss zoo and, in 1911, the first small colony was founded in the Canton of St. Gallen. This first release was not very successful because the winter habitat was not ideal. But, between 1914 and 1928, three colonies were established successfully in the cantons of Graubünden, Valais and Bern. As ibexes move easily on mountain tops, but avoid the valleys, they cannot spread across the Alps on their own. Therefore, animals from these well developing colonies were trapped and released at other sites (Meile *et al.*, 2003). So, the current distribution including major parts of the Swiss Alps and one colony in the Jura Mountains is the result of many releases (the latest 2004 in the Canton of Schwyz; Schnidrig-Petrig, 2005). Today the Swiss population is estimated at around 13 000 (BAFU 2006; Table 17.1). The ibex is still a species protected by federal law but for management reasons the cantons are given permission to cull a limited number of animals in colonies of 50 or more. In the last few years there has been a slight population decline in most colonies, for reasons that are still unknown. Reasons discussed are too high numbers culled, diseases, reproductive or genetic problems (bottleneck effect) and therefore a lack of possibilities for adaptation to changing environmental influences (e.g. global warming).

Two years ago, a programme with different ibex research projects was initiated: population genetics (Prof. Dr. Lukas Keller, University of Zurich), reproduction ecology (Dr. Peter Neuhaus, University of Neuchâtel), diseases (Dr. Marie-Pierre Ryser, University of Berne), winter ecology (Prof. Dr. Walter Arnold, University of veterinary medicine in Vienna) and population dynamics (Sæther *et al.*, 2002). The goal is to better understand these declines in population and based on the study results to adapt the ibex management strategies.

17.1.6 Mouflon

The mouflon is another non-native species which has colonised in comparatively recent times. Swiss populations derive, through natural colonisation the 1970s, from a population in the Department of Haute Savoie (France); the animals were themselves released there in 1954/1955 originating from Corsica. The Swiss animals live in two colonies near the French border in the Canton of Valais. For the first decade the immigrants spent the winter in France. The population is estimated to be about 250, with a tendency towards a slight increase. As the federal law does not consider them as an indigenous species, spreading should not be encouraged, but control is left to the cantonal hunting authorities (Lüps *et al.*, 2003). All the continental populations are suspected to cross-breed with domestic sheep (Tomiczek and Türcke, 1995). This might be the reason for deformation of horns, which is seen quite often (up to 30% of rams).

17.1.7 Wild boar

The wild boar disappeared from Switzerland in the early decades of the nineteenth century. Until about 1950, immigration from Germany, France and Italy resulted in only occasional presence of the species in Switzerland, but in the second half of the twentieth century, wild boar extended its range markedly, spreading from the northern border through the Jura Mountains and the Central plateau towards the Alps. As it is very difficult to estimate populations, no official numbers are available (BAFU, 2006), but increased culling and agricultural damage indicate that numbers are rising markedly.

17.2 Legislation

Until the beginning of the Middle Ages, everyone was free to hunt. Then it became a royal privilege which was later extended to the aristocracy and clergy near large towns, while, in practical terms, it remained somewhat free in rural and mountainous areas where enforcement of the law was more difficult.

From 1500 on, hunting became regulated in greater detail; first conservation measures were enacted (establishment of protected areas, persecution of poachers), as some of the most appreciated game species were seen to be gradually decreasing. When a more democratic system became established after the Napoleonic Wars, regulation of hunting was delegated to the cantons and rights to hunt were decoupled from private ownership of land. Nevertheless, the decline in Swiss ungulate populations could not be stopped until 1875, when the first Federal hunting law was enacted (Müller, 2005). Limited hunting seasons, protection of lactating females and young, and the creation of federal non-hunting areas permitted many species to recover within a few decades. Public game wardens were employed to control regular hunting and protected areas. Some animals such as the ibex became totally protected and could not be hunted at all. The aim of this first law was the protection of species and the re-establishment of exterminated populations for hunting.

The modern Federal Hunting Law, enacted in 1986, shifted the objective from the pure protection of animals to the protection of habitats and the regulation of populations. The main goals of this law are maintenance of biodiversity, protection of threatened species, limitation of damage caused by free-ranging animals, and sustainable culling of populations. The last of these objectives caused a transition from trophy hunting to culling of young and females, in order to influence population sizes sustainably, and this process is still in progress. The hunting seasons were extended, and even protected species such as ibex may now be hunted under certain conditions.

The Federal Hunting Law sets the basic directives for topics such as definition of protected species, management measures for protected species (ibex), protection periods for huntable species (Table 17.2), prohibited weapons and other aids, prevention and compensation for wildlife damage, etc. However, it requires the cantons to enact their own hunting laws and to work out management plans for all huntable species, naturally within certain limits such as for example the prevention of extinction, even on a local level. Therefore the cantons can extend (but not shorten) the protection periods, the list of protected species or prohibited weapons and ammunition, define the hunting examinations, permissions and permitted hunting types, draw up the shooting plan for each huntable species, etc. This federal approach can also cause difficulties because as a result of such devolution of responsibility to the regions, there are almost 26 different ways of managing wildlife in such a small country (Table 17.3). This can particularly become problematic for ungulate species with large home ranges such as red deer.

17.3 Management objectives

Modern wildlife management is the comprehensive management of wildlife species and their habitat. Another key factor in modern wildlife management is human

Table 17.2 *Minimal protection period for all ungulates as stated in the federal law*

Species	Protection period Start	End
Roe deer	1 February	30 April
Chamois	1 January	31 July
Red deer	1 January	31 July
Ibex	1 December	31 August
Wild boar	1 February	30 June
Sika deer	1 February	31 July
Mouflon	1 February	31 July

interests. To reach its objectives successfully, management cannot be isolated from its economic and societal surroundings. It has to respect regional traditions, the attractiveness of the landscape to tourists who like to observe animals and it has to meet ethical requirements regarding animal welfare.

In Switzerland hunting can best be described as a time consuming passion based on long standing traditions, although nowadays in some cantons there are very few young people willing to follow these traditions and the mean age of the hunters is therefore rather high. For the cantonal and federal authorities on the other hand, the main management goals are to have stable and healthy wildlife populations and to reduce wildlife damage to forestry and agriculture to a minimum.

17.4 Management structure

According to federal law the cantons are responsible for hunting and have to set up annual management plans for all huntable species. In all cantons these are discussed with commissions consisting of representatives from hunt, forestry, agriculture, communities, nature conservation and animal welfare. The cantons also have to keep records of hunting bag statistics and as far as possible of population numbers and to send these numbers to the Federal Office for the Environment every year, for their national statistics. Thus the Confederation is able to observe ungulate development in Switzerland and to intervene where necessary.

Two different administrative systems are operated for hunting in Switzerland: the licensing system ('Patentjagd') and the preserves system ('Revierjagd'). The licensing system is practised in 16 cantons by about 24 000 hunters on 70% of the national territory. Each hunter buys an annual licence from the cantonal hunting department, and the licence is valid throughout the canton (except in non-hunting areas). The number of animals culled is limited, depending on species and canton.

Table 17.3 Overview of the management system for roe deer, red deer and chamois in all 26 cantons in 2006

	Roe deer Hunting season	Quota	Red deer Hunting season	Quota	Chamois Hunting season	Quota
Federation	1 May–31 Jan		1 Aug–31 Jan		1 Aug–31 Dec	
Aargau 140 356 ha Plains, Jura	Buck: 1 May–30 Sep with rifle (sit and wait or stalking), 1 Oct–31 Dec with rifle or shotgun. Doe/Kid: 1–31 Oct with rifle (sit and wait or stalking), 1 Nov–31 Dec with rifle or shotgun (sit and wait or driven game shooting).	Shooting plan drawn up by hunter associations for each preserve.	No red deer population		Protected species	Culling of few animals causing damage.
Appenzell Innerrhoden 17 253 ha Prealps	4 Sep–21 Oct with rifle (sit and wait), 25 Sep–4 Nov with rifle or shotgun (sit and wait or driven game shooting).	In each year 1/3 of the hunters gets in alternating order permission for 1 buck and 1 doe, 1/3 for 1 buck and 1 kid, 1/3 for 1 doe and 1 kid.	4–23 Sep	No limits	Buck: 4–23 Sep Doe: 4 Sep–14 Oct Yearling: 25 Sep–14 Oct Kid: 16–21 Oct	2 animals per hunter until 14 Oct, max. 1 buck and 1 yearling. Number of kids not limited. Hunting can be closed for each category as soon as shooting plan is fulfilled. Milk does protected.
Appenzell Ausserrhoden 24 283 ha Prealps	8–30 Sep with rifle (sit and wait), 2 Oct–11 Nov with rifle or shotgun (sit and wait or driven game shooting).	1 buck, 1 doe and 1 kid per hunter or 1b, 1d and 2k, depending on region.	8–30 Sep and after hunt beginning on 13 Nov	In certain regions limited number, in others no limits, sex ratio 1m:2f.	8–30 Sep	Limited number per region, sex ratio 1:1, 1/3 yearlings, kids protected.

Bern 595 928 ha Jura, Plains, Prealps and Alps	1 Oct–15 Nov with rifle or shotgun (sit and wait or driven game shooting).	2 animals per hunter: 1k and 1b or 1d. In certain regions, additionally 1b (if before 1d culled) or 1 d (if before 1b culled). In few regions, a 4th animal possible (free choice).	1–20 Sep and 10–31 Oct	Culling only permitted in 4 regions, in these number of hinds/stags limited but not per hunter. In Oct only hinds and calves open. Milk hinds protected.	10–30 Sep	2 animals per hunter: b, d or y (not 2 from the same category). 3rd animal in 1 region (free choice). Kids and milk does protected.
Basel Land 51 755 ha Jura, Plains	Buck: 1 May–31 Jan Female yearling: 1 May–15 Jun and 15 Aug–31 Jan Yeld doe: 15 Aug–31 Jan Kid: 1 Oct–31 Jan. Driven game shooting with shotgun for all categories only from 1 Oct–15 Dec. At all other times sit and wait or stalking with rifle.	Shooting plan drawn up by hunting associations for each preserve.	No red deer population. Protected season all year round for single animals.		Protected species, but hunting permitted in certain regions from 1 Aug–31 Dec	Shooting plan fixed by cantonal authorities and not by hunting societies due to the protected status. Limited number per region, sex ratio 1:1, 2/3 yearlings.

(*cont.*)

Table 17.3 (cont.)

	Roe deer		Red deer		Chamois	
	Hunting season	Quota	Hunting season	Quota	Hunting season	Quota
Basel Stadt 3 700 ha city		Shooting plan drawn up by hunting associations for each preserve.	No red deer population.		No chamois population.	
Fribourg 167 059 ha Plains, Prealps, Alps	18 Sep–14 Oct with rifle or shotgun (sit and wait or driven game shooting).	Maximum 1 buck, 1 yeld doe and 1 animal <13 kg per hunter.	18–30 Sep. Hunt is stopped as soon as shooting plan is fulfilled or extended for 1 week if numbers are not attained.	1 stag or 1 yeld hind per hunter.	18–30 Sep, special hunt 2–7 Oct.	1 animal per hunter (b or yeld d). Special hunt: 1 animal (b, d, y or k) per chosen hunter.
Genève 28 235 ha city, plains	Hunting prohibited by cantonal law.					
Glarus 68 509 ha Prealps, Alps	Buck: 1 Oct and 7/8 Doe: 3–5 and 10–12 Oct Kid: 14 Oct–2 Nov All with rifle (sit wait or stalking).	3 animals per hunter (buck, yeld doe and kid). The number of bucks shot determines the shooting plan for the does and kids (ratio 1b:1d:0.66k).	4–18 Sep and after hunt in certain regions beginning on 1 Nov.	No quota per hunter, but total number per category is given.	Buck and Doe: 4–18 Sep Yearling: 4–8 Sep.	2 animals per hunter and not more than 1 per category (buck, yeld doe), although both could be yearlings.

Graubünden 71 547 ha Alps	9–26 Sep with rifle (sit and or stalking) and after hunt from 4 Nov–14 Dec in each region until number of hinds and kids culled = 50–65% of the total number culled (depending on the goal: reduction, stabilisation or raising of the pop.).	3 animals (roe deer or chamois) per hunter. Possibilities: 1 yeld roe doe; 1–3 yeld chamois does; 1 roe; or chamois buck or 1 chamois yearling (chamois buck only permitted if chamois doe shot first). For the after hunt roe kids are open, but bucks are closed.	9–30 Sep and after hunt in each region until number of hinds culled = 50% of the shooting plan. After hunt from 4 Nov–14 Dec, but gets closed in each region as soon as shooting plan is fulfilled.	No quota per hunter, but total number per region is given (sex ratio 1:1). Protected (except for 2 days) are hart royals with 3 top points on both sides and male yearlings with spikes longer than the ears. Milk hinds and calves are protected in Sep. At the after hunt all stags are protected.	9–26 Sep	3 animals (roe deer or chamois) per hunter. Possibilities: 1 yeld roe doe; 1–3 yeld chamois does; 1 roe; or chamois buck or 1 chamois yearling (chamois buck only permitted if chamois doe shot first). Chamois yearlings and does with horns >15 resp. 17 cm are protected over a certain height limit.
Jura 83 847 ha Jura	2 Oct–29 Nov with rifle or shotgun (sit and wait or driven game shooting).	3 animals per hunter: One from each category (buck, doe and kid).	No red deer population. Protected season all year round for single animals.		2–30 Sep	1 animal per hunter (b or yeld d). Milk does and kids are protected.
Luzern 149 349 ha plains, Prealps	Buck & Doe: 1 May–30 Sep with rifle (sit and wait or stalking), 1 Oct–15 Dec with rifle or shotgun (sit and wait or driven game shooting) Kid: 1 Oct–15 Dec.	Shooting plan drawn up by hunting associations for each preserve.	1 Aug–31 Jan	Shooting plan drawn up by hunting associations for each preserve.	1 Aug–31 Dec	Shooting plan drawn up by hunting associations for each preserve. Milk does and kids are protected.

(*cont.*)

Table 17.3 (cont.)

	Roe deer Hunting season	Quota	Red deer Hunting season	Quota	Chamois Hunting season	Quota
Neuchâtel 80 294 ha Jura	2 Oct–11 Nov with rifle or shotgun (sit and wait or driven game shooting).	One animal per hunter (buck, doe or kid) plus 1 kid from Oct 2–14.	No red deer population. Protected season all year round for single animals.		11–28 Sep	Half of the hunters: 1 b, other half: 1 yeld d (switches each year). Plus 1 yearling for each hunter from 11–15 Sep. Kids and milk does are protected.
Nidwalden 27 592 ha Alps	16 Oct–4 Nov with rifle or shotgun (sit and wait or driven game shooting).	One animal per hunter (buck, doe or kid).	4–30 Sep and possibly after hunt in certain regions in Nov/Dec.	1 stag and 3 hinds per hunter. From 21 Sep on only yearlings permitted. Hunting gets closed in each region as soon as shooting plan fulfilled.	4–30 Sep	2 animals per hunter: 4–23 Sep: 1 animal must be yeld doe, yearling or buck below 16 kg, 2 animals, free choice (except kids). 25–30 Sep: yearling, kid or buck below 16 kg, 2 animals, free choice (except does).
Obwalden 49 056 ha Alps	2–21 Oct with rifle or shotgun (sit and wait or driven game shooting).	2 animals per hunter: 1k and 1b, 1d or another kid.	1–23 Sep and after hunt in certain regions in Nov/Dec/Jan until shooting plan fulfilled.	1–16 Sep: 1 stag per hunter, yeld hinds and female yearlings not limited. 18–23 Sep: kids and 1 male yearling (if no stag shot before).	1–23 Sep	One animal per hunter (buck, doe or yearling).

St. Gallen 202 573 ha plains, Prealps, Alps	Buck, yeld doe and yearling: 1 May–15 Dec Milk doe & kid: 15 Aug–15 Dec. Driven game shooting only from 1 Oct–30 Nov.	Shooting plan drawn up by hunting associations and cantonal authority for each preserve.	15 Aug–15 Dec	Shooting plan drawn up by hunting associations and cantonal authority for each preserve. Hart royals with 3 top points on both sides are protected.	Buck: 15 Aug–31 Oct Doe, yearling & kid: 15 Aug–15 Dec	Shooting plan drawn up by hunting associations and cantonal authority for each preserve.
Schaffhausen 29 846 ha plains	Buck: 2 May–31 Dec Doe & kid: 1 Sep–31 Jan Yearling: 2–15 May and 1 Sep–31 Dec. Driven game shooting only from 1 Oct–31 Dec.	Shooting plan drawn up by hunting associations for each preserve.	No red deer population.		1 Sep–31 Dec	Shooting plan drawn up by hunting associations for each preserve.
Schwyz 90 816 ha Prealps, Alps	Buck and kid: 2–31 Oct Yeld doe and yearling: 2–14 Oct. With rifle (sit and wait or stalking).	2 animals per hunter: 1b or 1k and 1yd, 1y or 1k.	Stags and female yearlings: 1 Sep–21 Sep Yeld hinds: 1–9 Sep. Male yearlings and calves: 11–21 Sep.	No quota per hunter. Hart royals with 3 top points on both sides are protected.	1–21 Sep	One animal per hunter. If a hunter culls an animal <15 kg or a doe older than 10 years, he gets a second animal (yd or y). Milk does and kids are protected.
Solothurn 79 065 ha plains, Jura	Buck: 1 May–31 Dec Doe and kid: 1 Oct–31 Dec. Driven game shooting only from 1 Oct–15 Nov.	Shooting plan drawn up by hunting associations for each preserve.	No red deer population. Protected season all year round for single animals.		1 Aug–31 Dec	Shooting plan drawn up by hunting associations for each preserve.

(*cont.*)

Table 17.3 (cont.)

	Roe deer Hunting season	Quota	Red deer Hunting season	Quota	Chamois Hunting season	Quota
Thurgau 99 101 ha plains	1 May–31 Jan Driven game shooting only from 1 Oct–31 Dec	Shooting plan drawn up by hunting associations for each preserve. Milk does protected.	1 Aug–31 Jan. Only small population.	Shooting plan drawn up by hunting associations for each preserve. Milk hinds protected.	Protected species	
Ticino 281 221 ha Alps	Buck: 7–10 Sep Yeld doe: 7–14 Sep Kid: 15–23 Sep. With rifle (sit and wait or stalking).	1 animal per hunter (b, yd or k)	Stag: 7–14 Sep Yeld hind: 7–20 Sep Calf and spike stag: 22–23 Sep and after hunt in Nov/Dec	Maximal number per hunter per category: 1 stag with at least 2 points on one of the antlers; 3 yeld hinds; 2 calves; 1 spike stag	7–23 Sep	3 animals per hunter. Maximal number per category: 2 yeld does; 1 yearling; 1 buck (only permitted if doe shot first) or 1 male yearling with corns >16 cm.
Uri 107 673 ha Alps	Buck: 9–14 Oct. Yeld doe: 9–13 Oct. Kid: 14–21 Oct. With rifle or shotgun (sit and wait or driven game shooting).	2 animals per hunter: buck, yeld doe and kids. Maximum 1 buck and 1 doe per hunter. Milk does protected.	Male yearlings: 4–9 Sep. Stags, yeld hinds and female yearlings: 9–30 Sep and after hunt in each region beginning on 9 Oct until number of hinds culled corresponds to the shooting plan.	No quota per hunter, but total number per region and per category is given (sex ratio 1:1, 1/3 yearlings and calves). Milk hinds are always protected, calves only in Sep. At the after hunt all stags and male yearlings are protected.	Sep 4–16	2 animals per hunter: buck (corns $\geq$ 20 cm), yeld doe (corns $\geq$ 18 cm), yearling (corns $\leq$ 14 cm). Maximum 1 buck and 1 doe per hunter. Kids and milk does protected.

Vaud 321 194 ha plains, Jura, Prealps, Alps	2–31 Oct with rifle or shotgun (sit and wait or driven game shooting).	Alps and Plains: 3 animals per hunter. Jura: 2 animals per hunter, free choice, but at least 1 kid. Milk doe protected.	Alps: 6–13 Sep and 1 day per week in Nov Jura: 1 day per week from 25 Oct–3 Jan.	Hunters have to form groups of 6 (Alps) or 12 (Jura) people and to each group a certain number of animals is appointed. The hunt can be closed at all times (for a region, sex- or age-class) as soon as the shooting plan for this region/category is fulfilled. Milk hind protected.	14–22 Sep Special hunt Alps: 25–28 Sep Special hunt Jura: 11–15 Dec	1 animal per hunter, free choice. For the special hunt, the number of hunters is limited and 1 animal of a certain category is appointed to each hunter (shooting plan defines number of animals per category and casting lots decide which category for which hunter). Milk doe protected.
Wallis 522 442 ha Alps	Doe: 18–30 Sep with rifle (sit and wait or stalking). Buck: 2 days per week from 3–21 Oct with rifle or shotgun (sit and wait or driven game shooting).	1 yeld doe per hunter in Sep, 2 bucks per hunter in Oct. Kids are protected.	18–30 Sep and after hunt if necessary (did not take place until 2006).	Maximal number per hunter per category: 1 stag (no. of points ≥ 6) or 1 spike stag (spikes > 25 cm); 1 stag with 4 points; 1 spike stag (spikes < 25 cm); 1 hind or 1 female yearling; calves (no limits).	18–30 Sep	3 animals per hunter: 1buck, 1 doe and 1 yearling. If yearling's weight <14 kg or its corns <13 cm or yeld doe's age >13.5 years, then the hunter gets the permission for a 4th animal (b, d or female y).

(*cont.*)

Table 17.3 (cont.)

	Roe deer		Red deer		Chamois	
	Hunting season	Quota	Hunting season	Quota	Hunting season	Quota
Zug 23 870 ha plains, Prealps	1–31 Oct and 4 and 11 Nov with rifle or shotgun (sit and wait or driven game shooting).	1 animal per hunter, free choice. Permissions for 2nd animal are given out until shooting plan fulfilled. 2nd animal can be kid, buck (if 1st animal doe) or doe (if 1st animal buck). Milk does protected.	1–30 Sep	No limits. Calves only, from 18–30 Sep, milk hinds protected.	Chamois are protected	
Zürich 172 885 ha plains	Buck: 2 May–30 Nov Doe and kid: 1 Sep–31 Dec. Female yearling: 2 May–15 Jun and 1 Sep–31 Dec. Driven game shooting only from 16 Oct–30 Nov.	Shooting plan drawn up by hunting associations for each preserve.	2 Aug–31 Jan. Red deer are protected, but hunting societies are authorised to reduce numbers.	Shooting plan drawn up by hunting associations for each preserve.	Chamois are protected.	

> **Box 17.1**
> **Example of the success of modern wildlife management**
> **(Blankenhorn *et al.*, 1979)**
>
> The Swiss National Park was founded at the beginning of the twentieth century in the south-east of Switzerland, on the border with Italy. Still, today, it is the only national park in Switzerland. Since forestry, agriculture and hunting are prohibited in the park, it provides an attractive habitat for wildlife and soon after the park was established red deer numbers exploded in this region. In the 1970s the carrying capacity for the red deer population was surpassed; there were 4500 to 5500 animals in and around the park, i.e. an area of about 300 km^2.
>
> As deer use the park as their summer habitat and the region around it as their winter habitat, they caused severe damage to protection forests and to agriculture in the winter. Additionally, there was very high winter mortality (up to 600 dead individuals in one winter) due to the high population and consequent poor condition of the animals. Last, but not least, numbers of roe deer and chamois were declining as a result of competition. For all these reasons a management project, one of the first in Switzerland, was started with the goal of effectively, but sustainably, reducing the number of red deer. To attain this goal different measures were taken: first, intensive censuses were carried out to find more precisely where and when how many animals were to be found, and at what density. Based on these results, regulation measures were taken. A new approach to attain the desired reductions involved intensive culling of young and female animals and opening the culling of red deer after the regular hunting season, i.e. at a time when they are no longer in their summer habitat in the National Park. Despite the outcry of many hunters this management system has worked very well: by the beginning of the 1980s the red deer population had been reduced and it has since been kept at a stable level below the carrying capacity.

Game wardens that are appointed by the cantonal authorities are responsible for controlling hunting, and they also have policing rights. Depending on the canton, hunters either have to show the culled animals to the game warden or else the warden gives out a limited number of tags to each hunter and the hunter then has to attach a tag to each culled animal and fill in a form.

Ungulate hunting is normally limited to a few weeks in autumn (except roe deer in the plains; Table 17.3) However, if the harvest quota determined in advance by the cantonal hunting department is not fulfilled, a special hunt takes place in some cantons between November and January to cull the necessary additional numbers. Mostly, this after-hunt concerns red deer, as this species poses most damage problems to forestry and agriculture. As soon as the shooting plan has been fulfilled, the after-hunt is closed. In recent years some cantons have started to coordinate their management plans for red deer or wild boar to better be able to regulate and enhance a better distribution of these populations with home ranges covering several neighbouring cantons.

In nine cantons ungulates are managed according to the preserves system by about 12 000 hunters. In cantons with the preserves system, political authorities (canton or local authorities) lease the hunting rights for a certain preserve by contracts of normally eight years duration to a restricted number of people (hunter association). In general, non-members of the hunter associations are excluded from hunting in preserves but invitations are common. Each hunter association draws up its own management plan for its preserve or, as the preserves are rather small (mean size of preserve 8.2 km^2), for certain species with bigger home ranges such as wild boar one management plan is drawn up for several neighbouring preserves. These management plans have to be approved either by the cantonal authorities or by special regional hunting commissions. The associations communicate the numbers of animals culled and dead for other reasons at the end of the hunting season to the cantonal authorities. They can then intervene when necessary although this happens very rarely. The hunter associations are mostly self-regulated; only in one canton with the preserves system professional game wardens are employed.

Cantons with the licensing system are situated in the French-speaking and Italian-speaking parts of Switzerland and in the German-speaking Alps and Prealps whereas cantons with the preserve system are only situated in the German-speaking Central Plateau and Prealps. Further comparisons between these two hunting systems are given in Table 17.4.

In one canton (Geneva) hunting has been prohibited by law since a plebiscite in 1974 and management of ungulates is done exclusively by cantonal game wardens.

17.4.1 Non-hunting areas

There are currently 41 federal non-hunting areas, covering 1500 km^2, i.e. 3.6% of the area of Switzerland. Federal non-hunting areas were created after the first Federal Hunting Law in 1875. The main aim was the protection of game species. Today, this aim has been achieved; ungulate populations have reached stable numbers. In order to prevent numbers becoming too high, ungulates may now be hunted in these areas, following special management plans. Therefore, total protection of an area can be transformed into partial protection. However, culling is limited to a few species of special concern, such as red deer. Other species may not be hunted, and impacts on them must be limited to a minimum.

Although ungulate numbers have recovered, the status of the federal non-hunting areas is being maintained. Conservation measures taken originally for ungulates favour other species in the same habitat, for instance capercaillie (*Tetrao urogallus*), ptarmigan (*Lagopus mutus*) and black grouse (*Tetrao tetrix*). Furthermore,

Table 17.4 *Comparison between the two hunting systems practised in Switzerland: licensing system and preserves system*

	Licensing system	Preserves system
State administration and costs	high	low
Costs for hunter	rather low	average
Hunter's responsibility	average	high
Access to hunting	easy	sometimes difficult
Control	high (game wardens)	low (1 canton only with game wardens)
Hunting of roe deer, fox	efficient	very efficient
Hunting of red deer	efficient	difficult
Hunting of wild boar	efficient	difficult
Hunting of chamois	efficient	efficient
Hunting of ibex	efficient and even-handed	efficient but not every hunter gets the possibility to cull an ibex
Local hunting management	++	++++
Regional hunting management	++++	++
Supra-regional hunting management	++++	+
Collection of data for hunting management	+++++	+/−
Popular status	public hunt	traditionally gentleman's hunt, nowadays changing to public hunt

non-hunting areas are considered good refuges for the natural population development of ungulates, and they may also be a source for ungulate populations in neighbouring hunting areas. Apart from the federal non-hunting areas there are also many cantonal non-hunting districts and as noted, in one canton (Geneva) hunting has been prohibited by law since 1974.

Whereas most of the federal non-hunting areas were created in mountainous regions, cantonal ones are situated at any altitude. Most of them are only partially protected, depending on the species and the hunting season; in general they are rather small. In addition, new, so called wildlife protection zones ('Wildruhezonen') have been defined in certain cantons. Their main aim is to protect wildlife species from increasing disturbance due to recreational activities, especially in the winter, when disturbance can be fatal for ungulates. Therefore snowshoe hikers and skiers are asked not to enter these zones (Amt für Jagd und Fischerei Graubünden, 2005).

17.5 Management organisation

The size of management units differs according to the canton and the hunting system operated. The cantonal authorities set the directives for hunting. In some cantons with the licensing system, the territory of the canton is divided into wildlife management districts ('Wildräume'). For example the Canton of Bern (5959 km^2) is divided into 18 districts (mean size 331 km^2) according to the spatial distribution of ungulates (Mainini and Eyholzer, 2000). Management plans are drawn up separately for each district by the cantonal authorities in order to adjust ungulate populations in a more efficient and sustainable way.

In cantons with the preserve system, the management unit is the preserve (mean size of preserve 8.2 km^2), thus some populations are managed at a small scale level. This system causes problems for species with large home ranges, for instance, red deer and wild boar. Their management has to be coordinated between several preserves or management districts and in certain regions even between neighbouring cantons in order to be successful.

Whether drawn up by the cantonal authorities (licensing system) or hunter associations (preserve system) the minimum requirement for shooting plans was fixed by an agreement reached in 1995 between the Federal Office for the Environment and the cantonal forestry and hunting departments (see section 17.8).

17.5.1 Hunting licence

In Switzerland, anyone wishing to hunt must have a cantonal hunting permit. This permit is granted to applicants who show that they have the requisite knowledge, according to a test specified by the cantonal authorities. The test comprises a practical part (gun handling and shooting) and a theory examination.

In 2005, CHF 26 million (EUR 18 million) were paid to cantons or local authorities (communes) for annual licences or preserve leasing by in total 32 000 hunters (0.5% of Swiss population). In cantons with the licensing system there are around 20 000 ungulate hunters, in cantons with the preserve system there are 5500 preserve leaseholders and around 8000 hunters annually that are invited from the leaseholders to hunt in their preserve (BAFU, 2006).

17.6 Hunting practices

The types of hunting in Switzerland depend on the ungulate species and the cantonal laws. As regards arms, red deer, chamois and ibex are always culled with a rifle (ammunition: minimum 7 mm except in 1 canton 10.3 mm); roe deer either with a rifle or a shotgun and wild boar with a rifle or shotgun bullets, depending on the cantonal law. In general, roe deer in the Central Plateau are culled with a shotgun whereas roe deer in the Alps or Prealps are rather culled with a rifle. Regarding types of hunting, sit-and-wait hunting and stalking are used for red deer, chamois and ibex and sit-and-wait hunting or driven game shooting for roe deer and wild boar, again depending on the canton and hunting system (Table 17.1).

Roe deer is the ungulate species with the highest numbers culled. About 42 000 head are culled per year (30% of population, Fig. 17.1, Table 17.1), with an average sex ratio of 1 female: 1.2 male over the last five years (Fig. 17.2). About 15 000 animals are found dead, half of them having been killed by road traffic (Table 17.1).

Since 1990 population estimates for chamois have slightly decreased. Accordingly culling numbers have dropped from 20% to 17% of the population (Fig. 17.1, Table 17.1). The hunting of females only started in about 1960. Now, the culling of about 15 000 head per year is still male biased (overall sex ratio 1:1.4 over the last five years, Fig. 17.3). About 1800 animals are found dead per year, almost half of these can be accounted for by age or disease (Table 17.1).

In Switzerland, outbreaks of infectious keratoconjunctivitis (IKC) caused by *Mycoplasma conjunctivae* occur regularly in populations of both chamois and ibex (Giacometti *et al.*, 2000). Although the disease may kill up to 30% of a local population, IKC epidemics are not a threat to the presence of these species in Switzerland, because deep valleys turned out to be barriers preventing large scale spread of IKC (Tschopp *et al.*, 2005). Since there is not a strong correlation between outbreaks of IKC and the density of game species (Giacometti *et al.*, 2002) the main implication for management in infected areas would appear to be preserving affected individuals from disturbance rather than carrying out preventive reduction of population density. Furthermore, prevention of IKC in wild Caprinae should focus on hindering the spill-over of *M. conjunctivae* from livestock (Giacometti *et al.*, 2002).

For red deer, about 7000 head are shot per year (28% of the population, Fig. 17.1, Table 17.1). Culling is slightly male biased (1:1.2 over the last five years; Fig. 17.4). As for roe deer, a high proportion of animals found dead have been killed by road accidents (about 30%, Table 17.1).

Until the 1970s, prolific ibex populations were regulated by capturing animals to found new colonies throughout the Swiss Alps. Then the situation changed; increased winter mortality and complaints by farmers and foresters about damage restarted hunting of these animals which had been protected by the federal law (Fig. 17.5). The ibex is currently culled at a moderate level of 950 head per year (7% of the population, Fig. 17.1, Table 17.1). In the 1990s it was 12–14% of the population, which turned out to be a rather high percentage. Of some 500 individuals found dead per year, most can be accounted for by natural accidents (40%) or age and disease (35%, Table 17.1).

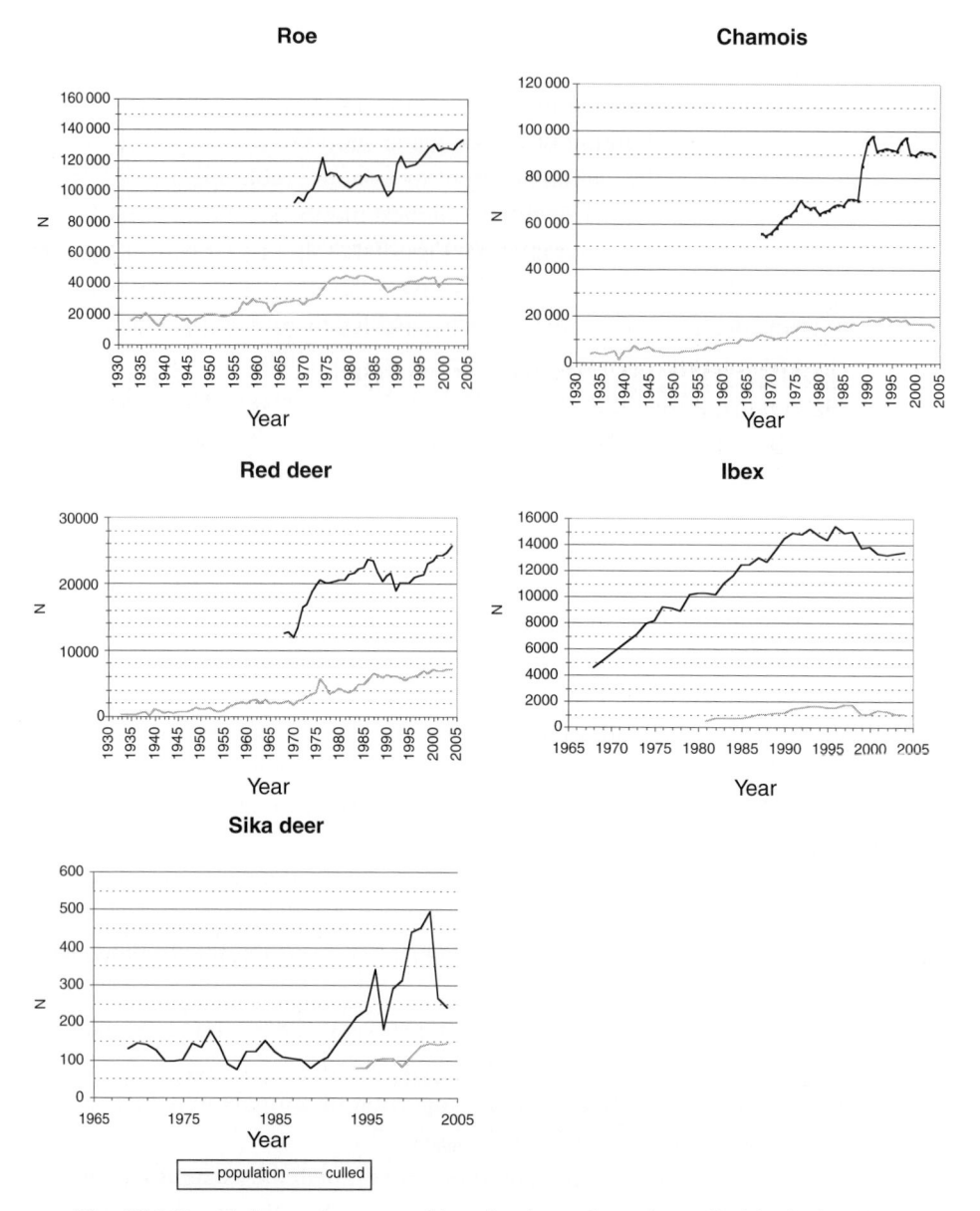

Fig. 17.1 Population estimates and hunting bag of species culled in Switzerland from 1933 to 2004 (BAFU, 2006)
Wild boar: no official population estimates, only culling numbers and details on deceased game. Mouflon: no official population estimates and regular culling numbers

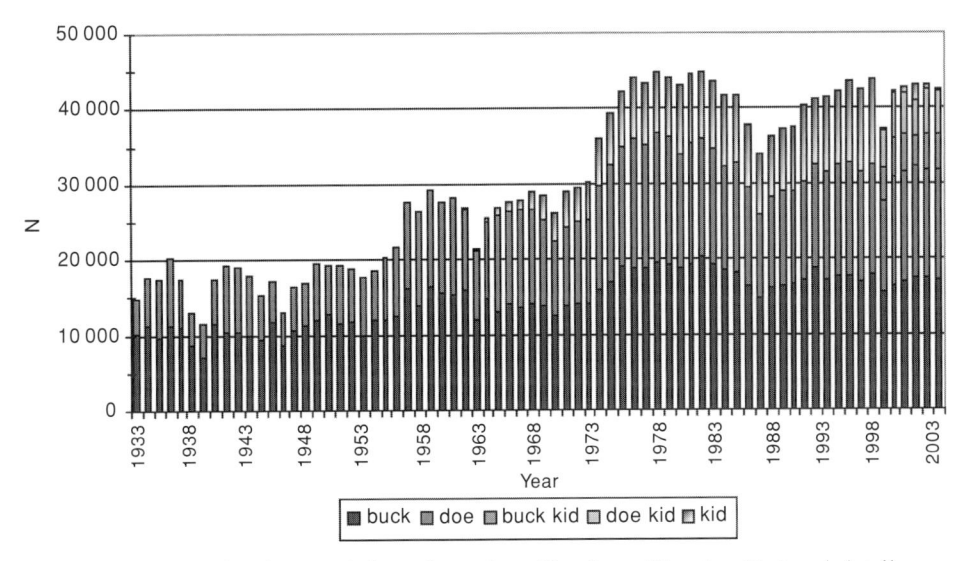

Fig. 17.2 Hunting bag statistics of roe deer. Number of head culled and details recorded since 1933 (BAFU, 2006)

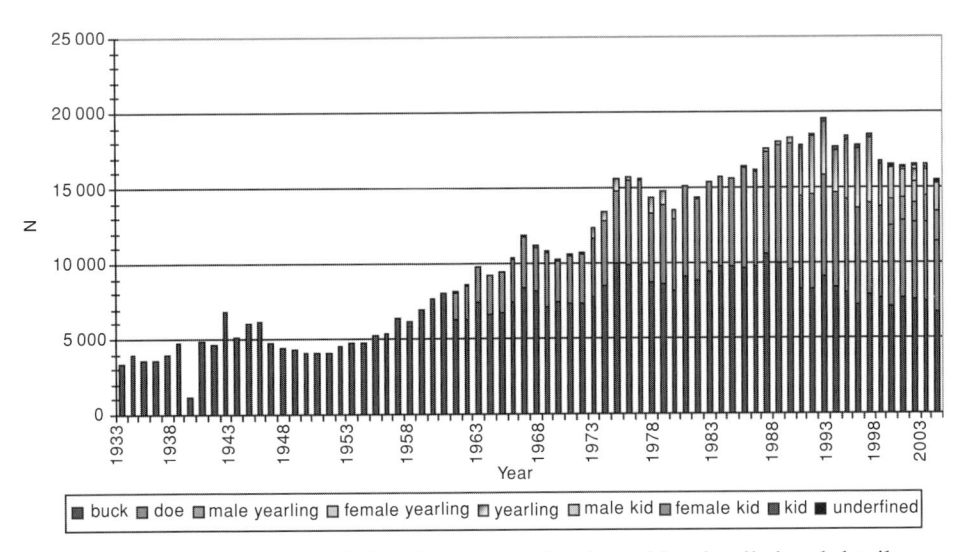

Fig. 17.3 Hunting bag statistics of chamois. Number of head culled and details recorded since 1933 (BAFU, 2006)

In those cantons where ibex populations are regulated by hunters, the hunters have to get a special licence – dependent on age, hunting experience and previously hunted ibex – in order to be allowed to cull one or two animals of a specific age- and sex-class.

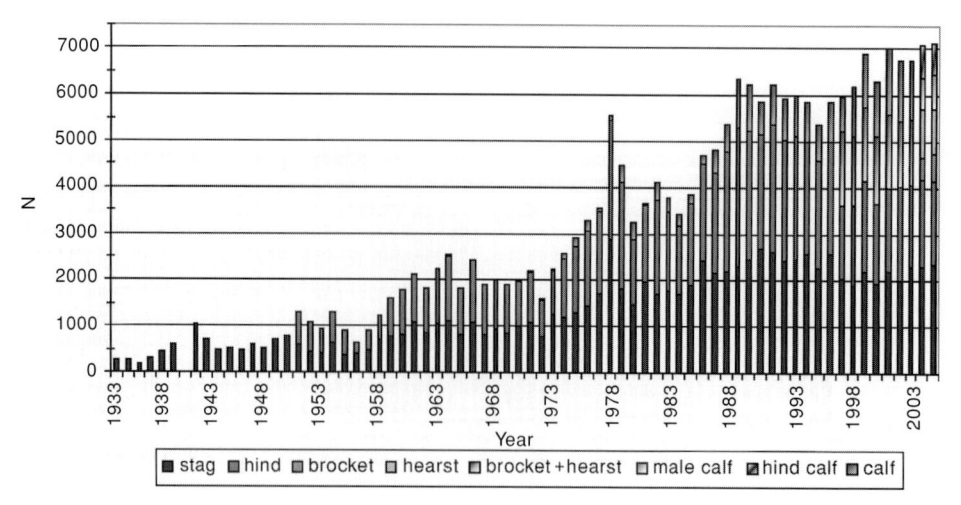

Fig. 17.4 Hunting bag statistics of red deer. Number of head culled and details recorded since 1933 (BAFU, 2006)

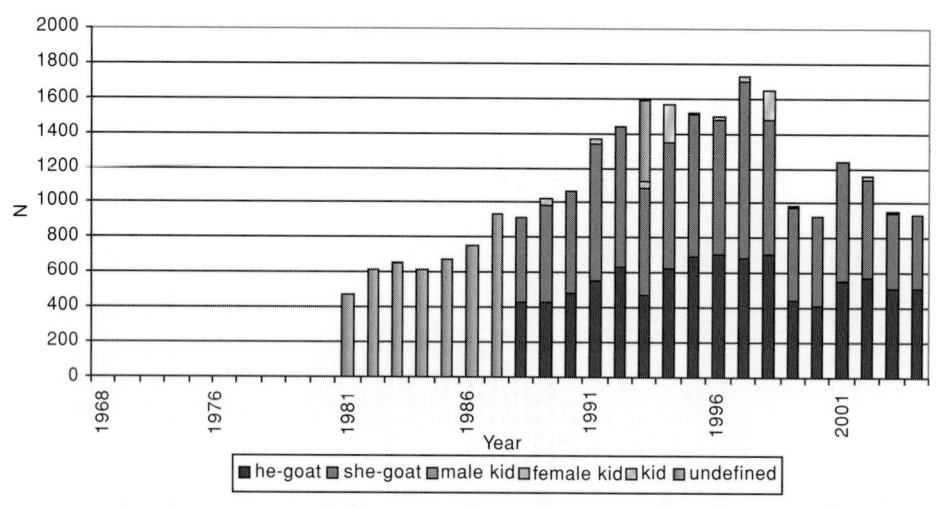

Fig. 17.5 Hunting bag statistics of ibex. Number of head culled and details recorded since 1981 (BAFU, 2006)

The management of wild boar is a rather special case because of the well-known fecundity of the animals. Cull levels were rather low until about 1975, reflecting the species' status in Switzerland. After a phase of slight increase the hunting bag increased from 1500 head in 1990 to currently 6000 per year (Fig. 17.1, Table 17.1). Wild boar caused a rapid increase in agricultural damage in some cantons. This situation could not be improved until a few years ago when population regulation started to be more effective due to common management plans over several

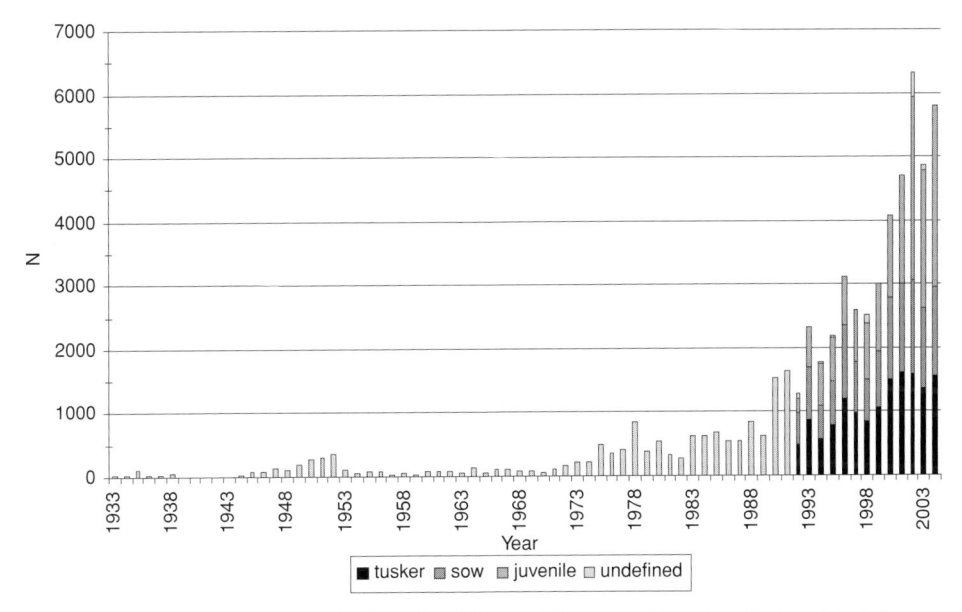

Fig. 17.6 Hunting bag statistics of wild boar. Number of head culled and details recorded since 1933 (BAFU, 2006)

preserves, the subsequent hunting of more females and piglets and more highly committed hunters. The sex ratio of the hunting bag is now balanced and includes a considerable amount of juveniles (50%, Fig. 17.6). According to Schnidrig-Petrig and Koller (2004) this proportion should be 70–90% to stabilise a population (culling of yearly offspring numbers) and if a population is to be lowered, then the sex ratio should even be clearly female-biased (0.9–0.5). Of about 600 animals found dead each year, two-thirds have been killed by road traffic (Table 17.1).

Populations of wild boar have in the past been susceptible to outbreaks of classical swine fever (CSF), and the incidence in free ranging animals may be underestimated because animals with the subacute, chronic form of the disease show rather unspecific symptoms. To protect domestic pigs from the disease and to limit economic damage, a specific management plan was used during the last outbreak of CSF in the Canton of Ticino in 1998/99, i.e. reduction in the number of susceptible animals in a defined area (Griot *et al.*, 2002). These measures were effective, so the disease was restricted to a small area, contamination of domestic pigs was avoided and the disease declined.

17.7 Census types and methods

Population numbers are indispensable for planning culling numbers. However, it is difficult to count ungulates. Thus, results of systematic counts cover a wide range of precision from rough estimate (roe deer, wild boar) to rather precise (e.g. ibex). In representing a relative population index rather than an absolute number, censuses provide valuable data, documenting chronological trends in population. Statistics on animals culled or found dead for other causes help check the accuracy of population estimates (cohort analysis).

In Switzerland, censuses are organised by the cantons, and are rather heterogeneous, but they can be summarised as follows: in cantons operating the preserves system, every hunter association estimates ungulate numbers in its preserve, whereas in cantons with the licensing system estimates are done by the game wardens. In general, ibex and chamois are counted with the vantage point method (e.g. Sæther *et al.*, 2002; Willisch, 2004; Struch, 2006), red deer are sampled by night lighting (partly coordinated between preserves/cantons) (e.g. Blankenhorn *et al.*, 1979), roe deer numbers are estimates based on night lighting, kilometric index or drive counting (e.g. Jäggi *et al.*, 2004; Rüegg, 2006) and wild boar are counted indirectly (culling number, tracks, damage) or by the capture–recapture method (e.g. Comte *et al.*, 2005).

The advantage of the licensing system is that counts are very systematic as they are done by the game wardens across the whole territory. The advantages of the preserves system are the high geographical resolution and the local knowledge of hunters. In both systems estimates are susceptible to manipulation, as has occurred in the past (Albrecht, 1989; Haller, 2002).

Beside the formal censuses other methods are used for further knowledge of spatial and seasonal distribution, social behaviour and activity budgets of ungulates. These include radio tracking of red deer (e.g. Righetti *et al.*, 2004; Zweifel-Schielly, 2005), ibex (e.g. Abderhalden, 2005) and wild boar (e.g. Comte *et al.*, 2005), tagging of roe deer fawns (e.g. Müri, 1999; Signer and Jenny, 2006) and genetic analyses (e.g. Haller, 2002).

17.8 Ungulate impacts and damage

Ungulate damage is mainly to agriculture (wild boar and red deer), forestry (red deer, roe deer, chamois and ibex) and in involvement in traffic accidents (roe deer, red deer and wild boar).

17.8.1 Damage to forestry

The Federal Forest Law of 1991 and the Federal Hunting Law of 1986 state that the natural regeneration of forests must be ensured using locally adapted tree species and without protective measures. According to an agreement (Kreisschreiben 21) made between the Federal Office for the Environment and the cantonal forestry and hunting departments in 1995 this has to be ensured on 75% of the forest area of each canton. To attain this goal, both hunting and forestry measures have to be taken. Hunting measures include the assessment of the distribution and recruitment rates of red deer, roe deer and chamois present and hunting plans designed to deliver the stabilisation or even reduction of the populations of these species.

The minimum requirement for shooting plans was fixed as follows in the agreement: (1) culling quotas must correspond at least to the annual growth rate of a population, (2) a minimum of 25% of the game bag must be kids/calves or yearlings, and (3) the sex ratio of the game bag must be at least 1:1 or even female-biased. Forestry measures include improvement of the food supply such as creating and maintaining stepped forest borders and open patches in the forest. In order to qualify for subsidies from the Confederation for the prevention of damage to forests, the cantons have to show that they fulfil the conditions stated in this agreement. This is especially the case for forests that protect features such as settlements and highways, as there forestry is subsidised by the Confederation.

Damage to forestry can be regionally or even locally very high, but there are no statistics kept on the economic costs of these damages. Additionally it is very difficult to estimate the real economic costs because there are still many open questions regarding the influence of nipping, fraying or stripping damage on forest dynamics (Weisberg and Bugmann, 2003). As stated above, the Confederation only pays prevention measures but does not compensate the immediate economic costs of these damages, i.e. replanting of trees, loss of valuable wood. They have to be paid by the forest owners themselves.

17.8.2 Damage to agriculture

Damage to agriculture is mainly caused by wild boar and red deer. Since 1990, wild boar populations have been markedly rising. This has resulted not only in a geographical extension of the spread of the animals, but also in local increases in wild boar densities. The main reasons for this change are the high mobility, adaptability and fecundity of the species, increased reproductive success due to increased natural food supply (mast years of beech *Fagus sylvatica* and oak *Quercus* spp.) and favourable climatic conditions. Also, populations benefited from the culling of fewer animals than the numbers of yearly offspring (Schnidrig-Petrig and Koller, 2004). For about 10 years, damage caused to agriculture by wild boar rose as populations increased (Fig. 17.7), mainly in the Central Plateau, and in the Canton of Geneva at the south-western end of Switzerland because in this canton hunting is prohibited and the 15 authorised game wardens have to regulate the increasing wild boar population by themselves. More intense culling and a reduction in the duration of the protected season – in 2003 from 1 March to 15 June

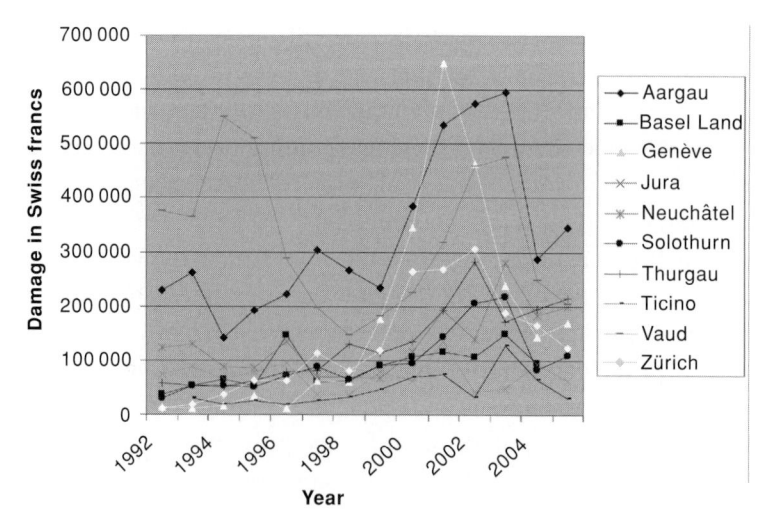

Fig. 17.7 Assessed and compensated wild boar damage in agriculture for the 10 cantons with highest damage costs in the years 1992–2005 (BAFU, 2006)

instead of 1 February to 30 June – finally resulted in most cantons in a decrease in damage caused to agriculture; from CHF 2.6 million in 2003 to CHF 1.7 million in 2004 (Fig. 17.7). Wild boar damage to agriculture is assessed either by the cantonal game wardens or special damage experts, authorised by the cantons.

The assessment is based in all cantons on a guidance from the Swiss farmer association (Schweizerischer Bauernverband, 2006) and then approved from the cantonal authorities. Regarding the damage compensation, the Federal Hunting Law states that small damages are not compensated and damages are only compensated if the farmer has taken some minimal prevention measures such as for example keeping a minimal distance of 5 m of unfenced cultivations from the forest or informing the relevant hunter association on the seeding of vulnerable crops, the time of harvest or the observation of wild boars in the vicinity. But again, it is up to the cantons to define the limit between small and considerable damage (in general CHF 100 or less) and the minimal prevention measures that have to be taken.

In terms of financing compensation, hunters have to pay at least part of the costs. Thus hunters have an interest in keeping damage at a minimum level. In cantons with the preserves system, the percentage paid by the hunter associations normally amounts to 20–50% of the total cost; the rest is paid by the canton. In cantons with the licensing system there is normally an annually adapted damage loading of the licence fees (Schnidrig-Petrig and Koller, 2004). Regarding red deer damage on agriculture, the damage is assessed and compensated in the same way, but there are no overall statistics kept on the economic costs of these damages as these are much less frequent then the wild boar damage.

Table 17.5 *Number of deaths of roe deer, red deer and wild boar due to traffic accidents in the last ten years (BAFU, 2006)*

	Roe deer	Red deer	Wild boar	Total
1995	7845	374	212	8431
1996	8036	435	264	8735
1997	8023	346	217	8586
1998	8776	430	206	9412
1999	9111	426	299	9836
2000	8311	465	426	9202
2001	8120	286	438	8844
2002	8237	439	527	9203
2003	8898	493	419	9810
2004	8557	414	445	9416
2005	8514	456	412	9382

17.8.3 Ungulate–vehicle collisions

The ungulate species concerned are mainly roe deer, wild boar and red deer. For roe deer and wild boar traffic accidents are by far the most common death cause in Switzerland (Table 17.1). Over the last ten years there are for these three species between 8000 and 10 000 deaths due to traffic accidents per year (Table 17.5; BAFU, 2006). The economic cost of damage caused is assessed only by the insurance companies but they do not give out official statistic data on these costs.

17.9 Supplementary feeding

The current Federal Hunting Law does not mention supplementary feeding, although, as in other countries, there is a long tradition of supplementary feeding of roe and red deer in Switzerland, especially during the winter. In recent decades this tradition has been subject to careful review. In many regions it has been reduced to emergency feeding (e.g. in very harsh winters), and in some cantons it has now been prohibited. The reason for this change is that most of the arguments in favour of feeding have not been verified, for instance compensation for lost winter habitat, decreased damage to forests, increased trophy quality, improved condition of the animals and control of the population distribution (Putman and Staines, 2004). In most regions it proved impossible to carry out winter feeding according to good practice.

Even the simplest requirements could not be fulfilled, such as no disturbance at the feeding site and the quality and quantity of the feed (Meile, 2006). The consequences of this are that the potential benefits (even if these were actually established) are never realised; on the contrary, provision of winter food in this way may actually be counterproductive in terms of assisting weak animals to survive over the winter period if daily drawn to feed sites and therefore to reduce the general condition of the population. Additionally, there may result an increased level of damage to forests around the feeding site and the adaptation of roe and red deer to winter conditions is not enhanced but hindered or even rendered impossible (Meile, 2006). In regions where they stopped feeding, it was found that after a few years the ungulates were more evenly distributed, that there was no increase in the number of deceased animals in cold winters or in the amount of forest damage (Meile, 2006).

Two special cases are diversionary feeding of wild boar to keep them away from agricultural fields and bait-feeding simply to cull the animals at the feeding sites. However, practical experience shows that such special feeding soon becomes normal feeding, which increases the population (Schnidrig-Petrig and Koller, 2004). Therefore, it is recommended to abandon such feeding except for cases with extremely high damage to agriculture. In that case, the canton should give temporarily and spatially restricted permission (Schnidrig-Petrig and Koller, 2004).

While provision of artificial feeds over winter may not be of significant value, in many areas hunters also undertake significant programmes of improvement of natural habitat structure and grazing quality within hunted areas. Those applying for a hunting licence have to do at least 50 hours of field work ('Hege'), depending on the canton, before being allowed to take the examination and in each preserve or region days of field work are organised on a regular basis by the local hunting communities. This field work includes improvement of food supply by diversifying monotonous forest border lines, by creating and maintaining open patches in the forest, by planting alternative tree species and by maintaining pastures that are no longer used by farmers.

17.10 Assessment of the present situation in Switzerland and challenges for the future

Compared with the situation in the nineteenth century, ungulate management in Switzerland is a success story, notably demonstrated by the re-establishment of exterminated populations such as red deer and ibex. Current legislation focusing on the maintenance of biodiversity, protection of habitats and regulation of populations reflects the change from trophy hunting to modern wildlife management, and is broadly respected and accepted by the public. Concerning population regulation, Swiss practice has reached a high level, despite the enormous diversity of management and hunting systems in such a small country. However, to manage animals such as red deer and wild boar successfully, cooperation between preserves or cantons should be enhanced.

In Switzerland, the three main natural predators of ungulates, wolf (*Canis lupus*), lynx (*Lynx lynx*) and brown bear (*Ursus arctos*) were all exterminated at the end of the nineteenth/beginning of the twentieth century. However, lynx have become re-established after reintroduction into two isolated areas in the western and central Alps and the Jura Mountains. The first animals were released in the 1970s and population estimates are today around 100 adults (Breitenmoser, 1998). Since 2001 nine individuals were moved to the eastern part of Switzerland to enlarge the population's range in the Alps (Robin and Nigg, 2005) and three to four individuals are still to follow in 2007/2008. However, due to the low numbers it is not sure that this subpopulation will survive in the long term. Individual wolves have entered Switzerland since 1900, and regularly since at least 1996 (Valière *et al.*, 2003). They are immigrants from the expanding Italian–French population in the western Alps. In 2005, at least three wolves were known to have their home range in Switzerland. However, several confirmed observations and traces in the Alps and also in the Jura mountains indicate a growing number of wolves in Switzerland.

In summer 2005, a single brown bear, immigrating from the reintroduced population in the Trentino (Italy), was seen sporadically in the canton of Graubünden, in the eastern part of Switzerland. This caused a great deal of hype, also because this young male bear came very close to humans and attacked livestock such as sheep and calves. It is likely that populations of all species will increase and the presence of predators, particularly lynx, may decrease ungulate numbers on a local scale and may also lead to a change in the behaviour of roe deer and sometimes chamois, making these species more secretive and elusive, and therefore more difficult to observe and to cull.

Increasing habitat fragmentation constitutes a major problem for ungulate species such as red deer, wild boar and roe deer. In the highly fragmented Central Plateau it causes, for example, wild boar populations to get stuck on the northern side of the main motorway between Zurich and Bern (Righetti, 1997), leading to increasing damage to agriculture. It also hinders the spreading of red deer populations from the Alps and Prealps to the Jura mountains and the Central Plateau (SGW, 1995; Righetti, 1997, Holzgang *et al.*, 2001) and leads to isolated roe deer populations beneath the minimum viable population size (Nunney and Campbell, 1993; Righetti, 1997). To improve the situation, ecological corridors are being restored by constructing fauna passages over motorways (Beier and Noss, 1998; Holzgang *et al.*, 2001; Oggier *et al.*, 2001). So far, 23 fauna passages have been constructed during the last years. They are used regularly by ungulates, especially roe deer and – if present – also by red deer and wild boar (Pfister 1997; PiU 2006 a, b, c, d). A total of 51 other fauna passages are planned on corridors of highest importance (UVEK Richtlinie, 2001).

Another increasing problem is disturbance. There is considerable evidence that outdoor recreational activities such as skiing, snowshoeing, paragliding and hiking have severe impacts on ungulates (Schnidrig-Petrig and Ingold, 2001; Ingold, 2005). Local conservation plans such as well marked wildlife protection zones and temporary restrictions on flying are now being implemented. Thus some causes can perhaps be addressed, but it is not easy to deal with the ultimate cause: increased access to remote areas by road and by cable cars.

The challenges in the future will certainly be to find sustainable solutions concerning wildlife damage and to counteract the increasing disturbance and habitat fragmentation of wildlife populations caused by recreational activities in the mountains and by increasing traffic and urban sprawl in the Central Plateau.

References

Abderhalden, W. (2005) Raumnutzung und sexuelle Segregation beim Alpensteinbock *Capra ibex ibex*. Nationalpark-Forschung in der Schweiz 92, 184 pp.
Albrecht, L. (1989) Die Geschichte des Steinbocks im Kanton Wallis. *Schriftenreihe Wildbiologie* 4(16), Wildtier Schweiz, 1–12.
Amt für Jagd und Fischerei Graubünden (2005) Wildschutzgebiete und Wildruhezonen. www.jagd-fischerei.gr.ch/wildasyl/. Accessed February 2006.
BAFU (2006) Eidgnössische Jagdstatistik. www.wild.unizh.ch/jagdst. Accessed January 2006.
Baumann, M. (2005) Native or naturalized? Validating alpine chamois habitat models with archaeozoological data. *Ecological Applications* 15(3), 1096–110.
Beier, P. and Noss, R. F. (1998) Do habitat corridors provide connectivity? *Conservation Biology* 12(6), 1241–52.
Blankenhorn, H. J., Buchli, Ch., Voser, P. and Berger, Ch. (1979) Bericht zum Hirschproblem im Engadin und im Münstertal. 160 pp. Unpublished report.
Breitenmoser, U. (1998) Large predators in the Alps: The fall and rise of man's competitors. *Biological Conservation* 83(3), 279–89.
BFS (2001) Bodennutzung im Wandel. Arealstatistik Schweiz. Bundesamt für Statistik (BFS), Neuchâtel. www.statistik.admin.ch. Accessed November 2005, 32 pp.
BUWAL (1994) *Rote Liste der gefährdeten Tierarten der Schweiz*. Bundesamt für Umwelt, Wald und Landschaft, 97 pp.
Comte, M., Fischer, C., Dändliker, D. et al. (2005) *Projet transfrontalier de marquage et suivis télémetriques de sangliers dans le bassin genevois*. Rapport intermédiaire. Service des forêts, de la protection de la nature et du paysage du canton de Genève, Service de conservation de la faune du canton de Vaud, Fédération départementale des chasseurs de l'Ain, Fédération des chasseurs de la Haute-Savoie, Office national de la chasse et de la faune sauvage de France, Office fédéral de l'environnement de la Suisse. Unpublished report, 84 pp.

Giacometti, M., Nicolet, J., Abdo, El-M. *et al.* (2000) Gemsblindheit. *Schweizer Archiv für Tierheilkunde* **142**, 235–40.

Giacometti, M., Janovsky, M., Jenny, H. *et al.* (2002) *Mycoplasma conjunctivae* infection is not self-maintained in alpine chamois in eastern Switzerland. *Journal of Wildlife Diseases* **38**, 297–304.

Giacometti, M., Janovsky, M., Belloy, L. and Frey, J. (2002) Infectious keratoconjunctivitis of ibex, chamois and other Caprinae species. *Revue scientifique et technique de l'Office international des Epizooties* **21**(2), 335–45.

Griot, C., Thür, B., Vanzetti, T. *et al.* (2002) Classical swine fever in wild boars in Europe; a disease still not under control. www.bvet.admin.ch/tiergesundheit. Accessed December 2005.

Haller, H. (2002) *Der Rothirsch im Schweizerischen Nationalpark und dessen Umgebung. Eine alpine Population von Cervus elaphus zeitlich und räumlich dokumentiert*. Nationalpark-Forschung in der Schweiz 91, 144 pp.

Hartl, G. B., Reimoser, F., Willing, R. and Köller, J. (1991) Genetic variability and differentiation in roe deer (*Capreolus capreolus* L) of Central Europe. *Genetics, Selection, Evolution* **23**, 281–99.

Holzgang, O., Pfister, H. P., Heynen, D. *et al.* (2001) Korridore für Wildtiere in der Schweiz. Schriftenreihe Umwelt Nr. 326, Bundesamt für Umwelt, Wald und Landschaft (BUWAL), Schweizerische Gesellschaft für Wildtierbiologie (SGW) & Schweizerische Vogelwarte Sempach, Bern, 116 pp.

Ingold, P. (2005) *Freizeitaktivitäten im Lebensraum der Alpentiere*. Bern: Haupt Verlag, 516 pp.

Jäggi, Ch., Gander, H., Baumann, M., Wasser, B. and Bieri, G. (2004) Waldverjüngung und Schalenwildbestand: Gutachterliche Verjüngungskontrolle und Kilometer-Index am Beispiel Honegg. Bern: WildARK, Unpublished report, 44 pp.

Kurt, F. (1991) *Das Reh in der Kulturlandschaft*. Verlag Paul Parey, 284 pp.

Lüps, P., Capt, S. and Crettenand, T. (2003) Der Mufflon *Ovis ammon musimon* in der Schweiz – eine geographische, wildkundliche und jagdliche Randerscheinung. *Beiträge zur Jagd- und Wildforschung* **28**, 99–104.

Mainini, B. and Eyholzer, R. (2000) Einteilung des Kantons Bern in regionale Wildräume RWR. Bericht zuhanden des Jagdinspektorats des Kantons Bern. WildARK. Unpublished report, 53 pp.

Meile, P. (2006) Wildfütterung in Theorie und Praxis. Schriftenreihe Wildbiologie 4/33, Wildtier Schweiz, 16 pp.

Meile, P., Giacometti, M. and Ratti, P. (2003) *Der Steinbock. Biologie und Jagd*. Bern: Salm Verlag, 269 pp.

Müller, K. (2005) Jagd. Von der Frühgeschichte bis zum Bundesgesetz von 1875. In *Historisches Lexikon der Schweiz*, www.dhs.ch. Accessed February 2006.

Müri, H. (1999) Veränderungen im Dispersal von Rehen in einer stark fragmentierten Landschaft. *Zeitschrift für Ökologie und Naturschutz* **8**, 41–51.

Nunney, L. and Campbell, K. A. (1993) Assessing minimum viable population size: demography meets population genetics. *Trends in Ecology and Evolution* **8**(7), 234–9.

Oggier, P., Rigetti, A. and Bonnard, L. (2001) *Zerschneidung von Lebensräumen durch Verkehrsinfrastrukturen* COST 341. Schriftenreihe Umwelt Nr. 332, Bundesamt für Umwelt, Wald und Landschaft, Bundesamt für Raumentwicklung, Bundesamt für Verkehr, Bundesamt für Strassen. Bern, 102 pp.

Pfister, H. P. (1997) Wildtierpassagen an Strassen. Schlussbericht zum Forschungsauftrag Nr. 30/92 des Bundesamtes für Strassenbau und der Vereinigung Schweizerischer

Strassenfachleute (VSS) (Hrsg.). Zürich und Sempach. Unpublished report, 29 pp.

PiU GmbH (2006a) Wildtierpassage Neu-Ischlag, Erfolgskontrolle 2001–2006. Im Auftrag des kant. Tiefbauamtes Bern. Liebefeld. Unpublished report.

PiU GmbH (2006b) Wildtierpassage Birchiwald, Erfolgskontrolle 2001–2006. Im Auftrag des kant. Tiefbauamtes Bern. Liebefeld. Unpublished report.

PiU GmbH (2006c) Wildtierpassage Stöck, Erfolgskontrolle 2001–2006. Im Auftrag des kant. Tiefbauamtes Bern. Liebefeld. Unpublished report.

PiU GmbH (2006d) Wildtierpassage Grauholz, Erfolgskontrolle 10 Jahre nach Bauabschluss. Im Auftrag des kant. Tiefbauamtes Bern. Liebefeld. Unpublished report.

Putman, R. J. and Staines, B. W. (2004) Supplementary winter feeding of wild red deer *Cervus elaphus* in Europe and North America: justifications, feeding practice and effectiveness. *Mammal Review* **34**, 285–306.

Righetti, A. (1995) Sikahirsch *Cervus nippon*. In Denkschriftenkommission der Schweizerischen Akademie der Naturwissenschaften, eds., *Säugetiere der Schweiz*. Birkhäuser, pp. 440–2.

Righetti, A. (1997) Passagen für Wildtiere. Die wildtierbiologische Sanierung des Autobahnnetzes in der Schweiz. Beiträge zum Naturschutz in der Schweiz 18. Unpublished report, 46 pp.

Righetti, A., Bebié, N. and Kamke, Ch. (2004) Interkantonales Rotwildprojekt der Kantone Bern, Luzern, Obwalden, Nidwalden und Uri: Schlussbericht 2004. PiU GmbH, Liebefeld b. Bern. Unpublished report, 24 pp.

Robin, K. and Nigg, H. (2005) Luchsumsiedlung Nordostschweiz LUNO. Bericht über die Periode 2001–2003. Schriftenreihe Umwelt Nr. 377. Bern: Bundesamt für Umwelt, Wald und Landschaft, 53 pp.

Rüegg, D. (2006) UVSL Bulletin Nr. 5: Untersuchungen über die Entwicklung der Verjüngung und das Verhalten von Schalenwild in Lothar-Sturmgebieten. Bundesamt für Umwelt, Bern. Unpublished report, 12 pp.

Sæther, B.-E., Engen, S., Filli, F. *et al.* (2002) Stochastic population dynamics of an introduced Swiss population of the ibex. *Ecology* **83**, 3457–65.

Salzmann, H. C. (1977) Gewicht, Schädelgrösse und Gehörnwachstum von Gemsen aus dem Jura und ein Vergleich mit anderen Populationen. *Zeitschrift für Jagdwissenschaft* **23**, 69–80.

Schibler, J. and Lüps, P. (2005) Fauna. In *Historisches Lexikon der Schweiz*, www.dhs.ch. Accessed February 2006.

Schmidt, K. and Hoi, H. (2002) Supplemental feeding reduces natural selection in juvenile red deer. *Ecography* **25**, 265–72.

Schnidrig-Petrig, R. (2005) Aufschwung der Huftierbestände im 20. Jahrhundert und Rückkehr der grossen Beutegreifer. In P. Ingold, ed., *Freizeitaktivitäten im Lebensraum der Alpentiere*, Haupt, pp. 54–61.

Schnidrig-Petrig, R. and Ingold, P. (2001) Effects of paragliding on alpine chamois *Rupicapra rupicapra*. *Wildlife Biology* **7**, 285–94.

Schnidrig-Petrig, R. and Koller, N. (2004) Praxishilfe Wildschweinmanagement. www.wildschwein-sanglier.ch.

Schweizerischer Bauernverband (2006) Wegleitung für die Schätzung von Kulturschäden. SBV Brugg, Bs0201. www.bauernverband.ch.

SGW (Schweizerische Gesellschaft für Wildtierbiologie, Hrsg.) (1995) *Wildtiere, Strassenbau und Verkehr*. Chur, 53 pp.

Signer, C. and Jenny, H. (2006) Rehkitzmarkierung im Kanton Graubünden 1972–2005. Amt für Jagd und Fischerei Graubünden, Chur. Unpublished report, 83 pp.

Struch, M. (2006) Gems- und Steinwild am Augstmatthorn: Bestandeserhebungen 2005. WildARK, Bern. Unpublished report, 12 pp.

Tomiczek, H. and Türcke, F. (1995) *Das Muffelwild*. Verlag Paul Parey, 126 pp.

Tschopp, R., Frey, J., Zimmermann L. and Giacometti, M. (2005) Outbreaks of infectious kreatoconjunctivitis in alpine chamois and ibex in Switzerland between 2001 and 2003. *Veterinary Record* **157**, 13–18.

UVEK (2001) *Richtlinie zu Planung und Ban von Wildtierpassagen an Verkehrswegen*. Bern: Eidgenössisches Department für Unwelt, Verkehr, Energie und Kommunikation, 1 p.

Valière, N., Fumagalli, L., Gielly, L. *et al.* (2003) Long distance wolf recolonization of France and Switzerland inferred from non-invasive genetic sampling over a period of 10 years. *Animal Conservation* **6**, 83–92

Weisberg, P. J. and Bugmann, H. (2003) Forest dynamics and ungulate herbivory: from leaf to landscape. *Forest Ecology and Management* **181**(1–2), 280 pp.

Willisch, Ch. (2004) Populationsökologische Untersuchung zu den Gämsen am Augstmatthorn: Ergebnisse der Bestandeserhebungen 1990–2004. WildARK, Bern. Unpublished report, 38 pp.

Zweifel-Schielly, B. (2005) Spatial and nutritional ecology of GPS-collared red deer in an Alpine region: the role of forage availability and quality. Unpublished thesis (nr. 16055), ETH Zürich.

18

Ungulates and their management in Portugal

JOSÉ VINGADA, CARLOS FONSECA, JORGE CANCELA,
JOANA FERREIRA AND CATARINA EIRA

18.1 History, distribution and current status

There are currently six species of wild ungulates in Portugal (red deer, roe deer, fallow deer, wild boar, mouflon and Iberian wild goat) and one semi-wild: the Garrano pony breed. While red deer, roe deer and wild boar are native to the country, fallow deer were introduced many centuries ago, and mouflon are a more recent introduction. Populations of Iberian wild goat (*Capra pyrenaica lusitanica*) went extinct and current goat populations derive from reintroductions of *C. p. victoriae* in Spain (Moço *et al.*, 2006). Populations of Garrano may result from the crossbreeding between ponies introduced by the Celts and ancient pony species descended from Palaeolitical glacial fauna (Portas *et al.*, 2001). The Portuguese Iberian wild goat populations as well as those of roe deer and Garrano are considered of high conservation importance.

18.1.1 Red deer

The red deer is the largest native cervid in Portugal. While the species was quite common throughout the country during medieval times, as described by Mendonça (2003) in the update of the *Livro da Montaria de El-Rei D. João I de Portugal*, by the end of the nineteenth century, red deer were already on the edge of extinction (Bugalho, 2002). Even by the 1970s, red deer still presented a reduced and scattered distribution. At that period, the red deer populations were largely confined to game parks and enclosures (such as Tapada de Mafra, Torre Bela, Tapada de Vila Viçosa) and virtually extinct in the wild. However, in the following decades, several deliberate attempts were made at restocking by releasing animals caught in different Portuguese enclosures (Vingada *et al.*, 1997; Fonseca, 2004a); in addition, several animals dispersed naturally from Spain into Portuguese territory.

Cervus elaphus hispanicus is generally accepted as the dominant subspecies in Portugal. However, the first breeding enclosures, and thus subsequent releases back to the wild, were performed using animals obtained from a number of different areas (Spain, Scotland, Hungary, etc.). Due to the lack of monitoring studies on the success of those early reintroduction efforts and due to the lack of a detailed study on red deer genetics, it is not currently possible to evaluate if any of these releases actually affected the genetic structure of native red deer populations. The majority of reintroductions occurred in Alentejo region in the Tejo Internacional and Lousã Mountain. Natural colonisations from Spain are primarily recorded in the Montesinho Mountains, Contenda-Barrancos region, once again in Tejo Internacional, and more recently in Gerês Mountains (see locations in Fig. 18.1).

The importance of this cervid as a game species has led to the deliberate promotion of red deer populations, resulting in further deliberate introductions into game reserves and fenced enclosures, so that in addition to the free-ranging populations there are also a number of captive herds. The total number of red deer in Portugal is probably of the order of 15 000–20 000 animals and nearly half of this amount is restricted to fenced or semi-fenced areas.

Currently, the red deer is roughly spread all over the country (Fig. 18.2), although the areas along the Portuguese–Spanish border present the most important populations. The largest red deer populations are located in Contenda Barrancos, throughout the Tejo Internacional region and also in Lousã and Montesinho mountains. According to the official game statistics, about 2000 red deer are harvested annually (considering the last three years) in Portugal (Direcção-Geral dos Recursos Florestais (DGRF) unpublished data) and annual values show an increasing pattern over the years. The largest proportion of harvested animals are from the South of Portugal (Tourist Hunting Reserves, Tapada da Contenda) and Tejo Internacional.

18.1.2 Roe deer

The roe deer is also a native species in Portugal where populations of this ungulate have always persisted in a few areas to the north of Douro river. During the twentieth century, there was a general expansion in both range and numbers of roe deer in the northern region of the country (deriving from the remnant populations in Peneda-Gerês Mountain, Larouco Mountain, Alvão-Marão and Nogueira Mountains). During its expansion, the roe deer was able to cross Douro river and subsequently colonise areas located to the south of this large river, which had always previously been considered as a potential geographical barrier.

Current distributions (Fig. 18.3) reflect this natural range expansion, but outside this immediate area, most population nuclei result from numerous reintroduction

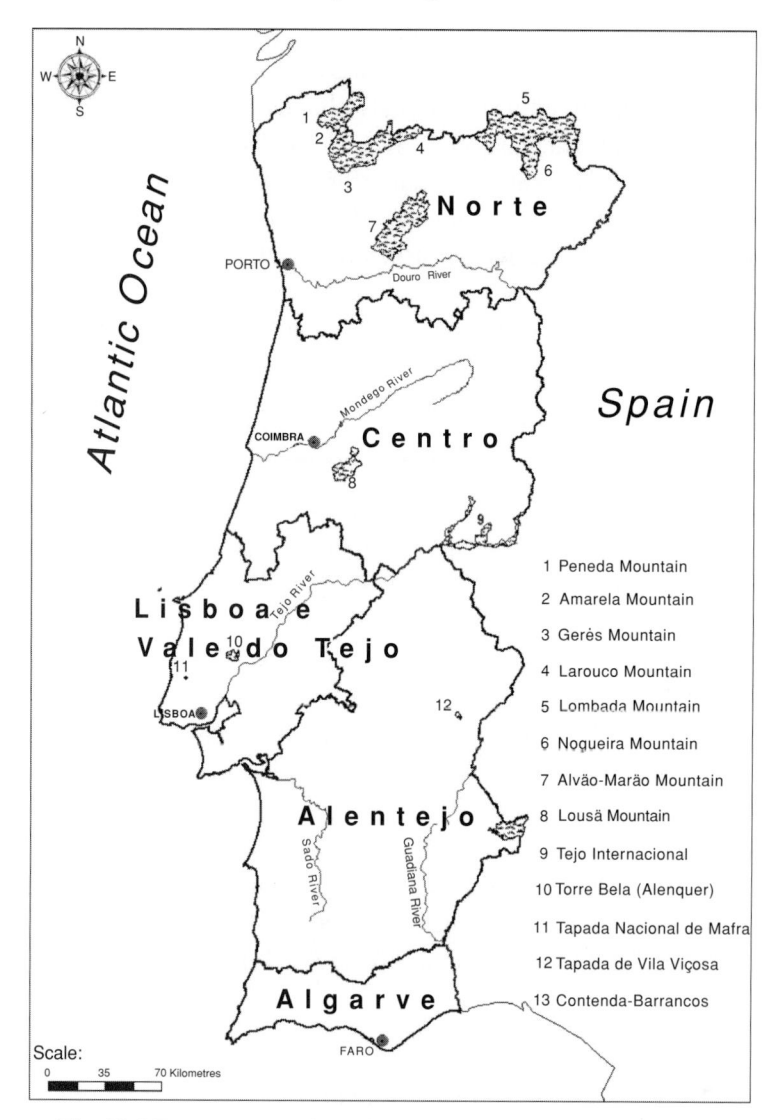

Fig. 18.1 Portuguese main regions and locations cited in the text

1 Peneda Mountain
2 Amarela Mountain
3 Gerês Mountain
4 Larouco Mountain
5 Lombada Mountain
6 Nogueira Mountain
7 Alvão-Marão Mountain
8 Lousã Mountain
9 Tejo Internacional
10 Torre Bela (Alenquer)
11 Tapada Nacional de Mafra
12 Tapada de Vila Viçosa
13 Contenda-Barrancos

attempts during the last decade. These reintroductions aimed at restoring this cervid to its original distribution area and, simultaneously, by increasing wild prey availability, reintroductions contributed to the conservation of the Iberian wolf population in areas located to the South of Douro river (Vingada et al., 1997; Fonseca and Carvalho, 2005). Most reintroduced animals at that time were translocated from Chizé and Trois-Fontaine (France) and a few animals were captured in the north-east of Portugal (Nogueira Mountain). Research on roe deer genetics in Europe (Randi et al., 2004; Lorenzini and Lovari, 2006; Royo et al., 2007) has emphasised the peculiar genetic structure of the roe deer in the Iberian

Fig. 18.2 Red deer distribution in Portugal

Peninsula. However, results on the genetic structure of Portuguese roe deer are inconsistent. Randi *et al.* (2004) propose that presently there is a single subspecies (*Capreolus c. capreolus*) and suggest that peripheral roe deer populations in Portugal may represent the remains of late glacial refugial populations that should be preserved and not artificially admixed with other geographical populations. Lorenzini and Lovari (2006) assumed that during the last glaciations the Iberian Peninsula was a roe deer refuge where they remained as a geographical isolate (rather than spreading northwards after the end of the glacial period) and were

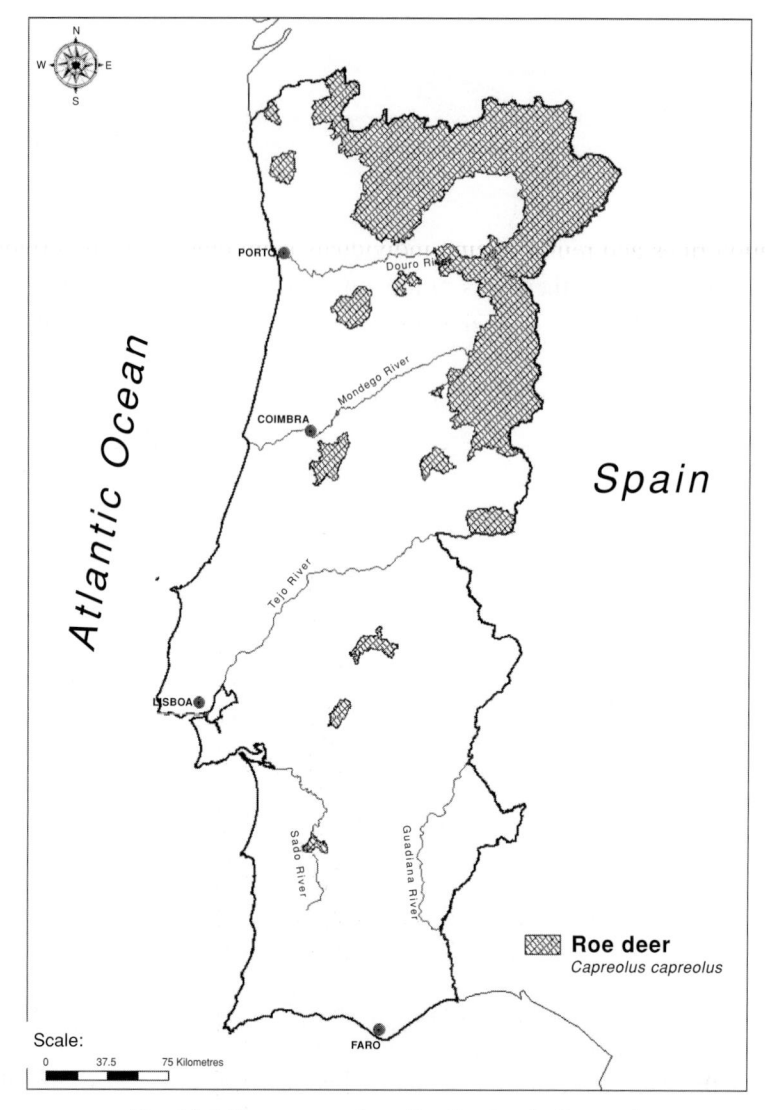

Fig. 18.3 Present roe deer distribution in Portugal

thus not involved as a source for wider postglacial re-colonisations. The same authors assume that roe deer populations in the north-western areas of Portugal may be a relict nucleus from a panmictic Pleistocenic population that survived in the region. Recently, Royo et al. (2007) analysed several roe deer nuclei in Spain and the analysis revealed that the Spanish roe deer populations are genetically heterogeneous. In fact, these authors propose a division between north-western (*Capreolus c. decorus*) and central-southern (*Capreolus c. garganta*) populations although acknowledging the need to pursue more analysis before defining a final subspecies division. Assuming the separation proposed by Royo et al. (2007),

Portuguese roe deer will be included in the north-western group (*Capreolus c. decorus*).

These three papers emphasise that research on roe deer genetics is still insufficient. Therefore, Portugal has assumed a conservative approach to roe deer management. According to the Legal Act no. 466/2001, from 8 May, the northern roe deer populations limited by the Douro river are managed according to specific conservation rules and reintroducing individuals from other areas is forbidden. It is thus urgent to evaluate the status of this relict population particularly given that Forestry and Game Services are being pressured into authorising restocking actions in such territories.

We estimate that current populations of wild roe deer in Portugal include between 3000 and 5000 animals, with the highest densities still belonging to the northern region of the country. Roe deer hunting is a minor activity, occurring in two hunting areas in the north of Portugal and also in fenced hunting areas in the rest of the country.

18.1.3 Fallow deer

The fallow deer has been present in Portugal for several centuries, although, nowadays, it occupies a rather restricted distribution, largely within fenced enclosures. Indeed, the present day distribution of fallow deer is confined to Tapada Nacional de Mafra (an 819 ha enclosure where the species is sympatric with red deer and wild boar) and to a number of other fenced game reserves scattered throughout the rest of the country (but in particular to the south of the Tejo river) (Fig. 18.4). Although several animals have already been observed outside these fenced areas, the only free-ranging population of any significance is located in the Sado river region. Presently, hunters do not consider fallow deer an attractive game species. Most enclosures in Portugal were designed primarily as recreational areas or for venison production and funds for establishing wild nuclei are small. The main reasons for this lack of interest towards fallow deer restocking could be the risk that a large proportion of animals would in any case be shot by poachers, and the possibility that they might cause significant damage to agricultural crops.

Unfortunately, there are no reliable figures for fallow deer population number, but we estimate that the total population is probably somewhere of the order of 500 free-ranging animals with a further 2500 in enclosures. The annual number of harvested fallow deer amounts to around 130 animals and most of this total refers to animals culled within fenced areas (see Table 18.3).

18.1.4 Wild boar

The wild boar used to be very abundant in Portugal. However, this ungulate suffered a severe decline in numbers and distribution during the early twentieth century,

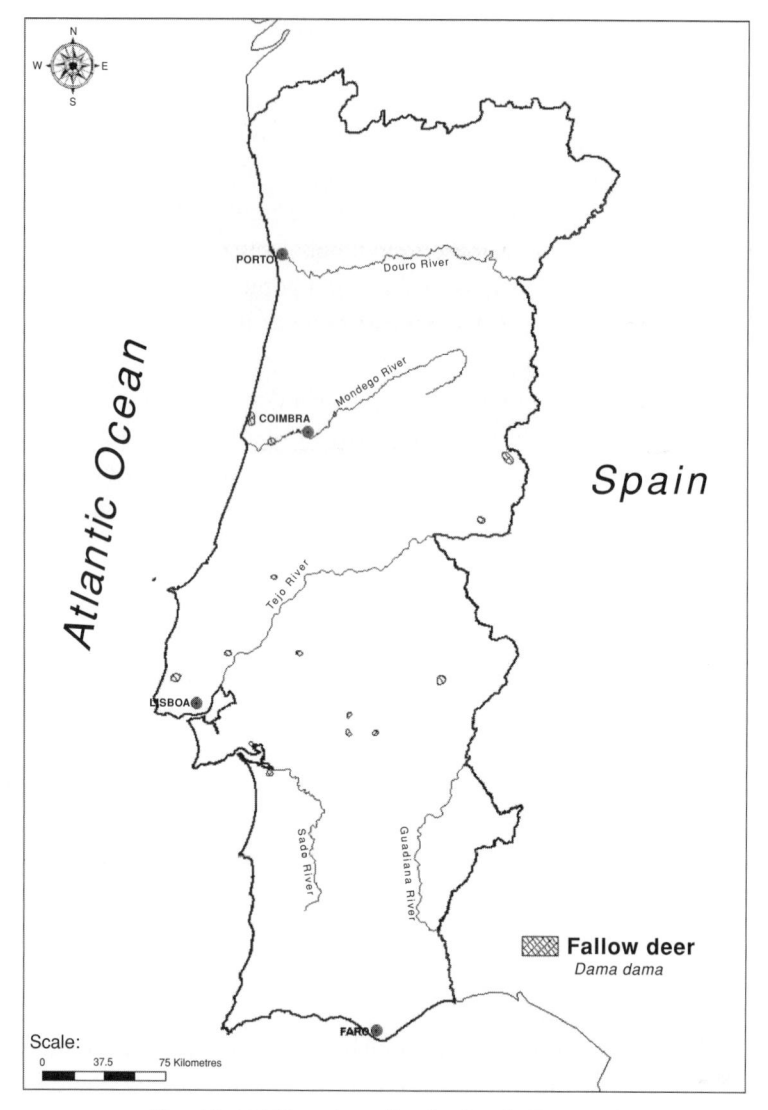

Fig. 18.4 Fallow deer distribution in Portugal

restricting populations to mountainous areas bordering Spain and some Royal Hunting Grounds. Wild boar hunting was forbidden outside fenced areas in 1967 (Act 47 847, 14 August) due to the reduced densities at that time. Indeed, in 1969 the wild boar was specifically designated an endangered species in Portugal during the VIIth IUCN and Resource Technical Meeting (Fonseca, 2004b).

The small pockets of population which persisted along the border of the country, especially those occurring to the South of Tejo river, allowed for a later expansion of the wild boar towards the north and other interior regions of the country. Presently,

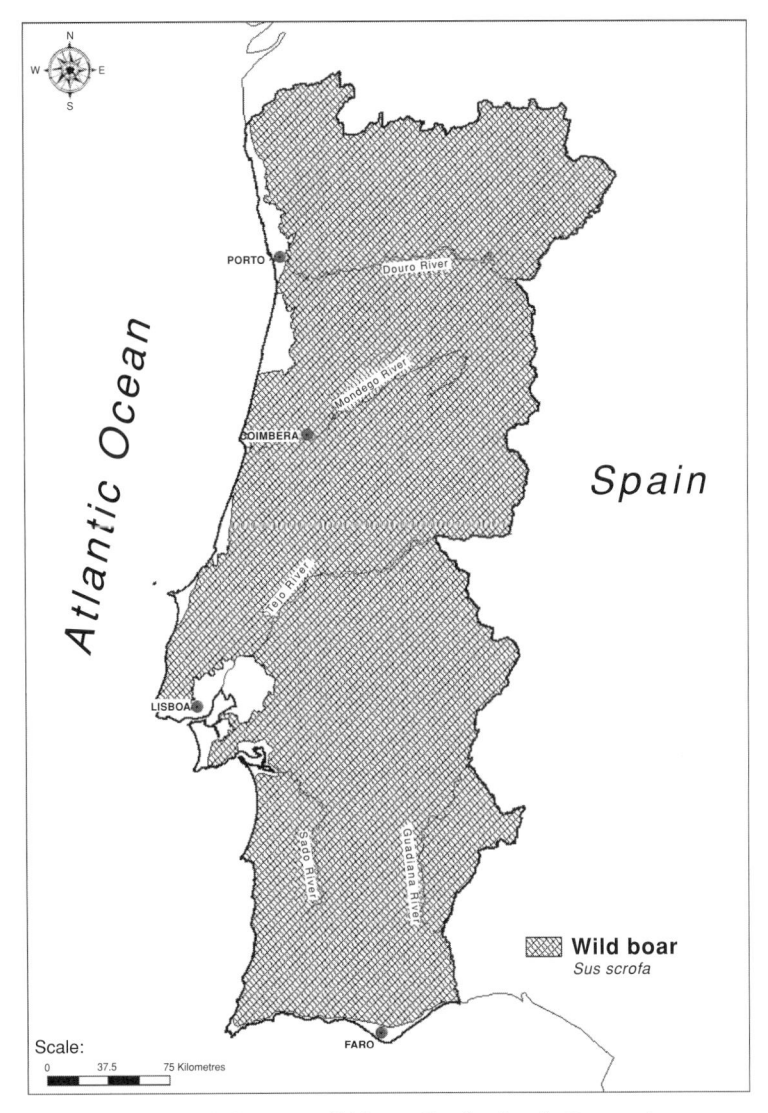

Fig. 18.5 Current wild boar distribution in Portugal

the wild boar is once more distributed throughout the country except for large urban settlements and some coastal areas (Fig. 18.5) (Fonseca *et al.*, 2004). Due to this recovery, the wild boar population has become an important species within the Portuguese fauna, particularly in view of its status as a prey species for Iberian wolf and its increasing importance as a game species. The annual number of wild boar harvested by hunters has increased steadily from around 423 in the 1989/90 game season to a total of 8000 animals shot in 2000/2001 (Fig. 18.6; Lopes and

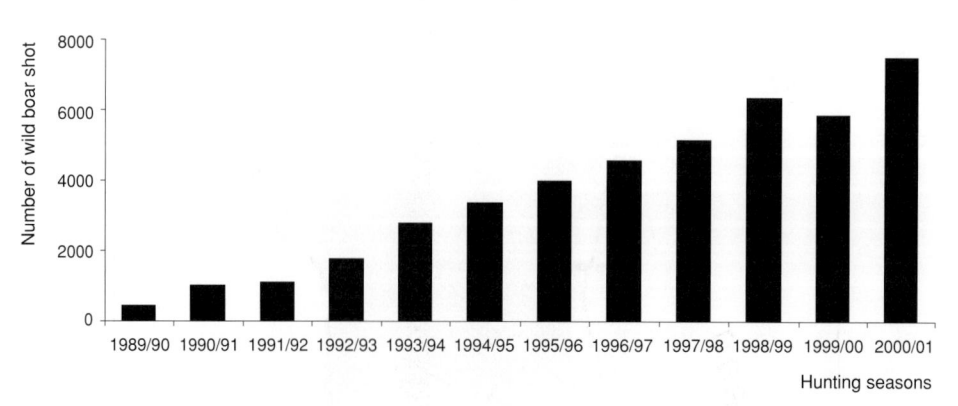

Fig. 18.6 Number of wild boar shot in Portugal between 1989/1990 and 2000/2001. Data referring to 1999/2000 do not include individuals shot in Alentejo (adapted from Lopes and Borges, 2004)

Borges, 2004). However, expanding populations also have their disadvantages due to an increasing significance of damage to agricultural crops.

18.1.5 Mouflon

The mouflon is an exotic species in Portugal, which was legally introduced (Act 43/90, 8 February 1990) exclusively for game purposes in 1990. Presently, the mouflon persists in some tourist hunting fenced areas in Alentejo and Tejo Internacional (Fig. 18.7). Currently, it is only possible to introduce this species into fenced areas. However, some animals have managed to escape from these areas and it is not yet possible to evaluate whether or not such escaped animals have been successful in the establishment of wild nuclei. Around 80 individuals are shot annually (see Table 18.3) out of the 2000 fenced mouflon estimated in Portugal.

18.1.6 Iberian wild goat

The Iberian wild goat is the only wild representative of the genus *Capra* in the Iberian Peninsula. Over the last millennium and particularly during the last 150 years, populations showed a severe decline along with the increasing of human population and excessive hunting (Pérez et al., 2002). In the past (according to fossil records) the species was originally distributed throughout the main mountain ranges in Portugal (Moço et al., 2006) and the continuity between Portuguese and Spanish mountains might have allowed for a wide distribution of this species. In Portugal, it is believed that those individuals occurring in Gerês Mountain belonged to a distinct subspecies *Capra pyrenaica lusitanica* Schlegel. However, the last capture of *C. pyrenaica* in Gerês mountain occurred in 1890 and the last

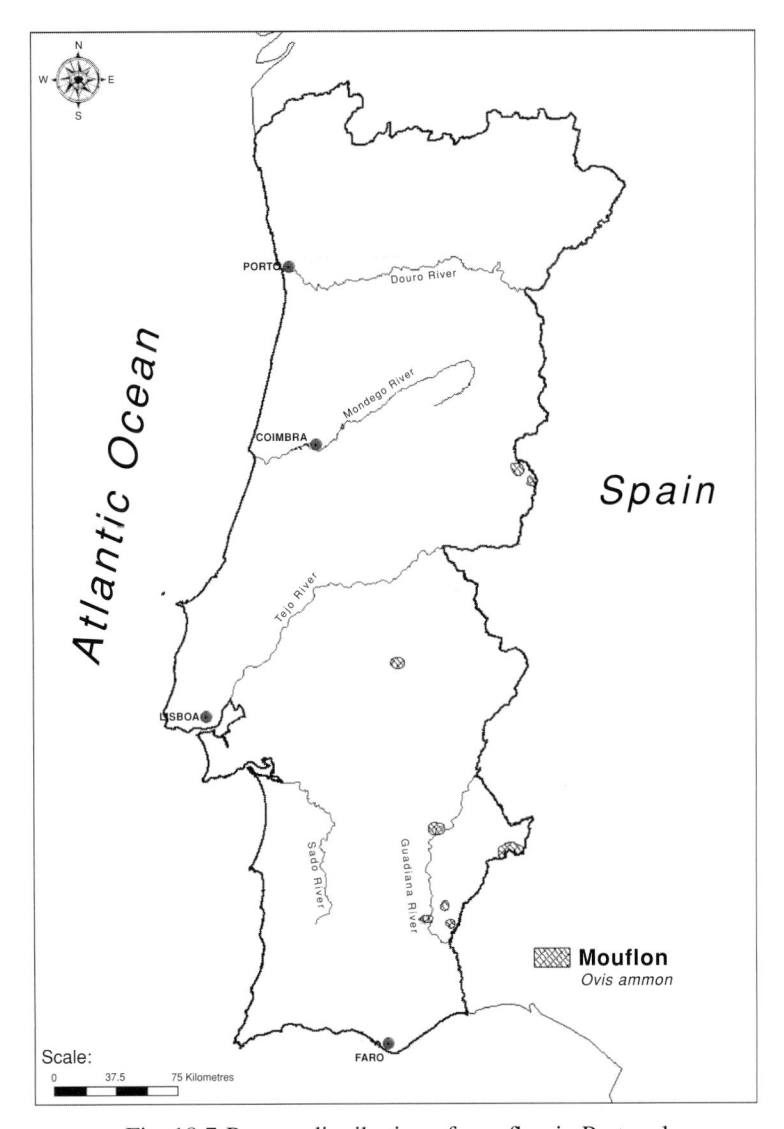

Fig. 18.7 Present distribution of mouflon in Portugal

reference to an observation of this species dates back to 1893 (Moço *et al.*, 2006), when this species was assumed extinct in Portugal.

In 1997, the Baixa Limia-Serra do Xurès Natural Park (Galiza, Spain), adjacent to the Peneda-Gerês National Park (united in a transboundary park), began an Iberian wild goat reintroduction programme in which 16 individuals (5 males and 11 females) were placed within enclosures (Santa Eufémia and Salgueiros enclosure, both near the Portuguese border). These animals belong to the subspecies *C. pyrenaica victoriae* Cabrera and they were brought from an enclosure located in the Montes do Invernadero Natural Park (Galiza, Spain). In turn, animals in the Invernadero Natural Park are also a result of a reintroduction programme started in 1992 with 12 individuals brought from Gredos National Reserve (Salamanca, Spain).

Six individuals escaped from the reintroduction enclosures between 1998 and 1999 and led to the first observations of Iberian wild goat in Portugal in 1999: three animals were observed in Amarela Mountain and three animals in Gerês Mountain (Moço et al., 2006). Subsequently, 25 individuals brought from the Spanish enclosure were deliberately released within the Baixa Limia-Serra do Xurès Natural Park (Spain) between October 2000 and September 2001 (Moço et al., 2006).

Presently, the Iberian wild goat distribution in Portugal is restricted to the Peneda-Gerês National Park, and it retains a strong connection to the population nucleus located in the Baixa Limia-Serra do Xurès Natural Park (PNBLSX) across the border in Spain (Fig. 18.8).

The expansion of this wild ungulate population appears to be promising and three main population nuclei have now been identified, resulting from the first releases. These nuclei include Portuguese areas in their ranges. Within these nuclei the overall estimates in 2003 suggests a minimum number of 75 individuals: 23 females, 20 males, 7 yearlings, 19 juveniles and 6 undetermined (Moço et al., 2006).

18.1.7 Garrano horse

The Garrano *Equus caballus* is a semi-feral native pony breed, from the north-west of Portugal where it is still bred in a semi-feral regime due to its robustness and resistance. The animals are left outdoors all the year around on a free-ranging regime with minor reproductive management. This breed also occurs in the Galicia Region where it is called Faco Galego (Royo et al., 2005). Animals of this breed have a straight, sometimes concave head profile, bay coat, and very dense mane and tail. The average height is 1.3 m at the withers (Oom, 1992). This general morphological type is represented in Palaeolithic paintings from North Iberian caves (Oom, 1992), suggesting the Garrano may originate from an ancient lineage harbouring genetic information relevant to conservation strategies.

Recent genetic studies have raised the hypothesis that Garrano might have a Celtic origin (Oom and Cothran, 1996; Morais et al., 2005). The work of Royo et al. (2005) supports the hypothesis that the present Northern Iberian pony breeds (Garrano included) may be the result of a male-mediated introgression of northern European ponies, probably linked with present British pony breeds. This is consistent with sex-biased ancient breeding practices (a small number of male ponies have probably been intensively used for reproduction purposes).

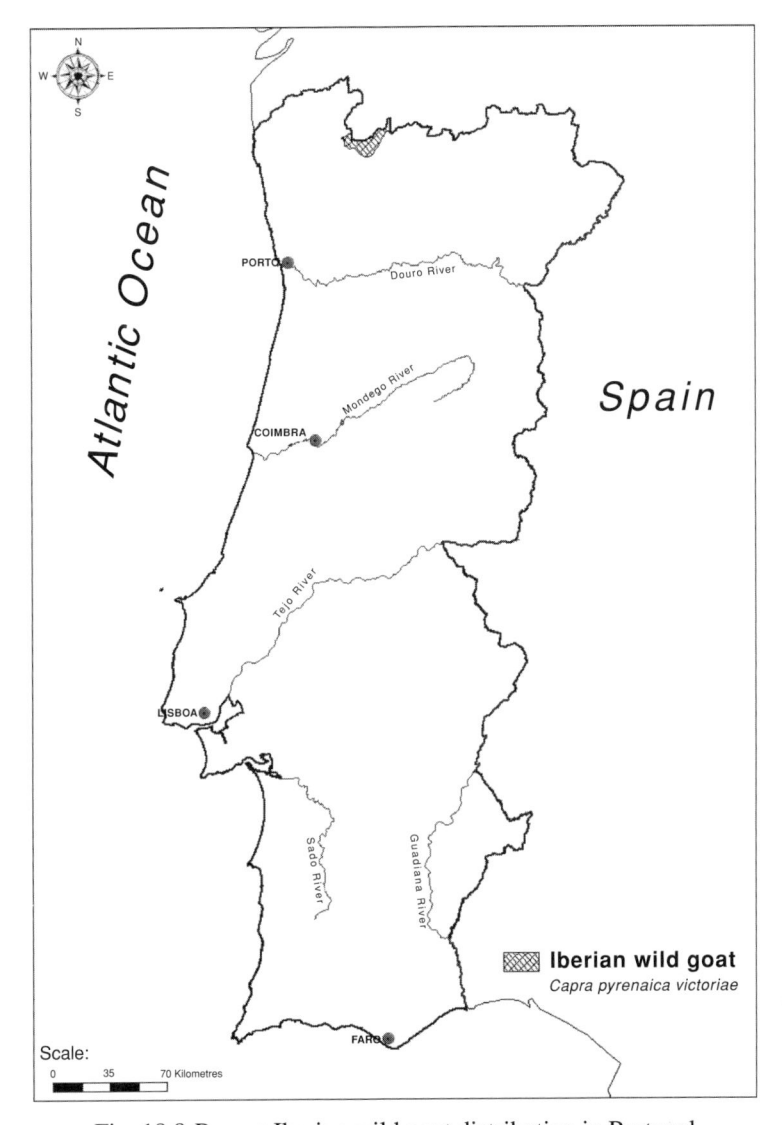

Fig. 18.8 Recent Iberian wild goat distribution in Portugal

Currently, the breeding population consists of almost 2000 animals, including 1500 adults with fewer than 1000 breeding mares and 30 breeding stallions. The average sex ratio is 1 male to 13 females (Portas *et al.*, 2001). This small population size can be explained mainly by wolves' predation of young animals. The Garrano breed is considered to be very important for the Iberian wolf (*Canis lupus signatus*) conservation, functioning as a preferred prey (Vos, 2000).

The decreasing economic interest in maintaining a pure Garrano line for agricultural purposes has been reflected in a progressive reduction of its effective number and in crossbreeding with other breeds for meat production. Due to its present status, according to the FAO (Food and Agriculture Organization of the United Nations), the Garrano is placed in the list of endangered breeds (Galal and Hammond, 1996).

18.2 Legislation

Hunting activity and game management are regulated by law (act n° 173/99 on 21 September 1999, which in turn relates to Act 202/2004, on 18 August 2004, subsequently updated to Act 201/2005, on 24 November 2005), and by a significant amount of legal directives, particularly the Annual Directive (defining which species are to be hunted in each game season) and the Directive which regulates reproduction and maintenance of game species in captivity. All legislation is available at www.dre.pt and www.dgrf.min-agricultura.pt.

Within the Portuguese territory, game affairs are dealt with in the Ministry of Agriculture, Rural Development and Fisheries and also in the Institute of Nature Conservation and Biodiversity, when concerned with management within protected areas or designated areas integrated in the Nature 2000 Network.

Portuguese nationals wishing to hunt game of any sort must hold a general hunter's licence. A hunter's licence (valid until the age of 60; after 60, renewed for 5-year periods), can only be issued to people over 16 years of age, after passing a theoretical and practical examination which evaluates the capabilities and knowledge on hunting activities.

In order to hunt large game species (ungulates) a General Game Licence is also required. This licence may be restricted to one game region (regional licence) or it may be valid for the whole country (national) and should be renewed annually. Finally, a Large Game Licence is also required, which is valid in those areas defined in the General Game Licence and is legal for all large game species. This licence is renewed annually and no examination is necessary.

In Portugal, the general game season starts on the 1 June and ends on the 31 May in the following year. However, large game species are hunted mainly between September and February. In areas managed under specific management plans, however (hence, 'Hunting Areas'), actual days on which hunting may occur are more closely specified in their respective management plans. Hunting is allowed between sunrise and sunset; however, hunting from a high seat (observation platform) may be permitted after sunset during the full moon period.

Ungulates may be legally hunted according to several procedures/methods:

1. By stalking – the hunter actively searches, pursues and takes game with or without the help of hunting dogs and a game guide;

2. Sit and wait hunting – the hunter remains in the same spot, usually high seat or observation platform, with or without decoys or hunting dogs that can find wounded animals, waiting for game;
3. Battue hunting – the hunter waits for game driven by beaters without hunting dogs;
4. Drive hunting – the hunter waits, in a previously designated location, for large game disturbed by dog packs driven by beaters;
5. Spear hunting – the hunter uses a spear to kill game with or without a horse or hunting dogs.

Within designated game areas following specific management plans (section 18.4), wild boar may be killed by any of the above-mentioned methods during the entire length of the game season, except for battue hunting and drive hunting, which are only allowed between October and February.

Fallow deer, red deer, roe deer and mouflon may be hunted by stalking, sit and wait hunting or spear hunting. Battue hunting and drive hunting are also permitted, but only from October to February. In Portugal, shotguns or rifles are used on large game hunting. However, hunting ungulates with shotguns requires the cartridge to be loaded with a single projectile (bullet). Bow and cross-bow ungulate hunting is also permitted.

18.3 Management objectives

The management objectives for wild ungulates in Portugal are principally for hunting activities, as is made explicitly clear when considering the several attempts to promote wild and captive populations by introduction and translocation. However, in the last few years, increasing attention has been paid to managing ungulates for conservation purposes, particularly in those areas where the conservation of large predators, such as the Iberian wolf, is a priority.

With respect to the red deer, the main thrust of management is linked to hunting activities. Hunting is considered as a sport/recreation activity, which is economically important in some regions of the country. Red deer are also managed for damage control and for venison production. In the north-western part of Portugal, the red deer is considered a key wild prey and the management objectives are clearly linked to the conservation of the Iberian wolf.

The management of roe deer populations is mainly directed towards encouraging expansion of current populations and the establishment of new population nuclei. Although management actions are patently directed with hunting in mind, current hunting activity is scarce and roe are not a major quarry in Portugal at the present time. In the northern part of its present distribution, management objectives are clearly related with conservation purposes, where it is assumed that roe deer contributes to the conservation of the Iberian wolf and also that roe deer presents a peculiar genetic structure, which must be preserved.

The management of the fallow deer population is based on hunting and recreational purposes. Hunting is carried out only in a few regions in Portugal (and only within enclosed areas, section 18.1). The management of wild boar populations is based mainly on hunting. Maintenance of populations to provide a prey base in conservation efforts directed towards Iberian wolf occurs in some areas of north and central Portugal. The very intense hunting activity (mainly in January and February) is considered as a sport/recreation, economically important in the countryside. Wild boar are also killed to control crop damage.

The management of the mouflon population is exclusively related to hunting objectives. The localised hunting activity is considered as a sport/recreation. In contrast, at the present moment, the management of the Iberian wild goat population is based on conservation objectives.

The management of the Garrano pony breed is clearly directed at venison production and recreational purposes, particularly as an equestrian breed. However, in areas such as the Peneda-Gerês National Park, part of the free-ranging herd is also managed in view of conservation purposes.

18.4 Management structure

In Portugal, game species belong to the Portuguese State, and the hunting activities are regulated by the Roman law *res-nullius*, which defines that the game species do not belong to the landowner. The management of game may be allocated to clubs or hunters associations or to private companies, which become responsible during a defined period for managing game species in accordance with the parameters established by the Portuguese State at the beginning of that period.

According to Portuguese law, two types of areas are defined in which hunting is permitted: areas which are not subject to any formal game management plan and other areas where hunting is more closely regulated according to defined game management plans. At the present time, the total number of unregulated hunting areas is very small and it is probably safe to assume that almost all areas representing potential game territories are required to produce management plans.

There are, in practice, two possible ways in which Hunting Areas may be allocated. One mechanism defines a given area as an Association Hunting Area or Tourist Hunting Area and rights to hunt within this area are leased to clubs, hunters associations or private companies in return for an annual fee. Game species and the right to hunt them belong to those organisations during the concession period. The other possible mechanism is direct management transference, in which the Portuguese State specifically delegates the management of a defined area with game potential to another organisation (Clubs/Hunters Associations or City Councils). This second mechanism of management transference is the one that allows the implementation of National or County Hunting areas, where hunters are allowed to hunt for a given number of days.

In the managed areas, the administrative organisations are required to produce a Game Management Plan (harvesting plan) for the agreed Hunting Area, which must be approved each year by the State Authorities. In most cases, those cull plans simply propose the total number of individuals to be killed. However, in game areas located in protected areas, as well as in National and County Hunting areas, these annual plans are more detailed and should include quota estimations based on age and sex classes for each species. The definition of hunting quotas in each Game Management Plan does not follow any general rule or legal recommendation. Each administrative organisation presents their quotas in the Game Management Plan, based on their perception of the amount of animals that can be culled in the next game season. However, the State Authorities have always the final say in terms of granting approval of these quotas.

The major obstacle in preparing a well-subtantiated harvesting plan is the lack of reliable ground-base information, population density values in particular. In the majority of hunting areas, the only available data are based on the harvest records or hunting statistics and thus the elaboration of a harvesting plan becomes a difficult task. Some Hunting Reserves are starting to implement monitoring programmes and soon it is expected that abundance estimates will become a routine management task, therefore helping to improve the quality of the harvesting plan. The best ungulate harvesting plans are prepared in National Hunting areas and in some Tourist Hunting areas where wildlife biologists or professional hunters are employed. The exploitation of specific trophy animals, sold at high prices, is the main goal of these hunting areas and consequently good harvesting plans are an indispensable tool.

18.5 Management organisation

With respect to game organisation and administration, Portugal is divided into five regions, where different measures may be adopted.

18.5.1 Size of management unit

On average, hunting areas comprise around 2500 ha, although those where red deer hunting occurs are significantly larger. Although hunting areas are effectively leased, or granted to hunting clubs by the state, the actual definition of a hunting area is usually initiated by the hunting clubs or associations who wish to take the

Table 18.1 *Annual costs (in EUR) associated with individual hunting licences during the 2006/2007 game season*

Licence types	Portuguese hunter	Non-resident hunter
Regional General Game Licence	12.47	–
National General Game Licence	24.94	–
General Game Licence for non-residents[1]	–	44.89
Large Game Licence	29.93	29.93
Total	42.40–54.87	74.82

[1] Valid for 30 days

lease, not by the state itself (only in the case of national hunting areas is the area concerned defined by the state). Because of that, in general the size and shape of any given hunting area is defined by the geographical location of the available ground, by the geographical connectivity of different parcels of land belonging to different owners and by the different agreements that it is possible to achieve between the landowners and the hunting clubs, associations or private companies in case of association or tourist hunting areas. Due to this fact, the size and the shape of the hunting areas is highly variable, creating a disorganised matrix that is clearly related with the pattern of land-ownership in Portugal. Hunting areas in the south tend in practice to be larger and involve fewer landowners, than the hunting areas in the centre and north of Portugal.

Within the geographical distribution range of red deer, hunting areas are larger both because most of such areas occur in the south of Portugal and also because the hunting clubs or private companies make specific efforts to increase the size of the hunting grounds by taking on larger areas.

18.5.2 Hunting licences

As noted above (section 18.2), in order to be permitted to hunt ungulates, a Portuguese national is required to have a hunter's licence, a general game licence and a large game licence (suitable for hunting all ungulates) validated according to areas referred by the General Game Licence. Licence fees (Table 18.1) are stipulated by the Portuguese State and licenses are provided by the state department responsible for game or, if requested, by hunter's federations and city councils, which retain 30% of the funds produced by the attributed licences.

An equivalency to the hunter's licence can be granted to foreign people living in Portugal, who hold a Hunter's Licence or an equivalent authority issued by another European Union country. In this case, the hunter may apply for a Portuguese hunter's licence, if their own national licence is considered valid and if

Table 18.2 *General Game Licences (a) and Large Game Licences (b) issued between 1999 and 2005 (DGRF, unpublished data)*

Game season	General Game Licence (a)	Large Game Licences (b)	(b/a) × 100
1999/2000	223 740	23 692	11
2000/2001	225 338	30 726	14
2001/2002	220 173	32 068	15
2002/2003	208 833	36 464	17
2003/2004	200 837	37 746	19
2004/2005	183 208	37 756	21

the hunter meets all the requirements demanded by Portuguese law (Act 173/99, 21 September).

Along with the costs of obtaining the licences provided by the Portuguese State, hunting areas are also entitled to charge for the right to hunt and for any of the obtained trophies.

18.5.3 Numbers of hunters and ungulate hunters

In Portugal (excluding Maderia and Azores), there are 294 055 hunters (DGRF, 13 May 2003) representing about 8% of the male Portuguese population over 16. The number of hunters purchasing the general licence has been continuously decreasing over the last six game seasons. However, the number of large game licences issued has doubled in the same period (Table 18.2).

18.6 Present management and hunting practices

As noted in section 18.2, permitted hunting methods include stalking, waiting in blinds or high seats, driven hunting with or without dogs, although different methods are permitted for different species. In practice, most common hunting methods are described below.

Drive hunting is the method most widely used for wild boar and red deer. It is a traditional hunting method in the south of Europe, and its widespread use clearly emphasises the social importance of hunting activities in Portugal. Generally, drive hunting is considered a non-selective hunting method. Hunting by waiting is used to kill wild boar, red deer and roe deer, particularly when hunters wish to obtain trophies. Stalking is mostly used in red deer and roe deer hunting where this seeks to be selective, in taking of trophies or directed at the elimination of old or sick animals or in order to balance the age structure and the sex ratio of a defined population. Wild boar may be hunted by any of the above-mentioned methods.

In Portugal, the hunting season for ungulates starts on 1 June and ends on 31 May in the following year. However, more than 90% of ungulate hunting in

Table 18.3 *Numbers of wild ungulates shot in Portugal over the years 1989–2004*

Species	Game seasons	Number of individuals shot[1]	Average number of individuals shot per year	Percentage of individuals shot per year in fenced enclosures or hunting parks
Wild boar	1989/1990– 2003/2004	80 480	5365	15–35%
Red deer	1989/1990– 2003/2004	8420	561	60–85%
Fallow deer	1989/1990– 2003/2004	1940	129	80–90%
Roe deer	1990/1991– 2001/2002	180	13	50–70%
Mouflon	1990/1991– 2002/2003	950	79	100%

[1] Direcção-Geral dos Recursos Florestais, unpublished data, May 2006

Portugal occurs between September and February. In areas managed under specific management plans, the numbers of days in which hunting may occur are more closely specified in their respective management plans. Managing organisations are required to record the number of animals harvested for each species within each game season and produce an annual report, which must be submitted to the Portuguese State. The Portuguese State records the number of animals shot annually in a national database. Although the data currently available refer to overall number of animals shot over relatively long time spans (Table 18.3), in the near future, it will be possible to enter data concerning the number of animals shot via the Internet thus allowing for a more thorough analysis of game statistics.

18.7 Census types and methods

In Portugal, wild ungulate densities have not been regularly monitored until recently, given the rather small number of areas which had significant ungulate populations requiring management. Early censuses aimed simply at gathering information on species distribution and often results were expressed in terms of presence/absence data.

The increase of some wild ungulate populations during the 1980s (roe deer in the north of Portugal and red deer in Alentejo) led the Game and Nature Conservation Services to implement systematic surveys aimed at estimating densities. However, the methodologies used were often rather basic, lacking standardisation, and the sampling effort was concentrated in defined periods.

Further, more regular monitoring is hampered by logistic difficulties and lack of personnel. In fact, in most of the Portuguese Hunting Areas, estimates of the number of animals to harvest are still based on guesswork or on managers and hunters' opinions. The lack of properly qualified game managers and the minor investment in research has led to the reduced use of adequate census techniques where ungulate populations occur.

Hunting bag analyses are the only nationwide ungulate census programme. However, this technique is not effective and produces misleading results. In most cases, data are not reliable due to errors during data collection.

In the last decade, it is possible to observe that there has been some increase in the use of direct census methods. However, these methodologies are merely applied in particular local areas such as: Peneda-Gerês National Park, Lombada, Nogueira and Lousã Mountains, Tapada Nacional de Mafra and Contenda-Barrancos. In spite of the efforts to implement monitoring programmes in these regions, census campaigns are not regularly applied. In some areas these census surveys are promoted by the administrative organisations or by the State Agencies that are responsible for Game Management or for Nature Conservation. However, in most cases, census programmes are closely associated with University research projects. In the last years, Universities working closely with the Game Management State Agency have been trying to propose a national system for an index of population size and trend at least for roe deer, red deer and wild boar. However, this effort is still in a very early stage, composed of field trials and essays of different methodologies.

In general, the evaluation of densities is based on methods that can be used simultaneously for several species. The most commonly used ungulate census methods (Table 18.4) in Portugal are: open hill counts or vantage point counts (Moço et al., 2006), drive counts or spotlight counts along transects (Fonseca et al., 2007), track counts (Ferreira and Diogo, 2006) or faecal pellet counts (Ferreira and Diogo, 2006; Carvalho, 2007).

18.8 Ungulate impacts and damage

Crop and forest damage caused by wild ungulates is widespread throughout Portugal. The main problems are related with the damage caused by wild boar in agriculture. However, in areas of recent colonisation by red deer (especially those areas where this species has reached relatively high densities) the number of complaints about damage caused by this species has increased significantly, accompanied by

Table 18.4 *Use of abundance estimate methods according to ungulate species occurring in Portugal: scarce (light grey), common (dark grey) and frequent (black)*

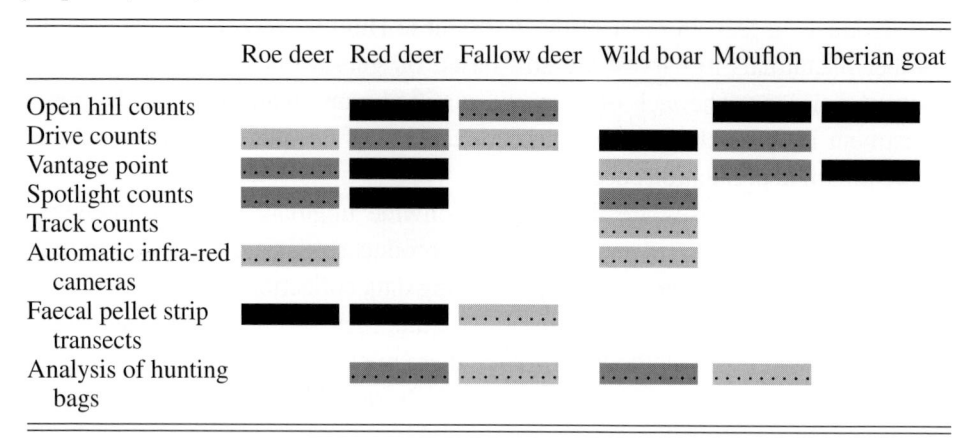

	Roe deer	Red deer	Fallow deer	Wild boar	Mouflon	Iberian goat
Open hill counts		■	▨		■	■
Drive counts	▨	▨	▨	■	▨	■
Vantage point	■	■		▨	▨	■
Spotlight counts	■	■		▨		
Track counts				▨		
Automatic infra-red cameras	▨			▨		
Faecal pellet strip transects	■	■	▨			
Analysis of hunting bags	▨	▨		▨	▨	

a significant reduction in the number of complaints regarding wild boar damage (Fonseca *et al.*, 2007).

The extent and type of damage differs according to region and at the present moment it is very difficult to have a clear and accurate overview of this problem on a national scale; there are no national statistics available on the distribution or economic cost of wildlife damage. As a result, it is not possible to present a clear national picture, but as a way of offering some information, we present here results from two specific case studies devoted to analysis of crop damage from ungulates: Lousã Mountain (Central Portugal) with reintroduced red deer and roe deer as well as established populations of wild boar (Fonseca *et al.*, 2007) and Peneda-Gerês Mountains (north of Portugal), with established populations of roe deer and wild boar (Diogo and Ferreira, 2006). These studies consider damage only to agricultural crops and do not provide data on other types of damage.

Agricultural damage caused by the red deer in Lousã Mountain (Table 18.5) is probably not of real economic significance, but occurs regularly throughout the year (except in September when the rutting season begins and animals move towards the most central and highest areas of Lousã Mountain, leading to a considerable decrease of damage to agricultural areas). As shown in Table 18.5, damage to horticulture crops such as beans, cabbages, pumpkins and onion represents 33.1% of all red deer damage to crops.

Impact of roe deer on agricultural crops is usually lower than that occurring on forest stands. In Lousã Mountain, where the distribution of this species is in any case rather restricted, significant damage to crops has not been reported.

Table 18.5 *Percentages of all crop damage due to red deer in Lousã Mountain (adapted from Fonseca et al., 2007)*

Crop types	Percentage damage
Horticulture	33.1
Potato	18.1
Vineyard	17.9
Chestnut trees	15.1
Fruit trees	12.1
Oak trees	3.7

Table 18.6 *Percentages of all crop damage due to wild boar in Lousã Mountain (adapted from Fonseca et al., 2007).*

Crop types	Percentage of damages
Maize	77.1
Potato	10.0
Horticultural	5.8
Wheat	3.2
Vineyard	1.4
Chestnut	1.3
Olive	1.2

It is clear that most of the damage reported in agriculture crops in this region is caused by wild boar. The wild boar is usually responsible for severe damage to crops throughout Lousã Mountain (Table 18.6), primarily through damage in cornfields (77.1% of all wild boar crop damage).

In spite of this qualitative evaluation of agricultural crop damage due to the three ungulates present in Lousã Mountain, no real economic assessment was carried out. Nevertheless, several mitigation measures were already implemented, such as the electric and wire fences (essentially used in agricultural fields over 1 ha), with good results (Fonseca *et al.*, 2007).

In the Peneda-Gerês Mountains, the wild boar is the only ungulate producing enough damage to cause complaints. In questionnaire surveys performed directly to farmers it was possible to detect 218 complaints in 2005 and 169 in 2006. The wild boar is usually responsible for severe damage to crops throughout these Northern Mountains, although in this area the main damages occurred in pastures, which

Table 18.7 *Percentage of complaints related to damage caused by wild boar in Peneda-Gerês Mountains*

Crop types	Percentage of complaints in 2005 and 2006
Pastures	33.3
Maize	24.3
Rye	4.7
Potato	1.3
Forest and chestnut	2.1
Others	34.4

produce fodder for livestock, while maize is the second most damaged crop type (Table 18.7).

Several types of crops such as olive trees, vineyards, wheat and horticulture products constitute the 'others' category. Independently, these items represent very small percentages but grouped in the same category they correspond to 34.4% of the total complaints.

Most damage was inflicted upon crops, which are usually used for local consumption and therefore it was not possible to estimate the economic value of damage. However, the increment of damage is closely associated with an increment of poaching with illegal traps (such as snares) that apart from removing the wild boar are also responsible for the killing of protected species such as the Iberian wolf. In order to promote mitigation measures and to demonstrate to the local communities the advantage of using deterrent devices, a trial with electric fences was performed. The obtained results emphasise that these equipments are effective in reducing the amount of damages produced by wild boars (Diogo and Ferreira, 2006).

18.9 Supplementary feeding

In Portugal, there is no established practice of providing artificial feedstuffs for wildlife populations at critical periods. However, in some areas there may be specific management efforts to provide increased availability of natural or semi-natural forages. The increment in food supply during the reproductive season and during summer is a major concern particularly where quality food is often scarce. Winter supplementary feeding of ungulates, as it is performed in other European countries, was initially implemented in some game areas occurring in mountain ranges. However, hunters found rapidly that the winter period is not critical to ungulates and presently this management practice is not very common.

In some cases, game crops may be sown in order to be used by ungulates and particularly by small game species. In addition, in fenced hunting areas, it is essential to provide supplementary food (sometimes throughout the year) considering that, in most cases, densities are well above the habitat's carrying capacity. The most common method used in these areas is dedicated wildlife crops. However, the use of artificial fodders has been increasing, particularly at the end of spring and summer when the extreme food scarcity leads to a decrease in densities or to a decline of the individuals' physiological condition.

In some regions of Portugal (especially in the south) and during extreme dry years (e.g. 2005) water availability is much reduced during the end of spring, summer and beginning of autumn. In most regions where wild ungulates occur, it is a common practice to increase the availability of water by providing artificial ponds or small dams, although in some areas it is frequently necessary to resort to more artificial methods to increase water supply.

Placing salt blocks for ungulates is also a common practice (either isolated or nearby dedicated wildlife crops) especially in fenced areas.

18.10 Effectiveness of current management strategies

At the present moment the management of ungulates in Portugal is in a state of transition from a somewhat trial-and-error system based on rather theoretical constructs to a more responsive system, where policies, decisions and management actions are supported by field data. However, there is still a long way to go in order to achieve a management system that is based on the long-term sustainability of the ungulate populations. In fact, in the next few years it will be necessary to study, improve and implement several management actions.

An important aspect that needs an improvement is the way in which data from hunting records are collected and analysed. The present system is not effective and produces misleading results. In most cases, data are not reliable due to errors during data collection. In the future, a strong education campaign towards hunters and managers is necessary to demonstrate that sustainable ungulate hunting requires a good system of collecting and analysing hunting bags.

Abundance or density estimates are also essential data in any ungulate management strategy. However, presently, these estimates are only produced in a small number of areas. So, there is an urgent need to implement a monitoring programme in order to improve the baseline knowledge for each ungulate species. It is suggested that it would be appropriate to link this to hunting bag statistics, allowing for the validation of the use of hunting bags as an index of ungulate population trend. This index could be a useful tool for state agencies to obtain a general picture of the status of different ungulates. A national monitoring programme will be initially located in key pilot areas, but in time, it will be necessary to spread the monitoring activities throughout a larger set of hunting areas.

The future management strategy must include a significant increase of scientific/technical studies. Our knowledge of almost all aspects of the biology and ecology of ungulates in Portugal is still rather incomplete and a special effort should be made towards the research into the ecological requirements of the different ungulate species. The need to produce and implement management strategies that successfully integrate ungulates and human activities (agriculture and forestry) strongly relies upon research results.

The overall consequences of habitat fragmentation constitute another severe problem, particularly those related to the increase in roads and road traffic. An evaluation of the effects of such fragmentation on the long-term survival of the wild populations is urgently required, to put into practice possible approaches to mitigate the effects of this problem.

Another problem of special concern is the extraordinary population increase of wild boar in Portugal. This must be properly monitored, both technically and scientifically, in order to ensure that increasing numbers do not result in any disruption of population structure or threaten the sustainability of this important resource. Recent genetic research emphasised a highly structured wild boar population, probably as a result of recent bottlenecks (Ferreira *et al.*, 2006). Another aspect that also needs constant surveillance is the increment of damage to agriculture crops. In fact, wherever wild boar numbers are seen to be increasing, this is followed by an increase of complaints, which must be carefully monitored in order to find adequate solutions. In some areas, the red deer is also achieving very high densities and consequently, similar problems to those caused by the high wild boar densities are being registered. So, the consequences of population increase should also be addressed in the case of red deer.

Finally, the size of the actual game areas and decision-making concerning game are crucial to the management of wild ungulates. In practice, each hunting area has the right to decide the number of animals that can be harvested, although these must be presented for official approval in annual management plans. However, bad management decisions or over-exploitation in small hunting areas can result in drastic declines in a wider geographical area outside the hunting area boundaries. The solution to these problems includes macro-zonation and aggregation of several hunting areas in a single ungulate management unit. The size of this new management unit should actually be related to the biological population range of each ungulate species, in order to achieve a better and efficient overall management programme.

References

Bugalho, M. N. (2002) *O veado na Tapada Real de Vila Viçosa*. Fundação da Casa de Bragança, 72 pp. (In Portuguese.)

Carvalho, P. (2007) *Ecologia de uma população reintroduzida de corços (*Capreolus capreolus *L.)*. MSc Thesis. FCTUC. Universidade de Coimbra, 117 pp. (In Portuguese.)

Diogo, H. and Ferreira, J. (2006) Damages caused by game species and essays of mitigation measures. In J. Ferreira, H. Diogo, L. Jorge et al., eds. *Relatório Final do Contrato de Comparticipação em projecto de Investigação e Desenvolvimento com o Parque Nacional da Peneda-Gerês para o ano de 2006*. Sociedade Portuguesa de Vida Selvagem, pp. 140–54. (In Portuguese.)

Ferreira, E., Souto, L., Soares, A. M. V. M. and Fonseca, C. (2006) Genetic structure of the wild boar (*Sus scrofa* L.) population in Portugal. *Wildlife Biology in Practice* **2**(1), 17–25.

Ferreira, J. (2003) Distribution and abundance of wild boar (*Sus scrofa* Linnaeus, 1758) in the Quiaios National Forest. Graduation Thesis, Universidade do Minho, 56 pp.

Ferreira, J. and Diogo, H. (2006) Monitoring and management of Iberian wolf wild prey. In J. Ferreira, H. Diogo, L. Jorge et al., eds. *Relatório Final do Contrato de Comparticipação em projecto de Investigação e Desenvolvimento com o Parque Nacional da Peneda-Gerês para o ano de 2006*. Sociedade Portuguesa de Vida Selvagem, pp. 63–139. (In Portuguese.)

Fonseca, C. (2004a) Berros na Serra (O regresso dos veados à Serra da Lousã). *National Geographic Magazine, Portugal* **38**, 11–21. (In Portuguese.)

Fonseca, C. (2004b) *Population Dynamics and Management of Wild Boar (*Sus scrofa *L.) in Central Portugal and Southeastern Poland*. PhD Thesis. University of Aveiro. Aveiro.

Fonseca, C., Santos, P., Monzón, A. et al. (2004) Reproduction in the wild boar (*Sus scrofa* Linnaeus, 1758) populations of Portugal. In C. Fonseca, J. Herrero, A. Luís and A. M. V. M. Soares, eds. *Wild Boar Research 2002. A Selection and Edited Papers from the 4th International Wild Boar Symposium*. Galemys, **16** Special Issue, pp. 53–65.

Fonseca, C. and Carvalho, P. (2005) Biologia e Gestão do Corço (*Capreolus capreolus* L.). Santo Huberto. *Boletim da Confederação Nacional dos Caçadores Portugueses* **2**, 14–18. (In Portuguese.)

Fonseca, C., Alves, J. and Silva, A. (2007) Plano Global de Gestão para a população de veados (*Cervus elaphus*) da Serra da Lousã. Aveiro: Direcção-Geral dos Recursos Florestais/Universidade de Aveiro, 87 pp. (In Portuguese.)

Galal, S. and Hammond, K. (1996) The global program for the management of farm animal genetic resources. In *Third Iberoamerican Congress on Native and Creole Breeds*, 25–30 November, Santa Fe de Bogota D.C., Colombia, available at www.corpoica.org.co/html/planes/cong3gan/galal.html.

Lopes, F. V. and Borges, J. M. F. (2004) The wild boar in Portugal. In C. Fonseca, J. Herrero, A. Luís and A. M. V. M. Soares, eds. *Wild Boar Research 2002. A Selection and Edited Papers from the 4th International Wild Boar Symposium*. Galemys, **16** Special Issue, pp. 243–51.

Lorenzini, R. and Lovari, S. (2006) Genetic diversity and phylogeography of the European roe deer: the refuge area theory revisited. *Biological Journal of the Linnean Society* **88**, 85–100.

Mendonça, M. (2003) *Livro de Montaria feito por El-Rei D. João I de Portugal*. Ericeira: Mar de Letras, 202 pp. (In Portuguese.)

Moço, G., Guerreiro, M., Ferreira, A. *et al.* (2006) The ibex *Capra pyrenaica* returns to its former Portuguese range. *Oryx* **40**(3), 351–4.

Morais, J., Oom, M., Malta-Vacas, J. and Luís, C. (2005) Genetic structure of an endangered Portuguese semiferal pony breed, the Garrano. *Biochemical Genetics* **43**, Nos. 7/8.

Oom, M. M. (1992) *O cavalo Lusitano: Uma raça em recuperação*. PhD thesis, Department of Zoology and Anthropology, Faculty of Sciences, University of Lisbon, Portugal.

Oom, M. M. and Cothran, E. G. (1996) Preliminary study of genetic variation of a feral pony from Portugal: the Garrano. *Animal Genetics* **27** (Suppl. 2), 17–42.

Pérez, J. M., Granados, J. E., Soriguer, R. C. *et al.* (2002) Distribution, status and conservation problems of the Spanish Ibex, *Capra pyrenaica* (Mammalia: Artiodactyla). *Mammal Review* **32**, 26–39.

Portas, M., Brito, N., Carvalho, I. and Leite, J. (2001) La conservación de la raza quina Garrana. *Archivos de Zootecnia* **50** (189–190), 171–179. (In Spanish.)

Randi, E., Alves, P. C., Carranza, J. *et al.* (2004) Phylogeography of roe deer (*Capreolus capreolus*) populations: the effects of historical genetic subdivisions and recent nonequilibrium dynamics. *Molecular Ecology* **13**, 3071–83.

Royo, L., Álvarez, I., Beja-Pereira, A. *et al.* (2005) The origins of Iberian horses assessed via mitochondrial DNA. *Journal of Heredity* **96**(6), 663–9.

Royo, L., Pajares, G., Álvarez, I., Fernández, I. and Goyache, F. (2007) Genetic variability and differentiation in Spanish roe deer (*Capreolus capreolus*): a phylogeographic reassessment within the European framework. *Molecular Phylogenetics and Evolution* **42**, 47–61.

Vingada, J. V., Ferreira, A., Keating, A. *et al.* (1997) *Conservação do Lobo (Canis lupus) em Portugal – Fomento e conservação das principais presas naturais do Lobo (Canis lupus signatus)*. Relatório final do protocolo com o ICN, no âmbito do Projecto LIFE "Conservação do Lobo em Portugal". Coimbra. Policopiado, 145 pp. (In Portuguese.)

Vos, J. (2000) Food habits and livestock depredation of two Iberian wolf packs (*Canis lupus signatus*) in the north of Portugal. *Journal of Zoology* **251**, 457–62.

19

Ungulates and their management in Spain

JUAN CARRANZA

As with many other facets of life in Spain, the recent history of wild ungulates has been largely conditioned by some key sociopolitical events. The main one was the civil war between 1936 and 1939. The war was followed by several years of economic privation. At this time, ungulate populations are believed to have become scarce and confined to the largest mountain chains and some particularly dense forests and shrub lands. It is likely that many populations disappeared or experienced bottlenecks at that time. When the national economy began to show some recovery, still within the dictatorial government of Franco, the national policy on environmental issues was essentially focused on productivity, with little concern for impacts upon natural habitats or animal species. Between the 1950s and the 1970s, the national administration for the 'conservation of nature' actively promoted the plantation of large production areas, planted with exotic trees, such as pines or eucalyptus. At that same time, ungulates such as fallow deer or mouflon were introduced or reintroduced in some areas directed to high-class sport-hunting. In some estates owned by the public administration, stocks of red deer, also, were deliberately caught up, and perhaps in some cases mixed with red deer from other origins, and used as seed populations to reintroduce the species in areas where it had become rare or extinct.

After the transition to democracy, in the late 1970s and early 1980s, most ungulate populations continued to increase both in size and in distribution. Some of them derived from reintroductions carried out in the 1960s and 1970s, but others increased from naturally occurring stocks. Among the main causes for this increment are probably the decline in economic land use in rural areas, such as extensive livestock and some traditional agriculture, together with the increase in use of these areas for hunting. Some species such as the wild boar and the roe deer have expanded their distribution ranges even more, particularly during the last two or three decades, perhaps associated with a trend for human migration to main cities and the complete abandonment of some rural areas (Sáez-Royuela and Tellería, 1986; Gortázar et al., 2000).

Hunting of ungulates has recently become more popular and more in demand, partly because of their expanded distribution areas and abundance, and also because of an increasing scarcity of smaller game species more generally. Under these circumstances, ungulates have increased their commercial value, and land use directed primarily towards production of game ungulates has increasingly become a feasible economic alternative to agriculture or livestock in many areas, especially in southwestern Spain.

19.1 Species present, status and distribution

There are eight wild ungulates in Spain. Native species are the red deer, roe deer, Spanish ibex, the Pyrenean chamois and wild boar. Mouflon and Barbary sheep are introduced species, and the origin of fallow deer is uncertain.

The actual status of ungulate populations mostly depends on the management practices, together with the type of hunting procedures. There are some differences in management practice between northern and southern areas in Spain. Northern areas are characterised by the increase of wild boar and roe deer populations, with the associated problem of damage in agricultural lands and increased road accidents. Wild boar and roe deer are the main big game species in these areas. Red deer populations are also increasing in some localities where this species was introduced from southern populations. Such increases in red deer populations usually result in the displacement of roe deer populations and further increase in impacts to crops and forests. Southern areas also experience the increase of wild boar and roe deer populations. The main feature of these areas is the growing tendency towards a more intensive game management with red deer targeted as the main species, many areas have been fenced, and red deer are maintained at relatively high population densities.

19.1.1 Red deer

Red deer is common and widely distributed in central-south-western Spain, with some populations in forested areas in the North (Fig. 19.1) (Carranza, 2004). In this latter case, red deer populations in the north of Spain almost disappeared in the twentieth century and were restocked with individuals from central and southern areas.

Although there are no complete census data of red deer for Spain, more than 70 000 stags were hunted per year during the last six years in Spain

Fig. 19.1 Distribution of Iberian red deer (*Cervus elaphus hispanicus*) in Spain. From Carrascal and Salvador (2004)

(J. L. Garrido, personal comunication) and total population must be over 800 000 individuals.

Red deer in Spain belongs to the subspecies *Cervus elaphus hispanicus* that may represent the remains of populations that occurred in Iberian glacial refugia during the Pleistocene. During the last 60 years, some introductions from different European origins have produced some admixture in local populations. The genetic situation of red deer is Spain is now a priority both in research and in legal regulations to protect native populations.

One of the most important threats to the conservation of Iberian red deer is the recent tendency to deer farming. Although deer farming is a common practice in many areas in the word, including European countries, in Spain this practice is very recent and there are still only a handful of deer farms. Most recent regulations tend to reduce farming since it carries significant risks of introducing foreign and artificially selected genes into natural populations.

19.1.2 Roe deer

The roe deer occurs mainly in the north of Spain (Fig. 19.2), in large areas predominately covered by deciduous Atlantic forests with *Quercus pyrenaica* and *Fagus sylvatica* as main overstorey species. These populations in the north of Spain are increasing and expanding their distribution range. Other populations occur in central Spain, in chestnut *Castanea sativa* woodlands of Villuercas Mountains and in Mediterranean ecosystems of Sierra Morena covered by holm (*Quercus ilex*)

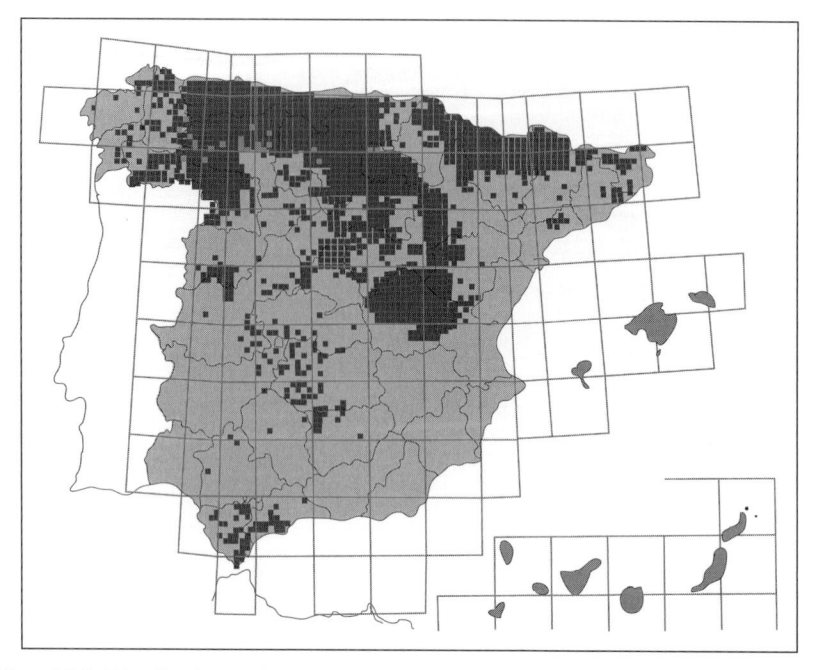

Fig. 19.2 Distribution of roe deer (*Capreolus capreolus*) in Spain. From Carrascal and Salvador (2004)

and cork (*Quercus suber*) oak forests and their associated Mediterranean shrubs. The southernmost roe deer population in Europe is in the mountains of Cadiz province, in Los Alcornocales Natural Park, a large mountainous area of some 167 000 hectares of protected cork oak forest that attracts the humidity of winds coming from the Atlantic Ocean eastwards through the natural passage of mountains that surround Gibraltar straits. During the last three decades, roe deer in Spain has increased both its abundance and distribution range.

The phylogeography of Iberian roe deer is still under study (Randi *et al.*, 2004; Lorenzini and Lovari, 2006; Royo *et al.*, 2007); molecular analyses suggest that some Iberian populations may be representative of refuge populations during the last glaciation and thus deserving of positive conservation efforts against genetic admixture. Even if at present we have no definitive evidence of genetic distinctiveness, genetic admixture is a serious potential threat to these roe deer populations, so that precautionary principles would suggest that any translocations are strongly discouraged.

19.1.3 Fallow deer

Fallow deer has a scattered distribution within Spain mostly deriving from recent introductions in a number of localities (Fig. 19.3). This species experienced a

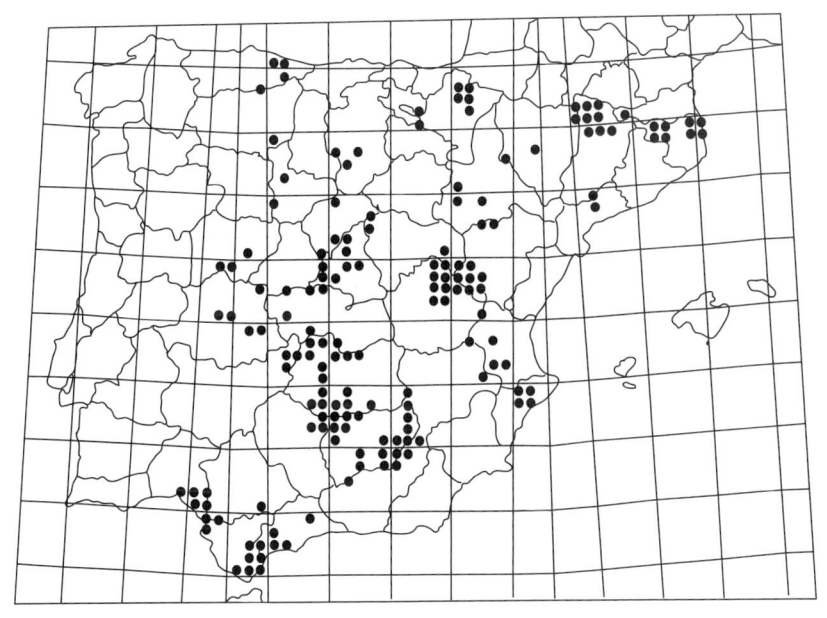

Fig. 19.3 Distribution of fallow deer (*Dama dama*) in Spain. From Carrascal and Salvador (2004)

general decrease in Europe during the last glaciation and disappeared from most of the continent, even if some small populations may have survived in southern Italy and elsewhere. Subsequently, fallow were distributed throughout the Mediterranean basin including Iberia by the Phoenicians and Romans. There are reports of its presence in the nineteenth century in some areas in the south of Spain (e.g. Sierra Morena: Cabrera, 1914). It became extinct and was reintroduced in Doñana National Park in the early twentieth century.

Later introductions from different origins promoted either by public administration or by private landowners have produced its current distribution. In most sites, fallow deer occurs in sympatry with red deer and displaces the latter from the best grazing patches (Carranza and Valencia, 1999).

19.1.4 Spanish ibex

The Spanish ibex (*Capra pyrenaica*) is an ungulate species endemic to Spain that includes two subspecies, *C. p. hispanica* along the mountain chains parallel to the Mediterranean coast, and *C. p. victoriae* in the central-to-northwest quadrant of peninsular Spain (Fig. 19.4). The whole population is estimated around 50 000 individuals (Alados and Escós, 2004). The subspecies *C. p. victoriae* only

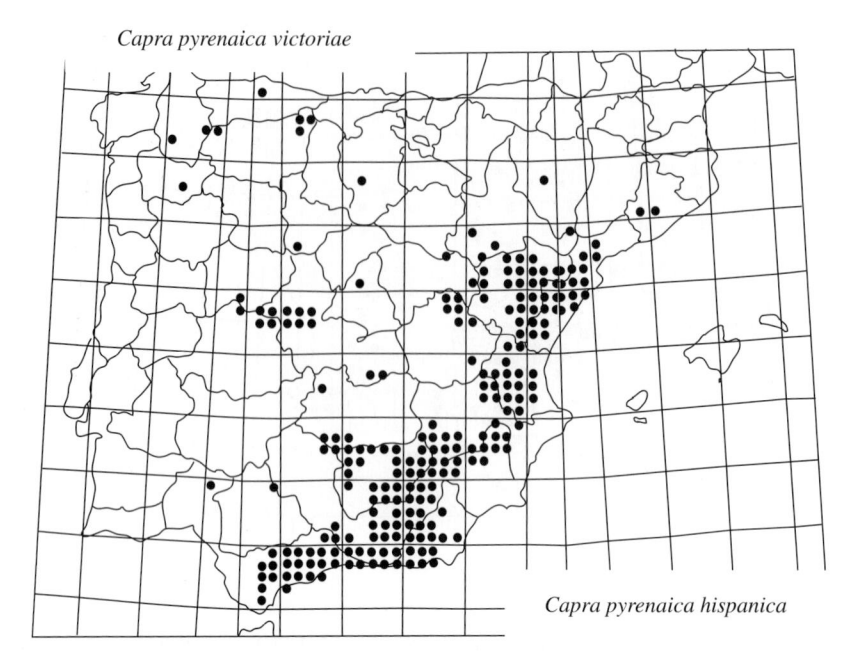

Fig. 19.4 Distribution of the two subspecies of Spanish ibex (*Capra pyrenaica*) in Spain. From Carrascal and Salvador (2004)

includes about 10 000 individuals and a small distribution area in Gredos mountains, central-west Spain. The subspecies *C. p. hispanica* extends throughout a large area in eastern and southern Iberian Peninsula and its populations are expanding. At this moment the subspecies *C. p. victoriae* is considered vulnerable (IUCN VU D2) due to its restricted distribution area while the *C. p. hispanica* subspecies is considered of lesser concern (IUCN LC/cd) and it is currently subject to management programmes by regional governments (Alados and Escós, 2004). Hunting bag in Spain is about 1500 individuals per year.

One main threat to Spanish ibex populations is the local increase of density that may result in an increased susceptibility to disease. In the Andalusian population of Cazorla Mountains, for instance, sarcoptic mange emerging in 1988 resulted in a 90% decrease in population size (Leon Vizcaino *et al.*, 1999, 2001). Further risks are population fragmentation, with the associated genetic effects, and sex ratio disequilibria caused by hunting on males with little control over females, which may lead to high female densities and increased impacts on natural vegetation and risk of disease.

19.1.5 Pyrenean chamois

Pyrenean chamois occurs in two separate areas in north Spain corresponding to two subspecies, *Rupicapra pyrenaica pyrenaica* in the Pyrenees and *R. p. parva*

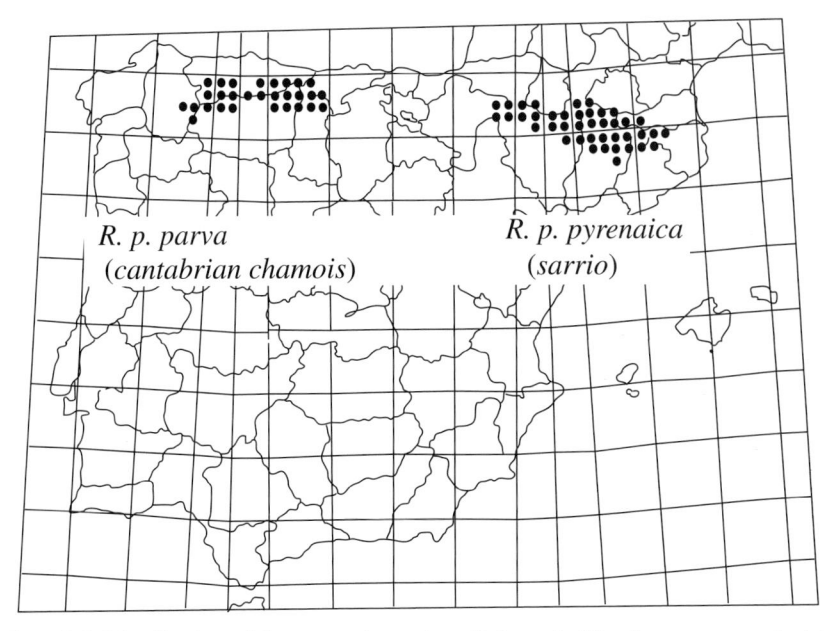

Fig. 19.5 Distribution of the two subspecies of chamois (*Rupicapra pyrenaica*) in Spain. From Carrascal and Salvador (2004)

in Cantabrian Mountains (Fig. 19.5). There is evidence that this species occurred throughout Spain during the Pleistocene, being relegated to higher mountains in the north of Spain during the Holocene, probably related to the warming of climate that favoured competing species in southern areas and lowlands.

Population size is about 50 000 individuals for the Pyrenean subspecies and about 15 000 for the Cantabrian chamois. About 2000 chamois are hunted every year in Spain.

The main predator for the chamois is the Iberian wolf, which occurs in the Cantabrian mountains, but not in the Pyrenean range. In practice however chamois appears to be the wild ungulate least selected as prey by wolves, at least in this area (L. Llaneza *et al.*, 1996). Thus, the effect of this large predator on chamois population dynamics may be very little.

Population regulation is crucial to control the prevalence of diseases. Sarcoptic mange was detected in 1993 in Pico Torres (Asturias) and from this date this parasitic disease has extended progressively throughout the Cantabrian population. In 1999, the disease reached the National Park Picos de Europa. Management efforts in Cantabrian Mountains are at this moment much oriented to control the advance of this disease. In the Pyrenees, the main disease since the 1980s has been keratoconjunctivitis (Loison *et al.*, 1996) and recently (by 2001) a new pathogen (pestivirus) is affecting some areas and seems to be producing local reductions of population census (Marco and Lavin, 2003; see also Perez-Barberia and Garcia-Gonzàles, 2006).

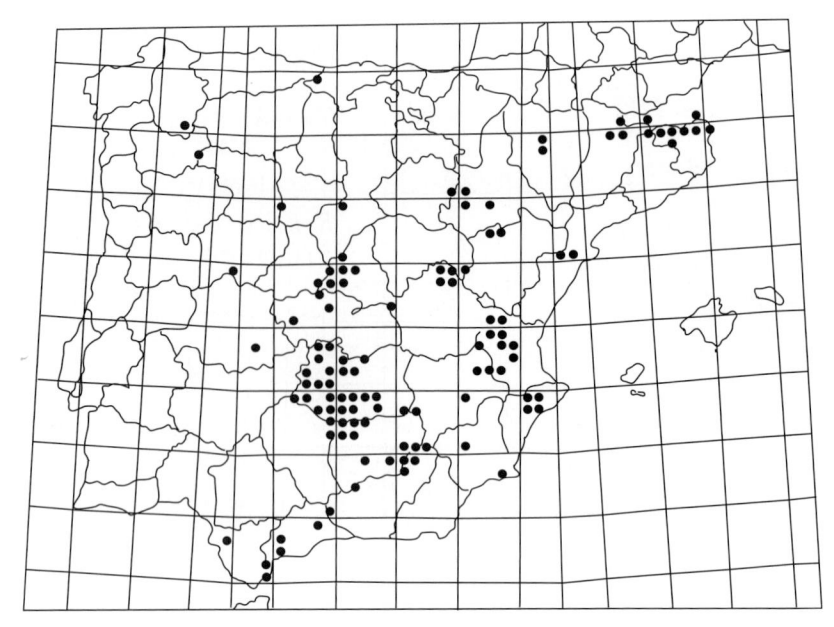

Fig. 19.6 Distribution of mouflon (*Ovis aries*) in Spain. From Carrascal and Salvador (2004)

19.1.6 Mouflon

European mouflon is generally considered a descendant of some domesticated ancestor of modern sheep that secondarily were released to the wild in some Mediterranean isles such as Sardinia (about 6000 BC) and Corsica. The species was introduced in many other parts of Europe during the mid-nineteenth century for hunting purposes. In Spain, it was introduced in Sierra de Cazorla (Jaen province) in 1954 by public administration. From this date, it has been introduced in many private lands (Fig. 19.6). Perhaps the most dangerous introduction has been the one in Canary Islands, in the National Park of Cañadas del Teide (Tenerife), where it currently constitutes a serious threat to endemic flora of this area. Mouflon is hunted in montería and by stalking, during the same period as red deer. It is now considered an exotic species in Spain and more recent regulations tend to reduce or eliminate its presence in most areas.

19.1.7 Barbary sheep

The Barbary sheep, Aoudad, or Saharian arrui (*Ammotragus lervia*) is the most recently introduced ungulate in Spain. Originally from mountainous areas of North Africa, it is differentiated into several subspecies to the north of Sahara, some of which may currently be in risk of extinction. It was introduced for hunting purposes in some southern states of the USA, and in Spain in Sierra Espuña

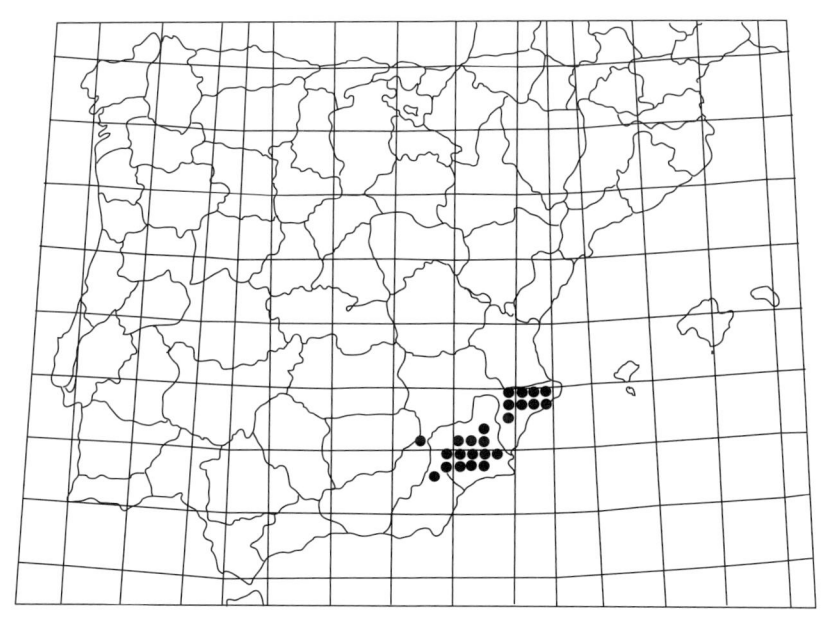

Fig. 19.7 Distribution of Barbary sheep (*Ammotragus lervia*) in Spain. From Carrascal and Salvador (2004)

(Cuenca province) in 1970 with 36 individuals coming from zoos (Fig. 19.7). From this original stock in south-eastern Spain, the population expanded to surrounding areas and grew up to 2000 individuals in the 1990s. The Arrui is hunted by stalking and its trophy is appreciated, perhaps because it is not too common in Spain. In its expansion to some areas it may produce the competition with other native ungulates, among which perhaps the main concern is for the Spanish ibex in the north-east of Andalusia.

The Arrui is considered a serious problem, especially by administrations of regions to where it is rapidly expanding, and in the future, policy may shift towards attempts at complete eradication. In Andalusia, for instance, its commercial hunting has been prohibited with the objective of making it unattractive for private owners. Despite the evident reasons to consider this species a threat for natural environments, it was, like mouflon, also introduced to the Canary Islands, in this case in La Palma, where again it has become a serious problem for insular endemic flora.

19.1.8 Wild boar

The wild boar is perhaps the most abundant and most widely distributed wild ungulate in Spain (Fig. 19.8). From a distribution area in the early twentieth century that extended in a diagonal axis from north-east to south-west Spain, this species

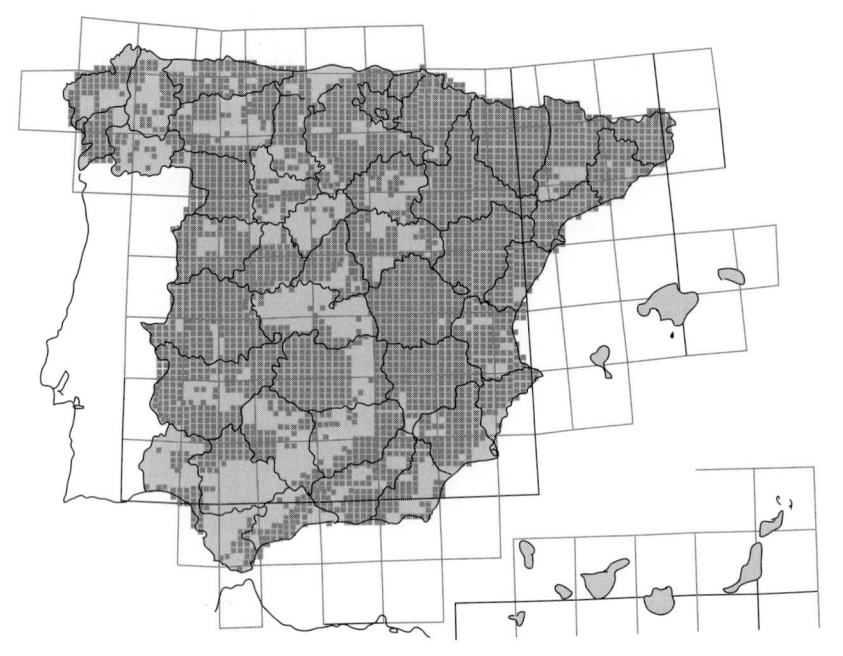

Fig. 19.8 Distribution of wild boar (*Sus scrofa*) in Spain. From Rosell and Herrero (2005)

has experienced a geographical expansion all over the Iberian peninsula, probably caused by the abandonment of many rural areas during the second half of the twentieth century and the associated increase of scrublands (Rosell and Herrero, 2005). There are new elements that may also contribute to its demographic expansion. Among them, recent climate change with generally milder winters may favour piglet survival; new overabundant resources have appeared from human activity such as rubbish dumps and large maize crops; finally some production of wild boars under farming conditions to satisfy hunting demand may have contributed to its presence in particular locations (Fernández-Llario, 1996). Wild boar populations fluctuate over cycles of several years but seem to follow a general increasing tendency. Although there are no formal estimates available for the whole population in Spain, hunting figures have increased and current bag is over 150 000 individuals of both sexes.

The popularity of the wild boar among Spanish hunters has increased during the last two decades. This is partly because the increase in numbers and distribution area, but, as noted more generally above, also because small game has become increasingly scarce.

Among its frequent parasites and pathogens, wild boar acts as reservoir for bovine tuberculosis and can disseminate this pathogen along movement routes throughout large areas, contributing to interspecific transmission to red deer and domestic cattle (Hermoso de Mendoza *et al.*, 2005; Vicente *et al.*, 2006).

19.2 Legislation

Game management and hunting in Spain is regulated by autonomous regional governments. As a result, there are 15 distinct regulatory and legal frameworks within continental Spain with little or no coordination at the level of the country.

19.2.1 Hunting seasons

The general season for hunting in most regions of Spain is between early October and late February. However, hunting periods for some species or hunting methods may lie outside this general season.

The first major general exception is the roe deer. Main hunting period for roe deer is from mid-April to the end of July in 12 out of the 13 regions where this species occurs. In five of them, there are additional hunting periods between September and October. Andalusia has a different schedule, with one period in March–April and another in July–August.

Red deer is hunted in the Spanish montería (driven hunt, see below and section 19.6) within the general hunting period from early October to mid-February, and by stalking during the rutting season (from September to the opening of the general season in October).

Permitted hunting methods for ungulates are stalking and 'montería'. Montería is a typical Spanish hunting procedure for big game, where several packs of dogs are released within an area of about 500 ha of forest or scrubland, from where they drive wild ungulates to the open fields around, where hunters wait at fixed points. Under the montería system each area is hunted only once (typically for about three hours) per year.

This system is used predominantly in south-western Spain, mainly for red deer and wild boar, together with some accompanying species such as fallow deer and mouflon. It is not normally used for roe deer (although there are some exceptions). Besides montería, the wild boar is also hunted in a stalking mode based on waiting for the animals at strategic sites, for instance, water and mud ponds, typically on full moon nights.

In the northern part of the country, red deer are hunted only by stalking. Hunting of roe deer also is generally by stalking and in some cases by beating, a procedure that is currently under debate. For Spanish ibex, Pyrenean chamois, and Barbary sheep, hunting is always by stalking.

19.3 Management objectives

Management of ungulate populations is mostly oriented to hunting, with the exceptions of protected areas where the main objective may be population regulation. In National Parks, hunting is prohibited by the current national law. There is an ongoing process of transference of National Parks to regional governments and the possibility of allowing some hunting within these parks is under consideration.

The main product with market value related to ungulates is sport hunting. Other items such as venison or cast antlers are only by-products that come to increase the profitability of the activity but that, by far, cannot maintain it without the income from hunting rights. Touristic value of ungulates is acknowledged especially in some natural areas, and it may tend to also increase in some private properties, although very slowly.

The Spanish ibex has become the most valuable big game trophy of the Spanish hunt. The exceptions to hunting management are those populations included in National Parks, such as Sierra Nevada in southern Spain that includes a population of about 16 000 individuals. In this area, population is controlled by the administration by selective culling.

Pyrenean chamois is hunted, except in the subpopulations included in Spanish National Parks. In protected areas management is mainly directed to control population size, which is a crucial factor for the conservation of natural vegetation in these areas and especially for the control of the prevalence of the diseases that affect this species such as sarcoptic mange, keratoconjunctivitis, or pestivirus (Loison *et al.*, 1996; Marco and Lavin, 2003).

Management of wild boar populations is also oriented to reduce impact on small game breeding (red-legged partridge nests and rabbit dens), crop damage and road accidents. These types of control may be somehow planned in hunting programmes of private owners or public administration, but they are normally based on special permits when some damage occurs.

The expansion of roe deer populations has been accompanied by an increase in the interest of hunters in this species; together with an increase of problems such impacts on forestry and road accidents.

Red deer management is a central activity in many rural areas in Spain, especially in south-western Mediterranean habitats. Some of these areas include the best-preserved remains of Mediterranean forest and scrublands, where some highly endangered species still survive, such as the Iberian lynx or the imperial eagle. One main challenge of red deer management in these areas is to ensure its compatibility with the conservation of valuable natural resources in these areas.

Main issues are the control of deer density to preserve natural vegetation and the whole ecosystem that depends on it, and, on the other hand, the maintenance of native populations of Iberian red deer in acceptable conditions that allow its natural behaviour and the operation of natural selection.

19.4/5 Management structure and organisation

In Spain, hunting regulation and the conservation of nature are under the administrative authority of autonomous regional administrations. As mentioned above, National Parks are the only protected areas that still depend on the central administration of Spain instead of on the regional administrations. Besides National Parks, all other protected areas, such as those called Natural Parks, and in general all the areas included in the Natura 2000 network, are under the administration of regional governments. In general, coordination between regional administrations is very low.

Roe deer is the only ungulate species that has an association in Spain founded around this small cervid to protect it, promote its hunting and advise about its management (www.corzo.info). As in the case of other species, every autonomous regional government has its own regulations, hunting periods, management policy, etc. for roe deer, but in this case at least, the Association for the Spanish Roe Deer (ACE) works in favour of some coordination between regional policies.

19.6 Actual management and hunting practices

As we have noted, hunting activities in Spain are independently regulated by each regional administration. Hunting licences are also specific for each region, so that several licences may be necessary to anyone who wants to hunt in several areas within Spain. Different autonomous regions may also differ in prerequisites and fees. In general, an examination (or a course as a substitute) is required to get a licence for the first time. Costs may vary, but as an example, 2007 taxes in Andalusia were EUR 25.17 for examination or EUR 50.33 for the course, and EUR 19.77 for one year licence for hunting ungulates.

The number of hunting licences in Spain is around 1 200 000 (for hunting in general, not only big game). This figure is likely to be slightly higher than the number of actual hunters since many hunters may have more than one licence to hunt in different regions. The number of licences for firearms was approximately 1 700 000 in 2004, of which 150 000 were for rifles used to hunt ungulates (RFEC, unpublished data). Many hunters (some 440 000) are associated in the Real Federación Española de Caza (RFEC), which is organized in regional federations (see www.fecaza.com/).

The general pattern of management of hunting areas and populations tends to be different between northern and southern Spain. In the north, ungulates are mostly within game reserves in large (> 30 000 ha) mountainous, forested areas managed by public administration. The density of ungulates is usually moderate compared to southern areas, and management is also of lower intensity than in the south.

In the case of Spanish ibex and Pyrenean chamois, management is done in most cases by regional governments, since these species are commonly in large mountainous areas, sometimes included in regional hunting reserves, rather than in private estates. For chamois, several regional administrations and three countries (Spain, France and Andorra) that share the distribution area do most censuses and management. Management includes annual censuses, commonly by linear transects, and elaboration of hunting quotas and culling plans.

Southern hunting areas are usually private estates that cover many well-preserved areas of Mediterranean shrub and forest usually with large areas of open savannah-like woodlands (dehesas), as well as traditional livestock lands. Main species in these areas are the red deer and the wild boar. Private estates are areas of relatively small size for ungulates (1000–4000 ha), where management tends to be more intensive because the owner may seek economic income from game ungulates. In many cases, these properties are fenced with 2 m high mesh fences that prevent the movement of ungulates and permit management of discrete populations in isolation from populations of neighbouring estates.

In most regions of Spain, for an area to be authorised for hunting exploitation, there is a prerequisite of the elaboration of a management plan. This plan is a project of management and hunting relating to the next several (typically five) years. The plan must include estimations of population size and dynamics, including the intended hunting quotas. Plans should be renewed for every period (e.g. five years) and approved by the administration. The main objective is the planning of the activities to guarantee that the use of hunting resources will be sustainable. The goal is indeed reasonable, but the practical application is not free of difficulties. One problem is the cost of elaboration for the landowner. In some cases, landowners' associations may provide members with such a service. However, whether produced by individual landowners or by consultants, these plans may be extremely variable in quality and rigour.

19.6.1 Actual hunting practices

Hunting in Spain includes some procedures used in other parts of the world, such as stalking, but also a mode that seems to be a genuine Spanish system: montería, where several packs of dogs are released within a portion of about 500 ha of forest or scrubland, from where they drive wild ungulates to the open fields around, where hunters wait at fixed points. A very special hunting practice is the use of lances in the horse-riding hunt of wild boars. This type of hunt was commonly practised during full moon nights in open dehesas in the southwest of Spain. Today it only remains in Doñana National Park, where it is practised in the morning when wild boars return from the marsh, where they spend the night foraging, to their resting places within the scrubland. Montería is used mainly in south-western Spain for red deer and wild boar, together with some accompanying species such as fallow deer and mouflon. It is not normally used for roe deer and in the northern half of the country almost all hunting is by stalking.

There are some animal welfare concerns on the use of dogs in hunting. In Spanish montería, the role of dogs is only to chase away game ungulates. However, dogs may sometimes catch some injured animal, or come into contact with large wild boars that on occasion, turn to face and threaten them. However, on the more positive side, under the montería system each portion of land is hunted only once per year, typically during three hours from 12.00 to 15.00, so the chasing by dogs of groups of ungulates is only a single event per year.

For Spanish ibex, Pyrenean chamois and Barbary sheep, hunting is always by stalking. Especially for Spanish ibex and Pyrenean chamois, stalking is usually performed accompanied by a warden who controls the number and type of animals shot. Wild boar may be hunted by montería in southern Spain, but is otherwise hunted in a stalking mode based on waiting for the animals at strategic sites, for instance water and mud ponds, typically on full moon nights.

Hunting is programmed in hunting plans (management plans, see above) for one or several hunting seasons, including the type of hunt to be used and the number of animals to be culled. Additionally, each hunting action should normally be authorised by the local government prior to its celebration in a particular date. Agents of regional administrations may register hunting bag data to check their agreement with the hunting plan, and for statistics. In Spain, meat from hunted ungulates can be used for commercial purposes. Veterinary inspection in the field is compulsory before transportation of carcasses, and data from these inspections become useful to know the health status of populations as well as to provide another source of hunting bag statistics.

19.7 Census types and methods

Each autonomous regional government has its own census policy and only some administrations do population estimations. In mountainous areas managed by public administration, censuses of ungulates are done mainly by linear transects (e.g. for ibex) or by counting the number of roaring males in the case of red deer. As noted earlier, estimates of population numbers of Pyrenean chamois are done by the several regional administrations of all three countries (Spain, France and Andorra) that share the distribution area.

In private estates, censuses are required to be included in game management plans every period of five years or so. In most private estates in south-western Spain, estimations of population size and composition are based on animal counts performed during late summer and early autumn, mostly in areas where ungulates gather at this time either because supplementary food is provided as forage availability in the field becomes more scarce at the end of the hot and dry summer or, in the case of red and fallow deer, because animals collect at some traditional mating areas during the rutting season.

The regional government of Andalusia has recently standardised the census procedure for all ungulates throughout the region, based on linear transects and the application of specific software, like the Distance program. Censuses carried out by following the standard procedure will be compulsory for private managers when presenting their management and hunting plans. Public administration will also use these methods to estimate ungulate populations in the whole region.

In areas where the predominant hunting system is montería, estimates of the size of populations of red deer and wild boar are generally based on hunting bags. In practice, under the montería system, the actual amount of animals to be harvested tends to be self-regulated by actual availability of animals rather than reliant on the calculation of fixed quotas. This is generally true for the wild boar and in most non-fenced areas for the red deer. In those cases, population tendencies become clearly evident from hunting data and it is also possible to estimate absolute population size, simply by having some estimation of the mean age of the individuals shot along consecutive years. A reduction in the mean age of the animals shot over the years is a useful tool to detect over-hunting.

19.8 Ungulate impacts and damage

The increase of ungulate densities in Spain during the last decades has been accompanied by the raising of associated impacts, which belong to two main types: damage to vegetation and road accidents. Impacts on vegetation include those on forest plantations, on agriculture and on natural woody vegetation.

Damage to forestry is almost exclusively confined to the north half of Spain, simply because forest plantations are scarce in the south. There are exceptions, mainly related to roe deer and red deer damage to young pine and chestnut trees in some southern woodland areas. In the north, most damage is caused by roe deer, whose populations have reached high densities in some areas traditionally used for wood production, either with deciduous or coniferous species. Protecting individual saplings and fencing whole plantations have been used in some cases to prevent damage, but they are expensive and none of them completely effective. Experience indicates that some changes in forestry activities based on the knowledge of browsing preferences and marking behaviour of deer may be highly valuable. The maintenance of a shrubby understorey within forested areas, as well as the amount of naturally regenerated sprouts after the cutting of a forest patch, can contribute to reduce the impact of ungulates on the forest plantation.

In the south, the highest ungulate densities (mainly red deer) occur in areas occupied by Mediterranean forest and savannah-like open woodlands called dehesas. In these areas, deer overabundance can jeopardise the persistence of natural shrub species, as well as seriously limit the natural regeneration of native tree species. Again, in these same areas (in the south) a single private landowner or manager may do all management over the territory; in managing primarily for deer production, he or she may show variable concern about conservation impacts. In this case it is the public administration who has to demand of managers the maintenance of acceptable densities of deer and the preservation of natural habitats.

Damage to agricultural and horticultural crops is mostly due to wild boar. In most cases, the compensation/solution by the administration is in the form of special permits to cull animals in the area where damage takes place.

The presence of ungulates on roads constitutes a grave, increasing problem in Spain. Most accidents involving ungulates occur in north and north-western Spain, and are mainly due to wild boar and roe deer. The National Head Office of Traffic in Spain performed a descriptive study on this problem covering one year (between February 2003 and January 2004). A total amount of 6227 accidents was registered, of which 316 resulted in victims, including 17 deaths, 76 serious injuries and 396 slight injuries.

Some of these accidents were due to domestic animals (mainly dogs 21.2%), but most of them (64.7%) were caused by wild ungulates. Wild boar were involved in 32.4% of accidents, roe deer in 22.0% and red deer in 4.4%. The report from the EU project COST 341 on the fragmentation of habitat in relation to transport infrastructures provides a useful analysis of causes and prevention measures, and it is also relevant to Spain.

19.9 Supplementary feeding

In Mediterranean ecosystems, the most severe shortage for herbivores usually occurs in late summer and early autumn, when several months with high temperatures and lack of precipitation dry up most herbaceous vegetation (Bugalho and Milne, 2003). In southern Spain, supplementary feeding is commonly used for red deer from mid summer (e.g. mid-July) to early autumn (e.g. late September), mainly in fenced estates where animals have no opportunity to undertake seasonal migratory movements. Supplementary feeding for red deer usually includes the rutting season that takes place from mid-September.

Supplementary feeding increases the spatial aggregation of females, which has knock-on effects on male–male interactions and on the distribution of matings among males (Carranza, 1995; Sanchez-Prieto et al., 2004).

Main types of food used are hay, alfalfa, cereals and commercial feed. Together with red deer, fallow deer and mouflon also use the same feeding points when they occur in the same estate. More recently there has been a trend for some estates to maintain feeding stations year round, a practice which is considered by some as becoming too interventional and making management more a matter of deer farming than supplementation of wild species. Such extended feeding may also lead to problems in creating an imbalance between winter and summer carrying capacity of the range. With feeding extending away from the two or three critical months and the amount of food increasing, ungulate densities may rise above the carrying capacity of natural habitats with the associated problems of elevated intraspecific competition and impact on the natural vegetation.

Supplementary feeding may be especially relevant for the wild boar. Food provided to red deer during the summer may be used by wild boars when it consists of grain (notably maize) or feed. Providing supplementary food during the summer may cause the undesirable effect of advancement of oestrus in wild sows, producing early births in late winter and increased piglet mortality due to their limited thermoregulation ability (Fernández-Llario and Mateos-Quesada, 1998).

Perhaps the main problems associated with feeding wild boars are to do with health. On one hand, the contact between wild boar and other species, such as red deer or even cattle, at the same feeding points increases disease transmission (Hermoso de Mendoza et al., 2005). On the other hand, some estates have recently begun to maintain permanent feeding points for wild boars. This produces the fixation of individuals, mainly females, around these points, increasing the prevalence of many diseases (Vicente et al., 2006; Fernández-Llario, *unpublished data*).

Supplementary feeding is not a common practice in large mountain areas managed by the public administration. Spanish ibex, chamois and roe deer are rarely supplementary fed. The exceptions are some private estates that have started to feed roe deer, mainly in the south of Spain, and in a few cases the Spanish ibex. As in other species, the common risks associated with these practices are disease transmission and the conservation of natural features of wild ungulate species, together with the increase of densities above carrying capacity of natural habitats.

19.10 Key points for the management of wild ungulates in Spain

The main challenge of ungulate management in Spain is to take advantage of the existing interest in hunting of these species, in order to promote the economic development of rural areas that may otherwise tend to be abandoned, but in this utilisation develop a form of land-use that is more compatible with conservation than alternative uses such as agriculture or livestock production. However, for this objective to be achieved, we need to implement adequate management procedures.

Criteria on adequate procedures have changed during the last decade. The presence of exotic species, for instance, was viewed as a way of improving the hunting offer based on increasing variety of game products. Now, a new tendency promoted by some private sectors and public administrations is towards a form of game management oriented to offer hunting of native species within a natural experience, which is likely to favour the maintenance of natural values. Main objectives are the maintenance of natural species in their natural habitats, and hunting by traditional procedures.

Ungulate management has become a main source of revenue in many marginal areas of south-western Spain. This has produced a tendency to increase the control by the owner over the populations occurring within his or her own estate. As a result, many properties have been fenced to prevent ungulate movements. Within fenced areas, management has to be more precise and based on technical knowledge, because animals cannot buffer environmental stress by migrating to other areas. Associated with fencing, supplementary feeding is widely practised, at least during the worst period of the year that in these habitats is the summer.

There is some concern that further progression along these lines could lead to still greater intervention: subdivision of parks by further fences to create separate paddocks for animals of different age- and sex-class, controlled (selective) breeding, use of artifical insemination, etc. Such intensification of management becomes akin to farming and distances management from that of the conservation of natural populations and habitats.

One main challenge for ungulate management in Spain is thus to be able to maintain the level of intervention within an acceptable range. Completely natural populations without any human intervention are not yet possible, but too intensive management and farming are incompatible with the preservation of natural characteristics of wild ungulates. The goal should then be to maintain management within an intermediate range of intervention and according to criteria that may make compatible economic productivity and conservation. Some initial steps have been taken such as genetic testing to check that red deer belong to the Iberian subspecies, recent legal regulations that tend to limit and constrain farming procedures, and a new system of certified quality for game management.

Some particular initiatives aimed at mitigating these problems have recently been implemented in Spain or are under consideration. For example, genetic introgression since 2003 is controlled by a genetic test that is applied to red deer trophies when they are submitted to the Spanish Trophy Commission where they are measured and catalogued according to the criteria of the International Game Council

(CIC). If genetic tests indicate that some trophies do not belong to pure Iberian red deer specimens, then the Spanish Commission rejects them as candidates to be included in the Spanish records (Carranza et al., 2003). This measure produces the effect of decreasing the value of hybrids as trophies and is producing the desired effect of reducing the introduction of foreign deer in Spain (CIC, unpublished report). At the same time, some public administrations have started using the genetic test as a prerequisite before authorising translocations, and some owners ask for the application of the genetic tests to samples of their live animals in order to implement programmes aimed at purging hybridisation from their populations.

In a further step, artificial selection is starting to be considered an undesirable process (Carranza and Martínez, 2002). For instance, the Administration of Andalucia, in the south of Spain, is implementing new legal regulations that prevent any procedures that interfere with the natural reproduction of game ungulates, such as artificial insemination or mating arrangements by direct choice of breeders (Ortega-Alegre and Rodriguez-Benavente, 2007).

Despite such initiatives, current market tendencies for game ungulates in Spain favour intensification, hybridisation, artificial selection and many other practices not compatible with conservation, particularly since so many populations are, in fact, enclosed within fences making such manipulations more feasible. Natural management as a global, integrated approach to game practice with ungulates is highly difficult to achieve simply through regulatory constraints. This problem is being faced in southern Spain with a new initiative called the 'Quality of game management system' (Vargas et al., 2005; Ortega-Alegre and Rodriguez-Benavente, 2007). This system is being implemented by regional administrations, and is aimed to encourage the retention of a more low-intervention management system, by adding a premium to 'naturalness'.

In those regions where the system operates, landowners can apply for a certificate of quality for their deer populations and trophies. These certificates are awarded by the regional government in agreement with a research institute (Carranza and Vargas, 2006).

Application for the certificate is voluntary for landowners, so that in order to encourage uptake, there must be some reward for doing so, hopefully in the longer term because hunters may set a greater value on the experience of hunting in these naturally managed areas. In the shorter term the incentive for owners to enter into such schemes is access to funds provided by the regional authority oriented to conservation and the launch of their products (game offer) to the market with a quality brand.

Award of the certificate is based on quite restricted management criteria based on conservation principles. Even among scientists and much more so among associations related to hunting or management, these principles and management criteria are clearly a matter of debate and potential disagreement. This concern motivated a group of scientists to organise a couple of workshops with the goal of promoting discussion and unifying criteria, first among research groups and then with representatives of the main associations and public administrations involved in hunting and game management in Spain. The result was a high level of agreement that appears in a publication resulting after these two workshops (Carranza and Vargas, 2007).

These measures are not enough, but they are at least first steps that mean a change in the direction that has dominated management policy during most of the last century.

References

Alados, C. and Escós, J. (2004) Cabra montés: Capra pyrenaica. In L. M. Carrascal and A. Salvador, eds., *Enciclopedia virtual de los vertebrados españoles*. Madrid: Museo Nacional de Ciencias Naturales, http://www.vertebradosibericos.org.

Bugalho, M. N. and Milne, J. A. (2003) The composition of the diet of red deer (*Cervus elaphus*) in a Mediterranean environment: a case of summer nutritional constraint? *Forest Ecology and Management* **181**(1–2), 23–9.

Cabrera, A. (1914) *Fauna Ibérica: Mamíferos*. Ed. Hipódromo, Madrid: Museo Nacional de Ciencias Naturales, 441 pp.

Carranza, J. (1995) Female attraction by males versus sites in territorial rutting red deer. *Animal Behaviour* **50**(2), 445–53.

Carranza, J. (2004) Ciervo: *Cervus elaphus*. In L. M. Carrascal and A. Salvador, eds., *Enciclopedia virtual de los vertebrados españoles*. Madrid: Museo Nacional de Ciencias Naturales, http://www.vertebradosibericos.org.

Carranza, J. and Martínez, J. G. (2002) Consideraciones evolutivas en la gestión de especies cinegéticas. In M. Soler, ed., *Evolución, la base de la Biología*. Proyecto Sur, Granada.

Carranza, J. and Vargas, J. M., eds. (2007) *Criterios para la Certificación de la Calidad Cinegética en España*. Universidad de Extremadura.

Carranza, J., Fernández-García, J. L., Martínez, J. G. *et al.* (2003) The preservation of Iberian red deer (*Cervus elaphus hispanicus*) from genetic introgression by other European subspecies. *IUCN Deer Specialist Group Newsletter* **18**, 2–4.

Carranza, J. and Valencia, J. (1999) Red deer females collect on male clumps at mating areas. *Behavioural Ecology* **10**, 525–32.

Carrascal, L. M. and Salvador, A. (eds.) (2004). Enciclopedia virtual de los vertebrados españoles. Madrid: Museo Nacional di Ciencias Naturales.

Fernández-Llario, P. (1996) *Ecología del jabalíes en Doñana: parámetros reproductivos e impacto ambiental*. Doctoral thesis, Universidad de Extremadura, Cáceres.

Fernández-Llario, P. and Mateos-Quesada, P. (1998) Body size and reproductive parameters in the wild boar Sus scrofa. *Acta Theriologica* **43**, 439–44.

Gortázar, C., Herrero, J., Villafuerte, R. and Marco, J. (2000) Historical examination of the status of large mammals in Aragon, Spain. *Mammalia* **64**(4), 411–22.

Hermoso de Mendoza, J. *et al.* (2005) Bovine tuberculosis in wild boar (*Sus scrofa*), red deer (*Cervus elaphus*) and cattle (*Bos taurus*) in a Mediterranean ecosystem (1992–2004). *Preventive Veterinary Medicine* **74**, 239–47.

León Vizcaíno, L., Ibañez, M. R. R. de, Cubero, M. J. *et al.* (1999) Sarcoptic mange in Spanish ibex from Spain. *Journal of Wildlife Diseases* **35**, 647–59.

León Vizcaíno, L., Cubero, M. J., González Capitel, E. *et al.* (2001) Experimental ivermectin treatment of sarcoptic mange and establishment of a mange-free population of Spanish ibex. *Journal of Wildlife Diseases* **37**, 775–85.

Llaneza, L., Fernández, A. and Nores, C. (1996) Dieta del lobo en dos zonas de Asturias (España) que difieren en carga ganadera. *Doñana, Acta Vertebrata* **23**, 201–13.

Loison, A., Gaillard, J. M., Gaillard, J. M. and Jullien, J. M. (1996) Demographic patterns after an epizootic of keratoconjunctivitis in a chamois population. *Journal of Wildlife Management* **60**, 517–27.

Lorenzini, R. and Lovari, S. (2006) Genetic diversity and phylogeography of the European roe deer: the refuge area theory revisited. *Biological Journal of the Linnean Society* **88**, 85–100.

Marco, I. and Lavin, S. (2003) WDA Section News: Pestivirus in chamois from the Catalan Pyrenees (NE Spain) in 2001 and 2002. *Journal of Wildlife Diseases* **39** (Suppl.), 14–15.

Ortega-Alegre, F. and Rodriguez-Benavente, J. (2006) Certificación de la Calidad Cinegética en Andalucía. In J. Carranza and J. M.Vargas, eds., *Criterios para la Certificación de la Calidad Cinegética en España*. Universidad de Extremadura.

Peŕez-Barberia, I. and Garcia-Gonzáles, R. (2004) Rebeco: Rupicapra pyrenaica. In L. M. Carrascal and A. Salvador, eds., *Enciclopedia virtual de los vertebrados españoles*. Madrid: Museo Nacional di Ciencias Naturales.

Randi, E., Alves, P. C., Carranza, J., Miloevi-Zlatanovi, S., Sfougaris, A. and Mucci, N. (2004) Phylogeography of roe deer (*Capreolus capreolus*) populations: the effects of historical genetic subdivisions and recent non-equilibrium dynamics. *Molecular Ecology* **13**, 3071–83.

Rosell, C. and Herrero, J. (2005) *Sus scrofa* Linnaeus, 1758. Jabalí. In L. J. Palomo and J. Gisbert, eds., *Atlas de los Mamíferos Terrestres de España*. Madrid: Dirección General de Conservación de la Naturaleza-SECEM-SECEMU, pp. 306–9.

Royo, L. J., Pajares, G., Álvarez, I., Fernández, I. and Goyache, F. (2007) Genetic variability and differentiation in Spanish roe deer (*Capreolus capreolus*): a phylogeoraophic reassessment within the European framework. *Molecular Phylogenetics and Evolution* **42**, 47–61.

Sáez-Royuela, C. and Tellería, J. L. (1986) The increased population of the wild boar (*Sus scrofa* L.) in Europe. *Mammal Review* **18**, 97–101.

Vargas, J. M., Carranza, J., Lucio, A. J. and Villafuerte, R. (2005) Caza certificada, un reto para el futuro. *Trofeo* **419**, 48–52.

Vicente, J., Höfle, U., Garrido, J. M. *et al.* (2006) Wild boar and red deer display high prevalences of tuberculosis-like lesions in Spain. *Veterinary Research* **37**, 107–119.

20

Ungulates and their management in France

DANIEL MAILLARD, JEAN-MICHEL GAILLARD, A.J. MARK
HEWISON, PHILIPPE BALLON, PATRICK DUNCAN, ANNE LOISON,
CAROLE TOÏGO, ERIC BAUBET, CHRISTOPHE BONENFANT,
MATHIEU GAREL AND CHRISTINE SAINT-ANDRIEUX

France (551 695 km^2) is situated in the south-west of Europe and is divided into 22 administrative regions and 96 departments (each on average 5500 km^2). The climate is temperate, with four biogeographical regions: Atlantic, Continental, Alpine and Mediterranean. The mean density of the human population is 112 inhabitants/km^2 and 76% of the French population lives in cities (www.insee.fr).

France's topography mainly consists of low-lying plains, with 67% of its area below 300 m a.s.l. Uplands (300–500 m a.s.l.) cover 14% and mountains (> 500 m a.s.l.) 20% of the country. Five mountain ranges can be found in France: the Vosges and the Jura in the north-east, the Alps in the south-east, the Massif Central in the centre and the Pyrénées in the south-west. In addition, high mountain areas occur in Corsica.

Open landscapes with various types of agriculture cover 54% of France's area (62% are arable fields, 34% meadows and pastures and 4% vineyards and orchards, www.insee.fr). Forests exploited for timber cover approximately 28% of the land area (15.2 million ha in 2005, Fig. 20.1). The diversity of climatic conditions and topography explains the great number of forest types present. Broadleaved forests occupy about 63.8% of the forested area (with the rest coniferous forests). Of the broadleaved trees, oaks (e.g. *Quercus robur*, *Q. petrae*) are the most common species (29.7%). Beech (*Fagus sylvatica*), chestnut (*Castanea sativa*) and other broadleaved species (maple, ash, black alder, birch) cover 9.3%, 3.6%, and 21.2%, respectively. Of the conifers, maritime pine (*Pinus pinaster*) is the dominant species, covering 9.7% of the forested area, mainly in the south-west of France. Other conifers present are: spruce (*Picea excelsa*), fir (*Abies alba*) 9.7%; other pines: scots pine (*Pinus sylvestris*), corsican pine (*Pinus nigra* ssp. *laricio*) 12.8%; Douglas fir (*Pseudotsuga menziesii*) 2.8% and larch (*Larix europaea*) 1.2%. There are three main types of forest ownership in France: state-owned forest (10%), other

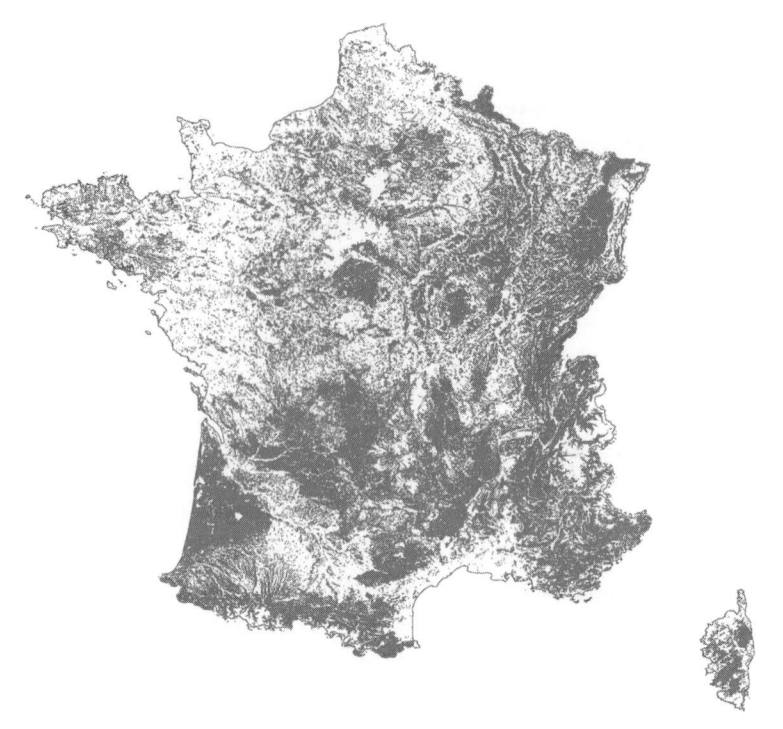

Fig. 20.1 Forestry map. Shaded areas represent forest (data IFN)

public forest (16%) and private forest (74%). The management of ungulates in France varies among these different types of land use and land ownership.

20.1 History, present distribution and genetic origin of ungulate species in France

Six species of native wild ungulates currently occur in France: the roe deer (*Capreolus capreolus*), red deer (*Cervus elaphus*) and the distinct Corsican deer (*Cervus elaphus corsicanus*), the wild boar (Sus scrofa), the Alpine chamois (*Rupicapra rupicapra*) and the related Pyrenean isard (*R. p. pyrenaica*), the mouflon (*Ovis gmelini musimon*) and the Alpine ibex (*Capra ibex ibex*). Three introduced species also occur in France: the fallow deer (*Dama dama*), sika deer (*Cervus nippon*) and Chinese water deer (*Hydropotes inermis*) (probably extinct in the wild). Of these species, all are hunted, except the ibex and the Chinese water deer.

As in most countries of Western Europe and North America (Gill, 1990; McShea *et al.*, 1997), there has been a marked increase in the number and geographical distribution of all ungulate species in France. This tremendous increase in ungulate numbers is likely to have had multiple causes. The most significant causes are likely related to direct management actions. Before 1979, populations of all ungulate species were strongly limited by the hunting pressure, and thus tended to occur at rather low densities. Two important changes in the legislation were made: in 1968 farmers were no longer allowed protect their crops from ungulates themselves, and any damage was compensated by the state (from income from hunters). Further, in 1979 specific management actions were taken to increase the size of ungulate populations:

1. Limitations of the hunting quotas were imposed by law for deer species. Similar rules were applied to mountain ungulates in 1990. Today, the only ungulate species whose management is not quota-based is the wild boar.
2. Selective shooting of young animals (30% of the bag) was recommended to the hunters in order to limit the shooting of adult females.
3. Translocations of ungulates from productive populations to low density populations were repeatedly and intensively carried out all over France for all ungulate species.

There is also clear evidence that the global climate is changing (IPCC, 2002) and this change has led to associated ecological changes (Stenseth *et al.*, 2002; Walther *et al.*, 2002). The negative influence of harsh winters on ungulate population growth has been well documented (see e.g. Sæther *et al.*, 2002; Jacobson *et al.*, 2004; Mysterud and Østbye, 2006), mainly through a decrease in the yearly survival of juveniles, yearlings and old individuals (Gaillard *et al.*, 2000). Consequently, in the case of ungulates in France, the lower frequency of severe winters in the 1990s may have contributed to an increase in the rate of population growth.

Changes in land use resulting in decreasing human presence in mountain and rural areas have also favoured ungulate populations. In the mountains, this situation occurs for all ungulate species resulting in an overlap of up to six ungulate species in certain areas (chamois, ibex, mouflon, roe deer, red deer, wild boar; Loison *et al.*, 2002).

20.1.1 Roe deer

The roe deer is the most abundant ungulate in France, but is absent from Corsica. Formerly restricted to forest habitats, until the 1970s roe deer occurred mainly in north-eastern, central and south-western parts of France. In the mid-1970s, two former NATO military camps (Chizé in the western part of France and Trois Fontaines in the eastern part of France) became National Hunting Reserves and were used as sources for roe deer translocations to other areas with low roe deer densities. In each of the two reserves, the populations of a few hundred adult roe deer were monitored intensively in order to keep the population size constant over time by removing the yearly recruitment (using drive-netting). From these reserves, more

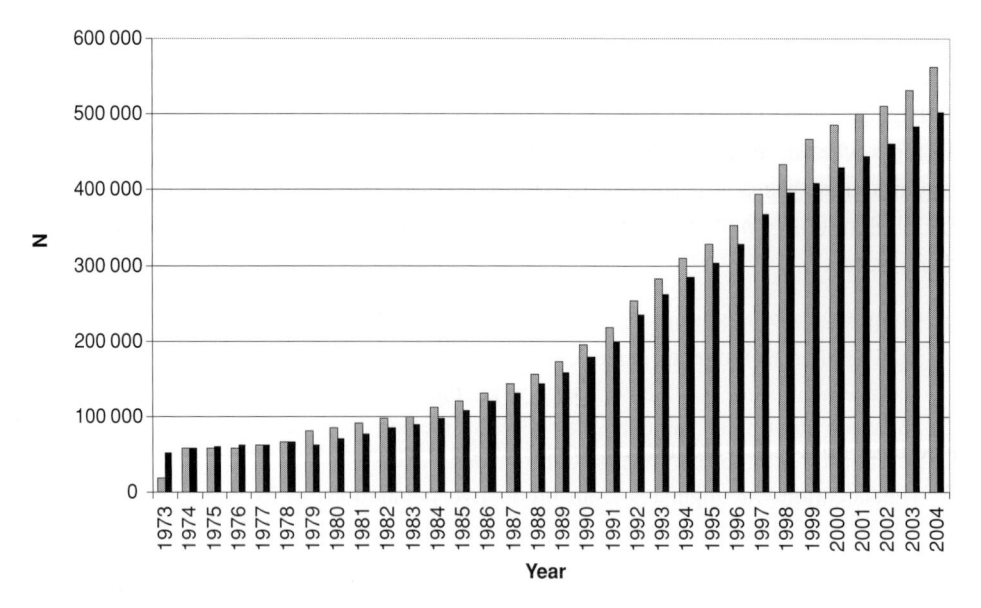

Fig. 20.2 Temporal changes of bag limits (grey bars) and the numbers of killed roe deer declared in each year (black bars) (data 'Réseau Ongulés Sauvages', ONCFS/FNC/FDC)

than 6000 roe deer have thus been captured and reintroduced elsewhere. In most cases, a management plan was set up, involving a non-hunting period immediately after the translocation (for 3 to 5 years) that allowed the populations to build up. Most translocations were highly successful, and have allowed not only an increase in numbers in areas with low density populations, but also the colonisation of new areas by roe deer.

During the 1980s and 1990s, roe deer colonised more open habitats in France. In particular, the number of roe deer markedly increased in agrosystems (field roe deer; Kaluzinski, 1982), in Mediterranean habitats (Maillard et al., 1999) and in mountain areas (Léonard et al., 2002a) in the north-west, south and east of France, respectively, so that roe deer are now present on more than 90% of the total land area of France (Boisaubert et al., 1999).

The spectacular increase in roe deer numbers is well illustrated when considering the number of animals declared shot every year: there has been a more than nine-fold increase from 52 849 roe deer killed in 1973 to 503 089 in 2004, with a mean yearly increase of 4.6% during the last 20 years (Fig. 20.2). We can clearly distinguish three different periods. Before 1979 and the application of the hunting quotas, the number of roe deer hunted was low and stable. Between 1979 and 1996, the number of roe deer hunted increased much faster. Since 1997, the growth rate has decreased markedly. This change in the growth of the declared hunting bag may reflect either a slower growth of roe deer populations, or reluctance among managers to set very high quotas.

However, the high frequency of forest damage attributed to roe deer, the high number of roe deer collisions with cars and the widespread occurrence of density-dependent responses in roe deer populations (Maillard *et al.*, 1989; Toïgo *et al.*, 2006; Zannèse *et al.*, 2006) indicate that there is room for further increase of roe deer quotas.

20.1.2 Red deer

Red deer numbers were at their lowest in the middle of the nineteenth century and red deer had almost disappeared from the south of France, in particular, as a result of the drastic reduction of the forests where they live (8 million ha of forest at the national level in 1800). Soon after the end of World War II, their numbers increased steadily owing to the release of animals from Chambord (80%) and the National Hunting and Wildlife Reserve of La Petite Pierre (respectively in the centre and north-eastern France) as well as from abroad (Germany, Austria and Hungary) in the 1950s and 1960s (Leduc and Klein, 2004). The setting up of a game harvest plan in 1979, limiting the bags, provoked a fast increase in numbers. In 1985, red deer numbers were estimated between 35 000 and 45 000 and in 2000 between 115 000 and 120 000 spread over 21% of France's area (Fig. 20.3), but half of them were concentrated on only 10% of the forested areas.

Originally, as for roe deer, red deer were primarily restricted to the lowest parts of forested areas, as in other countries (Mysterud *et al.*, 2002). As numbers started to increase, red deer also colonised mountainous areas. Nowadays, the highest red deer densities are found in mountain areas (up to about 40 individuals per km^2 in the Pyrénées). Red deer in France have a scattered distribution comprising a large number of small discrete populations (Fig. 20.3).

The number of red deer hunted has markedly increased from the early 1970s to the present: from 5510 in 1973 to 39 968 in 2004, corresponding to a seven-fold increase with a mean yearly increase during the last 20 years of 3.9% (Fig. 20.4). As for roe deer, several distinct periods can be distinguished. Before 1979 and the application of the hunting quotas, the exponential growth rate of the number of red deer hunted was 0.079. Between 1979 and 1983, the number of red deer shot did not show any trend. Between 1984 and 1997, the number of red deer hunted increased as fast as during the period prior to the hunting quotas. Since 1998, the growth rate of the number of red deer declared has decreased markedly. As for roe deer, this change in growth of the hunting bag is likely to reflect a reluctance among managers to set very high quotas.

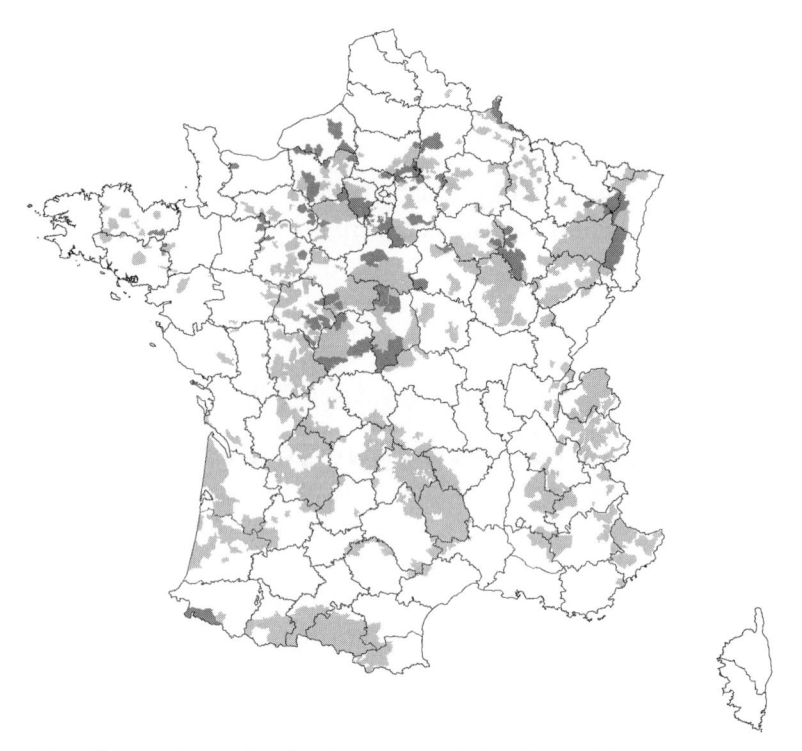

Fig. 20.3 Changes in spatial distribution of red deer from 1900 (in black) to 2000 (in grey) (data "Réseau Ongulés Sauvages', ONCFS/FNC/FDC)

The distinct Corsican deer, smaller than the red deer, may have been introduced to the island of Corsica by the Romans. However, the first records date only from the fourteenth century. Vigne (1992) documented the occurrence of Corsican red deer during the nineteenth century in most areas. It disappeared from Corsica in 1970 and was reintroduced in 1985–7 in the Quenza Park from a stock of animals belonging to the same subspecies from Sardinia. Because of high reproductive success in the park, a population has built up from the first deer released in 1998; hunting is still prohibited.

20.1.3 Fallow deer

The fallow deer was widely represented in Europe before the last glaciation (60 000 to 10 000 BC). It was probably reintroduced to Europe by the Romans from 150 AD (Schaal, 1981). In France, fallow deer mostly occur in enclosures. The largest wild population in France is located in the north-east, in the forest of Illwald (Alsace). This population dates back to 1854 and now numbers more than 1000 deer. Almost half of the national hunting bag (48%) is taken from this population.

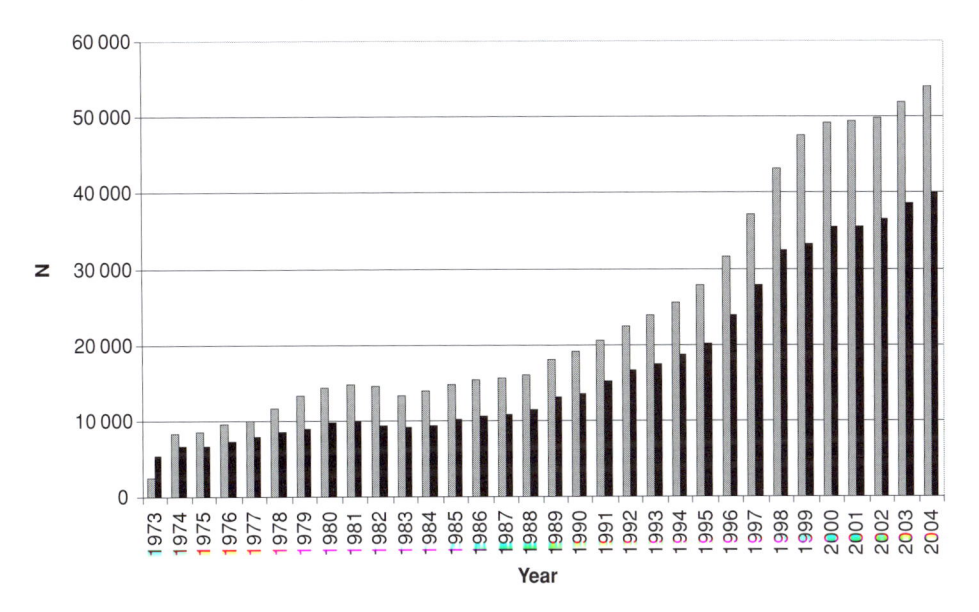

Fig. 20.4 Temporal changes of bag limits (grey bars) and the numbers of killed red deer declared in each year (black bars) (data 'Réseau Ongulés Sauvages', ONCFS/FNC/FDC)

Other populations are developing from animals that have escaped from enclosures throughout France, particularly since the hurricane that hit France in December 1999. However in most departments there is an accepted policy to try to eradicate such free-ranging populations (see Saint-Andrieux et al., 2006 for a recent review of status).

The fallow deer is currently present in 55 French departments (Fig. 20.5).

20.1.4 Sika deer

Native to the Far East (from Manchuria and Japan to Vietnam), the sika deer was widely introduced to Europe. The French populations came from a few individuals presented by the Mikado in 1980. Like fallow deer, sika deer are present in many enclosures, but wild populations are increasing as well (Saint-Andrieux et al., 2006). The largest population is located near Paris, and numbers about 200 deer. The sika deer is currently present in 16 French departments (Fig. 20.6). The development of wild sika deer must be proscribed owing to the risk of hybridisation with consequent loss of genetic integrity of red deer. Furthermore, sika deer enjoy dense forested areas and may cause important forestry damage. The requirement to eradicate escaped animals is very clear in all departments.

448   *European Ungulates*

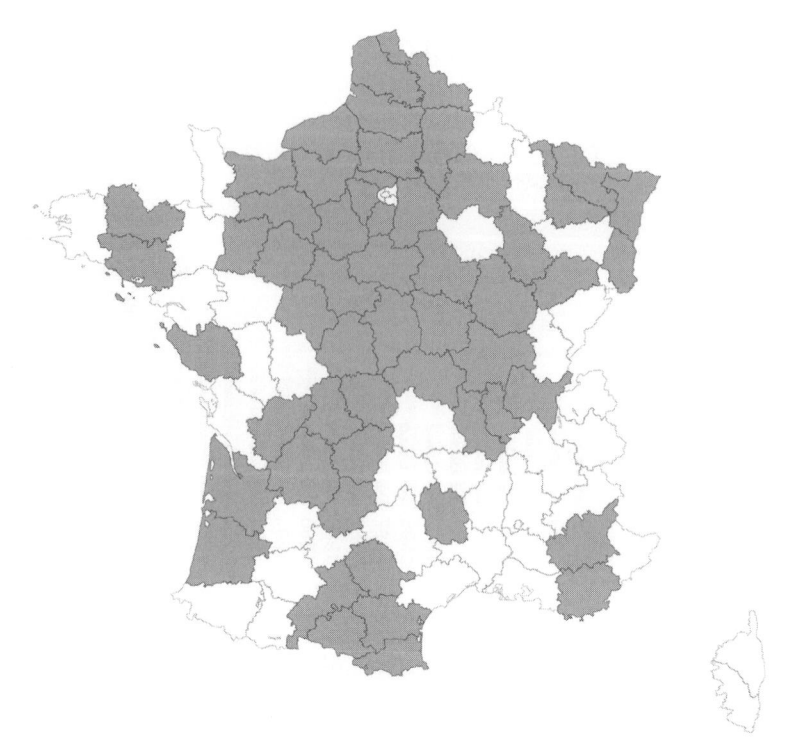

Fig. 20.5 Departments in which fallow deer has been present between 2000 and 2003 (in grey) (data 'Réseau Ongulés Sauvages', ONCFS/FNC/FDC)

20.1.5 *Chinese water deer*

Native to Asia, the first Chinese water deer were introduced in 1954 in an enclosure in western France (Haute-Vienne, near Poitiers). In 1960, a few escaped and formed a wild population which was reinforced between 1965 and 1970 (Duval and Boutin, 1988). The species has been protected since 1974, but the population has probably gone extinct, as there have been no records of them since 2000 in spite of efforts to locate them with the help of local hunters (R. Mauget *pers. comm.*).

20.1.6 *Chamois/Isard*

Originating from Asia, the first *Rupicapra* probably reached south-western Europe towards the end of the Mindel glaciation, 350 000 to 400 000 years ago. It is only during the second half of the Würm period (50 000 to 10 000 BC) that they likely colonised the major part of our continent. During the retreat of the glaciers, chamois reached the mountains. One encounters two species in France (Lovari and Scala, 1980): the chamois and the isard. The former species is naturally present in the

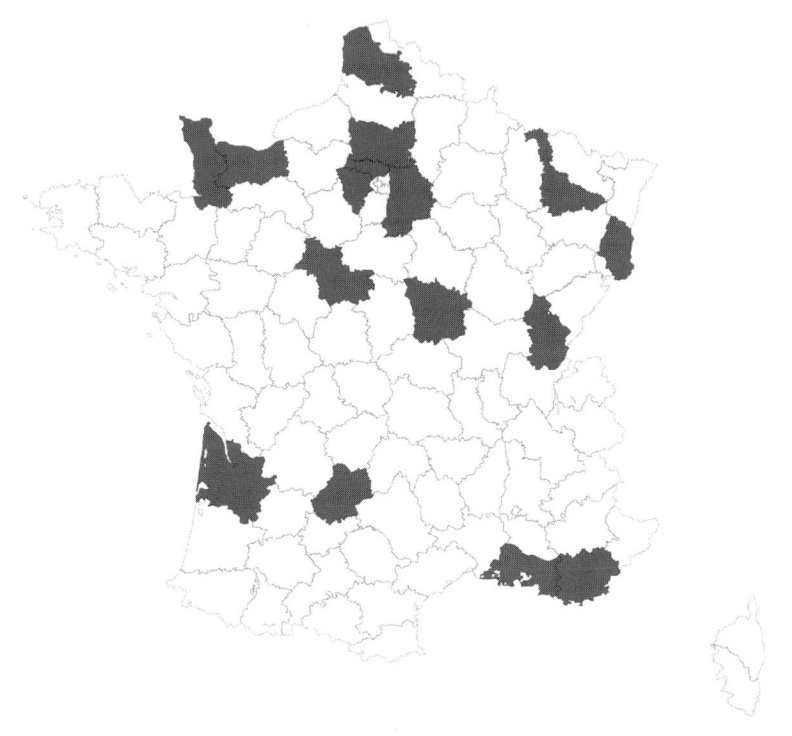

Fig. 20.6 Departments in which sika deer has been present between 2000 and 2003 (in grey) (data 'Réseau Ongulés Sauvages', ONCFS/FNC/FDC)

Alps (about 60 000 chamois), with a distinct subspecies in Chartreuse (*Rupicapra rupicapra cartusana*), and in the Jura (2500 chamois) and was re-introduced in the Vosges in 1956 and in the Massif Central in 1978. The latter species is naturally present in the Pyrenean range (about 25 000 isard) (Fig. 20.7). Chamois occupy a large diversity of habitats and can live at rather low elevations (200 m). However, these animals consistently select habitats with steep slopes.

Hunting quotas for this species have been in operation since 1990. The setting of hunting quotas has been consistently followed by a decrease in the number of animals shot in the first few years, and then by a rapid increase of the hunting bag in more recent years as populations increased in response to the more controlled harvest (Fig. 20.8). This is well exemplified by the management of chamois in the Department of the Alpes de Haute Provence. From 1973 to 1989, an average of 200 chamois were shot yearly but this dropped to 81 chamois in 1990. Afterwards, the number of chamois hunted grew at an exponential rate close to the expected rate for colonising chamois (Loison *et al.*, 2002) to reach 483 chamois in 1998. The application of hunting quotas has allowed chamois–isard to increase both in

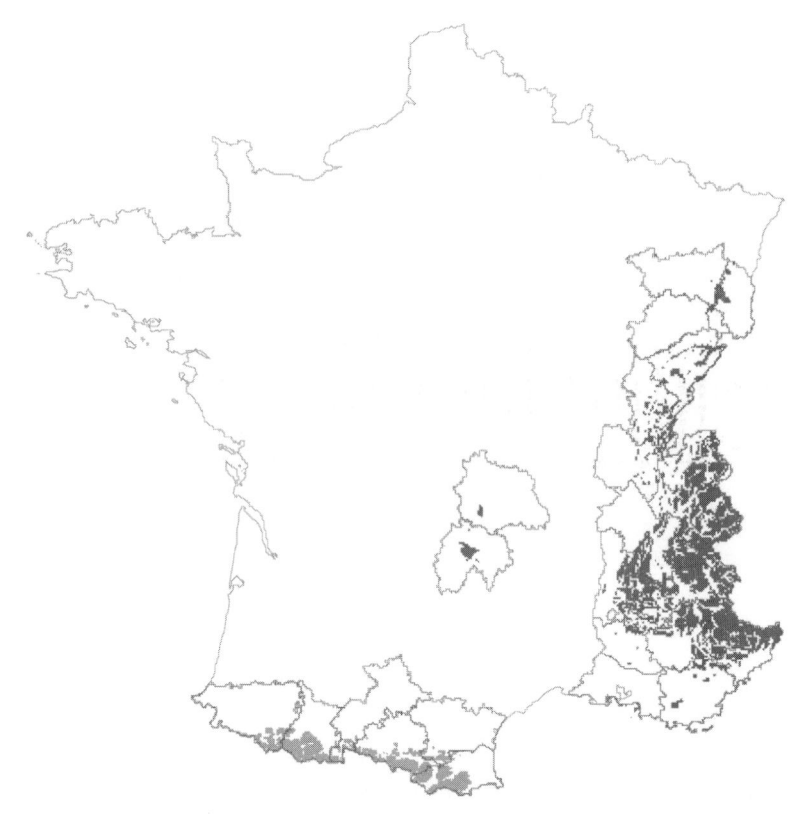

Fig. 20.7 Spatial distribution of Chamois (in light grey) and Isard (in dark grey) (data 'Réseau Ongulés Sauvages', ONCFS/FNC/FDC)

numbers and in spatial distribution. The harvesting of chamois in the Alps increased from 3645 in 1973 to 11 627 in 2004 (with a mean yearly growth during the last 10 years of 1.9%) and of isard in the Pyrenean region from 990 in 1973 to 2582 in 2004 (with a mean yearly growth during the last 10 years of 0.95%). This low growth rate in the Pyrénées could be due to the development of diseases (pestivirus, chlamydiosis, salmonellosis, erhlichiosis) in these populations.

20.1.7 Ibex

The ibex immigrated to France, along the edge of the Alps, during the Riss period (300 000 BC). Two species have occurred in France: *Capra ibex ibex* in the Alps and *Capra pyreneica* in the Pyrénées. This latter species disappeared during the nineteenth century and the former went close to extinction during the same period because of over-harvesting. The first translocation of ibex to the Alps occurred in 1963 in the Vanoise National Park from the Gran Paradiso National Park, in Italy.

(a) Chamois in Alps

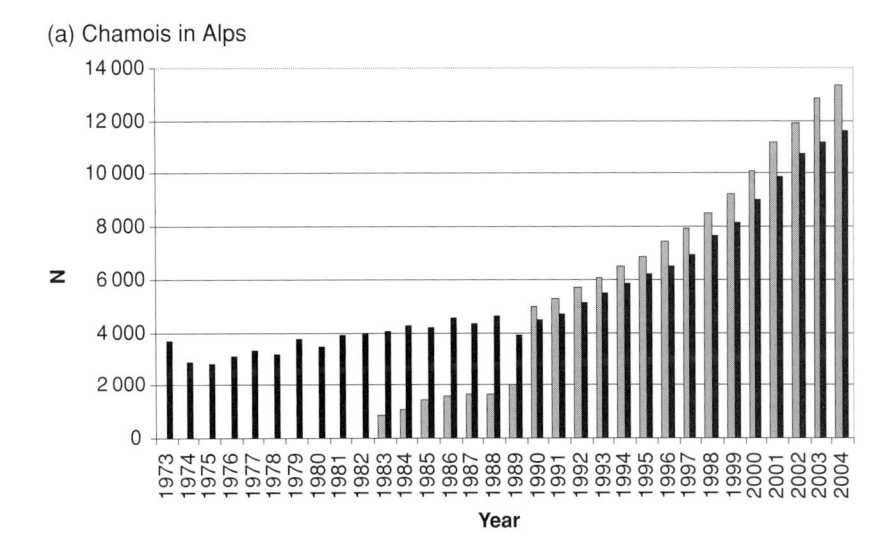

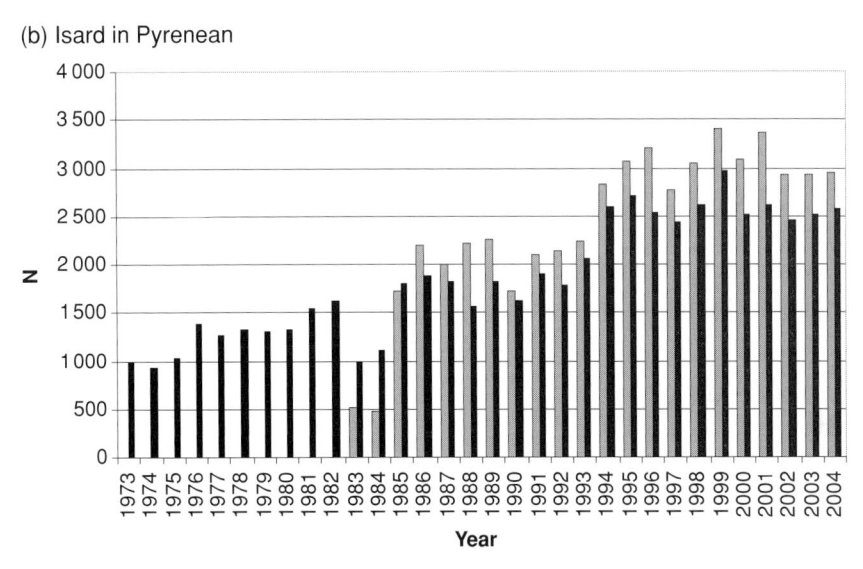

(b) Isard in Pyrenean

Fig. 20.8 Temporal changes of bag limits (grey bars) and the numbers of killed chamois/isard declared in each year (black bars) (data 'Réseau Ongulés Sauvages', ONCFS/FNC/FDC)

Ibex in France are now only found in the Alps and have been protected since 1981. Today, about 10% (3000 individuals) of all Alpine ibex live in France. They are distributed in 20 different populations (Gauthier and Villaret, 1990). Most ibex populations are increasing and their spatial distribution has increased markedly since the 1960s following successful translocations (Fig. 20.9). The success rate of ibex translocations is indeed very high (> 90%).

Fig. 20.9 Spatial distribution of ibex (data 'Réseau Ongulés Sauvages', ONCFS/FNC/FDC).

20.1.8 Mouflon

While all mouflon populations present in continental France today are derived from introductions (Cugnasse *et al.*, 2001), native populations are still present in Corsica. These latter mouflon are thought to originate from feral stock, and would have been brought to Corsica around 5000–6000 BC (Vigne, 1992). Before decreasing below 200 in the 1960s (Pfeffer, 1967), the Corsican populations had numbered more than 2000 mouflon. Hunting has been prohibited since 1953. In addition, the Corsican mouflon benefited from several protections (listed in Appendices II and IV of the European Habitat Directive, in Appendix III of the Bern Convention and Appendix II of the Washington Convention). Nowadays, two distinct populations occur in Corsica: at Bavella in the south with about 200 individuals and at Asco, in the north with about 400. These populations range over an area of 67 350 ha (Fig. 20.10).

The history of mouflon on the mainland is mainly defined by introductions for the purpose of establishing populations for hunting, although some scientists and naturalists have also considered these introductions as a valid way to protect the Corsican mouflon. Mouflon have thus been most often viewed as an additional game species that could occupy a vacant ecological niche. The first release occurred in 1949 in the area of Parc National of Mercantour (Cugnasse *et al.*, 2001). Most of

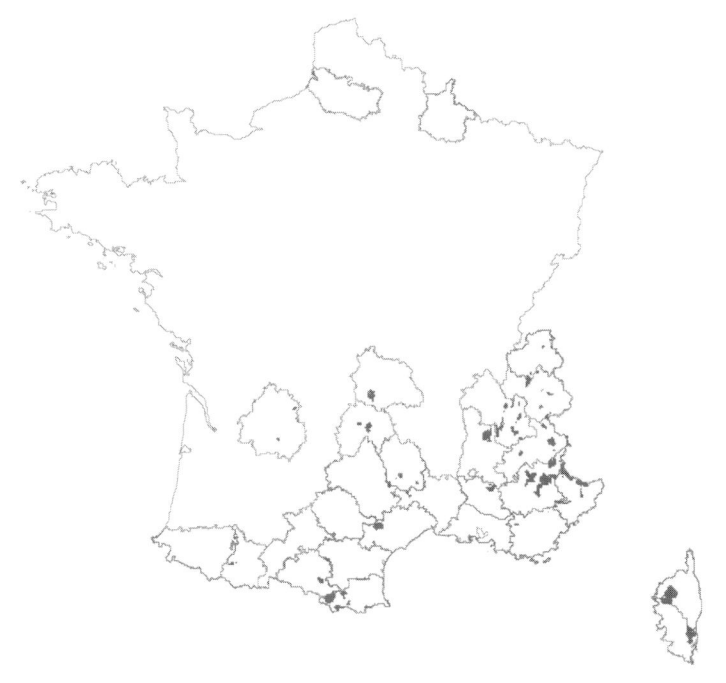

Fig. 20.10 Spatial distribution of mouflon (data 'Réseau Ongulés Sauvages', ONCFS/FNC/FDC)

the populations were founded with mouflon from three French national reserves. Mouflon used in translocations had a mixed genetic origin, including individuals from Sardinia and Corsica which had been crossbred with other domestic or wild sheep (Cugnasse *et al.*, 2001; Garel *et al.*, 2005a). Only three continental populations (one in an enclosure) are composed of pure-bred Corsican mouflon.

Mouflon have a limited geographical distribution in France. On the mainland, about 11 000 mouflon are distributed in 65 populations covering an area of 366 600 ha (Fig. 20.10). Among these populations, 44 range over less than 5000 ha. The largest population occurs in the Massif Central (more than 2500 individuals on 16 000 ha; see Garel *et al.*, 2005b), but the size of 31 populations is less than 50 mouflon, and only six populations number more than 500 animals, with a mean population size of about 200 (for further details see Cugnasse *et al.*, 2001). Indeed, in contrast to other ungulates, the translocations of mouflon have failed in several places, so that the growth of mouflon populations has been limited. Hunting quotas were first set in 1967 for the continental populations and now most populations (n = 46) are harvested. In 2004, more than 2000 mouflon were shot (Fig. 20.11).

The mean yearly increase during the last 10 years was only 1.3%. Two reasons might account for this low growth rate of most populations: introductions to unsuitable habitats which may keep the realised growth rate well below the r-max

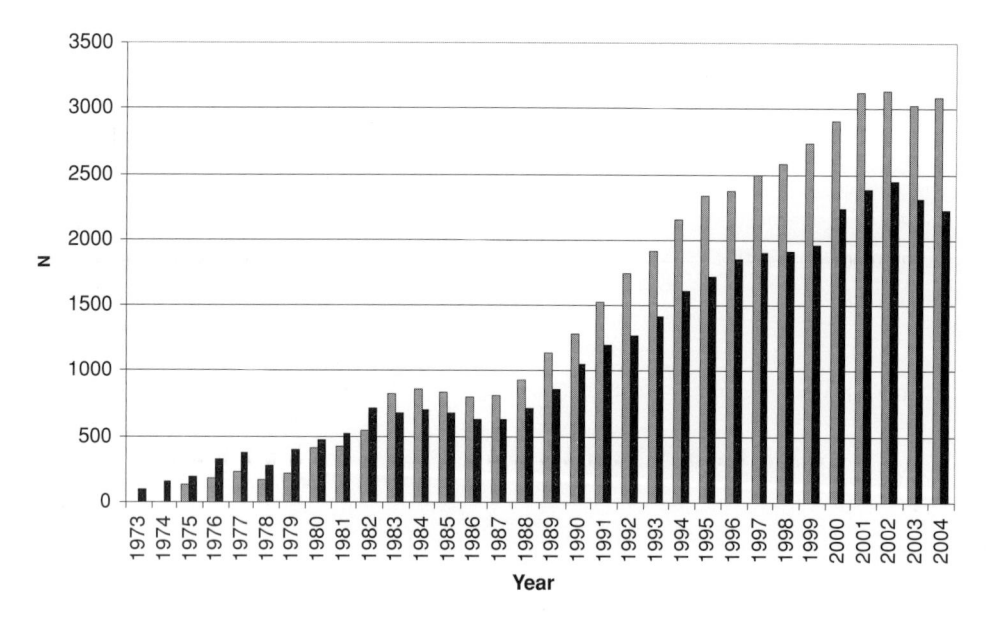

Fig. 20.11 Temporal changes of bag limits (grey bars) and the numbers of killed mouflon declared in each year (black bars) (data 'Réseau Ongulés Sauvages', ONCFS/FNC/FDC).

of mouflon, and conflicts with local interests (e.g. agriculture, forestry) which may lead to poaching.

The mixed origin of mouflon has generated atypical phenotypic and demographic characteristics as compared to native Corsican populations. Thus, the occurrence of hornless females or unusual conformation of horns in males, of twinning, of two lambing periods, and of a first mating at six months of age (Garel et al., 2005a) often characterises mainland populations of mouflon.

20.1.9 Wild boar

Wild boar are widespread in most parts of France, with the highest densities in north-eastern and south-western areas. The species is now common in mountain areas. All populations appear to share the same pattern of population growth, with a steady increase in numbers over time. In Corsica, wild boar are also very abundant. In contrast to deer species, the hunting quotas of wild boar are not required by the law but many departments set quotas for wild boar as well. The number of wild boar declared killed increased markedly from the early 1970s to now: from 36 429 in 1973 to 443 578 in 2004, corresponding to a twelve-fold increase with a mean yearly increase during the last 20 years of 5.1% (Fig. 20.12). Figure 20.12 shows clearly two different periods. From 1973 to 1989 the number of wild boar hunted

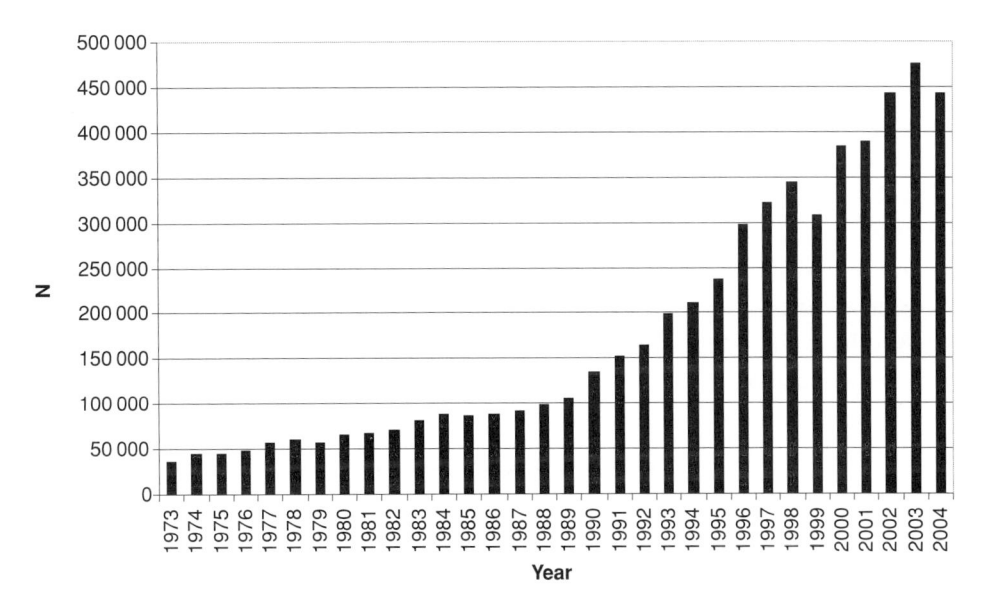

Fig. 20.12 Temporal changes of hunted wild boar (data 'Réseau Ongulés Sauvages', ONCFS/FNC/FDC)

increased slowly and since 1990 the increase has been very high. Many releases of animals from game parks, reserves or high density populations occurred in the 1980s.

The wild boar in France has 36 chromosomes, except in Corsica where it has 38 chromosomes. However, animals from breeding parks, and sometimes those crossed with domestic pigs (n = 38 chromosomes), have been released illicitly by hunting societies, thereby genetically polluting some populations.

20.2 Legislation

The two main laws regulating hunting in France are: the 'Hunting law' of 26 July 2000 and the 'Law on the development of rural territories' of 23 February 2005. These laws have been set to control the organisation of hunting, hunting areas, the shooting licence, the practice of hunting, game management, compensation for game-related damage, vermin, penalty clauses and other special clauses. In terms of management, the novelty of such laws involves the setting of regional guidelines for the management and conservation of wildlife and their habitats, as well as the setting of departmental plans for hunting management. Since 1979 (for deer) and 1992 (for chamois/isard), there has been a legal requirement to produce hunting plans. Since 2005, the new law requires each department to define regional wildlife policies and develop regional management plans for six years.

To be able to hunt, a French hunter needs to have a hunting licence. To obtain a hunting licence in France one should be over 18 and pass an examination organised by the National Hunting and Wildlife Agency (Office National de la Chasse et de la Faune Sauvage – ONCFS). The examination includes both theoretical and practical tests. A training course is required. Afterwards, the certificate is valid for one's entire life. The law also allows a young hunter (between 15 and 18 years of age) to hunt provided he or she is accompanied by a hunter with more than five years experience. Such authorisation is valid only for one year and the young hunter needs to have passed the theoretical examination. The two persons are allowed to carry only one gun.

To have the right to hunt, the hunter must also have subscribed to a Fédération Départementale des Chasseurs (FDC), by paying a federal contribution, variable from one department to another. He/she must have paid also the national or departmental contribution and have insurance. In addition to these compulsory contributions over the whole territory, he/she must contribute to the refunding of agricultural compensations set up by each FDC to balance accounts.

In France, hunting rights are attached to property rights; the hunter must therefore either be the owner of the hunting territory, or rent it for a given period, alone or as a member of a hunting society, or have permission to hunt there free of charge.

In general, all ungulates must be shot with a centre-fire rifle with a minimum of 5.6 mm diameter and a minimum energy (E100) of 1000 J. However, roe deer may be shot with a shotgun and lead shot (smaller than 4 mm) in certain, but not all, French departments (around 20 out of 90 or so) and in some areas, hunting with hounds and falconry or hawking. Use of bows has been authorised for hunting in France for a number of species (roe, fallow, mouflon, etc.) since 1995 (see section 20.6).

In France, the start of the global hunting season is 1 September. The end of all hunting is 28 February. There are specific hunting periods for ungulates (Table 20.1). Dogs can be used only during the global hunting season. Coursing starts on 15 September and ends on 31 March (red deer, roe deer and wild boar). Overall, these laws define a hunting period at the national scale. Within such a period, the exact hunting dates can vary quite a lot among Departments. The exact dates are selected by the 'Préfet de Region'.

20.3 Management objectives

The sustainable management of the fauna and its habitats is of general public interest in France. The practice of hunting, an important sport/recreation activity environmentally, culturally, socially and economically, contributes to the balance

Table 20.1 *Hunting seasons for wild ungulates in France*

Roe deer	15 May–31 Aug. (only stalking or fixed point hunting for bucks), 1 Sept.–28 Feb. (driving and other methods), 1–31 March (only coursing)
Red deer	23 Aug.–28 Feb. (all hunting methods), 1–31 March (only coursing)
Wild boar	15 April–14 August (stalking or fixed point hunting with special authorisation to limit damage), 15 Aug.–28th Feb. (driving and other methods), 1–31 March (only coursing)
Chamois	23 Aug.–28 Feb.
Isards	1 Sept.–28 Feb.
Mouflon	1 Sept.–28 Feb.
Sika deer	23 Aug.–28 Feb.
Fallow deer	1 June–28 Feb.

between the game species, their environment and human activities, by maintaining a balance between the interests of the farming, forestry and hunting lobbies "équilibre agro-sylvo-cynégétique". The principle of the sustainable use of natural resources is central: in return for the sustainable harvest of game species, the hunters have to contribute to the balanced management of the systems in which the game live.

Policies for the management and conservation of wildlife and their habitats are drawn up in each region, with a view to promoting sustainable management, while taking into account regional forestry plans and local agricultural priorities. Objectives to be reached are specified according to the conservation and sustainable management of the game or non-game species and their habitats, and to the coexistence of different uses of nature. An assessment of the main trends in population density and habitat suitability is thus required, as well as the identification of the threats posed to managed species by human activities, and the damage caused to human activities by the managed species.

In line with the regional wildlife policies, management plans are then set up for each department for a renewable period of six years. The plans include in particular:

1. hunting quotas;
2. actions proposed for improving the safety of hunters and non-hunters;
3. actions proposed for improving management of target species (regulation of game releases, supplementary feeding methods, etc.);
4. actions to conserve and/or restore natural wildlife habitats;
5. actions directed towards reaching a balance between hunting, farming and forestry interests.

The balance between these interests is currently a priority in France "équilibre agro-sylvo-cynégétique". This balance involves finding a good match between the sustainable presence of a rich and varied wild ungulate community and the sustainability and profitability of farming and forestry activities. In particular, the law on the development of rural territories (2005) makes provision not only for the compensation of agricultural damage, but also for the possibility of paying for forestry damage if the minimum game harvest quota has not been reached.

20.4 Management structure

The Office National de la Chasse et de la Faune Sauvage (ONCFS) is a public agency under the shared administration of the Ministry of Ecology and Sustainable Development (MEDD) and the Ministry of Agriculture. The ONCFS, created in 1972, ensures the development of wildlife stocks and promotes hunting in accordance with sustainable harvesting practices. The main role of the ONCFS involves:

1. the monitoring of wildlife and the environment by ONCFS employees (1760), as well as the control of hunting policies carried out by national wildlife protection officers;
2. technical support to administrations, associations and people involved in rural development to assess the distribution, the trends in numbers and the health status of wildlife, as well as the validation of hunting licences and the application of legal rules aimed to integrate wildlife better into public policies;
3. applied research and experimentation for the conservation, restoration and management of wildlife and their habitats, both at national and international levels.

In each department, there is a private association: the Departmental Hunters' Federation (FDC). The FDCs are concerned with the improvement of hunting conditions, as well as the protection and management of wildlife species and habitats. They (1) ensure the promotion and defence of hunting and the interests of their members, (2) lend their support to the ONCFS for the prevention of poaching, (3) provide information, education and technical support to land managers and hunters, (4) coordinate the actions of hunters' associations, (5) carry out actions to prevent game-related damage and solve problems of compensation, (6) train potential hunters to prepare for the hunter's examination certificate, and (7) coordinate specialised hunting associations (such as the National Big Game Hunters' Association, the Mountain Hunters' Association, the National Falconers' and Hawkers' Association, the National Wolf-hunting Lieutenants' Association, the Federation of Hound Hunters' Associations, the Archery Hunters' Federation, the Hunting Society, the National Union of Approved Trappers of France, the National Union for the Use of Bloodhounds).

Regional Hunters' Federations (FRC) ensure the representation of FDC members at the regional level. They lead and coordinate actions for the preservation of wildlife species and habitats. They contribute to the definition of the official policies of wildlife and habitat management of a given region (ORGFH).

The National Hunters' Federation (FNC) ensures the representation of the FDC and FRC at the national level. This association ensures the promotion and defence of hunting as well as the representation of hunting interests. The FNC coordinates the actions of the FDC and FRC and is involved in the compensation process for game-related damage.

To carry out rational management, the different partners sometimes gather together in voluntary structures which can include several neighbouring departments when management is focused on large species such as red deer, roe deer, wild boar, chamois/isard or mouflon. The 'Groupement d'Intérêt Cynégétique' (GIC, grouped local hunting association) are independent structures which pool together several hunters' associations (Approved Communal Hunting Associations or private associations depending on the department; see below) in order to apply the same management methods or actions across a wide hunting area. These structures may be financially supported by the FDC. The first GIC was set up in 1957 and since then 679 GICs have been created (268 to manage wild boar, 251 roe deer, 111 red deer, 38 chamois/isard and 11 mouflon, data from FNC-FRC-FDC). The GICs contributed significantly to the development of ungulate populations in France. Indeed, most of the releases were undertaken within the framework of these GIC which allowed populations to increase by prohibiting hunting for between three and five years just after the release.

20.5 Management organisation

The Regional Wildlife and Habitat Policies (ORGFH) required under the 2005 legislation are established by each Regional Environment Agency (DIREN) and the ONCFS after discussion with the local and regional authorities and are validated by the Government ('Préfet de Region').

The management plans at the department level are drawn up by the FDC in partnership with the owners, managers and users of the hunting areas, taking into account the departmental agricultural and forestry land management rules. After the assessment by the departmental hunting and wildlife council, the management plan is validated by the 'Préfet de Département'. The plans are implemented by the FDC under the supervision of the 'Préfets'.

In each department, a hunting commission has to fix the quota for a given species each year. Each holder of a right to hunt can ask to be assigned an individual shooting plan. This commission includes local administrators, hunters, farmers, foresters, conservationists and experts. The hunting quota areas are fixed in relation to the economic value of the forest in most areas and the population density in agreement with the Departmental plans of hunting management. The 'Préfet' has the legal power to take the final decision concerning the hunting quotas.

These quotas are numerical and, in some departments, may also specify numbers by age- or sex-class as well as overall quotas. It determines for each species the maximal number of animals that the hunter is allowed to kill, and the minimal number that he or she must harvest to control numbers and limit damage. Although the department may have management plans lasting six years, the shooting plan is usually annual but can also be valid for a period of three years. It is actually implemented and controlled by the issuing of the determined number of official tags that must be attached to the hindleg of the shot animal before its transportation.

The minimum charge for each tag (equivalent to a licence to cull an individual animal) is defined at the national level and depends on the species. However, each FDC can increase the cost of the tag to raise funds to be used to pay compensation for damage caused by ungulates (Section 20.8).

Management is usually carried out by management units covering many hunting territories. The departments are divided into management units that are monitored by the FDC, with the technical assistance from the ONCFS. Although these management units should ideally be defined based on the spatial distribution of the populations and the type of land use (i.e. agricultural versus forestry), they are mostly based on natural boundaries and administrative limits. These management units can differ among species, although a given management unit is sometimes used for very different game species (e.g. hare and roe deer). The management unit typically includes a set of communal associations or private groups of hunters.

As noted above, in France, hunting rights are attached to property rights; the hunter must therefore either: 'own the hunting territory (or must lease it for a given period, alone or as a member of a hunting society), or be a member of Approved Communal Hunting Associations (ACCA).'

This latter system, present in 29 departments (over a third of the country), requires hunters to join in a single association per commune, which potentially covers all the lands in the commune (private or public). It allows hunting to be coordinated in large areas, and to prevent management disintegration. All landowners are legally members of ACCA. The list of such departments is defined by the minister in charge of hunting based on proposals by the 'Préfets', ACCA aims to organise hunting in the commune, to develop game and wildlife while respecting the balance with farming and forestry interests, to contribute to the conservation of habitats, to educate the hunters, to regulate pests and to check that hunting quotas are respected. The FDCs coordinate the ACCA actions.

In the departments with ACCAs, the hunters do not pay for a hunting-lease, but pay a subscription to the association which gives them the right to hunt over the whole district, except on the 10% classified as refuges and on private grounds excluded from hunting. State lands include protected areas such as National Parks (mostly in mountain areas), Nature Reserves or Hunting and Wildlife Reserves in which the hunting is prohibited (the only notable exception being the National Park of Cévennes where deer quotas are fixed by the park). Areas bordering the national parks are quite heavily hunted. It was thought that such a system would function as a source–sink system (Pulliam, 1988), with individuals from the high density protected areas dispersing towards low density surrounding areas, hence allowing managers to control ungulate abundance within protected areas. However, contrary to this expectation, protected areas have played the role of refuges where ungulates have increased in density instead of dispersing.

As in the USA (see e.g. Wright, 1999) and also in some other European countries (Italy, Chapter 21), this situation has led to lively discussion on the question of whether or not culling ungulates within national parks should be permitted. The problem is especially critical for wild boar which has the highest reproductive output of all ungulates in France and thereby the highest potential yearly increase. In the departments organised into ACCA, the hunters must not hunt on 10% of the surface area and similar problems of very high local density of ungulates are likely to occur.

A certain number of National Hunting and Wildlife Reserves are maintained by law. In such areas, the ONCFS coordinates and carries out research and experimentation on wildlife and their habitats, often in partnership with other research organisms (Cemagref, CNRS, INRA, universities, etc.). Nine study sites focused on ungulates are currently managed by the ONCFS: Chizé and Trois-Fontaine (roe deer in lowland forest); La Petite Pierre (red and roe deer in upland forest: Vosges); Les Bauges (chamois, mouflon, roe and red deer in high mountains: Alps); Caroux-Espinouse (mouflon in a Mediterranean mountain environment); Orlu (Isard in high mountains: Pyrénées); Belledonne-Sept Laux (Ibex in high mountains: Alps); Asco and Bavella (mouflon in Corsican mountains).

During the last 30 years, the number of hunters has followed an inverse trend compared to the numbers of ungulates (Lecocq and Meine, 1998). The number of hunters in France has decreased from 2 000 000 30 years ago to 1 313 000 in 2005 (2.1 per 100 inhabitants). At the same time, the mean age of hunters has increased (50 years of age in 2002 versus 45, 20 years ago). In 2002, about three-quarters of hunters came from a family where hunting is traditional. These statistics clearly indicate that in the future, hunters will have increasing difficulties in controlling ungulate populations by themselves.

20.6 Hunting practice

Depending on the landscape features, different types of hunting are used. To hunt deer and wild boar that live most often in forested habitats, the most common hunting procedure involves drives with dogs. Generally, in the north of France, small dogs are used and they are replaced by big dogs in the south since the areas are larger, and the beaters are generally fewer. Few hunters use stalking or hunting from high blinds for these species. The hunting of mountain ungulates is usually done by stalking. Bows are increasingly used in France. Coursing is a traditional hunting method dating back to antiquity in which the animal is tracked down by a pack of hounds accompanied by a rider until exhaustion. This hunting method is mostly used in the large forests of Central and West France (formerly royal forests).

20.6.1 Roe deer

Drive hunting, silent or not, with many beaters sometimes accompanied by small dogs, is the most common hunting method in France to hunt roe deer. Techniques of 'silent hunting', (stalking or hunting from a fixed point), which were used mainly in the north-east, are now common elsewhere, in particular with the development of archery. Silent hunting is particularly common at the end of summer for trophy-hunting of adult males.

Shooting with bullets (or single balls from shotguns) is required by law in most departments, and shooting with lead shot is still authorised in some areas. Some 92 hunts are based on roe deer coursing with at least 30 hounds. Falconry with golden eagles is performed in south-western France, but only rarely. The largest roe deer harvests occur in the north-east and south-west of France (Fig 20.13a).

20.6.2 Red deer

As for roe deer, methods for hunting red deer are either drive hunting, stalking or fixed point hunting. Some 30 hunts do red deer coursing, with at least 30 hounds accompanied by two huntsmen. Coursing represents about 20% of the national harvest of the subadult and adult males. Females are not hunted using coursing. The largest harvests occur in the large productive forests of Central France (Fig. 20.13b).

20.6.3 Fallow deer

Since a management aim in most departments is to attempt to eradicate free-ranging populations of fallow deer, a large quota is commonly allocated to allow as many hunters as possible to shoot a fallow deer. In some departments there is no shooting plan for fallow deer because fallow deer have to be destroyed when they escape from enclosures. In 2004, a total of 1380 and 1420 fallow deer were hunted outside and within enclosures, respectively. Bow hunting is commonly used to hunt fallow deer within enclosures.

(a) Roe deer

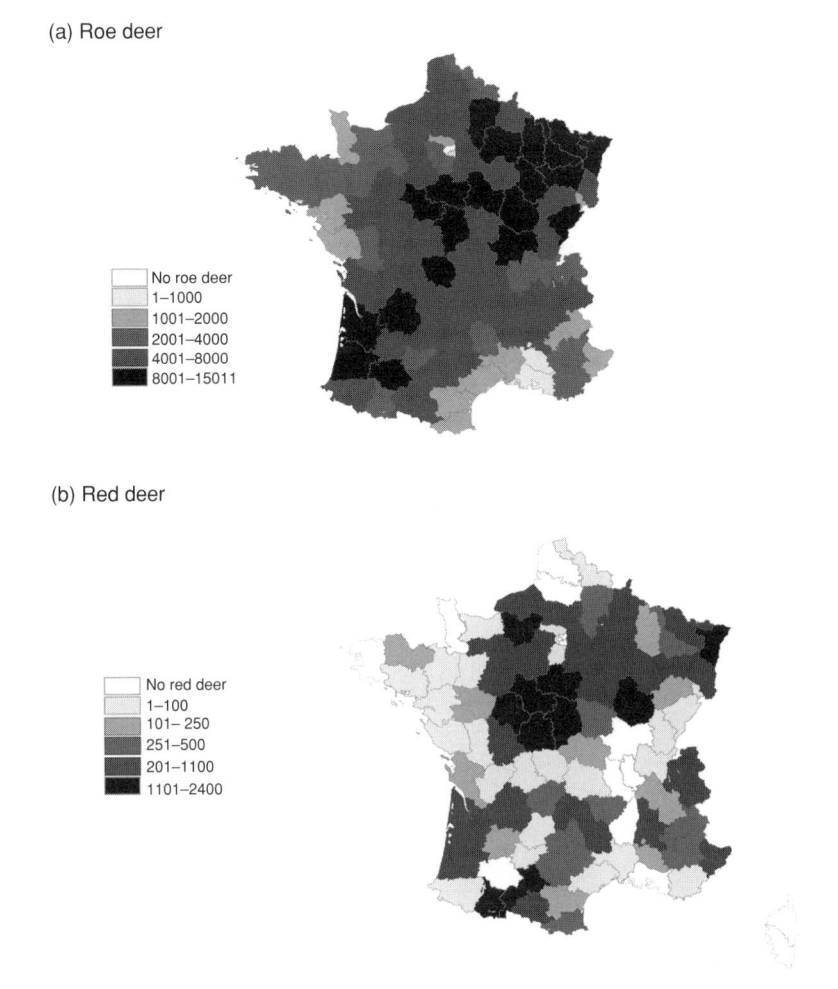

No roe deer
1–1000
1001–2000
2001–4000
4001–8000
8001–15011

(b) Red deer

No red deer
1–100
101– 250
251–500
201–1100
1101–2400

Fig. 20.13 Number of animals hunted per Department in 2005 (data 'Réseau Ongulés Sauvages', ONCFS/FNC/FDC)

20.6.4 Sika deer

In 2003, 145 sika deer were harvested outside parks or enclosures, corresponding to a 1.7-fold increase within 10 years. In parks and enclosures, a total of 146 deer were harvested in 2003.

20.6.5 Chamois/Isard

The most common way of hunting chamois and isard is stalking. However, in contrast to deer species, the hunting bags at the departmental level are consistently biased towards adult males (2.1 to 2.7 males:1 female in Alps) when no qualitative

464   *European Ungulates*

(c) Chamois/Isard

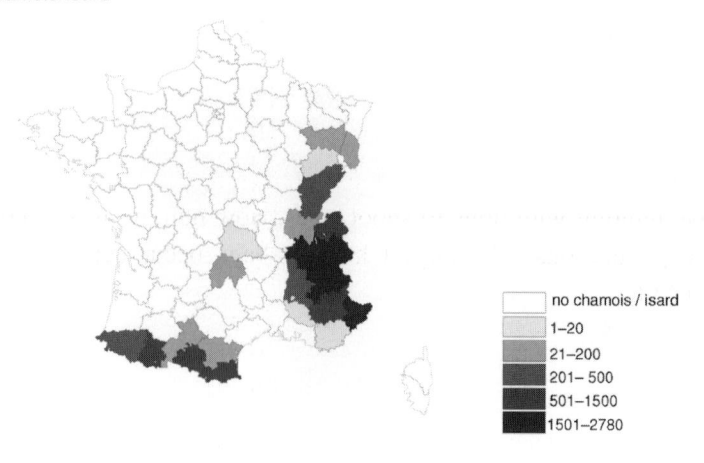

no chamois / isard
1–20
21–200
201–500
501–1500
1501–2780

(d) Mouflon

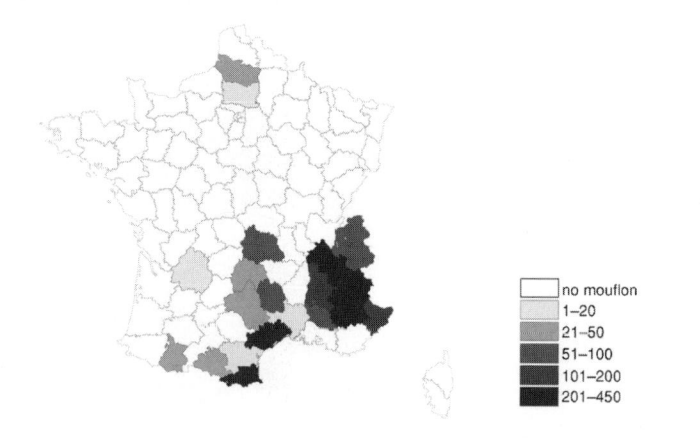

no mouflon
1–20
21–50
51–100
101–200
201–450

(e) Wild boar

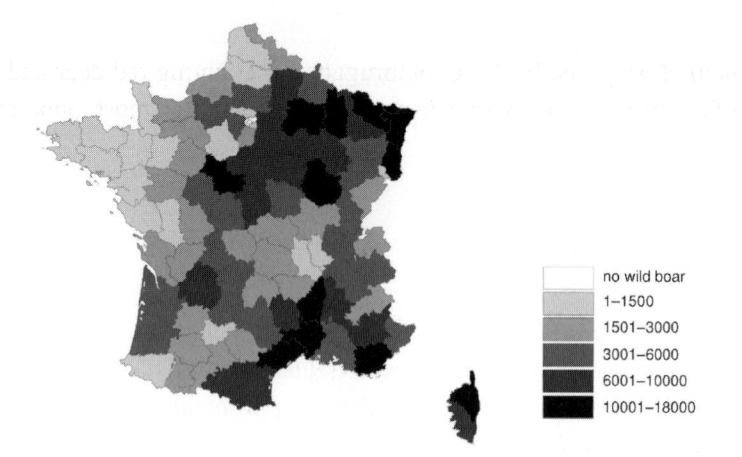

no wild boar
1–1500
1501–3000
3001–6000
6001–10000
10001–18000

Fig. 20.13 (*cont.*)

hunting plan is set (Léonard *et al.*, 2002b). Managers increasingly use sex- and age-specific quotas to correct for such biases (Fig. 20.13c).

20.6.6 Mouflon

Rams are shot for their trophies so the usual hunting procedure is stalking. Hunters use drive hunting with dogs to shoot ewes. Bow hunting is also commonly used in some populations. The largest hunting bags occur across four departments (Fig. 20.13d).

20.6.7 Wild boar

As for roe deer and red deer, methods for hunting wild boar are mainly drive hunting, and, exceptionally, stalking or fixed point hunting. As for red deer, 30 hunts do wild boar coursing. The analysis of the hunting bag reveals that 50% of shot animals are aged less than one year and 80% less than two years. While there is no annual shooting plan, an assessment of the harvests in each management unit is made in the middle of the hunting season (mid-November). This allows managers to assess the population trend as compared to previous years and, in relation to that, set an earlier or later date of closure for hunting. The largest bags occur in the south-east of France, in Corsica and in north-east France (Fig. 20.13e).

20.7 Monitoring methods: population abundance and condition

Traditionally, ungulates in France have been managed by censusing populations. Several hunting-related methods were thus used to assess the population size of ungulates in the 1970s and 1980s (see Cemagref, 1984 for a review).

The methods most commonly used derive from drives. Total or partial drives (Denis, 1985) and the *Approche et Affûts combinés* (combined stalking and observations) method proposed by De Crombrugghe for counting red deer and applied in a modified version to chamois/isard were among the most popular methods. Counting at feeding places was also used for wild boar (Vassant *et al.*, 1990).

Such ad hoc methods provided only a single yearly value, since replication of these counts is difficult due to logistical problems (large number of people involved and time required), hence no indication of sampling variation is generally available. Tests using known reference populations revealed the low accuracy of these methods for all species studied. In all cases studied so far, population size assessed using these counting procedures led to great underestimations. For example, in the enclosed population of Trois Fontaines, only 30% of the marked roe deer were counted during a total drive. Likewise, Siméon and Houard (1987) reported a marked underestimation (> 50%) with the *Approche et Affûts combinés* method for red deer as compared to helicopter censuses. Similarly, in Les Bauges reserve, Houssin *et al.* (1994) found a marked underestimation of the *Pointage-flash* method as compared to capture–mark–recapture estimates. Lastly, Toïgo (1998) found that population size was increasingly underestimated (by up to 60%) as population size of the ibex in Belledone increased. All these results clearly indicate that the use of such ad hoc methods for ungulates only provides a minimum number rather than an accurate estimate of the total population size, and the degree of underestimation increases with increasing population size. Such methods are obviously not appropriate when managers are dealing with high density populations.

The large increase of all ungulate populations in the 1980s can thus be linked to the strong underestimation of population size obtained from these counting methods that were very popular at that time. Indeed, hunting quotas were set in direct relation to estimates of population sizes which were strongly underestimated. Such an over-conservative management is partly the cause of the abundance of ungulates in France today.

The realisation of the problems inherent with these counting methods came as a result of the increasing economic problems posed by the high densities of ungulates present. We are now facing a situation requiring the management of high abundance in order to limit conflicts (such as car accidents, forest and crop damage, or diseases). This has led to an sharp change in management policies during the 1990s. After having recommended the use of very conservative management rules to hunters in the 1980s in order to increase ungulate populations in France (by using counts as a monitoring tool and also by recommending the shooting of young rather than of adult females), the management experts sought a change in management actions so as to limit the abundance of ungulates. Such a shift required new management tools, as the new situation cannot be managed by the use of the minimum size of a given ungulate population.

In response to this situation, two possible non-exclusive solutions are available: (1) using an accurate census method, or (2) focusing on both the overall performance of an ungulate population and the quality of its habitat, rather than focusing only on population size.

The concept of indicators of ecological changes is based on the observation that well-established populations of large mammals are often faced with decreasing per capita resources and, as a result, exhibit density-dependent responses in a predictable way (Fowler 1981, 1987; Eberhardt, 1977, 2002). At low density, an ungulate population increases at a rate close to the maximum r (r-max, see Caughley, 1977) that is defined by the species life history tactics. As it increases in size, the population has an increasing impact on its habitat. At some density threshold that depends mainly on the available resources (Van Horne, 1983), individual performance (phenotypic quality, reproductive output) will decrease. At a certain density, no more population growth is observed because mortality and recruitment compensate each other. Such changes of population dynamics with increasing abundance are well described (e.g. Gilpin and Ayala, 1973).

When moving along the population size trajectory from colonisation to saturation, several indicators will track ecological changes that occur either in the animal or in the habitat component of the system (see Morellet *et al.*, 2007 for further details). The potential number of such indicators is almost endless, but only some have been tested and validated empirically. As defined by Waller and Alverson (1997) indicators of ecological changes should be 'efficient and reliable indicators capable of serving as "early warning signs" of impending ecological change' (see also Cairns *et al.*, 1993). So far, those indicators of ecological changes which have been researched have been specifically those developed for roe deer (Cederlund *et al.*, 1998). The indicators which have been validated include measures of trends in population abundance (the kilometric index; Vincent *et al.*, 1991), in animal condition (winter fawn body mass; Gaillard *et al.*, 1996; hind foot length, Toïgo *et al.*, 2006; Zannèse *et al.*, 2006), in population productivity (recruitment in autumn; Vincent *et al.*, 1995), and in the browsing intensity (Morellet *et al.*, 2001).

20.8 Damage

In France, since 1968, the law requires that farmers receive compensation for agricultural damage caused by wild boar and cervids. In each department, the FDC is in charge of raising funds from hunters for this compensation. The damage is declared by the farmers and the compensation is estimated by experts employed by the FDC. The total amount of compensation for wild boar damage increased in close parallel with the number of wild boar hunted. From a total amount of EUR 2482042 in 1973, hunters had to pay EUR 21634000 in 2004/2005 (Figs. 20.14 and 20.15). Wild boar are responsible for 87% of the total amount paid for big game damage. Red deer can also very often be seen foraging on agricultural lands, and may cause high levels of crop damage (10% of the total amount paid). The spatial distribution of agricultural damage is not homogeneous in France (Fig. 20.16).

Red deer (a mixed feeder) and roe deer (a typical browser) damage trees (by bark stripping for the red deer and twig browsing for both roe and red deer). According to the law on the development of rural territories (2005), forest owners are now in a position to demand: (1) compensation for forest damage, or (2) funds to protect their trees. However, these compensations for the private foresters depend on some

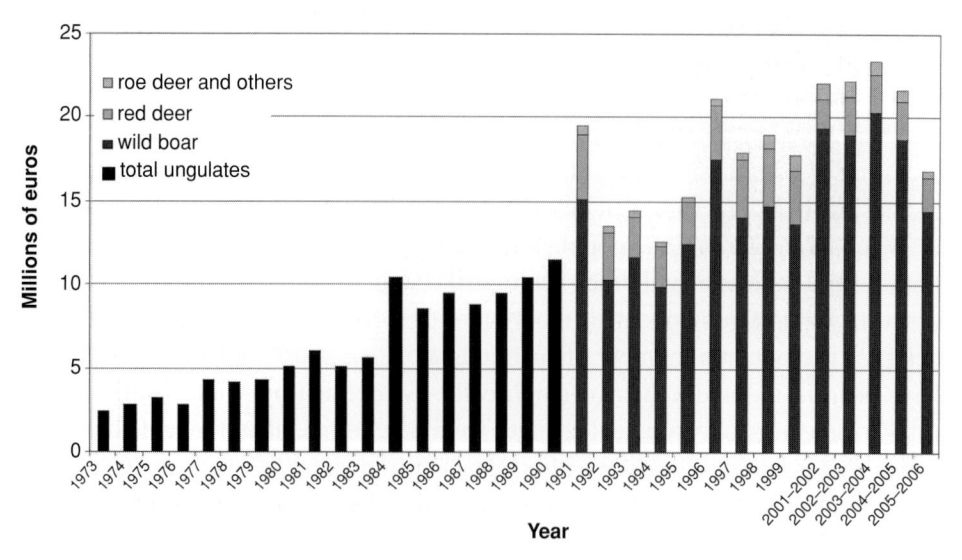

Fig. 20.14 Amount of damage compensation by animal species (data ONCFS/FNC/FDC)

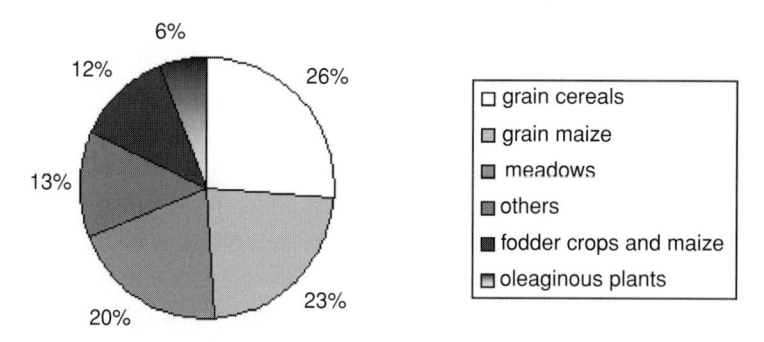

Fig. 20.15 Distribution of damage costs by type of crops in 2004–2005 (data FNC/FDC)

specific conditions: (1) damage to the trees by deer must be proved, and (2) the local hunters must have shot the minimum quota of deer for the year. This system is being set up; currently compensation for damage to forestry is provided in France only very rarely.

Estimates of the number of ungulate collisions with cars has increased from 3700 in 1984 to 23 500 in 2004 (6% red deer, 70% roe deer and 24% wild boar); this represents a minimum number because many (perhaps most) collisions are not even reported (Vignon and Barbarreau, 2008). Most of the collisions (62%) take place on departmental roads, 21% on the motorways and 17% on the national roads. The risk of collision differs on the different types of roads:

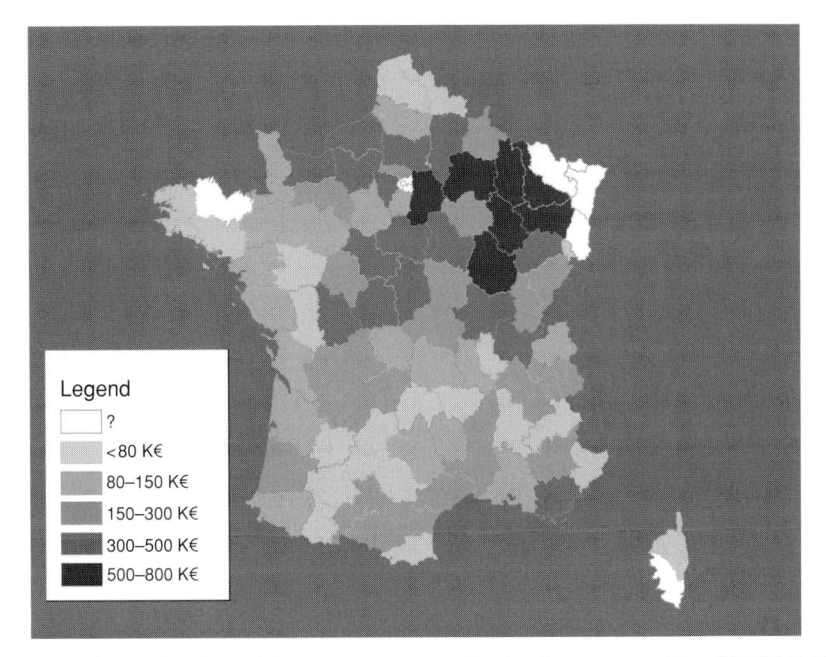

Fig. 20.16 Distribution of damage compensation by department (data FNC/FDC)

- 7 collisions/100 km on the motorways;
- 19 collisions/100 km on the national roads;
- 2 collisions/100 km on the department roads.

Total damage is >EUR 100 million/year; 20 people died in 2006 and 340 were injured.

20.9 Supplementary feeding

In France, supplementary feeding of big game species has two purposes: first, to reduce crop damage by wild boar. In this case, supplementary feeding is aimed at diverting animals from crops and can improve the balance between farmland and hunting activities (Vassant et al., 1992; Calenge et al., 2004). Feeding with grain is justified only during periods of crop vulnerability. It is used to limit damage to maize during the sowing period and when cereals are at the milky-pasty stage (April to October) and to prevent damage to vineyards (July to September). Grain is spread in the forest, more than 300 m away from the edge of any field. The supply must be adjusted to consumption, and thus to the number of wild boar. The method is effective and is very popular.

Secondly, supplementary food is provided as a complement to natural food resources so as to improve the population performance of a given population of big game. In some areas supplementary feeding can be used to compensate for especially poor habitat quality, for instance due to a very harsh winter or a very severe drought. Such practices should, however, be restricted to exceptional climatic events. The 'Préfets' are increasingly prohibiting supplementary feeding during the hunting season. Indeed, some managers feed wild boar simply to attract them on to their hunting grounds, thereby leading to an overabundance of wild boar and hence an increase in crop damage. The shooting of ungulates in the immediate proximity of artificial feeding sites is prohibited at the national level since 1 April 1986.

20.10 Future challenges

Two major lines of research are required in order to further develop practical management tools: first, we currently have several indicators of ecological changes that provide useful information on the relationship between ungulate populations and their habitat and that have been validated for roe deer and are being validated for red deer (Bonenfant et al., 2002), chamois/isard (Loison et al., 2006), ibex (Toïgo et al., 1996), and mouflon (Garel et al., 2005b). However, these indicators are interpreted in a sequential way, that is, the temporal variation of each indicator is analysed independently and at the end a synthesis is carried out in an empirical way. We still need to develop a multivariate quantitative synthesis that would integrate all the indicators measured within a single analysis in order to assess possible interactions among indicators. Moreover, most of these indicators of ecological change have been validated for single populations of ungulates, while more and more sympatric ungulate species are now developing in some contexts, mainly in mountainous areas.

Secondly, the approach based on the monitoring of indicators of ecological change has been validated in well-defined populations at a small scale (a few thousand hectares). Preliminary applications at the departmental scale have shown that changes in the sampling design (involving even more standardised procedures and lower sampling intensity) will be required. In addition, spatial heterogeneities, which are more pronounced at a large spatial scale, need to be accounted for in the sampling design. Lastly, to use this approach based on indicators of ecological change as an adaptive management strategy (see Williams et al., 2002), clear management objectives have to be set, and, ideally, experimental manipulations of population abundance should be carried out. Ungulates, at least in the French context, seem to be especially well suited to such an approach because the consequences of errors in management strategy (which cannot be avoided during the necessary trial–error process of the first years of monitoring) are expected to be very low (no risk of population extinction).

The general increase of ungulate populations has enabled the rapid development of large carnivore populations: the lynx in the Vosges and in the Jura and the wolf in the Alps. A study initiated by the ONCFS, the Mercantour National Park, the CNRS and the FDC of the South Alps (Mercantour National Park) is currently aiming to quantify the impact of wolf predation on the populations of wild ungulates (red deer, chamois, mouflon and roe deer). In the near future hunting quotas will have to be set taking into account the predation rates if population declines due to mortality caused by both hunters and large carnivores are to be avoided.

In a country so very diverse in terms of landscape, such as France, management should be context-specific and future recommendations may differ for different species and different areas. Such recommendations should be specific to a given management unit in the Departmental Hunting Plans, in line with the regional orientations for the management and conservation of wildlife and its habitats (ORGFH). One of the new challenges is the management of a guild of ungulate species rather than the management of a single species on a given area. This challenge is especially important in mountain areas, where the number of species coexisting is the largest (Loison *et al.*, 2002).

Monitoring must be maintained to prevent the development of diseases such as classical swine fever or brucellosis for wild boar, or keratoconjunctivitis, pestivirus infections and other abortive diseases for mountain ungulates.

References

Boisaubert, B., Gaultier, P., Maillard, D. and Gaillard, J. M. (1999) Evolution des populations de chevreuils en France. *Bulletin Mensuel de l'Office National de la Chasse* **244**, 6–11.

Bonenfant, C., Gaillard, J. M., Klein, F. and Loison, A. (2002) Sex- and age-dependent effects of population density on life history traits of red deer *Cervus elaphus* in a temperate forest. *Ecography* **25**, 446–58.

Cairns, J., McCormick, P. V. and Niederlehner, B. R. (1993) A proposed framework for developing indicators of ecosystem health. *Hydrobiologia* **236**, 1–44.

Cemagref (1984) *Méthodes de Recensement des Populations de Chevreuils*. Note Technique N° **51**, 1–65.

Calenge, C., Maillard, D., Fournier, P. and Fouque, C. (2004) Efficiency of spreading maize in the garrigues to reduce wild boar (*Sus scrofa*) damage to Mediterranean vineyards. *European Journal of Wildlife Research* **50**, 112–20.

Caughley, G. (1977) *Analysis of Vertebrate Populations*. Chichester, NY: Wiley and Sons.

Cederlund, G., Bergqvist, J., Kjellander, P. *et al.* (1998) Managing roe deer and their impact on the environment: maximising the net benefits to society. In R. Andersen, P. Duncan and J. D. C. Linnell, eds., *The European Roe Deer: The Biology of Success*. Oslo, Norway: Scandinavian University Press, pp. 337–72.

Crombrugghe S. A. De (1969) Modes de recensement du cerf (*Cervus elaphus* L.) en Belgique et portée pratique. *Proceedings of the IXth Congress of International Game Biologists*, 298–306.

Cugnasse, J. M. (2001) Mouflon (*Ovis gmelini musimon*) in France: past, present and future. In: Nahlik, A. Uloth, W. (eds.) *Proceedings of the Third International Symposium on Mouflon*, Sopron, Hungary, October 27–29, 2000:149–56.

Denis, M. (1985) Quelques méthodes pratiquées pour l'estimation de l'effectif d'une population de chevreuils (*Capreolus capreolus* L.). *Proceedings of the XVIIth Congress of International Game Biologists*, pp. 979–89.

Duval, B. and Boutin, J. M. (1988) Note sur le statut de l'hydropote en Haute-Vienne. *Bulletin Mensuel de l'Office National de la Chasse* **123**, 33–5.

Eberhardt, L. L. (1977) Optimal policies for conservation of large mammals, with special references to marine ecosystems. *Environmental Conservation* **4**, 205–12.

Eberhardt, L. L. (2002) A paradigm for population analysis of long-lived vertebrates. *Ecology* **83**, 2841–54.

Fowler, C. W. (1981) Density dependence as related to life history strategy. *Ecology* **62**, 602–10.

Fowler, C. W. (1987) A review of density-dependence in populations of large mammals. In H. H. Genoways, ed., *Current Mammalogy*. New York, USA: Plenum, pp. 401–41.

Gaillard, J. M., Delorme, D., Boutin, J. M., Van Laere, G. and Boisaubert, B. (1996) Body mass of roe deer fawns during winter in two contrasting populations. *Journal of Wildlife Management* **60**, 29–36.

Gaillard, J. M., Festa-Bianchet, M., Yoccoz, N. G., Loison, A. and Toïgo, C. (2000) Temporal variation in fitness components and population dynamics of large herbivores. *Annual Review of Ecology and Systematics* **31**, 367–93.

Garel, M., Cugnasse, J. M., Gaillard, J. M. *et al.* (2005a) Reproductive output of female mouflon: a comparative analysis. *Journal of Zoology* **266**, 65–71.

Garel, M., Cugnasse, J. M., Loison, A. *et al.* (2005b) Monitoring the abundance of mouflon in South France. *European Journal of Wildlife Research* **51**, 69–76.

Gauthier, D. and Villaret, J. C. (1990) La réintroduction en France du bouquetin des Alpes. *Revue d'Ecologie (Terre et Vie)*, Suppl. **5**, 97–120.

Gill, R. (1990) *Monitoring the status of European and North American cervids. GEMS Information Series global environment monitoring system*. Nairobi, Kenya: United Nations Environment Programme.

Gilpin, M. E. and Ayala, F. J. (1973) Global models of growth and competition. *Proceedings of the National Academy of Sciences of the USA* **70**, 3590–3.

Houssin, H., Loison, A., Jullien, J. M. and Gaillard, J. M. (1994) Validité de la méthode du pointage-flash pour l'estimation des effectifs de chamois (*Rupicapra rupicapra*). *Gibier Faune Sauvage* **11**, 287–98.

IPCC (2002) *Climate Change and Biodiversity*. H. Gitay, A. Suarez, R. T. Watson and D. Dokken, eds., Cambridge, UK: Cambridge University Press. http://www.gcrio.org/online.html

Jacobson, A. R., Provenzale, A., von Hardenberg, A., Bassano, B. and Festa-Bianchet, M. (2004) Climate forcing and density dependence in a mountain ungulate population. *Ecology* **85**, 1598–610.

Kaluzinski, I. (1982) Dynamics and structure of a field roe deer population. *Acta Theriologica* **27**, 385–408.

Lecocq, Y. and Meine, K. (1998) Hunter demography in Europe: an analysis. *Game and Wildlife Science* **15**, 1049–61.

Leduc, D. and Klein, F. (2004) L'origine du cerf français de 1900 à nos jours. *Faune Sauvage* **264**, 27–9.

Léonard, Y., Maillard, D., Suisse-Guillaud, T., Wanner, M. and Calenge, C. (2002a) La stratégie d'adaptation du chevreuil au milieu montagnard: premiers résultats d'une étude menée dans les Alpes du Sud. *Faune Sauvage* **257**, 6–12.

Léonard Y., Catusse, M., Dubray, D. and Maillard, D. (2002b) Le plan de chasse au chamois : état des lieux (1990–1998) et perspectives. *Faune Sauvage* **257**, 13–22.

Loison, A., Toïgo, C. and Gaillard, J. M. (2002) Large herbivore biodiversity in European mountain ecosystems: current status and challenges for the future. In L. Nagy, ed., *Alpine Biodiversity: Pattern, Process and Change in Europe*. Germany: Springer Verlag.

Loison, A., Appolinaire, J., Jullien, J. M. and Dubray, D. (2006) How reliable are total counts to detect trends in population size of chamois *Rupicapra rupicapra* and *R. pyrenaica*. *Wildlife Biology* **12**, 77–88.

Lovari, S. and Scala, C. (1980) Revision of *Rupicapra* Genus. I. A statistical re-evaluation of Couturier's data on the morphometry of six chamois subspecies. *Bulletin Zoologie* **47**, 113–24.

Maillard, D., Boisaubert, B. and Gaillard, J. M. (1989) La masse corporelle : un bioindicateur possible pour le suivi des populations de chevreuils (*Capreolus capreolus* L.). *Gibier Faune Sauvage* **6**, 57–68.

Maillard, D., Duncan, P., Gaillard, J. M. and Gaultier, P. (1999) Le retour des grands mammifères sauvages dans la région méditerranéenne française. *Forêt Méditerranéenne* **20**, 9–15.

McShea, W. J., Underwood, H. B. and Rappole, J. H. (1997) *The Science of Overabundance: Deer Ecology and Population Management*. Washington DC, USA: Smithsonian Institution Press.

Morellet, N., Champely, S., Gaillard, J. M., Ballon, P. and Boscardin, Y. (2001) The browsing index: new tool uses browsing pressure to monitor deer populations. *Wildlife Society Bulletin* **29**, 1243–52.

Morellet, N., Gaillard, J. M., Hewison, A. J. M. *et al.* (2007) Indicators of ecological changes: new tools for managing populations of large herbivores. *Journal of Applied Ecology* **44**, 634–43.

Mysterud, A. and Østbye, E. (2006) Effect of climate and density on individual and population growth of roe deer *Capreolus capreolus* at northern latitudes: the Lier valley, Norway. *Wildlife Biology* **12**, 321–9.

Mysterud, A., Langvatn, R., Yoccoz, N. G. and Stenseth, N. C. (2002) Large-scale habitat variability, delayed density effects and red deer populations in Norway. *Journal of Animal Ecology* **71**, 569–80.

Pfeffer, P. (1967) Le mouflon de Corse (*Ovis ammon musimon* Schreber, 1782) : position systématique, écologie et éthologie comparées. *Mammalia* **31** (Suppl.), 1–262.

Pulliam, H. R. (1988) Sources, sinks, and population regulation. *American Naturalist* **132**, 652–61.

Saint-Andrieux, C., Klein, F., LeDuc, D. and Guibert, B. (2006). Le Daim et le cerf sika : deux cervidés invasifs en France. *Faune Sauvage* **271**, 18–22.

Sæther, B. E., Engen, S., Filli, F. *et al.* (2002) Stochastic population dynamics of an introduced Swiss population of the ibex. *Ecology* **83**, 3457–65.

Schaal, A. (1981) Le daim en France (*Cervus dama* L.). *Mammalia* **45**, 512–13.

Siméon, D. and Houard, T. (1987) Méthode de recensement hivernal par hélicoptère de cerf élaphe (*Cervus elaphus*) en zone de montagne. *Gibier Faune Sauvage* **4**, 377–90.

Stenseth, N. C., Mysterud, A., Ottersen, G. *et al.* (2002) Ecological effects of climate fluctuations. *Science* **297**, 1292–6.
Toïgo, C. (1998) *Stratégies biodémographiques et sélection sexuelle chez le bouquetin des Alpes* (Capra ibex ibex). Unpublished PhD Thesis, University of Lyon, France.
Toïgo, C., Gaillard, J. M. and Michallet, J. (1996) La taille des groupes : un bioindicateur de l'effectif des populations de bouquetin des Alpes (*Capra ibex ibex*)? *Mammalia* **60**, 463–72.
Toïgo, C., Gaillard, J. M., Van Laere, G., Hewison, A. J. M. and Morellet, N. (2006) How does environmental variation influence body mass, body size and body condition? Roe deer as a case study. *Ecography* **29**, 301–8.
Van Horne, B. (1983) Density as a misleading indicator of habitat quality. *Journal of Wildlife Management* **47**, 893–901.
Vassant, J., Brandt, S. and Jullien, J. M. (1990) Essai de dénombrement d'une population de sangliers par observation sur places d'affouragements. *Bulletin Mensuel de l'Office National de la Chasse* **147**, 21–6.
Vassant, J., Brandt, S. and Jullien, J. M. (1992) Reducing wild boar damage to wheat and oats in summer: study of the effectiveness of maize distribution in the forest. In B. Bobek, K. Perzanowski, W. L. Regelin, eds., Proc.18th IUGB Congress, *Global Trends in Wildlife Management*, 79–88, Jagiellonian University, Krakow, Poland.
Vigne, J. D. (1992) Zooarchaeology and the biogeographical history of the mammals of Corsica and Sardinia since the last ice age. *Mammal Review* **22**, 87–96.
Vignon, V. and Barbarreau H. (2008) Collisions entre véhicules et ongulés sauvages : quel coût économique? *Faune Sauvage* **279**, 31–5.
Vincent, J. P., Gaillard, J. M. and Bideau, E. (1991) Kilometric index as biological indicator for monitoring forest roe deer populations. *Acta Theriologica* **36**, 315–28.
Vincent, J. P., Bideau, E., Hewison, A. J. M. and Angibault, J. M. (1995) The influence of increasing density on body weight, kid production, home range and winter grouping in roe deer (*Capreolus capreolus*). *Journal of Zoology* **236**, 371–82.
Waller, D. M. and Alverson, W. S. (1997) The white tailed deer: a keystone herbivore. *Wildlife Society Bulletin* **25**, 217–26.
Walther, G. R., Post, E., Convey, P. *et al.* (2002) Ecological responses to recent climate change. *Nature* **416**, 389–95.
Williams, B. K., Nichols, J. D. and Conroy, M. J. (2002) *Analysis and Management of Animal Populations*. San Diego, CA, USA: Academic Press.
Wright, R. G. (1999) Wildlife management in the National Parks: questions in search of answers. *Ecological Applications* **9**, 30–6.
Zannèse, A., Baïsse, A., Gaillard, J. M. *et al.* (2006) Hind foot length: an indicator for monitoring roe deer populations at a landscape scale. *Wildlife Society Bulletin* **34**, 351–8.

21

Ungulates and their management in Italy

MARCO APOLLONIO, SIMONE CIUTI, LUCA PEDROTTI
AND PAOLO BANTI

Italy is a complicated but fascinating mixture of different popular traditions, historical origins, dialects. The country ranges from the Alps to the large Mediterranean islands, and the nation itself is a composite mixture of many politically independent different areas, that were initially joined together in 1860. At this time unity as a single nation was only partially achieved, being further fulfilled during World War I but then reduced again after World War II. Innumerable political events and influences have left their mark and affected popular traditions during the first two millennia AD. The result of this process is a complex country, subdivided into 20 regions and 103 provinces, with a total land area of 30 210 000 ha and with a human density of 189 ind./km^2.

This is not only very interesting from a cultural and historical point of view, but leads to some complications in hunting management. Moreover, 5 out of 20 regions have been granted substantial autonomy by the Italian National Government, leading to still greater complexity in administration. For all these reasons it is extremely difficult to collect data on a large scale in Italy and, as will be remarked upon later in this chapter, this situation is also affected by the absence of any significant state control of management.

The present chapter is based in part on updating of previous works (Pedrotti *et al.*, 2001; Apollonio, 2004), but primarily tries to provide this missing overview by collating the results of new data collected between 2001 and 2004, on ungulate presence and management from all the 'traditional' 103 Italian provinces. More data on ungulate status and culling statistics come from Carnevali *et al.* (2007).

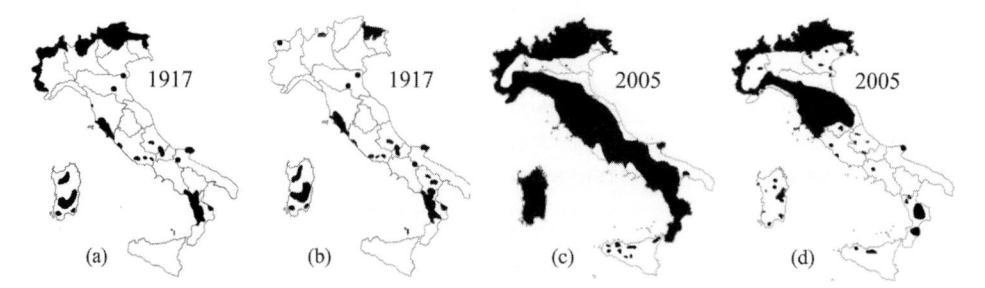

Fig. 21.1 History of ungulate presence in Italy in the last century. (a) Ungulate distribution at the beginning of the twentieth century (Ghigi, 1917, modified). (b) Ungulate distribution at the beginning of the twentieth century (without Alpine chamois) (Ghigi, 1917, modified). (c) Present ungulate distribution. (d) Present ungulate distribution (without wild boar)

21.1 Ungulate species and their distribution

There are eight different species of ungulates in Italy: wild boar, roe deer, red deer, fallow deer, Alpine chamois (*Rupicapra rupicapra*), Apennine chamois (*Rupicapra pyrenaica ornata*), Alpine ibex and mouflon.

The history of ungulate presence and distribution in Italy over the course of the last century has been reconstructed mainly thanks to the work of the grandfather of the Italian wildlife researchers, Alessandro Ghigi. In 1917 the only ungulates within the country were restricted to the Alps and a few other areas (Fig. 21.1a; Ghigi, 1917). If Alpine chamois (well represented in the Alps at the beginning of the last century) is excluded, the distribution of other ungulate species was restricted only to a few refuges (Fig. 21.1b). From this time until the present, the situation has changed significantly, as reported in Figure 21.1d, as ungulate distribution has increased dramatically especially in Central and Northern Italy, and, due largely to the spread of wild boar, also in the south of the country and islands (Fig. 21.1c).

This increase in distribution is probably largely the result of the contemporary abandonment of villages in the mountains and hills and of the growth of municipalities in lowlands. From 1870 to the present the Italian economy shifted from agriculture to industries and services after War World II (less than 10% of the total working population is now occupied in agriculture, and 42% of the total land area is used for such activity in 2005 – it was 67% in 1982). As a result, people left the hills and mountains and concentrated in big industrial areas. At the beginning of the twentieth century the Italian Gross Domestic Income was about one-third of that of France or the UK, now it is almost equal.

21.1.1 Red deer

This is one of the Italian ungulate species that was less well represented in the last century, as populations of this species in the mainland were completely

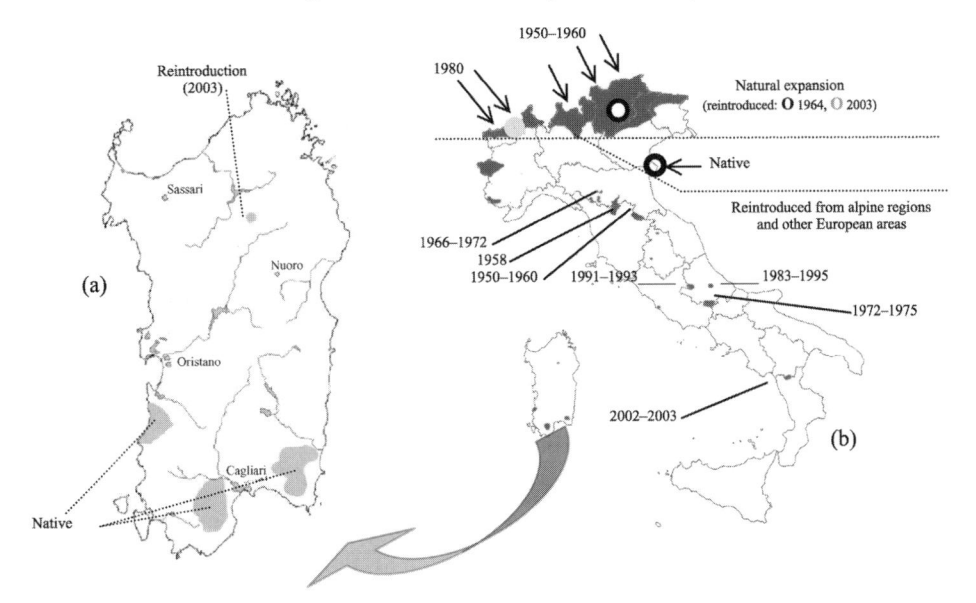

Fig. 21.2 Red deer distribution in Italy. (a) Sardinian red deer present distribution in Sardinia (IUCN status: *ENDANGERED*). (b) European red deer distribution in continental Italy

exterminated (with the possible exception of the population of Bosco della Mesola, below). Actually, only one mainland population is recognizable as truly native, the red deer from 'Bosco della Mesola', a small wooded area on the Northern Adriatic coast (Lorenzini *et al.*, 1998). This population probably represents a remnant stock, whose genetical isolation and low N_e have produced dramatic drift effects (Hmwe *et al.*, 2006). Otherwise the current distribution of European red deer (*Cervus elephus elaphus*) is entirely the result of several reintroductions performed between 1950 and 2003 and natural expansion in the Alps from the immediately neighbouring European countries (Fig. 21.2b) (Pedrotti *et al.*, 2001; Apollonio, 2004). Reintroduced populations in the central and southern Apennines are still isolated from each other (Acquerino Forest and Calvi mountain, Casentinesi Forest National Park, Abruzzo National Park, Maiella National Park, Velino-Sirente, Orecchiella Regional Park; Pedrotti *et al.*, 2001). Additionally, isolated and small populations are present in the Mandria and Castelporziano Estates (Turin and Rome provinces, respectively).

A distinct subspecies of red deer, the Sardinian red deer (*Cervus e. corsicanus*, IUCN status: *ENDANGERED*) is known to have been present on the island of Sardinia from about 6000 BC. However, geneticists have not yet reached an agreement about the geographical origin of this island population, which was in turn proposed to be in the Near East, in North Africa and in mainland Italy (Ludt *et al.*, 2004; Lorenzini *et al.*, 2005; Hmwe *et al.*, 2006). Even the hypothesis of a natural settlement of the population was not completely dismissed (Zachos *et al.*,

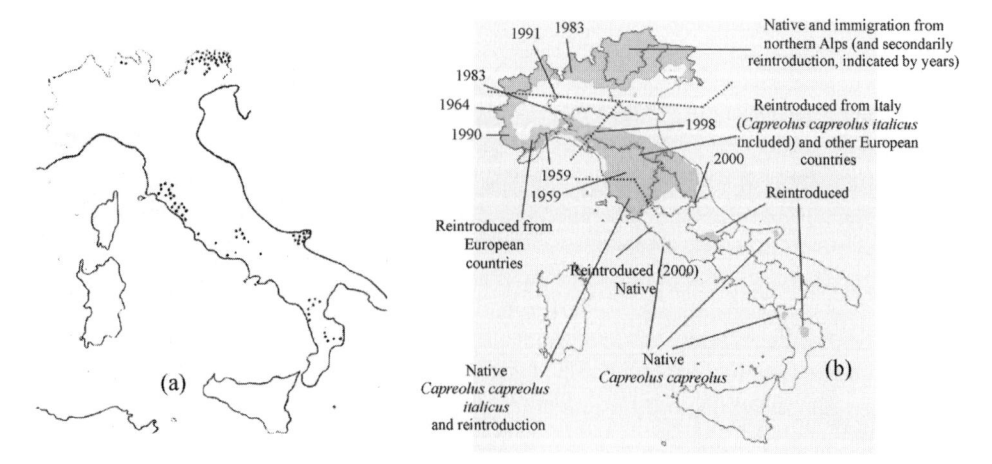

Fig. 21.3 History of roe deer distribution in Italy. (a) Roe deer distribution in 1917 (Ghigi, 1917, modified) and (b) present distribution with origin of different populations

2003). The distribution of the true Sardinian red deer is actually limited to the southern areas of Sardinia (Fig. 21.2a), as it has only recently been reintroduced in the northern part if this region.

21.1.2 Roe deer

This species, together with the wild boar, is the Italian ungulate which we feel may be most seriously compromised from a genetic point of view. Several molecular investigations have suggested that animals occurring in central-southern Italy appear to belong to a distinct native subspecies (*Capreolus capreolus italicus*) that split from a more widespread European clade during last glaciation (Vernesi *et al.*, 2002; Randi *et al.*, 2004; Lorenzini and Lovari, 2006). This presumed subspecies, however, now occurs largely in sympatry with various European roe deer stocks (*Capreolus c. capreolus*) of other origin, derived from several introductions/reintroductions (Lorenzini *et al.*, 2002). Although traces of the native lineage have been detected in many populations across the peninsula, the observed levels of genetic admixture with non-native roe deer have raised a big concern about the risk of genetic extinction of this relict taxon (Lorenzini *et al.*, 2002; Randi *et al.*, 2004).

As recorded for most Italian ungulate species, the overall distribution of this species has significantly increased from that recorded at the beginning of the last century by Ghigi (1917) when the species was limited to some spots on the Alps (Valtellina, Veneto and Friuli regions), to coastal south Tuscany and north Latium, and to some limited areas on Gargano promontory – Puglia region, on Orsomarso and Sila mountains – Calabria region and in central Abruzzo region (Fig. 21.3a).

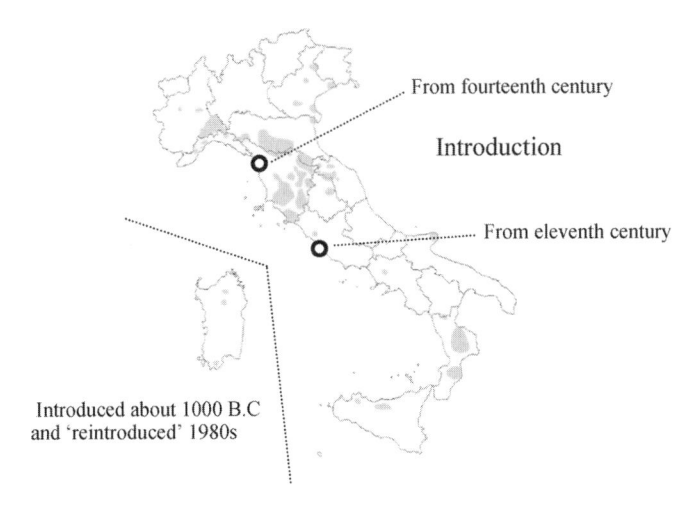

Fig. 21.4 Present fallow deer distribution

Origins of different stocks, as far as these are understood, are reported in Figure 21.3b, from which we may clearly see the actual distribution of the native roe deer, as just described, is restricted mainly to the coast of Tuscany or in a few other isolated populations in the southern part of Italy (Castelporziano – Rome, Foresta Umbra del Gargano – Foggia, Monti Orsomarso – Cosenza) (see also Festa, 1925). The other populations in the southern part of Italy were introduced in 1970 (Abruzzo National Park and Southern Apennine of Sila).

21.1.3 Fallow deer

The fallow deer was probably introduced to Sardinia by Phoenicians about 1000 BC, and was possibly moved afterwards by Romans to the mainland. This species is probably the Italian ungulate most commonly introduced by Forestry Authorities into Preserves and Hunting reserves, and there are two populations documented by historical notes from the eleventh and fourteenth centuries (Castel Porziano and San Rossore Estates, respectively). As consequence of its history (i.e. repeated bottlenecks), the species shows very low amounts of genetic variability (Hartl et al., 1986; Randi and Apollonio, 1988; Scandura et al., 1998).

Free-ranging populations are widespread in the northern and central Apennines (Fig. 21.4). Sardinian populations had become extinct by the late 1960s (Schenk, 1976), but this species was reintroduced in the early 1980s (Pedrotti et al., 2001) with fallow deer of mainland origin (especially from the San Rossore Estate). Recently fallow deer were also introduced to Sicily (Palermo province; Pedrotti et al., 2001).

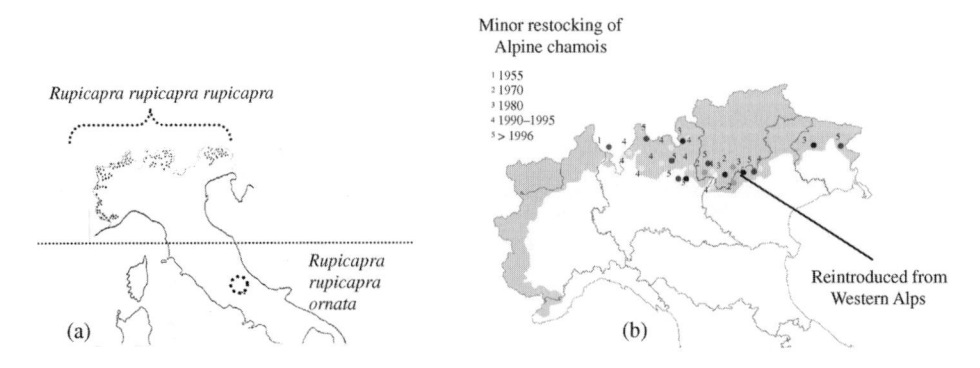

Fig. 21.5 History of the chamois distribution in Italy. (a) Chamois distribution at the beginning of the twentieth century (Ghigi, 1917, modified). (b) Present Alpine chamois distribution

21.1.4 Alpine chamois

Figure 21.5a reports the distribution of Alpine chamois at the beginning of the twentieth century (Ghigi, 1917). Actually, the distribution of this species has always been relatively widespread in the Alps (Fig. 21.5b), and the eastern population has also increased following several minor translocations performed with Western Alps stocks (from Gran Paradiso National Park).

Alpine chamois is the ungulate species whose distribution has been least affected by human pressure and that has remained wide even in the worst times for our wildlife. In a recent study, Crestanello *et al.* (2004) showed that the Western Alpine chamois population of the Gran Paradiso National Park includes several specimens belonging to a different mitochondrial lineage. Specifically, animals sharing a mitochondrial haplotype with the Spanish *Rupicapra pyrenaica pyrenaica* cluster were found. Although this result deserves further analysis to understand whether this is the consequence of recent translocation events or more ancient migration processes, this fact underlines the potential risk associated with reintroductions carried out with these stocks.

21.1.5 Apennine chamois

Figure 21.5a reports the distribution of Apennine chamois (*Rupicapra rupicapra ornata*) at the beginning of the twentieth century when it consisted of only one remnant population limited to a small area of Southern Abruzzo. The present distribution (IUCN status: ENDANGERED) remains very limited and localised mainly in the Abruzzo region, Abruzzo National Park, Gran Sasso-Monti della Laga National Park, Majella National Park; populations in these latter areas derive from reintroductions from the Abruzzo region at end of the last century (Fig. 21.6) (Pedrotti *et al.*, 2001).

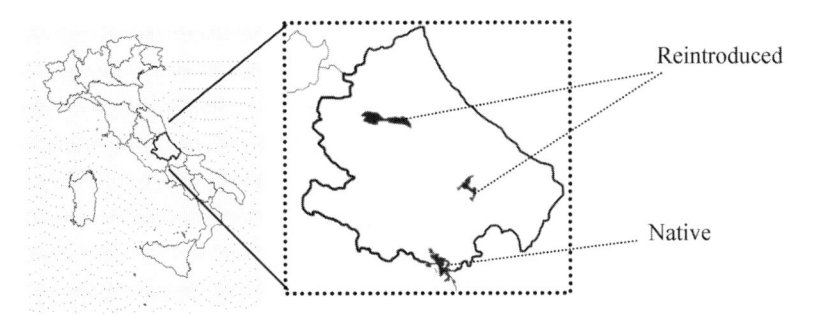

Fig. 21.6 Present Apennine chamois distribution (IUCN status: *ENDANGERED*)

21.1.6 Alpine ibex

The survival of the native Alpine ibex in Italy is totally linked to the stock which survived at the beginning of the twentieth century in the Gran Paradiso National Park (Ghigi, 1917) (Fig. 21.7a). Several reintroductions with ibex from this population and the natural expansion from reintroduced populations in bordering countries (Fig. 21.7b, Fig. 21.8) have resulted in the present distribution (Gauthier and Villaret, 1990; Pedrotti *et al.*, 2001) that includes all the Alps with a stronger presence within the Western Alps.

21.1.7 Mouflon

The mouflon was introduced to Sardinia in 6000 BC, where the species is commonly considered as 'native through long establishment' (Fig. 21.9, IUCN status: VULNERABLE). At the end of the last century its distribution significantly decreased (Beccu, 1993), and now the species is limited in Sardinia to the central mountainous area of the island (in the province of Nuoro) (Sacchi *et al.*, 2001). In contrast, several introductions were performed during the last century in the Alps (Bassano *et al.*, 1993; Pedrotti *et al.*, 2001), Northern Apennine, and coastal Tuscany as well as to a number of the smaller islands (Elba, Capraia, Giglio, Zannone and Marettimo), all using mouflon of Sardinian origin, leading to the establishment of more than 60 isolated populations (Pedrotti *et al.*, 2001).

21.1.8 Wild boar

The history of wild boar in Italy and its present distribution are affected by an enormous number of mistaken management actions, and its genetic purity is seriously compromised. At present, this species is widely distributed, as a result of a progressive expansion started at the beginning of the last century (Ghigi, 1917, 1950; Apollonio *et al.*, 1988) (Fig. 21.10). Two subspecies of wild boar were originally recognised in Italy (*Sus scrofa majori* in the coastal area of southern Tuscany

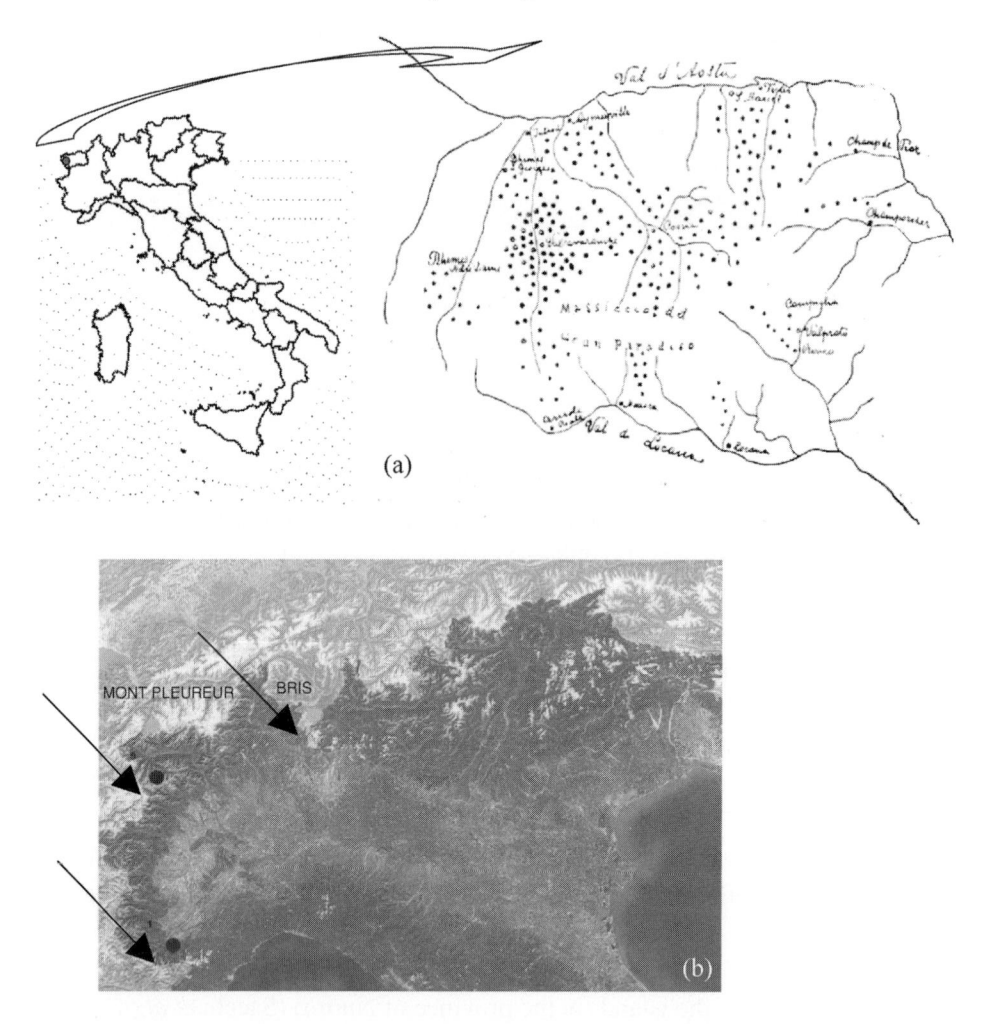

Fig. 21.7 Alpine ibex distribution at the beginning of the twentieth century (a) (Ghigi, 1917, modified) and in 1950 (b) (Bassano and Pedrotti, 2000, modified)

and Latium, *Sus s. meridionalis* in Sardinia; De Beaux and Festa, 1927; Apollonio *et al.*, 1988; Randi *et al.*, 1989; Apollonio *et al.*, 1992). At the beginning of the twentieth century this species was present only along the coast of Tuscany and Latium, in a large area in southern Italy across the Campania, Lucania, Puglia and Calabria regions, and in Sardinia.

Recent genetic studies have pointed out the presence of a separate mitochondrial DNA (mt-DNA) lineage in the extant Italian population of the last century (Larson *et al.*, 2005), which has been retained, at a not negligible frequency, by contemporary wild stocks (Scandura *et al.*, 2006).

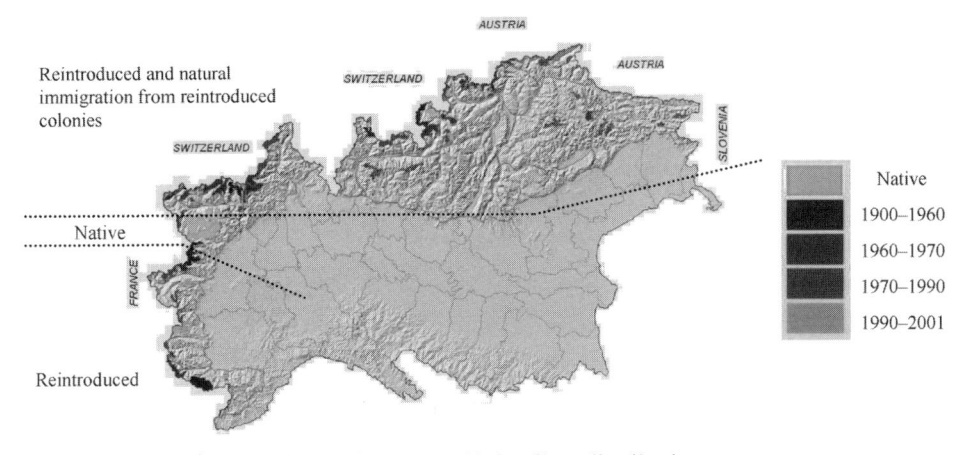

Fig. 21.8 Present Alpine ibex distribution

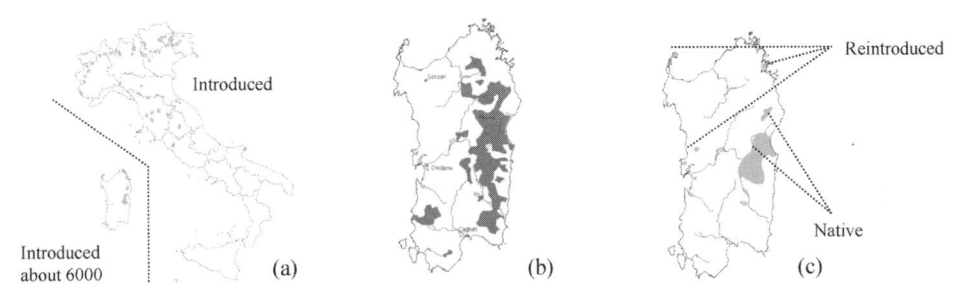

Fig. 21.9 Mouflon distribution (a), with particular reference to that recorded in Sardinia (b) distribution end of nineteenth century, Beccu, 1993, modified, (c) present distribution, Sacchi *et al.*, 2001, modified; IUCN status: *VULNERABLE*

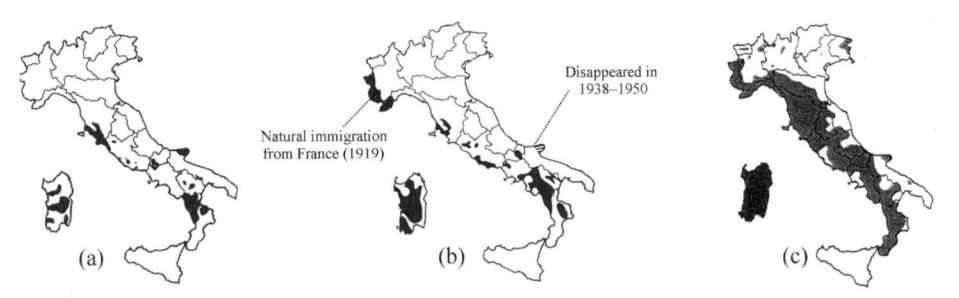

Fig. 21.10 History of the wild boar distribution in Italy. (a) Wild boar distribution in the first decade of the twentieth century (Ghigi, 1917, modified), (b) in the middle of the twentieth century (Ghigi, 1950, modified), and (c) in 1980 (Apollonio *et al.*, 1988)

Very little change to distribution occurred till 1950, but after this time extensive reintroductions dramatically changed this picture. This seems to have significantly affected the overall distribution of the species, leaving a signature on its genetic composition (Vernesi *et al.*, 2003; Scandura *et al.*, 2006).

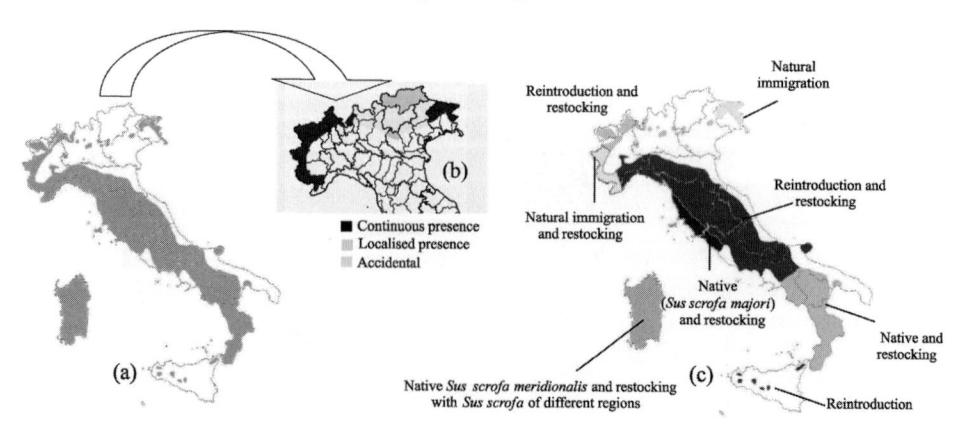

Fig. 21.11 Present wild boar distribution in Italy (a), with special reference to the evolving situation in Northern Italy (Monaco *et al.*, 2004, modified) (b). The map on the right (c) reports the present genetic status of the wild boar in Italy, as a result of both various human manipulations and natural immigration

Figure 21.11 shows both the present-day wild boar distribution, with special reference to the changing situation of Northern Italy (Monaco *et al.*, 2004), and also the presumed origin of different stocks. It is interesting to note how the native Sardinian subspecies *Sus scrofa meridionalis* was partially threatened by several separate reintroductions of continental wild boar from other regions of Italy, but its genetic status is further complicated by the presence of free-ranging domestic pigs maintained by local populations (Apollonio, 2003). Also the continental wild boar, presumably still partially of original native stock along the cost of Tuscany and Lazio regions, is geographically very close to or mixed with stocks introduced from East European countries.

21.1.9 Present status

As noted in the introduction, Italy is a very diverse country from an ungulate management point of view. Because, in consequence, it is sometimes very difficult to present a uniform picture, where hunting management may differ significantly in different areas, in the following paragraphs we will consider the country in five distinct regional areas (Fig. 21.12). Table 21.1 summarises the number of provinces within each of these main regions where each ungulate species is known to occur. In this case, one additional area is identified as the lowlands of the Po valley.

The actual Italian ungulate status is summarised in Table 21.2.

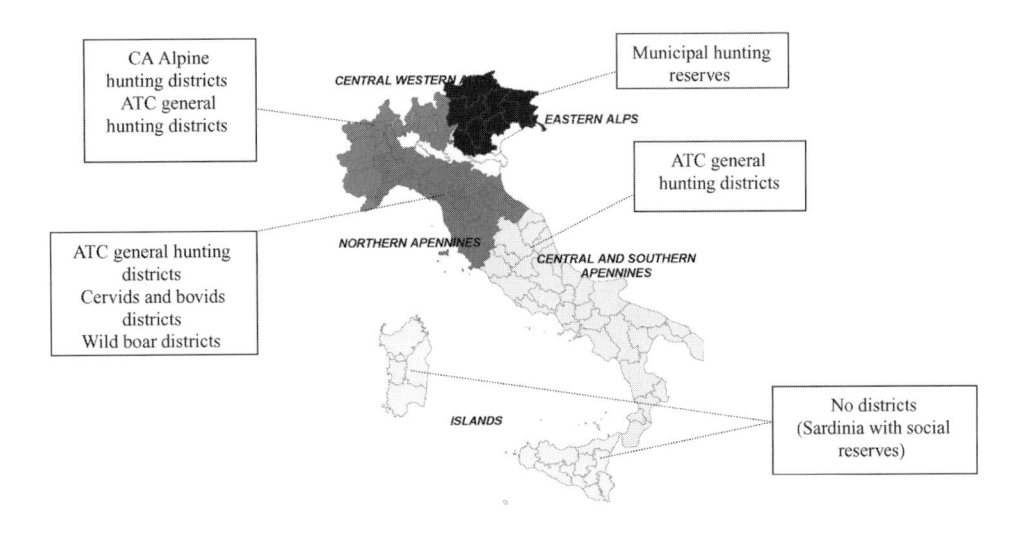

Fig. 21.12 Italy subdivided into five main regions. Boxes report main Italian hunting units

21.2 Legislation

Hunting of wild ungulates in Italy is primarily controlled by the provisions of the national hunting law 152/92; however much of the day-to-day administrative regulation has been devolved to regional byelaws that pass responsibility of actual management to provinces (103) and traditional General Hunting Districts or Alpine Districts smaller than a province. Individual hunters are linked to districts and are entitled to hunt only there. This kind of organisation creates a link of the hunter to the territory that can be loose in some cases due to the possibility of hunting in more than one General Hunting District (ATC) in the same hunting season or to benefit from very large sized ATCs.

Following the National law 157/92, the following ungulate species may be hunted in Italy: wild boar, Alpine chamois, roe deer, fallow deer, red deer and mouflon (although neither of these last two species may be hunted in Sardinia). The following species may not be hunted at any time: Apennine chamois and both mouflon and red deer in Sardinia. It is also not permitted in general to shoot Alpine ibex, but a few heads are legally shot every year for control operations in Bolzano province.

21.2.1 Permitted firearms

Firearms allowed in ungulate hunting by Italian laws are shotgun (single ball) and rifle for wild boar hunting, and only rifle for other ungulates.

Table 21.1 Ungulate presence in Italy (total number of provinces 102: Eastern Alps 10, Central Western Alps 14, Lowland 8, Northern Apennine 24, Central Southern Apennine 33, Islands 13)

Species	No. of provinces with species presence						TOTAL	RANK						Percentages of provinces with species presence						All provinces
	Eastern Alps	Central Western Alps	Lowland	Northern Apennine	Central Southern Apennine	Islands		Eastern Alps	Central Western Alps	Lowland	Northern Apennine	Central Southern Apennine	Islands	Eastern Alps	Central Western Alps	Lowland	Northern Apennine	Central Southern Apennine	Islands	
Roe deer	10	14	4	24	16	0	68	1	1	2	1	2	5	100	100	50	100	48	0	67
Fallow deer	3	4	6	20	10	4	47	7	7	1	3	4	3	30	29	75	83	30	31	46
Red deer	8	12	1	15	11	2	49	4	4	3	4	3	4	80	86	13	63	33	15	48
Mouflon	6	11	0	12	2	5	36	5	5	5	5	6	2	60	79	0	50	6	38	35
Wild boar	10	14	1	24	31	10	90	1	1	3	1	1	1	100	100	13	100	94	77	88
Apennines chamois	0	0	0	0	6	0	6	0	0	0	0	5	0	0	0	0	0	18	0	6
Alpine chamois	10	13	0	1	0	0	24	1	3	0	6	0	0	100	93	0	5	0	0	24
Alpine ibex	5	10	0	0	0	0	15	6	6	0	0	0	0	50	71	0	0	0	0	15

Table 21.2 Ungulate status in the last 25 years in Italy. (* = estimate; CNR = Research National Council)

Species	Status 1980 (Perco, 1981; Tosi and Perco, 1981)							Status 2005 (INFS, Carnevali et al., 2007)							Increase (%) 1980–2005
	Eastern Alps	Central Western Alps	Northern Apennine	Central Southern Apennine	Islands	TOTAL		Eastern Alps	Central Western Alps	Northern Apennine	Central Southern Apennine	Islands	TOTAL	
Roe deer	84 500	5 900	10 215	1 600	0	102 215		104 715	63 428	256 809	922	0	425 874	317
Fallow deer	250	100	3 800	2 230	50	6 430		566	1 274	16 054	2 152	950	20 996	227
Red deer	4 860	1 670	300	550	250	7 630		30 063	19 011	6 386	1 453	6 000	62 913	725
Mouflon	540	530	2 215	870	800	4 955		3 148	2 321	2 492	1 046	6 000	15 007	203
Wild boar	?	?	?	?	?	?		?	?	?	?	?	600 000*	?
Apennines chamois	0	0	0	234	0	234		0	0	0	1 120	0	1 120	379
Alpine chamois	33 602	25 300	present	0	0	59 902		67 419	69 350	0	0	0	136 769	128
Alpine ibex	170	4 180	0	0	0	4 350		2 185	12 707	0	0	0	14 892	242

21.2.2 Hunting practices

Wild boar is mostly hunted with dogs, all other ungulates are hunted only by stalking with rifles with the exception of, respectively, four provinces in North Eastern Alps where dog hunting for roe deer is allowed, and two for red deer. Stalking, single dog hunting and drives are also used to control wild boar. Hunting dogs are prohibited in chamois hunting.

21.2.3 Hunting seasons

Following National Law 157 (1992), wild boar can only be hunted for three months from October to January. All other ungulates which may be hunted at all can be hunted for two months (usually October–November, but the 60 days available can be moved before and after this time, i.e. they can be hunted in August–September and/or in February–March). Regional and Provincial Governments can apply to shift these time spans: once established any hunter in the province must respect these limits. There are some exceptions, with special reference to Eastern Alps and Emilia Romagna Region, where longer seasons are allowed. Detailed regional and provincial hunting times are summarised in Tables 21.3 and 21.4.

Very recently, a national decree (DL n. 203, n. 11) established that Autonomous Provinces and Regions can enlarge ungulate hunting times outside limits prescribed by National Law 157/92. Some regions like Liguria, Umbria, Marche and Tuscany allowed their provinces to make use of this possibility.

21.3 Management objectives

Because there are marked differences in the species present, in their distribution and local densities, and because in addition, there are marked cultural differences in attitude in the different Italian regions, management objectives vary widely between them. Generally, hunting in Italy is primarily for venison and for trophies, closely linked to a recreational aspect.

In central and northern Italy, management is also directed more specifically to the control of damage (especially in the case of wild boar in central and northern Italy, and sometimes red deer in north-eastern Italy). Almost all damage relates to agriculture and this is especially true for wild boar. Damage to forestry is sometimes estimated, but no compensation is paid. The purposes of habitat conservation have never featured as a major factor in ungulate management plans.

21.4/5 Management structure and management organisation

In Italy most hunting is open to anyone (over something between 90 and 99.5% of hunting areas), while the area where hunting is reserved by any one private individual is very limited (e.g Piemonte region: 5%; autonomous province of Trento: 0.4%; Tuscany region: 10%). This is because game is not considered the property of the landowner. Originally, from Roman Law game was seen as 'res nullius', but from 1977 (law 968) game is now declared 'res communitatis'. In addition, there is in effect little opportunity to reserve private hunting as the mean size of private landholdings is very small (e.g. less than 7 ha in the Tuscany region).

There are five different types of land organisation in Italy in relation to hunting (Fig. 21.12). The Eastern Alps has mainly municipal reserves within each province (mean size 3200 ha) where only the citizens of the municipality have the right to hunt. In the Central and Western Alps provinces are generally subdivided into ATC General Hunting Districts (ATC: *Ambito Territoriale di Caccia*) and CA Alpine districts (CA: *Comparto Alpino*) (mean size of these districts about 60 000 ha); in many cases these are further subdivided into ungulate hunting districts of about 5000–20 000 ha. For example, in the provinces of the Piemonte region, an ATC general hunting district is, on average, 68 053 ha, while a CA Alpine district is, on average, 59 834 ha. In this region, in all provinces (with the exception of Verbania) there is subdivision of CA Alpine districts into different hunting areas which relate to the management of specific different species (on average: roe deer 7661 ha, fallow deer 11 950 ha, red deer 27 911 ha, Alpine chamois 7007 ha, and mouflon 4154 ha). This is the general land organisation of the Eastern, Central and Western Alps. Figure 21.13a reviews four different settings, showing how nearby provinces may also represent different situations.

In Northern Apennine (including Tuscany and the province of Pesaro-Urbino) there are ATC general districts with special small hunting districts for each species like roe deer, red deer, fallow deer, mouflon and wild boar (average size between 6000 ha for roe deer and wild boar, and 15 000 ha for red deer; e.g. Tuscany region hunting district areas: roe deer 6651 ha, fallow deer 11 695 ha, red deer 14 657 ha, and wild boar 5398 ha). Figure 21.13b reports how the province of Pisa (Tuscany region) is subdivided into ATC and ungulate hunting districts.

In Central and Southern Apennines there are only ATC general districts of about 170 000 ha.

In Sicily and Sardinia there are no specific districts, and hunters are free to hunt on 2.4 and 2.6 million ha, respectively. Furthermore, in Sardinia there are 1500–3000 ha-wide social (public) reserves when only hunters associated with those specific areas can hunt.

From this more general description, it may be seen that management of ungulates in Italy is carried out by each management unit under the supervision of the game administration section of the provincial governments, and there is no overall state-controlled management. In fact, in Italy, there is no national level of control on

Table 21.3 *Hunting seasons in Northern and Central Italy*

	Species	\multicolumn{11}{c}{Month}
		May	June	July	August	September	October	November	December	January	February	March
Autonomous region of Friuli Venezia Giulia	wild boar									15		
	roe deer	15	15							15		
	red deer				15					15		
	fallow deer				15					15		
	mouflon				15					15		
	chamois				15					15		
Autonomous Province of Bolzano	roe deer	1							15			
	red deer	1							15			
	mouflon	1							15			
	chamois			1					15			
Autonomous Province of Trento *culling plan to complete hunting quotas (if necessary)	wild boar					7*	*	*	15*			
	roe deer M					7	26					
	roe deer F					7		6–11*	12*			
	red deer					5–19	10	24–29*	*			
	mouflon					19		18–24*	19*			
	chamois					19		18–24*	19*			
Veneto	wild boar					1				31		
	roe deer					+/– 60 days	1	30	+/– 60 days			
	red deer					+/– 60 days	1	30	+/– 60 days			
	fallow deer					+/– 60 days	1	30	+/– 60 days			
	mouflon					+/– 60 days	1	30	+/– 60 days			
	chamois					+/– 60 days	1	30	+/– 60 days			
Lombardia	wild boar					+/– 30 days				+/– 30 days		
	roe deer			1			1	30		31		
	red deer			1			1	30		31		
	mouflon			1			1	30		31		
	chamois			1			1	30		31		

Region	Species					
Autonomous region of Valle d'Aosta	wild boar					
	roe deer	21		20		29
	red deer	21		20		
	chamois	21		4	20	
Piemonte	wild boar		+/− 30 days	1	31	+/− 30 days
	roe deer	+/− 60 days		1	30	+/− 60 days
	red deer	+/− 60 days		1	30	+/− 60 days
	fallow deer	+/− 60 days		1	30	+/− 60 days
	mouflon	+/− 60 days		1	30	+/− 60 days
	chamois	+/− 60 days		1	30	+/− 60 days
Liguria	wild boar	21			21	
	roe deer	+/− 60 days		1	30	+/− 60 days
	fallow deer	+/− 60 days		1	30	+/− 60 days
	chamois	+/− 60 days		1	30	+/− 60 days
Emilia Romagna	wild boar	1	15	30	31	
	roe deer	1	15		1	10
	red deer					10
	fallow deer		10	5	1	10
	mouflon			5	31	
Toscana	wild boar		+/− 30 days	1	31	+/− 30 days
	roe deer	1				15 +/− 60 days
	red deer	1				15 +/− 60 days
	fallow deer	1				15 +/− 60 days
	mouflon	1				15 +/− 60 days
Umbria	wild boar	1		2	31	
	roe deer	1				15 +/− 60 days
	red deer	1				15 +/− 60 days
	fallow deer	1				15 +/− 60 days
	mouflon	1				15 +/− 60 days
Marche	wild boar	30		1	31	
	roe deer	+/− 60 days				15 +/− 60 days
	fallow deer	+/− 60 days				15 +/− 60 days

Table 21.4 *Hunting seasons in Southern Italy and Islands*

Species	May	June	July	August	September	October	November	December	January	February	March
Abruzzo wild boar					5			30			
Molise wild boar					19				18		
fallow deer					22	26					
Lazio wild boar							1		31		
roe deer						1	30				
red deer						1	30				
fallow deer						1	30				
mouflon						1	30				
Basilicata wild boar						1		31			
Calabria wild boar							1		31		
Campania wild boar						1		31			
Puglia wild boar						1		31			
red deer						1	30				
fallow deer						1	30				
mouflon						1	30				
Autonomous region of Sicilia wild boar							1	31			
Autonomous region of Sardegna wild boar							14,21,28	5,12,19,26	2,9,16		

hunting management beyond those overarching laws established by regulations 152/92 and 157/92.

In practice, differences in organisation relate largely to differences in distribution of ungulate species themselves. In Central and Southern Apennines and in the islands wild boar is the only hunted species: as a consequence no small hunting district below ATC size is appropriate in the provinces. Roe deer is the main species driving the organisation in Northern Apennines: the limits of its geographical distribution neatly coincide with, and in effect define, the limit of the area with a hunting organisation based on 'Provinces with small hunting districts for particular individual ungulate species'. Alpine chamois takes over this role in the Alps, where there has been a long-term tradition for the hunting of this species.

Throughout our country, all those wishing to hunt at all (whatever quarry) must pass a general hunting examination, but this is generally quite easy and there is a low selection threshold. This is not true for Trento and Bolzano provinces (Eastern Alps) where this examination is very much more testing than that of the other Italian provinces.

In the Eastern Alps there is no special examination specifically for those wishing to hunt ungulates, except for those who wish to become professional hunters (an obligatory escort that hunts with the ungulate hunter aiming to cull particular species, like Alpine chamois). In Central and Western Alps and Northern Apennine there are no special examinations for those wishing to hunt wild boar, but there are

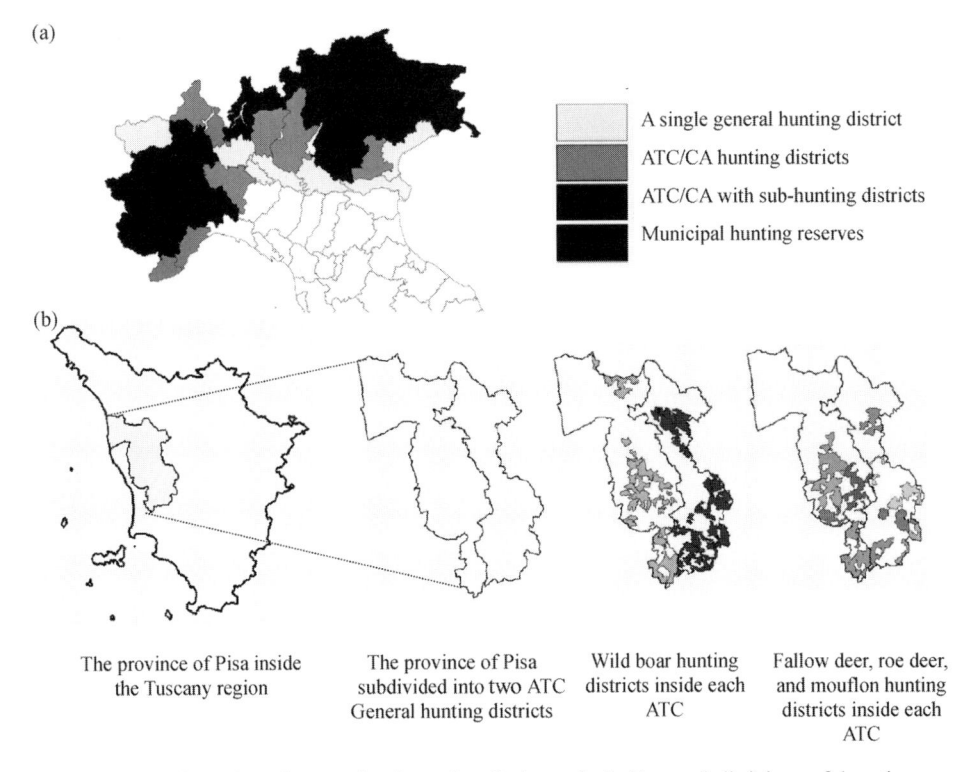

Fig. 21.13 (a) Land organisation: detailed north Italian subdivision of hunting units. (b) Example of land organisation in the northern Apennine main region: the example of province of Pisa

special ones for those who wish to hunt deer or bovids. No special examinations for wild boar hunters are required in Southern Apennine and the islands.

Hunting fees must be paid to provincial governments: fees for hunting wild ungulates may vary between EUR 200 and 400 per year but in some areas single heads are paid in relation to their market value up to EUR 2000 or more.

Amongst hunters, in general, those wishing to hunt ungulates range from 4% to 90%; the greatest proportion is in the Eastern Alps (e.g. Piemonte region, cervid and bovid hunters = 22.1%, total number of hunters = 27 536; autonomous province of Trento, cervid and bovid hunters = 90.5%, total number of hunters = 8000; Tuscany region, cervid and bovid hunters = 4%, wild boar hunters = 37%, total number of hunters = 120 000). Ungulate hunter number is rapidly increasing in Northern Apennines and includes 10% of all hunters in the better organised provinces (like Arezzo, cervid and bovid hunters = 44%, total number of hunters = 15 000) and is likely to increase almost everywhere due to a steady increase in ungulate number and a decrease in the number of small game. Figure 21.14 reports trends of roe deer

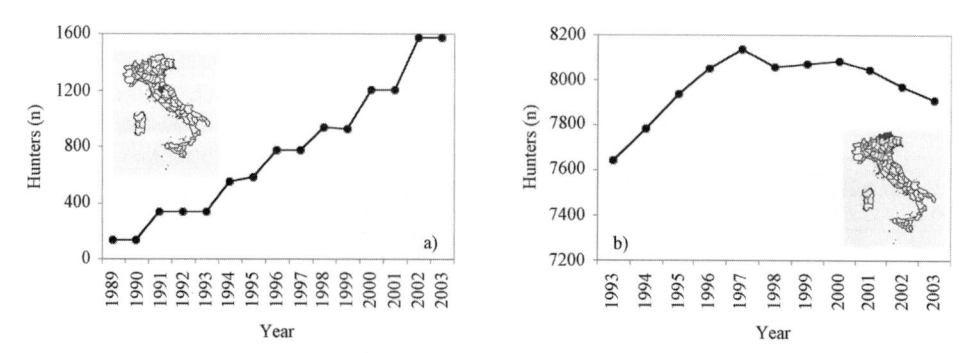

Fig. 21.14 Trend of roe deer hunters in (a) the Arezzo province between 1989 and 2003 (Mattioli, unpublished), and (b) of ungulate hunters in the Trento and Bolzano provinces from 1993 and 2003 (provinces of Trento and Bolzano, official data)

hunters in the Arezzo provinces (Mattioli, unpublished) and of ungulate hunters in the Trento and Bolzano provinces in the last decades (Trento and Bolzano provinces, official data).

21.6 Actual management and hunting practices

Table 21.5 reports the current situation of hunting in Italian provinces.

Shooting plans are mandatory to allow hunting of cervids and bovids: they must be prepared by ATC, CA or municipal reserve authorities, with detail as appropriate for any small hunting district defined within these larger areas and must be approved by the provincial government. They have to be detailed, prescribing not only the overall number of heads to be culled but also the number of individuals of each age- and sex-class to be shot. In some cases, there are official prescriptions related to the proportion of heads that can be hunted and the sex- and age-structure of such harvest: these apply on a provincial basis and can be suggested by the Italian Wildlife Institute.

When individual hunters apply for a licence to hunt, each will be allocated a specific number of animals within defined sex- and age-classes.

In contrast, shooting plans for wild boar, if present at all (only in 37% of provinces), are mainly referred to an overall number of boars to be culled without any indication of sex- and age-class.

In the case of wild boar if any quota is allocated at all, only overall hunting quotas are generally given with no assignment either to hunting teams or single hunters; in the absence of monitoring of the culling, this may lead to discrepancies between shooting plans and actual results.

Table 21.5 *Hunting in Italian provinces*

	\multicolumn{5}{c	}{Number of provinces with species presence}	\multicolumn{5}{c	}{Number of provinces with species hunting}	\multicolumn{5}{c}{Percentage of provinces with species hunting}
Species	Eastern Alps	Central Western Alps	Northern Apennine	Central Southern Apennine	Islands	Eastern Alps	Central Western Alps	Northern Apennine	Central Southern Apennine	Islands	Eastern Alps	Central Western Alps	Northern Apennine	Central Southern Apennine	Islands
Roe deer	10	14	24	16	0	10	13	20	2	0	100	93	83	13	0
Fallow deer	3	4	20	10	4	2	2	14	3	0	67	50	70	30	0
Red deer	8	12	15	11	2	6	9	6	1	0	75	75	38	9	0
Mouflon	6	11	12	2	5	4	7	9	1	0	67	64	75	50	0
Wild boar	10	14	24	31	10	9	13	24	31	9	90	93	100	100	90
Alpine chamois	10	13	1	0	0	7	12	0	0	0	70	92	0	0	0

Hunting is actually calculated to control population number of hunted species for wild boar (44 provinces), fallow deer (13), red deer (4), mouflon (3) and roe deer (2). In the Trento province, wild boar can be hunted only for control.

21.6.1 Hunting bag records

In most hunting regions, for cervids and bovids each hunter must record dressed weight for each animal shot, provide the lower jaw and display the trophy where appropriate. In some instances they also have to collect additional body measurements and information on reproductive status. In contrast, for wild boar, while hunting teams in a few limited instances must collect or estimate weight, age class, and sometimes reproductive tracts, where boar are hunted individually no data at all are collected. In consequence hunting bag records are available for cervids and bovids in all provinces but for wild boar in only 56% of them.

Table 21.6 reports number of heads hunted in Italy in 2004 and hunting bag distribution in the five main Italian regional areas. Records for wild boar must be considered a significant underestimate of actual numbers shot, and it is probable that numbers actually exceed 110 000 head per year.

Table 21.6 *Hunting bag in Italian main regions*

Species	Eastern Alps	Central Western Alps	Northern Apennine	Central Southern Apennine	Islands
Roe deer	18 355 (39%)	4 261 (9%)	23 891 (51%)	0 (0%)	0 (0%)
Fallow deer	7 (0%)	123 (3%)	3 766 (80%)	815 (17%)	0 (0%)
Red deer	5 572 (70%)	1 958 (25%)	446 (6%)	0 (0%)	0 (0%)
Mouflon	513 (59%)	193 (22%)	165 (19%)	0 (0%)	0 (0%)
Wild boar[1]	1 478 (1%)	16 051 (14%)	83 055 (72%)	9 927 (9%)	4 311 (4%)
Alpine chamois	8 338 (67%)	4 035 (33%)	0 (0%)	0 (0%)	0 (0%)
Alpine ibex[2]	75 (100%)	0 (0%)	0 (0%)	0 (0%)	0 (0%)

Hunting bag (number of heads) and distribution (%) (INFS, Carnevali *et al.*, 2007)

[1] total estimate = 115 000 head
[2] control only

21.7 Census types and methods

Because, as noted several times in this chapter, there is no formal coordination of ungulate management effort among provinces, there is likewise no formal agreement on methods to be used for population censuses of each species. As shown in Table 21.7, only Alpine chamois is censused in almost all the provinces where the species is present; by contrast, only about 40–60% of provinces perform deer censuses. The ungulate with the widest distribution in Italy, the wild boar, is censused only in about one-third of provinces.

Where some provincial supervision of hunting is present in a province, however, censuses are performed in most cases for each species, and this is because there is a legal obligation to produce shooting plans for all except wild boar. It is very clear that knowledge of the actual number, distribution and dynamics of wild boar populations in our country is extremely poor.

The lack of central coordination of management policy in Italy is underlined by the absence of uniformity in the use of different census methods (Table 21.8), especially evident for wild boar and deer, which have a distribution which includes most of the five main regional areas, in contrast to that recorded for other ungulate

Table 21.7 Censuses in the Italian provinces

Species	Number of provinces with species presence	Censuses: Number of provinces with censuses data	Percentage of provinces with censuses data	Provinces with hunting management	Hunting and censuses: Number of provinces with hunting management and censuses	Percentage
Roe deer	68	44	64.7	45	44	97.7
Fallow deer	47	21	44.6	24	21	87.5
Red deer	49	30	61.2	22	22	100
Mouflon	36	21	58.3	19	19	100
Wild boar	90	27	30.0	82	27	32.9
Alpine chamois	24	19	79.1	19	19	100

Table 21.8 *Censuses: methods used (percentage)*

Census methods	Roe deer	Fallow deer	Red deer	Mouflon	Alpine chamois	Wild boar
vantage point – block count – total count	26	39	18	48	82	8
vantage point – block count – sample area	30	21	18	24	14	35
transects	6	6	7	10	5	22
drive censuses	25	18	4	7	0	19
spotlight count	2	6	9	3	0	5
spotlight count – sample area	10	9	20	7	0	11
roaring stags count	0	0	25	0	0	0

Table 21.9 *Damage (gross underestimate but reliable proportion)*

Species	EUR (2004)
Wild boar	3 915 076 (90%)
Roe deer	171 133 (4%)
Red deer	219 558 (5%)
Fallow deer	60 906 (1%)
Mouflon	5 682 (<1%)
Chamois	0
Alpine ibex	0
Total	4 371 355

species such as chamois or ibex. In fact, census methods are very variable for all species (see Table 21.8) except for Alpine chamois for which total count by block counts is the most widely used method.

21.8 Ungulate impacts and damage

Reliable estimates of the amount of damage caused by ungulates to agriculture or forestry in our country are not available, being affected by the pattern of provincial administrations which collect data with different methods or do not have data at all.

However, an estimate is presented in Table 21.9. This is known to be a considerable underestimate, but the relative proportion of damage caused by the different ungulate species is thought to be more reliable. These data show that wild boar

Table 21.10 *Actual damage (EUR) in different Italian regions or provinces in 2004*

	Tuscany region	Autonomous Province of Trento	Aosta Valley	Palermo Province	Udine Province	Autonomous region of Sardegna
Wild boar	1 734 116	9 900	161 246	15 000	118 616	137 370
Red deer	69 350	8 163	70 006	\	3 555	7 800
Roe deer	162 650	8 163	\	\	14 742	\
Fallow deer	55 807	\	\	\	\	4 800
Total	2 021 878	26 226	231 252	15 000	136 913	149 970

is the most problematic species in Italy. Thus some 90% of damage attributed to ungulates is caused by wild boar with a total economic value probably somewhere in excess of EUR 10 million.

Table 21.10 reports some information from individual regions, where it is felt that data are more reliable. In particular, some regions collect a detailed picture of damage every year (for example, in Tuscany, in 2004, damage to crops was estimated at EUR 1 352 766, to olive trees and orchards was EUR 339 735, to vineyards was EUR 331 451, and to plantations or other was EUR 40 889; in all cases, the wild boar was recognised as responsible for more than 75% of damage caused, except in forestry plantations where cervids caused 50% of damage).

In general, damage to crops and orchards is the most serious form of damage in Italy. In the Alps, with special reference to the Eastern Alps, red deer may also cause considerable damage to woodlands through their browsing activities.

Problems related to ungulate involvement in traffic accidents are significantly relevant in northern Italy. Figure 21.15 reports number of traffic accidents between cars and roe and red deer recorded from 1993 to 2004 in the Trento province (Province of Trento official data): it is clear from these data that roe deer are the species most commonly involved in such accidents. Similar results were shown by Gazzola *et al.* (2005) in the Western Alps (Susa valley); in this Western Alps ungulate community, Gazzola *et al.* (2005) showed that traffic accidents were responsible for the death of 12.1% of all red deer while they represented the main cause of mortality for roe deer (77.7%).

In most areas, farmers receive compensation for damage to crops. Provinces pay compensation for the damage to agriculture, which can be high especially in central and northern Italy. Damage to trees and commercial forestry is, however, not normally compensated.

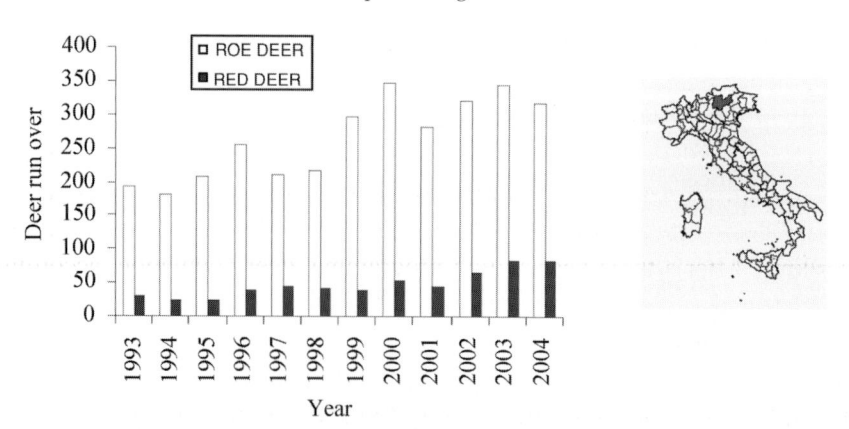

Fig. 21.15 Traffic accidents of cervids in the Trento province

21.9 Supplementary feeding

Supplementary feeding over winter is provided in Italy primarily for wild boar, roe and red deer which are fed in 14 provinces, 2 provinces, and 3 provinces, respectively. The two cervids are fed only in provinces of Eastern Alps, while the supplementary feeding of wild boar is more homogeneously distributed in our country (Eastern Alps 29%, Central Western Alps 7%, Northern Apennines 50%, and Central and Southern Apennines 14%).

Wild boar are fed primarily in order to limit damage to agriculture, even if many hunters actually supply artificial feed with the aim of increasing productivity and consequently the hunting bag. Cervids are fed in order to avoid damage to forest regeneration. In the Tarvisio Forest (Eastern Alps) red deer are also fed in winter but, in this case, this is done in order to avoid traffic accidents on the principal highway, as it is placed between red deer winter and summer ranges.

21.10 Ungulate management in Italy: crucial points for the future

21.10.1 Ungulates and protected areas: a major management issue

Over recent years the number of protected areas has increased in Italy. Before 1991 there were only four national parks in the whole country. Following law 394/1992, Italy now has 21 national parks. Altogether, protected areas in Italy comprise more than 10% of the total area of the country (Pedrotti *et al.*, 2001).

Ungulates cannot be hunted in protected areas in Italy (law n°394/1992) by the general public, but technically, they can be controlled by rangers or by hunters with special training and authorisation, under the control of rangers. In practice, the only culling programme for red deer is actually performed in the Stelvio National park (South Tyrol sector only). The first management/culling plan, from 2000 to 2002, aimed to reduce the red deer population in this park by half in order to reduce browsing impact on spruce forest regeneration (Pedrotti, unpublished). South Tyrol Stelvio National Park is divided into three different management units for red deer. The management plan was only carried out in one of these (Venosta and Martello Valley; 320 km^2, about 1400 red deer estimated) to reduce deer density from 8 to 4 deer/km^2. After a three-year culling programme, deer population, according to census data and abundance estimates, was reduced by 30% (Pedrotti, unpublished). A second triennial culling plan started in 2003 and, in 2007, reached the target density.

Italian hunter associations are pressing to have the opportunity to hunt inside protected areas, and this is may be the most complicated Italian management issue for the future. Studies performed with deer fitted with radiocollars in the Stelvio National Park and in other Italian protected areas have clearly shown the fundamental role played by these areas in ungulate conservation.

Stelvio National Park lies within the Val Di Sole red deer management unit (Trento province), which ranges over 720 km^2 in total. From 1993, hunting management aimed to limit red deer increase and to stabilise the population. The application of high culling regimes in the management unit as a whole (from 600 to 700 harvested red deer each year) meant that the deer population tended to concentrate in the only available sanctuary area: the Stelvio Park. The results showed a significant response of red deer behaviour to human induced disturbance and a growing disproportion between animals that consistently range only within the protected area and animals that move outside its borders (Pedrotti, unpublished). The same behaviour was recorded for female red deer in the Casentinesi Forest National park, with movement towards and from the protected area synchronised with times at which hunting with dogs is permitted (Apollonio, unpublished). Grigholio *et al.* (*in prep.*) recorded the same picture in the protected area 'Alpe di Catenaia' (a mountainous protected area in the Arezzo province surrounded by a district where various hunting practices are allowed, such as selective hunting on roe deer, hunting of wild boar with battues and hounds, etc.), where roe deer presence (n = 62) inside the protected area significantly increased when wild boar hunting with dogs was allowed outside (Fig. 21.16).

This suggests that these protected areas may play a very significant role in the overall dynamics of deer populations within the wider landscape area.

21.10.2 Wolf and ungulates

Wolf distribution in Italy has shown a marked increase during the last part of the last century, being only localised in central and southern Apennine in 1972

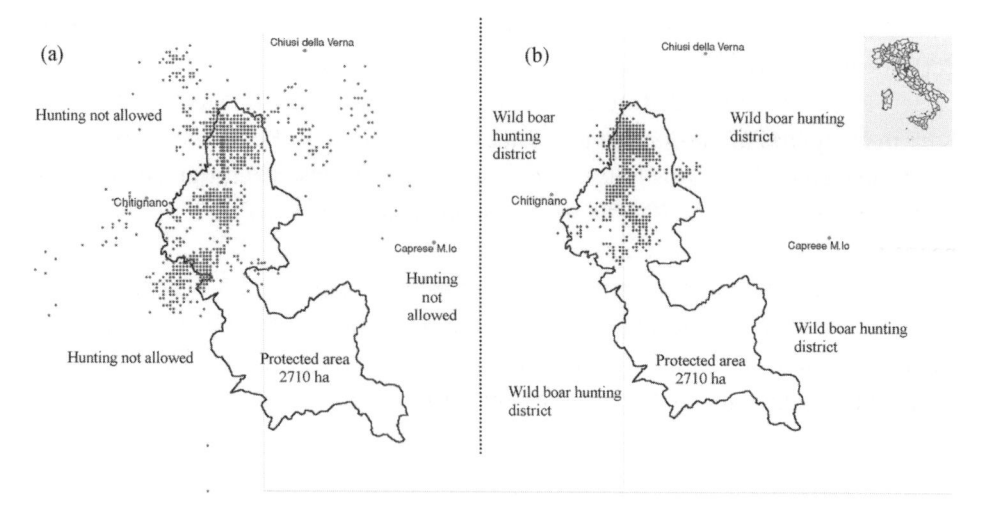

Fig. 21.16 Total roe deer fixes recorded in the 'Alpe di Catenaia' (Arezzo province) from March 2002 to August 2002 (no wild boar hunting with dogs) (a), and from September 2002 to January 2003 (wild boar hunting with dogs) (b) (Grigholio et al., in prep)

(Cagnolaro et al., 1974), whilst since that time this species has recolonised the Northern Apennines and Western and Central Alps.

This expansion is strongly linked to the increase in numbers and distribution of ungulate populations recorded in the last 30 years, as already described, and the simultaneous abandonment of villages in the mountains and hills. Wolf conservation is tightly linked to good ungulate management, as wolves in Italy have now reassumed a diet based on wild prey. Gazzola et al. (2005) showed in the Western Alps that the preferred prey of wolves is wild ungulates (87.2%). Cervids are the preferred prey (74.2%) and constitute the predominant food items both in winter and summer (Gazzola et al., 2005). The presence of domestic ungulates on high-altitude pastures during summer influences wolf diet but, despite the major density of domestic livestock, wolves still prefer wild ungulates (Gazzola et al., 2005). The same picture was seen in north-eastern Apennine (Capitani et al., 2004; Mattioli et al., 2004) where predation by wolves on wild ungulates was studied by scat analysis in five study areas. Also, in this case, wild ungulates constituted the wolf preferred prey, and in particular, wild boar was the main prey in almost areas. Establishing a network of protected areas with high ungulate diversity and abundance is proposed as the main factor for allowing a full recovery of the wolf population in Italy (Apollonio et al., 2004; Jędrzejewski et al., 2010).

21.10.3 Wild boar management

Wild boar is the most problematic species in Italy because it has such a wide distribution but is very badly managed; the practice of hunting with dogs is also considered to be very disturbing for all other ungulates and wildlife in general. It is disturbing that only one-third of provinces with wild boar hunting have censuses or even simple estimates. Only the same portion of provinces with wild boar hunting have shooting plans, and only a few more collect hunting bag data. Wild boar alone is responsible for 90% of damage caused by ungulates to agriculture, and a correct knowledge of the status of this species is therefore strongly needed.

Wild boar are artificially fed in 16% of provinces where present, and this is mainly done in order to increase productivity and supply food during hot and dry summers with lower food availability, these practices are only secondarily directed towards reducing damage to crops and orchards.

21.10.4 Collection of relevant management data

The general organisation of hunting and the collection of hunting data must be improved because there is too little cooperation and exchange of information between autonomous hunting districts/units. The effectiveness of current management strategies totally depends on the ability and experience of each provincial administration.

Provincial administrations usually maintain no information on the numbers and species composition of ungulates in protected areas on their territories: they are responsible for management within some areas where hunting is permitted and some local reserves, but their efforts are not coordinated with, or integrated with, management within regional or national parks which may occur in the same area.

Provinces usually do not gather data about damage because compensation is paid by ATC General Hunting Districts and thus only have data on areas they manage directly.

Some regions do not even delegate hunting management to the provincial level, so the latter do not have any data on hunting management.

Usually only a few provinces (or regions) make use of detailed data collected with selective ungulate hunting or have established long term data collection on consistency. Definitely, a common management strategy among provinces is urgently needed.

Acknowledgements

We gratefully acknowledge the help given during data collection by Beppe Meneguz, Guido Tosi, Damiano Preatoni, Michele Viliani, and Elena Rossi. We thank Silvano Toso who gave appreciable comments on the first draft of this manuscript. We thank very much all Italian provinces that during the period 2001–2004 provided us data on ungulate status of territories they managed. We are indebted to Rory Putman for accurate English revisions and invaluable comments on the first draft of this manuscript. S. C. was supported by Fondazione Banco di Sardegna.

References

Apollonio, M. (2003) *Sus scrofa* (Linnaeus, 1758). In L. Boitani, S. Lovari, A. V. Taglianti, eds., *Fauna d'Italia Mammalia III Carnivora-Artiodactyla*. Calderini Editore.

Apollonio, M. (2004) Ungulati in Italia: status, gestione e ricerca scientifica. *Italian Journal of Mammalogy* **15**, 21–34. (In Italian with English abstract.)

Apollonio, M., Randi, E. and Toso, S. (1988) The systematics of the wild boar (*Sus scrofa* L.) in *Italy. Bollettino di Zoologia* **3**, 213–21.

Apollonio, M., Randi, E. and Toso, S. (1992) A morphological and biochemical approach to some European wild boars' systematic problems. In B. Bobek, K. Perzanowski and W. Regelin, eds., *Global trends in wildlife management*. Trans. 18th IUGB Congress, Krakow, 1987. Krakow-Warszawa: Swiat Press, pp. 23–30.

Apollonio, M., Mattioli, L., Scandura, M. *et al.* (2004) Wolves in the Casentinesi Forests: insights for wolf conservation in Italy from a protected area with a rich wild prey community. *Biological Conservation* **120**, 249–60.

Bassano, B., Ferrario, G., Grimod, I. *et al.* (1993) Analisi della situazione e problemi di gestione degli ungulati nelle regioni alpine. Seminario interregioale *Gestione Faunistico: Venatoria degli Ungulati*, Bologna, 30 April 1993, Unpublished report. (In Italian.)

Cagnolaro, L., Rosso, D., Spagnesi, M. and Venturi, B. (1974) Investigation on the wolf (*Canis lupus*) distribution in Italy and in Canton Ticino and Canton Grigion (Switzerland). *Ricerche di Biologia della Selvaggina* **59**, 1–75. In Italian.

Capitani, C., Bertelli, I., Varuzza, P., Scandura, M. and Apollonio, M. (2004) A comparative analysis of wolf (*Canis lupus*) diet in different Italian ecosystems. *Mammalian Biology* **69**, 1–10.

Carnevali, L., Pedrotti, L., Riga, F. and Toso, S. (2007) *Banca Dati Ungulati. Status, distribuzione,consistenza, gestione e prelievo venatorio*. Rapporto INFS 2001–2005.

Crestanello, B., Pecchioli, E., Hauffe, H. C. *et al.* (2004) Genetic variation, divergence, and translocation in the chamois (*Rupicapra* spp.): implications for taxonomy and management. Atti del VI convegno FISV 30 September–3 October, Riva del Garda (TN).

De Beaux, O. and Festa, E. (1927) La ricomparsa del cinghiale nell'Italia settentrionale-occidentale. *Memorie della Società Italiana di Scienze Naturali. Museo Civico di Storia Naturale di Milano* **9**, 263–322.

Festa, E. (1925) Il capriolo dell'Italia Centrale. *Bollettino del Museo di Zoologia e Anatomia Comparata della Università di Torino* **40**, 1–2.

Gauthier, D. and Villaret, C. (1990) Réintroducion d'une espèce protégée: le Bouquetin des Alpes. *Revue d'Ecologie, La Terre at la Vie* **5**, 97–120.

Gazzola, A., Bertelli, I., Avanzinelli, E. *et al.* (2005) Predation by wolves (*Canis lupus*) on wild and domestic ungulates of the western Alps, Italy. *Journal of Zoology (London)* **266**, 205–13.

Ghigi, A. (1917) I Mammiferi d'Italia considerati nei loro rapporti coll'agricoltura. *Natura* **VIII**, 85–137.

Ghigi, A. (1950) *La vita degli animali. Il Mammiferi ed Uccelli sedentari delle terre continentali*. U.T.E.T., Milano.

Hartl, G. B., Schleger, A. and Slowak, M. (1986) Genetic variability in fallow deer, *Dama dama* L. *Animal Genetics* **17**, 335–41.

Hmwe, S. S., Zachos, F. E., Eckert, I. *et al.* (2006) Conservation genetics of the endangered red deer from Sardinia and Mesola with further remarks on the phylogeography of *Cervus elaphus corsicanus*. *Biological Journal of the Linnaean Society* **88**, 691–701.

Jędrzejewski, W. *et al.* (2010) Large carnivores and the impact of predation on populations of wild ungulates. In R. J. Putman, M. Apollonio and R. Andersen, eds., *Ungulate Management in Europe: Problems and Practices*. Cambridge, UK: Cambridge University Press.

Larson, G., Dobney, K., Albarella, U. *et al.* (2005) Worldwide phylogeography of wild boar reveals multiple centers of pig domestication. *Science* **307**, 1618–21.

Lorenzini, R. and Lovari, S. (2006) Genetic diversity and phylogeography of the European roe deer: the refuge area theory revisited. *Biological Journal of the Linnaean Society* **88**, 85–100.

Lorenzini, R., Mattioli, S. and Fico, R. (1998) Allozyme variation in native red deer *Cervus elaphus* of Mesola wood, northern Italy: implications for conservation. *Acta Theriologica* Suppl. **5**, 63–74.

Lorenzini, R., Lovari, S. and Masseti, M. (2002) The rediscovery of the Italian roe deer: genetic differentiation and management implications. *Italian Journal of Zoology* **69**, 367–79.

Lorenzini, R., Fico, R. and Mattioli, S. (2005) Mitochondrial DNA evidence for a genetic distinction of the native red deer of Mesola, northern Italy, from the Alpine populations and the Sardinian subspecies. *Mammalian Biology* **70**(3), 187–98.

Ludt, C. J., Shroeder, W., Rottmann, O. and Kuehn, R. (2004) Mitochondrial DNA phylogeography of red deer (*Cervus elaphus*). *Molecular Phylogeny and Evolution* **31**, 1064–83.

Mattioli, L., Capitani, C., Avanzinelli, E. *et al.* (2004) Predation by wolves (*Canis lupus*) on roe deer (*Capreolus capreolus*) in north-eastern Apennine, Italy. *Journal of Zoology, London* **264**, 1–10.

Pedrotti, L., Duprè, E., Preatoni, D. and Toso, S. (2001) Banca dati Ungulati: status, distribuzione, consistenza, gestione, prelievo venatorio e potenzialità delle popolazioni di Ungulati in Italia. *Biologia e Conservazione della Fauna* **109**, 1–132.

Perco, Fr. (1981) Daino, Cervo, Capriolo, Muflone. In M. Pavan and B. Boera, eds., *Distribuzione e biologia di 22 specie di Mammiferi in Italia*. Roma: C.N.R., pp. 129–59. (In Italian.)

Randi, E. and Apollonio, M. (1988) Low biochemical variability in European fallow deer (*Dama dama* L.): natural bottlenecks and the effects of domestication. *Heredity* **61**, 405–10.

Randi, E., Apollonio, M. and Toso, S. (1989) The systematics of some Italian population of wild boar (*Sus scrofa* L.): a craniometric and electrophoretic analysis. *Zeischrift für Säugetierkunde* **54**, 40–56.

Randi, E., Alves, P. C., Carranza, J., Milošević-Zlantanović, S. and Sfougaris, A. (2004) Phylogeography of roe deer (*Capreolus capreolus*) populations: the effects of historical genetic subdivisions and recent nonequilibrium dynamics. *Molecular Ecology* **13**(10), 3071–83.

Sacchi, O., Ziliani, U. and Posillico, M. (2001) Definizione dell'areale potenziale di cervo sardo *Cervus elaphus corsicanus*, muflone *Ovis orientalis musimon* e orso bruno *Ursus arctos marsicanus*. Progetto di monitoraggio dello stato di conservazione di alcuni mammiferi particolarmente a rischio della fauna italiana. Convenzione Università di Siena-Ministero dell'Ambiente.

Scandura, M., Tiedemann, R., Apollonio, M. and Hartl, G. B. (1998) Genetic variation in an isolated Italian population of fallow deer *Dama dama* as revealed by RAPD-PCR. *Acta Theriologica* Suppl. **5**, 163–9.

Scandura, M., Iacolina, L., Crestanello, B. *et al.* (2006) Genetic variation in the European wild boar: Italy as hotspot of diversity. *1st Congress of the Italiana Society of Evolutionary Biology* (S.I.B.E.), Florence, 4–7 September 2006.

Schenk, H. (1976) Analisi della situazione faunistica della Sardegna. Uccelli e mammiferi. In F. Pedrotti, ed., *S.O.S. Fauna. Animali in pericolo in Italia*. Camerino: Edizione W.W.F., pp. 465–556.

Tosi, G. and Perco, Fr. (1981) Stambecco Camoscio. In M. Pavan and B. Boera, eds., *Diztribuzione e Biologia di 22 Specie di Mammiferi in Italia*. Roma: C.N.R. In Italian.

Vernesi, C., Pecchioli, E., Caramelli, D. *et al.* (2002) The genetic structure of natural and reintroduced roe deer (*Capreolus capreolus*) populations in the Alps and central Italy, with reference to the mitochondrial DNA phylogeography of Europe. *Molecular Ecology* **11**, 1285–97.

Zachos, F., Hartl, G. B., Apollonio, M. and Reutershan, T. (2003) On the phylogeographic origin of the Corsican red deer (*Cervus elaphus corsicanus*): evidence from microsatellites and mitochondrial DNA. *Mammalian Biology* **68**, 284–98.

22

Ungulates and their management in Slovenia

MIHA ADAMIC AND KLEMEN JERINA

Slovenia, with a land area of about 20 000 km², is situated between the Eastern Alps, Dinaric Mountains, Adriatic Littoral and Pannonian flatland. Diverse landscapes provide habitats for an equal diversity of wildlife species. Among ungulates, typical Alpine species are represented e.g. chamois and ibex, as well other species which occur more widely from the lowlands to the mountains: roe deer, red deer and wild boar. According to the policy of the Hunters Association at the time, fallow deer and mouflon have been introduced in Slovenia in recent times (post-World War II).

About 60% of the land area of Slovenia is covered by forests – predominantly mixed deciduous and mixed coniferous–deciduous types of forests. The major tree species are beech (*Fagus sylvatica*), oaks (*Quercus* spp.), Norway spruce (*Picea abies*), silver fir (*Abies alba*) and red pine (*Pinus sylvestris*). The percentage of silver fir is decreasing due to problems with its natural regeneration, while spruce is decreasing due to bark beetle depradation. The area of forested land has increased over the last 100 years from 90 000 up to almost 120 000 km². Forests increased mostly due to changes in the socioeconomic situation, as well due to the changes in agricultural practices. Currently about 70% of Slovenian forests are privately owned (Slovenia Forest Service, www.zgs.gov.si/).

With the exception of north-eastern Slovenia, where larger blocks of arable land are found, agricultural areas in other parts of the country are scattered in small patches between the forests and urban areas and are thus suitable for small-scale farming only. Crop damage by ungulates occurs regularly within such landscapes with predominantly forest cover.

Slovenia is densely populated, with an average of 98.7 inhabitants/km². The pattern of settlements, scattered over the countryside, is not very suitable for the conservation management of large mammals. Few remote areas, except those in

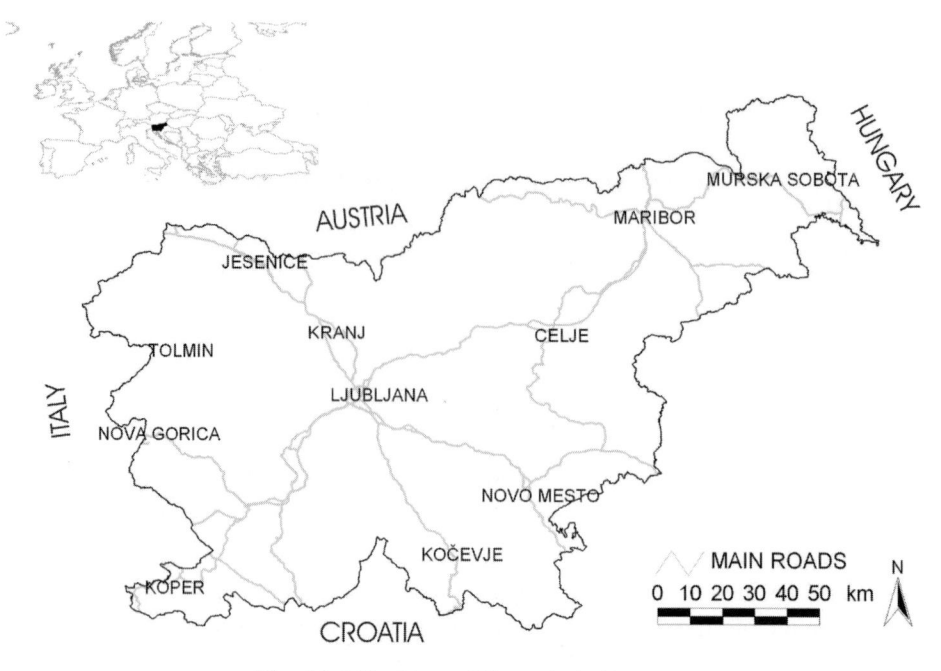

Fig. 22.1 Position of Slovenia in Europe

large forest blocks and high in the mountains, are free of human impact. The goals of wildlife management and human interests are thus often forced into conflict.

A network of fenced highways and regional motorways with a heavy traffic load pose serious barriers for the safe dispersal of large mammals. Red deer and wild boar are particularly affected by this problem of traffic. Until recently, few efforts were made to include effective mitigation measures during the construction of highways (Jerina *et al.*, 2005, but see also Pokorny *et al.*, 2007).

22.1 Status and distribution of ungulates in Slovenia

22.1.1 Red deer

Under the regimes of game management in the Austrian Empire of the eighteenth century, red deer populations in what is now Slovenia were hunted to extinction, probably by 1860 (Schollmayer, 1899; Valentinčič, 1958). At the end of the nineteenth century red deer were reintroduced to four locations in two distinct areas. In south-western Slovenia red deer from the Carpathians (unknown source), Austria (unknown source) and the Mecklenburg (Germany) were reintroduced to enclosures on two adjacent locations in Planina (Haasberg) in 1895 and on Sneznik (Schneeberg) in 1899. In northern Slovenia in the Karavanke Alps reintroductions took place in Kokra in 1888 (red deer from Hungary), and in Puterhof in 1894 (red deer from Poland and Lower Austria). A small number of North American wapiti

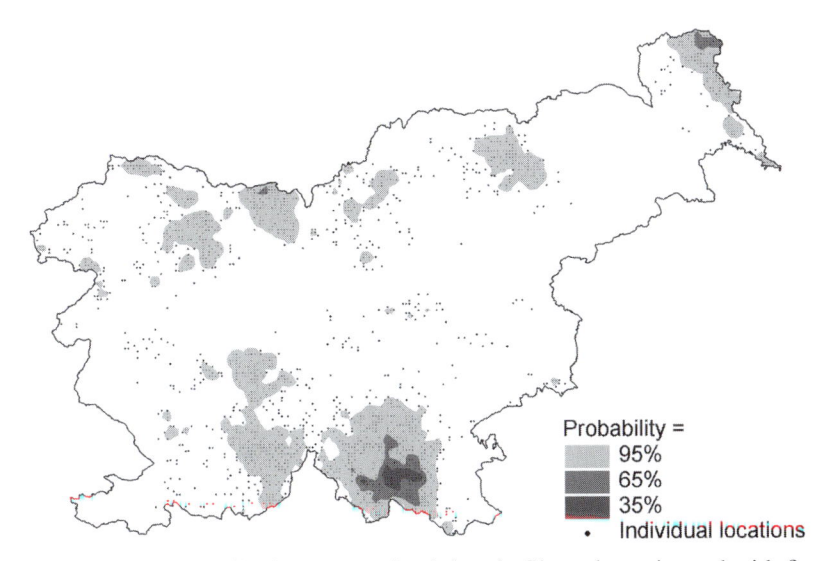

Fig. 22.2 Current distribution range of red deer in Slovenia, estimated with fixed kernel method based on data from the 'Central Slovene Register of Large Game Species and Large Carnivores' [see section 22.7]. Shaded areas show (cumulatively) 35, 65 and 95%, respectively, polygons enclosing the locations of all harvested red deer in Slovenia (see section 22.7 for further explanation), while points delineate individual locations of harvested red deer

(*Cervus canadensis*) were also released in the same area, but did not survive for long due to unsuitable, steep and rocky alpine terrain (Valentinčič, 1958).

Red deer from both reintroduction centres began to expand their range soon after the enclosures had been opened. But up to the end of World War II the extent of spread was limited, since the majority of dispersing individuals were soon shot by local hunters.

After World War II legal protection of red deer and other ungulates was strengthened; while, at the same time, the anti-wolf campaign in Slovenia was very active. Habitat improvements, supplemental feeding, extermination of wolves and strong legal protection triggered accelerated growth and spatial expansion of red deer populations (Adamič, 1990).

The red deer population in Prekmurje, north-eastern Slovenia, is now continuous with the red deer in Zala County (western Hungary), from where it spread naturally in the period after World War II. In the period of intensified red deer management and protection, additional restockings with red deer from Croatian Lowlands (Baranja) have been performed on Pohorje in 1962 and in Kocevje in 1962 (C. Štrumbelj, 2005, *pers. comm.*).

Currently about 80% of Slovenian forests are settled by red deer (Fig. 22.2). A crude estimation of the population size suggests somewhere between 10 000 and 14 000 animals. During the period 1998–2004 an average of 4174 ± 291

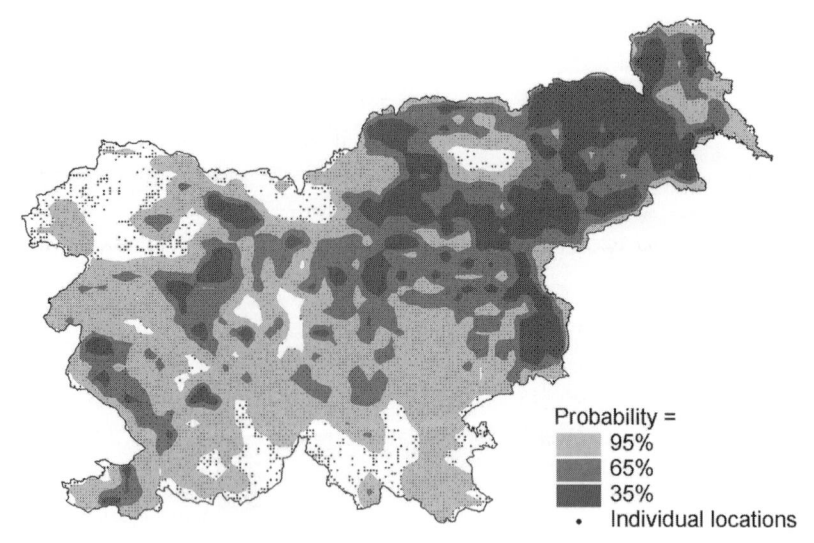

Fig. 22.3 Current distribution range of roe deer in Slovenia

red deer have been killed each year (as a total of both cull mortality and recorded non-cull mortality; Jerina, 2006b).

22.1.2 Roe deer

Roe deer is the most widespread and numerically abundant game species in Slovenia. It can be found from coastal to mountainous regions, in all vegetation zones and at all altitudes (Fig. 22.3). For these reasons roe deer has a very high value from the hunting aspect and for the majority of hunting clubs it represents the most significant economic income.

With the increase of forest cover, but also with modern forest management practices which influence relatively small coppices, the stock of roe deer in Slovenia has increased. In second half of the nineteenth century, roe deer was, for example, absent from a great part of the then deforested Littoral Karst in south-western Slovenia, but currently the same area with about 55% of forest cover sustains a yearly harvest 3–6 roe deer/100 ha of hunting surface (www.zgs.gov.si/).

After this period of increase and spread, however, the current population of roe deer in Slovenia appears to be stable and no further increase is expected. Indeed, to the contrary, it is more likely that numbers will decrease because of environmental changes and interspecies relations (mainly with red deer and other numerically increasing species).

About 35 000–45 000 roe deer are culled annually. Yearly harvest oscillates within 5-year amplitudes. Over the last decade (1996–2005) sex structure of the roe cull is as follows: 49.2% of males and 50.8% of females.

In the ten-year period from 1996–2005, total recorded mortality (cull plus non-cull mortality) was 417 550. That number is significantly higher than for other big game species; 79.2% of the overall mortality over that ten-year period was by hunting harvest, 4.8% from natural mortality (diseases) and 16.0% from non-natural mortality (other human caused but non-hunting mortality). The highest percentage of this comes from traffic losses; in the last decade some 5000 roe deer, on average, were killed each year in traffic collisions, mainly on the roads (Jonozovic et al., 2007; Kumelj and Orsanic, 2007). This is one of the major problems in roe deer management nowadays. Roads' heavy traffic burdens pose barriers in areas of previously continuous population, and in some areas the number of traffic-killed roe deer exceeds the number hunted.

22.1.3 Fallow deer

Fallow deer were first introduced into modern-day Slovenia at the beginning of the twentieth century. Previous to this wider introduction, at the end of the nineteenth century, a small herd of fallow deer was kept in a 60 ha large enclosure Pardovec in the foothills of the Pohorje Mountains in north-eastern Slovenia. The enclosure with about 10 animals was closed in 1923/24, and the animals were shot (Šivic, 1921, 1925).

The first official introduction (of six animals) took place in 1962, again on Pohorje (enclosure Šumnik). This was followed by a number of other introductions to different parts of Slovenia (Kocevje, Littoral Karst, Velenje, Goricko in north-eastern Slovenia, Krakovo Forest). The most successful introduction was performed in 1971 in the area of Sežana, western Slovenia, close to the border with Italy. The majority of introduced animals came from the Isle of Brioni and in Dubica (Croatia).

Releases in more mountainous areas in 1970 (Jelovica, Smrekovec) failed completely. Both types of release have been used: *hard release*, the animals have been released directly into nature; as well *soft release*, the animals have been kept in an enclosure and released later.

Currently there are several small enclosures in which fallow deer are kept for meat production, recreational hunting or just for viewing. Fallow deer are kept successfully in Game Enclosure Smuka, Kocevje with an area of approximately 1000 ha.

Current distribution is as shown in Figure 22.4. Estimates of total population number are not available, but numbers are not high: total recorded mortality over the

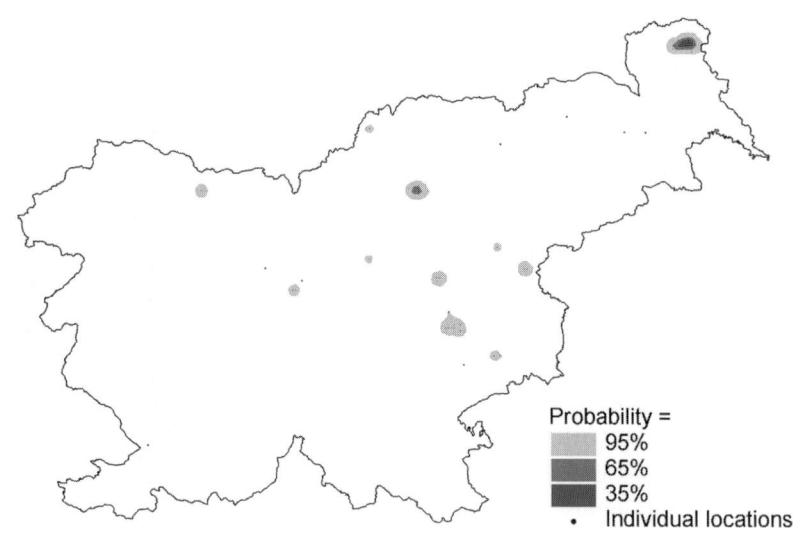

Fig. 22.4 Current distribution range of fallow deer in Slovenia

period 1996–2005 was of only some 140 animals on average per year (Jonozovic et al., 2007) (Table 22.2).

22.1.4 Alpine chamois

At the beginning of the twentieth century the chamois was widespread over the highest parts of the Alps and Pohorje Mountains. Small, isolated population units lived in Zasavje, central Slovenia, as well as in the Dinaric Mountains, e.g. in Borovniski Pekel, Kolpa and Iška Valley.

Additional introductions of chamois have been performed by the hunters on Sneznik in 1927, in Kolpa Valley in 1957 and on Nanos in 1959. In all three cases chamois from the Karawanke Alps have been used for restocking (Slovenian Hunters Association, 2007: www.lovska-zveza.si/).

Spontaneous colonisation by chamois and the establishment of new populations in new areas in forested sub-alpine regions was recorded in the pre-World War II period on Gorjanci and on Boč, both in south-eastern Slovenia. The recovery and natural spread of chamois was possible due to legal protection and the absence of large predators. Today's range of chamois (Fig. 22.5) encompasses continuous habitats in the Alps and Pre-alpine areas, as well small scattered habitat islands in the Dinarics, probably connected to the chamois range in Gorski Kotar in Croatia.

In the period after 1975, sarcoptic mange, a parasitic disease of chamois (and ibex) spread from Austria to the Karawanke and Julian Alps. The greatest part of

Table 22.1 *Estimated population sizes and the harvest of indigenous ungulate species in Slovenia given in five-year intervals (Statistical yearbooks of Slovene Hunters Association)*

	Red deer		Roe deer		Chamois		Wild boar	
Year	N est.	Bag	N est.	Bag	N est.	Bag	N est.	Bag
1975	5480	2264	75 850	22 596	12 950	1879	3200	1078
1980	6670	3098	88 050	27 661	11 950	2458	3700	1300
1985	6260	3472	91 500	36 301	10 900	1487	4200	2697
1990	7500	4713	98 600	42 736	11 000	1974	5000	5043
1995*	8830	3588	84 200	31 163	11 400	1805	4600	2925
2000	–	3686	–	31 080	–	1983	–	5068
2005	–	4923	–	42 393	–	2506	–	6569

* Estimations of population sizes have not been given after 1997

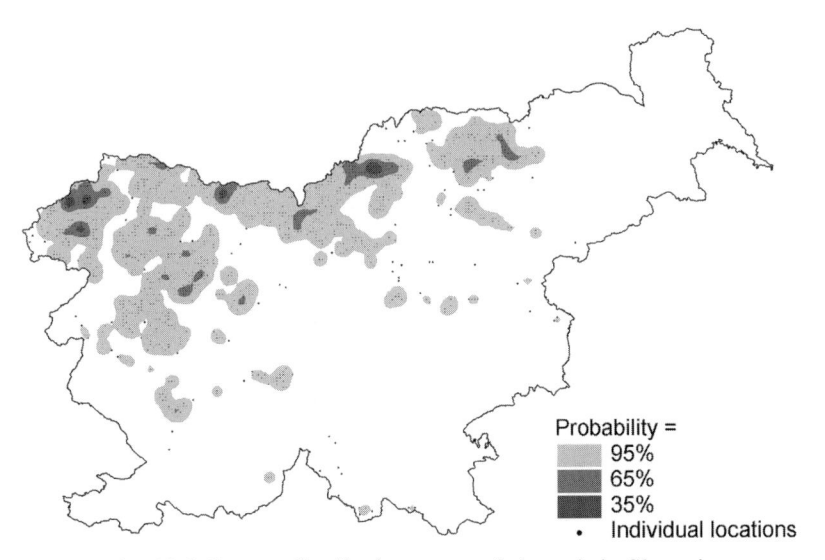

Fig. 22.5 Current distribution range of chamois in Slovenia

the chamois range was affected with up to 80% of the local chamois stock lost. Several preventative measures have been proposed and implemented, but with poor success. Occasional outbreaks of sarcoptic mange in local centres of the disease have to be accepted now as the long term reality of chamois population dynamics in Slovenia.

Over the ten-year period 1996–2005 total recorded mortality of chamois (cull and non-cull mortality, combined) averaged about 2500 head per year (Table 22.1).

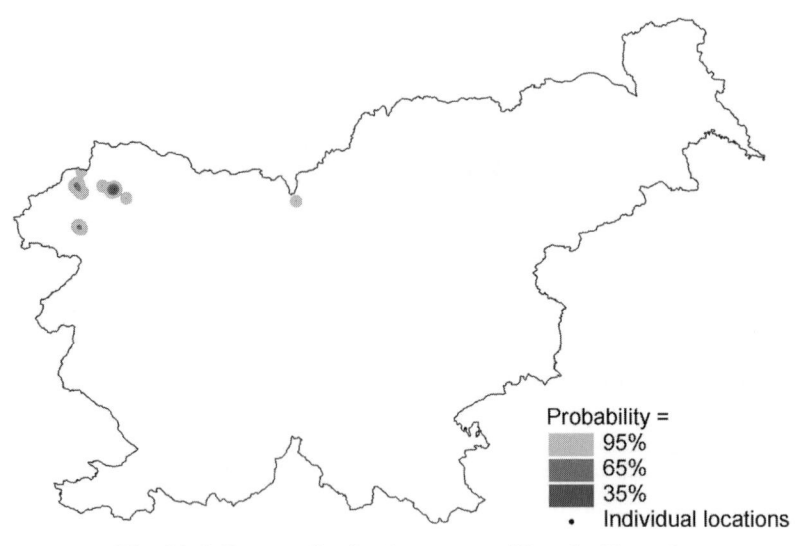

Fig. 22.6 Current distribution range of ibex in Slovenia

22.1.5 Ibex

Within the current land area of Slovenia there is no reliable evidence that ibex survived in post-Ice Age times. Thus, the introductions of ibex on Ljubelj in the Karawanke Alps by the estate-owner Dr Julius Born in the period 1890–6 can be taken as the time of establishment of ibex in the Slovenian Alps. Dr Julius Born, also known for the successful restocking of red deer in the Karawanke Alps, introduced 20 ibex, which he bought in Lausanne, Switzerland.

A second introduction of ibex in Slovenia took place in 1953 in Kamniška Bistrica, eastern Karawanke Alps when three ibex from Switzerland were released.

A further eight animals were released in the area in 1961 and 1965. The ibex moved to Mt. Brana and in 1975 about 95 ibex were recorded there.

A final introduction was performed in the period 1965–75 in Trenta Valley in Julian Alps, where ibex from Gran Paradiso National Park, Italy were introduced. In total, about 60 ibex have been successfully released there. In 1976 the population was estimated to be about 160 animals. The population area of ibex in Julian Alps is currently the part of the Triglav National Park (Adamič and Marenče, 1997).

The habitats of ibex are high alpine meadows and rocky terrain above the timberline (Fig. 22.6). Since Slovenian Alps peak up to 2864 m (the altitude of the highest mountain in Slovenia, Mt. Triglav), suitable habitats for ibex are few. Thus, the opportunities for successful dispersal and building of new colonies are limited. The outbreak of sarcoptic mange among ibex, being transferred from chamois in post-1980 period, also reduced their numbers, particularly in the Ljubelj area, where the colony vanished completely. Existing colonies, in Triglav National Park

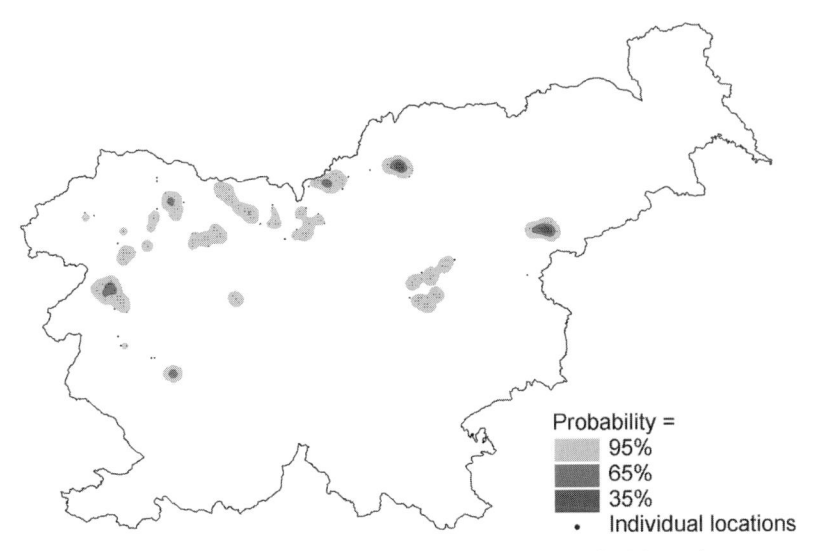

Fig. 22.7 Current distribution range of mouflon in Slovenia

and on Brana in Karawanke Alps, are isolated and separated each from another by more than a hundred kilometres. The prospect for long-term persistence of the ibex in Slovenian Alps is thus uncertain. The size of existing colonies of ibex in 2001 was estimated at 300 animals (Slovene Hunters Association, 2007: www.lovska-zveza.si).

22.1.6 Mouflon

The first mouflon were introduced in Slovenia in 1953, but the majority of introductions took place in the period 1965–70. The main source for released animals was from the Brioni Islands in Croatia, with a few also coming from Italy and Austria. Current distribution of mouflon in Slovenia is evident from Figure 22.7. Between 1996 and 2005, recorded mortality of mouflon (cull and non-cull mortality together) has averaged some 700 per year (Table 22.2).

The problem of introductions of mouflon and other non-indigenous ungulates is often presented as a concern about the increased extent of browsing damage from the additional species of newcomers. But in fact the key problem of introductions is rather in the diminishing interest in proper management of indigenous species. As a rule, the introductions of newcomers have taken a lot of money, but also additional management efforts of the local hunters, which have been previously invested in the management of native species. There is also clear evidence that browsing and bark peeling damage in young plantations by mouflon is not to be overlooked.

Table 22.2 *Estimated population sizes and the harvest of introduced (non-indigenous) ungulate species in Slovenia given in five-year intervals (Statistical yearbooks of Slovene Hunters Association)*

	Mouflon		Fallow deer		Ibex**	
Year	N	Bag	N	Bag	N	Bag
1975	1700	237	400	21		
1980	2430	277	620	82		
1985	2400	475	550	48		
1990	2140	549	450	118		
1995*	2100	567	400	227		
2000	–	623	–	94		
2005	–	718	–	140	–	20

* Estimations of population sizes have not been given after 1997
** Ibex was protected until last period

22.1.7 Wild boar

At the beginning of the twentieth century, the wild boar was a rare creature in what is modern-day Slovenia. It seems that this was the reason for the frequent articles published at that time on this species (Schollmayer, 1899; Zajc, 1907; Šašelj, 1911; Čebular, 1921; Donko, 1922).

In 1913, a small enclosure was erected at Radoha the Gorjanci mountains in south-eastern Slovenia. The owner of the estate brought in an adult sow with piglets, which he bought in Ulm, Germany. The sow and piglets escaped soon and were met by an adult boar which probably came from adjacent Croatian forests (Šavelj, 1933). To judge from the extent of reported crop damage in the period of the World War I, wild boar began to spread their range successfully.

Currently about 55% of Slovenian territory is settled by wild boar (Fig. 22.8), but according to Jerina (2006a) its potential range is larger – some 67% of the country. Although the forests in higher altitudes are not optimal habitats for wild boar, supplemental feeding provided by the hunters has attracted the species even into these more mountainous areas (e.g. Pohorje, Snežnik-Javornik, etc.).

Supplemental feeding with maize, organised by the wildlife managers over the whole range of the wild boar in Slovenia, is supposed to prevent crop damage by the species. But, according to the increasing extent of yearly reports on wild boar damage, it seems that the feeding interventions have only moderate effects.

The harvest of wild boar in Slovenia in the period 1970–2002 increased by 16-fold, from 472 in 1970 to 7500 individuals in 2002. Agricultural damage has

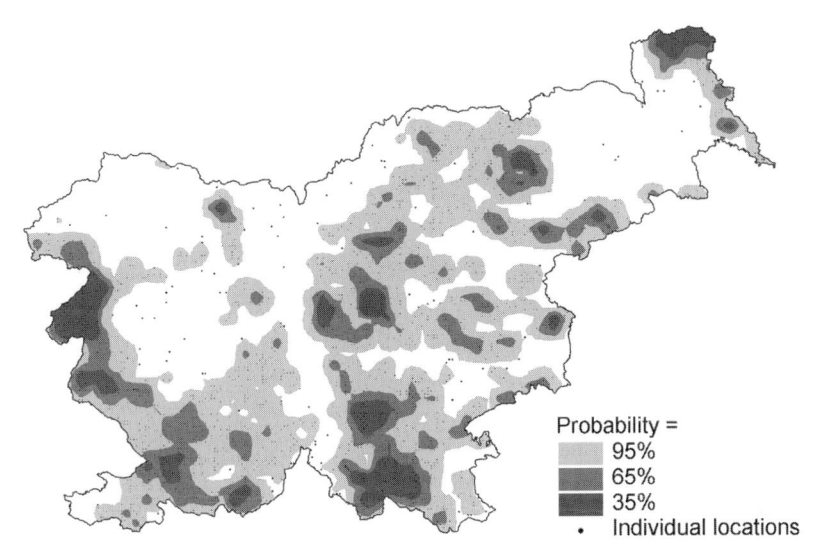

Fig. 22.8 Current distribution range of wild boar in Slovenia

been increasing simultaneously, all of which is strongly suggestive of a continuing increase in population.

In 2005, the harvest rate for wild boar was 0.35 individuals/km² of the total area of Slovenia, which according to Hell *et al.* (2004) was significantly lower than that in neighbouring European countries.

22.2 Legislation

The current wildlife management system in Slovenia is based on the Law on Wildlife and Hunting which was adopted in 2004.

Wildlife is declared as valuable natural resource and is the property of the state.

Several attempts to challenge this and link the right of hunting to land-ownership have been launched by groups of landowners, but this has been unsuccessful to this point.

Legal hunting seasons, for different wildlife species, were fixed in 2004 by the Act on Hunting Seasons and Wildlife (Table 22.3). Special permission for extended shooting seasons for red deer calves and yearlings (in late winter and in spring) are however regularly issued by the Slovenian Ministry of Agriculture and Forestry in areas of high damage to agricultural or forest crops.

Regulations on legal hunting practices and the use of hunting firearms, including regulations on the use of minimal rifle calibres, have been prescribed by the Regulation on the legal hunting firearms from 1 August 2005 (Table 22.4).

Table 22.3 *Legal hunting seasons for ungulates in Slovenia, according to the Law on Wildlife and Hunting (2004)*

		Legal hunting season	
Wildlife species	Sex/age class	*From*	*To*
Red deer	Hinds, calves	1 September	31 December
	Yearlings (M, F)	1 July	31 December
	Stags ≥ 2 y	16 August	31 December
Roe deer	Females ≥ 2 y, kids	1 September	31 December
	Yearling females	1 May	31 December
	Bucks ≥ 1 y	1 May	31 October
Fallow deer	Stags	16 August	31 December
	Hinds, calves	1 September	31 December
	Yearlings (M, F)	1 July	31 December
Chamois	Females, kids, yearlings	1 August	31 December
	Bucks	1 August	31 December
Ibex	Females, kids	1 August	31 December
	Bucks	1 August	31 December
Wild boar	Sows	1 August	31 January
	Males	1 May	31 January
	Piglets, yearlings (M, F)	1 January	31 December
Mouflon	Ram, yearlings, lambs	1 August	28 February
	Ewe	1 August	31 December

Table 22.4 *Minimal rifle calibres for the hunting of ungulates in Slovenia (Reg. 1.8.2005)*

Wildlife species	Calibre (mm (inches))	Bullet weight (grams)	E/100 m (J)
Red deer, ibex, fallow deer, wild boar – adults	6.5 (.257)	9.0	2500
Chamois, mouflon	6.0 (.243)	6.0	1800
Wild boar piglets+yearlings, red deer/fallow deer – calves	6.0 (.243)	6.0	1800
Roe deer	5.6 (.222)	3.2	1000

22.3/4/5 Management structure and organisation

For the purposes of wildlife management Slovenia is divided into 14 Wildlife Management Areas with areas of between 1000 and 1500 km^2.

The Wildlife Management Areas contain some 11 State Wildlife Reserves with an area of about 2595 km^2 (about 13% of Slovenia). State Wildlife Reserves are currently administered by the Slovenia Forest Service and function as centres for the conservation of rare and endangered wildlife species and their habitats (e.g. performing Natura 2000 Action, etc.) in Slovenia.

The rest of the Wildlife Management Areas are subdivided into 415 hunting units with a total combined area of 16 190 km^2, where hunting is performed by the members of local hunters' clubs (in Slovenia called hunters' families), currently with about 22 000 members. The area of each hunting unit varies between 20 and 90 km^2, and affords hunting opportunities for 40–100 member hunters.

Prior to the adoption of full membership in the hunters' families, the candidates have to pass a formal examination in wildlife management. Courses, run by the Slovene Hunters Association, include basic knowledge of wildlife and wildlife management, skills of handling the firearms and knowledge of current hunting legislation. Any citizen of Slovenia, aged ≥ 18 years, with the right to possess and carry the hunting firearms may compete for regular membership of the hunters' family.

Wildlife management plans covering a 10-year period are prepared by the District Wildlife Officers of Slovenia Forest Service, for each of the different Wildlife Management Areas. Yearly management plans, including harvest quotas for game wildlife species, the extent of interventions concerning the habitat improvement, etc., are then prepared for individual hunting units in collaboration with the Slovenia Forest Service and the members of hunters' families.

22.6 Actual management and hunting practices

As above, wildlife management plans covering a 10-year period are prepared by the District Wildlife Officers of Slovenia Forest Service, for each of the different Wildlife Management Areas. Yearly management plans, including the harvest quotas for game wildlife species, the extent of interventions concerning the habitat improvement, etc., are prepared for any of the hunting units in collaboration between the Slovenia Forest Service and members of hunters' families.

The system of legal hunting practices depends to some extent on the density of game species, as well the need to reconcile the requirements of wildlife management with those of other outdoor activities.

Wild boar piglets and yearlings of both sexes may be hunted all year (Table 22.3) and the largest proportion is shot on baiting places. Since wild boar is the species causing about 60% of all agricultural damage in Slovenia, the hunting system is flexible.

Another species involved in significant damage is red deer. Special permissions for extended the shooting season for red deer calves and yearlings (in late winter and in spring) in the areas of elevated crop and browsing damages have been regularly issued by the Slovenian Ministry of Agriculture and Forestry.

Shooting from the high-seats put on forest edges or in glades inside forests is the most common way of hunting red deer, roe deer and wild boar. Shooting close to the baiting stations is frequently the method of wild boar hunting. Hunting from the ground with beaters is also a legal way of wild boar and red deer hunting.

In the rutting period, the red deer stags are stalked on the ground. Sometimes also, calls imitating the roaring of rutting stags are used to attract animals to the hunter.

The use of dogs for coursing the game is generally prohibited. Only dogs used for seeking wounded animals are allowed.

22.6.1 Core Slovene Register of Large Game Species and Large Carnivores

In 2004, the so-called 'Core Slovene Register of Large Game Species and Large Carnivores' was established, which from that time has maintained individual records of all animals harvested by hunting (or otherwise recorded dead – from accident or disease). The register was established on the initiative of University of Ljubljana and it incorporates all organisations in Slovenia which are involved in hunting big game species including ungulates and large carnivores. The register thus covers the entire area of Slovenia. Within this register the following data are collected individually for every specimen shot, or otherwise found dead: species (for seven species of ungulates and three species of autochthonous large predators), sex, net body weight, estimated age, value of trophy, hunting district, geographical location (with a 1 km^2 spatial accuracy!), cause and date of death.

For determination of the exact geographic position of the place of death, maps on a scale of 1:25 000, showing a net of coded 1 km square grids, have been prepared for all hunting clubs in Slovenia. The main advantage of the register over the older methodologies of database gathering is its fine spatial accuracy. Each year approximately 55 000 new datasets on extracted specimens are added into the register.

Data gathered in the register were already used for a variety of purposes (see Adamič and Jerina, 2006b; Jerina, 2006a; Jerina, 2007 for details) including for assessing the distribution ranges of the ungulate species in Slovenia, which are shown in Figures 22.2–22.8.

22.7 Census types and methods

No scientific methods for density estimations have been widely used in Slovenia until now. Indeed, in the past, the usual method of obtaining estimates of ungulate populations on which to base management decisions has been to seek subjective estimations of each species density on the level of the individual hunting unit. These figures have been summed and the result was used as official data on population size.

However, data on bag size are now recorded in the Core Register, and in addition those data can be use to assess distribution of all ungulate species as in Figures 22.2–22.8. All harvest locations of an analysed species were included in kernel analysis (Worton, 1989); the smoothing factor was adjusted to the home range size of the particular species and polygons for 95, 65 and 35% probability were created for all ungulate species. Each of the created polygons encompasses 95, 65 or 35% of all harvested specimens in Slovenia.

In 1976, a sophisticated system of adaptive management of red deer population, named Kontrollmethode (Simonič, 1982), was launched on an area of about 140 000 ha of the Dinaric Karstland in west-central Slovenia. Browsing intensity of young trees, body weights of calves and yearlings of both sexes, reproduction rates of adult and yearling hinds, as well the general health conditions of the population have been registered as model parameters to inform future management strategy. Since the establishment of Slovenia Forest Service in 1994, browsing intensity surveys on a network of permanent sample plots was used as the main indicator of population status of ungulates in other parts of the country, too. Although the method used was critically evaluated and found to be incorrect (Stankovski *et al.*, 1998; Debeljak *et al.*, 1999) it is still in official use.

22.8 Damage

Crop damage by ungulates is widespread especially in areas where agricultural lands are patch-worked amongst major areas of forested cover. Compensation for the damage has to be paid to the farmers by local hunters' clubs. The extent of wildlife damage and related compensation claims have been increasing in Slovenia during the last 30 years. In practice, the damage caused by wild boar and red deer has increased, but the impact of roe deer and other wildlife species decreased in the same period.

In 1998–2000 the value of claims made in compensation for damage by wild boar reached EUR 460 000, which was about 60% of all agricultural damage claims in Slovenia in the same period. Calculated wild boar damage in 2005 was EUR 15 per km^2 within the entire are of Slovenia.

The actual breakdown of damage reimbursed in 2005, according to crop type, was: damage to cereal crops, 52.3%; damage to pastures, 42.4%; other types of damage (orchards, vineyards), 5.3%. Damage in vineyards caused by consumption of grapes will probably increase in the future, according to the expected climatic changes, e.g. extended summer droughts, elevated daily temperatures (Adamič and Jerina, 2006a; Gönter *et al.*, *in press*).

The current system of evaluation and compensation for crop damage by all species of ungulates was fixed in 2004 by the Law on Wildlife and Hunting in Slovenia. The damage has to be reported to the local hunters' family within a few days after being noticed. The hunter-representative, accompanied by the landowner, has to visit the damaged area within two days. Field inspection of the damage and the amount of compensation must be agreed and signed by both sides.

Browsing damage upon forest trees by ungulates is regularly checked by the Slovenia Forest Service on the state level. The extent of browsing is surveyed on the network of permanent sample plots, distributed systematically over the whole area of all managed forests in a 2 × 2 km square grid.

According to long term strategies for sustainable forest management, about 80% of the forests in Slovenia ought to be regenerated in natural way, with native tree species. The impacts of ungulates might thus seriously reduce the process of natural regeneration and affect strategic issues of forest management (Perko, 1982).

Until now the claims for ungulate damage in forests have not been reimbursed, except in a few cases of extreme browsing of young spruce plantations, and in the cases of repeated winter peeling of bark in spruce pole stands.

22.8.1 Road traffic accidents

The extent of traffic casualties among wildlife is increasing, with between 5400 and 6400 ungulates being killed each year on the roads in Slovenia and with the economic cost of such accidents (in terms of human injury, damage to vehicles and loss of hunting revenue) estimated to exceed EUR 10 million per a year (Pokorny *et al.*, 2007). Traffic accidents seem particularly to affect roe deer, with 27 731 deaths recorded over the period 2001–2005 and with road kill amounting to 61% of all non-cull mortality and 13% of overall losses from cull and non-cull mortality combined (Kumelj and Orsanic, 2007).

Until recently, few efforts were made to include effective mitigation measures during the construction of highways (Jerina *et al.*, 2005), but a number of research trials of different types of roadside deterrent are under way with promising results. Pokorny *et al.* (2007), for example, are investigating the effectiveness of three mitigation measures (ultrasound emitting devices, deer warning reflectors with additional sound deterrents and a combination of classic and acoustic reflectors) erected on 23 very problematic Slovene road sections in 2006. In total, the number of road-killed ungulates (primarily roe deer, representing > 95% of all reports) on protected road sections decreased in the 2006 study period (10 July–31 December) by an astonishing 83% in comparison either with a comparable period in the year before the trial or with the average value for the comparable periods in 2002–2005 (Pokorny *et al.*, 2007).

22.9 Supplementary feeding

Ungulates, particularly red deer, are fed supplementally during the winter months. Various fodders are used, but primarily the deer are offered hay, sugar beets, apples and maize. Specific feeding of chamois and roe deer is not allowed, but sometimes the feeding places in the vicinity are visited by both species, anyhow. Regulations on supplemental feeding of ungulates, concerning the periods of feeding and the use of different kinds of fodder, have been given as part of the 10-year Wildlife Management Plans for each of the 14 Wildlife Management Areas.

The main goal of red deer supplemental feeding in Slovenia is decreasing winter browsing on tree regeneration. After implementation of this rather expensive and time consuming measure, damage to regeneration is expected to decrease, because the deer get some food at the feeding places and therefore should need to feed less in the forests. However, extensive telemetric studies of red deer in Slovenia (Jerina *et al.*, 2002; Jerina, 2006b) showed that supplemental feeding results in a decrease in the home range size of the red deer, and markedly influences its annual and especially winter spatial distribution. During the winter time red deer strongly concentrate around feeding places; in consequence, the probability of using the areas which are less than 500 m away from nearest feeding place is increased by five- to ten-fold. In consequence the influence of the red deer on vegetation, and problems with forest regeneration, may be actively increased around feeding places (e.g. Schmidt and Gossow, 1991; Nahlik, 1995).

Supplemental feeding of wild boar, with maize, organised by the wildlife managers over the whole range in Slovenia is supposed to prevent crop damage by the species. But, judging by the increasing number of reports of wild boar damage, it seems that, here too, the feeding interventions have only moderate effects.

22.10 Effectiveness of current management strategies

Wildlife in Slovenia is state owned, therefore all Slovenian citizens are *de jure* the co-owners of wildlife. But few of them are aware of their rights to participate in all levels of the decision-making processes of wildlife management. The awareness of stakeholder rights of citizens became evident in few cases only. Extended shooting of large carnivores in last few years, according to the decision given by the Ministry of Environment, has triggered public protests. Since large ungulates in public concern are less charismatic than the carnivores, no pro-ungulate protests occur.

On the contrary, local extent of agricultural damages by ungulates provoked anti-wildlife and anti-hunter protests by local farmers and even got echoes in the Slovenian Parliament.

Efficient forms of partnership, particularly the cooperation among hunters and wildlife managers on one side and landowners on the other one, are lacking, too. No advance agreements on local crop policy have been established until now, although proper distribution of different crop areas might reduce the extent of wildlife damage. The problems of crop damage in Slovenia are increasing, particularly in the regions with less precipitation in the growing season, e.g. south-western Slovenia, and areas inside Pannonic climate type (Gönter et al., in press).

In 2005, the network of public roads of all types in Slovenia was estimated to be about 38 425 km, which is 1.9 km/km^2 of the area in total. As above (section 22.8), it is clear that the number of traffic casualties among wildlife is increasing. The network of fenced highways (named as Slovenian highway cross), which is currently in its final phase of construction, will pose new restrictions on the distribution of large mammals. According to the results of extended studies on wildlife–highway relations in south-western Slovenia in 1997–2000 (Adamič et al., 2000; Jerina et al., 2005), we can forecast that red deer and wild boar would be mostly affected by the highway network. Both species behave as highway shy and have avoided the vicinity of highways during our study, although the density of both species in the study area was satisfying.

Given the current (and still increasing) extent of forest cover in Slovenia, habitat conditions for large ungulate populations are favourable. But continuous expansion of urban areas (albeit small scale), as well intrusion of traffic networks inside forest blocks will doubtless affect the current situation.

New regulations, by which Slovenia will be divided into 14 (planned) regions, acting as new political units, will bring regional independence in economic development and in spatial planning relations. Lack of interest in conservation issues among local authorities, which became evident during the Natura 2000 Action will probably accelerate negative spatial trends. Current favourable habitat conditions might be thus seriously affected in the future and it may be more difficult to achieve wildlife management goals.

References

Adamič, M. (1990) Food habits as an element of the management of ungulate populations with the emphasis on the red deer (*Cervus elaphus* L.). Strokovna in znanstvena dela 105. Univerza v Ljubljani in Gozdarski inštitut Slovenije, Ljubljana, 203 str. (In Slovene with extended English summary.)

Adamič, M. and Jerina, K. (2006a) Populacijska dinamika divjega prašiča (*Sus scrofa*), vpliv notranjih in zunanjih dejavnikov nanjo in prognoza razvojnih trendov v

Sloveniji. [The population dynamics of wild boar in Slovenia, the impacts of intrinsic and extrinsic factors upon it and the predictions on its future development]. Final report of the project. Projekt V4-0980 (2004-2006)- zaključno poročilo. Univerza v Ljubljani, Biotehniška fakulteta. Str., pp. 1–17.

Adamič, M. and Jerina, K. (2006b). Monitoring – integralna sestavina odzivnega upravljanja s populacijami prostoživečih živali. [Monitoring as an integral part of adaptive management of wildlife populations]. In D. Hladnik, ed., *Monitoring gospodarjenja z gozdom in gozdnato krajino* (Studia forestalia Slovenica, št. 127). Ljubljana: Biotehniška fakulteta, Oddelek za gozdarstvo in obnovljive gozdne vire [Biotechnical Faculty, Department of Forestry and Renewable Forest Resources], pp. 247–59.

Adamič, M. and Marenče, M. (1997) Thirty years after the first ibex resettlement in Triglav National Park. In M. Marenče, ed., *Alpski kozorog (Capra ibex Linneaus, 1758) v Triglavskem Narodnem Parku in drugod po Sloveniji*. Razprave in raziskave 5. Triglavski narodni park, Bled, pp. 22–33. (In Slovene with English summary.)

Adamič, M., Kobler, A. and Jerina, K. (2000) Strokovna izhodišča za gradnjo ekoduktov za prehajanje rjavega medveda (*Ursus arctos*) in drugih velikih sesalcev preko avtoceste: (na odseku Vrhnika-Razdrto-Čebulovica): končno poročilo. [Expert backgrounds for the construction of ecoduct-green bridge for safer crossing of the highway section Vrhnika-Razdrto-Čebulovica by the brown bear and other large mammals.] Final report/Ljubljana: Biotehniška fakulteta, pp. 1–60.

Čebular, A. (1921) Divji prašiči v Belokrajini. *Lovec* (Ljubljana) **8**, 46–7.

Debeljak, M., Džeroski, S. and Adamič, M. (1999) Interactions among the red deer (*Cervus elaphus*, L.) population, meteorological parameters and new growth of the natural regenerated forest in Sneznik, Slovenia. *Ecological Modelling* **125**, 51–61.

Donko, I. (1922) Divji prašiči na Dolenjskem. *Lovec* (Ljubljana) **9**, 63–4.

Gönter, P., Kotar, M. and Adamič, M. (in press). Škoda od parkljaste divjadi v kmetijskem prostoru na območju Gojitvenega lovišča Kompas – Peskovci na Goričkem [Ungulate damages in agriculture area in Wildlife reserve Kompas-Peskovci, Goričko-northeastern Slovenia]. Ljubljana: Gozdarski vestnik.

Hell, P., Krajniak, D. and Kaštier, P. (2004) Analysis of wild boar management in Slovakia and preconditions of its improvement. *Folia Venatoria* **32** (Zvolen), 105–14. (In Slovak with abstract in English.)

Jerina, K. (2006a) Vplivi okoljskih dejavnikov na prostorsko razporeditev divjega prašiča (*Sus scrofa* L.) v Sloveniji. [Effects of environmental factors on the wild boar spatial distribution in Slovenia]. *Zbornik Gozdarstva in Lesarstva* **81**, 3–20.

Jerina, K. (2006b) Spatial distribution, home range and body mass of red deer (*Cervus elaphus* L.) in regard to environmental factors. PhD thesis, Ljubljana: Ljubljana. 172 pp.

Jerina, K. (2007) The effects of habitat structure on red deer (*Cervus elaphus*) body mass. *Zbornik Gozdarstva in Lesarstva* **82**, 3–13.

Jerina, K., Adamič, M., Marinčič, A. and Vidojevič, V. (2002) Analiza in prostorsko modeliranje habitata jelenjadi (*Cervus elaphus* L.) jugozahodne Slovenije v GIS rastrskem okolju [Analysis and spatial modelling of red deer habitat of south-western Slovenia in a raster GIS environment]. *Zbornik gozdarstva in lesarstva* **68**, 7–31. (In Slovenian with English abstract.)

Jerina, K., Adamič, M. and Krže, B. (2005) Influences of topography and highway as migration barrier on dispersal patterns of wild boar (*Sus scrofa*) in Slovenia. XXVIIth Congress of the International Union of Game Biologists: extended abstracts. Hannover: University of Veterinary Medicine, Institute for Wildlife Research & German Union of Game and Wildlife Biologists, pp. 133–5.

Jonozovic, M., Koren, I. and Marence, M. (2007) Roe deer management in Slovenia 1996 and 2005. 8th European Congress on Roe Deer Biology, Slovenia. Abstract.

Kumelj, M. and Orsanic, H. T. (2007) The impact of traffic on roe deer (*Capreolus capreolus* L.) populations in Slovenia. 8th European Congress on Roe Deer Biology, Slovenia. Abstract.

Nahlik, A. (1995) Browsing pressure caused by red deer and moufflon under various population densities in different forest ecosystems of Hungary; effects of supplementary winter feeding. Presentation to Symposium on *Ungulates in Temperate Forest Ecosystems*, Wageningen, The Netherlands, 23–27 April 1995.

Perko, F. (1982) Metode in prvi izsledki kvantificiranja vpliva divjadi na gozdno vegetacijo. Str. 121–160 v M.Accetto, ur.: Gozd – divjad. Gozdarski študijski dnevi 1980 – zbornik. Ljubljana: Biotehniška fakulteta.

Pokorny, B., Zalubersek, M. and Marolt, J. (2007) Ultrasound-emitting devices and acoustic deer-warning reflectors as useful deterrents for reducing the number of roe deer-vehicle collisions in Slovenia. 8th European Congress on Roe Deer Biology, Slovenia. Abstract.

Šašelj, I. (1911) Divjega merjasca je ustrelil. *Lovec* (Ljubljana) **2**, 113–14.

Šavelj, A. (1933) Divja svinja v kočevskih pragozdih. *Lovec* (Ljubljana) **20**, 22–30; 60–7.

Schmidt, K. T. and Gossow, H. (1991) Winter ecology of alpine red deer with and without supplemental feeding: management implications. *Proc. XXth Congress of the International Union of Game Biologists, 1991*, pp. 180–5.

Schollmayer, H. (1899) Die Jagd am Krainer Karste. (Schwarz-, Roth- und Raubwild im Besondern). Von Oberförster Schollmayer-Mašun. *Waidmans Heil* **9**(9), 109–14.

Simonič, A. (1982) Kontrolna metoda v gospodarjenju z divjadjo: Str. 161–213 v M.Accetto, ur.: Gozd – divjad. Gozdarski študijski dnevi 1980 – zbornik. Ljubljana: Biotehniška fakulteta.

Šivic, A. (1921) Podatki lovske statistike v Sloveniji za leto 1920. *Lovec* (Ljubljana) **8**, 264–9.

Šivic, A. (1925) Lovsko leto 1923 po statističnih in drugih podatkih. *Lovec* (Ljubljana) **12**, 60–7.

Stankovski, V., Debeljak, M., Bratko, I. and Adamič, M. (1998) Modelling the population dynamics of red deer (*Cervus elaphus* L.) with regard to forest development. *Ecological Modelling* **108**, 145–53.

Valentinčič, S. (1958) Iz zgodovine naše jelenjadi. *Lovec* (Ljubljana) **40**, 2–5.

Worton, B. J. (1989) Kernel methods for estimating the utilization distribution in home range studies. *Ecology* **70**, 164–8.

Zajc, F. (1907) Wildschweine in Krain. *Waidmansheil (Klagenfurt)* **27**: 112.

23

Ungulates and their management in Croatia

JOSIP KUSAK AND KREŠIMIR KRAPINEC

Croatia is a middle-European country bordering the Mediterranean, whose mainland area of 53 233 km² stretches from the Danube on the north-east to Istria on the west and to Boka Kotorska on the south-east; here offshore islands make up an additional 3286 km² of land. The mainland area itself consists of three different biogeographical regions: Pannonian and peri-Pannonian flatlands, Dinaric mountains and Mediterranean coastal areas with 866 islands.

Forest covers some 43.5% of the land, Mediterranean shrubland comprises a further 3.1%, while the remaining 53.4% of the land is covered by pastures, arable agriculture, roads, towns, etc. What forest cover remains in the Pannonian valley and peri-Pannonian area is isolated islands of forest, surrounded by agricultural lands. Dominant tree species are oaks (*Quercus robur, Q. petraea, Q. pubescens*) and beech (*Fagus sylvatica*). Forests are more continuous in the Dinaric mountains, which, with some 65% forest cover, are the most forested part of Croatia. Here, the dominant forest community is mixed beech and fir (*Abies alba*) forest, with embedded 'beech only' stands. In the Mediterranean region any forested areas were subject to intensive exploitation in the past, used for firewood and as forest pastures. At the end of the twentieth century this use was mostly abandoned (Rauš *et al.*, 1992). Natural stands of submediterranean and epimediterranean, termophyle decidous forests of Mediterranean oak (*Q. ilex*) with white and black hornbeam (*Carpinus orientalis, Ostrya carpinifolia*) are regenerating and covering what was bare rock areas 40 years ago.

Native ungulate species occurring in Croatia are: red deer, roe deer, wild boar and chamois, while mouflon, axis and fallow deer have been introduced; the last occurs only within fenced enclosures and on some islands (Raguž and Grubešić, 1992).

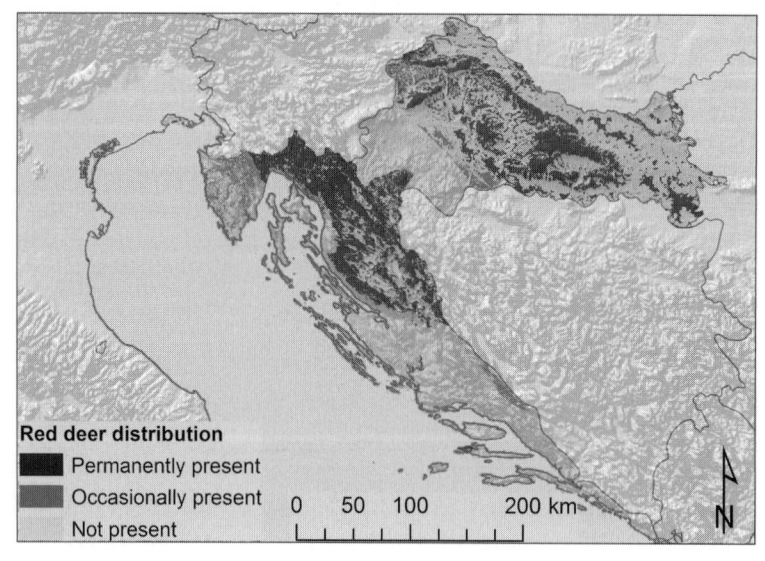

Fig. 23.1 Red deer distribution in Croatia at the beginning of twenty-first century

23.1 Ungulate species and their distribution

23.1.1 Red deer

Red deer is a native species, but the genetic purity and origin are not known. According to Grubešić and Krapinec (2003) and Vratarić *et al.* (2005) red deer is widespread throughout forested areas of the lowland Pannonian part of Croatia. This game species occupies common beech (Grubešić and Krapinec, 2003) and Dinaric karst forests (Grubešić and Krapinec, 2001) with a total area of 15 770 km^2. It is recorded occasionally on an additional 1730 km^2, and it is absent from the remainder (8855 km^2) of continental Croatia (Fig. 23.1). Based on a presumption that distribution is connected to forest cover (and thus with unforested parts of Croatia not included in calculations) the total number is estimated at about 9600 animals (as of 1 April 2002).

23.1.2 Roe deer

Roe deer is also a native species, but again the genetic origin is unknown, nor is it known if the species may have suffered admixture with introductions of other genetic provenance. According to Grubešić and Krapinec (2001, 2003) and Vratarić *et al.* (2005) roe deer is permanently present in the whole forested continental parts of Croatia, on the island Krk and on the Pelješac Peninsula, with total distribution range of 21 121 km^2. It is occasionally present in Dalmatia over 2362 km^2 (Fig. 23.2). On the rest of the Croatian mainland (2872 km^2) roe deer is absent. On the same assumptions as used for red deer (23.1.1), the total number is estimated

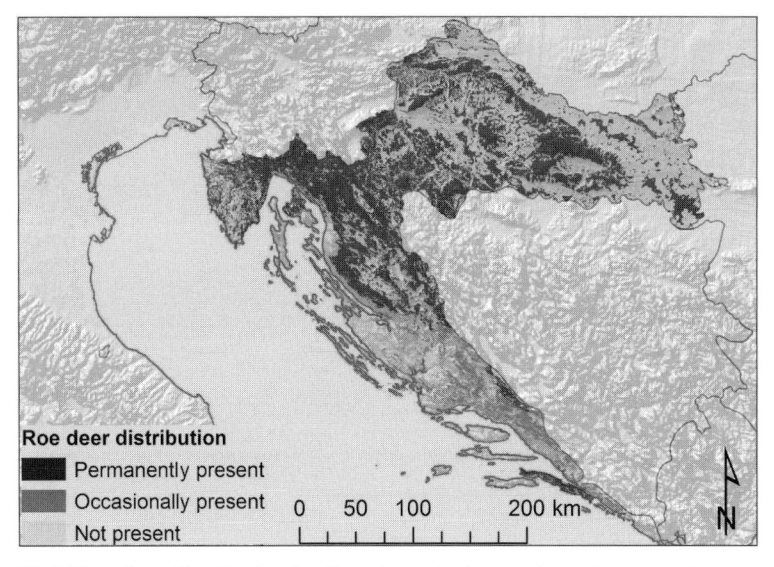

Fig. 23.2 Roe deer distribution in Croatia at the beginning of twenty-first century

to be 41 500 animals (as of 1 April 2002). Roe deer is a game species whose management is oriented to sport and recreation (tourism).

23.1.3 Fallow deer

Fallow deer were first introduced to Croatia in the Suhopolje area (eastern Slavonia region) in 1850, and their genetic origin is not known. Fallow deer are now present on the Croatian mainland in this same general area around Suhopolje, on part of Istria peninsula across Brijuni island, and on parts of Cres, Lošinj and Grgur islands (Fig. 23.3). The entire distribution covers 25 km^2, with an estimated 1200 individuals (1 April 2003). Fallow deer is a game species with management oriented primarily to sport and recreation.

23.1.4 Axis deer

Axis deer were introduced by Carl Hagenbeck to Brijuni island (near the southwest coast of the Istria Penninsula) in 1911. The genetic origin of introduced animals is unknown. Croatian hunters subsequently tried to introduce this species to continental parts of Croatia, but without success because axis deer could not adapt to a continental climate (Krapinec, 1998, 2001, 2005). Today, axis deer can be found on two islands; Brijuni and Rab (Fig. 23.4), with a total of 200 individuals. Some animals are observed to swim sometimes from Brijuni to the mainland in the estuary of Mirna river.

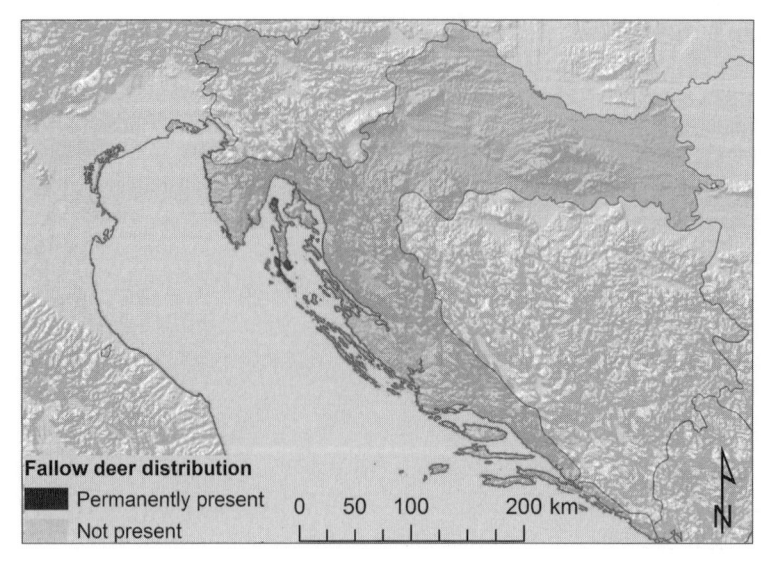

Fig. 23.3 Fallow deer distribution in Croatia at the beginning of twenty-first century

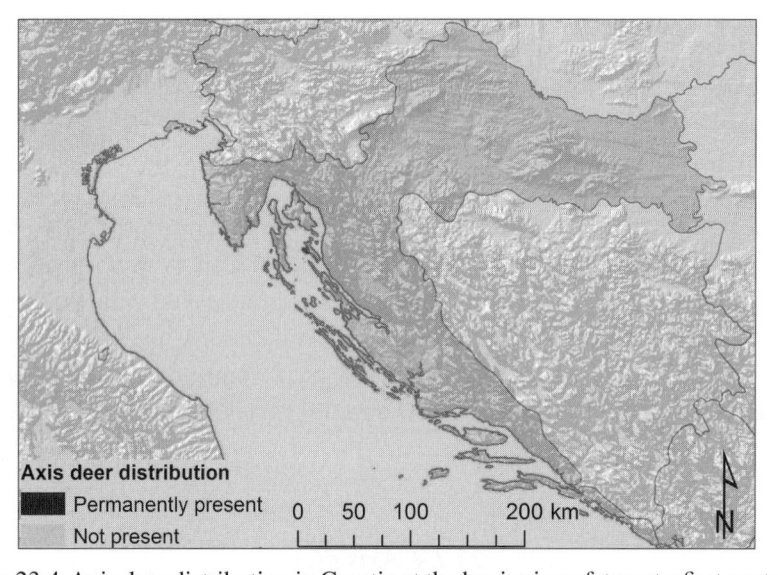

Fig. 23.4 Axis deer distribution in Croatia at the beginning of twenty-first century

23.1.5 Alpine chamois

Chamois are native to Gorski kotar (northern part of Dinarids) and have been more recently reintroduced to an area of northern Velebit (1964) and the Biokovo mountain (1974). The genetic status of introduced animals is unknown. Chamois are currently present in parts of Gorski kotar along Kupa river canyon, and on

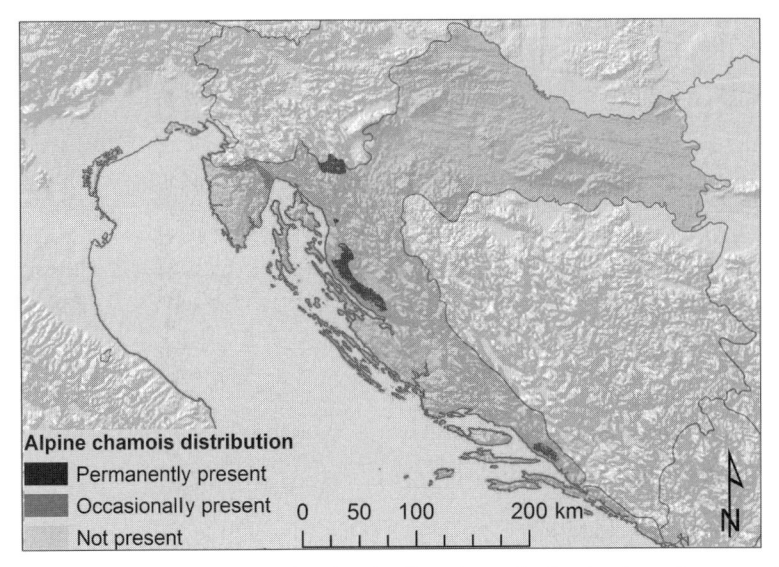

Fig. 23.5 Alpine chamois distribution in Croatia at the beginning of twenty-first century

Velebit and Biokovo mountains (Fig. 23.5) with a total number estimated to be 400 individuals (1 April 2004). The size of their distribution range is 1010 km^2.

23.1.6 Mouflon

According to Krapinec (2001, 2005), mouflon was first introduced in Novi Marof region (north-west part of Croatia) in 1900. This population was exterminated after World War I. A second introduction was made in 1908 on the island of Veliki Brijun near Istria. The origin and genetic status of introduced animals is unknown.

Today, mouflon can be found on islands: Brijuni, Cres, Lošinj, Rab, Dugi Otok, Brač, Hvar, Pelješac Peninsula, on four coastal hunting grounds, and in one hunting ground in Slavonia (Panonian mainland, Fig. 23.6). The total distribution area is 1347 km^2, with a total of 1600 individuals (1 April 2003). Mouflon is a game species with management oriented primarily to sport, recreation and control of damage.

23.1.7 Wild boar

Wild boar is a native species in Croatia, present on the all areas of the mainland (Grubešić and Krapinec, 2001, 2003) which are forested, on the islands of Krk, Cres, Šolta, Brač and on Pelješac Peninsula with total distribution range of 23 712 km^2 (Fig. 23.7). The estimated number of individuals is 18 200 (as of 1 April 2003).

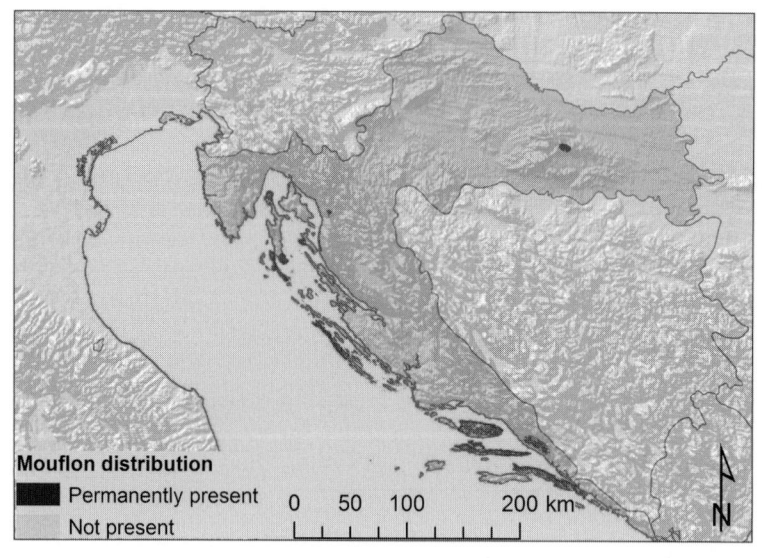

Fig. 23.6 Mouflon distribution in Croatia at the beginning of twenty-first century

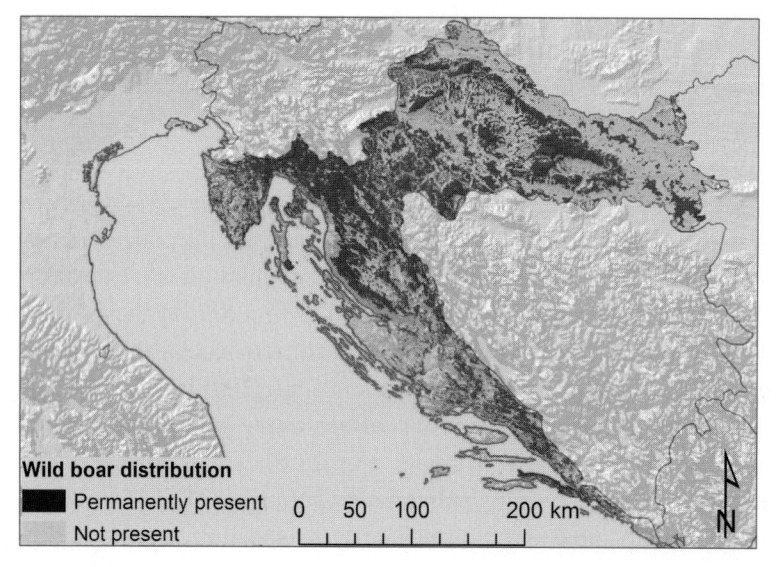

Fig. 23.7 Wild boar distribution in Croatia at the beginning of twenty-first century

Hybridisation with the domestic pig is common in the Pannonian region of Croatia where traditional extensive domestic pig husbandry includes free ranging pigs, foraging in lowland oak forests (Grubešić & Krapinec, 2003; Vratarić et al., 2005). Wild boar is considered a game species with management primarily oriented to control of damage, sport and recreation.

Table 23.1 *Hunting seasons for wild ungulate species in Croatia (Official Gazette, 155/2005)*

Game species	Sex and age	Hunting season
Red deer	Stags	from 16 August to 14 January
	Hinds and calves	from 1 October to 14 January
Fallow deer	Stags	from 16 September to 14 January
	Hinds and calves	from 1 October to 31 December
Axis deer	Stags	When antlers are not in velvet
	Hinds and calves	When hind is not heavily pregnant or accompanied by young fawns
Roe deer	Roebucks	from 1 May to 30 September
	Fawns and calfs	from 1 October to 31 January
Mouflon	Rams	Through year
	Eves and lambs	from 1 August to 31 December
Alpine chamois		from 1 September to 31 December
Wild boar	Boars, farrows, yearlings	Through year
	Sows	from 1 July to 31 January

23.2 Legislation

Wildlife is the property of the state. Any individual may gain the right to hunt as long as they have passed the appropriate hunting examination (section 23.5). Management of actual hunting grounds (or game management areas) is, however, carried out by individuals or organisations who are formally registered for hunting in that area (see section 23.4).

All ungulate species can be shot by rifle. An exception is wild boar which can be also shot by shotgun (gauge 12, 16 or 20) but only with a single ball (Breneke, Paradox, Ideal, etc.) (Official Gazette, 140/2005 and 68/2006).

23.3 Management objectives

Hunting in Croatia is primarily oriented to sport and recreation, although with attention paid to conservation of stocks of native species. Management of chamois is entirely directed towards conservation. Management of wild boar and mouflon are equally oriented towards sport and recreation, but with a strong emphasis also on control of damage.

Attempts to establish hunting management on a commercial basis have had variable success. While small game hunting usually returns a moderate profit, big game hunting management in Croatia tends overall to run at an economic loss. One of the most important reasons for this is the rather low game densities permitted.

Table 23.2 *Permitted energy, weight of bullet and shooting distance for wild ungulate species in Croatia (Official Gazette, 68/2006)*

Game species	Minimal energy at 100 m – E100 (J)	Minimal weight of bullet (g)	Maximal shooting distance (m)
Roe deer and young of other ungulate species	1000	3.24	150
Mouflon, Alpine chamois and axis deer	2000	4.80	200
Red deer, fallow deer and wild boar	2500	8.20	150

23.4 Management structure

Management of hunting grounds is caried out by licensed hunting ground holders, who have the obligation of maintaining the numbers of game species at an economically acceptable level. They also have an obligation to pay compensation for all damage caused by ungulates on the hunting ground they manage. While primarily tasked with maintaining stable populations they may also apply to reduce the numbers of animals if they become 'too numerous'. They can do this, however, only with the explicit permission of the ministry responsible (Ministry of Forestry, Agriculture and Water Management) by submitting a request supported with receipts for compensation paid or with the signature of subjects who had the damage (Official Gazette, 140/2005).

Since 1994, a new hunting law introduced the dominal system in Croatia, where hunting ground holders have to pay for leasing or concession rights for hunting grounds. Two different types of hunting grounds were formed; state controlled and county controlled. The minimal size of the area which can be formed as hunting ground is 10 km^2 on the mainland and 5 km^2 on the islands.

A total of 317 state-controlled hunting grounds were established, covering a total of 17 000 km^2. A total of 39 state hunting grounds were let for management by Croatian Forest Enterprise. In addition, a total of 724 county-controlled hunting grounds were established, extending to a total combined area of 33 000 km^2.

State hunting grounds can be given for short-term lease over 10 years or let as concessions for a longer period of 30 years (Official Gazette, 140/2005). Concessions are granted only within state hunting grounds which manage red deer or brown bears.

The new hunting law anticipates the establishment of 'management regions' which will cover several hunting grounds or whole mountain ranges where bears or red deer live. In those cases, quota sizes are centrally established and subsequently subdivided between hunting grounds (Grubešić, 2006). This system has been applied for bears since 2005 (Official Gazette, 140/2005).

23.5 Management organisation

There are about 55 000 registered hunters in Croatia. They are organised by the 'Croatian Hunting Association'. There is no specialisation among hunters in Croatia – all hunters hunt ungulates as well. Every hunter has to pass a hunter's examination, which includes both a theoretical part and one year of practical (field) work.

Each hunting ground is obliged to send census data and records of numbers of animals shot or otherwise 'lost' (e.g. due to road traffic accidents or predators) to the Statistical Department of the Croatian state, every year. Each hunting ground also receives at least one inspection per year. If it is found that the hunting ground holder has not been managing the ground according to the agreed contract, the contract is cancelled, and the hunting ground offered again for lease/concession; the former lessee may not apply.

Each hunting ground given on lease/concession must have an approved management plan. That management plan must be approved 90 days after concluding a contract of hunting district concession (or leasing). The management plan can be prepared by professional companies specialising in preparation of such plans and which employ forest engineers, agriculture engineers or vets (Official Gazette, 40/2006).

Croatia is divided into different management regions for red deer, chamois and wild boar (Grubešić, 2006). Each management region consists of a number of hunting districts. As a result there is some variation in the size of management areas for these game species (section 23.6). The Ministry of Agriculture, Forestry and Water management approves quotas for these three species. The size of management units is from 91.7 km^2 to 986.6 km^2 for red deer. The size of management units for chamois is from 14 km^2 to 567 km^2, while that for wild boar varies from 30 km^2 to 987 km^2.

Mouflon, fallow deer, axis deer and roe deer do not have management regions but must be censused in management plans. However, the minimum permitted size for a hunting ground in Croatia is 1000 ha (10 km^2). In consequence the minimum hunting ground for these four species is 10 km^2, and the maximum is, by default, the largest hunting ground where these four species occur. For roe deer, this means that in practice, the size of management unit may be from 10 km^2 to 458 km^2; for fallow deer and axis, the size of management units is from 2.1 km^2 to 14 km^2. And for mouflon, management areas may vary from 2.1 km^2 to 260 km^2.

Table 23.3 *Permitted hunting methods for ungulates in Croatia (Official Gazette, 140/2005; 62/2006)*

Game species	Permitted hunting methods
Roe deer, fallow deer, axis deer, mouflon, chamois	Stalking, tracking, stand hunting (sitting up on high-seats or from the ground)
Red deer	Stalking, tracking, stand hunting (sitting up on high-seats or from the ground), calling
Wild boar	Stalking, tracking, stand hunting (sitting up on high-seats or from the ground), driving, baiting

23.6 Actual management and hunting practices

Permitted hunting methods for red deer and roe are stalking or luring of animals to bait sites. Hunting by dogs is not allowed, although each hunting ground that manages large game animals is obliged to have a trained bloodhound for following up injured animals (Official Gazette, 140/2005). Management is done by hunting ground holders but, as above, overall the management is coordinated at a national level by the state. Each trophy must be measured (CIC propositions) and for each trophy hunting ground the user must issue a trophy card (Official Gazette, 92/2008).

For fallow and axis deer, the size of management units is, as above, from $2.1\,km^2$ to $14\,km^2$. Management is by hunting ground holders, but again, the overall management is controlled at the national level. We should repeat at this point that populations of these species are always within fenced exclosures or on islands.

Chamois is a game species with management oriented to conservation only. However, conservation objectives do not necessarily exclude hunting, like preservation. Chamois can be hunted on each hunting ground where they can be found, but this should be done in accordance with management plans, which are oriented to conservation.

For mouflon, the size of management units is from $2.1\,km^2$ to $260\,km^2$. Mouflon compete with domestic sheep and the hunting ground holder must pay for all damage done by game animals. In the same way, for wild boar, damage to agriculture and through involvement in traffic accidents must be compensated by the hunting ground holder who must pay all damages.

23.7 Census types and methods

Approved methods for game censuses are formally laid out in the Rules on Contents and Methods of Development and Approval of Hunting Management Programs, Programs for Game Breeding and Programs for Bear Protection (Official Gazette,

40/2006). For large game animals, this means year-round observations, on trunks, feeding places, etc., but the numbers are given as of 1 April.

As a condition of the lease, the user of each hunting ground is obliged to send census data for each ungulate species present to the Statistical Department of the Croatian state, on an annual basis (hunting year: from 1 April to 31 March).

For most species, the census is done by direct observations on feeding sites and other places through the year, but numbers are given as of 1 April.

23.8 Damage caused by large ungulates

An estimate of the total yearly damage done by game animals is EUR 685 000. This includes damage to agricultural and forest crops and damage to vehicles involved in traffic accidents with game animals. There is in fact no national inventory of game damage and figures presented above derive from detailed data available in four specific counties in Croatia where damage occurs regularly (see below).

The true amount of damage is very difficult to measure because hunters compensate amounts of damage by venison or crops rather than by cash. Insurance companies do undertake some check for damage levels because each hunting district with a hunting lease or concession must take out insurance to cover costs of game damage and compensation payments. However, the insurance companies are unwilling to release information about sums involved due to client confidentiality. Grubešić *et al.* (2005) studied game damage in four Croatian counties and concluded that actual levels of damage were of the order of:

1. *Agriculture* from EUR 0.5 to 3 per hectare of hunting area
2. *Forestry* (insignificant)
3. *Road traffic accidents* (from EUR 0.14 to 0.71 per hectare of hunting area)

Damage from ungulates in forestry is generally considered to be negligible (above). Damage to agricultural crops is mostly due to wild boar (95%), then red deer (4%) and other game animals including bears (1%). The most important reason for negligible forest damage is probably the fencing of old stands (stands which are in regeneration). The practice of fencing these stands is increasing, and foresters do this in lowland pedunculate oak forests. Ungulates do not cause significant damage in beech stands (Grubešić *et al.*, 2005).

23.9 Supplementary feeding

Hunting ground holders have a requirement to feed game animals 'ad libitum', throughout the whole year. Besides providing artificial supplements (mostly grain), hunting ground holders can establish additional fields where they grow specific game crops. Supplementary feeding is obligatory and the amount of food to be

Table 23.4 *The effectiveness of current management strategies varies over three different biogeographical regions*

Animal species	Pannonian	Mountainous	Mediterranean
Wild boar	+	+	+
Red deer	+	0	0
Fallow deer	0	0	+
Roe deer	+	−	+
Axis deer			0
Mouflon	0	−	+
Chamois		0	+

+ increasing
0 stable
− decreasing

provided for each big game species must be presented in the management plan presented for each year.

23.10 Ungulate management in Croatia: crucial points for the future

Hunters have a vested interest in seeing populations increase – if they pay for hunting grounds they would like to have a large population of game species and, because of that, higher hunting quotas. Most Croatian hunters still hunt primarily for venison and not for trophies. Wild boar is a species with high fertility and large amount of meat and is thus encouraged – hence the expansion in numbers especially of this species. In Germany as an easy control of wild boar they encourage shooting of piglets (young pigs under 30 kg weight), but in Croatia this part of the wild boar population has very low bag rate.

Another problem is controlling sex ratios in populations. Because of higher quotas, hunters avoid shooting females. That is why Croatia has sex ratios of 1:5 or higher, males to females. This causes trophy values and body weight to decrease.

A national big game inventory is still impossible to compile because of the high cost. There is an obligation for hunters to record weights of all animals shot, but it is difficult to enforce this or check the validity of statistics returned. Starting in 2005, there is a new 'Hunting Law' in Croatia and, from that point, hunting legislation has a higher level of control. In a couple of years we will see the results of these new hunting law measures.

Finally, a recent Act Official Gazette 33/2006 prescribes that mouflon breeding is not allowed on Croatian islands. All recent mouflon must be eliminated from the islands! This will have a big impact on hunting in this Croatian area because mouflon is a Mediterranean species and belongs in these habitats.

Generally, for better management of wild ungulates in Croatia, we must conduct several investigations: origin of game species, movement patterns, population ecology (fecundity, mortality) and feeding ecology. With better information on these topics we could develop a good management plan.

References

Grubešić, M. (2006) *Growing Districts for Red Deer, Alpine Chamois and Wild Boar in Republic of Croatia.* Zagreb: Ministry of Agriculture, Forestry and Water Management.

Grubešić, M. and Krapinec, K. (2001) Fir forests as hunting grounds and habitats of animal species. *Silver Fir in Croatia. Zagreb*, 649–55.

Grubešić, M. and Krapinec, K. (2003) The significance of beech forests for fauna and hunting. *Common Beech in Croatia. Zagreb*, 599–622.

Grubešić, M., Krapinec, K., Budor, I. and Kovačević, M. (2005) Länderbaricht über Wildschäden in Kroatien. *Internationale Symposium "Wildschäden durch Großwild"*. Wien, Östereich 25. und 26. February 2005, pp. 103–16.

Krapinec, K. (1998) Axis deer is also game of our hunting grounds. *Lovački vjesnik broj* **6**, 18–20. (In Croation.)

Krapinec, K. (2001) *Diet structure of mouflon* (Ovis ammon L.) *and axis deer* (Axis axis Erx.) *on the island of Rab*. Masters thesis, Faculty of Forestry University in Zagreb, 107 pp.

Krapinec, K. (2005) *Mouflon* (Ovis ammon musimon *Pallas, 1811*) *diet in the Eu-Mediterranean zone of the northern Adriatic Sea*. Dissertation thesis, Faculty of Forestry University of Zagreb, 252 pp.

Official Gazette, 40/2006 (2006) Rules on Contents and Methods of Development and Approval of Hunting Management Programs, Programs for Game Breeding and Programs for Game Protection.

Official Gazette, 140/2005 (2005) Hunting low.

Official Gazette, 155/2005 (2005) Rules on closed season.

Official Gazette, 33/2006 (2006) Amendments of Islands low.

Official Gazette, 62/2006 (2006) Rules on requirements that must be achieved for hunting and hunting techniques.

Official Gazette, 68/2006 (2006) Rules on allowed hunting weapons and ammunition.

Official Gazette, 92/2008 (2008) Rules on trophy measurement, trophy measurement form, evidence of trophy measurement and report of trophies which are measured.

Raguž, D. and Grubešić, M. (1992) Lovna fauna hrvatskih šuma. In Đ. Rauš, ed., *Šume u Hrvatskoj*. Zagreb: Šumarski fakultet Sveučilišta u Zagrebu i "Hrvatske šume" 181–96.

Rauš, Đ., Trinajstić, I., Vukelić, J. and Medvedović, J. (1992) Biljni svijet hrvatskih šuma. In Đ. Rauš, ed., *Šume u Hrvatskoj*. Šumarski fakultet Sveučilišta u Zagrebu i "Hrvatske šume" J.P., Zagreb. 33–78.

Vratarić, P., Grubešić, M., Krapinec, K. and Getz D. (2005) Hunting management in floodplain forests. *Floodplain Forests in Croatia*, 352–76.

24

Ungulates and their management in Greece

HARITAKIS PAPAIOANNOU

The total land area of Greece (including the various islands) extends to 132 000 km^2; the largest part of this (59.6%; approx. 78 600 km^2) lies between 0 and 500 m and is covered by Mediterranean vegetation, such as phrygana, maquis, evergreen shrubs (*Quercus coccifera, Q. ilex, Phillyrea latifolia, Pistacia lentiscus, Arbutus unedo, Juniperus oxycedrus*, etc.), deciduous shrubs and trees (*Fraxinus ornus, Quercus* spp., etc.) and forests of Mediterranean pines (*Pinus halepensis, P. brutia* and in a few cases *P. pinea*). It is worth mentioning here, that the greater part of the most intensively cultivated land also falls within this zone.

A further 38 000 km^2 (28.8%) of the land surface lies at medium altitude, between 500 and 1000 m. This is covered by sclerophyllous evergreen and deciduous shrubs, oak forests, with a smaller number of cultivated areas. The upper zone (1000–1500 m) extends to 11 600 km^2 (8.8%) and is more or less completely covered by mixed or pure forests, comprising mainly deciduous species (oak or beech (*Fagus* spp.)) and coniferous tree species (black pine *(Pinus nigra)*, fir *(Abies borisii-regis, A. cephalonica)* and, in a few cases, spruce *(Picea abies)* and Scots pine *(Pinus sylvestris)*).

The high altitude zone (1500–2000 m) is characterised by the presence of pure or mixed forests of coniferous and deciduous tree species (Balkan pine *(Pinus leucodermis)* or fir; beech), interspersed with smaller areas of pasture, steep bare slopes and cliffs. This altitude zone covers only 2.7% (3600 km^2) of the total land area. Finally, the highest altitude zone (2000–2917 m), which covers only 0.1% (160 km^2) of Greek land surface, includes mainly sub-alpine meadows, high altitude pastures, steep bare slopes and high cliffs above the tree line.

Fig. 24.1 Black pine (*Pinus nigra*), Balkan pine (*Pinus leucodermis*), beech (*Fagus sylvatica*) forests and calcareous cliffs constitute the northern part of Balkan chamois habitat on Mt. Timfi (2497 m) (Vikos-Aoos National Park, northwest Greece). July, 1990. Photo by Haritakis Papaioannou

24.1 Ungulate species and their distribution

Six wild ungulate species exist in Greece: the red deer, roe deer and fallow deer, the Balkan chamois *(Rupicapra rupicapra balcanica)* the Cretan wild goat *(Capra aegagrus cretica)* and the wild boar. An additional ungulate species, the European mouflon, has been introduced in very few – mostly private – enclosures and in one state controlled hunting reserve (Sapientza Island). This exotic species does not form free-ranging populations in Greece, except on Sapientza and, therefore, it is not taken into account in the present chapter.

All species, except one – wild goat – are native and even the Cretan wild goat is of ancient origin, considered to have been introduced by Neolithic humans (Kahila Bar-Gal *et al.*, 2002). Current populations of fallow deer, which are largely restricted to islands, are also considered to have been introduced by Neolithic humans (Masseti, 2002). In addition, we may note that the majority of the current red deer populations have derived from introduction, reintroduction or restocking of local populations with animals from other countries, albeit that, in some cases, individuals from adjacent countries were used. Four of the six species (Balkan chamois, wild goat, red deer, fallow deer) are considered rare and have a restricted

Fig. 24.2 Male Balkan chamois at the most southern area of *Rupicapra* genus distribution in Europe (Mt. Giona, Central Greece). February, 2006. Photo by Haritakis Papaioannou

and localised/fragmented distribution; in most cases their population densities are very low. The roe deer has a wider distribution but, again, at rather low densities. Only wild boar has a relatively widespread distribution and occurs sometimes at medium or relatively high abundance in several parts of the country.

All the ungulates, with the exception of the wild boar, are protected by national law and their hunting is forbidden, at least during the last 40 years. Data on population status is largely lacking, although some recent survey work provides estimates for the Greek populations of Balkan chamois (Hatzirvasanis, 1991; Papaioannou, 1991, 2003, 2005; Adamakopoulos *et al.*, 1997; Sfougaris *et al.*, 1999, 2003;

Papaioannou and Kati, 2003, 2004, 2007; Sfougaris and Giannakopoulos, 2005), Cretan wild goat (Adamakopoulos *et al.*, 1997), red deer (Adamakopoulos *et al.*, 1991) and fallow deer (Bousbouras *et al.*, 1991; Masseti and Theodoridis, 2002). Results of these surveys suggest that populations of none of these four species exceed 1000 individuals at a national level. With respect to the roe deer and wild boar, no reliable estimates at a national level are currently available.

24.1.1 Red deer

In general, scientific data on red deer distribution at national level before the nineteenth century are lacking. Remains have been found in several prehistoric (Paleolithic and Neolithic) human settlements, revealing a wide distribution of the species during the early and mid-Holocene (Gamble, 1997). Comparing present status with that of former times (as may be deduced from scant anecdotal reports from the recent past; nineteenth century–first decades of the twentieth century), it is evident that a considerable shrinkage, both in distribution and in population size, has occurred at national level. The decline of the species was rapid during the second half of the nineteenth century and the first half of the twentieth century and, apart from remnant populations in three to four small isolated areas, it was already extinct in most of its former distribution by the middle of the twentieth century.

Current species distribution includes only three geographically isolated populations: Mt. Parnitha – Parnitha National Park, Rhodopi mountain range and Koziakas Controlled Hunting Reserve (Adamakopoulos *et al.*, 1991), whereas another one (Sithonia area in Halkidiki peninsula) has become extinct only recently (1980s) (G. Douros, *pers. comm.*).

The population on the Rhodopi mountain range is presumed to be the only pure native Greek population. However, it is unknown whether introductions or restocking have ever taken place on the northern slopes of this mountain in the adjacent country of Bulgaria. On the other hand, both populations of Mt. Parnitha – Parnitha N.P. and Koziakas Controlled Hunting Reserve – seem to have derived from introductions, reintroductions or restocking.

Thus the Mt. Parnitha–Parnitha N.P. population has derived either from the occasional restocking of the native population with individuals from other countries (Central Europe (Germany, Denmark) and Balkans (Former Yugoslavia, Bulgaria)) (S. Papika, *pers. comm.*; G. Douros, *pers. comm.*) or exclusively from reintroductions from these countries (Adamakopoulos *et al.*, 1991) following the extinction of the native population. The population of the Koziakas Controlled Hunting Reserve has derived exclusively from reintroductions with animals from Mt. Parnitha–Parnitha N.P. (G. Douros *pers. comm.*; S. Papika, *pers. comm.*), as

Fig. 24.3 Red deer (*Cervus elaphus*) on Mt. Parnitha (Parnitha National Park) near Athens, Greece. Photo by Panagiotis Latsoudis

the extinction of the native population in this area had occurred long before any attempt at restocking.

The Mt. Parnitha–Parnitha N.P. population is the only one in Greece that has shown an increasing population size and expanding distribution during the last decade (S. Papika, *pers. comm.*; G. Douros, *pers. comm.*). There was an initial estimation of about 120–140 individuals in 1995. Nowadays, the same population is considered to be of around 500–520 individuals, revealing a 400% increase (S. Papika, *pers. comm.*). Population estimates regarding the other two populations are absent but, unofficially, they are considered to number fewer than 30 individuals each. Recent anecdotal evidence from the Koziakas Controlled Hunting Reserve shows that the introduced population has declined to fewer than five free-ranging individuals, presumably due to regular poaching, whereas more individuals are kept in an enclosure in this area (S. Zogaris, *pers. comm.*, A. Sfougaris, *pers. comm.*).

In addition to these free-ranging populations, a few red deer, with more or less unknown origin, are kept either in private collections and zoos or in state and private game enclosures. Inevitably, a few individuals have occasionally been released into the wild by the local Hunting Clubs and Federations – or other state and private bodies – during unsuccessful efforts to establish free-ranging populations.

Small population size, fragmentation, poaching, disturbance due to tourism activities, increased road accessibility close to or inside the species habitat are some of the current problems the species faces in Greece. While red deer is not a rare species elsewhere in Europe, it is classified as an Endangered (E) species in the Red Data Book of Threatened Vertebrates of Greece (Karandinos and Paraschi, 1992). The current total national population size, regarding all the free-ranging populations – excluding those in enclosures – is considered to be about 600–650 individuals (G. Douros, *pers. comm.*; S. Zogaris, *pers. comm.*; S. Papika, *pers. comm.*; A. Sfougaris, *pers. comm.*).

24.1.2 Roe deer

There are no accurate records regarding roe deer distribution at a national level before the twentieth century. Scant anecdotal reports on the distribution of this species in recent times (first half of the twentieth century) exist; by comparison, current species distribution is considered fairly restricted at a national level. Roe deer has, for example, been extirpated from the Peloponnese, where the species occurred before World War II.

In general, distribution extends throughout areas with medium altitude, usually associated with large mountain massifs and their foothills within the Greek mainland, excluding the Peloponnese. Although distribution may have diminished in recent years, roe deer still maintain a relatively wider distribution on the Greek mainland than those of all other ungulates, except wild boar. Populations present local fluctuations in numbers and densities over several years (Adamakopoulos *et al.*, 1991), however in no case are numbers or densities as high as in other areas of Central and Western Europe (Pielowski, 1982; Vincent *et al.*, 1991; Prior, 1995; Gill *et al.*, 1996; Lovari and San-Jose, 1997; Monaco *et al.*, 2001; Sfougaris, 2005b).

Detailed studies regarding population distribution and population size and density are generally lacking, with the exception of a few recent case studies, regarding certain areas. A 4-year research project concerning roe deer ecology and management was carried out in the Epirus region, covering 6.7% of the area of Greece (but a much higher proportion of the roe deer distribution area) (Sfougaris, 2005a; Sfougaris and Giannakopoulos, 2005). According to this project, mean autumn roe deer density in Epirus is 1.82 ind./km^2 and winter density 2.22 ind./km^2. Other detailed studies regarding the species status include the 2-year Egnatia Project in the north-eastern Pindus mountain range (Sfougaris, 2005b) and a project conducted in Parnassida Controlled Hunting Reserve, where population density does not seem to exceed 1 ind/km^2 (Monaco *et al.*, 2001).

Genetic analysis of Greek roe deer populations has shown that populations may represent the remains of late glacial refugial populations, which means they may constitute a distinct subspecies and should be preserved and not artificially mixed with other geographical populations (Randi *et al.*, 2004). It is classified as Vulnerable (V) in the Red Data Book of Threatened Vertebrates of Greece (Karandinos and Paraschi, 1992).

Low density, poaching, disturbance due to legal hunting and recreation/ tourism activities, increased road accessibility close to or inside the species habitat and lack of an effective wardening system are some of the current problems the species faces in Greece.

24.1.3 Fallow deer

Fallow deer used to be native in continental Greece, where it survived the last glaciation (Trantalidou, 2002). It is considered that wild fallow deer populations still occurred in mainland continental Greece (in Boetia, Akarnania and on the Pindus Mountains) until the nineteenth century (Heldreich, 1878; Ondrias, 1965; Chapman and Chapman, 1975, 1997; Yannouli and Trantalidou, 1999; Masseti, 1999, 2002), but by the first quarter of the twentieth century those populations had all been extirpated (Serva, 1927; Wettstein, 1942; Masseti, 1999, 2002).

The only remaining free-ranging population of fallow deer in Greece occurs on the island of Rhodes. It is believed that humans introduced fallow deer in the eastern-south-eastern Aegean (on Lesbos, Rhodes, Lemnos, Chios and Crete) for hunting purposes during Neolithic times and the Early Bronze Age (Trantalidou, 2002). All these populations became extinct in historical times except that on the island of Rhodes.

Fossils of fallow deer have been found on the island dating from the late sixth–early fifth millennium (Halstead, 1987; Halstead and Jones, 1987; Masseti, 1999, 2002; Trantalidou, 2002). Genetic evidence from recent mtDNA analysis verifies an ancient fallow deer introduction to the island. According to these data, the Rhodian fallow deer seems to be distinct compared to the populations of Turkey and other European countries (Masseti *et al.*, 2002). While systematic studies on population size are not available, it is thought that the fallow deer population on the island of Rhodes has increased from around 30–40 individuals in 1988 (Bousbouras *et al.*, 1991) to 70–300 individuals a few years later (Masseti and Theodoridis, 2002) and currently numbers at least 400 individuals (D. Mertzanidou, *pers. comm.*).

Captive or enclosed fallow deer populations also occur in private and state reserves, collections and game enclosures in a few sites in continental and insular Greece. The exact origin of most animals in these collections and game enclosures is unknown. An exception is the nearly free-ranging population confined in the promontory of the castle of Myrina on Lemnos, which derived from Rhodian ancestors. Most other captive or confined populations come from reserves from other European countries (Masseti, 1999; D. Mertzanidou, *pers. comm.*).

Fallow deer is classified as Vulnerable (V) in the Red Data Book of Threatened Vertebrates of Greece (Karandinos and Paraschi, 1992). Current total free-ranging national population size – excluding those in enclosures – is considered to be at least 400 individuals, restricted to the island of Rhodes.

24.1.4 Balkan chamois

Scientific data regarding species distribution at a national level before the twentieth century are lacking. Species remnants have been found in a few prehistoric (Paleolithic and Neolithic) human settlements (rock shelters), revealing a wider distribution of the species in the distant past than nowadays. Presumably the species was widespread during the early Holocene, even in southern Greece. According to the few non-scientific reports available, some of the remaining populations have more recently become extinct or are suffering from a considerable shrinkage either of their distribution or of their population size (Papaioannou and Kati, 2007). In general, species distribution at a national level is considered to be severely restricted, compared to the situation before the middle of the twentieth century.

Current distribution of the species includes 18 distinct subpopulations, together forming at least six discrete and isolated populations at the following mountain ranges: Northern & Central Pindus (10 subpopulations), Eastern and Central Rhodope (2 subpopulations), Central Sterea Ellada (3 subpopulations), Mt. Olympus (1 subpopulation), Mt. Tzena-Pinovo (1 subpopulation) and Mt. Nemertsika (1 subpopulation) (Hatzirvasanis, 1991; Papaioannou, 1991, 2002, 2003, 2005; Adamakopoulos *et al.*, 1997; Papaioannou and Kati, 2003, 2004; Sfougaris *et al.*, 1999, 2003, 2007; Sfougaris and Giannakopoulos, 2005). Besides, the species may form five additional very small subpopulations on Mt. Pindus and one extremely small population on Mt. Varnountas) (Papaioannou and Kati, 2007).

The size of each individual subpopulations ranges from 10 to 130 individuals, with the majority between 10 and 60 individuals in most of the cases (Papaioannou and Kati, 2007).

Despite the fact that genetic status has been ascertained only in few cases of subpopulations (Perez *et al.*, 2002; Hammer *et al.*, 2003), it is considered that all populations belong to the same subspecies of Balkan chamois (*Rupicapra r. balcanica*). Introductions, reintroductions or restocking of native populations with individuals of the same or other subspecies have never been attempted in Greece,

Fig. 24.4 Balkan chamois group on Mt. Timfi (Vikos-Aoos National Park, northwest Greece). December, 2003. Photo by Haritakis Papaioannou

even between subpopulations in the same area (Papaioannou, 2005). Consequently, all Greek chamois populations are considered genetically pure.

The subspecies belongs to IUCN category LR/lc. It is classified as Rare (R) in the Red Data Book of Threatened Vertebrates of Greece (Karandinos and Paraschi, 1992). The total national current population size is estimated at 480–750 individuals (Papaioannou, 2005; Papaioannou and Kati, 2007). The main threat for the species is poaching. All the subpopulations suffer from regular poaching to a greater or lesser extent (Hatzirvasanis, 1991; Papaioannou, 1991, 2003, 2005; Adamakopoulos et al., 1997; Sfougaris et al., 1999; Papaioannou and Kati, 2003, 2004, 2007) Geographical isolation in small population sizes, disturbance due to legal hunting, competition with livestock, disturbance due to livestock presence, increased road accessibility close to or inside the species key habitats and lack of an effective state wildlife management system at a national level are a few of the additional current problems.

24.1.5 Cretan wild goat

The Cretan wild goat is considered to have been widely distributed on Crete – and probably on other islands – during prehistoric and ancient times. It was originally

Fig. 24.5 A young adult male agrimi (*Capra aegagrus cretica*) on abandoned farmland on Mt. Lefka Ori in Crete (Greece). 2004. Photo by Alkiviadis Geskos

thought that this species was derived from a primitive domestic goat, which, after its introduction in Crete during the Aceramic Neolithic period (7000 BC), became feral (Kahila Bar-Gal *et al.*, 2002). However, more recently Kolska Horwitz and Kahila Bar-Gal (2006) have suggested that they may, after all, be wild in origin (even though introduced by humans to Crete) but have subsequently partially interbred with domestic animals.

Until recently the Cretan wild goat occurred in all three of the highest mountain regions of Crete (Lefka Ori, Idi and Dikti moutains) (Sfougaris, 1995; Sfougaris *et al.*, 1996). Nowadays, there is only one long-established wild population in Greece (totaling about 500–600 individuals), restricted to an area of approximately 72 km^2 in south-west Crete, on the Lefka Ori Mountains and in the Samaria National Park (Sfougaris, 1995; Adamakopoulos *et al.*, 1997).

An additional population exists on the small island of Theodorou (68 ha), close to the north coast of the western part of Crete (Husband and Davis, 1984). This population was more recently established during the first half of the twentieth century as a result of introductions with a few founder individuals from Mt. Lefka Ori, and now totals around 100 individuals – a level which is believed to approximate to the carrying capacity of the area (Husband and Davis, 1984; Sfougaris,

1995; A. Sakoulis, *pers. comm.*). There are a few other, introduced populations – all originating from Theodorou island – on Moni island (160 ha) near Aegina, Sapientza Island (880 ha) offshore of the south-western Peloponnese (Sfougaris, 1995; Sfougaris *et al.*, 1996).

There is a further population on the Agii Pandes Islands off northern Crete as well as on Atalandi Island, but all these are known to be hybrids between founders from Theodorou Island and domestic goats (Sfougaris, 1995; Sfougaris *et al.*, 1996). A further hybrid population existed on Dia Island, Crete, but was exterminated sometime between 1997 and 2004 (A. Geskos, *pers. comm.*).

In addition to these populations of Cretan wild goat and their hybrids, there are also a further three additional island populations of wild goats which have arisen as hybrids between local forms of wild goats – existing there from ancient times – with domestic goats. These populations, which occur on the islands of Erimomilos (Antimilos), Samothrace and Gioura, had been classified in the past as separate subspecies (*C. a. pictus* Erchard, 1858; *C. a. dorcas* Reichenow, 1888 or *C. a. jourensis* Ivrea, 1899) (Sfougaris, 1995; Adamakopoulos *et al.*, 1997).

A number of other populations of wild goats (fewer than 100 individuals each) are kept in private areas (for hunting or recreation) and in most of the State Controlled Hunting Reserves. It is considered that most of these animals have been derived from the Theodorou population (Husband and Davis, 1984), but actually their origin is unknown. One of these populations, probably originating from Mt Lefka Ori, is free-ranging on Mt. Parnitha, near Athens (G. Douros, *pers. comm.*; S. Papika, *pers. comm.*).

The main problem affecting conservation of wild goats is hybridisation with feral domestic goats, which is considered to occur even within the unique long-established wild population of the species, located on Mt. Lefka Ori (Adamakopoulos *et al.*, 1997). A further conservation problem is inbreeding which inevitably takes place in the introduced populations – all originating from three Leuka Ori pairs introduced to Theodorou Islet in 1928, 1937 and 1945 (Husband and Davis, 1984; A. Geskos, *pers.comm.*).

Poaching of the native population, food competition with livestock and road accessibility, which in turn increases disturbance from tourism and possible poaching, are some additional problems.

The subspecies is included in the VU D1+2 IUCN category. It is classified as Endangered (E) in the Red Data Book of Threatened Vertebrates of Greece (Karandinos and Paraschi, 1992). The total national population size of pure origin wild populations (Mt. Lefka Ori and Samaria N.P., Theodorou Island and possible Mt. Parnitha) is at least 600–750 individuals (Adamakopoulos *et al.*, 1997; S. Papika, *pers. comm.*; A. Sakkoulis, *pers.comm.*).

24.1.6 Wild boar

Scientific data on wild boar distribution within Greece before the twentieth century are absent. However, reports on the local presence, by several travellers and historians since ancient times, show a wide distribution range of the species across the country. Although its current distribution status is considered to have declined, compared to the situation in the recent past (nineteenth century), the wild boar still presents a relatively wide distribution, mainly in the areas of the continental part of the country which are located in medium altitude zones.

During the twentieth century the species was exterminated from the Peloponnese and part of the low altitude zone of the mainland due to redistribution of cultivated lands and other intensive human activities, although in some parts it has recently been reintroduced or recolonized appropriate habitats naturally (G. Giannatos, *pers. comm.*; G. Iliopoulos, *pers. comm.*; A. Sfougaris, *pers. comm.*; S. Zogaris, *pers. comm.*). In general, current species distribution range extends over areas with medium altitude (400–1200 m a.s.l.), usually inside or close to large massifs and their projections on the mainland. Although formerly the species was widespread in wetland areas (e.g. Amvrakikos wetlands) it is currently very rare in the lowlands, especially in the southern half of the Greek mainland.

Although the wild boar is the only ungulate that may be legally hunted in Greece, scientific data on population size and density are few. Detailed data on wild boar ecology and management are derived from a research project carried out in the Epirus region, covering 6.7% of the area of Greece (Sfougaris, 2005a, 2005b; Sfougaris and Giannakopoulos, 2005). According to this project, mean autumn wild boar density in Epirus is 3.21 ind./km^2 and winter density 2.44 ind./km^2. Other detailed studies regarding the species status include the 2-year Egnatia Project in the north-eastern Pindus mountain range (Sfougaris, 2005b).

Due to the hunters' interest in maintaining satisfactory wild boar population densities for hunting purposes, several introduction, reintroduction and restocking operations have been carried out by the Greek Hunting Clubs and Hunting Federations. Actually, most of these operations, which were a common practice during the last three decades, often failed, as they were neither based on a clear scientific plan nor had the necessary guidance and monitoring at a national or regional level.

Although the genetic stock of the introduced wild boars in the Peloponnese is suspect, the animals are now widespread especially in the river valleys (i.e. Alfios river) (S. Zogaris, *pers. comm.*). It must be stressed that there is no scientific documentation on the origin of the individuals used for reintroductions, introductions and population restocking. Therefore, such operations may cause problems such as genetic impoverishment, especially in case of isolated subpopulations. In conclusion, many wild boar populations are considered to carry genes from populations from other regions, even from other countries.

Wild boar is commonly kept in several private collections or private and state game enclosures. The total wild boar population size at a national or regional level is not known.

24.2 Legislation

Several protected areas, with various levels of protection, exist throughout the country. According to Hellenic legislation, hunting is totally forbidden within the following categories of protected areas: (1) Wildlife Sanctuaries (former Game Sanctuaries), (2) core areas of National Parks, as they were established under the former regime, and (3) 'Nature Protection Areas' in more recently established National Parks (under national law 1650/86 in combination with 92/43 EU Habitat Directive). This means that hunting is forbidden over some 8% of the total national land area. In addition, there are two private and nine State Controlled Hunting Reserves (1% of total land area), where special measures regarding game and hunting are in force. Different management systems are in effect within the few state and private game enclosures, and some of these are of particular significance as breeding grounds for particular species.

Under European legislation, Balkan chamois, Cretan wild goat and fallow deer are listed in Annex III of the Bern Convention (Convention for 'the conservation of wild life and natural environment of Europe'). Moreover, Balkan chamois and Cretan wild goat are listed in Annex II ('Species with community interest, whose conservation involves the determination of special conservation zones') and in Annex IV ('Species of community interest which demand strict protection') of the Habitat Directive 92/43 EU 'for the conservation of natural habitats as well as wild flora and fauna'.

In consequence, under Greek national law, hunting of most ungulate species in natural ecosystems is forbidden. Therefore, hunting of Balkan chamois, Cretan wild goat, red deer, roe deer and fallow deer has been officially forbidden since 1969, according to presidential decree 86/69 and its following modifications. Very low quotas of some of these species are allowed to be shot within the State Controlled Hunting Reserves (Cretan wild goat, red deer, roe deer) or within the state and private Game Enclosures (Cretan wild goat, red deer, roe deer, fallow deer).

The wild boar is the only ungulate game species that is hunted legally during a defined period every year throughout most of its distribution. The wild boar hunting period is limited to the period between 15 September and 20 January, three days per week (Wednesday and weekend).

24.3 Management objectives

As mentioned above, hunting of the majority of ungulates (Balkan chamois, Cretan wild goat, red deer, roe deer and fallow deer) in natural ecosystems in Greece is forbidden and management is directed primarily towards conservation. Only wild boar may be hunted for sport/recreational purposes.

Culling for prevention of crop damage has never been carried out, even when locals' claims of crop damages are very strong – usually at the end of summer. The most likely explanation of this is that any problem due to high local density of wild boar – which is rare – will be solved during the following hunting period, as, in practice, there are no quotas regarding total regional or national wild boar harvesting.

24.4 Management structure

The Hellenic Forestry Service, attached to the Ministry of Rural Development and Food (former Ministry of Agriculture), is responsible for wild ungulate management in Greece. As noted above, hunting is forbidden in certain protected areas which together make up some 8% of the national areas; limited numbers of red deer, roe deer, fallow deer and wild goat (as well as wild boar) may be shot under licence in Controlled Hunting Reserves (1% of total land area). Of all the species of ungulates, only wild boar may be widely hunted outside these areas.

Hunting is permitted for all citizens over 18 years who have obtained a hunting permit. A general annual official circular is issued yearly by the Ministry of Rural Development and Food, specifying the particular regulations for every hunting season: (1) duration of the annual hunting period (August–February), (2) species of birds and mammals allowed to be hunted, including only wild boar among the ungulates, (3) particular hunting periods (and days of the week) regarding several species of birds and mammals, again including only wild boar among the ungulates, (4) maximum quotas (number of individuals allowed to be shot per hunter or per hunting group in case of wild boar during a whole day of hunting activity).

Greek hunters who renew their hunting permit yearly are estimated at about 225 000. They were obliged, until quite recently, to be members of Greek Hunting Clubs, which, according to the legislation, should cooperate with the Ministry of Rural Development and Food. Although nowadays this obligation has been abolished, the majority of Greek hunters continue to be members of the hunting clubs. There are 241 hunting clubs throughout Greece, which belong to seven hunting federations. All Greek hunting federations are placed under the Greek Hunting Co-federation. In addition, there are a few hunters who do not belong to any official hunting club but may be members of the recently established, independent hunting clubs, which are not officially obliged to cooperate with the Ministry of Rural Development and Food.

The Hellenic Forestry Service, under the Ministry of Rural Development and Food (former Ministry of Agriculture) is the state authority responsible for wild ungulate management in Greece. Consequently, the Forestry Service is responsible for the enforcement of hunting bans for wild ungulates.

Wild boar shooting is carried out only by private amateur individuals. Introductions, reintroductions and restocking of natural wild boar populations were carried out, until recently, by the Hunting Federations and Clubs under the supervision of the Forestry Service. Although nowadays such activities have been banned, there is a high pressure from hunting clubs, hunting federations and the owners of private breeding grounds for this to be allowed again.

Data regarding number of wild boar hunters and quotas (number of animals shot) in particular areas as well as age, sex and morphometric data of shot animals are not kept systematically either by Forestry Service nor by any hunting club or federation.

24.5 Management organisation

Management units regarding wild ungulates or other species of wild fauna do not exist in Greece. Hunting permit cost varies and does not depend on the game species. There are three categories of hunting permits allowing the shooting of any mammal or bird species listed on the general official game species list. This list remains more or less the same for the whole country during the annual hunting period.

Hunting permit categories comprise: prefecture (local HP), regional (regional HP) and state levels (general HP). Fees/prices are EUR 98.5, 119.5 and 141, respectively, for a hunter who is member of a hunting club under cooperation with the Ministry of Rural Development and Food – annual subscription cost for the hunting club and federation is included. In case of non-membership status, hunting permit fees are EUR 71, 92 and 112 respectively. The quota per hunter's day, for each species, is limited. Wild boar is usually hunted by hunters organised in groups, using the traditional 'drive-hunt' method. No more than ten hunters are allowed to participate in each hunting group and the allowed quota is maximum two wild boar per day for each group.

Obtaining a hunting permit in Greece is relatively easy. Examinations take place once in a hunter's lifetime. It is a simple procedure consisting of the completion of one or more standard questionnaires. A health certificate and a clean personal criminal record are also required. Special training regarding use of guns or a practical examination for the hunting permit acquisition are not required by law. However, most of the Greek male citizens have a basic knowledge of the use of guns, which was obtained during their mandatory army service. Renewal of the hunting permit must be done on a yearly basis, prior to the hunting season, and it is a routine procedure, usually carried out by the hunting clubs.

The total number of hunters specialising in wild ungulate (wild boar) hunting, at a national level, is not precisely known. While all Greek hunters are potential wild boar hunters, only a proportion of them is specialised in this game species. The total number of hunting permits issued/renewed every year at a national level is approximately 225 000. As a consequence approximately 2% of Greek citizens (or 6% of men between 18 and 75 years old) own a hunting permit for boar and could be considered potential wild boar hunters.

24.6 Actual management and hunting practices

Regarding the majority of ungulate species, for which hunting is banned within natural ecosystems, management practices aim at the enforcement of the relevant legislation in order to prevent/control poaching. The following information, therefore, relates only to the wild boar, as it is for the most part the only ungulate species which may legally be hunted.

According to Greek legislation, it is not necessary to compile and apply censuses or shooting plans before each hunting period. As a consequence, neither the Forestry Service, the hunting clubs and federations nor any other body, related with game and wild fauna carries out such surveys. Data/records on the results of each hunting day (number of shot animals, sex, age, weight, etc.) are not kept, not even by the several hunting groups, which – as they do not have any official status – may in any case change either geographically or in member composition without the obligation to declare it to any authority. Consequently, neither the hunting groups nor any official authority (Forestry Service or hunting clubs and federations) collect reliable data on annual harvests of wild boar in Greece.

However, the Greek Hunting Federation has been carrying out a project (Artemis Project), since 1994, regarding annual hunting activities and annual harvest of some game species, including the wild boar. This project is based on questionnaires, distributed to the hunters through their associations. However, most organisations, institutes, individual scientists and wildlife and game specialists, even the Greek Forestry Service, which is the state authority responsible for wild fauna and game species in Greece, have not yet obtained access to the data.

'Drive-hunt', with or without dogs, is the typical and traditional method applied for wild boar hunting. Up to ten hunters may participate in each wild boar hunting group. There is no obligation to register with any authority either the composition of the hunting group or the hunting ground. Two wild boar are allowed to be shot daily by each hunting group, independent of the total number of hunters participating.

No restrictions exist regarding the total number of animals shot or the number of hunting days that an individual hunter or hunting group can spend during a hunting period. In practice, therefore, an individual hunter is allowed to shoot as many animals as he or she can, within the restrictions regarding the quota per day (up to two animals) and the particular hunting days (Wednesday, weekend), during all the weeks of the hunting period (15 September–20 January). Shotguns are used for wild boar hunting, as the use of rifles is totally forbidden across the country. Likewise, shotguns are used for additional ungulate species hunting within the Controlled Hunting Reserves.

24.7 Census types and methods

Censuses of wild ungulate populations are not carried out systematically in Greece. Efforts to estimate wild ungulate populations have very rarely been carried out. State services are not usually involved. So far, the only censuses performed concern the Cretan wild goat population in Lefka Ori, roe deer populations in three areas – based on abundance index – (Monaco *et al.*, 2001; Sfougaris, 2005a, 2005b; Sfougaris and Giannakopoulos, 2005), the red deer population located in Parnitha N.P.–Mt. Parnitha (S. Papika, *pers. comm.*) and a few Balkan chamois populations (Hatzirvasanis, 1991; Papaioannou, 1991; Papaioannou and Kati, 2007). In addition, there is only one case of a Balkan chamois population in Mt. Timfi and Vikos–Aoos National Park where a systematic annual census has been carried out during the last six consecutive years (Papaioannou and Kati, 2007). This count consists mainly of simultaneous estimations of the total number of animals occurring/observed above the tree line during autumn.

In general, therefore, systematic censuses regarding ungulate populations in Greece are not regularly carried out. As a consequence, essential data for ungulate management in Greece are still lacking, even for wild boar, which is both the most abundant and the most popular hunting species.

24.8 Ungulates impacts and damage

There are no official records of any kind of damage related to wild ungulates in Greece. The national and local media sporadically report limited damage to corn crops, caused by wild boar. Such cases usually occur in areas where wild boar have been previously released by the local hunting clubs and federations or the hunters themselves. It is worth noting that the state authorities have recently banned releases of wild ungulates for population restocking purposes.

In general, according to Hellenic legislation there is not any compensation system regarding damage caused by wild ungulates, except for the damage to crops caused by wild boar within the Controlled Hunting Reserves. The local Forestry Service is responsible for compensation in the latter case.

In addition, damage caused by fallow deer to crops has been reported over the last two years on the island of Rhodes. The damage occurs mainly on young olive trees and on summer crops. Damage to olive trees is related to de-barking and scraping/fraying by male fallow deer during the rut, and is generally limited. However, damage to summer crops and especially to melon and watermelon crops, even if quite local in distribution, can be severe and by far exceed EUR 1000 per farmer. For these reasons, the creation of a compensation system for damage caused by fallow deer on summer crops is in progress (Mertzanidou, 2005). Moreover, during the last four years, six road traffic accidents involving fallow deer have occurred on the island of Rhodes. In all cases, the animals died (D. Mertzanidou, *pers. comm.*).

In general, apart from the sporadic cases of low scale damage mentioned above, wild ungulate populations in Greece neither cause damage to agricultural production, habitats and productive forests nor are responsible for road accidents and other actions that can cause problems to humans, crops, habitats or ecosystems. Low population sizes and densities of wild ungulates in Greece are considered to be the main reasons for this.

24.9 Supplementary feeding

Supplementary feeding regarding the majority of wild ungulate populations and especially those belonging to the following species: roe deer, Balkan chamois and fallow deer, has never been implemented officially by the state authorities. On the other hand, Greek hunting clubs and federations occasionally carry out supplementary feeding of wild boar populations, mainly in those cases where individuals, brought up in captivity, have been released by them. Besides the direct food supply, cultivation of abandoned agricultural lands with maize is a practice sometimes implemented for wild boar by the hunting clubs and federations. The total extent and intensity of supplementary wild boar feeding operations are not clearly known, since it is not part of any official management plan. In general, it is not carried out systematically and it seems to be restricted on an annual basis in small areas defined by the strategies of the local hunting clubs and federations.

Concerning the other ungulate species, supplementary feeding is implemented in one case of a red deer population (located in Parnitha N.P–Mt. Parnitha) (S. Papika, *pers. comm.*) and to few small, usually artificial and/or insular populations of wild goat (Husband *et al.*, 1986; Sfougaris, 1995). Likewise, supplementary feeding is carried out, more systematically, in small populations in artificial, semi-captive conditions, like the fallow deer population in Lemnos.

24.10 Ungulate management in Greece: crucial points for the future

The main problem of the current management strategies regarding most of the Greek ungulate species populations is that, more or less, management strategies do not exist at all. Apart from a few specific measures taken inside the Controlled Hunting Reserves and within the Parnitha N.P., practically nothing is done in the majority of the whole national territory, even inside the rest of the protected areas in Greece (national parks, wildlife sanctuaries). Actions, such as occasional and ad hoc releases of wild boar, supplementary feeding of wild boar populations and (unsuccessful) releases of red deer, often implemented by hunting clubs and federations, cannot be considered as organised management actions as they do not fall under any general and officially approved management plan, based on systematic and scientific data.

In general, without taking into account the few exceptions mentioned above, hunters themselves – and sometimes poachers – 'manage' wild ungulate populations without applying a specific scientific management plan. Thus, the author considers that the following basic measures and actions are required:

- Develop and implement a Species Action Plan for each species at regional and national level.
- Define an efficient state authority responsible for wild ungulate management.
- Establish defined management units and develop specific management plans for each defined area with management policy informed by annual censuses and monitoring.
- Make the proper changes to the distribution and the range of the established wildlife sanctuaries or establish new ones – if needed – according to the results of recent or future research projects on wild ungulates.
- Control poaching by establishing an efficient state-managed warden body.

Besides, the following statements could be considered by whoever is responsible for developing the individual Species Action Plans in the future:

- Follow specific measures for the conservation of wild ungulates, with priority ungulate populations within the protected areas (Natura 2000 areas, national parks, wildlife sanctuaries, Controlled Hunting Reserves), where it is easier – because of the legislation – to apply additional conservation measures.
- Establish additional Controlled Hunting Reserves as the current responsible authority (Forestry Service) seems to pay much more attention to such areas than in the rest of

the Greek territory. Thus some of the proposals stated here could be applied more easily within the Controlled Hunting Reserves.

- Establish management units, and define and implement harvesting quotas for the wild boar in each according to carrying capacity, and in the future to the rest of the ungulate species in case their populations increase.
- Carry out management actions, based on scientific data, in order to improve crucial habitats.
- Assess the feasibility and requirements for possible organised reintroduction operations of wild ungulates, based upon scientific data and criteria at a national and/or regional level.
- Create a database of the genetic structure of all captive and free-ranging ungulate populations with priority to those living in subpopulations or in very low numbers and restricted ranges.
- Eliminate the existence of Cretan wild goat hybrids and feral goats within Cretan wild goat habitats.

Acknowledgements

The author is grateful to the following scientists who showed great interest in the theme and eagerly provided useful comments (Dr G. Mertzanis, D. Mertzanidou, S. Zogaris, S. Papika, D. Bousbouras, Dr V. Kati, Dr A. Sfougaris and R. Tsiakiris) or additional information (A. Geskos, G. Giannatos, G. Douros, G. Handrinos, G. Iliopoulos, A. Sakoulis) and especially to Prof. R. Putman for his valuable comments on the manuscript.

References

Adamakopoulos, P., Adamakopoulos, T., Bousbouras, D. *et al.* (1991) Les grande mammiferes de Grece (Carnivores et artiodactyes): Situation actuelle, repartition, habitat – les especes menaces, perspectives de protection. *Biologia Gallo-Hellenica* **18**(1), 107–26.

Adamakopoulos, T., Hablutzel, Ch. and Hatzirvasanis, V. (1997) Status and distribution of Caprinae in Greece. In D. Shacleton, ed., *Wild Sheep and Goats and their Relatives. Status Survey and Conservation Action Plan for Caprinae.* IUCN/SSG Caprinae Specialist Group, pp. 104–8.

Bousbouras, D., Ioannidis, Y. and Matsakis, J. (1991) Queles informations recentes sur le daim (*Dama dama*) de l ile de Rhodos. *Biologia Gallo-Hellenica* **18**(1), 7–12.

Chapman, D. I. and Chapman, N. G. (1997) *Fallow deer.* Machynlleth: Coch-y-bonddu Books, 280 pp.

Chapman, D. I. and Chapman, N. G. (1975) *Fallow Deer: Their History, Distribution and Biology.* Lavenham, Suffolk, UK: Terence Dalton Ltd., 271 pp.

Gamble, C. (1997). The animals bones from Kleidi. In G. Bailey, ed., *Kleithi: Palaeolithic Settlement and Quaternary Landscapes in Northwest Greece. Vol. 1: Excavation and intra-site analysis at Kleithi.* Macdonald Institute Monographs, pp. 207–44.

Gill, R. M. A., Johnson, A. L., Francis, A., Hiscocks, K. and Peace, A. J. (1996) Changes in roe deer (*Capreolus capreolus* L.) population density in response to forest habitat succession. *Forest Ecology and Management* **88**, 31–41.

Halstead, P. (1987) Man and other animals in later Greek prehistory. *Annals of the British School in Athens* (BSA) **82**, 71–3.

Halstead, P. and Jones, G. (1987) Bioarchaeological remains from Kalithies Cave, Rhodes. In A. Sampson, ed., *The Neolithic Period in the Dodecanese*. Athens: Ministry of Culture, pp. 135–52.

Hammer, S., Suchentrunk, F., Herrero, J. *et al.* (2003) Complex evolutionary scenario for the molecular phylogeny of chamois (genus *Rupicapra*), inferred from mitochondrial and nuclear DNA sequences. 26th Congress of International Union of Game Biologists *Integrating Wildlife with People* and 10th International Perdix Symposium, Sept. 1–6, 2003, Braga, Portugal.

Hatzirvassanis, V. (1991) The status of chamois *(R. r. balcanica)* in Greece. *Biologia Gallo-Hellenica* **18**(1), 31–44.

Heldreich, T. (1878) *La faune de la Grece. Premiere partie. Animaux vertebras*. Expositions dela Universite de Paris en 1878.

Husband, T. and Davis, P. (1984) Ecology and behaviour of the Cretan agrimi. *Canadian Journal of Zoology* **62**, 411–20.

Husband, T., Davis, P. and Brown, J. (1986) Population measurements of the Cretan agrimi. *Journal of Mammology* **67**(4), 757–9.

Kahila Bar-Gal, G., Smith, P., Tchernov, E. *et al.* (2002) Genetic evidence for the origin of the agrimi goat (*Capra aegagrus cretica*). *Journal of Zoology (London)* **256**, 369–77.

Karandinos, M. and Paraschi, L. (1992) *The Red Data Book of the Threatened Vertebrates of Greece*. Greece: Greek Zoological Society and Greek Ornithological Society.

Kolska Horwitz, L. and Kahila Bar-Gal, G. (2006) The origin and genetic status of insular caprines in the Eastern Mediterranean: a case study of free-ranging goats (*Capra aegagrus cretica*) on Crete. *Human Evolution* **21**, 123–38.

Lovari, S. and San-Jose, C. (1997) Wood dispersion affects home range size of female roe deer. *Behavioural Processes* **40**, 239–41.

Masseti, M. (1999) The European Fallow Deer, *Dama dama* L. 1758, in the Aegean region. *Contribution to the Zoogeography and Ecology of the Eastern Mediterranean Region*, Vol I: 17–30.

Masseti, M. (2002) *Island of Deer. Natural History of the Fallow Deer of Rhodes and the Vertebrates of the Dodecanese (Greece)*. Rhodes, Greece: City of Rhodes, Environment Organization.

Masseti, M. and Theodoridis, N. (2002) Recording the data on the former and present distribution of the free-ranging deer populations on Rhodes. In M. Masseti, ed., *Island of Deer. Natural History of the Fallow Deer of Rhodes and the Vertebrates of the Dodecanese (Greece)*. Rhodes, Greece: City of Rhodes, Environment Organization.

Masseti, M., Cavallaro, A. and Vernsei, C. (2002) The population genetics of the fallow deer of Rhodes. In M. Masseti, ed., *Island of Deer. Natural History of the Fallow Deer of Rhodes and the Vertebrates of the Dodecanese (Greece)*. Rhodes, Greece: City of Rhodes, Environment Organization.

Mertzanidou, D. (2005). *Damages Caused by Fallow Deer to Crops on the Island of Rhodes*. Aethrea, Greece: Agro-Environmental Research and Action Team.

Monaco, A., Pedrotti, L., Facoetti, R. and Lovari, S. (2001) *Conservation and Management of Wild Ungulate Populations in the Controlled Hunting Reserve Area of the Prefecture of Fokida*. ARCTUROS. Technical report.

Ondrias, J. C. (1965) Die Saugetiere Griechenlands. *Saugetierk. Mitt.* **13**, 109–27.
Papaioannou, H. (1991) The chamois *(Rupicapra rupicapra)* in the Epirus mountains. *Biologia Gallo-Hellenica* **17**, 53–66.
Papaioannou, H. (2003) *Habitat Use, Population Status and Conservation of the Balkan Chamois* (Rupicapra rupicapra) *on Mt Timfi and in the Vikos-Aoos National Park.* MSc Thesis, Manchester Metropolitan University, UK.
Papaioannou, H. (2005) *Chamois, at the Limits of Survival: A Monograph for Chamois in Greece.* 104 pp. (In Greek.)
Papaioannou, H. and Kati, V. (2002). The status and conservation of Balkan chamois (*Rupicapra rupicapra balcanica*) in Greece. *Proceedings of the Third World Conference on Mountain Ungulates.* IUCN. Caprinae Specialist Group. Saragossa (Aragon, Spain), June 10–15.
Papaioannou, H. and Kati, V. (2003) *Management and Conservation of the Balkan chamois* (Rupicapra rupicapra balcanica) *on Mt. Timfi and Vikos-Aoos National Park.* WWF–Greece. Technical report. (In Greek.)
Papaioannou, H. and Kati, V. (2004) Distribution and status of Balkan chamois *Rupicapra rupicapra balcanica* in Greece. *Proceedings of the 11th Congress of the Hellenic Zoological Society and Hellenic Ecological Society.* Mytilene, 18–21 November, 2004. (In Greek.)
Papaioannou, H. and Kati, V. (2007) Current status of the Balkan chamois *(Rupicapra rupicapra balcanica)* in Greece: Implication for conservation. *Belgian Journal of Zoology* **137**, 33–9.
Perez, T., Albornoz, J. and Dominguez, A. (2002) Phylogeography of chamois (*Rupicapra* spp.) inferred from microsatellites. *Molecular Phylogenetics and Evolution* **25**(3), 524–34.
Pielowski, Z. (1982) Population characteristics of roe deer inhabiting a small forest. *Acta Theriologica* **27**(28), 409–25.
Prior, R. (1995) *The Roe Deer. Conservation of a Native Species.* Shrewsbury, UK: Swan Hill Press.
Randi, E., Alves, P. C., Carranza, J. *et al.* (2004) Phylogeography of roe deer (*Capreolus capreolus*) populations: the effects of historical genetic subdivisions and recent nonequilibrium dynamics. *Molecular Ecology* **13**, 3071–83.
Serva, P. J. (1927) *On the hunt.* Athens: S.K. Vlastos, 288 pp. (In Greek.)
Sfougaris, A. (1995) The distribution, ecology and management of goats *Capra aegagrus* in Greece: An outline. *Caprinae* **8**, 5–9.
Sfougaris, A. (2005a) Population-habitat relationships for the roe deer (*Capreolus capreolus* L.) and the wild boar (*Sus scrofa* L.) in Epirus Region, Greece. *Book of Extended Abstracts of XXVIIth Congress of the International Union of Game Biologists*, Hanover, Germany, 28 August–3 September 2005.
Sfougaris, A. (2005b) *Study on Ungulates: Roe deer and Wild boar. Project on monitoring and assessment of the effects on large mammals and their habitats of the construction and operation of Egnatia highway.* (Part 4.1 Panagia-Grevena). Laboratory of Ecosystem Management and Biodiversity, University of Thessaly. Technical report. (In Greek.)
Sfougaris, A. and Giannakopoulos, A. (2005) Population density and habitat parameters relations for three ungulates: roe deer (*Capreolus capreolus*), wild boar (*Sus scrofa*) and Balkan chamois (*Rupicapra rupicapra balcanica*), in Epirus region, NW Greece. *Proceedings of the Joint Conference of the Greek Ecological Society and the Greek Zoological Society*, Mytilene 2004. Greece: Greek Ecological Society and University of the Aegean. (In Greek with English summary.)

Sfougaris, A., Nastis, A. and Papageorgiou, N. (1996) Food resources and quality for the introduced Cretan wild goat or agrimi (*Capra aegagrus cretica*) on Atalandi Island, Greece, and implications for ecosystem management. *Biological Conservation* **78**, 239–45.

Sfougaris, A., Giannakopoulos, A., Goumas, H. and Tsachalidis, E. (1999) Status and management needs of a Balkan chamois population in the Rodopi Mountains. *Caprinae News*, May 1999.

Sfougaris, A., Giannakopoulos, A., Goumas, H. and Koutsikos, N. (2003) Conservation of low and isolated Balkan chamois populations in Epirus region, western Greece. 26th Congress of International Union of Game Biologists *Integrating wildlife with people* and 10th International Perdix Symposium, 1–6 September, 2003, Braga, Portugal.

Trantalidou, K. (2002) The Rhodian fallow deer: game and trophy since prehistoric times. In M. Masseti, ed., *Island of Deer: Natural History of the Fallow Deer of Rhodes and the Vertebrates of the Dodecanese (Greece)*. Rhodes, Greece: City of Rhodes, Environment Organization.

Vincent, J., Gaillard, J. M. and Bideau, E. (1991) Kilometric index as biological indicator for monitoring forest roe deer populations. *Acta Theriologica* **36**(3–4), 325–8.

von Wettstein, O. (1942) Die Saugetierwelt der Agais nebst einer Revision des Rassenkreises von *Erinaceus eurpaeus*. *Annales Naturalist Museum Wien* **52**, 245–78.

Yannouli, E. and Trantalidou, K. (1999) The fallow deer (*Dama dama* Linnaeus 1758): Archaeological presence and representation in Greece. In N. Benecke, ed., *The Holocene History of the European Vertebrate Fauna*. Berlin: Springer Verlag, pp. 247–81.

25

Ungulates and their management in Serbia

MILAN PAUNOVIĆ AND DUŠKO ĆIROVIĆ, WITH JOHN D. C. LINNELL

There are four native ungulates species in Serbia; red deer, roe deer, chamois and wild boar, and three introduced species; fallow deer, white-tailed deer and mouflon. There has been little scientific investigation of ungulate populations in Serbia. Therefore, the material used in this chapter is drawn from a range of secondary sources, including the records of the Hunting Association of Serbia (Šelmić *et al.*, 2001; Anonymous, 2007), the database of the Natural History Museum, the national official statistical data, as well as data collected by the authors' own research. The few national and relevant international publications were also studied (Bjedov *et al.*, 1997; Bradvarović *et al.*, 1994; Jovanović *et al.*, 1983; Kryštufek *et al.*, 1997, Milošević-Zlatanović *et al.*, 2005; Popović *et al.*, 2002; Randi *et al.*, 2004; Savić *et al.*, 1995; Vasić *et al.*, 1991; Živančević, 1956, 1960). In order to present the legal regulations and laws about ungulates in Serbia, we consulted current official legal documents (Službeni glasnik, 1993a, 1993b, 2002).

25.1 Distribution and population status of ungulates in Serbia

25.1.1 Red deer

Historically, red deer were widely distributed in Serbia in both the lowland and mountainous forests. The native lowland populations have been continuously present in only a few localities in Srem and Bačka (parts of Vojvodina province). The native Balkan and Carpathian populations of red deer in the mountainous parts of Serbia are extinct (Bojović, 1967). Individuals from the lowland populations were reintroduced into the mountain forests in the 1950s and 1960s, with animals mostly coming from the region of Belje (in nearby Slavonia, Republic of Croatia). The reintroductions were made into large enclosures, but many animals escaped

Table 25.1 *Estimates of population size for ungulates in Serbia (1991–2007) according to the official data collected by the Hunting Association of Serbia*

Species	1991	1995	1997	1999[1]	2001[1]	2007[1,2,3]
Red deer	5 538	4 949	3 926	3 020	3 748	5 000
Roe deer	104 177	78 046	75 176	78 995	93 296	120 000
Fallow deer	834	945	1 223	1 065	978	3 000
White-tailed deer	?	?	?	?	?	100
Chamois	1 070	836	808	163	608	600
Mouflon	1 265	649	600	678	877	1 000
Wild boar	18 834	12 395	11 920	10 837	12 648	30 000

(1) Data for 1999, 2001 and 2007 are incomplete, as there were no reports from the province of Kosovo and Metohija.
(2) Population numbers for 2007 were roughly estimated and officially published in the handouts of 54th CIC general assembly, held in early May 2007 in Belgrade (Anonymous, 2007).
(3) Data for American white-tailed deer are believed to be overestimated according to Miodrag Strnad (*pers. comm.*) who indicates that no more than 40 individuals remain.

and established free-ranging populations. At present, the largest area of red deer distribution is situated in the central parts of eastern Serbia. Red deer are currently bred within fenced hunting areas at more than seven localities in Serbia. During the 1990s, the population decreased, but this trend has changed in the last seven years (Table 25.1) and the range has slightly increased. The total abundance today is estimated at more than 5000 individuals. Most of these individuals are present in the hunting areas of the state owned enterprise 'PE Srbijašume', while fewer than 10% belong to the hunting areas owned by other hunting clubs (during the 1990s, the average number of specimens shot in areas managed by these other hunting clubs has been around ten per year as opposed to >500 for the hunting grounds of PE Srbijasume). In Serbia, red deer are classified as a Vulnerable (VU) species (Savić *et al.*, 1995). They are also included in the preliminary Red List of Vertebrates of Serbia (Vasić *et al.*, 1991), and will be included in the Red Book of Vertebrates of Serbia, which is presently being prepared.

25.1.2 Roe deer

Of all the ungulates, this species (together with wild boar) has the widest distribution and the most permanent presence in Serbia. As in other species, the population numbers significantly decreased during the 1990s. According to Šelmić *et al.* (2001), the reasons for the decrease were overhunting, poor harvest management and a reduction in supplementary winter feeding. In the mid 1990s, the Hunting

Association of Serbia suggested that hunting clubs should stop hunting if they estimated the population to be fewer than two individuals per km². It is believed that the implementation of this measure greatly influenced the renewal of the population and there has been a significant increasing trend during the first seven years of the twenty-first century. This is an interesting phenomenon due to the continuous presence of hunting pressure and significant and stable presence of predatory species, primarily wolves (*Canis lupus*). In Serbia, roe deer were placed into the category Lower Risk: conservation dependent (LR:cd) (Savić *et al.*, 1995). They were also included in the preliminary Red List of Vertebrates of Serbia (Vasić *et al.*, 1991).

25.1.3 Fallow deer

This species is exclusively bred in large fenced hunting areas, although there are known cases of escapees and short-term formation of free-ranging herds. Although fallow deer were introduced to hunting areas in Serbia a long time ago, they disappeared after World War II. Other introductions were made in 1958 near Belgrade, in 1961 in central Serbia, and in 1967 in western Serbia. All these sites were fenced hunting areas (Bojović, 1967) owned by PE Srbijašume and protected military nature reserves. Small-scale breeding (around 70 individuals) also happens in the fenced hunting areas of several other hunting clubs. Due to their breeding in protected fenced areas, the population numbers fluctuated only slightly at around 1000 specimens during the critical period of the 1990s. Since 2000, there has been an increasing trend. In the fenced hunting areas they are almost exclusively kept in mixed groups with mouflon. Fallow deer are in the threat category Lower Risk: conservation dependent (Savić *et al.*, 1995), and were also included in the preliminary Red List of Vertebrates of Serbia (Vasić *et al.*, 1991).

25.1.4 White-tailed deer

The introduction and acclimatisation programme for this species in Serbia was initiated in the period 1970–5 (Jovanović *et al.*, 1983). This programme was attempted at several localities in the former Yugoslavia, but it was most successful in the fenced hunting area of Karađorđevo, in the northern Serbian province of Vojvodina. A group of 14 specimens was introduced during 1970 and 1971. In 1983, the population numbered 150 individuals. Several individuals escaped from the fenced area and were observed for several years in neighbouring areas, but they never maintained any significant numbers outside the fenced area. Today the population within the fenced hunting area is about 40 individuals, and the official annual harvest is about two individuals. The annual illegal harvest is estimated at about ten individuals. This species was placed in the threat category Lower Risk: conservation dependent (Savić et al., 1995), and it was also included in the preliminary Red List of Vertebrates of Serbia (Vasić et al., 1991).

25.1.5 Chamois

The native populations of Balkan chamois (*Rupicapra rupicapra balcanica*) persisted only in the western and south-western parts of Serbia. In 1963, chamois were introduced into three localities, one in each of three following regions: north-eastern Serbia (Djerdap National Park, Donji Milanovac), central Serbia (Stolovi, Kraljevo, PE Srbijašume), and south-western Serbia (Dubočica, Prokuplje, PE Srbijašume) (Bojović, 1967). The only population that experienced any success was the one in north-eastern Serbia, and individuals from this population were used in 1982 for another successful introduction in eastern Serbia (gorge of Mikuljska Reka river, Bor) (Kryštufek et al., 1997). According to the official data, the total current population numbers of chamois at these three localities in Serbia is about 600 individuals. However, data are missing for the populations in the southern parts of the province of Kosovo and Metohija, although there are some indications of a very poor situation there. The official data indicate a catastrophically decreasing trend of chamois populations during the 1990s, although the present data show some signs of regeneration since 2000. In recent years, some spontaneous increase in range has been recorded. Chamois are in the category of Vulnerable (VU) (Savić et al., 1995), and will also be included in the updated Red Book of Vertebrates of Serbia, which is presently being prepared.

25.1.6 Mouflon

Individuals from this species were introduced into the Lipovica hunting area near Belgrade in 1958, and into the Vratna hunting area near Negotin, Eastern Serbia in 1967 (Bojović, 1967). In central Serbia (Rudnik Mt.) there was a spontaneous range spread in 1999 from the neighbouring fenced hunting area, and this herd is currently believed to have 20 individuals. As this species is bred in fenced areas, its population numbers have been stable during the last 15 years (Table 25.1). As with the fallow deer, the main challenges of breeding in natural conditions are harsh winters and the significant presence of predators, primarily wolves and feral dogs. Mouflon were placed into the threat category Lower Risk: conservation dependent (Savić et al., 1995), and were also included in the preliminary Red List of Vertebrates of Serbia (Vasić et al., 1991).

25.1.7 Wild boar

Together with the roe deer, this species has the widest distribution and the most permanent presence in Serbia. However, it is absent in a few areas where the agriculture is very intensive. As in other species, the population numbers significantly decreased during the 1990s, while there has been a significant increasing trend and range expansion during recent years. This has been assisted by the constant removal of swine plague vectors (domestic pigs). Wild boar are exposed to heavy hunting and poaching pressure and are also the main prey base for wolves. The main challenge in their management is large-scale crop damage. In Serbia, wild boar were placed into the threat category Lower Risk: least concern (LR:lc) (Savić et al., 1995). They were also included in the preliminary Red list of Vertebrates of Serbia (Vasić et al., 1991).

25.1.8 Unsuccessfully introduced ungulate species

The literature also mentions several other species of ungulates, whose representatives lived for a short time in the territory of Serbia.

25.1.9 European bison

Several individuals of this species, originating from Poland, were released in the fenced hunting area Karađorđevo (Bačka, province of Vojvodina) in 1974. During the 1980s the herd included about 20 individuals, but the last specimens were hunted down in the early 1990s (Sreten Kućančanin, *pers. comm.*).

25.1.10 Wild goat

One male and two females, originating from Persia and the southern Caucasus, were released in June 1965 in the stony areas of National Park Đerdap (Bojović, 1967). They were observed as a group for several years, and then they completely disappeared.

25.1.11 Ibex

In 1959, two male and two female ibex, originating from the Swiss Alps, were released at the mountain massif Koprivnik, at 2460 m a.s.l., on the northeastern slopes of Mt. Prokletije above Peć, in the province Kosovo and Metohija (Živančević, 1960). This group was observed only for a few years.

Table 25.2 *Official records of ungulates harvested in Serbia, 1991–2005 (data for 2000 and 2005 are not complete)*

Species	1991	1995	1997	1999[1]	2000[1]	2005[1]
Red deer	916	696	489	529	?	?
Roe deer	8 048	4 240	3 632	2 310	3 334	> 5 145
Fallow deer	54	78	16	296	?	?
White-tailed deer	?	?	?	?	?	1–2 (∼10)
Chamois	46	23	17	4	?	?
Mouflon	139	53	72	47	?	?
Wild boar	3 783	1 365	1 741	2 325	∼ 3 000	2 366

(1) Data for 1999, 2001 and 2005 are incomplete, as there are no reports from the province of Kosovo and Metohija.

25.1.12 Status and population trends

The only indications of total population size for the various species (Table 25.1) are the population estimates published each year by the Hunting Association of Serbia (Šelmić et al., 2001; Anonymous, 2007). They pertain to the whole territory of Serbia, including the hunting grounds managed by hunting societies, hunting grounds managed by the State Enterprise 'Srbijašume', as well as the national parks. The methodology is not very scientific, but has been more or less continuous such that it represents a good picture of trend as well as an approximation of the true size. The decrease in population numbers during the 1990s was most probably caused by the bad economic situation in Serbia and the war activities in surrounding countries, when poaching was widespread and in some areas the most basic breeding activities in fenced hunting areas were discontinued.

Since 1998, the data are almost completely lacking for the province of Kosovo and Metohija, which used to host important fenced breeding and open hunting grounds. Therefore the data for this period almost exclusively pertain to central Serbia and the province of Vojvodina. Since 2000, the socioeconomic situation has gradually stabilised, resulting in application of active management practices, as well as recovery and increasing population trend in almost all ungulate species in Serbia (Table 25.1). The trend in harvest (Table 25.2) represents a fair depiction of the population trends. Only four shot chamois in 1999 indicates both the bad state of the population and the weak participation in hunting activities due to the war situation in Serbia. From 2000, official data on legal harvest are incomplete, so they are not presented here.

25.2 Legislation

All ungulate species are protected by a closed season according to the present Hunting Law (Službeni glasnik, 1993a), while the accompanying regulations determine

Table 25.3 *Current closed season periods for Ungulata in Serbia (according to the Order on close season, Službeni glasnik (2002))*

Species	Period of closed season
Red deer	Males and calves: 15 February–31 July
	Females: 1 February–15 August
Roe deer	Males: 1 October–30 April
	Females and fawns: 1 February–30 September
Fallow deer	Males: 1 February–15 September
	Females and calves: 1 February–30 September
White-tailed deer	Males: 1 February–15 September
	Females and calves: 1 February–30 September
Chamois	Males: 1 February–15 September
	Females: 1 February–31 August
	Kids: whole year
Mouflon	Males and females: 1 January–30 September
	Lambs: whole year
Wild boar	Males: 1 February–30 April
	Females: 1 January–30 June
	Piglets: 1 February–30 June

the closed season periods, according to trends and the state of populations. In order to avoid any contradictions between the Hunting Law and the present Ordinance on Natural Rarities (Conservation Law) (Službeni glasnik, 1993b), the latter does not include ungulates in any of its protected species lists, although the current status of some of these species indicates an urgent need in the future to put in place appropriate conservation measures including the protection of these species and their habitats. The present dates of closed season for each species, prescribed by the regulation on closed seasons (Službeni glasnik, 2002), are included in Table 25.3.

Article 2 of the same regulation prescribes closed season throughout the year for all ungulate species except wild boar, if the basic stock at the hunting grounds is less that 50% of the optimal game stock determined by management plan of hunting grounds. For the wild boar, the close season throughout the year is prescribed if the basic stock is less than 30% of the optimal game stock determined by management plan of hunting grounds. Article 3 of the same regulation allows within the period 16 May–31 July only the selective hunting of male roe deer, except in case postulated in article 2 of this regulation.

25.3 Hunting practice in Serbia

The hunting clubs (grouped under the Hunting Association of Serbia as an independent non-governmental organisation), the Public Enterprise 'Srbijašume' and certain national parks (Tara in western Serbia, Fruška Gora in the province of Vojvodina, and Šarplanina in the province of Kosovo-Metohija) have their own hunting areas where they conduct wildlife management. In the hunting clubs, members pay an annual fee, which allows them to hunt a certain number of individuals (determined by the annual management plan) at a lower cost. For other foreign and native hunters, there are officially determined prices for killing the animal, as well as for services provided during hunting. Therefore, the local hunters are in their respective areas provided with ungulate hunting at special lower cost and/or with special ways of paying, but only within the frames of the annual management plan. This plan includes the number of individuals to be shot, their age, sex and trophy value. In the hunting areas owned by PE Srbijašume and national parks, the ungulates are also hunted according to annual management plans, but the prices are equal for all potential users.

25.4 Conclusions

The status of Serbia's wild ungulates has fluctuated in synchrony with its political and socioeconomic situation. The 1990s were a difficult period, but present trends indicate that the situation is improving. There is still a need for further modernisation of the wildlife management system, and, especially, for some modern scientific research into the status and ecology of these species in Serbia.

Acknowledgements

The first author was supported by the Ministry of Science (and Environmental Protection) of Republic of Serbia in the frame of project #146023. The work was also supported by a cooperative grant from the Norwegian Research Council. The authors are grateful for very valuable information to Svetislav Tatović, Aleksandar Ćeranić, Miodrag Strnad and Sreten Kućančanin. The chapter was initiated, evaluated and reviewed by John Linnell.

References

Anonymous (2007) Briga o životinjama, razumevanje među ljudima. 54. Generalna skupština CIC-a, Međunarodni savet za lov i očuvanje divljači (CIC), katalog, 1–35, Beograd. [Passion for Wildlife means Caring for People]. (In Serbian.)

Bjedov, V., Bradvarović, J., Savić, I. and Ćirović, D. (1997) Taksonomski aspekti reintrodukcije jelena (*Cervus elaphus* L., 1758) na području južno od Save i Dunava. Zbornik radova sa savetovanja u Požegi, Beograd. [Taxonomic aspects of Red Deer (*Cervus elaphus* L, 1758) reintroduction in the area to the south from Sava and Danube]. (In Serbian.)

Bojović, D. (1967) Later Works on Settling Big Game on the Territory of Serbia Southerly of the Sava and the Danube. *Les travaux des VII Congress de l'Union Internationale des Biologotes du gibier*. Belgrade, pp. 359–64.

Bradvarović, J., Savić, R. I. and Milošević-Zlatanović, S. (1994) Taksonomski i ekološki status jelena (*Cervus elaphus* L) na prostoru Deliblatske peščare. In: *Deliblatski pesak. Zbornik radova* **6**, 483–8. [Taxonomic and ecological status of red deer (*Cervus elaphus* L) in the area of Deliblato Sands]. (In Serbian with English abstract.)

Jovanović, V., Ćirić, D, Bojović, D. and Šmit, Ž. (1983) Američki belorepi jelen *Odocoileus virginianus* Zimmermann, novi član naše faune. *Second Symposium on fauna of Republic of Serbia*, Proceedings, pp. 189–92, Belgrade. [American white-tailed deer (*Odocoileus virginianus* Z.), a new member of our fauna]. (In Serbian with English summary.)

Kryštufek, B., Milenković, M., Rapaić, Ž. and Tvrtković, N. (1997) 6.16 Former Yugoslavia. In D. M. Shackleton, ed., and the IUCN/SSC Caprinae Specialist Group. 1997. *Wild Sheep and Goats and their Relatives. Status. Survey and Conservation Action Plan for Caprinae*. Gland, Switzerland and Cambridge, UK: IUCN, pp. 138–43.

Milošević-Zlatanović, S., Crnobrnja-Isailović, J. and Stamenković, S. (2005) Allozyme variability and differentiation in Serbian roe deer populations *Capreolus capreolus*. *Acta Theriologica* **50**(4), 429–44.

Popović, Z., Bogdanović, V. and Gajić, I. (2002) Estimation of parameter distribution of trophy in roe deer. *Biotechnology in Animal Husbandry* **18**(5/6), 291–8.

Randi, E., Alves, P. C., Carranza, J. *et al.* (2004) Phylogeography of roe deer (*Capreolus capreolus*) populations: the effects of historical genetic subdivisions and recent nonequilibrium dynamics. *Molecular Ecology* **13**(10), 3071–83.

Savić, I. R., Paunović, M., Milenković, M. and Stamenković, S. (1995) Diverzitet faune sisara (*Mammalia*) SR Jugoslavije, sa listom vrsta od međunarodnog značaja. In V. Stevanović and V. Vasić, eds., *Biodiverzitet Jugoslavije, sa listom vrsta od međunarodnog značaja. Biološki fakultet i Ecolibri*. Belgrade, pp. 517–54. [Diversity of mammal (*Mammalia*) fauna of Yugoslavia, with list of species of international importance. In: Stevanović, V., Vasić, V. (eds.), *Biodiversity of Yugoslavia*, with list of species of international importance]. (In Serbian.)

Šelmić, V. (ed.) *et al.* (2001) *Program razvoja lovstva Srbije 2001–2010. Lovački savez Srbije*. Belgrade, pp. 1–241. [Serbian Hunting Development Program 2001–2010]. (In Serbian.)

Službeni glasnik (1993a) Zakon o lovu. 39, Belgrade. [Hunting Law]. (In Serbian.)

Službeni glasnik (1993b). Uredba o zaštiti prirodnih retkosti. 50, Belgrade. [Ordinance on conservation of natural rarities]. (In Serbian.)

Službeni glasnik (2002) Naredba o lovostaju. 19, Beograd. [Order on closed season on game animals]. (In Serbian.)

Vasić, V., Džukić, G., Janković, D. *et al.* (1991) Preliminarni spisak za Crvenu listu kičmenjaka Srbije. *Zaštita prirode* **43–44**, 121–32. [Preliminary Red List of Vertebrates of Serbia]. In Serbian with English summary.

Živančević, V. (1956) *Uzroci propadanja lovne faune u Srbiji i uslovi za njenu obnovu u rezervatima i nacionalnim parkovima. Zaštita prirode, Zavod za zašt. prir. i nauč. prouč. prir. retkosti NR Srbije*. Beograd, pp. 1–72. [Threat factors for game animals in Serbia and conditions necessary for their recovery in reserves and national parks]. (In Serbian with English summary.)

Živančević, V. (1960) Introdukcija i aklimatizacija kozoroga *Capra ibex* L. na Prokletije. *Vesnik (organ muzejskog i konzervatorskog društva NRS)*, 1960 (1–2) pp. 13–20. [Introduction and acclimatization of Ibex *Capra ibex* L. at Prokletije]. (In Serbian.)

26

Ungulates and their management in Macedonia

ALEKSANDAR STOJANOV, DIME MELOVSKI
AND GJORGJE IVANOV, WITH JOHN D. C. LINNELL

At present, there are six species of wild ungulates in Macedonia: wild boar (*Sus scrofa*), roe deer (*Capreolus capreolus*), red deer (*Cervus elaphus*) and chamois (*Rupicapra rupicapra*) are native species, while fallow deer (*Dama dama*) and mouflon (*Ovis orientalis*) have been introduced. Currently, wild boar, roe deer and chamois occur in free-ranging populations, while red deer, fallow deer and mouflon are bred only in fenced hunting grounds and reserves. Until now, no formal scientific work on the estimation of population size of ungulates in Macedonia has been conducted. Due to this, there is a lack of data on population size.

26.1 Ungulate species and their distribution

26.1.1 Red deer

Native populations of red deer became extinct in Macedonia at the beginning of twentieth century. After World War II, the species was reintroduced from different sources (Slovenia, Croatia and Serbia). Today, they can be found in fenced reserves on Bistra mountain and in fenced hunting grounds in the Osogovo Mountains (Petkovski, 1998). Red deer are managed as a game species and hunting is allowed only in hunting grounds during the hunting season, from 1 September to 31 January.

No data are available on the size of red deer harvest.

26.1.2 Roe deer

Roe deer in Macedonia are believed to belong to the subspecies *Capreolus capreolus grandis* Bolkay, 1925 (Petkovski, 1998). Roe deer inhabit deciduous and mixed

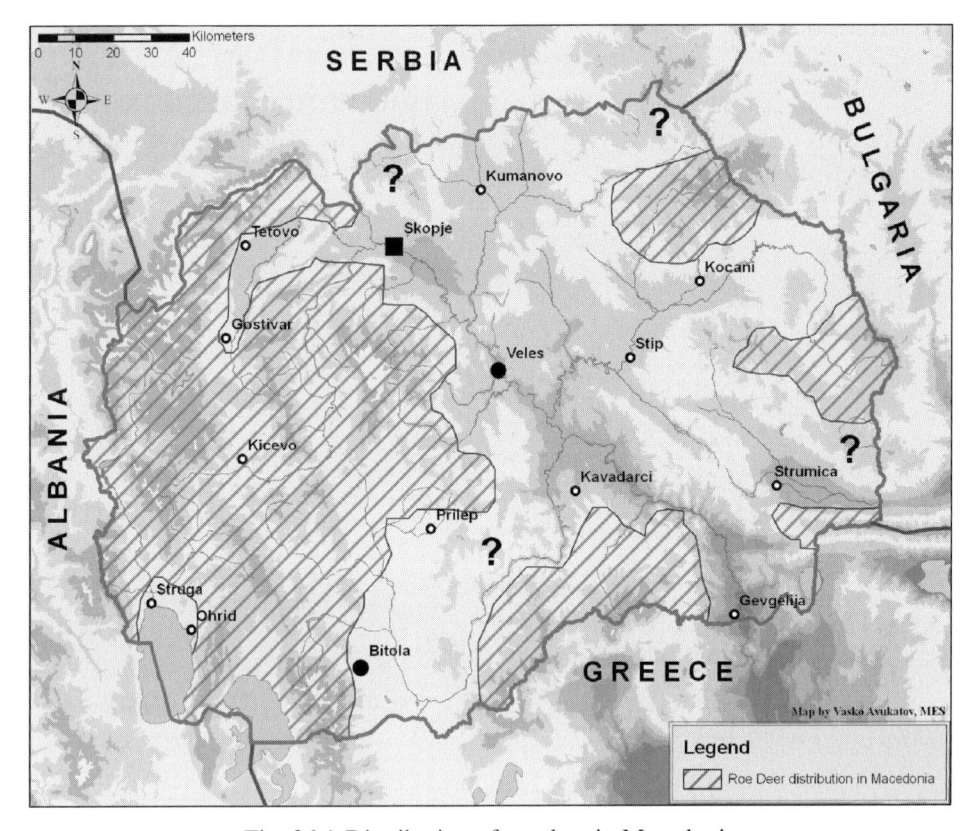

Fig. 26.1 Distribution of roe deer in Macedonia

forests in all mountain ranges in Macedonia. They are protected by law and hunting is prohibited. The population is believed to be decreasing, mainly due to poaching (author's own data).

26.1.3 Fallow deer

The fallow deer population in Macedonia was introduced from individuals brought from Bulgaria. They are currently bred in a fenced reserve on Bistra Mountain and in a fenced hunting ground on Osogovo Mountain (Petkovski, 1998). Fallow deer are managed as a game species and hunting is allowed only in hunting grounds during the hunting season, from 16 September to 31 January. No harvest data exist.

26.1.4 Wild boar

Wild boar in Macedonia are belived to belong to the subspecies *Sus scrofa reiseri* Bolkay, 1925 (Petkovski, 1998). Wild boar occur in all mountainous areas of

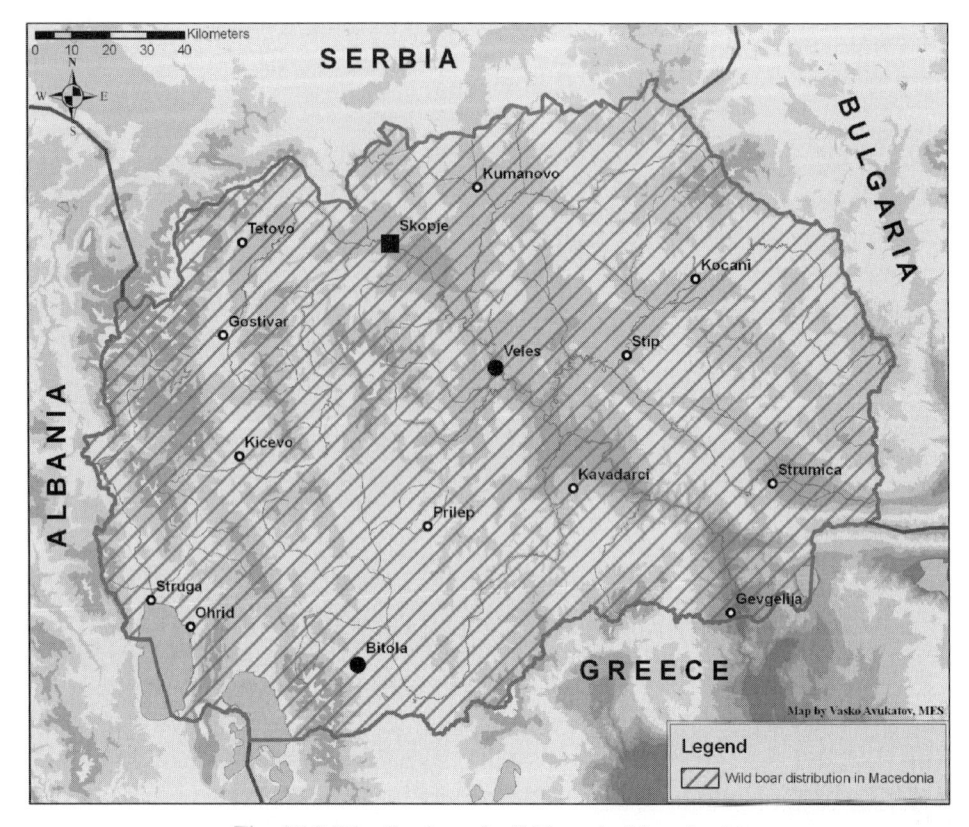

Fig. 26.2 Distribution of wild boar in Macedonia

Macedonia. They mainly inhabit open, deciduous forests. Wild boar are classified as a game species and hunting is allowed during the hunting season, starting from 1 October to 31 January. The number of wild boar harvested in 2005 was reported as 712 (Statistical Review, 2005). The population of wild boar in Macedonia is believed to be stable.

26.1.5 Chamois

Macedonian chamois are believed to belong to the subspecies *Rupicapra rupicapra balcanica* Bolkay, 1925 (Petkovski, 1998). The chamois population is distributed mainly in the mountainous areas in western, central and southern Macedonia, including the Shar Planina, Bistra, Korab, Deshat, Stogovo, Jablanica, Galichica, Kozhuf and Jakupica mountains and they are mainly confined to alpine areas above the treeline. Chamois are managed as a game species and hunting is allowed during the hunting season, from 1 October to 31 December. The reported number of chamois shot in 2005 was 47 (Statistical Review, 2005). The population is believed

Table 26.1 *Harvest records for chamois and wild boar in Macedonia 2000–2005*

	2000	2001	2002	2003	2004	2005
Chamois	12	55	4	35	8	47
Wild boar	737	663	575	525	667	712

Fig. 26.3 Distribution of chamois in Macedonia

to be decreasing during the last few years. The main threat to chamois population appears to be poaching (author's own data).

26.1.6 Mouflon

The mouflon population in Macedonia was introduced and can be found in the fenced hunting ground on Osogovo Mountain (Petkovski, 1998), as well as in the strict reserve 'Jasen' on Jakupica Mountain. They are managed as a game species

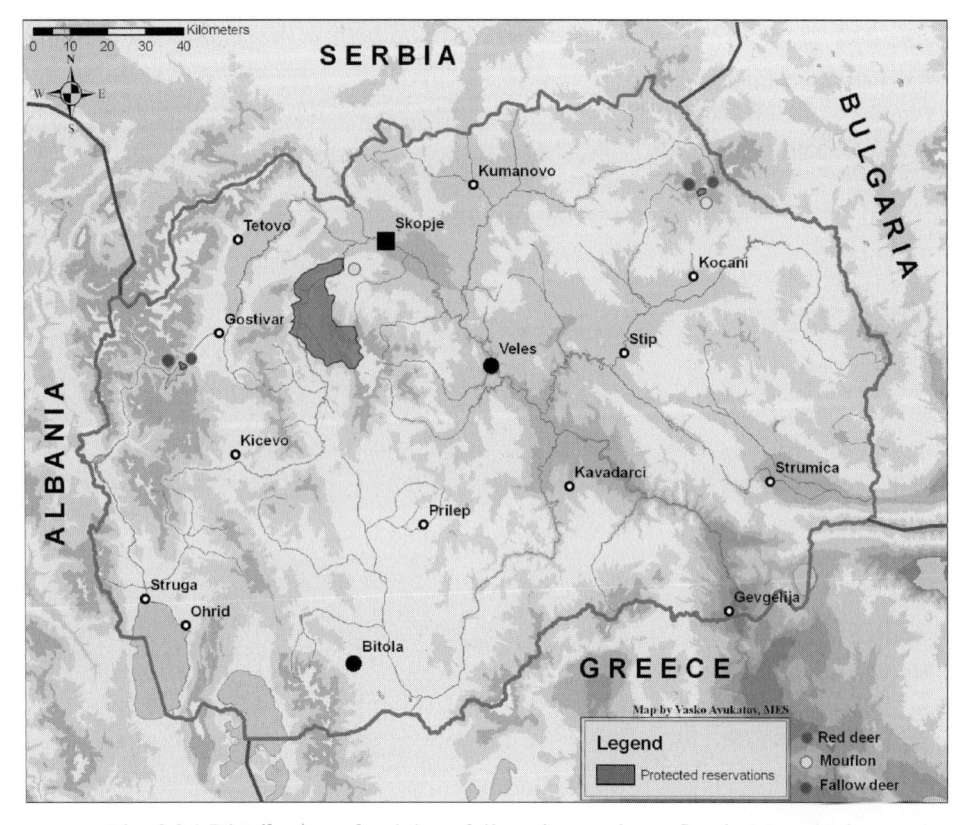

Fig. 26.4 Distribution of red deer, fallow deer and mouflon in Macedonia

and hunting is allowed only in hunting grounds during the hunting season, from 1 October to 31 January (Official Gazette of the Republic of Macedonia, 20/96). No harvest data exist.

26.2 Legislation

The government of Macedonia establishes the hunting grounds in Macedonia according to the physical plan of the country. The hunting grounds are assigned to the legal entity that conducts forestry activities, hunting or protection of the environment in the area. Game hunting in specific hunting grounds is allowed only with the given permission from the owner of the game in that hunting ground. Hunting permission is given only to a person who has already passed the hunting examination or to a foreign person who has the necessary papers for hunting.

References

Official Gazette of the Republic of Macedonia 20/96 [Law on hunting].
Petkovski, S. (1998) *Project: Mammals in Macedonia, Final report 1995–1997*. Skopje: Macedonian Museum of Natural History, 131 pp.
State Statistical Office of the Republic of Macedonia (2005) *Forestry, 1998–2005*, 30 pp.

27

Present status and future challenges for European ungulate management

Managing large ungulates in Europe is no easy task. There are some 20 species, each living under a great variety of environmental conditions across their full distributional range, and as such, their population biology is affected by a complex suite of influencing factors. Populations of most species are increasing in nearly all European countries (Gill, 1990 and chapters in this book) – and in consequence, they are having a profound effect on the ecological dynamics of both natural and human-made ecosystems of which they are a part.

Extracting figures from the various chapters presented in this book (see Tables 27.1 and 27.2), we estimate that at present the total number of ungulates in Europe adds up to more than 15 million. This represents a standing biomass of more than 0.75 billion kg. As these animals have an estimated annual consumption of nearly 20 million tonnes of green vegetation, nobody will question their impact on the landscape and their keystone role in the functioning of ecological systems.

Showing such a great variety in body size, appearance and habitat use, they represent in themselves an immense potential resource – both in terms of biodiversity, and in economic terms. Although their value as an energy resource is huge (Tables 27.3 and 27.4; the more than 5.2 million animals harvested each year represents more than 120 000 tonnes of meat, and a potential hunting revenue of several hundered million Euros), they also have inestimable aesthetic and cultural value as country-specific carriers of a whole range of cultural and hunting traditions.

Clearly, nobody reading this book can fail to appreciate the significance of maintaining a proper, well-functioning and well-integrated management of this hugely valuable resource. In this concluding chapter we first review the successes and failures of ungulate management in the twentieth century apparent in the different 'country chapters' of this book, in an attempt to learn something from both successful and less successful approaches in the past. We then describe some of the

Table 27.1 *Estimated number of Cervidae in Europe (in thousands). Estimation techniques vary throughout Europe, as do their precision and accuracy. Thus figures should be used as approximations to actual numbers. Most figures are estimates in 2004 and 2005, except Slovenia (1995)*

	Roe deer	Red deer	Fallow deer	Reindeer	Moose	White-tailed deer	Sika deer	Axis deer	Muntjac	Chinese water deer
Austria	1 050	190	1.5		0.01		2.7			
Belgium	60	10	0.2							
Czech R.	292.8	23.3	19		0.03	0.4	6			
Croatia	41.5	9.6	1.2					0.2		
Denmark	200	14	5.8				0.5			
Estonia	48.4	1.55			11.9					
Finland	30			1.2	93	55				
France	1 200	120	0.6				1			
Germany	2 400	150	12		0.05		3			
Greece		0.65	150							
Hungary	316	74.1	0.4							
Ireland		4	21.6				25			
Italy	425	63	10							
Latvia	129.5	28.4	21		14.5					
Lithuania	81.3	12.6			3.9					
Netherlands	60	2.7	1.15						0.1	
Norway	90	130		25	110					
Poland	692	141	13.1		3.9		0.1			
Portugal	5	20	3							
Romania	158.7	36.1	5.9							
Serbia	120	5	3			0.1				
Slovakia	35	38	7.5							
Slovenia	150	14	0.3							
Spain	600	900	100							
Sweden	800	10	?		200					
Switzerland	130	25					0.25			
UK	450	420	152				27		118	1.5
Total	9 616.15	2 443.035	529.25	26.2	437.27	55.5	65.55	0.2	118.1	1.5
Mean BW kg	20	100	50	50	200	50	50	50	15	10
Total biomass (tonnes)	192 323	201 523.5	26 462.5	1 310	87 454.4	2 775	3 277.5	10	1 771.5	15

Table 27.2 *Estimated number of Bovidae, Ovidae and Suidae in Europe (in thousands). Estimation techniques vary throughout Europe, as do their precision and accuracy. Thus figures should be used as approximations to actual numbers. Most figures are estimates in 2004 and 2005, except Slovenia (1995)*

	Alpine ibex	Spanish ibex	Alpine chamois	Pyrenean chamois	European bison	Barbary sheep	Mouflon	Wild goat	Musk ox	Wild boar
Austria	4		150				7.5			60
Belgium							0.4			21
Czech R.			0.4			0.03	17			48
Croatia			0.4				1.6			18.2
Denmark							0.08			0.1
Estonia										16.9
Finland							0.1			0.4
France	3		62.5	25			13			1000
Germany	0.4		20				13			1000
Greece			0.8					0.75		?
Hungary							8.3			78.1
Ireland										
Italy	14.9		136.7	1.12			15			600
Latvia										46.8
Lithuania					0.045					29.5
Netherlands							0.3			2.3
Norway									0.2	
Poland			0.08		0.65		1			600
Portugal		0.075					2			?
Romania			6.8				few			56.7
Serbia			0.6				1			30
Slovakia			0.6				8			28
Slovenia	0.3		15.6		0.007		2.1			10
Spain		70		50		?	50			600
Sweden	13						1		0.006	40
Switzerland			90				0.25			?
UK										0.3
Total	35.6	70.075	484.41	76.120	0.702	0.03	142.230	0.75	0.206	3858.9
Mean BW kg	60	50	25	25	400	60	30	40	150	50
Total biomass (tonnes)	2136	3503	12110.25	1903	280.8	1.8	4266.9	30	30.9	192945

Table 27.3 Estimated number of Cervidae harvested in Europe (in thousands). Axis deer is not being hunted in any European country. Most estimates are figures from 2005

	Roe deer	Red deer	Fallow deer	Reindeer	Moose	White-tailed deer	Sika deer	Muntjac	Chinese water deer
Austria	280.5	49.6	0.55				0.83		
Belgium	20.47	3.18				0.03			
Czech R.	121	18.5	9				6.8		
Croatia	8.13	1.16	0.23						
Denmark	103.3	3.34	3.13				0.36		
Estonia	5.46	0.14			3.85				
Finland	2.4			0.09	70	22			
France	503.1	40	0.2				0.29		
Germany	1077	62.9	2.8				1.2		
Greece			52.2						
Hungary	86	43	9.1						
Ireland			2						
Italy	46.5	8	4.7		2.58				
Latvia	18	3.47			0.09				
Lithuania	15	0.57							
Macedonia									
Netherlands		0.34							
Norway	30	24		6.5	37				
Poland	151	39	3				0.03		
Portugal	0.02	2	0.13						
Romania	4.3	0.83	0.93						
Serbia	5.1	0.53	0.3			0.01			
Slovakia	18	10	2						
Slovenia	42.4	4.92	0.14						
Spain	17.85	90.05	7.6						
Sweden	155	3			100				
Switzerland	42.5	7.1					0.14		
UK	108.05	81.5	64.6				11	23.5	1.5
Total	2 861.05	497.16	162.62	6.59	213.52	22.04	21.35	23.5	1.5

Table 27.4 Estimated number of Bovidae, Ovidae and Suidae harvested in Europe (in thousands). Barbary sheep, wild goat and musk ox are not regularly hunted in these European countries

	Alpine ibex	Spanish ibex	Alpine chamois	Pyrenean chamois	European bison	Mouflon	Wild boar
Austria	0.46		22.7			2.4	27.2
Belgium						0.07	14.37
Czech R.			0.03			6.3	121
Croatia			0.009			0.37	9.82
Denmark							0.03
Estonia							7
Finland						0.005	0.03
France			11.6	2.6		2.2	443.6
Germany			4				476.6
Greece							
Hungary						2.8	86.7
Ireland							
Italy	0.075		12.4			0.9	114.8
Latvia							17.2
Lithuania							13.02
Macedonia			0.05				0.7
Netherlands							
Norway							
Poland					0.065	0.3	136
Portugal						0.08	8
Romania			0.2				10
Serbia			0.004			0.05	2.37
Slovakia						2	22
Slovenia	0.020		2.5			0.72	6.57
Spain		1.85		2		4.3	161.5
Sweden						0.1	20
Switzerland	0.95		15.5				5.8
UK							
Total	1.505	1.85	68.98	4.6	0.065	22.57	1704.28

new challenges that will have to be dealt with by management in a rather different future. Considering these, we then attempt to suggest some general principles that we believe will be required for successful management of Europe's various ungulate populations in the twenty-first century.

27.1 Success and failures of ungulate management in the twentieth century

It is not difficult to find examples from previous chapters where ungulate management in the twentieth century has been successful in delivering its objectives. However, it is also easy to find many examples of failures to achieve declared aims, and unfortunately the failures outnumber the successful management stories in the last part of the past century. But let us briefly summarise some of the success stories first.

Numbers or range of threatened species or subspecies have been increased and stabilised in many countries. One unquestionable success story has been the conservation of Alpine ibex. From a single source population in Gran Paradiso National Park in Italy (where at the beginning of the nineteenth century just a few hundreds of ibex survived), there are now more than 130 populations in Italy, France, Switzerland, Germany, Austria and Slovenia with a total population numbering more than 34 000 ibex.

In the Mediterranean islands of Sardinia and Corsica, Italy and France have managed to improve the conservation status of mouflon and Sardinian red deer. Numbers of mouflon in Sardinia were fewer than 1000 in the 1970s and have now increased up to about 6000, while in Corsica mouflon have increased from fewer than 200 individuals to more than 2000 at present. Sardinian red deer was extinct in Corsica and hung on with only about 200 individuals in Sardinia at the beginning of the 1970s: now, thanks to a successful conservation programme Sardinia harbours more than 6000 deer and some of them have been translocated to Corsica where a new population has been successfully established. Elsewhere, Poland reports to have secured its native moose population. From a population numbering only eight animals in the 1930s, the population is now estimated at more than 2000 individuals. In the same country the last free-ranging European bison was killed in 1919. However, after reintroductions of animals surviving in zoological gardens and private parks, we can now find five populations in Poland, numbering more than 650 individuals in total.

For some, it may come as a surprise that also species that today are among the most numerous ungulate species had, in the relatively recent past, an unfavourable conservation status in many European countries. Roe deer, the most abundant large ungulate in Europe, numbers nearly 9 million animals today. Yet many countries report in these pages severe declines in numbers over past centuries due to overhunting, from which numbers have only relatively recently recovered; the species even went extinct in England and Wales by the beginning of the eighteenth century and has been re-established only by deliberate reintroduction. In France, more than 6000 roe deer have been translocated to former distribution areas in the last 30–40 years, now allowing an annual harvest of 0.5 million animals.

Ranking third in abundance among large ungulates, the estimated number of red deer in Europe adds up to more than 2 million. However, at the start of the twentieth century, red deer populations were dramatically reduced and regionally extinct in many European countries. After World War II, reintroductions of red deer were carried out throughout Europe.

These reintroductions are reported to be successful in the Apennines in Italy, and in many Departements in France, where hunting bags have increased from 5000 to 40 000 in the last three decades after the implementation of game harvest plans in 1979. In Portugal the red deer was already on the brink of extinction at the end of the nineteenth century, but their recovery after reintroductions now allows an annual harvest of 2000 individuals. In Hungary the story is the same. Here red deer were introduced to several game parks or released into the wild in order to establish new stocks or to improve local populations, resulting in a five-fold increase in population size from 1960 to 2005, and an annual harvest increasing from 3800 to 43 000 animals.

One of the largest ungulates in Europe, the moose, was once very scarce in Scandinavia; in fact, the famous Swedish naturalist Linné never saw a moose. However, implementation of new management principles, e.g. age- and sex-specific quotas putting pressure on males and young unproductive animals, has prompted a substantial increase in moose populations in Norway, Sweden and Finland. We have chosen examples only and many other 'success' stories are recorded in these pages.

At the same time as numbers and distributions of threatened taxa have been increasing, so there has also been a clear increase in numbers of more established species and subspecies (e.g. Gill, 1990; chapters in this book) with this increase often deliberately encouraged to support sporting interests. Unfortunately, this increase in large ungulate numbers has perhaps overshot its target and is now seen by many commentators of wildlife management as a problem. Perhaps because objectives have changed over the years, and because of growing concern about the impact of ungulates on natural and man-made ecosystems, current population densities and continuing increases in number in many areas are now commonly regarded as a demonstration of failure of current management to control ungulate populations and control impacts.

To be fair, there are numerous examples where management has been ineffective in terms of reducing damage caused to agriculture or forestry. For example, wild boar, ranked second in abundance among large ungulates (estimated to be nearly 3 million animals in Europe), accounts for nearly 90% of the damage to agriculture and forestry in Italy and France, and causes an economic loss of more than EUR 30 million. In addition, there are many other examples in these pages where damage by ungulates to agriculture, or more particularly forestry, is of serious economic consequence.

In a similar vein, there are few reports of successful efforts to reduce the increasing numbers of ungulate–vehicle collisions, estimated to be more than 750 000 incidents per year, each representing a cost to society of EUR 2000 simply in terms of material damage, and causing a large number of human injury accidents, which thus add further economic loss of twice that figure (J. Langbein, *pers. comm.*).

In many cases, therefore, we may suggest that current management strategies adopted in particular cases are not proving successful in reducing population growth, or reducing the impact of large ungulates to levels accepted by society; in other cases, such as in Sweden, Norway and Belgium, inappropriate selection of harvested individuals by age- or sex-structure within the cull is reported to have exacerbated damage through disrupting social organisation, threatening the sustainability of sporting (trophy) harvests, or critically lowering the effective population size.

Different problems may have resulted from past introductions or reintroductions. In every European country there are ungulate species that are not native to the country. In fact, between 20 and 64% of all wild ungulate species that could be found within the countries are introduced species. Most extreme are the Czech Republic and UK, where only four of eleven species, and two of six species, respectively, are native to the country.

Further, even reintroduction of species to parts of their former range – or, in other cases, attempts to introduce new individuals from elsewhere to bolster up existing native populations – may have unforeseen and undesirable consequences. Reintroductions of red deer in northern Spain have resulted in the displacement of other ungulates, and led to a significant increase in damage to agriculture. Further, in many reintroduction programmes, animals are brought in from a number of different sources, producing a mongrel population of uncertain provenance. France has used red deer from Germany, Hungary and Austria; Austria has used a mixture of breeds from Asia, America and Carpathian countries, while reintroductions in Portugal were animals obtained in Spain, Scotland and Hungary. No European country seems to harbour red deer populations that are completely native.

Were not this enough of a problem, perhaps even more insidious is the effect such introductions may have had on population genetics where individuals of outside (often unknown) origin are introduced into areas where there remain existing populations of endemic species or subspecies – resulting in an erosion of the genetic integrity of such native taxa. Such problems threaten the integrity of native Italian roe deer or those of the Iberian peninsula (Lorenzini *et al.*, 2002; Vernesi *et al.*, 2002), while red deer populations of Scotland, widely used in reintroduction programmes in other countries (above), have themselves been subject to various 'subsidies' over the years from animals of a diverse range of Continental origins and are of somewhat questionable genetic provenance (Hmwe *et al.*, 2006).

As noted also in Chapter 1, the situation is even more complicated where the introduction of novel species (let alone subspecies) may lead to hybridisation. The genetic integrity of many populations of red deer in Scotland, England and the Republic of Ireland is seriously compromised through past and ongoing hybridisation with the introduced sika deer (Harrington, 1973, 1982; Ratcliffe *et al.*, 1992; Goodman *et al.*, 1999; Pemberton *et al.*, 2006) – and fears of similar hybridisations are already a matter of concern elsewhere within their range (Czech Republic: Bartoš *et al.*, 1981; Bartoš and Žirovnický, 1981; Zima *et al.*, 1990, Germany; these pages)

So, despite some successes, management of ungulate populations and their impacts has, in many instances, failed to deliver what was desired.

Several factors may be responsible for the shortcomings; these include:

1. lack of clarity of management objectives and lack of coordination between different land-use interests to agree on appropriate management objectives;
2. lack of coordination of management objectives between neighbouring (local or regional) management units;
3. lack of coordination between countries in cases where ungulates roam across borders;
4. problems related to scale, i.e. mismatch of management areas with actual biological range of ungulate species, so that management is not coordinated across the population biological range;
5. problems caused by inappropriate legislation;
6. inadequacy of monitoring systems of ungulate numbers and their impact;
7. failure to set adequate hunting quotas in relation to population densities and dynamics;
8. failure of management units to achieve hunting quotas, even when these are set;
9. lack of knowledge regarding possible effects of selective harvesting.

We will briefly explore some of these, and pinpoint some of the future needs.

27.1.1 Lack of clear definition of precise management objectives

As is abundantly evident from the various country chapters, large herbivores may have a huge impact on their habitats, and affect a variety of societal values. Consequently, it is crucial that some effective management policy shall be determined.

Effective management of any ungulate population requires clear definition of objectives. Those objectives need to be translated in terms of actual management needs before a specific management strategy directed towards satisfaction of those defined objectives can be implemented. The final management 'package' adopted will of course differ markedly in different situations and will depend very heavily on the varying objectives of that management (or different priority of objectives, in situations where a number of separate interests must be satisfied).

It is clear, however, that at present there is a large variation in the degree to which the responsible authorities, or in some cases even private stakeholders, show an interest in developing such policy or in sharing their objectives with the public. Furthermore, in several countries we find that specific interest groups are able to influence political decision-making processes and cause rapid changes in the game management system, prioritising their own particular objectives. Under such circumstances, we are unlikely to be able to manage ungulate populations in a manner that is balanced and sustainable and delivers an appropriate integration of all end-user objectives.

Since it aims to effect changes in the future, inevitably management aims at a moving target; circumstances and external conditions change; management prescriptions themselves cannot always be sufficiently precisely defined a priori to deliver exactly the objectives sought. The influence of stochastic factors is pronounced in most populations, and the predicted increased frequency of extreme weather conditions is likely to increase their influence on population dynamics. For all these reasons, it is essential to monitor the effects of *any* management policies adopted in order to check that they are achieving broadly what is required of them and, in the light of experience, to refine or adjust them, so that they more closely deliver the desired objectives, i.e. adopt a more adaptive management approach.

27.1.2 *Lack of coordination of management over a larger geographical scale*

Very few European countries report a satisfactory coordination of management activities. That is, coordination between neighbouring geographical areas may be lacking, and commonly coordination between the various management levels may also be inadequate. This lack of coordination of management effort over a sufficiently large area is cited by most authors in this volume as a serious constraint making it difficult to deliver management objectives.

For effective management, culling effort must be coordinated over the entire population range. This is currently the exception rather than the rule, with the result that the overall impact of any management effort at a local level may be diluted or even countermanded at a national, or even regional level if neighbouring areas are undertaking no management at all or are undertaking management directed towards some different objective. Even at the local level, each management block is commonly surrounded by areas of land where no management may be undertaken at all, or where management is directed towards completely different objectives, clearly reducing any individual manager's chances of achieving his own or her management aims.

Even more complicated is the situation when ungulates perform seasonal migrations between different countries. The Alps offers a good illustration of these inconsistencies between neighbouring countries in relation to a whole range of different management practices. Even in regard to practices such as supplementary feeding, it is astonishing to note that such supplementation is compulsory in countries on the northern side of this mountain chain (Austria and part of Germany) but not in those to the south (e.g. Italy, France and Slovenia). The outcome is that in some border localities red deer populations often behave in an unexpected and unwanted way – attracted into certain areas by winter feeding on one side of the border – but with this increase in local densities causing significant damage to forestry interests on the other side. A different example may be given for the same area in relation to the different strategies adopted to deal with mite infestation in chamois (and ibex). While in Austria, the policy is to shoot any infested animal, in most neighbouring Italian provinces, policy is diametrically opposite: that is, hunters are discouraged from shooting any chamois with signs of infestation, instead allowing the population's own dynamics to respond to this natural challenge. Thus, lack of coordination between the countries sharing the same populations is hardly well designed to ensure effective control. Clearly effective management for the future will demand administrative structures, and biological management units, which ensure proper coordination of objective and management effort over an appropriate spatial scale.

27.1.3 *Inadequate scale of management units*

A related problem to that of populations roaming across borders, concerns the common 'mismatch' between actual management areas, or hunting units, inside a specific country and the biological range size of the species to be managed. A very common characteristic of most European countries is the small size of hunting units of ungulate species. This is often the case even for large species like red deer or moose, whose individual home range may comprise up to many thousands of hectares, while the size of hunting unit may be as low as 5–20 ha for a moose in Sweden (B and E licences, respectively), or 250–500 ha for all ungulates in Germany.

In general, mismatch of management areas with actual biological range results in uncoordinated management across the population's total range. This may lead to serious problems where conflicting interest between different hunting units may hinder the achievement of large-scale management objectives like a reduction of the population.

It is now increasingly recognised that management units should be established with due regard to the biological range size of the species to be managed, but this very often conflicts with an established link between land ownership and the right to shoot game on that land. Even where state or regional authorities determine management units, it is common experience that these are, for purely practical reasons, often considerably smaller than the effective population range – or are determined as the same area for all species, irrespective of ranging patterns.

Extreme variants can be found in, for example, Spain, where ungulate management has become the main economic use in many marginal areas of the south-western part of the country. This has produced a tendency to increase the control by the owner over the populations occurring within his/her own estate; as a result, many properties have been fenced to prevent ungulate movements.

27.1.4 Problems with inappropriate legislation and law enforcement

Careful management, well designed to deliver its defined objectives, can be rendered ineffective if there is significant loss of animals to illegal hunting (or illegal hunting practices). It is noted that, in many countries, losses to poaching still constitute the biggest threat to conservation of rare or threatened taxa and it is clear that effective legislation (and law enforcement) are required.

Finally, it is also clear that there is a wide diversity between different countries in Europe in relation to permitted hunting practices (e.g. in some countries use of dogs is permitted, in others it is strictly forbidden), permitted firearms, calibres of weapons and permitted seasons. Indeed, it is remarkable how little consistency is observed in the different areas. However, all these elements of management may have implications for animal welfare which themselves warrant careful review.

Although all European countries have specified permitted seasons for the different game species (exception Portugal, where technically the season lasts from 1 June in any year to 31 May of the following year, although most hunting activity is carried out between September and February), there is, however, an enormous diversity in length (and actual time of year) of the permitted season, which shows little consistency between, and even within, countries and often little relation to actual biological breeding seasons (i.e. timing of rut, parturition, period of dependency of young). The mismatch between hunting and biological seasons, and the implications of this for welfare, social dynamics – and the ability (or failure) of hunters to regulate prey populations, reflects an inappropriate legislation in many countries.

In many countries, seasons for males and females are the same, or show significant overlap perhaps, at first glance, suggesting little regard for biological season. While it is difficult to extrapolate too widely, as the different countries of Europe span a wide range of latitudes and timing of the rut and juvenile dependency may vary, we see from the country chapters that the earliest permitted time for culling red deer females is 1 August (Netherlands) and the latest 31 March (France, England), and 31 May in southern Spain. Correspondingly, the earliest permitted time for culling roe deer females is 1 May (Austria, Switzerland) or 15 August (Latvia), while the latest is 31 March (Scotland, England) and 31 May (Spain). If we assume (over the latitudinal range) that the period of parturition for roe deer is from late April/early May to end of June (Linnell and Andersen, 1998; Linnell *et al.*, 1998) and that for red deer is from mid-May to the end of June (e.g. Fletcher, 1974), we may speculate that neonates not accompanying the mother may be orphaned if mothers are shot before say mid-June (roe) or mid-July (red), while unless culled with the mother, juveniles nutritionally dependent on lactating dams will have an increased risk of dying if mothers are shot before their third month of life.

On such a basis, it is clear that with seasons for mature red deer females in most countries not opening until September (Croatia, Slovenia, Hungary Romania – all central European, with earlier breeding seasons anyway) or October (Denmark, Sweden, Wallonia, Poland, Estonia, Lithuania) cull seasons may be considered outside the period of maximum welfare risk. Some countries delay the commencement of the season even further (November in England and Eire). However we may note that seasons in the Netherlands, Latvia, the Czech Republic, Slovakia and Switzerland open as early as the beginning of August. Seasons for roe deer are generally restricted to a period well before parturition (e.g. 1 January to 15 March, or 15 January to 15 March in the Netherlands or Flanders) or do not commence until September or the beginning of October (the majority of countries). Only in Spain, Austria and Switzerland is the season for mature females open from April (Spain) or May. Females culled at this time may well be near-term or actually have given birth. While in France the season for roe does finishes at the end of March, we may note that for the final month (1–31 March), roe may only be hunted by coursing!

For males, the earliest date for the opening of the permitted season for red stags is 1 July (Scotland), while the more general start of the season is August or September. In the majority of countries the season extends through to the end of January or February, and only in France and England does it continue to the end of March. The start of the roe buck season (1 April) in Scotland and England is also one of the earliest in Europe, but in many countries/states, buck shooting may continue to the end of November, December, or even into January (Switzerland). Also evident from the country chapters (e.g. Poland), male seasons extend through the rut in the majority of countries, with an associated potential for disruption of breeding, or social 'distress'. In some few countries (e.g. Norway), the season starts after the rut, and only in Denmark and Wallonia does the roe buck season appear deliberately 'broken' to accommodate an undisturbed rut.

Length and timing of hunting season may also have other implications, less related to welfare of the animals themselves, as impacting on the actual effectiveness of management. Where seasons are too short (or timed inappropriately in relation to biological seasons), managers may simply be unable to achieve the necessary cull numbers to control problem populations. Problems experienced in controlling wild boar populations in many of the European countries in which they occur provide a particularly clear illustration of this. The story is clearly a complicated one and failure to control numbers (and damaging impacts) is, in some part, simply due to lack of willingness of hunters to kill sufficient numbers (many of them are actually happy to see an expansion in range and abundance of this economically valuable game species and so do not actively seek to reduce numbers); nonetheless, it is clear that a major contributing factor in many cases is the lack of adequate time in which to carry out an adequate cull.

In most European countries wild boar hunting stops between December and February with some exceptions in relation to culling of adult males and juveniles of both sexes. While this may in itself be constrained because of welfare issues (as from March onward sows are heavily pregnant and/or have recently given birth), this is not compatible with the need of strong limiting action to stop the general increase in numbers of wild boar. In many cases, in addition, sows accompanied by piglets are protected, still further reducing the potential for controlling numbers.

27.1.5 Inadequacy of monitoring systems of ungulate numbers and their impact

Accurate estimation of ungulate numbers whether at a local or regional level is extremely difficult, particularly when those ungulates occupy forest or other concealing habitats. Despite the number of reviews which have been offered of the possible direct and indirect methods available (e.g. Mayle and Staines, 1998; Mayle *et al.*, 1999; Morellet *et al.*, 2007) the problem of properly estimating ungulate numbers is still unresolved in most European countries.

Many countries indeed do not undertake any coordinated census at all, simply relying on harvest numbers ('bag numbers') to indicate trend. Yet this is done, commonly, with no validation that bag numbers are in fact closely related to population size (rather than simply related to hunter effort) and no attempts to calibrate bag number with true population size.

In other cases, even where some system of census is attempted (whether co-ordinated at a national level or at the level of Departments or hunting units) such censuses commonly rely on old and unverified methods and thus often fail to deliver any truly realistic figure of population size (or trend) so that cull numbers may actually exceed census numbers of the previous years – and do so consistently for many years.

There is a great deal of active discussion going on at the moment about the accuracy of the various different census methods in current usage, the utility of using census methods of unknown (or at least unquantified) accuracy, or those known to have poor levels of accuracy. Much of the debate depends on whether one seeks absolute estimates of animal number or simply a relative index sufficiently robust to reflect population trend (increase or decrease).

At the extreme, some would argue (e.g. Morellet *et al.*, 2007) that in many instances management does not actually require a detailed knowledge of actual animal number, but management decisions can be based on 'derived' measures of population condition, or measures of environmental (habitat) impacts. In reality, the 'solution', as usual, probably depends on the objectives of management, and where management aims to deliver a particular quota of animals for harvest, some idea of numbers is probably required. Even where management objectives are to reduce impacts on agriculture, forestry or native vegetation, we should be aware that impacts of even a constant ungulate population vary stochastically from year to year – and that there is often a considerable time-lag in vegetational response to changing density.

But the main point is that, whatever methods are to be adopted – whether in monitoring ungulate populations, population condition, or vegetational indicators – it is crucial that some programme of consistent monitoring is undertaken, to assess the effectiveness of any management action and inform appropriate future management decisions. Without some form of monitoring, how do we have any idea if current management approaches are delivering their objectives – or what changes in management may be required? It is also important that consistent methods are adopted throughout (consistent within any given country or group of countries and consistent over time).

Methods however should be 'fit for purpose' – simple and robust, designed to give the information required in an economical manner without excessive complexity. Methods must be robust and must be applicable on a large scale with an acceptable precision. It is also essential that methods used are ones which which can be readily used or at least understood by landowners and hunters, as well as by professional managers and wildlife rangers, so that any management decisions which are made on the basis of such figures are transparent and understood by all parties. It is not useful to advocate methodologies with perhaps the level of precision that might be required for detailed academic research, since these give a level of precision which is commonly not required as a basis for management decisions and the complexity of method (or amount of sampling required in order to generate acceptable levels of accuracy) may mean that they are not widely used, or used improperly.

The social importance of inclusivity in census and decisions arising from that census should not be underrated. It is of utmost importance that those who are actually involved in implementing management decisions feel intimately involved in those decisions and not just end-users with no responsibility apart from shooting. Active involvement in censuses or population estimation can be part of this process, as examples from Scandinavia (Moose Obs. scheme) or central Italy may show.

27.1.6 *Failure to set adequate hunting quotas and achieve these when set*

In all countries, except the UK, quotas are set or must be approved by regional or state authority. However, partly in direct consequence of lack of adequate information on ungulate numbers/densities, whether at local or even at regional scales, but also through ignorance of the basic biology and population dynamics of many European ungulates, there is a widespread problem of proper setting of hunting quotas for different species.

In countries where it is the managers themselves who undertake population estimates and where hunters or hunting organisations suggest a quota (e.g. Romania), they often deliberately overestimate the number of animals in the area in order to secure for themselves an increase in hunting quota or as an insurance, so that they still retain adequate hunting opportunities even if the authorities reduce the allocated quota from what is applied for.

Furthermore, setting proper quotas may become even more complicated where large predators are present or are recovering their former distribution, exerting a parallel predation pressure on ungulate populations. Although, for example, wolves may exert a low predation pressure at a regional scale, the predation pressure at a local scale may be high and unpredictable, making proper setting of the quotas difficult, as reported from Norway, Sweden and the Baltics.

This seems to be mainly true for northern ecosystems with low ungulate biomasses and with populations at medium-low densities.

Even where appropriate quotas are established, it is further apparent that, for any of a variety of reasons, the targets set are not always achieved in actual practice, and thus management fails, simply due to the fact that management actions prescribed are not actually carried out.

In Germany, for example, it is suggested that increased shyness of many ungulate, species, as a result of long hunting seasons and high hunting pressure, has a significant effect on hunting success. In Romania, a number of predators (bear, wolf, lynx), are reported to affect the behaviour and space use of game species, chasing prey animals away from their normal range for weeks. If this period coincides with the hunting season, hunting will be unsuccessful and quotas difficult to achieve.

It is, in fact, extremely difficult to assess actual cull harvests against quotas awarded since hunters will of course ensure that returns match the quota allocated under the licence granted (and there is no obvious way of 'checking'). Thus,

1. if a hunter has shot more than his/her permitted quota this will not be admitted; numbers by age and sex on any return will be presented to match the quota allocated and more detailed statistics, if required (for weight, reproductive condition, antlers, etc.), will simply be presented for the 'correct' number of animals declared;
2. if a hunter has shot less than his/her permitted quota, this may be honestly represented if no penalties attach (and simply the licensing authority subsequently 're-lets' the shortfall under another licence to ensure that the total cull level is maintained). However, in many situations, the licensing authority applies penalties if the required cull is not taken and, in this case, cull returns may be inflated to avoid such penalty.

Even where actual tagging of the carcase after death is mandatory, this does not wholly resolve the issue of accuracy. Animals taken in excess of quota will not be tagged or declared, while in the case of a shortfall on quota, surplus tags, where issued, can simply be disposed of.

For all these reasons, we can assume that the allocated quotas of animals which may be hunted in different areas are not really related to any preplanned wildlife management objectives and we may note that even those allocated quotas are not necessarily adhered to in practice. Many countries (e.g. Germany, France, Italy and Romania) report that they are unable to halt the general increase in wild boar populations, which again are causing huge damage to agriculture.

Reasons are reported to be inappropriate hunting season (above) and hunting techniques (i.e. mostly night hunting close to feeding places in Germany), but, in fact, failure correctly to estimate actual population size may be the most important factor.

27.1.7 Problems arising from inappropriate age- and sex-structure in the cull

So far, most management-oriented research has primarily been focused on population dynamics, particularly questions of density dependence and time lags in population and habitat responses, or on the relationships between herbivores and predators. Only recently, the effects of non-random hunting mortality have been brought up as an important management issue.

As documented in the country chapters, some selectivity of harvest (in terms of a 'bias' in the age- or sex-structure of animals selected for harvest) is apparent in most countries throughout Europe, either through the selection of 'trophy males' in recreational harvest, a concentrated focus on culling of females and juveniles in management programmes designed to cause population reduction, or some other imposed selection of specific age-classes.

As sport hunting is the principal cause of death in most populations (>90% in most managed populations of red and roe deer (Putman, 2008)), the actual age- and sex-distribution in hunted populations will be radically different from what we could find in populations not managed by humans. The age distribution in the live population will be heavily skewed toward younger animals, and, where hunting is primarily directed towards trophy shooting of males, the sex ratio will be biased in favour of females. Although proper selective harvest is not wrong in principle, we must be aware of unintended changes in population genetics and demography that may, in the short term, have undesirable effects on the behaviour of the population (and the sustainability of future harvests) and may, in the long term, have significant ecological and evolutionary consequences if there is heritable genetic variation for the target characteristic and harvesting occurs before the age of maturity.

A cull concentrating on the wrong age- or sex-class of animals may not only fail to achieve any reduction in numbers at all but may distort the social structure of the population, resulting in the appearance of abnormal behaviours or an increase in the frequency of aggressive interaction and of associated damage like bark-stripping and fraying (Putman, 1989). Distortion of the normal balance of social structure may also encourage emigration, while the disturbance caused by shooting may, in its own right, cause fragmentation and dispersal of the population (and the associated damage) to new areas. Finally, regular shooting over a protracted period may cause a shyness of behaviour that makes future control even more difficult (Challies, 1985; Putman, 1989).

Although several studies have significantly contributed to a broader knowledge regarding the effects of selective harvest (e.g. Ginsberg and Milner-Gulland, 1994; Coltman, 2008; Fenberg and Roy, 2008), we still need more precise answers to the following questions, which all will be of significance when developing future, more refined, management strategies:

- As post-hunt sex ratios of fewer than 5 males per 100 females have been reported in some populations, will this lead to a strong decrease of effective population size?
- Is this likely to influence the rate of genetic drift and lead to rapid loss of genetic variation?
- Will a biased age structure towards younger males lead to an increase in reproductive investment in young males, causing a higher mortality in this age group?
- Will a larger involvement of young males affect the sex ratio at birth (as we have seen more female moose calves born)?

- Given that a proportion of the variability in horn and antler size is genetically determined, and that their size influences sexual selection, will trophy hunting create the paradoxical situation of selecting against a genotype that otherwise, in absence of hunting, should be favoured?
- Does trophy hunting disturb natural mate selection and affect social structure stability?

27.1.8 Lack of science-based management

In many countries the pressure from society for a proper science-based ungulate management is increasing and this need for science-based management is indeed a recurring theme in many of the preceding chapters. The reasons are obvious; large populations of ungulates often affect other societal values and needs, and as we have already remarked, there is an increasing public awareness of (and involvement in) wildlife management issues, whether it is directed towards conservation, damage control or exploitation. In fact, the whole debate about wildlife and their management is, in so many countries, much more out in the public arena than previously.

Serious questions are now being voiced about both the need for management in some circumstances and the methods to be used, with frequent concerns being expressed that both objectives and means of achieving those objectives are not in line with the societal needs and values. The amount of recent research devoted to the exploration of immunocontraceptive techniques in the control of populations of deer and other larger wildlife (e.g. Putman, 1997a, 2004; Curtis et al., 2007) makes clear the increasing groundswell of public opinion questioning the methods of established 'tradition'. Those charged with responsibility for management of deer populations thus need to be more sensitive in approach and more publicly accountable for their decisions. All of this requires that our management is not only properly informed and based on good objective analysis of situations and solutions, but that the management is also transparent and actively seen to be well founded.

There is an increased pressure for more precise management methods. That is, we need to either develop better census methods, or develop management systems that pay more attention to animal–vegetation relationships, and to make use of more sophisticated management tools (modelling, population genetics, satellite-derived data coupled to GIS methods). However, the management methods used need to be accepted by and simple enough to be adopted by the people that actually undertake that practical management. This means that not only do we need to develop relevant and robust techniques which are acceptable to all practitioners, we also need to develop a proper understanding of the management principles among all parties involved in management.

As is apparent from the majority of chapters in this book, management of large ungulates in most cases is carried out primarily by those interested in hunting for sport or recreation. It is unlikely that management directed primarily towards recreational hunting will continue indefinitely to be tolerated by the rest of society. Increasingly, there will be a need for a management approach which, while it may still include elements of recreational hunting, will also be directed towards controlling damaging impacts to agriculture and forestry, will be directed towards minimising damaging impacts on natural vegetational communities, towards promoting wider biodiversity targets and ensuring sustainability both of the ungulates themselves and their environment.

Adopting more adaptive management principles seems to be an essential way forward. Including indicators of environmental change in an adaptive management strategy (see Walters and Holling, 1990), will ensure that management of ungulates is seen as a part of a wider environmental management that includes both the animals and their habitats. Whatever methods are to be adopted in monitoring ungulate populations, population condition, or vegetational indicators (section 27.1.5), it is crucial that some programme of consistent monitoring is undertaken, to assess the effectiveness of any management action and inform appropriate future management decisions. Without some form of monitoring we can never truly assess whether current management approaches are delivering their objectives, or what changes in management may be required better to reach those objectives – nor can we justify our actions to an ever-increasingly wildlife-conscious public.

27.2 Future challenges

These are all problems experienced in current management, which need to be addressed in developing better management for the future. But management in the twenty-first century will also need to address additional new issues arising from:

1. Likely changes in land-use patterns and priorities across Europe;
2. Climate changes and their effects on large herbivore populations;
3. The likely increase in number and distribution of large-carnivore populations and the effect that this may have on large herbivores and human management needs.

27.2.1 Likely changes in land-use patterns

Europe has experienced a strong decline in its agricultural activities in the last 50 years. After World War II most countries of the 'western' block showed a common pattern of increase in industrialisation and service provision with a concomitant abandonment of rural areas, especially in the mountains and hills. This pattern was followed some decades later by the eastern countries, which are now experiencing a fast development of their economies.

All this had, and continues to have, a powerful influence on habitat quality and availability for wild ungulates: it seems probable that such changes were the primary factor behind the large increase in numbers and distribution of almost all wild ungulates in Europe.

It seems unrealistic to expect that in the future this pattern will change: despite the efforts made within the European Community to encourage, at least, the maintenance of the present status in rural areas with a very supportive economic policy, it seems unavoidable that more marginal areas will be abandoned by agriculture. Within such context, it is possible to predict a further increase of ungulate populations in Europe that may be paralleled by new forms of exploitation of once marginal agricultural areas, most of which will be represented by tourist activities and rural housing development. Ungulates may be beneficial to ecologically oriented tourism as much as they were in the past (and can still be now) to hunting tourism. Conversely, in many European parks, wild ungulates are becoming the main source of attraction and 'deer watching' an interesting activity for visitors.

However, the increase of natural areas harbouring ungulates (together with an increased colonisation by the ungulates themselves of peri-urban and even urban areas) has brought also new problems: together with the increase of traffic accidents (this volume and e.g. Groot Bruinderink and Hazebroek, 1996; Romin and Bissonette, 1996; Putman, 1997b; Hedlund *et al.*, 2004; Putman *et al.*, 2004), we are now experiencing in many heavily industrialised countries a number of events in which the presence of wild ungulates close to or sometimes in the outskirts of large cities is increasing the potential for disease transmission to domestic stock (e.g. Bouvier, 1963; Delahay *et al.*, 2002; Huitema, 1972 for bovine tuberculosis; Smith and Roffe, 1992 for brucellosis). Two recent articles in *Science* and *Nature*, respectively, state that 'emerging infectious diseases (EIDs) pose a substantial threat to the conservation of global diversity' (Daszak *et al.*, 2000), and that 'zoonoses from wildlife represent the most significant, growing threat to global health of all EIDs' (Jones *et al.*, 2008). Generally, in the future wild ungulates will become more a part of everyday life than they are now, their presence not only familiar to hunters or foresters but also to the public at large.

27.2.2 Large herbivores and climate change

Despite inconsistency in predicting the magnitude, a wide range of theoretical models agree in the basic direction of climate change: both winter and summer temperatures in Europe are expected to increase, there will be larger spatial and temporal variation in precipitation, and the fluctuations in climatic conditions will be more extreme. This will inevitably affect population dynamics and distribution of large ungulates. As the climatic changes are expected to be most pronounced in the northern parts of Europe and on mountain chains, mountain-dwelling species like wild reindeer, Alpine ibex, musk ox and Alpine chamois subspecies living on Central European mountain chains are likely to be affected first. As populations of these species already have restricted distribution areas, increased frequency of freeze–thaw episodes may cause local extinctions.

However, as a corollary we may imagine an overall increase of population productivity of forest and plains-living species in most European countries where winters will become milder, if wetter, and the selective capacity of the harsh climate will be limited by the higher temperature and scarcity of snow cover. Species like roe deer and wild boar will further increase their distribution and abundance in many European countries and reach higher latitudes, as it is already the case for Scandinavia.

However, maybe most importantly, it is the actual fluctuations in climate which may have greatest impact, in imposing a greater instability in population dynamics. This will jeopardise the stability in harvest outcome that we often have a tendency to strive for. If pronounced, the temporal variation in ungulate population dynamics will increase the need for more refined management strategies in heavily harvested populations, to ensure that there is no time-lag between population growth rate responses and harvest quotas.

As the response of ungulates to climate change will be mediated through changes in their habitats, we need to have a more 'multivariate' focus when setting both management objectives and strategies, reinforcing our suggestions in the previous sections that we must look for more holistic management approaches which are responsive and adaptive to monitored changes both in animal numbers and distribution and in vegetation quality. Moreover our skills to foresee the trends of the environmental changes and the consequent changes in distribution and abundance of ungulate species will be a deciding factor in the success or failure of a European management strategy.

27.2.3 Interactions between large carnivores and large herbivores

As a result of a gradual introduction of wider protection, and active reintroduction, European populations of large carnivores are either stable or growing. Reintroduction programmes have been undertaken for brown bear and/or lynx in France, Italy, Slovenia, the Czech Republic, Germany, Switzerland and Austria. In addition, wolverines have been reintroduced to central parts of Finland, and programmes of reintroduction of lynx and wolf are actively being debated in the UK.

In addition, natural recolonisation has occurred in many areas. Wolves are now increasing in Spain, northern Italy, Norway and Sweden, and have recently begun colonising France, Germany and Switzerland. In many of these areas, the expansion is facilitated by the increase in ungulate numbers and distribution. Establishing a network of protected areas with high ungulate diversity and abundance is therefore proposed as a strategy for allowing a full recovery of the wolf population in several countries.

However, since these larger carnivores have been absent from their former distribution areas for so many years, both animal and human populations have lost their knowledge of how to deal with this new situation. Inevitably the increasing number of large carnivores will affect population growth rate of large ungulate populations as well as population size (i.e. reducing overall population densities and the proportion of the production that could be harvested by humans), but according to standard predator–prey models this is supposed to have a strong effect only in areas with low ungulate densities (e.g. Messier, 1994). However, such models are generally 'naturalistic' and do not normally take into account the additive 'predatory effect' of humans. Thus, even in areas with relatively high densities of ungulates the effect of large carnivores may be substantial if combined with excessive pressure of hunting. For example in south-central parts of Sweden, the lynx have been reported to cause a decrease in the roe deer populations to such an extent that the lynx themselves are now facing a decline as an effect of prey scarcity. Consequently, in areas where the management objective is to increase ungulate populations (e.g. moose in Lithuania), it would be vital to adjust the hunting quotas. Conversely, in areas where management aims at reducing ungulate numbers (e.g. wild boar in many European countries) allowing large carnivore populations to increase (most effectively wolves) may only partly solve the specific management goal, but create several others.

Europe does not have natural reserves or other protected areas big enough to establish 'natural' ecosystems involving all ecological processes related to predator–prey interactions. Furthermore, within their distribution areas most populations of large carnivores will be managed by humans to a large extent. Despite that, there will be an increased demand for management strategies that take into account the presence of the carnivores. As the presence of large carnivores may impose locally high predation pressure on ungulates, this will increase the need for defining management units of proper sizes, i.e. like presumed climatic changes and changes in land use regime, the presence of large carnivores should promote a discussion regarding the scale of management units. Large carnivores may also induce behavioural responses in ungulates, like the increase of group size (Bobek et al., 1984 but see Creel and Winnie, 2005) and the avoidance of risky habitats (Winnie and Creel, 2007), which may affect both their activity rhythm and habitat selection.

27.3 Ungulate management in the twenty-first century?

While we must address all the management problems of the twentieth century, we also need to develop systems which will enable us to deal with the new challenges.

In both cases we need to develop a more holistic and responsive management system, which

1. attempts to integrate management of ungulates in relation to all land-use interests where ungulates themselves may have an impact. This means the management of the ungulate populations themselves, whether objectives are control, exploitation or conservation, but also management of their impacts on other land-use interests: agriculture, forestry, habitat conservation, recreation, access to the countryside;
2. properly declares and defines management objectives (transparency);
3. includes more extensive (and science-based) monitoring systems which record trends in ungulate populations and impacts in order to assess effectiveness of management strategies in the short or medium term and allow refinement or adjustment of management policy so that it better delivers the declared objectives of that management;
4. explicitly recognises the value of wild ungulates as a natural resource both in terms of their value as living organisms and part of the wider biodiversity of an area, but also as a resource that can be managed in order to provide better living conditions for the people living in the same area, and ensures greater coordination of management both within and between countries.

To this final end, we should perhaps consider the need to develop a European policy directed to regulate the use of this important natural resource.

We believe that this book is a contribution to this refinement of management strategy in each Member State and across Europe as a whole, by highlighting problems faced by different European countries in management of their ungulate populations, considering current management practices and exploring where current management successfully delivers the objectives required (solves the problem) and where it might appear that the problem is, by contrast, a direct consequence of the management policy adopted in that particular situation. By learning from each other's successes and failures we can more easily establish management approaches in our own countries that will help us to reach our management objectives.

References

Bartoš, L. and Zirovnicky, J. (1981) Hybridisation between red and sika deer. II. Phenotype analysis. *Zoologischer Anzeiger Jena* **207**, 271–87.

Bartoš, L., Hyanek, J. and Zirovnicky, J. (1981) Hybridisation between red and sika deer. I. Craniological analysis. *Zoologischer Anzeiger Jena* **207**, 260–70.

Bobek, B., Boyce, M. S. and Kosobucka, M. (1984) Factors affecting red deer (*Cervus elaphus*) population density in Southeastern Poland. *Journal of Applied Ecology* **21**, 881–90.

Bouvier, G. (1963) Transmision possible de la Tuberculose et de la Brucellose du gibier a l'homme et aux animaux domestiques et sauvages. *Bulletin de l'Office Int. des Epizooties* **59**, 433–6.

Challies, C. N. (1985) Establishment, control and commercial exploitation of wild deer in New Zealand. In P. F. Fennessy and K. R. Drew, eds., *Biology of Deer Production. Royal Society of New Zealand Bulletin* **22**, 23–36.

Coltman, D. W. (2008) Molecular ecological approaches to studying the evolutionary impact of selective harvesting in wildlife. *Molecular Ecology* **17**, 221–35.

Creel, S. and Winnie, J. A. (2005) Response of elk herd size to fine-scale spatial and temporal variation in the risk of predation by wolves. *Animal Behaviour* **69**, 1181–9.

Curtis, P. D., Richmond, M. E., Miller, L. A. and Quimby, F. W. (2007) Pathophysiology of white-tailed deer vaccinated with porcine zona pellucida immunocontraceptive. *Vaccine* **25**, 4623–30.

Daszak, P., Cunningham, A. A. and Hyatt, A. D. (2000) Emerging infectious diseases of wildlife: threats to biodiversity and human health. *Science* **287**, 443–9.

Delahay, R. J, de Leeuw, A. N. S., Barlow, A. M., Clifton-Hadley, R. S. and Cheeseman, C. L. (2002) The status of *Mycobacterium bovis* infection in UK wild mammals: a review. *The Veterinary Journal* **164**, 90–105.

Fenberg, P. B. and Roy, K. (2008) Ecological and evolutionary consequences of size-selective harvesting: how much do we know? *Molecular Ecology* **17**, 209–20.

Fletcher, T. J. (1974) The timing of reproduction in red deer (*Cervus elaphus*) in relation to latitude. *Journal of Zoology* **172**, 363–7.

Gill, R. M. A. (1990) *Monitoring the Status of European and North American Cervids*. GEMS Information Series, 8; Global Environment Monitoring Systems, Nairobi: United Nations Environment Programme, 277 pp.

Ginsberg, J. R. and Milner-Gulland, E. J. (1994) Sex-biased harvesting and population dynamics in ungulates: implications for conservation and sustainable use. *Conservation Biology* **8**, 157–66.

Goodman, S., Barton, N., Swanson, G., Abernethy, K. and Pemberton, J. (1999) Introgression through rare hybridization: A genetic study of a hybrid zone betweeen red and sika deer (genus *Cervus*) in Argyll, Scotland. *Genetics* **152**, 355–71.

Groot Bruinderink, G. W. T. A. and Hazebroek, E. (1996) Ungulate traffic collisions in Europe. *Conservation Biology* **10**, 1059–67.

Harrington, R. (1973) Hybridisation among deer and its implications for conservation. *Irish Forestry Journal* **30**, 64–78.

Harrington, R. (1982) The hybridisation of red deer (*Cervus elaphus* L. 1758) and Japanese sika deer (*C. nippon* Temminck, 1838). *International Congress of Game Biologists* **14**, 559–71.

Hedlund, J. H., Curtis, P. D., Curtis, G. and Williams, A. F. (2004) Methods to reduce traffic crashes involving deer: what works and what does not. *Traffic Injury Prevention* **5**, 122–31.

Hmwe, S. S. , Zachos, F. E., Sale, J. B., Rose, H. R. and Hartl, G. B. (2006) Genetic variability and differentiation in red deer (*Cervus elaphus*) from Scotland and England. *Journal of Zoology* **270**, 479–87.

Huitema, H. (1972) Tuberculosis in animals other than cattle domesticated and wild: its relation to bovine tuberculosis eradication and its public health significance. *First International Seminar on Bovine TB for the Americas* **258**, 79–88.

Jones, K. E., Patel, N. G., Levy, M. A. *et al.* (2008) Global trends in emerging infectious diseases. *Nature* **451**, 990–3.

Linnell, J. D. C. and Andersen, R. (1998) Timing and synchrony of birth in a hider species, the roe deer *Capreolus capreolus*. *Journal of Zoology* **244**, 497–504.

Linnell, J. D. C., Wahlstrom, K. and Gaillard, J.-M. (1998) From birth to independence: birth, growth, neonatal mortality, hiding behaviour and dispersal. In R. Andersen, P. Duncan and J. D. C. Linnell, eds., *The European Roe Deer: The Biology of Success*. Oslo, Norway: Scandinavian University Press, pp. 257–84.

Lorenzini, R., Lovari, S. and Masseti, M. (2002) The rediscovery of the Italian roe deer: genetic differentiation and management implications. *Italian Journal of Zoology* **69**, 367–79.

Mayle, B. A. and Staines, B. W. (1998) An overview of methods used for estimating the size of deer populations in Great Britain. In C. R. Goldspink, S. King and R. J. Putman, eds., *Population Ecology, Management and Welfare of Deer*. UK: Manchester Metropolitan University and Universities' Federation for Animal Welfare, pp. 19–31.

Mayle, B. A., Peace, A. J. and Gill, R. M. A. (1999) *How Many Deer? A Field Guide to Estimating Deer Population Size*. Forestry Commission Field Book 18. Edinburgh, UK: Forestry Commission.

Messier, F. (1994) Ungulate population models with predation: A case study with North American moose. *Ecology* **75**, 478–88.

Morellet, N., Gaillard, J. M., Hewison, A. J. M. *et al.* (2007) Indicators of ecological change: new tools for managing populations of large herbivores. *Journal of Applied Ecology* **44**, 634–43.

Pemberton, J., Swanson, G., Barton, N., Livingstone, S. and Senn, H. (2006) Hybridisation between red and sika deer in Scotland. *Deer* **13**, 22–6.

Putman, R. J. (1989) *Mammals as Pests*. London: Chapman and Hall, 271 pp.

Putman, R. J. (1997a) *Chemical and Immunological Methods in the Control of Reproduction in Deer and Other Wildlife: Potential for Population Control and Welfare Implications*, RSPCA Technical Bulletin. Horsham: Royal Society for the Prevention of Cruelty to Animals, 50 pp.

Putman, R. J. (1997b) Deer and road traffic accidents: options for management. *Journal of Environmental Management* **51**, 43–57.

Putman, R. J. (2004) *The Deer Manager's Companion: A Guide to Deer Management in the Wild and in Parks*. Shrewsbury, UK: Swan Hill Press.

Putman, R. J. (2008) *A Review of Available Data on Natural Mortality of Red and Roe Deer Populations*. Inverness: Research Report to the Deer Commission for Scotland.

Putman, R. J., Langbein, J. and Staines, B. W. (2004) *Deer and Road Traffic Accidents: A Review of Mitigation Measures, Costs and Cost-effectiveness*. Contract report RP23A. Inverness, Scotland: Deer Commission.

Ratcliffe, P. R., Peace, A. J., Hewison, A. J. M., Hunt, E. J. and Chadwick, A. H. (1992) The origins and characterization of Japanese sika deer populations in Great Britain. In N. Maruyama *et al.*, eds., *Wildlife Conservation: Present Trends and Perspectives for the 21st Century*. Tokyo, pp. 185–90.

Romin, L. A. and Bissonette, J. A. (1996) Deer-vehicle collisions: status of state monitoring activities and mitigation efforts. *Wildlife Society Bulletin* **24**, 276–83.

Smith, B. L. and Roffe, T. (1992) Diseases among elk of the Yellowstone ecosystem. In W. van Hoven, H. Ebedes and A. Conroy, eds., *Wildlife Ranching: A Celebration of Diversity*. South Africa: University of Pretoria Press, pp. 162–6.

Vernesi, C., Pecchioli, E., Caramelli, D. *et al.* (2002) The genetic structure of natural and reintroduced roe deer (*Capreolus capreolus*) populations in the Alps and central Italy, with reference to the mitochondrial DNA phylogeography of Europe. *Molecular Ecology* **11**, 1285–97.

Walters, C. J. and Holling, C. S. (1990) Large-scale management experiments and learning by doing. *Ecology* **71**, 2060–8.

Winnie, J. A. and Creel, S. (2007) Sex specific behavioural response of elk to spatial and temporal variation in the threat of wolf predation. *Animal Behaviour* **73**, 215–25.

Zima, J., Kožená, I. and Hubálek, Z. (1990) Non-metrical cranial divergence between *Cervus elaphus, C. nippon nippon and C. nippon hortulorum. Acta Scientiarum Naturalium. Brno* **24**(3), 1–41.